Memory, Learning, and Higher Function

Frontispiece: *The Doubter,* by Yves Tanguy. (Reproduced with permission from The Hirshhorn Museum and Sculpture Garden, Smithsonian Institution, Washington, D.C., U.S.A. Photo by John Tennant.)

C. D. Woody

Memory, Learning, and Higher Function

A Cellular View

With 143 Figures

Springer-Verlag New York Heidelberg Berlin

Charles D. Woody, M.D.
Anatomy and Psychiatry
University of California, Los Angeles
The Center for the Health Sciences
760 Westwood Plaza
Los Angeles, California 90024, U.S.A.

Library of Congress Cataloging in Publication Data
Woody, Charles D.
  Memory, learning, and higher function.

  Bibliography: p.
  1. Psychology, Physiological.   2. Memory—Physiological aspects.
3. Learning—Physiological aspects.   4. Higher nervous activity.   I. Title.
QP360.W66   153   80-25185

Typeset by Publishers' Service, Bozeman, Montana, U.S.A.
Printed and bound by Halliday Lithograph Corporation, West Hanover, Mas-
sachusetts, U.S.A.
Printed in the United States of America.

9 8 7 6 5 4 3 2 1

ISBN 0-387-90525-1   Springer-Verlag   New York   Heidelberg   Berlin
ISBN 3-540-90525-1   Springer-Verlag   Berlin   Heidelberg   New York

Prologue

Memory, learning and higher function cannot easily be treated analytically. The subjects are so broad and complex that any attempt to incorporate them within a physical science, as herein, seems likely to fail. Quite apart from the complexities of the subject matter, the descriptive terminology itself is flawed. Even the simplest definitions of terms suffer because they are generated by a system to which the terms pertain (i.e., the brain). Given these limitations, perhaps the most useful way to improve our knowledge of memory and learning would be to develop an awareness of the constraints that affect these processes [1102]. In this way, at least, it might be possible to avoid a few misunderstandings about the subject. A physicalistic approach to this subject should consider the cellular and molecular substrates on which learning and memory are based and how these substrates might constrain our abilities to learn and remember. This book represents an attempt to catalog these and other presently known constraints and describe the physical context within which they function.

The significance of molecular processes as substrates for memory, learning, and higher function needs little justification in light of present knowledge. For those who find such justification necessary, perhaps the most convincing evidence is that of complex innate behavior, behavior that is not acquired through experience, but instead through genetic expression. Such behavior must have a cellular and molecular basis. One can imagine that if innately "programmed" behavior can have a molecular basis, so too may behavior that is acquired through experience.

Three examples of innate behavior come readily to mind. One is that of distance perception in rats. Lashley found that rats reared in darkness from birth encountered little more difficulty in judging a specified distance in performing a conditioned jump than did normally reared rats [579]. Lashley argued that some ability for distance perception was present at birth in these animals and could be transferred to learned behavior.

A second example is the ability of parasitically nested birds, reared in the presence of a foreign species, to perform a complex mating pattern successfully with their own species at maturity. Since there would be no opportunity to learn this behavior after birth, the potential for performing it must be assumed to be present innately.

Finally, a large number of highly stereotyped behavioral reactions appear to be based on genetically transmitted information. These include the catnip response, other pheromone-released mating behavior, imprinting, nest-building, and web-building. They, too, appear to have a molecular basis.

Cellular views of behavior tend to focus on molecular processes, but the manner in which the involved cells are interconnected into a transmission network is also important. If we are to extend our comprehension of adaptive processes, we need an analytic methodology for handling the network as well as its adaptive elements. This book describes such a methodology. The descriptions are of necessity abbreviated, but references are provided for those who wish to read further or would explore the rationale for a particular assertion. As a more formal methodology is generated, it will almost certainly lean heavily on the mathematics of geometry, probability theory, and systems engineering as applied to the analysis of neuroanatomical and neurophysiologic systems. Only in this way can it deal descriptively, predictively, and rigorously with complex biophysical substrates of learning and memory. The approach envisioned should complement and extend the recently established communication and informational sciences of Wiener [1085], Shannon [884], and Von Neumann [1049], perhaps in a direction anticipated by work of Minsky and Papert [672].

Los Angeles, California   C.D. Woody

Acknowledgments

Sources of information for this text includes works by Pavlov, Hilgard, Marquis, and Kimble, Denny-Brown, Gormezano, Kandel and Spencer, Minsky and Papert, and others who generated the 1150 works referenced herein. A smaller type font designates material that quotes or closely follows the original source. I thank these authors and others such as J. Bureš, F. Ervin, K. Frank and D.O. Hebb for inspiring my interest in these areas. I am grateful to the following for permission to reproduce material: D. Aidley, K. Akert, T. Bartfai, T. Bullock, J. Dowling, D. Goodenough, W. Haymaker, J. Heuser, H. Jasper, E.R. John, G.A. Kimble, G. Kreutzberg, R. Llinas, S. Locke, M. Minsky, J. Nicholls, G. Pappas, W. Rall, H. Rasmussen, T. Ruch; Academic Press, Inc., Cambridge University Press, Grass Instrument Co., Hadassah University Press, Little, Brown & Co., MIT Press, C.V. Mosby Company, Raven Press, W.B. Saunders Company, Sinauer Associates, Inc., Springer-Verlag New York, Inc., John Wiley and Sons, Inc., *Ann. N.Y. Acad. Sci., Electroenceph., Clin. Neurophysiol., Exper. Neural., J. Exper. Psychol., J. Neurophysiol., Neurosci., Res. Prog. Bull.* The Smithsonian Institution, Hirshhorn Museum, granted permission to reproduce *The Doubter* by Yves Tanguy as the frontispiece.

Special thanks are due to T. Bartfai, L. Bindman, J. Bureš, O. Burešova, B. Dadourian, D. Denny-Brown, R. Doty, Sr., I. Gormezano, I. Krekule, J. Křivanek, M. Letinsky, R. Pay, J. Schlag, B. Swartz, and L. Vyklicky for reviewing entire chapters or the whole book. D. MacKay, A.M. Uttley and others at UCLA, ČSAV (Inst. Physiol.), and elsewhere were kind enough to comment on material related to their own research or research interests. The contribution of those in Prague was made possible by an exchange fellowship awarded to me through the CS and US National Academies of Science. Much of the original research of myself and colleagues described herein was supported by NSF, NICHD, and AFOSR. The illustrations were done under the direction of Bill Fulton, the editing by Rex Pay. The cover photomicrograph was taken by Dr. Gijs Vrensen of the Netherlands Interuniversity Opthamological Research Institute from material supplied by Dr. Woody.

I express my deep appreciation to those named above, to my students, and to my family.

Memory, Learning, and Higher Function: A Cellular View, by Charles D. Woody

ERRATA

Page 21 (Table 2.2): ^{c} (or latent <u>facilitation</u>)

Page 53 (Legend, Fig. 2.12): appetitive jaw movement <u>UR</u>
aversive nictitating membrane <u>UR</u>.

Page 69 (Lines 12-13): For nictitating membrane conditioning, the effects of ISIs between –50 and 200 msec . . .

Page 110 (Line 25): (2) <u>responsive to the stimulus,</u>

Page 168 (Line 37): stimulation of the cortex at rates of 10-20/sec <u>[929]</u>.

Page 203 (Section 3.b.): g K$_{Ca}$ ❭b. Slow K^{+}-calcium dependent . . .
depends on . . .
(Section 4.): <u>g Cl</u>   4. **Chloride conductance**

Page 243 (Fig. 5.19, left): Transpose Nos. <u>1</u> and <u>2</u> on interior $\mu A/nA$ axis.

Page 254 (Fig. 5.26): pronase (delete L.C. "P")

Page 262 (Line 19): then . . ." (see Fig. 7.4). Parallel circuits may be more redundant and <u>less efficient.</u>

Page 290 (Line 26): be perceived as curved; the figure in C appears to have three distinct <u>extensions.</u>

Page 306 (Line 7): <u>nomy</u> (see p. 401).

Page 391 (Line 16): r is in X,   (delete t)

Page 400 (Footnote, line 1): *Minimizing $\Sigma_j C_{jk} \cdot B_j \cdot \Pi_i (P_{ij}/q_{ij})^{\varphi} \underline{i}$,

Page 452: 996. <u>Tasaki I, Warashina A (1975) Changes in light absorption, emis-</u><u>sion</u>

Page 463 (Line 31, **Inactivation**): near the limiting <u>value</u> of conductance change.
(Line 37) **Instrumental conditioning** See page <u>46</u>.

Page 466 (Line 39, **Transmittance**): ship between <u>node</u> variables (see page 369).

© 1982 *Springer-Verlag New York, Inc.*

Contents

Introduction

The basis of learning appears to be a network of interconnected adaptive elements (such as those found in the brain) by means of which transforms between inputs and outputs are performed. By adaptive I mean that the element can change in some systematic manner and in so doing alter the transform between input and output. In living systems, transmission within the neural network involves coded nerve impulses and other physical chemical processes that form reflections of sensory stimuli and incipient motor behavior. The properties of the transmission network become significant determinants of behavior and depend on the mechanisms of neuronal adaptation, the means by which the connectivities between different neurons are modified. Particular paths through the network become labeled with reference to specific inputs and outputs. The network then operates through labeled interconnections linking specific elements within the network and through the mechanisms that underlie each element's adaptation. The adaptive features are crucial to learning and imply some associated, underlying mnemonic process. The labeling is of consequence with regard to the resulting specificities of stimulus reception and motor performance that characterize adaptive behavior.

Memory involves time-dependent information processing relying on encoding and retrieval as well as storage itself. In the brain, engrams can be defined as those elemental adaptive changes that take place when learning and memory storage occur. Persistent engrammatic modifications of neuronal structure commonly arise through the same associative mechanisms responsible for learned behavior [397, 486, 759, 1020]. An appreciation of the critical associative contingencies between stimulus inputs that lead to these changes may be as useful to neurophysiologists seeking laws of cellular change as to behaviorists seeking laws of behavior. Some of the principal attributes of the mnemonic process also involve reproducing or recalling what has been learned and retained. This aspect of the mnemonic process is termed recollection.

One goal of any science of learning and memory would be to provide a useful description of molecular physiology acting within its broader neuroanatomical context to support higher function. Such a goal requires integration and extension of present knowledge from several existing scientific disciplines. Most of these disciplines concern the brain and its function, but others concern informational networks in general and have emerged from studies of machines only recently, in the last half century. The present treatment begins with the philosophical background to studies of higher functions, proceeds to the psychophysiology of the reflex as a basic component of behavior, dwells on the neurophysiology of simple networks, examines the properties of complex neural networks revealed by neuropathology, and concludes with the cybernetics of informational networks in general. The treatment is based on the premise that a general relationship can be established between neuronal operations and complex function. This can be done in a formal analytic sense as in systems engineering. Cellular operations can be mapped in terms of reflex outcomes as well as molecular mechanisms such as those governing ionic conductances across nerve membranes. These operations are central to the production of memory, learning, and higher function.

The forms of learning that support higher functions then emerge as the sums of the properties of the nervous system at the subcellular, cellular, and network levels, i.e., the physical characteristics of the adaptive elements, their sensitivities to change, the numbers involved in specific reflex operations, and the organization of their interconnections.

Chapter 1

Commonsense Views of Memory and Learning Obtained from Philosophy

It is memory ... that makes the past and the future real and therefore creates true duration and true time.

(Bergson, 1908)

The earliest understandings of memory, learning, and higher function were acquired by direct observation and based on common sense. Reflection followed observation and led to the elaboration of philosophies. As philosophy progressed, the need for better understanding of the biological processes supporting memory, learning, and higher function was recognized. This conclusion followed the realization that these processes were interdependent. The biological processes of memory and learning influenced higher functions such as thought, and higher functions, in turn, governed our conceptualization of the processes of memory and learning.

Because of this interdependency it would be foolish to ignore philosophic foundations in discussing memory, learning, and higher function and so they are treated first. However, it should be kept in mind that the early philosophers lacked detailed knowledge of the physical and physiologic sciences.

Knowledge, Recollection, Perception

Knowledge involves recollection. Knowledge represented as memory within the organism is subject to distortion by noisy biological processes. Knowledge represented outside the organism, in the form of graphics or writing, is more stable and provides a unique basis for commonality in communication between organisms. Even this extrinsic knowledge evolves from recollective knowledge, and requires the organism for expression. Thus, it, too, depends on the characteristics of biological processes.

Recollection is implicit in memory. The recollective aspect of memory affords a description of past events. In memory, the past survives into the present, and the mnemonic process therefore requires some physical form that is stable over time.

Perception is a more difficult matter. Perception joins recollections of the past with the experience of the present. Empirical knowledge is derived from perception. Perceived events may or may not be remembered; unperceived events cannot be remembered.*

The thesis herein is that recollective constructs and related phenomena arise from cellular processes. Thus, physiologically speaking, perception and recollection are effects not only of stimuli (the objects perceived or recollected) but also of the elements perceiving and recollecting. Neurons may be said to perceive, though not in the same sense of Leibnitz' monads or in any anthropomorphized manner. To speak of perception at the neuronal level simply acknowledges the primacy of the fundamental physical processes supporting information transfer through which perception is constituted.

Analytically, one can separate the phenomena of perception into at least three variables: (1) the effects of the physical stimulus; (2) the effects of the apparatus of the central† nervous system (CNS) involved with processing information related to that stimulus; and (3) feedback effects from previous perturbations *of* the apparatus *on the apparatus itself.* The environment also provides feedback, but consideration of this variable, herein, is confined to effects manifested within the nervous system.

By dealing with these matters physiologically, it is possible to describe memory, learning, and higher functions such as perception as characteristics of nervous tissue. Thus, in considering these phenomena one need not depart from physicalistic interpretations.

Inference and Experience

The position maintained in this book admits the assumption that knowledge is derived or can be inferred from experience, the fourth of the philosophic positions described below.

---

*"Unconsciously" perceived events constitute a subclass of perceived events that also may be remembered, though sometimes with difficulty. Some learning processes can even take place under anesthesia, for example, the formation of associatively induced adaptations supporting conditioned taste aversion and the encoding of information pertaining to the noxious US (LiCl) used in this paradigm [130].

†The apparatus of the peripheral nervous system is involved as well.

Russell [856] discusses the philosophic question of whether we can infer any other events from our own perceptions, i.e., events that we know without inference or know alone from memory. He says that four positions are possible:

1. One may deny the validity of all inferences from present percepts and memory to other events.
2. One may adopt solipsism (recognition of only the "I am" in "I think, therefore I am"), which allows some inference from one's percepts, but only to other events in one's own biography.
3. One may admit inferences to events analogous to those in one's own experience.
4. One may admit commonsense and traditional physics with the assumption that there are also events that no one experiences. When this point of view is scientific, it bases the inferences to perceived events on causal laws.

It is assumed that the same causal laws that govern our inferences govern the molecular substrates within the nervous system on which experience and inference depend.

Sensation, Neural Activation, Neural Adaptation

Sensation requires neural activation and may be considered as being equivalent to the immediate activation of certain afferent neurons. Perception links immediate with past activation. Activation may follow (1) stimuli extrinsic to the organism, (2) stimuli extrinsic to the activated neuron but arising within the organism, as from memory, or (3) events generated spontaneously within the neuron, as in pacemaker activity. Thus, inputs reflecting the physical world apart from the organism must interact at the cellular level with inputs reflecting memory and other internal processes within the organism. Bergson [68] reached an analogous conclusion on philosophical grounds. He argued for two conceptualizations of memory. One, which he called habit, represented undistorted recollective reproduction of sensation. The other, a more realistic view, represented more complex recollection and consisted of habit and its surrounding, distorting context of other events and memories. Bergson therefore grasped the possibility that a memory of the past might interact with and distort perception of the present.

Sensation and perception will then be influenced by events at the cellular level, where sensation and perception are represented by the dawning activation of neural elements. Different combinations of inputs will potentially distort the reception of each separate, single input. Moreover, if the cell adapts, the adaptation will further modify reception.

Feedback: Orderly Learning and Memory

Learning requires adaptation. In fact, the changes in function that distinguish complex learning from simpler forms of adaptation require adaptations that are sensitive to the environment and lend themselves to self-organization. The problem is to produce orderly adaptations that will favor the production of specific outputs, given particular inputs. Then, sensory perception, though still somewhat "distorted" by repeated transmissions, will be orderly rather than chaotic, and perhaps beneficial rather than adverse. An orderly mnemonic process will favor useful recollection.

A most difficult question is how neural adaptations might depend on contingencies arising both intrinsic and extrinsic to each single neuron and yet maintain organization within a dynamic neural system of complex architecture. Two possibilities are suggested. One is based on a preprogrammed response to a particular input. This type of adaptation will occur regardless of the remaining system state or other variables. The contingencies for its occurrence are preestablished and fixed. As a result, it may not support learning in the broadest sense, but only close facsimiles. To appreciate this point of view, the reader may wish to reflect for a moment on the relation or nonrelation to learning of (1) the control of room temperature by a thermostat, (2) the control of room temperature by a person operating a heater directly, (3) the performance of genetically transmitted mating behavior, and (4) the performance of mating behavior by trial and error. Few would describe the first as learning. Most would describe the last as learning. The ambiguity surrounding the remaining two examples as much exposes the limitations of ourselves as of the term learning itself.

The other type of adaptation admits further modification based on feedback of information concerning the effect of prior adaptation. This information may come, in part, from the adaptive element itself, providing an update of the local system's state, or it may arise extrinsically, from the environment. Without feedback, the state of the system, including the success or failure of previous adaptations, is not considered. Feedback to elements within the system permits a kind of evolutionary adaptation based on past system performance. In addition, it allows interaction between past and present events. The cellular processes supporting memory and learning may therefore by expected to have some aspects of feedback incorporated into their design. They will also be predisposed to adapt to certain stimulus contingencies. The adaptations will reflect a continual exchange between the organism and its environment. Over generations, adaptations that have survival value will predominate. Thus, some adaptations will evolve in the Darwinian sense, whereas others will change only during the existence of the organism. While it can be argued that the environment and the organism interact and that both change physically, the present treatment concentrates only on changes within the organism.

Cybernetic Analysis

The cellular processes supporting memory, learning, and higher function are potentially formulable. In effect, this requires a description of the anatomical and physiologic functions of the cellular elements, their interconnections, and the network states. In addition, attention must be paid to genetic (preprogrammed) and environmental influences. Such a formulation is considered throughout this book, but most particularly in the last chapter under the subject of cybernetics.

The goal of cybernetic analysis of adaptive cellular processes is to provide probabilistic descriptions of element and network states and the means by which the changes therein are controlled. Neural adaptations are controlled by determinable physical events and their contingencies. A probabilistic knowledge of states of brain as transfer functions between inputs and outputs can lead to predictions of incipient motor activity as a consequence of sensory input, adaptation, and recollection. Such a conceptualization is not entirely foreign to earlier views of higher function. For example, the living being has been described philosophically as a sum of contingencies or possible actions with respect to the rest of the world [68].

Chapter 2

The Reflex and Behavior

The task of physiology ... is to account for causal relations between input and output which are the special concern of a science of behavior.

(B. F. Skinner, 1956)

The fire touching the foot of the boy causes him to withdraw his foot. The mechanism acts through ... the lower end of the nerve ... is transmitted upwards to the brain ... travels back down the nerve ... and causes the foot to be pulled back.

(Rene Descartes, 1662)

The Reflex

The Concept of the Reflex in Relation to Behavior

Memory, learning, and higher function arise from operations of networks of adaptive elements. Physiologically, in terms of brain function, the elements are neurons and the networks may be considered as reflex pathways linking inputs and outputs by way of specifiable transforms. There are many reflex systems—some as simple as those in the spinal cord described by Sherrington [887], others much more complex. Means of influencing the transforms of adaptation in these systems have been known for years. Remarkable insights into reflex processes supporting memory and learning were gained within this century by I. P. Pavlov [759] and B. F. Skinner [908,910]. Their insights arose from an appreciation of the fundamental significance of the reflex as a mediator of behavior. The next few pages describe how this view evolved.

Three hundred years ago, Descartes elucidated the idea of the reflex [213, 214]. He regarded every activity of the organism as a necessary reaction to some external stimulus. The connection between the stimulus and the response was made through a particular neural path. This connection, he stated, was the main purpose of the neural structures of the animal's body. In effect, sensorimotor integration, if not behavior in its entirety, arose from the operation of reflex pathways.

Sherrington [887] provided physiologic documentation of the neural pathways that connected stimulus with response. A knee jerk elicited by tapping the tendon below the patella was found to be mediated by two types of neurons (Fig. 2.1). One, the sensory or afferent neuron, had a stretch

Knee Jerk Reflex

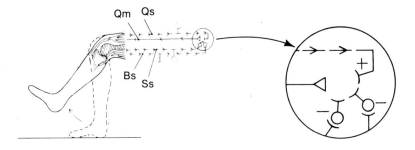

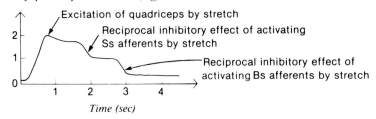

Fig. 2.1. *Neural control of the knee jerk. Extension at the knee is facilitated by activating the motor neurons (axons designated by Qm) to the quadriceps muscle. The muscle contracts and the knee is extended. Stretch of the quadriceps muscle, as by brisk tapping, activates the sensory neurons (axons designated by Qs) of the muscle stretch receptors. This type of neuron has its cell body in the dorsal root ganglion, but synapses on the Qm motor neurons in the ventral horn of the spinal cord. Activation of this synapse excites (+) Qm, leading to contraction of the quadriceps and a knee jerk.*

Reciprocal innervation exists wherein sensory neurons from opposing, antagonist musculature such as the biceps (Bs) or the semitendinosus (Ss) also project, interneuronally, to the Qm motor neuron. When activated by stretch as in knee extension, they may discharge and inhibit (-) Qm activation and quadriceps contraction through an interneuron as shown in the graph to the right. (After Liddell and Sherrington [601] in Mountcastle [693].)

receptor* located within the tendon, a cell body located in the dorsal root ganglion, and its axon terminations located in the ventral horn of the spinal cord. The other, the motor or efferent neuron, had its dendrites and cell body located in the ventral horn and received synaptic inputs from the sensory neuron. When excited, the motor neuron emitted an impulse down its axon, producing extension of the knee joint by virtue of its terminations on the muscle.

This two neuron arrangement has remained the basic example of a reflex circuit because of the ease with which the interaction between sensory input and motor output can be described. However, such reflex circuits are rare in the brain because any single neuron is likely to receive synaptic inputs from more than one other neuron. Interneurons are also typically inserted between sensory neurons and motor neurons, and each neuron usually finds itself within an extensive network of interconnected neurons in which there are various alternative paths and feedback loops. The resulting gain in sophistication of reflex processes in going from the two neuron pathway to multiple neuron circuits is immense.

Sherrington grasped the significance of the cellular processes illustrated in Fig. 2.1 in the production of reflex behavior. However, although both Descartes and Sherrington conceived of the reflex as a fundamental property of the organism, their appreciation of the implication of complex reflex processes was somewhat restrictive. Both were dualists [214,887,889].

It was Pavlov [759] who recognized the role of *adaptive* reflex pathways in connecting a stimulus with a response. He documented the contribution of internal, reflex-mediated memory to learned behavior by the experiments shown in Fig. 2.2.

In light of present knowledge, the role of adaptive reflex pathways may be described as follows. Reflexes depend on the properties of neural tissue, and adaptations of reflexes occur as a result of changes in that tissue. Given appropriate contingencies between presented stimuli, changes in reflex pathways occur and the response to stimulus presentation is altered. Learned behavior arises in the context of adaptive, reflex mechanisms such as are seen with conditioning. Complex behavior then depends on significant numbers of reflex adaptations occurring in the cortex and elsewhere [e.g. 111,651,1110, 1122]. As Pavlov has summarized it [759], *all conditioned reflexes and much adaptive behavior have a distinct representation within the central nervous system[†] in one or another set of cells.*

One set is linked with one activity; another set is linked with another activity. Subsets of this mosaic that are involved initially in one particular learned activity enlarge their functional role and become "connected" with additional learned activity of the animal. In this process, the original connections and functional representations are not necessarily lost; rather, the full [multiple] transmission properties of the neural network and its mosaic components are realized [759].

*See glossary for definitions of unfamiliar terms.
†The peripheral nervous system also adapts; in addition, other parts of the body can influence the nervous system.

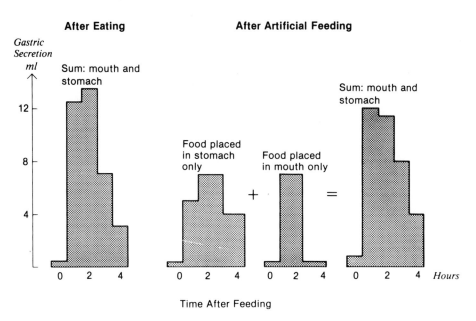

Fig. 2.2. *The contribution of internal memory to behavior. Food placed in the mouth adds to the flow of gastric secretion beyond that produced on reaching the stomach. Pavlov termed this added component the "psychic" response [758]. It was later redefined as a conditioned response (CR). The other component is the unconditioned response (UR). (After Pavlov [758] in Rachlin [795].)*

Skinner, too, grasped this fundamental significance of reflex operations in linking stimulus (S) with response (R), even though he elected to treat the reflex network performing these linkages as a "black box." He attempted to quantitate reflex behavior resulting from operant conditioning [908]. Pigeons were taught to peck repetitively for food as a reward and the rate of pecking was measured. The rate of pecking depended on such features of behavior as motivation, hunger, and satiation, and could be varied as a consequence of the schedules of reinforcement. In effect, these experiments indirectly measured consequences of neural adaptation, brought about by delivery of a reinforcing food stimulus, on the production of motor responses.

This focus on reflex adaptation need not be overly restrictive; it can be used to describe most behavioral events. Thus, for example, for the physiologist, walking can be described in terms of muscular contractions resulting from a reflex network that involves the motor cortex, the vestibulocerebellar system, the nucleus reticularis of the brainstem, and the motoneurons of the lumbosacral spinal cord. Patterned walking is possible with only the latter two neuron populations intact [891]. Coordinated, purposeful locomotion requires all the above neural populations and still others. Adaptive locomotion depends on adaptations within these neurons. Skinner suggested that the operations of [reflex substrates supporting] * S-R linkages might transcend a great many of our behavioral and philosophic conceptions [910]. The latter would then be secondary and consequential to the more primary physiologic operations. Thus, freedom, dignity and the like would arise out of reflex operations and be thereby constrained.

In summary, adaptive reflex operations are central to the production of memory and learned behavior. Neurons, their interconnections, and the mechanisms by which they adapt form the basis of reflexes. The result of these processes is the ability to respond adaptively to different stimuli, a property common to all organisms that learn, remember, and are capable of higher function. Accordingly, it will be useful to construct a taxonomy of reflex functions by which some simplified forms of behavior can be discussed, physiologically. The remainder of this chapter is devoted to this task. Those who wish to skip the preliminaries dealing with necessary but somewhat tedious terminologies may continue on p. 16, preferably inspecting the figures and italicized material in between. An outline of the taxonomy is presented later in Table 2.2.

Partitioning the Reflex

Stimulus-response (S-R) systems consisting of complex adaptive neural reflexes can best be understood if partitioned in terms of their function. Three separate functions can be specified:

1. *The system should possess an analytic means* by which it can select, out of the whole complexity of the environment, those inputs that are of significance.

2. *The system should possess a synthetic means* by which the inputs of individual elements within the neural mosaic can be assembled into a particular functional complex.

3. *Adaptive changes should take place within one portion of the system without unduly disrupting the functions of other portions of the system.* Such adaptations need not require completely independent operation of adaptive elements involved with different analytic or synthetic functions. Examples can be found of automata (e.g., Rosenblatt's Perceptron [838]; see Chapter 7) that use parallel processing through interdependent adaptive elements to perform tasks involving learning and memory. Some of these automata are quite successful at image recognition and game-playing strategies.

One requirement of the S-R operation of the nervous system is that there be some interconnections between elements representing common analytic or synthetic functions. This permits utilization of the full capacity of the net-

*Added by this author but implicit in Skinner's formulations.

work. However, elements with functional commonalities need not be restricted to one focal region of the network. They may be scattered throughout, as long as their connections are maintained. Simple economy will preclude too diffuse a representation within the network. Also, the speed of operation of these elements and their connections must be greater than that of the function performed.

Describing the Reflex

Adaptive reflex systems and their outcomes can be described at several levels. The most basic of these (apart from molecular reactions) is the *cellular level*. Neural components act as the substrate of the reflex to mediate sensory analysis and motor synthesis and to permit adaptation. A different level of description reflects the outcome of *integrated reflex operations*. Adaptations facilitate or suppress stimulus reception and the production of a motor response. The overall operation of the reflex is then changed by the adaptive process. The third, or *behavioral level*, is the most holistic and concerns commonalities between different reflex operations and outcomes. The commonalities must be linked, descriptively, in some manner. Observably similar outcomes are the usual linkages, e.g., appetitive behavior, preparatory reflexes, etc. Other linkages involve common features between processes used to bring about reflex adaptations, such as the parameters of stimulus-contingent adaptation discussed in Chapter 3.

Descriptions at other than the primary, cellular level are intuitively appealing but are likely to be imprecise and may be biased by conceptualizations that obscure the nature of the observations. For example, the Freudian concepts of the id, ego, and superego suffer for want of a physiologic substrate. This is because the concepts were defined more on the basis of descriptive observations than on the underlying reflex operations. Although the behavioral effects of cellular adaptations are seen most easily at the second and third levels of description, the cellular processes governing these adaptations remain their primary determinants.

Behavioral taxonomies may fail because they ignore the reflex substrate and define the reflex system as consisting of simply a stimulus and a response. In contrast, the present attempt to relate memory, learning, and higher function to brain processes recognizes the primacy of the cellular operations themselves. Many neural adaptations supporting learned behavior are likely to involve persistent changes in conductance across the nerve membranes via channels admitting ions such as potassium and calcium, as explained in Chapter 5. The generation of persistent conductance changes will depend on specific chemical interactions and on frequencies of transient currents within the cells [c.f. 410,411,1116,1117,1124,1126]. The parametric sensitivities of the persistent conductance changes are likely to resemble those of the learned behavior they support. As we better understand the primary neural adaptations and the parameters by which they are controlled, so then must our understanding of the causes and nature of the resulting functions be modified. It is this priority of basis in establishing proper definitions of behavior to which the reader's attention is directed.

Adaptive Reflexes

My proposed taxonomy of behavioral reflex adaptation focuses on physical features controlling the adaptations, such as the frequency of the applied stimuli. In constructing a taxonomy of the operations of adaptive reflex systems, the following positions are maintained: First, it is possible to establish a general relationship between neuronal operations and complex function. Second, this can be done in the formal analytic sense, as with a complex engineering system. Third, this requires that the cellular operations be partitioned into analytic, synthetic, and adaptive terms. Fourth, it will be useful to map these operations in terms of neural adaptations and reflex outcomes. Fifth, the results will be consonant with behavioral descriptions, although the latter are likely to change in their formulation as the main cellular effects are recognized. This taxonomy prefers definitions based on physically quantifiable formulations to those based on ambiguous descriptions. By using this approach, it may be possible to make descriptions of reflex outcomes more isomorphic with the underlying cellular and molecular processes that serve as their building blocks. An example of such a potential isomorphism is shown in Fig. 2.3.

Reflex adaptations may be divided into those induced by simple stimulus presentation, those induced by repetitive stimulus presentation, and those induced associatively by the presentation of different stimuli. Repetitive stimulation involves presentation of the same stimulus repeatedly. Associative stimulation involves presentation of two different stimuli in temporal relationship to each other. In search of relationships between reflex adaptation and molecular neurochemistry, the description of repetitively induced reflex adaptations in this chapter is succeeded by a description of effects of various types of stimulation on neural activity and excitability (Chapter 4) and then by a description of the frequency dependency of certain ionic conductance mechanisms that might engrammatically modify the transfer properties of single neurons (Chapter 5). A corresponding description of the associative processes is given in Chapters 3-5. The exposition that follows assumes that the reader is familiar with behaviorally oriented taxonomies of simple forms of learning such as may be found in Kimble [519] or Rachlin's [795] texts.

Facilitated Reflex Outcomes

Facilitated reflex outcomes are herein defined as those in which the adaptations facilitate a motor response to a sensory stimulus. The adaptations may be termed "facilitatory."* The definition does not distinguish enhanced

---

*The adaptations need not be excitatory at the physiologic level since reflex facilitation can be achieved by inhibiting reflex inhibition.

**Effects of Interstimulus Interval on Conditioning (Left)
and on Neuronal Calcium Conductance (Right)**

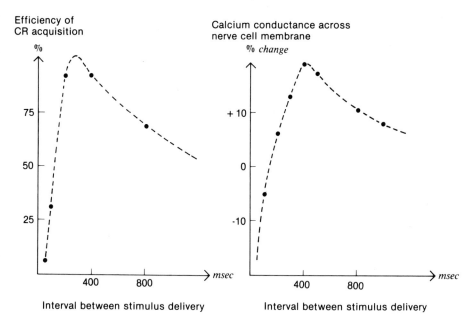

Fig. 2.3. Note the similarities between the curves on the left and right and
their abscissas. The ordinate of the graph to the left reflects conditioned
reflex behavior, whereas that to the right reflects a molecular process involving a change in conductance of ions across a nerve cell membrane to be
described further in Chapter 5. See Figs. 3.10 and 5.6 for further details.

stimulus reception from facilitated motor performance and says nothing of
the time duration of the adaptation—matters best resolved by cellular studies
—but it will serve for the present.

Pavlov notes that any novel stimulus produces distinct neural excitation
and potential reflex facilitation. Neural excitation may occur at the cessation
of the stimulus as well as at its onset. The extent of the excitation is widespread within the neural network and commonly reaches the level of final
motoneurons, even with weak stimuli [1113].

Thus, a weak stimulus can produce the following effects:

1. A gross peripheral motor response
2. A slight, but visible, muscle twitch or fasciculation
3. A visually subliminal muscle activation, a fibrillation, measurable only by
   the EMG except in the tongue, where fibrillations may be seen
4. Excitatory postsynaptic potentials (EPSPs) but no action potential in
   groups of motoneurons
5. Activity in more proximal neurons

Effects 1–4 simply reflect gradations of excitation within a group of motor
units, and effect 5 represents termination of the progression of excitation at

a different point in the reflex network of which this group is a part. Physiologically, there are other significant differences in the outcomes of effects 1-4. Effect 1 will likely activate all three types of nerve afferents that are sensitive to muscle contraction or stretch: the Golgi tendon organs (group Ib or II) as well as muscle spindle fibers containing the annulospiral (group IA) and flower-spray nerve endings (group II) [cf. 693,849]. Effect 2 may fail to activate the Golgi tendon organs or related fibers which are sensitive to loads on the muscle tendons. Effect 3 may activate the low threshold group IA afferents, but not the higher threshold group II afferents. Effect 4 may activate none of these. Behaviorally, it is noteworthy that conditioned learning of the Pavlovian type can occur in the absence of effects 1-3. That is, an unconditioned, peripheral motor response to the US is unnecessary for this type of conditioning to occur [54,198]. (The terms US and CS are discussed below.)

In the example shown in Figure 2.4, an animal was presented with a weak, 70 db click stimulus. A neural response was observed at the level of the facial motoneurons even though a gross facial movement was absent. The animal was untrained. After conditioning with the click as CS and glabella tap as US, the size of the neural response increased and a conditioned facial movement was produced. With extinction of the conditioned reflex, the movement was lost. The neural response diminished but was larger than that in the naive state. Thus, a reflex effect of the weak auditory stimulus was seen regardless of whether an overt motor response was produced. Moreover, the effect was subject to modification by the animal's experience.

It is important to recognize the significance of this observation for the usual taxonomies of behavioral outcomes of reflex adaptation [480,486,519, 795,1016]. First, the fact that weak stimuli perturb the organism's nervous system as far as the final motor elements suggests that most neurons can potentially adapt by admitting transient, polysynaptically transmitted perturbations evoked by innumerable environmental stimuli. Though recognized by Pavlov [759], this was forgotten by some of his successors. If weak stimuli can produce such neural adaptations, unpredictable forms of stimulation should be avoided if a steady state is to be reached against which other changes may be compared. Second, the fact that motoneurons are activated, if not discharged, by weak, natural stimuli reveals liminal muscle activation to be an arbitrarily selected criterion of "response". Activation of the entire chain of neurons between sensory receptor and muscle end plate without liminal muscle contraction is itself a significant response. Definitions of conditioning based on whether or not the CS produces an overt peripheral movement are of questionable validity. (It has long been known that EEG activation can replace muscle activation as an accurate index of conditioned behavior.) One must focus on changes in the probability of neural activation as well as muscle contraction, and I shall do this later, in Chapters 3, 4, and 7. In this way a more precise formulation of reflex and behavioral change can be obtained.

Pavlov also recognized in his studies of conditioning that it was the reflex substrate that changed and *not* the stimuli which provoked the change. Hence, the terminologies condition*ed* stimulus and uncondition*ed* stimulus

Brain Activity Changes with Conditioning

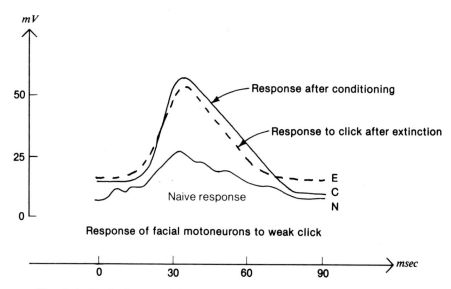

Fig. 2.4. Evoked potentials recorded monopolarly from the facial nucleus during development and extinction of a conditioned eye blink in a cat. Each trace is the average of 128 responses to a 70 db, 1 msec click (CS): N, initially in naive animal; C, after establishment of the conditioned reflex; E, after extinction. The traces begin 8.4 msec before arrival of the click (0 msec) at the ears of the animal. Calibrations are as shown; positive up. Note that a response to the stimulus is present in the naive animal. The facial nucleus contains the motoneurons for producing the eye blink. (Woody and Brozek [1113].)

were not his and are misnomers. Better terms would be condition*al* stimulus and uncondition*al* stimulus because they reflect the need (or not) of contingencies for the production of certain degrees of response to various extrinsic stimuli. Herein, the terms CS and US are used, and the reader may construe them as desired.

Suppressed Reflex Outcomes

Suppressed or "inhibited" reflex operations are defined as those that suppress motor responses to sensory stimuli, the responses ranging from evoked neural activity to overt movement. The corresponding adaptations are termed inhibitory. Again, the spike activity of any single neuron within the reflex network may be increased or decreased so long as the consequence is to promote suppression of the neural effect in question.

Note that the nature of the nervous system is such that it is possible to facilitate or suppress transmission along neural pathways* by a variety of

---

*A pathway is a set of functionally related neural elements consisting of integrative components such as dendrites and somas and their all-or-none axonal connections.

excitatory or inhibitory mechanisms. Spinal reflex pathways use facilitatory and inhibitory mechanisms, simultaneously and reciprocally, to control posture and movement [632,887]. Flexion and extension reflexes are mediated at the spinal level by preexisting reciprocal neural connections and synaptic functions. Thus, facilitation of knee extension is typically accompanied by inhibition of knee flexion and then followed by inhibition of knee extension (Fig. 2.1), and learned movements such as a conditioned leg withdrawal may involve both facilitatory and inhibitory adaptations.

This complexity of underlying reflex processes poses a problem for any taxonomy of adaptive reflexes. The taxonomy must either be so specific as to suffer when used descriptively or must risk being physiologically imprecise. The proper solution to this dilemma lies in a detailed analysis of the reflex network as suggested later in Chapter 7. However, since we cannot afford the time spent in making these detailed analyses at this stage of our exposition, let us push on using admittedly imprecise descriptive indices of reflex outcomes such as: (1) augmentation or reduction of motor performance elicited by a CS, (2) augmentation or reduction of motor performance elicited by a US, (3) extent of generalized motor performance, (4) level of spontaneous motor performance, (5) extent of generalized stimulus receptivity, and (6) rate of acquisition of conditioning, extinction, or other alterations in behavioral states.

Simple Facilitatory Adaptations

In effect, all stimuli that are capable of producing neural activation are potentially capable of producing facilitatory reflex adaptations. This assertion is made because most simple stimuli produce reflex outcomes such as orienting and alerting that visibly facilitate subsequent reception and transmission of stimulus inputs [759]. The passage of information related to these stimuli can be observed through virtually all levels of the central nervous system ranging from the sensory receptors to the motoneurons themselves (e.g., Fig. 2.4). The question then arises if any reflexes do not adapt. Probably few fail to adapt, at least in the sense of being transiently perturbed as described earlier. However, some reflexes return to their original state following adaptation, while others undergo a change of state wherein their transfer properties are persistently altered.

The simple adaptations are herein defined as being of the former type (that admit transient perturbations). They arise de novo from the reflex substrate itself on presenting single or simple stimuli (Table 2.1) and therefore represent the innate or preprogrammed response of the neural system to a stimulus input. At the cellular level, these adaptations are likely to be uncomplicated and transitory. Many occur simply from activating a set of convergent nerve terminals. Transmission through neurons that are on the "subliminal fringe" of the set's zone of discharge may thereby be altered [612], either facilitating or suppressing the reflex operations that they mediate, depending on the type of alteration and its location within the reflex circuitry (Fig. 2.5).

Table 2.1. Pavlov's Means of Inducing Simple Facilitatory and Inhibitory Adaptations and Evaluating Their Induction With Test Stimuli

	Simple Facilitatory Adaptation	Simple Inhibitory Adaptation
TEST BASELINE RESPONSE TO STIMULUS, S_1	S_1 → NO RESPONSE	S_1 → RESPONSE (Unconditioned or conditioned with training)
INTERPOSE STIMULUS, S'	S'	[a]S' (According to Pavlov, the stimulus, S', that induces the inhibitory adaptation should be presented *with* rather than separate from the test stimulus, S_1. Sometimes, however, inhibitory adaptations will occur when S' is given *apart* from S_1.)
TEST RESPONSE TO S_1 AGAIN	S_1 → RESPONSE (Unconditioned)	S_1 → NO RESPONSE

[a] S' may block production of the response to S_1 perhaps by masking reception of S_1. (See Tables 2.2 and 2.3 for nearly similar instances, depending on associative linkages.)

A Reflex Circuit Capable of Facilitation and Occlusion

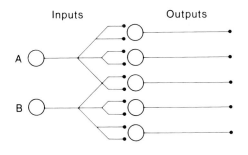

FACILITATION	versus	OCCLUSION

Assuming 2 inputs required to fire O—▸ :

Input A fires 2 outputs
Input B fires 2 outputs
Inputs A + B fire 5 outputs

$5 > 2 + 2$

(firing A + B together *facilitates*
reflex outcome since $5 > 2 + 2$)

Assuming 1 input required to fire O—▸ :

Input A fires 3 outputs
Input B fires 3 outputs
Inputs A + B fire 5 outputs

$5 < 3 + 3$

(firing A + B together *occludes*
reflex outcome since $5 < 3 + 3$)

Fig. 2.5. Schema of facilitation and occlusion produced by summatory effects. Analogous processes are involved in temporal and spatial summation. For further details and definitions of terms, see text and glossary.

The simplest alterations in neuronal function are then attributable to effects of temporal and spatial summation. Though transient, they may last long enough to produce temporary alterations in transmission along neural pathways. Classically, temporal summation was thought of as the augmented effect on one postsynaptic neuron of repeated activation of a single input. Spatial summation was thought of as the effect of activating several inputs to the same postsynaptic neuron at the same time. In fact, *temporal summation* represents *any* augmentation of synaptic transmission by temporally close neural events, such as successive postsynaptic conductance changes and the resulting postsynaptic potentials (PSPs). *Spatial summation* represents any augmentation of synaptic transmission by spatially close neural events. Physiologically speaking, both temporal and spatial summation may be influenced by (1) the time constant of the cell membrane, (2) the duration of postsynaptic potentials resulting from different transmitter-induced conductance changes, (3) changes in the input resistance of the cell, including that at the peak of the action potential effects, and (4) by the numbers of different axons that converge upon a neuron as well as by where along the dendritic processes of the neuron these axons terminate. The effects are manifest in terms of the cable properties of the postsynaptic cell [805-807] described in Chapter 4.

Simple Inhibitory Adaptations

Simple inhibitory adaptations are the counterpart of the facilitatory adaptations described above. They, too, arise de novo out of preexisting connections and functions of the neural network [781]. Simple inhibition is equivalent to the *external inhibition* of Pavlov in that the adaptations are produced by simple, single stimuli, are transient, and result in the suppression of reflex outcomes.

> Pavlov trained a dog to perform a conditioned salivatory response using a bell as the conditional stimulus (CS) and food as the unconditional stimulus (US). After stable conditioning had occurred, he found that presenting certain novel stimuli other than the CS concurrently with the CS could inhibit performance of the conditioned response to the original CS for short periods of time. The performance of unconditioned responses to a US could also be suppressed by such means [759].

The results indicate that reflex-suppressive adaptations can be produced by single presentations of certain novel stimuli. The effect represents an innate, inhibitory adaptive response of the nervous system to these stimulus inputs.

While most of Pavlov's terminologies were devised remarkably shrewdly despite his lack of our present day neurophysiologic understandings, the term external inhibition was not. It incorrectly implied an external effect of the stimulus rather than an internal prepotential of the reflex substrate. Although his terminologies have been maintained where possible, they have been revised to fit more recent developments, where necessary, in the expositions that follow.

That either simple facilitation or simple inhibition may involve reciprocal reflex pathways is quite clear. With simple inhibition, the suppression of the conditioned reflex (CR) or unconditioned reflex (UR) is frequently accompanied by production of an investigatory response. This represents inhibition with reciprocal facilitation of another motor response. Thus, one reflex pathway is facilitated while another is suppressed. Which response is facilitated or inhibited depends on the locus of the adaptations. This, in turn, depends on the physical characteristics of the applied stimulus. Usually, simple facilitation and inhibition occur rapidly, act reciprocally, and are of brief duration. As a result, the possibility is suggested that many adaptations of this type* arise from summatory occlusion or facilitation among reciprocally linked neural populations.

---

*Exceptions are those adaptations, such as imprinting, which are also preestablished genetically. They are triggered by a particular (though not necessarily simple) stimulus, and probably involve more substantial cellular adaptations.

A variant of simple adaptation is found that is persistent. This variant was termed *permanent external inhibition* by Pavlov. In this instance, presentation of the novel stimulus leads to a long-term, and presumably more substantial, neural adaptation supporting a persistent suppression of reflex behavior. An example would be "gun shyness" following a single exposure to the loud sound of a gunshot. One can argue, however, that this is a compound adaptation, resulting from the combination of auditory and nociceptive manifestations of a single stimulus.

Other examples of relatively persistent reflex facilitation arising from single stimulus presentation can be found, as in the phenomenon of sensitization. Sensitization involves a more substantial adaptation than temporal or spatial summation and probably involves a physical change in the presynaptic terminals of neurons called presynaptic facilitation (see Chapters 4 and 5). A behavioral description of this phenomenon may be found later in this chapter.*

Compound Reflex Adaptations

Compound reflex adaptations are defined herein as adaptations arising from compound features of stimulus presentation such as the frequency at which a stimulus is presented repetitively, the physical differences between two presented stimuli, or the temporal relationship within which two different stimuli are presented. Whereas a single application of a stimulus usually suffices to initiate cellular processes leading to simple facilitation or inhibition, compound adaptations require multiple or otherwise complex applications of stimuli. They are categorized in the present taxonomy according to whether they are induced by repetitive or associative stimulus presentation (Table 2.2).

The differences between simple and compound adaptation result from differences in cellular processes that mediate the reflex effects. Not only are the processes induced differently (e.g., by repeated or associated versus single stimuli), but many cellular changes supporting compound adaptation appear to be more substantial and endure longer than those supporting simple adaptation.

Returning briefly to the earlier discussion of analysis of sensory inputs and synthesis of motor outputs, it is not conclusively established which of the simple and compound cellular adaptations primarily affect reception of the stimulus and which affect production of the motor response. However, some evidence suggesting that certain repetitively induced adaptations inhibit the production of motor responses is provided in the following descriptions.

---

*Further justification for classifying sensitization as a simple adaptation and distinguishing it from reflex dominance and pseudoconditioning is found in that sensitization arises nonassociatively and nonrepetitively, and often exhibits a broad generalization gradient, being initiated nonspecifically by a variety of stimuli.

Table 2.2. A Guide to the Simple, Repetitively Induced, and Associatively Induced Neural Adaptations

	Facilitatory	*Inhibitory*
Simple	Orienting Alerting	Arrest
	Imprinting[b]	
	Sensitization	
Repetitive[a]	*(CS repeated)*	
		Extinction, Latent Inhibition Differentiated inhibition Conditioned inhibition Inhibition-produced delay
	(US repeated)	
	Reflex dominance[c] Pseudoconditioning	Habituation Habituatory adaptation
Associative[a]	Conditioning[b] Sensory preconditioning[b] Second-order conditioning[b]	

[a] (Compound)
[b] (may be facilitatory or inhibitory)
[c] (or latent inhibition)

Repetitively Induced Inhibitory Adaptations

Adaptations of the repetitively induced type were among the earliest recognized reflex changes. Although both facilitatory and inhibitory adaptations could be induced by repeated stimulation, the usual reflex outcome was inhibitory, resulting in the suppression of motor responses. The first characterization of compound inhibitory reflex operations in the central nervous system was made by Pavlov [759]. He observed that every extraneous stimulus that fell upon the cerebral hemispheres and remained without any further consequence to the animal, *if repeated,* caused the spontaneous development of a cortical* inhibition. Thus, *repetition changed the reflex effect of presenting a stimulus from facilitation to suppression.* Evidently, the neural adaptations supporting reflex suppression were initiated by the repetitive aspect of the stimulation.

"In many . . . experiments," said Pavlov [759], "the positive alimentary conditioned reflexes diminish . . .This diminution is due to the repetition of the conditional stimulus and not to any other factor."

*The role of the cortex was inferred rather than experimentally confirmed.

This is a remarkable observation, for it implies a specific neural consequence of a specific parameter of stimulus presentation. If repetition is critical, then some kind of temporal contiguity of the neural effects of stimulation must be required for these adaptations to occur. Storage or feedback within the nervous system must provide a time delay to permit contiguity between stimuli presented at different times.

Four types of repetitively induced inhibition were identified by Pavlov: (1) *extinction,* (2) *differentiated inhibition,* (3) *conditioned inhibition,* and (4) *inhibition-produced delay.* They are summarized in Table 2.3 and will each be discussed after a few introductory remarks concerning the stimuli used to produce them.

Their common feature is that all result from repeatedly presenting a CS or a CS-like stimulus. The latter may be a *neutral stimulus* (NS) not previously paired with the CS or US or a *discriminative stimulus* (DS) paired with CS and US (either nonassociatively or following US presentations). The inhibitory effects of presenting such stimuli repetitively are readily observed upon attempted elicitation of a conditioned response previously elicited by the stimulus.

Pavlov measured the reflex suppression resulting from repetitively induced inhibition in the context of a previously acquired conditioned response and thought that prior conditioning was necessary for these forms of inhibition to be manifest. However, more recent studies have shown that this inhibition develops irrespective of previous conditioning. It is latent, awaiting usage of the repeated stimulus as a CS in conditioning or some other associative context. Then, the acquisition of the conditioned response is retarded. Thus, it is repetition* of the stimulus (not previous conditioning) that is essential for the development of this form of inhibition.

Two other types of compound inhibition—*habituation* and *habituatory adaptation*—can also be distinguished. They arise from repeated presentation of a US rather than a CS and their inhibitory effects can be observed directly as they suppress production of the unconditioned response. Usually, CSs are distinguished from USs in that the latter produce overt peripheral motor responses. However, this distinction is not very reliable. As noted earlier, some weak stimuli that serve quite well as CSs produce weak motor responses initially that are supplanted by stronger responses after conditioning. Conversely, some stimuli (such as electrical stimuli delivered directly to the brain) can serve as effective USs even though overt peripheral responses are not observed. Clearly, a physiologic analysis is needed to distinguish the significant differences between the consequences of these stimuli on neural adaptation (i.e., the salient features involved in their repetitive and associative interactions). Again, one must bear in mind that it is not the stimuli alone that produce learning, but rather the prepotential of neural elements to adapt to specific stimuli and to specific patterns of stimulation. Nonetheless, one notes

---

*The frequency of repetition may be critical, slow frequencies sometimes resulting in facilitation (e.g., reflex dominance) rather than inhibition.

Table 2.3. Pavlov's Forms of Compound Inhibition

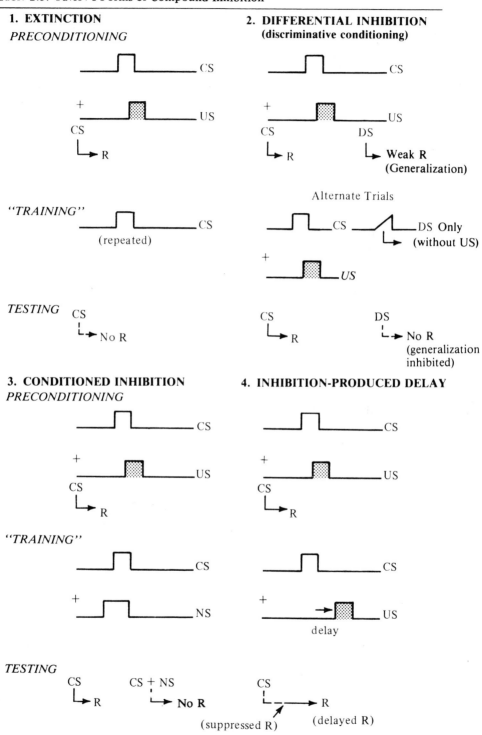

1. **EXTINCTION**

PRECONDITIONING

CS

+
CS
US
R

"TRAINING"

CS
(repeated)

TESTING CS
No R

2. **DIFFERENTIAL INHIBITION**
   (discriminative conditioning)

CS

+
CS   DS
US
R   Weak R
         (Generalization)

Alternate Trials

CS   DS Only
         (without US)

+
US

CS   DS
R   No R
         (generalization
         inhibited)

3. **CONDITIONED INHIBITION**
PRECONDITIONING

CS

+
CS
US
R

"TRAINING"

CS

+
NS

4. **INHIBITION-PRODUCED DELAY**

CS

+
CS
US
R

CS

+
US
delay

TESTING
CS   CS + NS   CS
R   No R   R
          (suppressed R)   (delayed R)

that stimuli such as CSs and USs, when presented repetitively, frequently produce inhibitory effects in addition to whatever effects result from their associative presentation with other stimuli. The latter are important and may overshadow the inhibitory effects, sometimes even producing facilitation (see p. 33). They may arise from unappreciated compound features of the US (e.g., it produces a motor response *and* is noxious).

Accordingly, whereas the similarities in response suppression among the four types of compound inhibition described by Pavlov arise from the common feature of repetitive stimulus presentation, their differences, described below, arise from different associative contingencies among the paradigms such as those illustrated in Table 2.4.

> As will be seen, it may be exceedingly difficult to distinguish exactly which of the different types of adaptation occur and are responsible for the overt reflex outcomes without performing the appropriate cellular studies. Yet some taxonomy of simple learned behavior is required, even before such studies are performed, in order to provide some basis for an orderly discussion of the subject. As this Sisyphean task is pursued (over the next 16 pages), the reader's tolerance is sought.

Extinction and Latent Inhibition. Extinction involves the suppression of an established (learned or conditioned) motor response to a CS. After Pavlov's dog learned to salivate at the sound of the bell, repeated presentation of the bell-CS in the absence of food as US led to the disappearance of the conditioned salivatory response. Repetitive presentation of a CS, without reinforcement, typically produces this effect. When this is done prior to the establishment of a conditioned response, *latent inhibition* occurs and subsequent development of a CR is retarded when the CS is used later as part of an associative pair [629,630]. The inhibition is latent, awaiting the acquisition or training period for the suppression of response performance to be manifest.

There is no evidence that the neural adaptations supporting latent inhibition differ from those supporting extinction. The possibility that extinction arises associatively from a negative correlation between CS and US, as has been postulated for other forms of compound inhibition [820], seems unlikely since it occurs in the (uncorrelated) absence of presenting the US. Here, the correlation coefficient is not -1, as it would be if the US were being presented steadily except at the time when the CS was delivered, but is effectively 0.

Extinction appears to be an active process, counteracting rather than erasing the effect of conditioning. Although there is reduced electrical excitability of the motor cortex during extinction [1003,1064,1125] and other forms of compound inhibition [107,109], the increased excitability of neurons of the motor cortex that supports conditioning has been shown to persist through extinction, together with learning savings of the conditioned response [110,111]. Thus, extinction involves separate adaptations. After cessation of the extinction procedure, CRs that have been fully established initially may return spontaneously, sometimes even to their full strength [759]. The return may be hastened by presenting single stimuli that facilitate conditioning or inhibit extinction, such as the loud noise in Pavlov's experi-

Table 2.4. Associative Aspects of Conditioned Inhibition[a]

I. THESE ASSOCIATIONS EASILY PRODUCE CONDITIONED INHIBITION.

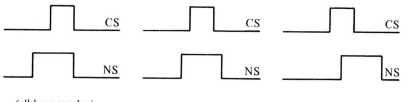

(all have overlap)

II. THIS ASSOCIATION PRODUCES CONDITIONED INHIBITION WITH DIFFICULTY (MANY PAIRINGS REQUIRED).

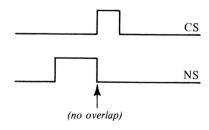

(no overlap)

III. THIS ASSOCIATION HAS NO EFFECT (OTHER THAN LATENT INHIBITION).

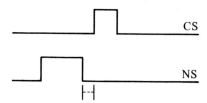

< *10 sec* (in some cases a shorter interstimulus interval can effectively produce second-order conditioning)

IV. THIS ASSOCIATION USUALLY PRODUCES SECOND-ORDER CONDITIONING.

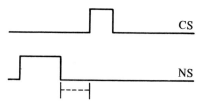

≥ *10 sec* (according to Pavlov's classical experiments [759], but see Fig. 3.13 on sensory preconditioning)

[a]All of the above associations are done *after* the animal has learned a conditioned response to the CS.

ments in which the salivatory response to the bell was extinguished. This restoration of an extinguished reflex was termed "disinhibition" by Pavlov. The recovery of some conditioned reflexes after extinction may require further presentations of reinforcing or associative stimuli.

Experimentally, extinction weakens not only the particular CR that was directly subjected to extinction (primary extinction), but also other conditioned reflexes (secondary extinction). Secondary extinction can involve CRs that were based on a different unconditioned reflex (heterogeneous CRs) as well as those that were based on an unconditioned reflex common with the primary extinguished reflex (homogenous CRs). Thus, there is generalization of the inhibitory effects of extinction.

The maintained effect of conditioning subsequent to extinction is termed a *learning savings* because the conditioned behavior is only temporarily suppressed rather than being permanently erased. Extinction itself has learning savings, its first establishment taking more time than any succeeding establishment. Both types of learning savings are illustrated in Fig. 2.6.

Differentiated Inhibition (Discriminative Conditioning). Pavlov's second type of repetitively induced inhibition, *differentiated inhibition*, is characterized by the suppression of a generalized response to a discriminative stimulus (DS). First, conditioning is accomplished by pairing a CS with a US in the usual manner. The CS eventually comes to evoke a CR. Then, the generalized response is determined to a second stimulus, the DS, which was never paired with the US. Next, the animal is given alternate trials of CS-US pairing and of DS presentation alone (Table 2.3). Thereafter, the generalized response to the DS is suppressed.

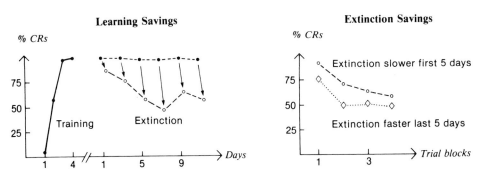

Fig. 2.6. *Learning savings of conditioning and extinction. Left: Rabbits were trained to perform a conditioned nictitating membrane response. Then conditioning (CS-US) was alternated with extinction (CS alone) as indicated by the arrows. There is recovery of the CR after extinction (learning savings of conditioning) as well as a steady progression of the extinction effect (extinction savings). Right: Data from 4 successive blocks of 20 trials, shown separately for first five and last five days. Extinction savings were manifest by a reduced level of CR performance over the last five days and an increased rapidity of extinction between block 1 and 2 over the last five days. (Smith and Gormezano [914].)*

In this form, differentiated inhibition resembles the outcome of *discriminative conditioning.* There, the CS, US, and DS are presented in consecutive order; on each trial the CS precedes the US, and the DS succeeds the US.* There, too, a conditioned response to the CS develops, but any response that occurred initially to the DS is suppressed. This inhibition of response to the DS that occurs with differentiated inhibition or discriminative conditioning is indistinguishable from that of extinction and latent inhibition and is attributable to repetitive presentation of the DS.

The other features of discriminative conditioning such as the reduction of some conditioned responses and enhancement of others, relative to those learned without discriminative training, derive from associative parameters of the presented stimuli (Chapter 3). Pavlov noted that presentation of the DS just prior to CS-US presentation might potentiate the response to the CS (he called this positive induction). However, careful examination of Pavlov's report [759] reveals great variability in the occurrence of these phenomena, indicating that the associative processes are more complicated than might be thought. As shown later in Table 2.9, quite different outcomes can result from small differences in the orders and intervals of stimulus presentation as well as in their relative intensities and durations. Corresponding differences in the induction of the underlying neural adaptations may be expected to occur.

Conditioned Inhibition. The third type of repetitively induced inhibition, *conditioned inhibition,* results in suppression of a conditioned response to a NS-CS pair but not to the CS alone. It also differs from extinction in that stimuli inducing the effect are presented associatively as well as repetitively (Tables 2.3, 2.4). One stimulus is the CS. The other is called the "neutral" stimulus (NS), though in order to induce conditioned inhibition, this stimulus may actually elicit some antagonistic or inhibitory response. Taking Pavlov's conditioned dog once again as an example, repeated† presentation of a loud sound at the time of presentation of the bell CS leads to temporary suppression of the conditioned salivatory response. The suppression of response represents a conditioned inhibition.

Typically, presentation of the NS is begun a few seconds before giving the CS and is continued so that it overlaps presentation of the CS. This is done repetitively, without other reinforcement. Thereafter, although the conditioned response is suppressed consistently when the stimuli are presented together, it still occurs when the CS is presented alone.

Pavlov provides a further characterization of the associative parameters required for certain forms of conditioned inhibition to occur. As stated above, the neutral stimulus should begin before the CS and overlap it. If the two stimuli never coincide, the development of conditioned inhibition is

---

*Or the DS may be presented "randomly."

†The question arises whether conditioned inhibition is repetitively or associatively induced. Also, single stimuli may produce analogous effects (see simple inhibitory adaptations and "external" inhibition). The present taxonomy classifies conditioned inhibition as a repetitively induced, inhibitory adaptation because repeated presentation of the NS-CS pair appears to be the key feature in its development.

difficult and may be accompanied by restlessness and various defense reactions of the animal. If, finally, a pause of several seconds is introduced between the termination of the neutral stimulus and the beginning of the CS, no inhibition develops at all. An even more contrary effect is seen in most cases when this pause reaches a duration of about 10 seconds. The additional stimulus itself acquires the properties of the CS, and a second order, facilitatory conditioned reflex develops. However, with very intense neutral stimuli, such as a motor car horn, the pause can be increased to as much as 20 seconds and a conditioned inhibition will still develop [759].

These parametric features are summarized in Table 2.4.

Inhibition-Produced Delay. The fourth type of compound inhibition is *inhibition-produced delay*. We will again use Pavlovian conditioning as an example. Normally, since food is given promptly upon ringing the bell, the conditioned salivatory response occurs promptly when the bell is presented alone. If, however, presentation of the food US is gradually delayed for seconds or even minutes after the bell is rung, a corresponding delay ensues in performance of the conditioned salivatory response to the bell alone [759]. This lengthening of CR latency, as it is called, is attributed to an inhibition that delays performance of the CR. In fact, the inhibition suppresses performance of early, short latency CRs, and in their absence longer latency CRs are manifest. Hence, the delay reflects inhibition followed by the appearance of a separate motor response.

Again, repetitive stimulus presentation controls development of the inhibition. Interestingly, the lengthening time interval between CS and US, which occurs repeatedly during the trials of CS-US pairing, appears to influence this type of compound inhibition. The immediate absence of the US permits extinction of the short latency response to the CS, while its later presentation leads to development of the longer latency CR. Conditioning with a long interstimulus interval is not very efficient (Fig. 3.9), and, as might be expected, the rate of formation of a delayed conditioned reflex is variable. In fact, in most animals, it is difficult to develop a delayed reflex without first establishing the corresponding simultaneous conditioned reflex.

That a repeated time interval can constitute an effective stimulus for producing a repetitively or associatively induced adaptation has been established by Pavlov [759] and confirmed by later Soviet researchers [540]. Their experiments showed that, with slow, repetitive presentation of a stimulus eliciting a motor response, it was possible to see a similar response performed at times when stimulus presentation was omitted. This effect is called "time conditioning" in the Soviet literature.

Inhibition-produced delay, then, results in suppression of the performance of a conditioned response for a period of time. The delay period can range from milliseconds [341] to minutes [759]. The likelihood that the originally facilitated reflex process remains intact during the delay period is supported by the observation that if another novel stimulus is presented during the inactive delay period, a motor reaction analogous to the conditioned response can be produced.

Pavlov's original "inhibition of delay" represents a specific variation on this general theme. Pavlov distinguished between "simultaneous" and "delayed" conditioned reflexes. In conditioned reflexes in which the interval between CS and US presentation was short, say 1 to 5 seconds, the CR almost immediately followed the beginning of the CS. In contrast, in reflexes with a longer CS-US interval, the onset of the CR following CS presentation was delayed. The delay was proportional to the CS-US interval and could last several minutes [759].

In summary, repetitive presentation of a stimulus often leads to the induction of inhibitory adaptation akin to that found with extinction and latent inhibition. The additional types of inhibition described by Pavlov also depend on this parameter and differ only in additionally associatively induced features which modify other aspects of their reflex outcomes.

Habituation. The two types of compound inhibition arising from repetitive presentation of a US are habituation and habituatory adaptation. *Habituation* involves a decrease in the magnitude and frequency of a response following repetitive presentation of a single stimulus. The stimulus has the characteristics of a US and normally elicits a peripheral motor response. For example, in the intact mammal, an eye blink is the usual unconditioned response to a tap on the glabella, the bridge of the nose. As the tap stimulus is presented repetitively, at frequencies exceeding one per second, the eye blink habituates readily and visibly; that is, the blink response decreases in frequency or fidelity of following the stimulus as well as in strength or amplitude. Interestingly, this response may not habituate in humans suffering from Parkinson's disease [202].

Thompson and Spencer [1018] have characterized nine phenomenologic features or outcomes of habituation:

1. *Response decrement*—as described above.
2. *Response restoration*—which occurs spontaneously a variable time after cessation of repetitive stimulation.
3. *Dishabituation of habituation*—the response decrement of habituation is interrupted by presentation of a novel stimulus.
4. *Habituation of dishabituatory stimuli*—habituation of this latter effect occurs when the novel stimuli are presented repetitively.
5. *Greater habituation with weak than with strong stimuli.*
6. *Greater habituation with short than with long stimulus intervals.*
7. *Generalization of habituation to other stimuli.*
8. *Prolongation of recovery to repeated stimulation* as the number of repetitions increases, even after decrement has abolished the response.
9. *More rapid decrement with repeated periods of habituation and rest.*

Many of these features appear to be served by cellular mechanisms that alter the efficacy of synaptic transmission at the level of subcortical motoneurons or interneurons. This conclusion is supported by investigations in cat and frog spinal cord (Farel et al. [279] ; Spencer and Thompson [931-933]), in peripheral ganglia of invertebrate mollusks (cf. Kandel and colleagues in *Aplysia* ganglia [480,484]), and in the crayfish (cf. Kennedy and colleagues [509] ; Krasne [551], where neurons at primary afferent levels are also shown to be involved). Most of the cellular changes are thought to occur directly at presynaptic terminals (see Chapters 4 and 5).

Habituatory Adaptation. Some investigators distinguish another phenomenon resulting from repeated presentation of an unpaired US. This phenomenon has been called adaptation, but should be termed *habituatory adaptation,* or *H-adaptation*, to avoid confusion with physiologic terminology. If one introduces a series of trials of repetitive US presentation alone before conditioning, the rate of CR acquisition indicated by the percent CR performance per unit of training may thereafter be reduced (Fig. 2.7). This represents habituatory adaptation, and the inhibitory effect of H-adaptation persists well into the conditioning-training period.

With H-adaptation as with habituation, response strength and frequency diminish. However, H-adaptation resembles latent inhibition in that a period elapses between the stimulus presentations and the response diminution. This differs from habituation, in which stimulation is concurrent with the reduction of motor response. Another difference between habituation and H-adaptation is the relative persistence of the effects seen with H-adaptation.

Two other examples of behavioral adaptation are given by Kimble [519] :

MacDonald [637] ... conditioned the eyelid reflex and finger retraction in human subjects with and without a series of 50 prior adaptation trials with the US airpuff or shock for the two different procedures. By comparison with control groups which received no adaptation trials, she found that the effect of the adaptation trials was to reduce the [mean] number of conditioned responses from 27.7 to 6.0 in the case of the eye blink, and 27.1 to 10.0 in the finger retraction experiment.

Taylor [1002], using three adaptation groups and a control group in an eyelid conditioning experiment, studied the effectiveness of different US intensities during 50 adaptation trials. The higher the intensity of the US during adaptation, the lower the percentage of CR in 50 subsequent conditioning trials.

The difference between habituation and H-adaptation in the persistence of effect need not mean that the two processes have completely dissimilar underlying mechanisms. Some types of habituation are long-lasting [146,151, 480]. Moreover, both habituation and H-adaptation occur after presentation of a US, a stimulus that ordinarily elicits an observable motor response. The same mechanisms supporting some of the nine phenomenologic features of habituation described by Thompson and Spencer may also support aspects of H-adaptation (Table 2.5). Presumably, however, the mechanisms that support the transient changes are different from those that support the persistent neural changes.

Effects of H-Adaptation

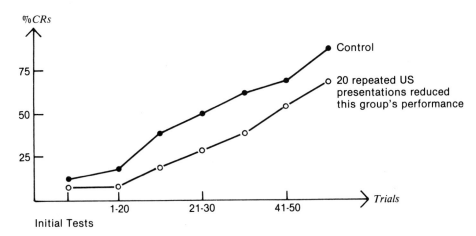

Fig. 2.7. Rate of eyelid conditioning without H-adaptation trials (control) compared with that after 20 H-adaptation trials (○). US presentations were given during initial test trials. The CS was a light; the US was an air puff. (Kimble and Dufort [520].)

Extinction and latent inhibition are analogous to habituation and H-adaptation in that they also depend on repetitive processes for their development. They differ, however, in that they are typically evoked by presentation of a CS rather than a US as summarized in Table 2.6.

In terms of persistence of effect, extinction and latent inhibition are usually closer to H-adaptation than to habituation* (Table 2.7).

Receptor Adaptation and Fatigue. Receptor adaptation as well as diminution of response as a function of simple fatigue also occur after presenting repetitive stimuli but should be separated from the phenomena discussed above. *Receptor adaptation* involves changes in the input-output transfer function through a receptor element and is generally transient rather than persistent. As a cellular effect, it occurs, by definition, at the specialized sensory endings of the nervous system. Mechanisms of adaptation may depend on the compliant properties of the specialized tissue surrounding the neural ending (as with the capsule of the Pacinian corpuscle) or on changes in ionic conductances (e.g., Na^+, Cl^-, K^+, or Ca^{2+}) that influence the ability of the neural element to reach firing threshold from its resting state. Simple *fatigue* is usually thought of as a motor phenomenon in which there is a reduction in response performance. Commonly, it is attributed to a buildup of metabolites or to the exhaustion of available chemical energy supplies that can influence muscle contraction. More complex forms of fatigue can affect the operation of the central nervous system, but their details are poorly understood.

*Except in mollusks, where long lasting habituation is seen.

Table 2.5. *Possible*[a] Differences Between Habituation, Habituatory Adaptation, Extinction, Latent Inhibition, Reflex Dominance, and Pseudoconditioning[b]

	Habit	H-Adapt	Ext.	Lat. Inhib.	Ref. Dom.	Pseudocond.
1. Response decrement/inhibition	++	++	++	++	(facilitation)	(facilitation)
2. Spontaneous restoration of response	++	(+)	+	+	–	–
3. Dishabituation	++	?	++	?	?	?
4. Habituation of dishabituation	++	?	+	?	?	?
5. Strong stimulus more effective than weak stimulus	++	+	++	+	++	++
6. Short stimulus more effective than long stimulus	++	?	?	?	+	?
7. Effect generalizes to other stimuli	++	++	++	++	++	++
8. Prolonged recovery with repeated stimuli	++	++	++	++	?	?
9. More rapid response decrement with repeated habituation	++	?	++	?	?	?
10. Effect is typically shortlasting	++	0	0/+	0	(+)	(+)
11. Effect typically develops rapidly	++	0	0/+	0	+	+

[a]A comparison of features of habituation with those of other forms of adaptation is desirable but, at best, conjectural. The ambiguities herein reflect a scant literature and the limitation of other-than-cellular taxonomies. A taxonomy based on cellular considerations occurs later (Table 4.3).

[b]Shows effect very strongly ++, strongly +, weakly (+), not at all 0, inconsistently 0/+, not known?, doesn't apply –.

Table 2.6. Adaptations of the Repetitive Inhibitory Type

	US	CS
Stimuli given before response established by training	Habituatory adaptation	Latent inhibition
Stimuli given with response established	Habituation	Extinction

Repetitively Induced Facilitatory Adaptations

Facilitatory reflex adaptations may also result from repetitive stimulus presentation. Two types are recognized: (1) the reflex dominance of Ukhtomsky or latent facilitation and (2) pseudoconditioning. Both characteristically appear after repeated presentation of a "strong" stimulus like a US, which produces an overt motor response, but they can also be seen after presentations of CS-like stimuli or even weak, direct electrical stimulation of the brain [231].

It is unclear if these adaptations produce only direct reflex facilitation or if the facilitation reflects the suppression of reflex inhibition. Available evidence suggests that facilitatory neural adaptations occur in combination with separate inhibitory adaptations [107-111,1108,1110]. Why slow repetition of some stimuli leads to latent facilitation, whereas repetitive presentation of other stimuli (at comparable rates) leads to latent inhibition is not presently known. This curious inconsistency only serves to support the remarks made earlier concerning the limitations of descriptive (as opposed to systems analytic) taxonomies of adaptive reflex operations and to reinforce our pursuit of the cellular and molecular basis of these processes. Latent substrates from earlier reflex adaptations could play a key role in the development of these disparate effects. If this were the case, or if the repetition took on the character of a second-order stimulus, the facilitatory effect might arise as a latent, associative adaptation. Otherwise, different stimuli would presumably address two characteristically different pathways, each containing different neurochemicals that would be activated by repetitive stimulation and produce facilitation or inhibition, respectively.

Reflex Dominance. Ukhtomsky's [1030] phenomenon of *reflex dominance* occurs after repetitive stimulation of motor pathways and results in facilitation of a specific motor response. This conclusion can be drawn from Ukhtomsky's observation that a reaction which is repeatedly elicited by a strong stimulus (i.e., a US) may become dominant over other reactions so that it is elicitable by a much wider range of stimuli than is normally the case. Recent studies [111,651,1109] show that repeated presentation of a US such as glabella tap results in an increased excitability of neurons along the pathway between the motor cortex and the musculature involved in producing the unconditioned motor response. These excitability changes appear to support the latent facilitation responsible for reflex dominance.

Table 2.7. Features of Some Simple and Repetitively Induced Adaptations

	Single (S) or Compound (C) Stimulus	Learning Savings	Requires Rapid (R) or Slow (S) frequency of repetition	*Persistence*		
				Brief	Intermediate	Permanent
Simple Adaptation						
Facilitatory						
Alerting-orienting	S	No		+		
Sensitization	S	No		+		
Inhibitory						
Arrest	S	No		+		
(Reciprocal inhibition)						
Imprinting	S	Yes				+
Repetitively induced adaptation						
Inhibitory						
Extinction, latent inhibition	C[a]	Yes	S		+	
(other variations depend on associative factors)						
Habituation			R	+	(+)	
H-Adaptation			S		+	
Facilitatory						
Reflex dominance[b]	C[a]	Yes	S		+	
Pseudoconditioning			S		+	

[a] (repetitive)
[b] (equivalent to latent facilitation)

Pseudoconditioning. As defined behaviorally, *pseudoconditioning* involves the "strengthening of a response to a previously neutral stimulus through the repeated elicitation of the response by another stimulus without paired presentation of the two stimuli" [cf. 359,519,1016]. Grether [359] produced pseudoconditioning by the following procedure. The experimental animal was first presented with a weak sound which failed to produce a response. Then the animal was exposed to a loud sound, a gunshot, which elicited a startle response, including eye blinking. Subsequently, presentation of the weak sound elicited an eye blink response.

It is not known if pseudoconditioning differs in any substantial way from reflex dominance. The same types of adaptations may be involved with pseudoconditioning as with reflex dominance. After repeatedly presenting the glabella tap US described above [107,108,110,111], *electrical* stimulation of single neurons of the motor cortex was more effective than before in producing motor activity in the musculature supporting production of the unconditioned response. However, no CRs to click CS followed similar presentations of glabella tap. In this instance, then, "behavioral" pseudoconditioning did not occur but reflex dominance did, and the absence of "behavioral" pseudoconditioning depended solely on the type and location of the stimulus used to elicit the pseudoconditioned response.

Pseudoconditioning does differ from simple facilitation and sensitization in that it is more persistent and may be more specific. Sensitized responses are elicited by very many stimuli, whereas pseudoconditioned responses seem to be elicited by a narrower range of stimuli. Pseudoconditioning still does not show the specificity of elicitation shown by the associatively conditioned responses, much less the greater specificity of the discriminatively conditioned responses. Usually, pseudoconditioning requires many repetitive presentations for its development; although, as Grether's original description suggests, certain stimuli that serve as USs with conditioning can produce pseudoconditioning upon a single presentation (cf. Kimble [519]). More typically, however, increasing numbers of presentations produce increasing amounts of measurable pseudoconditioning effects.

These effects may be as robust as those of conditioning (see Table 2.8). Kimble [519] reports that

> 10, 20, or 30 shock trials produced increasing amounts of pseudoconditioning in cats, with the function reaching a plateau after 20 trials (Harlow and Toltzein [384]). In this study, tests were delayed for 5 min., 3 hours, or 24 hours after the shock trials. Pseudoconditioning occurred to about the same degree in each of these conditions.

In summary, repetitive presentation of stimuli, either CSs or USs, commonly leads to inhibitory reflex effects. At slow rates of repetition, facilitatory effects can also occur as indicated in Table 2.7.

The tendency of repetitive presentation of a CS to produce inhibitory adaptations leading to reflex suppression is further supported by experi-

Table 2.8. Percentage of Responses to Tone Following Various Training Procedures

Paradigm	Extinction Trials					
	1	2	3-4	5-6	7-8	9-10
Forward Conditioning	90.0	70.0	60.0	35.0	30.0	35.0
Backward Conditioning	84.6	46.1	30.7	23.0	26.8	23.0
Random Presentation	44.4	33.3	22.2	16.6	22.2	22.2
Pseudoconditioning[b]	100.0	80.0	30.0	10.0	20.0	10.0

[a]From Harris [386] in Kimble [519].
[b]The highest percentage of responses was found in the groups given pseudoconditioning. These responses were also the most easily extinguished.

ments of Kimble and colleagues (Fig. 2.8) in which *omission* of the repetitive CS in the course of conditioning facilitated acquisition and retention of the conditioned response.

These effects were not replicated in still different experiments in which presentations of the CS were given before training was begun [972]. There was a separation between the performance of this group and that of a group given repeated US presentations prior to training. The *latter* showed slightly retarded acquisition of the CR (Fig. 2.9). However, the animals given CS did show lower response levels in the pretraining period.

Another effect noted in this study was an increased rate of extinction in the group given CSs. Thus, some inhibitory effects were seen in the group given repeated presentations of the CS. Other experiments described later in Fig. 2.10, in which the effects of CS presentation were tested during the course of repeated CS-US trials, confirm the inhibitory effects disclosed in Fig. 2.8. The response to the US is greater if the CS is omitted. The onset and duration of persistence of different repetitively induced adaptations also vary. Some are quite transient; others are nearly as prolonged as associatively induced adaptations.

Three conclusions may be drawn from studies of this type made at both behavioral and physiologic levels. They are that (1) the behavioral methods for measuring adaptations are often too imprecise to be adequate, (2) cellular methods of measuring adaptive effects promise greater precision, and (3) taxonomies based on behavioral results should be revised as cellular results yield further insight into the physical phenomena underlying behavioral changes. While little can be done at present beyond separating the simple, repetitively induced, and associatively induced adaptations, this may be preferable to less accurate alternatives.

Associatively Induced Adaptations

The other types of compound adaptations are associatively induced, arising from temporal associations between different stimuli. Although many presentations of the associated stimuli are usually required to induce these adaptations, some adaptations such as those supporting conditioned taste aversion

Omitting CS Facilitates Acquisition and Retention of the CR

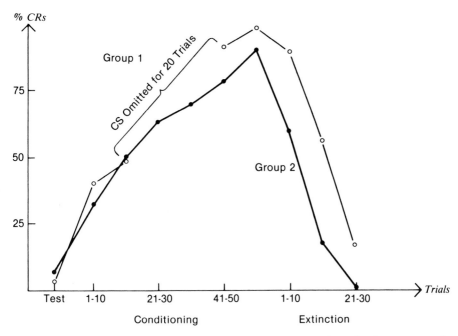

Fig. 2.8. Effect of omitting CS on learning and extinction curves. Both groups received trials in which CS and US were paired. In group 1, the CS was omitted on Trials 21-40. (Kimble, Mann, and Dufort [521].) These results could not be replicated in some other experiments [338].

[316-318], may be induced by one or two pairings. The common associatively induced reflex adaptations such as conditioning, sensory preconditioning, and second-order conditioning are described behaviorally at the end of this chapter. What information is available at the reflex or cellular levels concerning these adaptive processes can be found in Chapters 3-5.

The associative processes are complex, and it is likely that more than one adaptation arises to support the different behavioral outcomes. Consider, for instance, the degree to which reflex suppression resulting from repetitively induced inhibition can be modified associatively. In the experiments outlined in Table 2.9, all groups received presentation of CS_1, CS_2, and US on alternate training trials. On the other trials Group 1 received CS_1, US; Group 2 received neither CS nor US; and Group 3 received CS_1 alone.

The results suggest that the repetitive inhibition from repeatedly presenting CS_1 alone was counteracted by associating it with presentation of the US. This association had an inverse effect on the response to CS_2; it was suppressed.

If these experiments are performed slightly differently, with a series of trials of CS_2, CS_1, US and a series of trials of CS_1, US (see Table 2.4 and

Effects of Pre-Training Presentations of CS or US

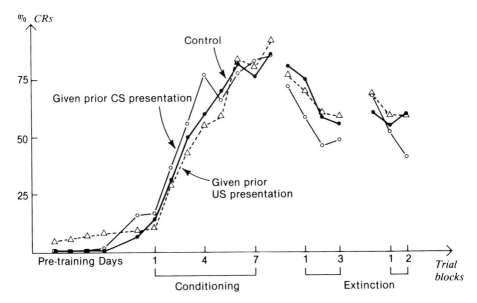

Fig. 2.9. Acquisition of nictitating membrane CR in rabbits after pretraining exposure to repeated presentations of (i) CS alone, (ii) US alone, and (iii) nothing (○). Animals that received the CS alone had lower response levels in the pretraining and extinction period than animals receiving US alone, but had slightly higher * response levels during the acquisition training period in which all animals received CS followed by US. During pretraining, groups i and ii received 70 stimulus repetitions per day. During training, each group received 210 CS presentations per day. (Suboski et al. [972].)

Fig. 2.13), then a second-order conditioned response to CS_2 develops in addition to the conditioned response to CS_1. In that case, associative conditioning has overshadowed the repetitive inhibition of presenting both CS_2 and CS_1. Clearly, the order and timing of stimulus presentations are important. Much of Chapter 3 is devoted to further discussion of this point.

Generalization as a Means for Distinguishing Altered Sensory Reception from Altered Motor Performance

One way to penetrate this complexity might be to distinguish adaptations that altered sensory reception from those that altered motor performance. Despite the interdependence of reception and performance (adaptations that alter one may affect the other), some of these effects could potentially be

---

*It was not possible to demonstrate statistical significance conclusively on an interval scale. The lack of larger differences may itself be of significance.

Table 2.9. Complex Outcomes of Associative Pairing[a]

	Group I	Group II	Group III
Training:	CS_1	CS_1	CS_1
	+	+	+
	CS_2	CS_2	CS_2
	+	+	+
	US	US	US
alternatively	⌐ – – ·(R)	⌐– – ·(R)	⌐ – – ·(R)
each trial	CS_1		CS_1
	+	(No CS or US	(No US or R)
	US	given)	
	⌐ – – ·(R)		
Testing with:	CS_2	CS_2	CS_2
Result:	Low R	Medium R	High R
Testing with:	CS_1	CS_1	CS_1
Result:	High R	Medium R	No R

[a] Modified from Rachlin [795] (R = response)

separated. For example, the ability to play the same musical composition with the left hand that was learned with the right would suggest that homologous motor adaptations occurred in the contralateral hemisphere. Analogously, the manner in which the primary effects of reflex inhibition generalize to other reflex operations may reveal the sensory or motor consequence of the primary reflex adaptation. Are responses to a fixed class of stimuli inhibited? Or is there a specific class of motor responses that is suppressed? The former would suggest an inhibition of sensory reception, the latter an inhibition of motor performance.

With extinction, conditioned responses of peripheral skeletal musculature are typically reduced, while conditioned autonomic responses to the same CS are maintained. Since some responses to the original CS are possible, this type of inhibition may be said to involve local suppression of motor activity rather than generalized inhibition of receptivity to the CS. This conclusion is further supported by the fact that motor responses other than the original conditioned response can also exhibit the inhibitory effects of extinction or conditioned inhibition.

Although neural adaptations serving repetitively induced inhibition may affect motor performance as above, it is likely that adaptations influencing receptivity to the CS also play a key role in the inhibitory process. This is because inhibition occurs after repetitive presentation of the CS and subsequently inhibits conditioned responses formed associatively between that CS and other USs. Since adaptation requires input from the CS, cells that adapt must be receptive to the CS in some sense. Adaptations supporting extinction may then involve neurons (1) addressed by the repetitive stimulus, (2) responsive to the stimulus, and (3) of significance for production of a motor response.

Inhibition of stimulus reception may depend, in part, on the formation of second-order associations. Conditioned inhibition generalizes to other CS-CR combinations, provided the generalization is consonant with the discriminative effects of the associative part of this paradigm. Further evidence regarding this possibility is introduced in Chapter 3 with reference to generalization of associatively induced adaptations.

Behavioral Outcomes of Simple Adaptive Reflex Operations

Let us now examine some behavioral descriptions of simple adaptive reflex processes. These are descriptions of the outcomes of reflex operations, grouped according to their commonalities. Outcomes with common features are frequently perceived as entities, e.g., sensitization, habituation, and pseudoconditioning, but this is incorrect. They are rather reflections of cellular processes. Specifically, the critical cellular processes are the adaptations mentioned earlier and their locations within the neural network. With the production of multiple adaptations at multiple loci, the multiple facets of phenomena such as habituation can be accounted for. Which adaptive processes are involved depends on the physical characteristics of the initiating stimuli, the parametric features of their presentation, the state of the neural substrates over which information regarding the stimulus is transmitted, and the adaptive properties of these substrates.

Phenomena Resulting from Simple Facilitation

Simple facilitation follows the presentation of simple stimuli and results in an enhanced responsiveness of the organism. When the enhancement is general, the behavioral phenomenon is called alerting or arousal. When the enhancement is somewhat more specific or persistent, the behavioral phenomenon is called sensitization.

Alerting and Arousal
Alerting and *arousal* involve a heightened sensitivity of the organism to stimulus inputs. Alterations in brain activity occur. Startle and orienting responses frequently accompany these alterations. They involve stereotyped movements such as turning the head and eyes, cocking the ears, and analogous motor responses. All these appear to improve the animal's ability to receive extrinsic stimuli and to respond. There are also systemic changes including respiratory, cardiovascular, and other autonomic effects such as those described in Table 6.1.

Sensitization
The following examples are representative of *sensitization*: (1) After the level of fear or alertness of an animal is increased by presenting a painful stimulus, the animal may acquire the ability to respond to stimuli, such as a weak click, that would not normally elicit an overt behavioral response [348,379].

(2) After a single photograph is taken, using a flashbulb, the subject may experience an increased rate of eye blink before the next shot is taken. In this example, it is not the receptivity to the flash that is enhanced, but blink performance that is facilitated. Receptivity may actually be diminished by retinal aftereffects or reduced by performance of the facilitated response (eyelid closure).

Sensitization can be characterized as follows:

1. Sensitization involves an increase in responsiveness to a stimulus, S_1, as a consequence of simple, nonrepetitive presentation of another, usually intense stimulus, S_2.
2. There may or may not be an overt response to the S_1 stimulus initially, before sensitization (for another view, see [349,485]).
3. There is usually a response to the S_2 stimulus.
4. A distinguishing feature of sensitization is the low degree of stimulus and response specificity. That is, after sensitization has occurred, many stimuli will be effective as the S_1 stimulus in producing a response. The response produced may be generalized (as in arousal), and the extent of generalization will vary with the initiating stimulus.
5. Another distinguishing feature is that sensitization effects typically are acquired rapidly and habituate rapidly, although sometimes less rapidly than the effects of alerting or arousal.
6. Alerting and arousal may represent a subclass of sensitized, stereotyped responses.
7. With sensitization, it is unclear whether receptivity to stimuli is enhanced or the production of motor responses is facilitated. However, since EEG arousal can be sensitized in curarized animals, it is likely that stimulus receptivity is enhanced in at least some instances.

Phenomena Resulting from Simple Inhibition

Though inhibitory as well as facilitatory behavior can result from simple adaptation, there is as yet no evidence to point to a separate adaptive cellular phenomenon linked solely with the production of inhibitory behavior. Thus, it is likely that the same class of cellular events supporting simple facilitation is involved in the production of simple inhibition by means of reciprocal reflex effects or differences in neurotransmitters serving the reflex pathways.

Arrest-Freezing*

Arrest reactions in which responses to a variety of stimuli are suppressed can be produced by simple stimuli. Thus, a distinct motor arrest can be produced upon hearing a simple warning rattle of a snake, without the snake ever being seen. This type of inhibitory response is concurrent with the facilitatory response of arousal. Thus, while a motor arrest occurs upon hearing the snake, there is also simultaneous alerting. This may simply reflect reciprocal reflex

*Also see avoiding, catatonia (Chapter 6).

effects, or, as Pavlov believed, a single CS may simultaneously have "excitatory" and "inhibitory" potential within the CNS, depending on its past history of associative reinforcement or nonreinforcement.

Phenomena Resulting from Innate Adaptive Processes

Innate, preprogrammed neural substrates exist in which adaptations await their obligatory release upon presentation of a particular stimulus. These changes may be either facilitatory or inhibitory, but the neural effects of stimulus presentation are ramified according to a latent, preprogrammed chain of events. Because these adaptations are commonly released by a specific stimulus and have a predetermined, uncomplicated course of development, they may be included among the simple adaptations. Their underlying mechanisms may, however, be complex.

Facilitatory Preprogrammed Adaptations

Perhaps the best known example of an innate, facilitatory preprogrammed process is imprinting. The stimulus specificity for eliciting the programmed adaptation with imprinted behavior is great, though not so great as to preclude certain humorous errors in stimulus recognition—for example, the imprinting of goslings to Lorenz instead of to the mother goose as described in his book *King Solomon's Ring* [625]. In this case, the adaptations facilitated following behavior directed to Lorenz rather than the goose, and the goslings followed him.

Another phenomenon, that of preestablished mating behavior in parasitically nested birds, was cited earlier. Presumably, a genetically transmitted, neurally coded response awaits release by a particular stimulus-cue delivered from a similar species after maturity.

"Inhibitory" Preprogrammed Adaptations

Aversive imprinted responses, such as flight from a potential predator, differ qualitatively from responses that support the tropismic following behavior described above, but they may not differ physiologically in any substantive sense. Flight can hardly be described as reflex suppressive. *The ultimate fallacy of any inhibitory-facilitatory classification is exposed at the physiologic level.* Only by identifying and properly labeling each component of the reflex effects can this problem be circumvented.

Another adaptation that may require latent, innate, preprogrammed processes for its development is that involved with a one-trial, conditioned aversion to food. Here, the ingestion of a noxious food stimulus leads to nausea or vomiting. This contingency results in aversive conditioning and, subsequently, the stimulus produces inhibition of the feeding response [316-318]. Motor activity normally elicited by the food stimulus is suppressed.* One-trial associations with long delays between initial ingestion and the pre-

---

*Some, but not all, motor activity is suppressed. The salivatory response may remain.

sentation of the negative reinforcer must act through preestablished neural channels with preestablished mechanisms for producing reflex adaptation. Whether this type of innate preprogramming differs substantially from that which serves as the substrate for other associative adaptations described below remains to be seen.

Review of Behavioral Outcomes of Repetitively Induced Reflex Adaptations

In summary, all liminal stimuli produce simple reflex effects, many with overt motor manifestations. In addition to the direct motor effects, there may be adaptive effects. Single stimuli usually result in facilitating the performance of motor responses and represent simple reflex facilitation. Sometimes, presentation of single stimuli results in suppressing the performance of motor responses. This represents simple reflex inhibition. Reciprocal reflex effects contribute to both simple reflex facilitation and inhibition and may be the primary determinant of whether motor facilitation or inhibition predominates. In addition to simple adaptations of this type, more complicated effects of stimulus presentation, called compound adaptations, can be distinguished (Table 2.2). Compound adaptations induced by repetitive stimulus presentation at rates > 1 Hz usually produce motor inhibition. Several different types of repetitively induced inhibition can be distinguished, including habituation, habituatory adaptation, and the four inhibitory processes described by Pavlov: (1) extinction (or latent inhibition), (2) differentiated inhibition (or discriminative conditioning), (3) conditioned inhibition, and (4) inhibition-produced delay.

Some differences between the types of inhibition described by Pavlov depend on whether or not associative stimulus presentations are combined with repetitive stimulation. The associative features of conditioned inhibition lead to stimulus-specific inhibition, e.g., suppression of the response to the NS-CS pair (Table 2.3) but not to the CS alone. The associative features of differentiated inhibition (discriminative conditioning) lead to a potentiation of the response to the CS, the repetitive features leading to a suppression of response to the DS.

Not all repetitively induced adaptations are inhibitory. Those supporting reflex dominance and pseudoconditioning appear to be facilitatory. While these outcomes could conceivably result from inhibitory adaptations located in such a way as to produce reciprocal reflex effects, present physiologic evidence (see Chapter 4) suggests that they are produced by direct reflex facilitation. Spontaneous neural activity may provide sufficient CS-like information to permit "pseudo"-associative adaptations to take place.

In general, compound adaptations differ from simple adaptations in that they are more substantial and are produced by compound stimulus presentations. There are learning savings. Compound adaptations therefore require prolonged neural changes involving the formation of engrams. Those changes supporting compound inhibition alter motor performance and, in some instances, stimulus reception. With habituation, some changes inhibiting motor performance occur in interneurons as they terminate on motoneurons that, in turn, innervate the reflex musculature [480,931-933].

Cellular changes serving simple adaptation may involve facilitation or occlusion of subliminal fringes of reciprocally connected neural pathways. It has been demonstrated that such pathways exist at the level of spinal motoneurons. They primarily affect motor performance but can also influence sensory receptivity.

The neural substrates mediating compound repetitively induced inhibition typically require the contingency of repetitive stimulation for adaptation. This frequency dependent cellular property characterizes this adaptive process and the neurons that adapt. Different frequencies of repetition will trigger different neural adaptations. Rapid repetition* leads to habituation, while less rapid repetition leads to extinction, latent inhibition, or habituatory adaptation as described above. Slow rates of repetition may also lead to facilitatory effects. These differences in the effects of different frequencies of repetition are mirrored at the cellular level (Chapter 5).

Behavioral Outcomes of Associatively Induced Reflex Adaptations

Compound reflex adaptations commonly result from paired or associative presentation of different stimuli as opposed to repetitive presentations of the same stimulus. Adaptations resulting from associative processes can involve either facilitatory or inhibitory processes, and often both [107-111,120, 1110,1118]. Multiple, serially chained second and third-order adaptations can also occur.

Complicating Factors of Compound Stimuli

Associatively paired stimuli will produce the unpaired and repetitive effects described earlier, unless some specific mechanism is initiated to suppress these effects. For example, "although the normal effect of pairing the CS and US is to produce conditioning, the procedure is known to have two other effects: (1) a suppression of the response to the US and (2) a sensitization of the response to the CS" [519]. Suppression of the response to the US is illustrated in Fig. 2.10.

During paired presentations of CS and US, a latent inhibition appears to occur with repeated presentation of the CS, and results in reduction of the amplitude of the unconditioned response. Removing the CS restores the full magnitude of the unconditioned response, indicating, says Kimble [519], "that the response diminution resulted, not from . . . reflex fatigue, but from

---

*Some stimuli may have such rapid repetitive frequencies that they may best trigger these adaptations when their presentations are reduced to slightly lower frequencies.

Amplitude of Unconditioned Response Is Reduced by Presence of CS

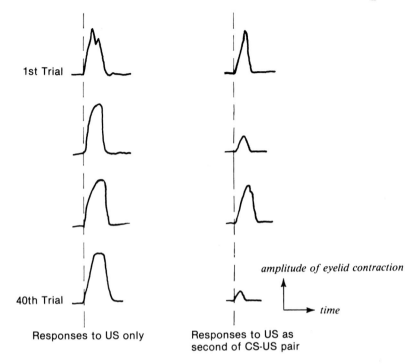

1st Trial

40th Trial

amplitude of eyelid contraction

time

Responses to US only

Responses to US as
second of CS-US pair

Fig. 2.10. Effect on unconditioned motor response (eyelid movement) of presenting CS and US versus presentation of US alone. The size of the response is smaller when preceded by paired presentation of CS and US. (From Kimble and Ost [522].)

an inhibitory process under the control of the CS." This multiplicity of effects complicates analysis of the associative consequences of pairing the compound stimuli. In view of this complication, one may wish to consider the use of several explicitly paired and unpaired patterns of stimulus presentation as controls for associative behavior. The intervals between the CS, US, and DS should be specified as well as their order of presentation. This will enable one to avoid use of randomization, i.e., "random" temporal pairings of stimuli, as a "control" for associative behavior. The "random" paradigm is either unsystematic or biased, and can potentially produce a broad range of simple, repetitive and associative effects. Which will predominate will depend on the band width of temporal frequencies of the selected "random" presentations or upon chance. Properly random processes such as are discussed in Chapter 7 occur over an unrealizably long time period (i.e., an infinite one) and not over the short periods that are used for training.

Before further considering the many parameters to which the associatively induced adaptations exhibit sensitivity, let us look at some of their outcomes.

Conditioning

The best known outcome of associative presentation of compound stimuli is conditioned behavior.

Taxonomy

The presently accepted taxonomy of conditioning is outlined below. It embraces a variety of different reflex operations and subjective observations. Although it is descriptive and largely devoid of basic physical considerations from which laws of adaptive processes might be derived, it somehow remains widely used. A more useful set of descriptions, drawn upon parameters of the associated compound stimuli, is presented in the next chapter.

Classical and Instrumental Conditioning

Classical conditioning is the associative conditioning of Pavlov. Here, reflex adaptations occur after compound stimuli are presented in close temporal association with each other. One of the stimuli, the US, typically produces a motor response de novo.* It is called the unconditioned response (UR). Most often, the other stimulus, the CS, does not initially produce a consistent gross motor response. It does, however, produce widespread neural activity and this can result in inconsistently produced peripheral motor responses. After pairing the CS with the US, repeatedly, in close temporal relationship with the US following CS, the CS consistently begins to elicit a motor response much like that to the US. This response is called the conditioned response (CR) and is equivalent to that conditioned classically by Pavlov.

Instrumental conditioning involves all conditioning in which, says Thompson [1016], "The response of the animal is instrumental in determining whether or not the US or 'reinforcing stimulus' will occur." With this type of conditioning, the frequency or probability of the response is altered by the contingent occurrence of the reinforcing stimulus. It is the motor response† of the animal contingent upon delivery or production or cessation of this stimulus that is crucial [538]. This provides the basis for an associatively induced "closed-loop" adaptation (Chapter 7, p. 384) that may differ in consequence but not necessarily in mechanism from an associatively induced "open-loop" adaptation. The term "instrumental" can give rise to the mistaken belief that introduction of an instrument such as a lever to be pressed is the important associative variable. It is not.

The physiologic basis of the induction of instrumental conditioning appears to be equivalent to that of operant conditioning, escape conditioning, and avoidance conditioning since all depend on the contingency between motor response and the occurrence of some reinforcement-like stimuli. Ordi-

---

*Note, however, the remarks made earlier (p. 22) concerning the reliability of this characterization.

†The response need not be overt or externalized in instrumental conditioning, nor is this aspect of instrumental conditioning substantially different from Pavlovian conditioning except for certain parametric features of the association between motor response and reinforcement.

narily, the response of the organism influences the probability of occurrence of these stimuli. Some of these contingencies are illustrated in Table 2.10.

Two questions arise concerning the neural adaptations that underlie associative conditioning. The first is whether different adaptations are necessary to support the various subcategories of instrumental conditioning. The second is whether different adaptations are necessary to support classical versus instrumental conditioning.

Table 2.10. Types of Instrumental Conditioning[a]

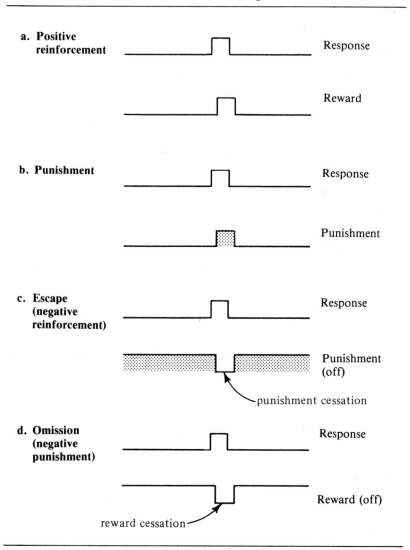

[a] There is usually some temporal contiguity between the events (or event cessations) and the response of the animal. After Rachlin [795].

Neither question is easily answered. Let us consider the different subcategories of instrumental conditioning:

1. *Operant conditioning* is synonymous with instrumental conditioning. Typically a bird pecks a button or an animal presses a level to secure a food reward. As the co-occurrence of pecking and food reward increases and as hunger is maintained, so will the probability of pecking increase. As careful studies have shown, neither the button or lever nor a peripheral motor response is needed for this type of conditioning to occur. Operant conditioning can even occur when cortical neuronal activity is monitored by the investigator and used to trigger the release of food (e.g., Disterhoft and Olds [222]). In this case, the instrument and the peripheral motor response are dispensed with. Thus, neither is necessary for this type of conditioning.

2. *Passive avoidance conditioning* introduces an aversive stimulus in place of a positively reinforcing or appetitive stimulus. For example, shock instead of (or in addition to) food follows the lever press or the neural activation. As a result, the animal learns to suppress the response to avoid occurrences of the noxious event.

3. *Escape conditioning* introduces a noxious stimulus which the animal can escape by moving. The animal learns to escape from the stimulus that is delivered. Anticipatory escape would be equivalent to active avoidance.

Although the same adaptive mechanism could serve as the basis for any of the above examples of conditioning, several different mechanisms could serve just as well. Differences in conditioned motor performance need only require that the adaptations occur along different neural pathways. (Some of these pathways may be expected to utilize different neurotransmitter chemicals.) The occurrence of each class of adaptations would be contingent on neural activation (the initial response of the organism) being associated with subsequent neural activation (the later stimulus from the environment). Whether the probability of occurrence of the environmental stimulus is increased or decreased may be important to activating the mechanism of adaptation but may not serve to distinguish the three different forms of conditioning described above. This is because reflex facilitation and suppression can simultaneously involve reciprocal neural pathways and antithetic neural transmitters. Detailed cellular and molecular studies are therefore required to answer the first question.

The second question is whether the associative contingencies of instrumental conditioning and resulting adaptations are similar to those of classical conditioning. Some investigators suggest that intrinsic stimuli are generated within the organism in the course of instrumental conditioning and that such "phantom" stimuli serve as a basis for adaptations similar to those of classical associative conditioning (see Gormezano and Tait [346]).

Others hold that the differences are more substantial. They point out that the classical conditioned reflex is typically a copy of the unconditioned reflex, whereas the instrumental conditioned reflex may be any reaction of the animal, quite unrelated to the reinforcing agent (Konorski, cited by

Buresova [132]). Careful examination discloses that the classical conditioned and unconditioned reflexes are *not* identical but differ physiologically. For example, even superficially similar blink reflexes will be mediated by different, though partly overlapping, pools of motor neurons projecting to the eyeblink musculature [111,1110,1118]. Thus, differences in conditioned and unconditioned motor response do not distinguish conclusively between different forms of conditioned adaptation.

The following examples are interpreted by some as requiring still different, bidirectional associative reflex adaptations, atypical of either first-order classical or instrumental associative processes, for their explanation.

Konorski and Miller [c.f. 539] "trained a dog to perform a classical CR using passive raising of one hind limb as a CS and presentation of food as the US. After the CR had been established, the dog often raised the leg spontaneously. If such active movement was reinforced by food in the same way as the passive movement, the dog started to use it as a 'self-induced' CS" [132]. "Pavlov suggested that these results might be explained by bidirectional connections between the kinesthetic and gustatory centers. This conception", says Buresova [132], "represents the CR as a synthesis of two unconditioned reflexes and may help to bridge the gap separating classical and instrumental conditioning". Other experiments also support this assertion. In studies by Struchkov [970], dogs received small portions of food, and when eating it, their hind limb was passively placed upon a low pedestal. After elaboration of the CR, the animals placed the hind limb on the pedestal whenever they started to eat. To test for the presence of the backward connection, the limb was moved passively. In all cases, the movement triggered salivation and search for food in the feeder. In other experiments, Rudenko [850] "used corneal air puff as a CS and food as the US. After elaboration of the CR, presentation of food elicited repetitive eye blinks. Under the above conditions when each stimulus elicited a clearcut UR," says Buresova, "the association led to formation of bidirectional connections. Any member of the pair could then serve as the CS for the other reaction" [132].

Of the above results, those of Konorski and Miller can be explained as well by overlap of enduring stimulus effects at the cellular level as by the bidirectional reflex connections suggested above. Those of Rudenko are more problematic. However, Rudenko's results could also be associatively explained if more than one type of adaptation were formed on the basis of either classical or instrumental stimulus-response contingencies. The linkage of stimulus to new response (CS to CR) in classical conditioning would then not need to differ substantially from the linkage of response-to stimulus-to altered response in instrumental conditioning, given intermediary linkages served by multiple cellular adaptations. That these secondary types of adaptations can occur with classical conditioning is supported by evidence cited earlier (e.g., Table 2.4) as well as by more recent studies of sensory preconditioning and second-order conditioning of chain reflexes [107,120]. Other, nonassociatively or pseudoassociatively induced adaptations may also occur, such as those found with reflex dominance and pseudoconditioning [111, 1122].

Comparison of Pseudoconditioning and Conditioning. If one compares the behavioral consequences of pseudoconditioning (p. 35) with those of associative conditioning, one finds more similarities than differences. Levels of CR performance after pseudoconditioning procedures can surpass those found after conditioning procedures (Table 2.8). Moreover, the pseudoconditioned responses can be learned as rapidly as the conditioned responses [383], although they appear to extinguish more rapidly (Table 2.8). The difference in persistence is replicated by neurophysiologic findings described in Chapter 4.

Kimble suggested that pseudoconditioning may be a part of all conditioning in which a noxious stimulus is employed [519]. Wickens and Wickens [1083] interpret pseudoconditioning as a case of true conditioning with transference from a noxious to a neutral stimulus. The transfer occurs because of some similarity between the noxious and the neutral stimuli. Physiologically, the critical similarity may be that the neutral stimulus has access to the reflex pathway facilitated by the nonassociatively induced adaptation of pseudoconditioning. Still another explanation could account for the similar effects of nonassociative pseudoconditioning and associative conditioning. With pseudoconditioning (or, for that matter, reflex dominance) the US could react with preexisting, intrinsic neural substrates similar to those produced as a consequence of presenting a CS. Thus, a pseudoassociative rather than a repetitive adaptation could result, and the outcome would be very much like that of conditioning.

Other Definitions. Other definitions of conditioning have been proposed that depend on the conditioned response being performed after a long latent period following delivery of the CS or on the failure of the CS to produce motor responses before conditioning [351,480,485,486]. They are unsatisfactory. Differences in CR latency may depend as much on the conduction times of involved reflex pathways as on transmission delays arising from the types of involved neural adaptations. The idea that conditioning requires long latency responses seems to have arisen from early observations of short latency sensitized responses that were confused with conditioning. It would be foolish, however, to assume that all short latency responses represent sensitization. Reaction time, the latency for performance of a rapid skeletal response to a selected stimulus, is commonly between 100 and 150 msec, and the response latency of some Pavlovian *conditioned* reflexes has been shown to be as short as 20 msec [1113]. Short-latency CRs meet the same criteria of associative conditioning as do long latency CRs. They arise from associative pairing, extinguish on reversing the order of CS-US presentation, and are elicited discriminatively by the associated CS as opposed to other, unpaired stimuli [1128]. Conditioned responses may also develop to CSs that initially produce motor responses analogous to those produced after conditioning. Often, these preliminary responses are produced weakly or inconsistently and disappear after the first few presentations of the CS. Pavlov recognized the occurrence of preexisting unconditioned responses to the CS in some of his own classical, associative conditioning paradigms. The idea that a stimulus such as dilute broth, which produces weak salivation, cannot be paired with a US such as steak to produce copious conditioned salivation is demonstrably incorrect.

Sensory Preconditioning

Another consequence of associative presentation of compound stimuli is *sensory preconditioning*. Sensory preconditioning results from associatively pairing two stimuli that resemble CSs, i.e., stimuli that typically do not produce consistent, overt motor responses. Subsequently, one of the stimuli is paired associatively in the usual manner with a motor-effective US to produce a conditioned response. Then, as a consequence of the original associations, the other CS-like stimulus, though never paired with the US, is able to evoke the CR.

According to Kimble [759] (see Fig. 2.11), the basic paradigm for producing sensory preconditioning involves three stages:

1. Two neutral stimuli, S^1 and S^2, a tone and a light, for example, are presented together, usually for a large number of trials (although a large number of associative trials is not *always* required).
2. A response is conditioned to one of these stimuli, say S^2.
3. The other stimulus, S^1, is then presented to determine if the conditioned response transfers automatically to it or if there is transfer of learning savings, another indication of conditioning.

The implication is that some association is formed in the first, preconditioning phase of the experiment that facilitates the performance of the subsequently acquired motor response to either of the originally paired stimuli. This effect, when it occurs, is termed sensory preconditioning. Brogden [103,104] is credited with a particularly clear demonstration of the phenomenon and for the name.

Kimble points out the need to employ control groups in which the sensory stimuli, S^1 and S^2, are not paired in order to control for effects of stimulus generalization that could complicate the experiment. If the group in which S^1 and S^2 were previously paired showed superior responding to S^1 as compared to the control group, that would be considered evidence for the establishment of sensory preconditioning.

Sensory preconditioning can occur when the associative procedure is instrumental rather than classical [37,494,882] and also when responses are intentional or influenced by instructions [104,161].

The effects of pairing two USs have also been studied [346]. The results indicate that greater than 90% CR performance levels can readily be acquired, the initial US becoming effective in eliciting the response elicited by the second US in addition to its own normal unconditioned movement. The results also suggest the possibility of some enhancement of response performance by US_1-US_2 pairing akin to that of sensory preconditioning. This is indicated in Fig. 2.12 by the relatively high rate of response performance in the unpaired "control" group.

Sensory Preconditioning

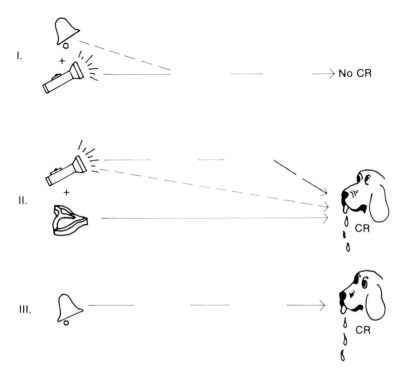

*Fig. 2.11. S-R explanation of sensory preconditioning. Solid lines are uncon-
ditioned connections. Dashed lines are conditioned connections. In the above
example, the bell (S¹) comes to evoke the salivatory CR without ever having
been paired explicitly with food US. Kimble [519] suggests that this is due to
proprioceptive stimulation produced by the UR in response to the light as
US. In Stage I an unmeasured response to light with its hypothetical proprioceptive stimulus, designated by the empty spaces, is conditioned to a tone. In
Stage II, both light and its response-produced stimulus are conditional stimuli
for salivation elicited by food. In Stage III, the proprioceptive stimulus
(evoked when the tone elicits its previously conditioned response to light)
now elicits the salivation. (Modified from Kimble [519].)*

Second-Order Conditioning of Chain Reflexes

The effect produced by pairing two USs associatively mirrors the phenomenon of chain reflexes formed by *second-order conditioning* (Fig. 2.13). After
conditioning a dog to salivate to a bell as CS, the animal can then be taught a
second conditioned response to the original CS using food presentation as a
CS! The bell will then be effective in producing both salivation and the
second CR. This second-order effect is attributable to a chained linkage between two reflex pathways in which separate adaptations have occurred. This
type of phenomenon could explain the results of pairing two USs described

Effects of US$_1$-US$_2$ Pairing

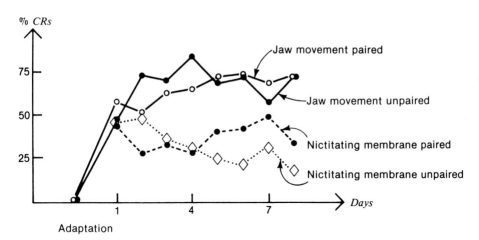

Fig. 2.12. Acquisition of conditioned motor responses following US$_1$-US$_2$ pairing. Rabbits were trained by pairing oral injection of water (US$_1$)—producing an appetitive jaw movement US and air puff to the cornea (US$_2$)—producing an aversive nictitating membrane US. Experimental groups received US$_1$-US$_2$ pairs followed by US$_1$ test stimuli. Control groups received separate, unpaired train presentations of US$_1$ and US$_2$ followed by test stimuli as in the respective experimental groups. Although no differences attributable to the experimental backwards associative pairing were found (see ref. 346 and Chapter 3 for further explanation), there was a surprisingly high level of acquired response performance in both experimental and control groups. The response that was counted as acquired was that of the UR to the nontest stimulus. (Gormezano and Tait [346].)

above. As mentioned earlier, chain reflexes may also be formed with repetitively induced adaptations, as with conditioned inhibition.

Other Taxonomies
Other taxonomies of reflex behavior tend to be based on anthropomorphized perceptions of the taxonomist rather than on knowledge of the underlying physiologic processes.

Appetitive and Defensive Reflexes and Preservative versus Protective Behavior. Approach or appetitive reflexes are often separated from defensive or avoidance reflexes. This may be done irrespective of whether the reflexes are unconditioned or conditioned. The problem with making such a separation is that exactly the same reflex activity can be construed as being either appetitive or defensive. An animal can learn merely to eat food in order to avoid a noxious stimulus. The eating of food becomes an appetitive *and* a defensive reflex. If the motor response is one and the same, so may be the reflex adaptations supporting its acquisition. It seems unlikely that the neuron cares a

Second-Order Conditioning

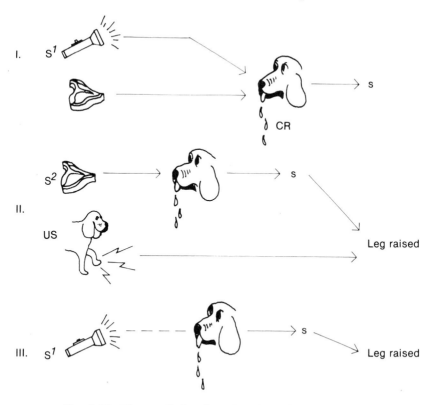

Fig. 2.13. The mediational explanation of second-order conditioning. Here, the mediator is the salivatory response or its response-produced stimulus, S, depending on one's view. Classical conditioning has been shown to develop in the absence of both the peripheral motor response to the US and proprioceptive feedback therefrom [54,198,997]. (After Kimble [519].)

whit if the ultimate outcome of its adaptation is preservative or protective except in so far as it lies along a pathway of particular receptive, motor, or pharmacologic significance. Adaptations promoting each of the above types of behavior can be induced by direct electrical stimulation of neural tissue as CS or US, which need have no preservative or protective significance at all! The same argument holds for unconditioned reflexes. Basically, the issue is between a semantic versus a physiologic definition of behavior.

Preparatory and Consummatory Reflexes. Preparatory reflexes are said to provide the organism with attractive stimuli, such as food, or to forestall aversive stimuli as a consequence of motivation or drive. Consummatory reflexes are said to be elicited by specific stimuli requiring an appropriate adaptive response. Thus, contraction of the internal sphincter to avoid micturition is, in housebroken pets, both a preparatory and consummatory reflex.

Again, the taxonomy is unsatisfactory because of its linguistic imprecision and a tendency to anthropomorphize impersonal or unconscious reflex operations. There are, of course, certain reflex networks that lend themselves to the production of feeding, predation, flight, mating, and other fundamental behaviors as discussed later in Chapter 6. However, there is at present no reason to believe that the cellular adaptations or reflex pathways supporting motivation, consummation, preparation, and the like are uniquely different from those supporting specific sensory reception or specific motor performance. Classification of many forms of functions of neurons and their pathways should primarily be a matter of physical chemistry, geometry, and probability (Chapter 7) rather than of linguistics.

Developmental Considerations

One might attempt to distinguish between different adaptive reflex processes on the basis of their development. For example, some adaptations might be functional at an earlier developmental stage than others. With this in mind, three aspects of development can be considered with specific reference to conditioning. The first is the course of development of the conditioned response itself. The second is the ontogenetic development, i.e., How early in the age of the animal can the response be conditioned? Third is the development of the conditioned reflex under certain abnormal conditions, as for example, in Korsakoff's syndrome (see Chapter 6).

Course of Development of the CR. Typically, the conditioned response develops gradually, rather than abruptly. There is a classical, *S*-shaped curve that describes the acquisition of increasing levels of CR performance over time (see Fig. 2.9). This could mean that the underlying neural adaptations occur slowly. Or it could mean that they occur rapidly, but it takes a long time to produce enough adaptations in different neurons to influence reflex motor performance significantly and reliably.

What cellular adaptations are known (Chapters 4 and 5) appear to occur fairly rapidly, but require 5-30 min to become fixed or permanent. More than one adaptive process appears to be involved. The possible involvement of *separate* short and long term memory processes should also be considered. (Bures' points out [125] that as early as 1900 Müller and Pilzecker [696] hypothesized that an experience first persists in the brain in labile form and then gradually changes or "consolidates" into a fixed, permanent memory trace.)

Pavlov also noted that a sequence of different, overt behavioral manifestations occurred in the course of conditioning. First, there was a period of orienting and increased exploratory behavior (or arrest in the case of conditioning with aversive stimuli). Then, with the initial development of conditioned behavior, the responses were elicited nonspecifically. Many stimuli other than the CS were effective in producing the CR. Finally, with further conditioning, the response to the CS became discriminative. Responses were not performed to other stimuli, a phenomenon attributed by Pavlov to the supplemental acquisition of conditioned inhibition. The sequence may reflect the formation of different neural adaptations serving conditioning and, conceivably, some classification of adaptive reflex processes based on these sequences might be designed.

Some attempts have been made to study the development of conditioning at the neurophysiologic level. For example, Adey and colleagues [6] investigated the effects of the development of conditioned behavior on EEG activity in the region of the hippocampus. The results of these studies did not lead to a conclusive electrographic index of the developmental stages of conditioning. However, some alterations in rhythmic electrical activity of the hippocampus in the frequency range of 3-5 Hz (theta) were observed in the course of conditioning.

One concludes that these kinds of "developmental" considerations could lead to an improved taxonomy of adaptive reflex processes, but that, at present, the evidence is insufficient for this to be accomplished.

Ontogenetic Development of the CR. Much the same conclusion may be drawn about applying ontogenetic considerations to taxonomies of simple learned behavior. Surprisingly little is known concerning the ontogenetic development of conditioning, yet what is known is of taxonomic relevance. In mammals, many conditioned reflexes to noxious exteroceptive stimuli cannot be acquired prior to about two or three weeks of age. On the other hand, a few conditioned reflexes, such as those involving changes in heart rate, are said to be formed prepartally, and alimentary CRs can be learned in the first day or two of life [461,698,924]. In rats, aversive reflexes can be obtained at age 2 days instead of age 10 days by using intraperitoneal instead of peripheral shock as the US [385]. Thus, several factors, yet unknown, determine the earliest age at which a particular type of conditioning can be acquired. A compendium of articles on this subject has just appeared [924], as has a comprehensive review written in Czech [698].

Abnormal Development of the CR. The development of conditioning can also be studied in the face of abnormality. Usually, the abnormality represents a reduction in the amount of available neural substrate, i.e., brain damage of some sort or another. Experimentally, the effect of this abnormality can be assessed by studying conditioning in animals from which various portions of the central nervous system have been removed.

Lashley [578] showed in 1929 that "cortical lesions influence acquisition or retention of a maze habit in rats according to the size of the damage, but the impairment is relatively independent of the location of the injury. Even as small a portion of the visual cortex as 2% could maintain its mnemonic function for tasks such as pattern discrimination" [125]. This observation holds for many types of conditioning in which the cortex is involved, i.e., extensive lesions are required for acquisition to be impaired.

Conditioning has also been attempted in humans who have suffered natural lesions of portions of the prosencephalon, particularly involving the hippocampus and other parts of the limbic system that make up Papez' circuit (see Fig. 6.1). Many of these studies were done in chronic alcoholics with thiamine nutritional deficiency and an amnestic-confabulatory syndrome of the Korsakoff type (Chapter 6). The results indicate that some conditioning occurs. In 1911, Claparede [171] was able to condition a woman with Korsakoff's syndrome to painful stimulus (pinprick) in a two trial session of a few minutes each. The woman was unable to verbalize what the CS (handshake) or the US (concealed pin) was, but she avoided the experimenter when he held the pin. She explained her otherwise peculiar avoidance behavior by saying that she "just thought something bad might happen if she did not act that way." In 1942, however, Gantt and Muncie [315] unsuccessfully attempted to produce shock avoidance conditioning in three Korsakoff patients. In 1954, Linskii [605] reported that the speed of conditioning in Korsakoff patients was the same as that in normal humans, although the Korsakoff patients showed faster rates of extinction. Talland [988] investigated this using a buzzer (CS), an air puff to the eye (US), and an eye blink (UR, CR), and confirmed that Korsakoff patients took a much shorter time than normal to extinguish. In separate experiments, he found that lists of ten or more words appeared to exceed the learning capacity of Korsakoff patients. Perhaps they extinguished too rapidly to learn the entire sequence.

Attempts have been made to study conditioning in decorticate preparations. Decorticated animals are able to learn some types of conditioned behavior. However, it is unclear whether subcortical learning occurs normally in the intact brain or whether this type of learning appears only as compensation for damaged cortical mechanisms. Bures [125] points out that whereas decorticated man becomes a vegetative preparation with complete loss of postural reactions, posture and locomotion are preserved in neodecorticated dogs or cats [773] and such preparations can acquire simple conditioned reactions. Generally, learning in decorticated animals is slow and limited to the more primitive reactions and to elementary processing of sensory signals [55]. Thalamic or diencephalic cats and rats are hyperactive and exhibit a wide range of behaviors, but are unable to feed themselves. They can acquire simple, classically conditioned reactions and can increase the frequency of movements reinforced by rewarding stimuli. Recent studies confirm this and show that even mesencephalic preparations with most of the telencephalon and diencephalon removed can learn [444,661,721,722].

Conversely, conditioning is also possible in chronic cats sectioned at the midcollicular or pretrigeminal level. Here, the opposite of the above occurs, and structures supporting learning are isolated from the mesencephalic and rhombencephalic structures below. The pretrigeminal cat [1146] displays orienting reflexes to visual stimuli consisting of fixation and following eye movements, dilation of the pupils, accommodation, and EEG arousal. These responses can be habituated or conditioned just as in normal cats. Even ocular instrumental reactions can be acquired rapidly in pretrigeminal cats [868]. Thus, many areas of the brain have the capacity to learn independent of their connections to other regions.

Classical conditioning in the spinal cord of frogs and cats appears to be quite difficult, but is possible [280]. For a review of this literature, see Morgan [683]. Bures [125] maintains that most of these effects cannot easily be distinguished from nonspecific changes of threshold caused by repetitive application of the US (as by Ukhtomsky [1030,1031]).

Parametric Features—An Introduction
More useful distinctions between different types of associative conditioning derive from the parametric features of the associative paradigms by which they are induced. These include order, interval, rate, duration, character, and intensity of the paired stimuli. The time delay between stimulus presentations or pairings was also treated by Pavlov virtually as though it were a physical feature of the stimulus.* With reinforcement, as in instrumental conditioning, the timing between response and reinforcer, the ratio of reinforcement, and the character of the reinforcer are they key parametric features. The correspondence between these variables and the induction of cellular adaptations may help us distinguish among adaptations supporting classical Pavlovian conditioning, instrumental conditioning, sensory preconditioning, second-order conditioning, extinction, chain reflexes, etc. In fact, these commonalities among the associative processes used to bring about reflex adaptations may prove better descriptors, analytically, than the commonalities among behavioral outcomes described above.

---

*However, this time delay should be considered as a parametric feature of the associative process.

Chapter 3

Associative Processes and Behavioral Psychology

The fundamental requisite is that any external stimulus which is to become the signal in a conditioned reflex must overlap in point of time with the action of an unconditional stimulus.

(I. P. Pavlov, 1927)

An understanding of behavior requires an understanding not only of the involved reflex pathways, but also of the mechanisms of neural adaptation and their associative sensitivities.

(Author, 1982)

The associative processes (temporal and spatial) are significant factors to be accounted for in learning. By examining the behavioral evidence of the outcomes of associative stimulus presentation, it is possible to infer some of the changes, correlated with such stimuli, that must necessarily occur in nerve cells when reflex learning takes place. Much learning depends on the contingencies between presented stimuli such as their order or timing. When met, these contingencies trigger "open loop" adaptations, as, for example, those arising from Pavlovian presentations of CS and US or different CSs. Analogous contingencies resulting from instrumental association of stimulus and response trigger "closed loop" adaptations. The latter admit feedback from prior adaptations or from the environment by which the course of self-organizing adaptations may be guided. Since instrumental responses express their effects through secondary stimuli or analogous neuronal input parameters, we may consider all associatively induced adaptations as if they arose from presenting two or more different stimuli. The stimuli range from those consciously perceived to those as subtle as artificial electrical stimulation of a few neurons [233]. Internal visceral autonomic reactions and other involuntary motor responses as well as peripheral motor responses can be acquired by these means [132].

The temporal relationship between stimulus presentations is the most prominent associative factor leading to adaptive changes and has led to parametric definitions of conditioning such as those shown in Fig. 3.1.

Significant temporal variables include the order and interval between presentations of stimuli and their frequency of presentation. Thus, Pavlov found that if too long an interval elapsed between the sound of the bell (CS) and the sight of food (US), conditioned salivation failed to develop.

The spatial consequences of associatively presented stimuli are also important. It is difficult to visualize the representation of the stimulus effects within the neural reflex network, but they do occur over a space within the brain and spinal cord. Neural adaptations supporting conditioned reflexes occur at selected loci. Their spatial representation depends on a number of

Parametric Definitions of Conditioning

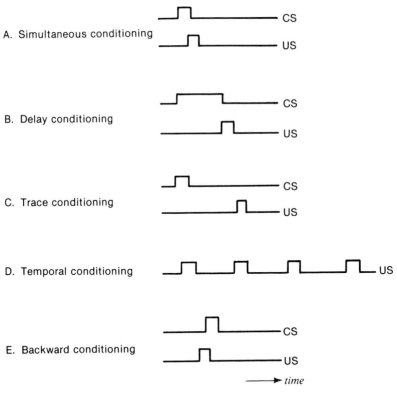

Fig. 3.1. Some parametric definitions of conditioning based on order, overlap and interval between stimulus presentations. Ambiguities in the terminologies are not easily avoided. As illustrated herein, only portions of the stimuli need coincide to be considered "simultaneous" (A) and only part of the US need precede the CS to be considered "backward" (E). Such complications are considered further in Fig. 3.8 and in the text. (After Rachlin [795].)

factors. These factors include the repetitive and associative parameters of stimulus presentation, the remaining physical characteristics of the stimuli, and the specific neural pathways that are receptive to the stimulus inputs and will transmit this information.

Mechanisms of neural adaptation are then sensitive to certain specific parameters of neuronal inputs. These sensitivities, as addressed from moment to moment, form the basis of the associative processes that not only control the induction of neural adaptations but help impart their locations within the neural network. As a result, highly specific behavior may be induced by selected combinations of stimuli. Consider the following example. Stimuli such as a click and glabella tap are presented associatively, the click CS preceding the tap US by 400 msec. Repeated presentations lead to acquisition of a conditioned eye blink in response to the click stimulus [1113]. The response is selectively elicited by the CS as opposed to some other, unpaired stimulus [273]. The behavior induced by this associative paradigm is discriminative with respect to sensory reception. In addition, the myographic pattern of the learned motor response is specific [1118]. An eye blink is performed as opposed to a tail wag or a knee jerk. Therefore, the motor performance that is acquired as a result of this associative paradigm is selective.

It is the spatial representation of adaptive changes within the neural network that leads to the specificity of stimulus reception and motor performance which characterizes conditioned and other learned behavior. The parametric features of stimulus association described below and the intrinsic properties of the neural network described in Chapters 4 and 5 control adaptations within neuronal elements in such a way as to promote specific reflex operations and specific behavior. An understanding of the behavior therefore requires an understanding not only of the involved reflex pathways but also of the mechanisms of neural adaptation and their associative sensitivities.

Philosophic Significance of Association

Associative processes have a fundamental significance philosophically as well as physiologically. Philosophically, the principle of association is said to replace the principle of causality in inductive logic [856]. That is, in reasoning inductively, it is the associative or conditional relationships between facts or other sets of variables that lead us to some general conclusion. If events A and B are found to be associated often enough, one can infer that some dependency or conditional relationship exists between these or related phenomena. Either the appearance of one event is conditional on the other, or the appearance of both events is conditional on a third, common variable.

Conditional relationships of this type lead to logical induction* scientifically as well as philosophically. (In science, says Russell [856], such

---

*Beware, for given a conditional probability of <1, it is by no means certain that event B will follow event A. Formal logic has long taken note of this.

propositions as A causes B are never to be accepted, but our inclination to accept them is explained by habit and the association of events.) Given the habitual concurrence of events A and B, the principle of causality implies that the probality of occurrence of event B is particularly high when event A occurs. Scientifically, causality represents a high conditional probability between positively correlated variables. Formal analysis of "causality" requires probablistic consideration of conditional relationships with the establishment of a coefficient of correlation between two variables or functions.

Interestingly, it is the probabilistic association between stimulus variables that profoundly influences reflex adaptation and behavior. Hume [440] recognized the significance of this association, philosophically, when he said that the connection between two objects or actions "arises from a repetition of their union . . . that has influence . . . on the mind." This view is remarkably analogous to that of Pavlov concerning the establishment of neuronal adaptations as a consequence of the effects of repetitive association of two objects that serve as the CS and the US. The important difference between Hume's and Pavlov's views of the associative principle is that Pavlov's principle is physiologic and can potentially be mapped in terms of chemistry, physics, and mathematics.

Critical Variables Controlling Associatively Induced Adaptations

The principal variables controlling the induction of neuronal adaptations by stimulus association are the timing between presentations of associated stimuli and the physical features of the stimuli, particularly their similarities, differences, frequencies, and intensities.

Stimulus Timing

Several features of the timing of stimulus presentation influence the development of associatively induced neural changes:

1. The duration and overlap of the stimuli.
2. The interval between stimulus associations [*interstimulus interval* (ISI)].
3. The rate of stimulus presentation [*intertrial interval* (ITI)].
4. The order of stimulus presentation.

Duration and Overlap of the Stimuli
The duration and temporal overlap of associated stimuli will affect neural adaptations that are contingent on the order, interval, or frequency of stimulus presentation. Repetitively induced inhibitory adaptations can be elicited by stimuli of long duration, as well as by stimulus presentations with short intervals in-between. With shorter durations or longer intervals, facilitatory adaptations may occur.

The effects of stimulus order on neural adaptations are also far-reaching. Conditioning ordinarily depends on the CS preceding the US. When the same stimuli are presented in reverse order, US preceding CS, extinction usually occurs, the repetitive effects of presenting the CS outweighing any facilitatory associative effects. When presentation of the CS overlaps and outlasts that of the US, either conditioning or extinction can occur, or sometimes, combinations of both. The outcome depends on which neural adaptations predominate—those arising from forward CS-US pairing such as shown in Fig. 3.2 or those arising from backward (US-CS) presentation.

The Stimulus Trace. The trace paradigm of stimulus presentation (Fig. 3.2) admits no temporal overlap between associated stimuli. This paradigm is named after the physiologic constraint it imposes on any neural adaptations induced associatively by it: i.e., some enduring physical chemical reflection of the initial stimulus must be maintained until the cellular effect of the second stimulus manifests if there is to be contiguity between stimuli. Otherwise, there could be no basis for a neural adaptation contingent on stimulus association to take place.

Although the concept of the stimulus trace has long been recognized in psychology (Fig. 3.2), there has been little physiologic evidence by which the concept could be made more meaningful. Recently, however, evidence has been found for several mechanisms by which time-delayed traces could be represented at the molecular level within the nervous system. These mechanisms range from regenerative activity within loops of neurons to molecular mediators of transmitter effects in single neurons, as shall presently be seen.

Complex Attributes of the Stimulus. Attributes of the stimulus can affect the consequences of its being paired with other stimuli. Each physical attribute shown in Fig. 3.3 has its own representation within the nervous system. The features that characterize the stimulus proper (i.e., frequency, intensity, and physical modality) are reflected in each attribute. When these variables are encoded for transmission by networks of neurons, they may produce effects that take on the property of ancillary stimulus features. For example, the stimulus offset may produce a characteristic pattern of unit discharge different from that of the stimulus onset. Thus, onset and offset of a CS can act differently in inducing associative adaptations supporting conditioning or other learned behavior (Fig. 3.4). In the above experiments, turning the intermittent tone on as a CS was more efficacious in producing conditioning than was turning it off.

Transformation of physical parameters of the stimulus during reception and neural transmission must also be taken into account, as must perceptual factors. Are certain frequencies of the stimulus filtered out at the receptor? Does the stimulus contain a set of separate substimuli, each with an onset and offset? Is there a perceptual fusion, so that only one onset and offset are perceived no matter how long an oscillating stimulus is continued? For example, at flicker fusion frequency or above, a flickering light is perceived as a steady stimulus, whereas below that frequency it is perceived as intermittent.

The different associative effects of presenting a steady versus an intermittent stimulus are shown in Fig. 3.5. Here, an intermittent auditory CS was more efficacious than a steady CS in producing conditioning.

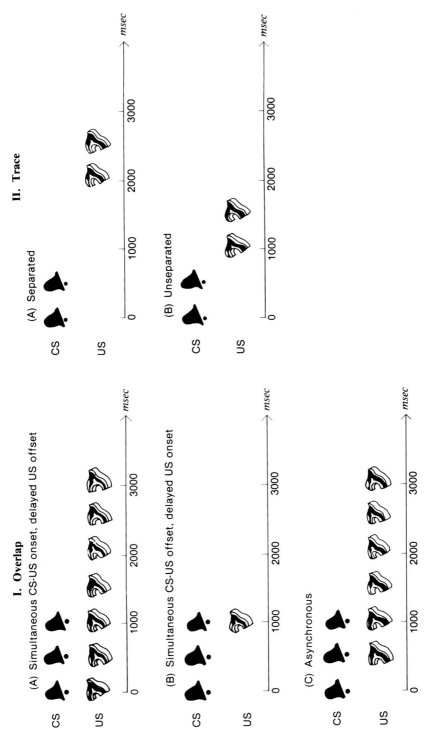

Fig. 3.2. Examples of different timings between "forward" associative presentations of stimuli such as bell (CS) and food (US). Backward presentations involve presenting some part of the US before the CS. Thus, the example shown in I(C) involves both forward and backward presentations.

Physiologic Complexities

**Physical Attributes
of the Stimulus**

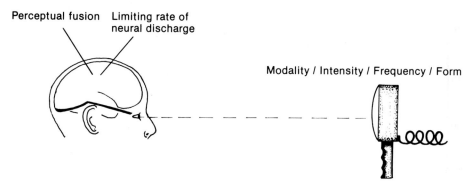

Onset - Offset

Perceptual fusion   Limiting rate of
                     neural discharge

Modality / Intensity / Frequency / Form

Fig. 3.3. Physiologic complexities complement the physical attributes of the stimulus.

Effect of Stimulus Onset-Offset on Conditioning

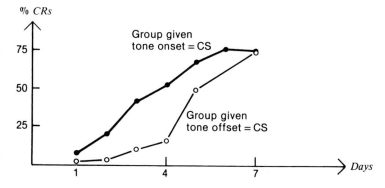

% *CRs*

75

50

25

Group given
tone onset = CS

Group given
tone offset = CS

1   4   7   *Days*

Fig. 3.4. Conditioned nictitating membrane response produced in rabbits by pairing tone onset as CS (with air puff—US) versus tone offset as CS. The same intermittent tone (1000 Hz, 50 msec on—50 msec off) was used as CS, but in one group, it was turned on 1000 msec before the US and discontinued at US offset; in the other, it was discontinued (off) 1000 msec before the US and turned on at US offset, continuing during the intertrial interval. See Fig. 3.5 for further results (Gormezano [341].)

Effect of "Steady" Versus Intermittent CS on Conditioning

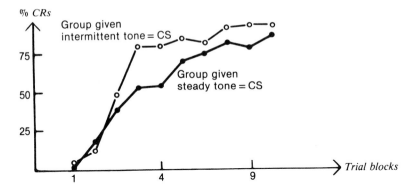

Fig. 3.5. Conditioned nictitating membrane responses produced in rabbits by pairing a steady versus intermittent tone CS with an air puff US. The steady, 1000 Hz tone lasted 1100 msec and terminated with US offset. The ISI was 100 msec. The intermittent tone was the same stimulus, interrupted for 50 msec of every 100 msec during CS delivery. (Gormezano [341].)

Efficacy of Trace versus Overlap Conditioning. As mentioned earlier the efficacy of neural adaptations supporting conditioning is influenced by the duration and overlap of the associated stimuli, i.e., of the CS and the US. A number of different configurations of stimulus duration and overlap are shown in Fig. 3.2. The effects of some of these configurations on associative processes have been studied experimentally (Fig. 3.6). Most investigators have examined the production of conditioned responses rather than the direct cellular effects of the stimulus presentations. Nonetheless, the results are revealing. Gormezano and colleagues [342] studied overlap versus trace conditioning of an eyelid response (Fig. 3.7). They compared conditioning with a prolonged CS-delayed US onset, a simultaneous CS-US offset (and delayed US onset), and a trace paradigm, and they also studied extinction.

1. When the duration of the CS outlasted that of the US, conditioning was impaired. The impairment is attributable to repetitively induced inhibition arising from CS presentation that was not counteracted associatively due to the partial backward presentations.
2. Both the prolonged CS-delayed US onset and the simultaneous offset-delayed US onset procedures were more efficacious than was trace conditioning. Whether this was a consequence of the longer duration of associative stimulus combination during the overlap period was unclear. Different combinations of ISIs arose from the overlap than from the trace paradigm. The efficacy of conditioning could have been influenced by these differences. In both instances, the CS endured long enough to include a number of associatively effective CS-US intervals. Either a prolonged dura-

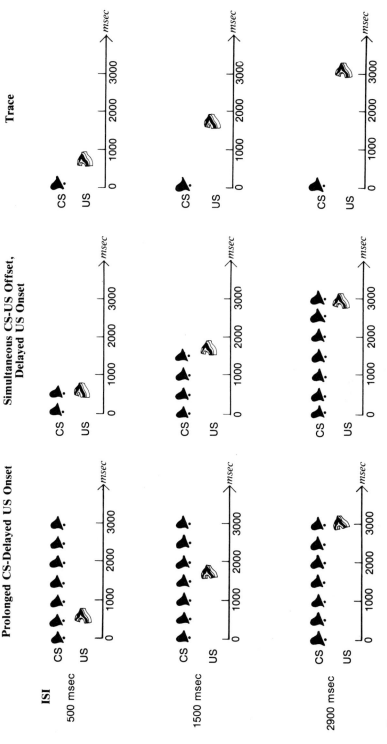

Fig. 3.6. A comparison of three associative paradigms with ISIs of 500, 1500, and 2900 msec used for the conditioning in Fig. 3.7.

Effects of CS-US Interval, Duration and Overlap on Conditioning and Extinction

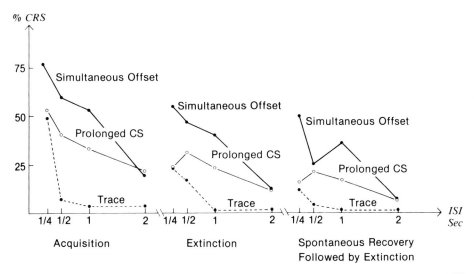

Fig. 3.7. The mean percentage of CRs as a function of CS-US interval and CS duration (simultaneous CS-US offset-delayed US onset, prolonged CS-delayed US onset, and trace). (Gormezano [342].)

tion in which more, equally effective ISIs occurred or the inclusion of ISIs of superior inductive efficiency may have led to the production of additional neural adaptations that facilitated conditioning. Note that with overlap of stimuli arising from prolonged stimulus duration (Fig. 3.8), an ISI of 2900 msec contains effective ISIs of 400 msec, 1400 msec, etc. A trace associative paradigm with an ISI of 2900 msec is shown for comparison. Generally, fewer overlap than trace presentations are required for the acquisition of high levels of CR performance, but the quantification of rates of acquisition is not normalized to discount the "extra" pairings within the overlap paradigm.

3. Conditioning was more efficacious when the CS terminated at the end rather than at the beginning of the US [778]. Most of Pavlov's associative pairings were performed in a short-trace fashion. Both stimuli were presented close together (up to 5 sec), but the CS was usually terminated a few seconds before the US began. Although some of his "simultaneous" pairings fell into the overlap category, the resulting reflex operations closely resembled those found with short-trace conditioning. Pavlov separated short-trace ("simultaneous") from long-trace ("delayed") conditioned responses. In the latter, the interval between the cessation of the CS and the beginning of the US was a minute or longer. Long-trace conditioned responses were said to be formed with greater difficulty than short-trace conditioned responses. In view of current knowledge, these variables are better studied as effects of the interval between presentation of CS and US (or the interstimulus interval-ISI) on the efficiency of acquisition of learned behavior.

(A) Overlap paradigm

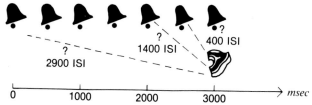

(B) Trace paradigm

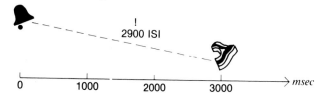

Fig. 3.8. *Different ISIs arising from overlap (A) and trace (B) associative paradigms.*

Optimal Interstimulus Intervals

Conditioning. The efficiency* of CR acquisition, that is, the number of conditioned responses performed per number of associative training exposures, is now known to be a function of the time interval between CS and US delivery. Intervals between 200 and 500 msec are commonly found to be most effective for many forms of classical conditioning. The optimal intervals have been determined with increasing precision by a number of investigators. When Spooner and Kellogg's results [946] are shown together with those of Wolfle [1095,1096] (see Fig. 3.9), peak effects are found with ISIs of 300 and 500 msec.

Gormezano and colleagues have conducted the most extensive investigations of the efficacy of conditioning as a function of the ISI. For nictitating membrane conditioning, the effects of ISIs between - and 200 msec were studied particularly carefully. The results, shown in Figs. 3.10 and 3.11, can be generalized to many, though not all, associative processes.

A nictitating membrane response [341] was conditioned in rabbits using ISIs of 800, 400, 200, 100, 50, 0, and -50 msec, the last figure representing backward conditioning with the US preceding the CS. The CS was a 50 msec, 1000 Hz tone; the US was a 50 msec shock.[+] Figure 3.10 shows the averaged levels of CR acquisition. Control studies in which the CS and US were presented in an unpaired manner showed response levels comparable to those with an ISI of -50 msec.

---

*Efficacy (a related variable) is defined as the level of performance (% CR) after a certain number of trials—the usual form of quantification.
[+]See earlier comments regarding ambiguities arising from the duration of the stimulus.

Effects of Order and ISI on Conditioning

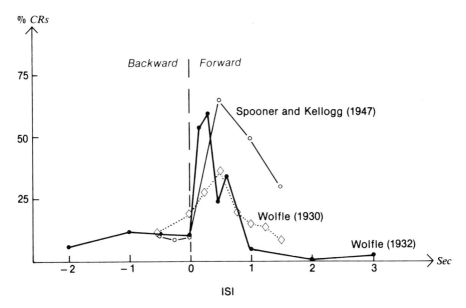

Fig. 3.9. Acquisition of conditioning (mean percent CR) as a function of ISI between CS and US. (After Spooner and Kellogg [946].)

Another study of nictitating membrane conditioning used electrical stimulation of the inferior colliculus as the CS and shock as the US. In this way, short ISIs of 50 and 100 msec could be more accurately studied. As shown in Fig. 3.11, an ISI of 100 msec was more efficacious than one of 50 msec or simultaneous presentation of CS and US (0 msec). The results of control pre-

Effect of ISI on Conditioning

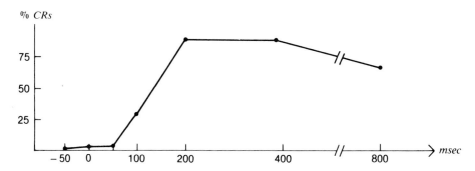

Fig. 3.10. Efficacy of acquisition of an associatively conditioned response as a function of ISI between auditory CS and shock US. (Gormezano [341].)

sentations of unpaired CS and US and extinction giving the CS alone are also illustrated.

Gormezano and colleagues also determined CS-US interval conditioning functions under three associative procedures affecting the duration of the CS (Fig. 3.7). Two of these were delay conditioning procedures. One employed a tone with duration held constant as 3000 msec. The other employed simultaneous offset of CS and US. The third was a trace procedure with a CS of 200 msec duration. The percentages of conditioned responses for all three associative procedures were found to be monotonic, decreasing functions of the CS-US interval. Altering the duration of the CS affected levels of conditioning, extinction, and spontaneous recovery. As shown in Fig. 3.7, the trace procedure involving the briefest presentation of the CS produced the lowest levels of responding at each CS-US interval, with the disparity being least at 250 msec and greatest at 2000 msec. In the two delayed conditioning procedures, extending the CS past the offset of the US lowered the levels of conditioning. The differences in levels of responding were greatest at the shortest CS-US interval and least at the longest CS-US interval. The manipulation of CS duration gave empirical outcomes consistent with stimulus trace accounts of classical conditioning [342].

Further information on optimal CS-US intervals for various types of Pavlovian conditioning is summarized in Table 3.1.

The optimal CS-US intervals of 200-500 msec appear to hold for a great variety of conditioned peripheral motor responses ranging from conditioning of galvanic skin responses (GSR) to conditioning of skeletal responses such as finger withdrawal and eye blink. However, for aversive conditioning of an appetitive reflex (e.g., bait shyness and other forms of conditioned taste

Effects of ISI on Conditioning and Extinction

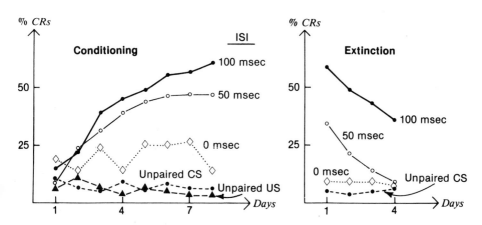

Fig. 3.11. *Nictitating membrane conditioning with brief ISIs. Electrical stimulation of the inferior colliculus was the CS (see text for further details). (Patterson [756].)*

Table 3.1. Summary of Optimal ISIs for Acquisition of Various Conditioned Responses[a]

Response	Optimal ISI (msec)	
	Median[b]	Minimal[c]
Eyeblink	390	250
Finger withdrawal	400	235
GSR	500	440
Nictitating membrane	—	200

[a]From material in Gormezano and Moore [345] and Kimble [519].
[b]Medians are median optimal ISIs from all data cited below.
[c]Minimal ISI is the shortest optimal ISI reported, and may reflect improved techniques for measurement.

aversion), a much wider range of intervals (ISIs of many minutes) is effective (Fig. 3.12). This is also true for other conditioned autonomic-visceral responses: salivary conditioning, 16 sec optimal ISI [270]; cardiac conditioning, 20 sec optimal ISI [169]; conditioned emotional response, 3 min optimal ISI [345, 478]. In addition, latent learned behavior such as sensory preconditioning is produced, optimally, by ISIs of more than 1 sec.

The optimal CS-US intervals of 200-500 msec for skeletal conditioning also generalize across stimuli of different functional significance, holding for aversive or noxious stimuli as well as for positive stimuli. Moreover, short ISIs are also efficacious for the development of instrumental conditioning. Unfortunately, the variable latencies of most instrumental procedures do not permit precise quantitation of ISI effects in the range of less than 500 msec.

The same parametric considerations apply to the offset of stimuli. Parenthetically, unconditional stimuli associated with *cessation* of a noxious stimulus function much the same as unconditional stimuli associated with the *onset* of a positive reinforcer in producing instrumental conditioning [48,339, 478,695].

In sum, with the exceptions noted above, short ISIs are generally more effective in producing conditioning than long ISIs, irrespective of most physical characteristics of the applied stimuli, and the generalization holds for many different types of conditioning. The mechanisms reflected by the present relationships thus appear to have wide usage. Moreover, the different relationships found with ISIs for conditioned taste aversion and sensory preconditioning imply other mechanisms being involved with those processes.

Sensory Preconditioning. The efficacy of acquisition of sensory preconditioning is also a function of the time interval between the delivery of the first stimulus (S_1) and delivery of the second (S_2). Acquisition is measured in terms of learning savings tested by means of transfer to a conditioned response acquired to the S_2 stimulus. Differences in acquisition of sensory preconditioning as a function of different ISIs were identified by Hoffeld and colleagues [422].

Optimal ISIs for Conditioned Taste Aversion

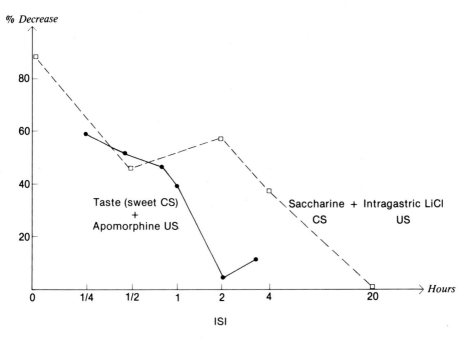

Fig. 3.12. Effects of the interstimulus interval (ISI) between taste CS (saccharin) and nausea-producing US (LiCl) on conditioned taste aversion. (Garcia et al. [316] and Palmerino et al. [748].)

They used tone as S_1 and light as S_2 separated by 0, 0.5, 1.2, 2.0, or 4.0 sec for different groups of cats. A control group was included. All the cats were then trained to avoid a shock in a wheel-turning apparatus with light as the CS, using a criterion of 90% CR performance. Then, levels of sensory preconditioning were measured as the number of responses that occurred until extinction using S_1 as the CS. In these tests, the control group gave no CRs, but all the experimental animals gave at least one response.

The results (Fig. 3.13A) showed that an ISI of 4 sec was more effective than shorter ISIs. Also of interest was the observation that four associative presentations were more effective than either fewer or greater numbers of presentations over the range of 1-800 pairings (Fig. 3.13B). This means that the neural adaptations that support this phenomenon are not only induced optimally by unusually long ISIs, but that they are inhibited, either in being formed or by the formation of other adaptations, by too many pairings. The inhibition might arise simply from repetitive stimulus presentation.

Berman [70] studied effects of presenting paired auditory or somato-sensory stimuli (i.e., CSs) on the amplitude of evoked potentials recorded from the anterior ectosylvian gyrus of anesthetized cats. *The pairings*

Optimal ISIs and Numbers of Pairings for Sensory Preconditioning

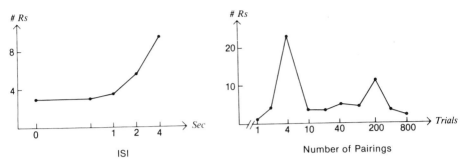

Fig. 3.13. Left: effectiveness of different ISIs in producing sensory precon-ditioning. Right: effectiveness of different numbers of pairings on the same phenomenon. (Hoffeld et al. [422].)

generally led to reduction in the amplitude of the evoked response in com-parison with the amplitude evoked by a single stimulus (Fig. 3.14). Repeti-tive presentation of each auditory stimulus was also studied for ISIs between 33 and 110 msec. The evoked responses were usually abolished with repetitive ISIs less than 33 msec. In general, the shorter the ISI, the greater was the reduction in response amplitude.

Somewhat more complex effects resulted from pairing auditory (click) with somatosensory (electrical shock to the contralateral radial nerve) stimuli (and vice versa by reversing the order of stimulus presentation). As shown in Fig. 3.14, *the response amplitude diminished* as the ISI decreased from 60 to 10 msec, but then increased toward normal size at shorter ISIs or upon simultaneous presentation of the two stimuli.

Repetitively Induced Inhibition–Habituation. As indicated by the material in Fig. 3.14, the efficacy of reflex inhibition produced by repetitive stimu-lation is also a function of the interstimulus interval. Here, the ISI is that between repeated presentations of the same stimulus. Another experimental study of this effect involved habituation of the electrical activity of the brain evoked by a click [1017]. The plots of response size versus ISI (Fig. 3.15) showed a strong interdependency. Conclusions vis-à-vis the location of the underlying neural adaptations must be tempered by electrophysiologic con-siderations that will be discussed in Chapter 4.

Rate of Stimulus Presentation and Optimal Intertrial Interval
Optimal Intertrial Interval. The interval between trials of associative presen-tations influences the development of conditioned reflexes. There is, in general, an optimal intertrial interval (ITI) at which conditioning will be most efficacious. Thus, in certain instances, fewer optimally spaced trials can be more efficacious than more numerous, massed trials (Fig. 3.16). As shown, stimulus pairings presented 90 sec apart led to more rapid acquisition of conditioning than did more frequent presentations. Reduced acquisition with

Changes in Cortical Evoked Potentials with Repeated Stimulus Presentations

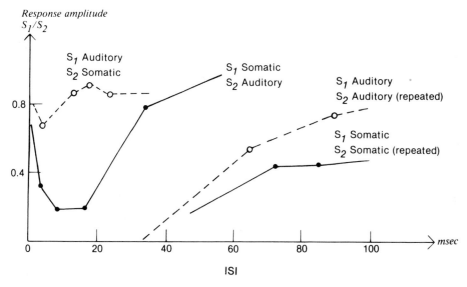

Fig. 3.14. Effect of stimulus pairing on the amplitude of evoked potentials recorded from the anterior ectosylvian cortex of the cat. (Berman [70].)

Effect of Frequency of Click Repetition on Cortical Evoked Potentials

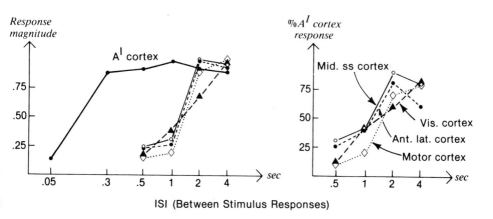

Fig. 3.15. Effect of click-stimulus repetition rate on auditory evoked field potentials recorded in the cortical areas as designated. Size (left) is defined as the sum of amplitudes divided by the number of records taken. Percent A^I (right) is defined as the sum of amplitudes divided by the number of response occurrences, taken relative to the percent from A^I (primary auditory) region. (Thompson and Sindberg [1017].)

Effects of ITI on Conditioning

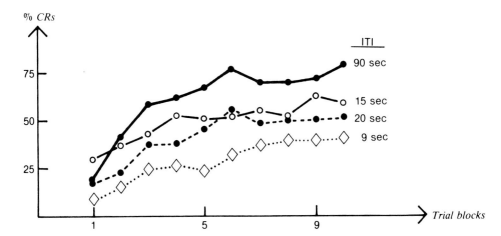

Fig. 3.16. *Acquisition of a conditioned eyelid response using different inter-trial intervals (ITIs). Acquisition is faster with longer ITIs; however, very prolonged ITIs may retard acquisition (Fig. 3.37). (Spence and Norris [926].)*

more frequent pairings may be attributable to a decrement in response due to repetitively induced inhibition. With extremely prolonged ITIs, a greater number of training trials may be required because of learning decay.

Effect of Intermittent Reinforcement or Association. Prolonged intermittence between associative pairings or reinforcements slows the development of conditioned behavior. Sometimes the slowdown can be attributed to intervening exposures to extinction-producing stimuli. Studies of associative conditioning of nictitating membrane and jaw movement responses have consistently shown reduced rates of acquisition when nonassociative trials were interspersed between associative pairings [344,423,777]. Studies of operant conditioning have shown that if reinforcement is given in only part of the trials, conditioning takes place more slowly [338]. However, slower rates of acquisition were not found in the experiments shown in Fig. 3.17 [521]. Conditioning with intermittent reinforcement is also said to be more resistant to extinction [1015]; however, no consistent effect on extinction was found in studies done by Gormezano's group [344,432,777]. Thus, these effects bear further clarification.

Use of Time Interval as an Associative Variable. The time interval between stimulus presentations can itself be used as a dependent variable in associative conditioning. For example, presentation of a US at regular, fixed time intervals can lead to the production of a motor response at the time that such a stimulus is omitted. As noted in Chapter 2, this phenomenon is called time conditioning in the Soviet literature [540].

Effects of US Absence on Conditioning

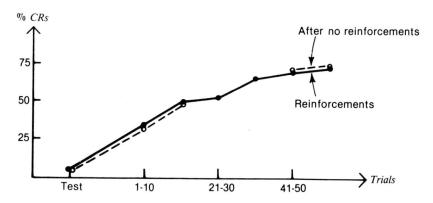

Fig. 3.17. Graph showing effect on conditioning of interpolated trials without presentations of US. (Note the increase in CRs despite the absence of reinforcements, putatively as a consequence of the reduced inhibitory effects of repeated US presentations.) In the experimental group, no reinforcements were given between control trials 20-40. These results may be complicated by the phenomena illustrated earlier in Figs. 2.7 and 2.8. (Kimble et al. [521].)

Other uses of time intervals or delay as an associative variable are more familiar to many psychologists. They include:

1. *Delayed response performance.* The animal is given a cue that it must remember for a certain delay period to receive a reward or avoid punishment.
2. *Delayed alternation performance.* This is a variant of delayed response performance in which the animal has to choose between two performances to secure reward or avoid punishment. It must alternately perform each response on successive trials. A delay between trials determines the time over which it must retain a memory of the previous correct response.
3. *Delayed reinforcement.* The animal may delay receiving a shock by lever pressing or some other kind of performance. Appreciation of the delay itself becomes a kind of positive reinforcer.
4. *Differential reinforcement of low-rate (DRL) performance.* The animal is reinforced only for delaying appropriate performance for a particular time period; a variation is that it must stop pressing the lever after a particular time period (simple hold DRL) or must stop and then press again within a restricted time period (complex hold DRL).
5. *Fixed interval conditioning.* Reinforcement is applied at regular time intervals, resulting in anticipatory motor activity prior to reinforcement.

These tasks are useful in evaluating the time constants of trace effects, retention, and the like. The specific way in which the memory of the time interval interacts associatively is not known physiologically, and merits further clarification.

Order of Presentation of CS and US (or of Response and Reinforcer)

As mentioned earlier, a significant aspect of the temporal relationships between CS and US presentation is the order of presentation. Backward associative pairing, in which the US precedes the CS, usually fails to produce conditioning. Pavlov was perhaps the first to appreciate this. He noted that presenting the odor of vanilla *after* the introduction of a dilute acid into the dog's mouth failed to produce conditioned salivation. In addition, presenting an electric bell following administration of food as the US failed to produce a salivatory CR. The evidence from a variety of other studies (Figs. 3.7, 3.10, and 3.11) also weighs against associative conditioning resulting from backward pairing of CS and US. This may, however, be an oversimplification. Some reports have appeared in which backward conditioning does result in increased performance [227].

The latter observations may be explained in the following manner. First, since repetitive presentation of the CS is known to induce inhibitory adaptation, it is reasonable to find less performance with US-CS pairing than with US presentation alone. This would also explain the observation that attempts at backward conditioning are more successful when fewer rather than greater numbers of pairings are used [227-229]. Second, some experiments in which backward conditioning has succeeded may be explained by effects of the US that persist long enough to overlap and even outlast presentation of the CS. Then, forward conditioning can occur. For example, light used as a US may produce retinal afterimages that last for hundreds of milliseconds, exceeding the interval between US and CS. Indeed, when "random" pairings of the same stimuli are used with longer ISIs, lower rates of performance are found [229]. Similarly, air puff to the eyes as US may have irritative aftereffects. One must try to select stimuli that will avoid these ambiguities.

It should also be remembered that strong pseudoconditioned responses may arise from presenting the US alone. Experiments in which a small amount of conditioning was thought to occur when delivery of the US preceded that of the CS [979] have later been interpreted to represent pseudoconditioning, arising from repetitive application of the US rather than from backward association of US and CS. Barlow [48] and Konorski [538] have suggested that the backward conditioning procedure leads to associative conditioning of a response antagonistic to the CR, but this view had not been borne out. Finally, either facilitatory or inhibitory consequences of the repetitively applied US can occur, latent facilitation sometimes resembling conditioning.

A comparison of several complex associative effects of trace, interval, and order of stimulus presentations can be found in the studies of Mowrer and Aiken [695] (Fig. 3.18). Their experimental parameters included trace and nontrace pairing with CS preceding US delivery, as well as pairing of stimuli in reversed or backward order with US preceding CS.

As summarized by Kimble [519], Mowrer and Aiken taught rats to press a bar to obtain food in the first stage of an experiment. In the second stage, they paired a 3 sec flickering light with a 10 sec shock under the five arrangements shown in Fig. 3.18 in which the CS (1) terminated as the US came on, (2) came on with the US, (3) came on 3 sec before US termination and went off with the US, (4) came on as the US went off, and (5) came on 2 min after the offset of shock, thus following rather than preceding the US. The effect of these different procedures was tested later by turning on the CS when the rats were pressing the bar to obtain food. In general, the flickering light tended to depress the rate of bar pressing. The extent of this effect differed for the five groups as shown in Fig. 3.18.

Similarities and Differences between Associated Stimuli

Similarities and differences between presented stimuli have profound effects on the induction of neural adaptations. Consider the following attributes of the stimuli:

1. *Their similarities.* Repetitive presentation of the same stimulus generally inhibits the response to the stimulus, whereas repetitive presentation of different stimuli generally facilitates the production of a new response.
2. *Their differences.* Differences in character or intensity between two stimuli can amplify associative effects.
3. *Their functional attributes.* Appetitive stimuli such as food commonly have different associative consequences than aversive stimuli requiring some defensive reaction for the preservation or survival of the organism.

Effects of Stimulus Order and Overlap on Conditioning

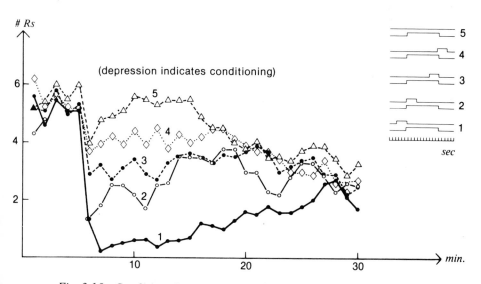

Fig. 3.18. *Conditioned suppression of a hunger motivated response. The usual reduction in response performance (group 1) is found after pairing a blinking light (CS) with a succeeding electric shock (US). The other patterns of stimulus presentation are as shown to the right. In group 5 the CS was presented nonassociatively 2 min after the US had terminated. In the inset CS is upper trace; US is lower trace. (Mowrer and Aiken [695].)*

Other, intermediary stimuli support associative reinforcement of the organism by the environment, as in instrumental conditioning.

4. *The background noise** surrounding stimulus presentation. Aspects of these noisy stimuli may be incorporated with the relevant stimulus in producing associative effects.

Each of these attributes can be more precisely described in terms of physical features of the stimuli.

Physical Features of Stimuli

The physical features of stimuli include their (1) frequency and (2) intensity relative to that of (3) the environmental noise, and their (4) modality (pressure, light, sound, etc.), and (5) form (boundaries, movement-vector, location, etc.). Each of these variables can affect associatively induced neural adaptations.

Frequency
The effects of stimulus frequency on associatively induced neural adaptations were discussed earlier under effects of stimulus timing (Figs. 3.5, 3.8–3.15).

Stimulus Intensity
The intensity of the stimulus will have direct neural effects. It will influence the probability of postsynaptic potential and spike generation as well as the extent of the set of synapses and neurons activated. So will frequency, modality, and intensity of background noise, but the effects of stimulus intensity may be the most obvious.

The effects of the intensity of the CS and US on Pavlovian conditioning can be summarized as follows:

CS Intensity [†]

1. Conditioning may be facilitated by increased CS intensity (Figs. 3.19 and 3.20).
2. The ratio of intensity to background level or degree of stimulus change is more important than absolute CS intensity. Thus, if the background or intertrial stimulation is quite intense, the weaker CS will yield to the stronger stimulus, and the latter will become the CS. CS offset, which is as effective as CS onset in producing conditioning, is more effective if the stimulus is strong than if it is weak [345].
3. Unconditioned performance (simple adaptation) is usually influenced more than conditioned performance (associatively induced adaptation) by relative or absolute CS intensity.
4. Weak stimuli are particularly effective in conditioning components of the orienting reflex.

*C.f. p. 328 for definition of "noise."
[†]See Gormezano and Moore [345] for further details.

5. Extinction may be influenced by CS intensity (Fig. 3.20).
6. Stimulus generalization and CR performance may be greater when the test stimulus is more intense than the CS than vice versa (Fig. 3.21).
7. CS intensity effects vary with ISI.

The effects of CS intensity on nictitating membrane conditioning (Fig. 3.20) were examined in the following manner. All subjects received 100 conditioning trials per day at a CS-US interval of 500 msec for 10 days of acquisition training. One group of subjects (Group L) was conditioned to an 86db tone, another (Group S) to a 65db tone, and a third group (LS-L and LS-S subjects combined) received 50 conditioning trials per day to each tone intensity presented in random order. The major findings, shown in Fig. 3.20, indicate that the more intense CS yielded higher levels of response. Moreover, the magnitude of the effect was virtually identical whether the subjects received a single CS intensity or both CS intensities within the conditioning session [866]. This finding was in contradiction to earlier results of Grice and Hunter [361], which showed an augmented effect within subjects.

The effects of US intensity on nictitating membrane and eyelid conditioning were examined separately as described in Fig. 3.22 and 3.23. The results are summarized below.

1. Increased US intensity is correlated with increased efficacy of conditioning (Fig. 3.22).
2. Associative effects of US intensity should be separated from effects of motivation or drive (Fig. 3.23).

Effects of CS Intensity on Conditioning

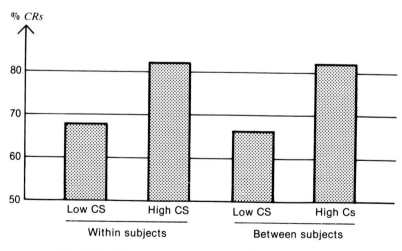

Fig. 3.19. *The mean percentage of CRs to a low-intensity (65 db) and high-intensity (86 db) tone CS for subjects exposed to both intensities (within subjects) and those exposed to only 1 CS intensity (between subjects). (Gormezano [341].)*

Effect of CS Intensity on Conditioning and Extinction

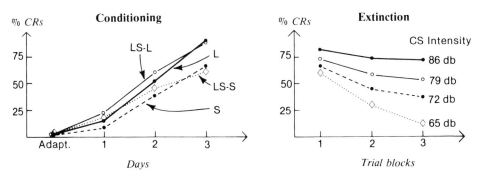

Fig. 3.20. Left: nictitating membrane conditioning obtained by pairing tone CS of different intensities with shock US. L = 85 db tone, S = 65 db tone; LS-L = trained with both L and S, tested with L; LS-S = trained with both L and S, tested with S (see text for further description). Right: extinction of conditioned nictitating membrane response as a function of CS intensity. During extinction, tones of intensities ranging from 65 to 86 db were presented to the combined LS-L and LS-S groups. (Scavio and Gormezano [866].)

3. Increasing the duration of the US may fail to improve the efficacy of conditioning or may actually decrease it (e.g., conditioned inhibition).
4. The intensity of the US may affect the types of associative adaptations that are produced. With nictitating membrane conditioning as in general, the stronger the intensity of the US, the more efficacious the conditioning

Generalization of Conditioning as a Function of CS Intensity

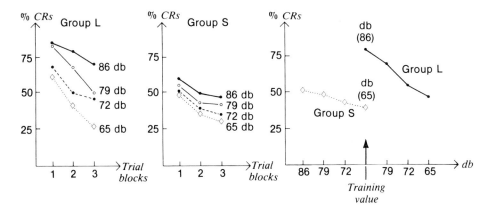

Fig. 3.21. Generalization of conditioned nictitating membrane response as a function of CS intensity. Group L trained with 85 db tone, as in Fig. 3.20; Group S trained with 65 db tone. Response to generalization test stimuli of different intensities as indicated. (Scavio and Gormezano [866].)

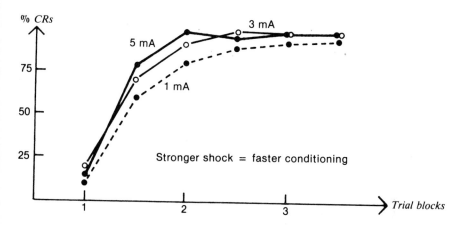

Fig. 3.22. *Effects of US intensity on acquisition of a conditioned nictitating membrane response in rabbits. CS = tone; US = 5 mA, 3 mA, or 1 mA shock. (Gormezano and Coleman [344].)*

(cf. Fig. 3.22). However, as the intensity increases to the point of becoming noxious, a different, more generalized conditioned motor response may develop. Finally, with further increases in the intensity of the US, there may be inhibitory effects on the development of the conditioned response.

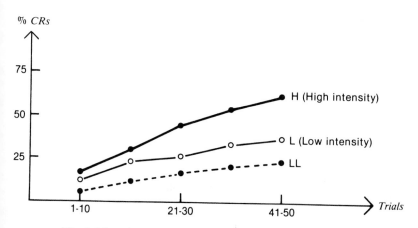

Fig. 3.23. *Effects of US intensity on eyelid conditioning. Group H received a strong air puff in association with the CS and a weak air puff for an equal number of nonassociative presentations. Group L received the weak air puff associatively and the strong air puff nonassociatively. Group LL received a weak air puff both associatively and nonassociatively. (Gormezano [341].)*

Environment–Background Noise.

Another variable that affects associatively induced reflex adaptations is the environment or background noise in which the associative process takes place. Pavlov thought this variable sufficiently important to construct a special, environmentally restricted laboratory, the Tower of Silence, in which noisy extraneous stimuli could be reduced or eliminated during associative pairing for the production of conditioned reflexes. He believed, quite properly, that the interaction of the environment and the investigator with the animal was an important consideration. He noted that the environment changed continually and attempted to reduce this variability. However, isolating the organism from normal stimulus exposure can itself lead to significant alterations in behavior. Thus, the noise-reduced type of training chamber may not be universally useful, and may sometimes provide a more artificial and artifactual background than a quiet, natural environment.

What Happens To Networks of Adaptive Reflexes as a Consequence of Stimulus Association?

What happens to adaptive reflexes as a consequence of stimulus association? Note that in the example of eye blink conditioning used earlier, the same physical stimulus (the CS) that failed to produce a specific motor response before association with a US, did so afterward. In order for this to have happened, some physical changes must have occurred within the CNS. These changes, or neural adaptations, are the consequence of stimulus association at the reflex level. They facilitate at least two separable reflex operations: reception of the CS and performance of the CR. They can cause changes in the latencies of overt reflex behavior as well as in qualitative reflex performance. *The changes in the latency of reflex response may reflect alterations in the pathway used to perform overt reflex behavior.* These alterations are highly sensitive to the parametric features of stimulus association.

Latency of the CR Varies as a Function of Parametric Features of Stimulus Association

The latency of conditioned responses will vary as a function of parametric features of stimulus association. For example, short-latency conditioned blinking results from pairing a weak click as a short-trace CS with glabella tap as the US. The latency of performance of this conditioned response is 20 msec after CS delivery. In contrast, a longer-latency conditioned eye blink (latency of 80 msec or more) can be produced by using a different CS and US [722]. This occurs when a tone CS is paired in temporal overlap with a US consisting of air puff to the eye or electrical stimulation of the angle of the eye. The parametric differences between these types of conditioning include that between trace and nontrace pairing as well as the degree of unpleasantness of the unconditional stimulus.

The conditioned response latency may also change in the course of development of the conditioned reflex to approach that of the ISI used in training. Boneau [91] studied the distribution of response latencies in eyelid conditioning as a function of training (Fig. 3.24). He found that they decreased initially and then subsequently increased toward the latency of the interstimulus interval. Millenson and colleagues [666] studied nictitating membrane conditioning in rabbits with ISIs of 200 and 700 msec. They used tone as the CS and shock as the US. Nictitating membrane responses of two different latencies were acquired, each being near that of the ISI used during acquisition training. Comparable observations were made in later investigations (Fig. 3.25) by Gormezano and colleagues [180,341,342,912].

The question arises whether the different conditioned response latencies are attributable to different neural pathways involved in their production or if, instead, more efficacious use is made of the same pathway. It may be a mistake, physiologically, to assume that variability of tens and hundreds of milliseconds will reflect changes in the efficacy of transmission rather than substantial differences in the pathways conducting information linking CS with CR. Synaptic transmission typically ranges between 0.3 and 0.6 msec per synapse. Even if full range changes of 0.3 msec occurred and were all in the same direction, a change in a reflex pathway of 30 serial neurons* would produce only a 9 msec change in response latency. Thus, alterations in the speed of synaptic transmission should not be expected to alter reflex latency greatly.† Conduction delay along the reflex pathway consumes most of the time required for message transmission. Response latency primarily represents the time of transit of all-or-none action potentials along the axons making up the reflex pathway. A change in the transmission pathway may therefore be expected to produce a greater change in response latency than a change in the efficacy of synaptic transmission.

A taxonomy of latencies of conditioned reflexes is shown in Table 3.2 based on observations such as those of Fig. 3.26. Levels of conditioned response performance can be as high with CRs in the alpha range of latency as with longer latency CRs [1113,1122]. Moreover, both long- and short-latency CRs can be performed discriminatively to a CS as opposed to another neutral or previously unpaired stimulus.

---

*This is actually a *large* number relative to known, *serial* pathways from receptor to cortex (frequently but three or four serial neurons) or from cortex to peripheral musculature (frequently two or three neurons).

†Changes in postsynaptic integrative properties of neurons (the membrane time constant or modulators of slow postsynaptic potentials; c.f., Chapter 6) could more greatly alter transmission times through a single neuron, but there is no evidence for changes of sufficient selectivity or precision of timing between neurons to change the latency of a reliably transmitted message without effectively changing the reflex pathway. (Also see the discussion of serial and parallel pathway message transmission in Chapter 7.)

Latencies of CRs

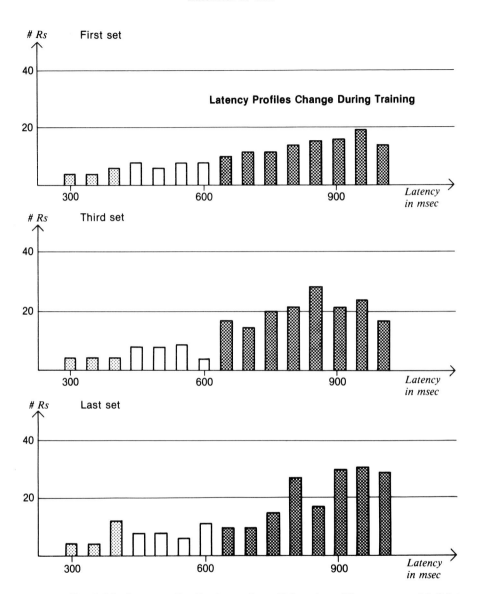

Fig. 3.24. Latency distributions of conditioned eyelid responses with light as CS and air puff as US. Interstimulus interval 1 sec. Conditioning sessions are divided into fifths, with first, third, and fifth sets as shown. (Boneau [91].)

Qualitatively Different Behavior Results from Different Parametric Features of Stimulus Association, with Possible Exceptions

The postulate that different behavioral outcomes ordinarily result from differences in associative or repetitive parameters of stimulus presentation is strongly supported by the material presented in this and the preceding

CR Magnitude as a Function of Latency and ISI

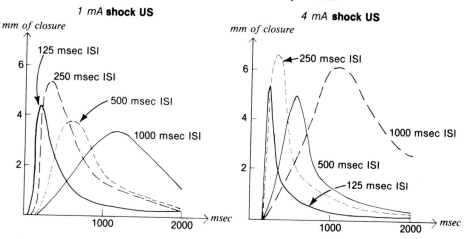

Fig. 3.25. The mean latency of conditioned responses determined on test trials for the tenth day of acquisition. The CR was closure of the cat nictitating membrane. The mean membrane extension is plotted in millimeters as a function of time after CS onset in milliseconds. The topographies plotted are for 8 experimental groups that varied as a function of CS-US interval (125, 250, 500, and 1000 msec) and shock US intensity (1 and 4 mA). Each topography function consists of 100 means, 20 msec apart, plotted over a 2-sec observation interval. Note how the peaks of the distributions fall near the time of US delivery (ISI) and even nearer as the intensity of the US is increased. (Gormezano [341,342].)

chapter. However, as the following examples will indicate, exceptions to this principle can be found: similar behaviors can be produced by dissimilar parameters, and dissimilar behaviors by superficially similar parameters of stimulus presentation.

Simple Extinction (Similar Behavior Produced by Dissimilar Parameters)
Simple extinction can be produced by superficially dissimilar procedures. After conditioning, the frequency and intensity of the response elicited by

Table 3.2. Response Latencies in Associative Conditioning[a]

Response nomenclature	Latency range (msec)
Alpha	12-115
Beta	116-245
Gamma	246-500

[a]Derived from experiments of Grant and Norris [351] with eyelid conditioning and of the author and colleagues with eyeblink conditioning [1113,1125,1127]. The range assignments are descriptive and are *not* absolute. Thus, some monogenic CRs may have latencies in both beta and gamma ranges, etc. For proper determination of early latency CRs, a short duration CS must be used. Responses with latencies of 12 msec and less may be evoked by direct stimulation of the motor cortex used as a CS.

Latencies of CRs

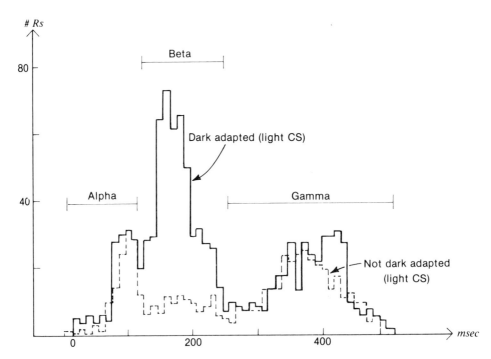

Fig. 3.26. Latency distributions of conditioned eyelid responses elicited by light as a CS in subjects adapted to the dark or not, as indicated. (Grant and Norris [351] with modifications of some definitions by this author.)

the CS will decrease, i.e., undergo extinction, under the following circumstances:

1. If there is no further training.
2. If the CS is presented repeatedly without association with the US.
3. If the US is presented with the CS but in backward order, US preceding CS.

Procedure 1 differs from procedures 2 and 3 in that the CS is not presented repetitively. Thus, in *this* case, extinction results either from spontaneous decay of the neural adaptations supporting conditioning or from cumulative, inhibitory effects of repetitive environmental stimuli other than the CS.

There are dissimilarities in the extinction produced by these means. It takes longer to produce a comparable degree of extinction with procedure 1 than with procedures 2 and 3. Presumably, commonalities between adaptive changes engendered by the dissimilar procedures explain why the different associative parameters lead to superficially similar behavior.

Extinction of Chain Reflexes (Dissimilar Behavior Produced by Superficially Similar Parametric Procedures)

Dissimilar extinction of chain reflexes can result from applying the same extinction procedure if the associative procedures leading to the initial development of the chain reflexes are themselves dissimilar.

Two different types of chain reflexes are recognized: sensory preconditioning and second-order conditioning. Both are called chain reflexes because the establishment of one reflex is linked, subsequently, to the establishment of a second reflex.

With sensory preconditioning, one stimulus (S_1) is initially paired with another (S_2). Then, S_2 is independently paired with a US to produce a conditioned response (cf. Fig. 2.11). Because of the chain reflex effect, S_1 (which was never associatively paired with the US) is also able to elicit the conditioned response.

The other type of chain reflex, second-order conditioning, is formed on the basis of a slightly different associative procedure. With second-order conditioning, S_2 is originally paired with a US to produce a conditioned response. Then, S_1 is paired with S_2 (without the US). Because of the chain reflex effect, S_1 is also able to elicit the conditioned response (cf. Table 2.4; another means of accomplishing second-order conditioning is illustrated in Fig. 2.13). The following example of Pavlov's describes the former procedure [759].

After developing a salivatory CR to a metronome CS, presentation of the metronome (S_2) was associated with some neutral stimulus (S_1) without introducing food as a US. The new stimulus (S_1) then acquired the ability to produce the salivatory CR without having been paired with an alimentary US. Pavlov termed this type of CR a secondary or second-order conditioned reflex. An essential parametric feature, he said, was that the new stimulus be withdrawn some seconds before the primary stimulus was applied. Pavlov found it impossible, in the case of alimentary reflexes, to use the secondary conditioned stimulus to establish still another chain reflex of the third order. However, conditioned reflexes of the third order could be obtained with the help of second-order conditioned reflexes involving defense reactions following stimulations of the skin with a strong electric shock.

Second-order reflexes may also be formed through repetitively induced, conditioned inhibition, as noted earlier.

Differences in Extinction of Sensory Preconditioning and Second-Order Conditioning. Differences in extinction of sensory preconditioning and extinction of second-order conditioning are as follows. With second-order conditioning, there is retention of conditioning to a second-order CS (S_1) despite extinction of conditioning to the first-order CS (S_2) on which it is based. However, with sensory preconditioning, extinction of the first-order stimulus eliminates the response to the secondary stimulus [826]. Thus, extinction after sensory preconditioning gives no response to S_1 or S_2 while extinction after second-order conditioning gives a CR to the new CS (S_1) despite extinction of the CR to the original CS (S_2).

Why extinction is linked to both stimuli with sensory preconditioning and to one stimulus with second-order conditioning must be explained by differences in the reflex adaptations supporting the two processes.* We will examine some clues to the way in which the different adaptations might be generated.

Differences in Associative Parameters Leading to Sensory Preconditioning and Second-Order Conditioning. Sensory preconditioning and second-order conditioning differ in the optimal associative parameters leading to their development. The main difference is that simultaneous or even backward pairing is frequently effective in producing sensory preconditioning.

Silver and Meyer [904] compared the effects of simultaneous, forward (CS-US interval 1.5 sec), and backwards (US-CS interval 1.5 sec) presentation of stimuli in the preconditioning phase of a sensory preconditioning experiment, using light and buzzers as the two stimuli and using rats as subjects. After 3000 presentations of the stimuli (perhaps too many), they conditioned a running response to one stimulus until 7 conditioned responses occurred in a series of ten trials. Finally, there was a test consisting of 100 reinforced trials with the other stimulus. In this test, the forward conditioning group was superior to the simultaneous and backwards conditioning group, which were themselves indistinguishable. All of the preconditioning groups were superior, however, to the appropriate control groups [519].

Coppock [184] performed analogous studies in humans using tests of galvanic skin response, GSR, in five groups as outlined in Table 3.3. Note that there were two preextinction groups: one for the purpose of extinguishing associations established in preconditioning, and an inverted preconditioning group for which the procedure corresponded to Silver and Meyer's [904] backward conditioning. The results of Coppock's experiments are shown in Fig. 3.27. Here, the three preconditioning groups were all superior to the control and inverted (backward) conditioning groups. Moreover, there was no significant difference between the latter two groups or among the first three. Thus, although backward pairing is frequently effective in producing sensory preconditioning, it is not always effective [519].

Whether the differences in chain reflexes are mediated by generalization from comparable adaptations in different networks or by the induction of different basic adaptations is a difficult question to resolve. One of the more interesting attempts to make such an analysis is as follows:

---

*Though perhaps by very specialized differences, since this result is not duplicated in some other experiments.

Table 3.3. Summary of Conditions in Coppock's [184] Experiment[a]

Group	Preconditioning	Preextinction	Training	Test
Control	Tone and light each presented alone	—	Light–shock	Tone
Preconditioning	Tone–light	—	Light–shock	Tone
Standard preextinction	Tone–light	Tone only	Light–shock	Tone
Inverted preextinction	Tone–light	Light–tone	Light–shock	Tone
Inverted preconditioning	Light–tone	—	Light–shock	Tone

[a] Tone-light conditions represented were reversed for half of the subjects. (From Kimble [519].)

A light flash was paired repeatedly with a tap to the cheek as US. The UR and CR were an eyelid movement. Next, cheek tap was paired as a CS with a shock that caused finger withdrawal. Then, presentation of the original light flash CS not only evoked the eyelid CR but also the finger withdrawal, although the light had never been paired, specifically, with the

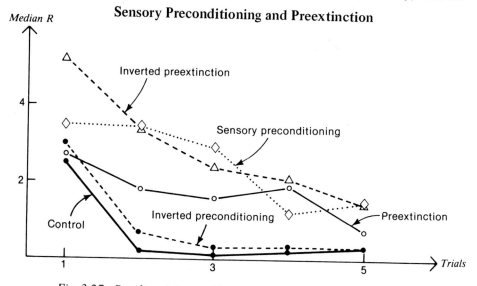

Fig. 3.27. Results of Coppock's experiment on sensory preconditioning. The groups (from Table 3.3) are: (1) inverted preextinction; (2) sensory preconditioning; (3) standard preextinction; (4) inverted preconditioning; (5) control. Note that groups 4 and 5 are inferior in performance to the other three groups. The inferiority of the inverted preconditioning group supports the hypotheses: (a) that for optimal sensory preconditioning to occur, the order of stimuli during the preconditioning phase of the experiment should be in the forward-conditioning sequence, but (b) that some sensory preconditioning will still occur in backward sequence. (After Coppock [184] in Kimble [519].)

shock US. Interestingly, if the eyelid response was absent during performance, so was the finger response [631].

This demonstrates that two motor reflex pathways were linked to production of the second-order CR, but it does not establish whether they were linked serially or in parallel nor whether the adaptations along each pathway were similar or different.

Kimble [519] implies that some mediator (such as proprioceptive feedback)* mediates second-order conditioning in the manner shown in Fig. 2.13. On the basis of this mediation hypothesis, he predicts that the amount of generalization between two stimuli will increase if the subject makes the same initial response to them. Grice and Davis [360] tested this possibility using a conditioned eye blink procedure.

> Three tones of different pitch were used as CSs. Only the middle tone was reinforced. Another response, pushing and pulling a lever, had also been conditioned to each of the CSs. "For one of the non-reinforced stimuli, the lever response was the same as to the reinforced CS. For the other negative stimulus, it was different. The subjects made significantly more generalized CRs to the non-reinforced stimulus involving the same motor response as [that to] the CS, than they did to the stimulus requiring a different reaction" [519].

These results support the theory that motor-coded neural adaptations serve as the basis for the generalizations (irrespective of whether or not they are induced by proprioceptive feedback) and suggest that comparable motor-coded adaptations in different reflex networks play a key role in generalization across conditioned chain reflexes. Further descriptions of the generalizations or "dynamic stereotypes" of such reflex cascades can be found elsewhere, particularly in the Soviet literature [33,572].

What Happens to Adaptive Reflexes as a Consequence of the State of the Organism?

The state of the organism can also affect adaptive reflex operations resulting from associative processes by affecting levels of neural excitability, receptivity, and the like. For example, it is generally accepted that little or no learning takes place during sleep† and that a certain degree of arousal facilitates learning. Thus, adaptive processes supporting learning are likely to be state dependent.

The organism can influence its own behavioral "state," so it is not surprising that one can "instructionally" influence neural adaptations arising from associative processes. Conditioned responses increase when attempts to

---

*Proprioceptive feedback is not required for conditioning [198,997]; hence, the mediator may have a different physiologic basis.
†Exceptionally, linkages to CS and US can be formed under anesthesia as in conditioned taste aversion [cf. 130,133].

prevent their development are reduced. They may also increase when attempts are made to enhance their development.

Norris and Grant [723] (Fig. 3.28) showed that conditioning was acquired more rapidly after instructing their subjects not to control their natural reactions to the stimuli than after instructing them to suppress their reaction. Further support for the efficacy of verbal (or other) instructions in influencing conditioned responses is found in the work of Miller [667] (Table 3.4). Additional evidence is provided by Hilgard and Humphries [414] (Table 3.5) [519]. Nonetheless, some conditioned responses can still be acquired or can persist despite instructions to the contrary (Tables 3.4 and 3.5).

Specific Behavior as a Consequence of Specific Reflex Operations Altered by Specific Neural Adaptations

Physiologically speaking, behavioral specificity is equivalent to a change in the probability of discharge of certain neurons along specific sets of reflex pathways. With discriminative conditioning, specific reflex changes support enhanced receptivity to the CS and related stimuli. Receptivity to the discriminative stimulus is reduced and that to other stimuli is either unchanged or is altered reciprocally. Other changes support performance of the conditioned motor response. They are also specific. Both types of change depend critically on parametric features of the associative process.

Effects of Modulatory Instructions on Rates of Conditioning

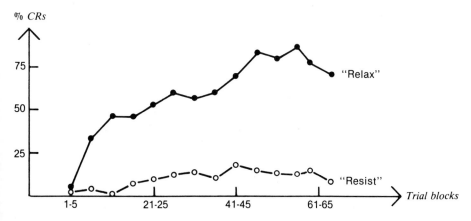

Fig. 3.28. Effects on rate of conditioning of instructions to alter behavioral state. Relax = "Do not attempt to control your natural reactions to these stimuli. Simply behave naturally and let your reactions take care of themselves." Resist = "Be sure you do not wink before you feel a puff." (Norris and Grant [723].)

Table 3.4. Effect of Supplementary Instructions on Frequency of Conditioned Responses[a]

Group	Instructions	% trials on which conditioned responses appeared
(1) Inhibitory	"Be sure that you do not wink or start to wink before you have felt the puff" ($n=20$)	26
(2) Instructed antagonism	"Open your eyes each time the air puff strikes your eye" ($n=20$)	28
(3) Noncommittal	Only minimum instructions necessary for photographic recording ($n=25$)	38
(4) Informed	Told that light would be followed by air puff ($n=20$)	44
(5) Facilitatory	"In case you feel your eyes closing or starting to close, do nothing to prevent it" ($n=20$)	71

[a]Conditioned stimulus, light; unconditioned stimulus, air puff to one eye; interval 400 msec. The groups are arranged in order of increasing success of conditioning. (From Miller [667] in Kimble [519].)

Some endure; others do not. The poststimulus time (PST) histogram provides one useful index for studying these changes at the neural level [900]. Alterations in neural excitability to injected current provide another [1107]*. Generalization furnishes a means for studying these changes at the overt behavioral level, and it is this latter index to which the next portion of this chapter is addressed.

Specificity of Stimulus Reception

It is both the specification or "labeling" of a reflex pathway receptive to the particular stimulus and changes in neurons along that reflex pathway contingent on parameters of stimulus presentation that lead to the specificity of altered stimulus reception. Adaptive changes supporting enhanced sensory reception will occur somewhere within the set of neurons receptive to the CS.

Generalization of Stimulus Reception

Sensory generalization develops as a function of the overlap of sensory representation between the set of neurons receptive to the novel stimulus and the set labeled by the CS[†] and adapted by the associative process. The generalization gradient is a function of the overlap and the degree of adaptation

---

*Further details concerning PST histograms and measurement of neural excitability can be found in Chapters 4 and 5.
[†]For a definition of the term "line labeled," see p. 110 ff.

Table 3.5. Effect of Instructions on Characteristics of Conditioned Eyelid Responses to Positive Stimulus within a Discrimination Experiment

Groups in order of amount of voluntary supplementation of response (10 subjects in each group)	Characteristics of responses to positive stimulus		
	frequency (%)	amplitude (mm)	latency (msec)
Instructed to refrain from responding to either stimulus	55	13	448
Instructed to refrain from responding to positive stimulus but instructed to respond to the negative stimulus	71	16	404
Without instructions with respect to response	74	19	401
Instructed to respond to positive stimulus, not to negative stimulus	90	35	319

(From Hilgard and Humphries [414] in Kimble [519].)

within elements receptive to both stimuli. Thus, sensory generalization reflects not only commonalities between various physical qualities of the stimuli but also reflex circuitries, adaptations intrinsic to the neural network, and their dependence on parametric features of the original stimulus presentations. As adaptations occur and evolve, reception of the original stimulus by the receptive elements may be altered much as though the physical character of the stimulus were changed. These changes will greatly influence perception of the stimulus.

The principal studies of sensory generalization have been of the effects of associatively induced neural adaptations on generalization, but baseline studies of preexisting generalization gradients or stimulus discriminability have also been performed. Their conclusions will be examined below.

Simple Discriminability

Discriminability is defined by Kalish as "a measure of the sensitivity of the organism to stimulus differences" [473; also see 472]. A liminal stimulus will have a coded representation within that part of the nervous system that is receptive to it. Discriminability will be a consequence of the uniqueness* of this representation vis-à-vis that of another stimulus.

Tests comparing receptivity to one particular stimulus with that to other, different stimuli reveal the discriminability of the nervous system to those stimuli, but the results are usually described in terms of generalization to motor performance evoked by the stimuli (Fig. 3.29). Thus, the tests determine to what degree the different stimuli will evoke the same motor response. Figures 3.29 and 3.30 illustrate the results of such tests in man and pigeon. They suggest that:

*This can be defined more precisely, both physiologically and mathematically, but for the present "uniqueness" will suffice.

Generalization Gradients

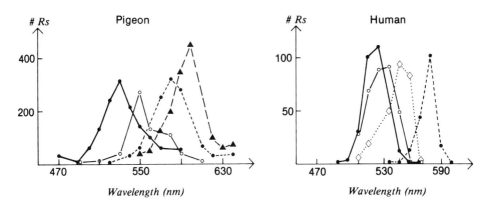

Fig. 3.29. Generalization to motor performance in pigeons (left) and humans (right) between a light CS used during training and light stimuli of other frequencies used in testing. (Kalish [472].)

1. Discriminability is much the same for light stimuli of frequencies between 530 and 600 nm. Within species, the gradients of generalization and the functions of discriminability often look similar for different (modality-related) stimuli.
2. Generalization gradients (the slope of the number of responses elicited as the stimulus is changed) or, more properly, discriminability functions, are different in human and pigeon: that for light in the human is somewhat steeper (better discriminability) near 530 nm, and that in the pigeon is steeper near 590 nm. Thus, discriminability may differ between species.
3. Within the same sensory modality, generalization across physically similar or related stimuli is greater than across physically dissimilar or unrelated stimuli. That is, the closer the frequency of the test light to that of the light used as the CS, the greater the performance elicited.
4. Generalization across the same sensory modality is greater than that across a different sensory modality. Figure 3.31 shows levels of CR performance in animals trained to a CS alone (a tone), to a tone CS presented with an auditory discriminative stimulus (DS_s), and to a tone CS presented with a nonauditory (visual) discriminative stimulus (DS_d). There was a higher percentage of responding to the discriminative stimulus of the same sensory modality (DS_s) than to that of a different sensory modality (DS_d).

Changes in the generalization gradients of sensory reception from those predicted by simple discriminability reflect adaptations within the underlying reflex networks. For example, in Fig. 3.31 the rates of CR acquisition in the groups trained with CS and DS are reduced in comparison with the rate in the group trained with CS alone. In terms of neural adaptations, this may reflect an inhibitory effect of presenting a discriminative stimulus associ-

Stimulus Generalization in Human and Pigeon

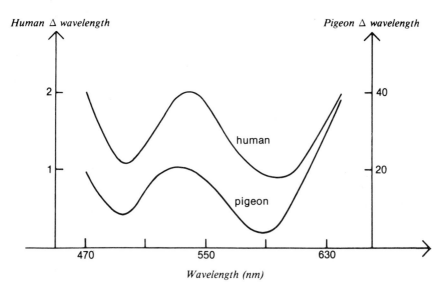

Fig. 3.30. Comparison of hue discrimination as a function of wavelength for pigeons and humans. (Kalish [472].) Each ordinate is the ratio of the difference thresholds for discriminating between different wavelengths.

atively with a CS, attributable to the repetitive exposures during training. After acquisition, performance may actually be enhanced by introduction of a DS perhaps as a consequence of second-order, associatively induced adaptations.

Sensory generalization is also influenced by the type of motor activity performed. High levels of performance with cross-modal sensory generalization (i.e., generalization with a stimulus of entirely different modality) signify the accessibility to the novel stimulus of the reflex network supporting that motor performance. Levels of performance arising from cross-modal generalization have been reported to be as high as 38% of performance to the original stimulus, Razran [816] (cited by Martlatt et al. [649]), and levels as high as 60% have been reported by Martlatt et al. (in Gormezano [340]) for classical human eyelid conditioning.

Learned discrimination
Learned discrimination is the behavioral outcome of neural adaptations that link discriminability with motor performance. The adaptations may alter either the discriminability function of sensory reception or the accessibility of motor performance. Together with the circuitry of the reflex network, these two types of adaptation (i.e., sensory and motor) support learned discrimination. Each will be reflected in the changes in generalization gradients found after conditioning. The gradients can be studied during extinction. Determining whether the changes are in the gradients of stimulus reception or

Discriminative Conditioning

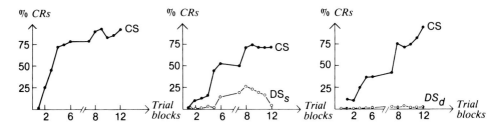

Fig. 3.31. Discriminative conditioning of a nictitating membrane response to a tone CS in rabbits. Left: control training without DS. Middle: training with reinforcement of CS and no reinforcement of a DS$_s$ of similar sensory modality. Right: training with reinforcement of CS and no reinforcement of a DS$_d$ of different sensory modality. (Moore [679].)

in those of motor performance may help us decide which type of adaptation has occurred.

Effects of Extinction on Stimulus Generalization. How does extinction itself affect stimulus generalization? An example is shown in Fig. 3.32. Here, seven groups of pigeons were trained using a light of 550 nm as the CS. Then, in six groups, the conditioned responses were extinguished using a different stimulus. The frequencies of the stimuli used during extinction (ESs) ranged between 490 and 560 nm. Generalization gradients were obtained across the entire frequency range for each group. The results suggest that:

1. Extinction reduces sensory reception to the ES. This effect generalizes to other stimuli, as shown.
2. Extinction either reduces reception of the original CS or inhibits performance of the CR, as the ES increasingly resembles the original CS.

Effects of Discrimination Training on Generalization Gradients. The effect of discrimination training on sensory generalization is shown in Fig. 3.33. Here, groups of pigeons were trained with both a CS and a DS. The CS was positively reinforced; the DS was negatively reinforced. The CS was a light of 550 nm. The DSs were lights of 555, 560, 570, and 590 nm, respectively. A control group that was trained without a DS was included. After conditioning was established, generalization gradients were determined in each group for light stimuli ranging between 480 and 620 nm.

The results of Figs. 3.31 and 3.33 indicate that:

1. Discrimination training can sharpen generalization gradients. The gradients of sensory generalization in the discrimination groups were sharper than those in the control group (Fig. 3.33).
2. Discrimination training can shift the preferred stimulus frequency for inducing a response from that of the original CS to another frequency; the

Generalization of Extinction

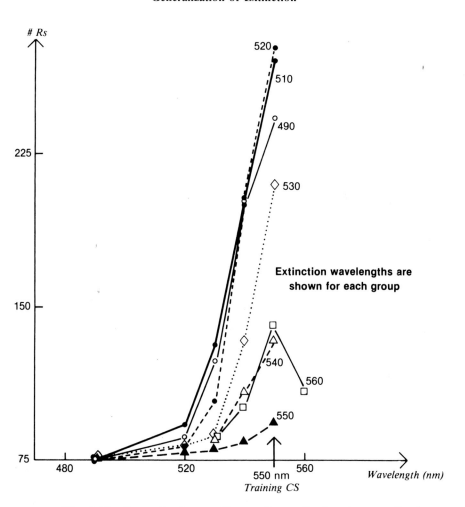

Fig. 3.32. Generalization gradients after extinction to one stimulus wavelength indicated by the numbers beside each curve. The wavelength of the training CS was 550 nm in all groups. (Kalish and Haber [474].)

displacement is away from the negatively reinforced DS and the gradient is skewed. Repetitively induced inhibition may be responsible for these effects.

The remarkable skewing effect of discrimination training is more obvious when the gradients of Fig. 3.33 are compared with those obtained in the absence of discrimination training with a DS of common modality (Fig. 3.34). In the latter example, an auditory stimulus, a 1000 Hz tone, was used as the CS. Periods of silence were associated with nonreinforcement [458]. Compare these data with the null performance levels shown

Generalization After Discrimination Training

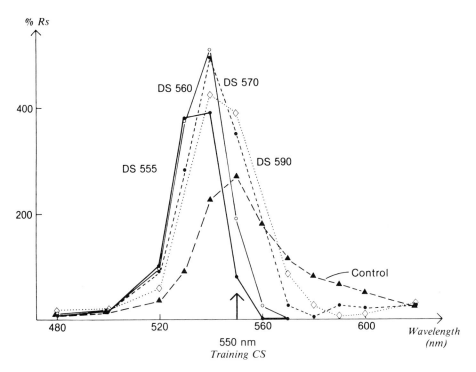

Fig. 3.33. Generalization following discrimination training (pigeons pecking to cue stimuli, CSs, and not to discriminative stimuli, DSs, of different wavelengths). Training CS = 550 nm in all groups. DSs are as indicated by numbers. No DS used in control group. (Hanson [382].)

in Fig. 3.35. There, the tone was delivered continuously, during nonreinforcement as well as during reinforcement. It was therefore of no significance to the response of the organism (again pigeons).

3. Discrimination training can reduce the rate of conditioned response acquisition (Fig. 3.31).

4. Discrimination training can either enhance or reduce performance levels relative to those learned without discrimination training depending on the paradigm used.

   The discrimination-trained groups of Fig. 3.33 showed enhanced performance levels compared to the control group. In other studies operant responding to a cue signaling positive reinforcement was enhanced by introducing a second cue signaling nonreinforcement [639,821]. When a cue signaling greater reinforcement was introduced, operant responding was reduced [639].

5. Discrimination training produces learning savings that subsequently generalize to produce faster learning of similar responses to different stimuli or different responses to similar stimuli.

Generalization After Discrimination Training With Tone as CS, No Tone as DS

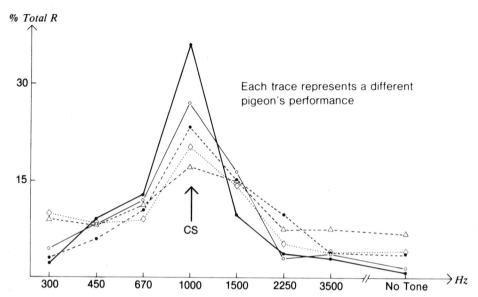

Fig. 3.34. Generalization gradients after discriminative training of pigeons with a 1000 Hz tone as CS; no tone as DS. The means of three generalization tests are plotted separately for five different subjects. (Jenkins and Harrison [458].)

Generalization Without Discrimination Training

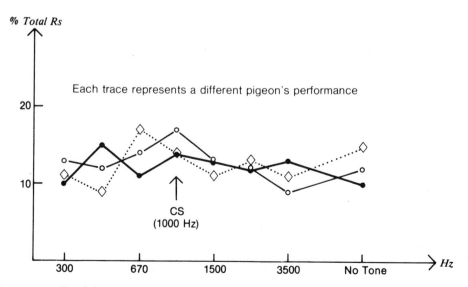

Fig. 3.35. Generalization gradients following nondifferential training with a 1000 Hz tone as CS. Data from three pigeons, based on the same tests of generalization as in Fig. 3.34, are shown. (Jenkins and Harrison [458].)

Successive discriminations to new stimuli are learned more rapidly by animals that have experienced discrimination training than by control animals given equivalent exposure to a nondiscriminative experimental situation [79,260,642,1011]. This difference is found both with novel discriminative stimuli whose modality differs from that of the original and with tasks that involve learning different instrumental responses. For example, monkeys trained to make serial visual discriminations will learn subsequent discriminations increasingly rapidly, sometimes in a single trial, even if the relevant stimuli differ considerably from the original stimuli [872].

Other experiments (Fig. 3.36) have explored generalization gradients during extinction after discrimination and nondiscrimination training using a compound CS [281].

Three groups of pigeons were trained to peck for food using a vertical line plus a color as the compound cue stimulus. In one group, the DS (nonreinforcement) was the same color (there was no line). In a second group, the DS was a different color (also no line). In a third group, no DS cues were presented during periods of nonreinforcement.

After training, the pigeons were given generalization tests:

Test A: Rotation of the line between $0°$ and $67°$ (i.e., generalization to variation of half the compound stimulus).

Test B: The compound (line plus color) stimulus including rotation of the line between $0°$ and $67°$.

The findings (Fig. 3.36) suggest:

i. The response to training with *a compound CS plus a physically analogous DS* is greater than (or extinction is less than) the response to training with *a compound DS plus a physically different DS,* which, in turn, is greater than (or extinction is less than) the response to training with *a compound CS with no DS.* (This is the same skewing effect of discriminative training that was observed earlier in Fig. 3.33.)

ii. The same results were found for the (generalized) response to the nondiscriminative half of the compound stimulus. (This indicates that the effect generalizes to half of the compound stimulus.)

iii. The generalization gradient to the half stimulus is sharper than that to the whole compound stimulus. (This suggests that not all gradient sharpening with discrimination training is due to the discrimination per se. Rather, the pairing of CS and DS (as S_1 and S_2) may have an effect.)

iv. Interestingly, the group trained with both line tilt and color relevant (the second group) did not show sharper generalization gradients than the first group trained with only half of the compound stimulus relevant.

The studies of generalization indicate that both sensory and motor adaptations are acquired in the course of discrimination training. They influence learning and subsequent generalization of stimulus reception and motor performance and have many of the same parametric sensitivities as the other associative phenomena discussed earlier. The evidence concerning the parametric sensitivities of generalization will now be summarized.

Generalization Test Results

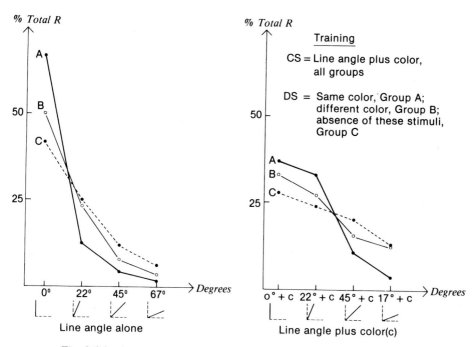

Fig. 3.36. *A comparison of generalization gradients tested during extinction (nonreinforced trials) between discriminatively and nondiscriminatively trained groups. (Farthing [281].)*

Stimulus Intensity
Generalization gradients vary as a function of the intensity of the CS (see Fig. 3.21). Rabbits classically conditioned to lid closure to a loud sound as a CS show steeper generalization gradients than do those trained to a softer CS. Also, animals trained to a soft sound as a CS show increased numbers of responses when tested with louder stimuli (cf. [866] and Fig. 3.21). Also see [984] for effects of shock intensity on discrimination performance.

Intertrial Interval
Generalization gradients vary with the intertrial intervals used during training. An example is shown in Fig. 3.37. Here, pigeons were trained to a 550 nm light CS using reinforcements at intervals of 15 sec, 1 min, and 4 min. The group with the shortest reinforcement intervals had the greatest number of responses and the steepest generalization gradients.

Testing Exposure (Number of Extinction Trials)
Generalization gradients may be maintained in the course of extinction while the overall-percent response gradually declines. An example is shown in Fig.

Generalization Varies with ITI

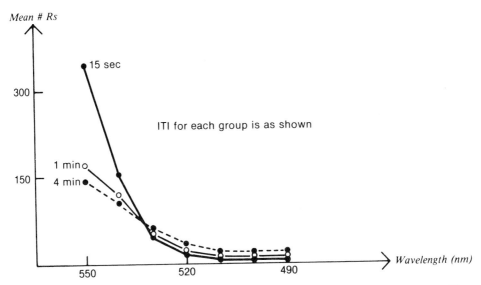

Fig. 3.37. Generalization gradients as functions of ITI used in training. The training cue stimulus was 550 nm. (Haber and Kalish [375].)

3.38. Here, pigeons were again trained to peck to a light CS.* The frequency of the training CS ranged between 530 and 600 nm in four groups of birds. Generalization gradients were determined for stimuli ranging ± 60 nm from the CS. The results were combined across groups and then divided according to the number of extinction trials.

Extrinsic Background
Generalization gradients vary according to the environmental background in which training occurred. An example is shown in Fig. 3.39. Ducklings raised in a monochromatic (589 nm) light environment showed flatter generalization gradients than did ducklings raised in a polychromatic (100 Watt, tungsten) light environment. The operant task used a 589 nm CS. The birds with the flat generalization gradients were able to learn visual discriminations in these frequency ranges if given discrimination training.

Intrinsic Background
Generalization gradients vary according to factors intrinsic to the organism such as hunger and fear. These factors are commonly called effects of drive. Fatigue, arousal, drowsiness, etc. also contribute to the intrinsic background.

---

*CS used here as cue stimulus (in operant conditioning) is not distinguished from use of this term as conditional stimulus in classical conditioning within this section. Both stimuli elicit learned motor behavior, although the timing between CS and CR may be looser with the operant task.

Generalization Gradients During Extinction

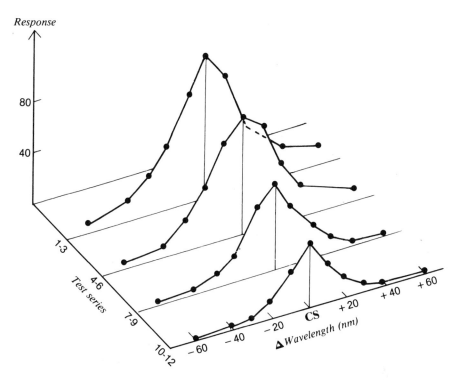

Fig. 3.38. Generalization gradients averaged for successive fourths of an extinction test series in groups of pigeons. See text for further details. (Guttman and Kalish [374] in Kalish [473].)

The effects, though poorly characterized, should be considered in evaluating generalization. Examples of differences in generalization gradients attributable to drive are shown in Fig. 3.40. Here, feeding weights during training and testing were varied from 60% to 90% of the normal ad libitum value. The effects on stimulus generalization are as illustrated.

In summary, the gradients of sensory generalization appear to be functions of (1) stimulus relatedness, (2) parametric features of associative processes leading to neural adaptations (discrimination training, stimulus intensity, intertrial interval, and testing exposure), (3) the preexisting reflex circuitry, and (4) background influences such as drive and distraction. One may reasonably assume that neuronal adaptations of the associatively or repetitively induced types support some of these generalization functions just as they support conditioning, habituation, and the like. The gradients of generalization also reflect the reflex context within which the adaptations have occurred. Studies of the generalizations, both behavioral and physiologic, may reveal whether the adaptations primarily support sensory reception, motor performance, or both.

Developmental Environment Affects Generalization

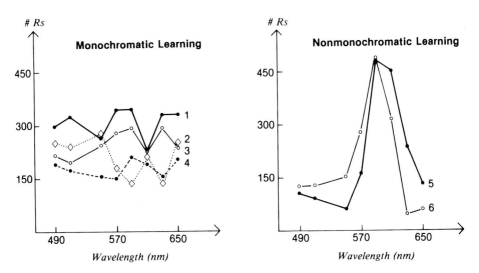

Fig. 3.39. Stimulus generalization gradients for individual ducklings raised in a monochromatic environment (left) versus ducklings raised in a nonmono-chromatic environment (right). (Peterson [765].)

Effects of Hunger/Drive on Stimulus Generalization

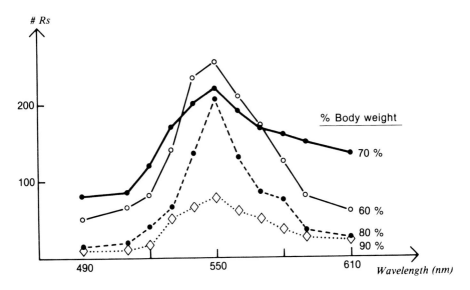

Fig. 3.40. Effects of hunger on generalization gradients. Subjects were trained to feed after receiving a 550 nm CS. Both training and testing were done with body weight maintained at the percentages shown. (Thomas and King [1010].)

Specificity of Motor Performance

Much motor performance that is acquired through associative adaptation is specific. Either a specific motor response is acquired, or a specific motor response is suppressed. Usually, the response resembles that elicited by the US or reinforced by (contingent on) one of the associated stimuli. Such performance requires that the neural adaptations be located with great specificity along motor pathways.

The specificity of learned motor performance may be quantitative as well as qualitative. Consider the variation in pressure of the motor response learned for food reward shown in Fig. 3.41. This variation forms a statistical distribution reflecting the characteristic output of an underlying set of motor units activated to perform the response. Analysis of the specificity of learned motor performance requires corresponding stochastic considerations of the sort described in Chapter 7.

Whenever a specific learned response is acquired, the properties of some neurons that project, many polysynaptically, to the target musculature of this response must be selectively altered. An altered probability of discharge in this set of neurons will constitute the neural form of the learned motor response.

Generalization of Motor Performance

Motor generalization gradients develop as a function of the overlap of motor projection between the set of neurons performing the novel response and the set "labeled" by the adaptations. How this labeling might occur is a matter of separate interest and will be discussed shortly. Where it takes place along the motor pathways responsible for production of the learned response is also of interest, since generalization will arise from commonalities between different pathways for motor performance.

Responses performed by reciprocally innervated musculature often show paradoxical latent facilitation. Thus, the generalization may sometimes be to opposing rather than to synergistic responses. For example, a person who has been conditioned to extend his resting index finger to a CS in order to avoid a shock to the finger pad will flex his finger to the CS when his hand is turned over [413,1082].

The production of conditioned and unconditioned responses involves different neural pathways supporting common motor functions [111,1110,1118]. Even when responses to the CS and the US have qualitative similarities, as in Pavlovian conditioning, the form of the CR will differ somewhat from the form of the UR both in terms of motor unit representation, measured electromyographically, and in latency [111,1110,1112,1113]. The latencies of the CR and UR will be expected to differ because of their different initiating stimuli and characteristic neural pathways linking stimulus with response.

Transposition gradients, the generalization gradients of motor performance, will then reflect:

Motor Generalization

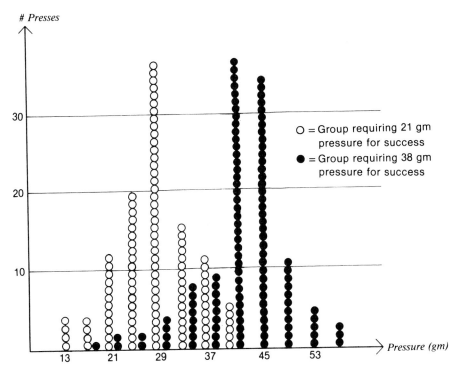

Fig. 3.41. Generalization of learned motor performance. The distributions of pressures used in two different bar press tasks (○, requiring 21 gm pressure for success; ●, requiring 38 gm for success). The distributions represent motor generalizations. Note the efficient grouping of modal pressures just above those needed for success. (Data from R. Hays and C. B. Woodbury, presented by Hull [439] and illustrated in Kimble [519].)

1. Physiologic commonalities between movements performed (do they involve the same or different muscle groups?).
2. The circuitries of preexisting reflex pathways such as those responsible for complex, species specific stereotyped movements.
3. Adaptations of these reflex pathways. (Just as with sensory processes supporting discriminability versus learned discrimination, transposition gradients of preexisting, simple motor performance may differ from those of learned motor performance.)

Preexisting Reflex Pathways
Certain neural pathways present in the organism from birth are preconnected in such a way as to support the production of complex, stereotyped movements. Numerous examples can be found, ranging from the reciprocal innervation of Sherrington (Chapter 2) to species-specific web building in spiders (Prologue).

Some consider these stereotyped movements to be fixed-action motor responses. However, defining a fixed-action response as a response "played out independently of the input" [480], takes too narrow a view of this behavior. Apart from the intrinsic contradiction of terms implying that action can somehow be fixed, motor responses in mammalian systems generate self-modifying sensory feedback, even at the most peripheral levels, and are often correctable in the face of injury. They are therefore not independent of their generating input or of the inputs that they themselves generate. This is so even for highly stereotyped movements such as stepping or more complex locomotor activity [891]. Exceptionally, some ballistic movements are thought to be relatively free of self-modifying sensory feedback, but their complete independence from their generating input, once begun, has not been conclusively demonstrated.

Fixed-action responses are, in fact, stereotyped motor activities that have highly specific, motor labeled reflex pathways. They may result from genetic preprogramming of specifically connected networks, or from disproportionately large numeric representations of these pathways within the nervous system. Because of the latter, complex patterns of motor behavior may be maintained with minimal new learning after destruction of some portions of their motor pathways. The spider will build its stereotypic web even though one or more of its legs is injured, and the cockroach will clean its antennae after loss of a leg (even though some postural adjustments must be made to do so) [205]. Thus, different, interdependent sets of motor reflex pathways can contribute to the support of analogous, highly sterotyped behavioral outcomes.

The dependence of some learned, stereotyped motor responses on modifying inputs is demonstrated by the fact that they vary adaptively. Consider the acquisition of a slice in golf! Such motor behavior must involve adaptations beyond those primarily related to the originally learned, specific motor task. Motor behavior, even the most highly stereotyped, then depends not only on preexisting reflex pathways, but also on neural adaptations that influence transmission through those pathways.

It may be difficult to separate generalizations depending on the new adaptations from those depending on older adaptations or on the fundamental, preexisting circuitry. Take, for example, the generalization of a learned right leg flexion withdrawal to a left leg flexion withdrawal. Does this transposition gradient mainly reflect the use of already existing pathways that are ordinarily available for simple rerouting of learned movement? Or does it reflect neural adaptations along pathways that were not previously used to perform this movement? The answers must be provided by physiologic investigation.

Differences in Motor and Sensory Adaptation Inferred from Patterns of Motor and Sensory Generalization

Were the psychological approach more precise and the physiologic system less complex, it would be possible to infer accurately whether adaptations were of the sensory or motor type on the basis of whether the related behavior showed sensory or motor generalization. Instead, the inferences in Table 3.6 must be drawn but speculatively. They require confirmation or rejection by neurophysiologic studies of the types described in Chapters 4 and 5.

During extinction, receptivity to the CS is altered by repetitively induced inhibition. Where a repetitive input from a CS is required for adaptation to occur, cells receptive to the CS must adapt.

It can also be inferred that repetitively induced inhibition generates adaptations by which motor performance is selectively suppressed, although all components of learned motor performance are not suppressed by repetitively induced adaptations. For example, during extinction, skeletal motor responses may be reduced, but conditioned autonomic responses to the same CS may be maintained. Since this cannot be explained simply by inhibition of receptivity to the CS, one must hypothesize the additional occurrence of some type of motor inhibition. Studies of generalization indicate that the inhibitory effects of extinction spread to involve secondary motor responses. So do those of conditioned inhibition. Thus, on this basis, too, it appears that some neural adaptations serving repetitively induced inhibition primarily affect motor performance.

While repetitively induced inhibition following presentation of USs may be manifest by a suppression of motor performance, one may also find a latent facilitation of motor performance following repetitive presentation of some USs. The underlying adaptations can be triggered in those motor neurons* that are reached by the repetitive US. It can be inferred then that adaptations such as these involve neurons that are (1) addressed by the repetitive stimulus, and (3) of significance for the production of the motor response.

Associatively induced adaptations are more difficult to characterize on the basis of generalization, but some inferences, drawn from the earlier descriptions of generalization in this chapter, are included in Table 3.6.

Mapping the Reflex Through Sets of Adaptive Neurons

Line Labeling

Line labeling [123,291,693] defines the representation of stimulus-specific and motor-specific information along networks of neurons and within the cable space of single neurons. Further reference to current flow within passive neuronal cables is made in Chapter 4, p. 128 and Fig. 4.8. The contribution of changing ionic conductances to transmission through this cable space is considered in Chapter 5.

---

*A simple term is needed to describe one neuron of a set that has a common polysynaptic motor projection. In this book, that term shall be "motor neuron." Confining use of the term to spinal motoneurons takes an unduly parochial view of the motor system. Motor neurons may not only have polymodal projections, i.e., be involved in more than one functional motor set, but may also have polymodal sensory receptive properties [111,273,1110,1118]. This property may lend itself to supporting some of the sensory and motor generalizations described earlier.

Table 3.6. Postulated Sensory and Motor Significance of Neural Adaptations

Cause	Postulated Adaptation	Behavior
ES presentation^a (ES only, repetitively, without any other stimulus being presented)	S^- (S^-, M^-) M^-	**1. Extinction/Latent Inhibition** a. Reduces sensory reception to ES b. Reduces sensory reception to original CS and performance of CR c. Accounts for selective inhibition of non-autonomic CR (with retention of autonomic CR, see p. 110)
US presentation^{b,c}	M^+ M^-	**2. Discrimination Training** a. Enhances response performance b. Sharpens transposition gradients of motor response
Associative CS (+ US) presentation	S^+	c. Shifts receptivity in favor of CS
DS presentation (repetition)	S^-	d. Reduces receptivity to DS and sharpens generalization gradients

Key: CS - Conditional stimulus S^- - Adaptation inhibiting stimulus reception
      DS - Discriminative stimulus S^+ - Adaptation facilitating stimulus reception
      ES - Extinction-producing stimulus M^- - Adaptation inhibiting motor performance
      US - Unconditional stimulus M^+ - Adaptation facilitating motor performance

^{a} plus latent effects of US presentation as below
^{b} if presented in association with CS, the M^+ effect persists
^{c} plus latent effects as above

A neural set is defined in terms of the representation of specific inputs or outputs within the network (see Fig. 3.42) and within the neuron itself, the latter as related to a space constant, λ, between different synaptic inputs and the locus of spike initiation within the cell.

There are two types of labeling: sensory (stimulus) labeling and motor (response) labeling. *Sensory labeling* involves the representation of stimulus-specific information along a set of neurons receptive to that stimulus. *Motor labeling* is the representation of a to-be-performed motor response among a set of neurons whose polysynaptic motor projection will mediate the performance of that response. Examples of both kinds of labelings within the same neural network are shown in Fig. 3.42. These definitions, though simple, are by no means trivial in light of analytic approaches that are made possible by such means (Chapter 7).

Functional Representation

The representation of an item of line labeled information in the network defines the reflex function of a set of neurons. It reflects a parametric feature of association-dependent neural events, i.e., the spatial variable in associative processes (see p. 60). The extent of a particular neural set will influence the associative variables of stimulus timing and intensity by summatory facilitation and occlusion as described earlier.

Further significance of sensory and motor labeling for the generation of different reflex behavior may be inferred from the different outcomes of the following associative paradigms:

1. CS-US pairing leads to conditioning.
2. CS_1-CS_2 pairing leads to sensory preconditioning.

These differences may well arise because presentation of USs produces strong motor labeled effects*, whereas presentation of CSs produces primarily sensory labeled effects (see Tables 3.6 and 4.3). The differences between CS and US are often spoken of in terms of "salience" [795], but terminologies more oriented to reflex anatomy, and the physiology of neuronal adaptation and message transmission may be preferable.

Space of the Neural Set

Different stimuli, when received, will "map" on different neural spaces or functionally different neural sets. The extent of neural activation, even by simple stimuli, is widespread. Most neocortical units have polysensory receptive fields e.g. [1122], and, in the pericruciate cortex, polymodal motor projections [1110]. There will be functional overlap between different elements within particular line labeled neural sets as well as within single elements. The overlap and redundancy are intrinsic to the known organization of the nervous

---

*and probably some sensory labeled effects as well.

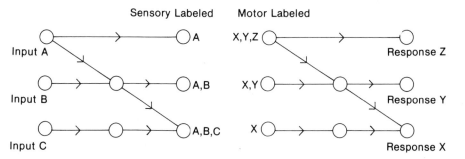

Fig. 3.42. Diagram of identical sensory (left) and motor (right) labeled networks.

system. It may be possible to deal with such complex interdependencies mathematically using linear systems analysis [582,704,1087] and conditional probabilities [282]. The object would be to analyze associations and substrate adaptations according to sensory and motor labeling and to map these functions as inputs, transforms, and outputs of single neurons. (A detailed description is given in Chapter 7.)

The space or extent of the neural set activated by a particular stimulus will have profound consequences on neural adaptation. If a neuron is to participate in an adaptation, it must first be activated, though not necessarily to spike threshold. Commonalities or differences in the spatial effects of different stimuli within single cells [807] can then play a critical role in determining whether associatively or repetitively induced adaptations will occur.

Neuronal Specificity

Another variable that will influence neural adaptation is the specificity of the involved neurons. Some relevant attributes of neuronal specificity are whether the cell has dendritic spines, electrical synapses, particular neurotransmitters, receptors, messengers, and ionophores, and whether or not the dendrites can support actively propagated action potentials. These attributes are described in detail in Chapter 5. Neuronal specificity will determine what kinds of adaptations a particular neuron can potentially undergo.

In summary, consideration of the above variables allows one, in principle, to map the reflex through sets of adaptive neurons. The first variable, *functional representation*, concerns identification of those neurons in the reflex that can respond to appropriate stimulation and influence production of the desired motor response. The second variable, *the neural set*, defines the network architectures within which elements identified by the first variable are contained. In effect, the interconnection between elements is considered by this variable. The third variable, *neuronal specificity*, defines the adaptations that elements identified by the first variable are capable of undergoing. Knowledge of the second variable can provide information concerning feedback effects on these adaptations.

In conclusion, critical parametric features of associative processes play a key role in controlling neural adaptation. Cellular, subcellular, and molecular specificities underlying these adaptations contribute to the changes and are sensitive to parametric features of stimulus presentation such as order, interval, duration, and intensity. As learning occurs, enhanced receptivity to specific stimuli and enhanced ability to perform specific responses develop, together with gradients of stimulus and motor generalization. The critical variables influencing these generalization gradients are:

1. Overlap of multiple sensory representations along a particular network line labeled by the CS (responsible for discriminability). Enhanced transmission along these pathways will facilitate reception of all stimuli which these pathways can receive.*
2. Overlap of multiple motor representations along a particular network line labeled by the US (responsible for simple transposition gradients). Enhanced transmission along these pathways will facilitate activation of all muscles to which these pathways project.*
3. The representation of adaptive changes within the network.

The possibility that the significance or meaning of a stimulus lies within its line labeled representation over selected neural networks seems preferable to other possibilities based on philosophic or syntactic constructs. Acceptance of this view can lead to considerations that bear significantly on traditional views of society concerning phenomena such as freedom, dignity, and the like. The reader is referred elsewhere for discussions of these questions [910].

---

*Subject to exclusion by reciprocal inhibition, lateral inhibition, and the like.

Chapter 4

Cellular Correlates of Learned Behavior

What appears to be a skilled musician, is a brain in action . . .

(Anonymous)

How have scientists attempted to study memory and learning at the cellular level? Anatomists have sought changes in the morphology of cell structure in relation to learned behavior with variable success. The results of their investigations are described in the next chapter. Others, primarily electrophysiologists, have attempted to establish relationships between neural activity and simple forms of learning. Fine microelectrodes have been designed that can be positioned within or just outside simple neurons to accomplish this purpose. Cell activity is then assessed in relation to some experimentally produced behavior. For example, patterns of spike discharge elicited by a CS are studied before, during, and after conditioning, or activity elicited by a US is studied during habituation.

Some neural responses show changes isomorphic with the development of behavior, and some responses are produced associatively or repetitively, thus mimicking, parametrically, the induction of learned reflexes. Other neuroelectric responses can be conditioned and habituated apart from the animal's immediate, overt behavior. They affect the organism's behavior subliminally. However, when cumulative, they, too, may have overt behavioral consequences.

Quite different approaches have also succeeded in linking brain and behavior. For example, both electrical and chemical stimuli have been used directly in the brain to change neural function. The object has been to produce learned behavior as well as neural isomorphisms thereof.

This discussion of cellular aspects of learning and memory begins by considering the established relationships, or correlates, between neural activity and learned behavior. The more useful correlates meet the following criteria:

1. Direct measurements of cellular function are obtained, such as the rate or probability of spike discharge over a fixed time period following CS presentation and prior to CR performance.
2. A specific behavioral state or a simplified aspect of behavior is identified and studied.
3. A specific relationship is demonstrated between the neural changes and particular behavioral alterations. For example, after conditioning, increases in the electrical excitability of neurons are found to occur selectively in neurons that project to muscles performing the CR.

Electrophysiologic Correlates of Behavior

What are neural correlates of behavior and how are they measured electrophysiologically? To an electrophysiologist a neural correlate of behavior is a change in potential, or other electrical parameter referable to neurons, the time course, magnitude, and induction of which relate directly to measurable features of the behavior.

Most electrophysiologic measurements of neural activity are those of potential differences between two points. The potentials change from moment to moment so that instead of measuring the potential difference at a single time (Fig. 4.1A), it is measured continually, again and again, as a time function (Fig. 4.1B,C). This function is equivalent to that seen on a recording instrument such as an oscilloscope (Fig. 4.1D). When the potential difference between the scalp and some other point such as the ear is measured, it is found to vary with a magnitude of 50-100 μV or more, and is called the electroencephalogram (EEG) (Fig. 4.2). The potential difference between the cortex or dura and elsewhere is greater in magnitude (500 μV), and this time function is called the electrocorticogram (ECG).

The EEG and ECG measure fields of neural activity generated over distances of millimeters, but if the size of an electrode tip placed within the brain is small, i.e., of the range of 0.2-40 μm in diameter, one begins to discern spikelike action potentials of single neurons (Fig. 4.3A). These unit impulses range in magnitude from 100 μV (extracellular recording, e.g., Fig. 4.14) to 70 mV or more (intracellular recording, e.g., Fig. 5.17) with some variability depending on the location of recording and type of electrode used. Recordings of unit activity may be thought of as functions of time, much like unit-impulse functions (see refs. 200, 240, 582 and Fig. 4.3B). Means for assessing these time functions, statistically, are described at length later.

Gross Potential Activity

Gross potentials were the first measures of neural activity to be correlated with learned behavior. The gross potential is the electric field potential re-

Brain Potentials Are Functions of Time

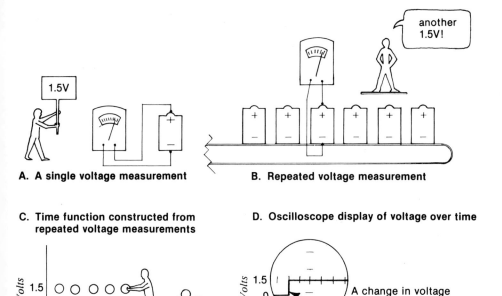

A. A single voltage measurement

B. Repeated voltage measurement

C. Time function constructed from repeated voltage measurements

D. Oscilloscope display of voltage over time

Fig. 4.1. Measures of potential difference over time. (A) A single measurement; (B) repeated measurements; (C) time function; (D) the same measurements displayed on an oscilloscope as a time function. While a voltmeter can be used to measure one or more steady potentials, an oscillograph or oscilloscope is needed to study rapidly varying potentials as functions of time, f(t). Thus, in part D, where voltage (V)=f(t): at t_o, V=0; at t_2, V=1.5; at t_4, V=1.5.

Measurement of EEG and ECG

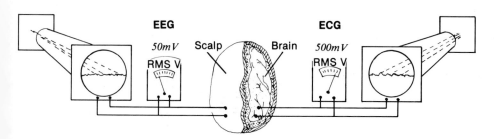

Fig. 4.2. Measurement of EEG and ECG differs with respect to the location of the two points at which the potential differences are measured. RMS is the root mean square of the fluctuations in voltage.

Unit Activity is Also a Function of Time

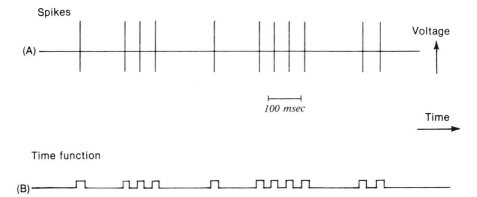

Fig. 4.3. Thinking of unit activity as a time function will make it easier to understand the analytic approaches described in Chapters 5 and 7.

corded extracellularly from the brain* by macroelectrodes with tip sizes generally ≥ 0.1 mm. The potential difference may be measured between two, immediately adjacent points within the brain (bipolar recording) or between a single point in the brain and some remote location (monopolar recording) as shown in Fig. 4.4.

Bipolar recordings will reject noise common to both electrodes when led to a differential amplifier (an advantage) but may admit great variation in signal size due to minute positional differences in electrode placement, as with small, unintentional movements of an electrode tip (a disadvantage). Recordings may be made in a similar manner from the brain, brainstem, and spinal cord or from peripherally located structures such as the skeletal musculature (electromyogram-EMG).

Although the gross potential activity of the brain varies as a function of behavioral state almost irrespective of where the potential is recorded, not all variations are reproducible even if recorded sequentially at the same locus. This is because gross potentials reflect irrelevant electrical signals, or "noise," as well as neuronal information transmission. Muscle contractions, body movement, changes in blood flow, and respiration can each contribute artifactual noise to field potentials recorded from the nervous system. Thus, even those changes in potential that are isomorphic with behavior may be difficult to interpret. They may reflect changes in muscle activity instead of changes in neural events! It is also difficult to determine where the sources of the neural potentials are located because their generating current leaves the neuron along the entire extent of the soma and dendritic branches and may then be distorted during transmission through the extracellular space, not to

---

*Or spinal cord or skull, changes in CS evoked EEG activity being among the earliest correlates of learning [1132-1135].

Bipolar versus Monopolar Recordings

(A)

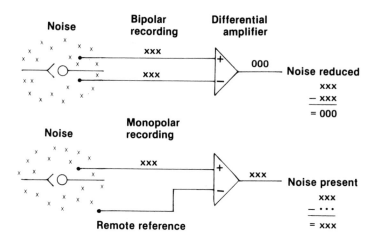

(B)

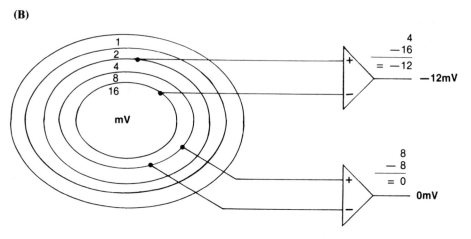

Fig. 4.4. Differences in measurements made with monopolar and bipolar recordings led to a differential amplifier. (A) Noise at the recording location is reduced when it is common to both recording electrodes, as with bipolar recording. (B) Small changes in electrode position along the gradients of voltage emanating from a voltage source (mV) can lead to big differences in the potentials measured by bipolar recording.

mention through the skull. Despite these limitations gross potentials have been used by many investigators to study learning and memory. In addition, the EEG is used clinically as an index of brain function.

As one might expect, gross potentials can be altered by procedures employing simple, repetitive or associative parameters. However, in learning to perform a conditioned movement, the movement sometimes leads to a change in brain potential regardless of whether it is performed as a conditioned or unconditioned response. Therefore, some changes in gross potentials attributed to learning may reflect simply the performance of a motor response. Other changes in gross potentials occur directly as a consequence of associative parameters and reflect neural processes mediating learning. For example, the changes in potentials after eyeblink conditioning that were shown in Fig. 2.4 mainly reflect alterations in local postsynaptic potentials arising from associatively altered excitability of brainstem motor nuclei and the cortical projections thereto [111,467,651,1110,1113]. These increases in the excitability of single neurons to intracellularly injected current that are co-incidental with conditioning can be measured in the motor cortex as well as in the facial nucleus. The increases persist if the CS and US are paired associatively, but are transient in duration after presentations of USs alone [111,651].

Arousal, Fear, Vigilance, and Wakefulness

The amplitude and frequency of the EEG and other spontaneous gross potentials vary as a function of arousal, fear, vigilance, wakefulness and other aspects of behavioral state [cf. 456,689,1133]. Some frequencies may reflect characteristic transmission times along specific neural circuits such as those connecting the thalamus and the cortex [771,772]. Other frequencies may reflect characteristic discharge patterns of certain pacemaker neurons.

There are well-established behavioral correlates of certain EEG frequencies. For example, in the resting, inattentive state with the eyes lightly closed, the predominant frequency is alpha, i.e., between 8 and 14 Hz (Fig. 4.5). Upon arousal or alerting, a decrease in amplitude and an increase in frequency occur (low voltage, fast desynchronization—Fig. 4.6A). During sleep, slow waves of 3 Hz or less are seen, often with superimposed sleep-spindle bursts of 10-12 Hz.

Some changes in field potentials occur so abruptly following delivery of a particular stimulus that they are termed *evoked responses* or, synonymously, *evoked potentials*. They are thought to reflect currents arising from postsynaptic conductance changes (PSPs) during neurotransmission. Such changes can be produced by almost any perceptible stimulus since most areas of the brain receive inputs of every sensory modality.

Often, analysis of these potentials is based on the assumption that the latency of the response is fixed. This may not always be the case. Sometimes the onset of the evoked potential change is not abrupt because the stimulus onset is gradual. In other instances the onset latency may vary because the stimulus information is transmitted indirectly, through a number of parallel pathways with different conduction times. Given alterations in the involved

EEG Activity

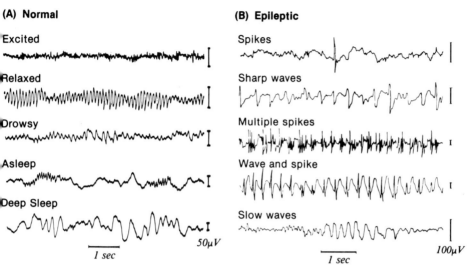

Fig. 4.5. *Some characteristic patterns of EEG activity. (From Jasper, reproduced in Ruch et al. [849], and Penfield and Jasper [761] in [393].)*

transmission pathways, the latencies of the predominant response may be expected to change. If this is recognized, matched filter analysis [1103] can be performed to separate and identify responses of different latency.

Evoked potentials, just as spontaneous potentials such as the EEG, may change in amplitude as well as latency as a function of arousal, fear, or vigilance [323,379,644,768]. An example is shown in Fig. 4.6B.

It is quite common, then, for either the spontaneous activity or the evoked response of the nervous system to a particular stimulus to change as a function of behavioral state. The changes that occur in relation to learned behavior such as habituation and conditioning are described below. However, as will be seen, many results have been a disappointment for those who wished to link changes in brain potential to the information content of specific stimuli or to the underlying physiology of learning processes.

Habituation

Gross potentials may vary as a function of habituation. Repetitive presentation of stimuli that at first produce arousal and enhancement of evoked potentials can result in decreases in the size of evoked potentials and failure of desynchronization of the EEG [404]. This type of habituation, according to John [462], "has been uniformly reported for a wide variety of structures." However, Hall's evidence [378] suggests that this uniformity is not consistent throughout the brain. It shows that while habituation-like effects occur in late components of evoked responses to auditory stimuli recorded from auditory cortex and medial geniculate body, habituatory changes do not occur at all in recordings from other portions of the auditory system. These regions include

Changes in Brain Potential with Arousal

(A) Arousal reduces the amplitude of brain activity.

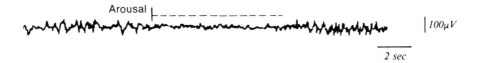

(B) Arousal increases the amplitude of *some* changes in brain activity evoked by stimulation.

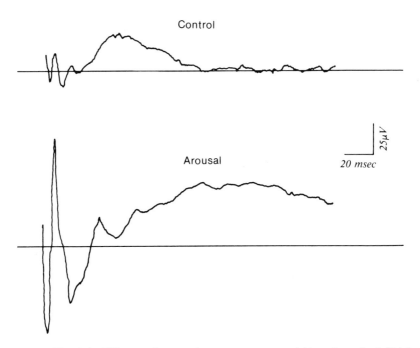

Fig. 4.6. Effects of arousal on spontaneous (A) and evoked (B) brain potentials. The traces in (B) are averages of 550 responses to an electrical stimulus. The arousal there is attributable to fear of the experimental paradigm. After Moruzzi and Magoun [690] (A) and Hall and Mark [379] (B).

the inferior colliculus, ventral cochlear nucleus, and portions of the reticular formation. In a separate study [1004] Teas and Kiang failed to find changes in early or late components of evoked potentials at the auditory cortex. Thus, the variation in evoked potentials with habituation is inconsistent. As an explanation for this inconsistency, Hall points out that some of the positive results may be secondary to changes in the level of arousal rather than direct reflections of cellular processes serving habituation.

Conditioning

Gross potentials can be modified by conditioning. The acquisition of conditioned behavior is associated with changes in evoked potential activity. Increases in the amplitude of responses evoked by the CS [29,290,310,513, 780,1104,1113] are somewhat more frequently observed than decreases [166,395,456,832]. The changes vary from locus to locus [310], and their differences cannot be resolved on the basis of the types of conditioning used [644,686].

It can be argued that the changes in potential most closely related to conditioning should be those occurring at an appropriate time in relation to performance of the conditioned response [1104,1113]. There should be correspondence between latency and conduction time along neural pathways that lead to production of the conditioned movement. There will be an onset latency or time delay between stimulus presentation and the evocation of a neural response and then another latent period before the movement itself. The briefer and less variable the latency of the CR, the more likely the possibility of detecting a specifically related neuroelectric response in the midst of the surrounding background noise. In the example shown earlier in Fig. 2.4, short-latency eyeblink conditioning was associated with a significant increase in the amplitude of a short-latency evoked response to click CS recorded at the facial nucleus of the cat [1113]. This nucleus contains the motoneurons supporting performance of the blink movement. Analogous increases were also found at the motor cortex [1104]. They are shown in Fig. 4.7 together with the increases recorded from the facial nucleus. The definition of each recorded response was improved by using variable latency detection and averaging procedures [1103].

The onset latency of the eyeblink CR, relative to the arrival of the click CS, averaged 20 msec in the orbicularis oculi muscles. The onset latency of the field potential evoked at the facial nucleus was 17 ± 3 msec following arrival of the click CS at the ears of the preparation [1113]. (Conduction delay between the facial nucleus and the peripheral musculature is 2-3 msec.)

The amplitude of the response at the facial nucleus was greater in conditioned animals than in naive animals. With extinction, the amplitude decreased, though not completely to the level found in the naive state. This reduction is not attributable to changes in fear or alertness because extinction was accomplished simply by reversing the order of CS-US presentations. Specificity of the CS in eliciting the eyeblink response and normal behavioral extinction following reversal of the order of CS-US presentation indicate that the behavioral response was that of conditioning and not that of sensitization or pseudoconditioning.

At the motor cortex [1104], the amplitude of evoked responses also increased with the development of the conditioned eye blink and decreased with its extinction (Fig. 4.7). The onset latency of the cortical response to click-CS was 13 ± 4 msec, while the onset latency to light-CS was significantly longer. This represents a difference of 7 msec between the latency

Evoked Potentials and Behavioral State

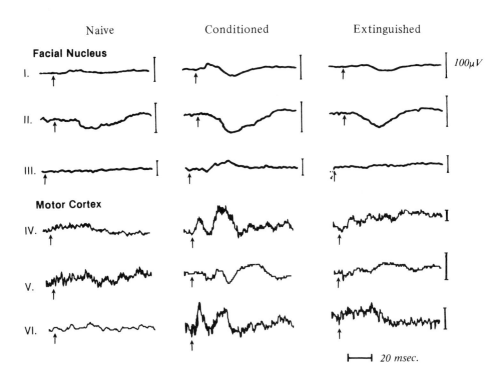

Fig. 4.7. Averages of evoked potentials to click (arrows) recorded mono-polarly (positive up) from the facial nucleus and the motor cortex (within coronal-pericruciate gyri) or six cats during different behavioral states. The click was used as CS to condition an eyeblink response. (From Woody and Brožek [1113] and Woody [1104].)

of cortical activation and that of activation of the orbicularis oculi muscles. Conduction delay between electrical stimulation of the motor cortex and evoked contraction of the eye blink muscles is also 7-8 msec [1125].

In conditioned animals, there is a strong correlation between the magnitude of the response evoked at different areas within the motor cortex and the threshold at these same areas for eliciting an eye blink by electrical stimulation [1104]. The higher the amplitude of the evoked response at a particular locus, the lower was the corresponding threshold to electrical stimulation. Evoked potential changes were of the smallest magnitude at areas at which eye blink representation was not found (for stimulating currents up to 3 mA).*

*With glass-coated, Pt-Ir electrodes of 40 μm tip.

These studies show changes in gross potentials that are correlated with conditioning and are referable to neural circuitry supporting performance of the conditioned response. They demonstrate that:

1. The latency and wave shape of field potentials evoked at the motor cortex of blink-conditioned cats depend on the sensory modality of the CS used to produce the CR. (Electrical activity evoked by a click CS could be distinguished from that evoked by a light CS [1104].)
2. Peak latencies of responses evoked by a particular CS appear to be nearly the same in naive and conditioned animals.* This suggests that much the same pathways may be used to transmit this message in the conditioned animals as in the naive animals. Since the potentials seen at the motor cortex and facial nucleus of conditioned animals are principally larger versions of those found in naive animals, the results support Jasper's view [456] that conditioning opens up preexisting neural transmission pathways rather than forming completely new connections.
3. Although the response amplitudes are much smaller in the naive animals, some responses to click can still be recognized at the cortex and at the facial nucleus. Thus, even CSs of low intensity (65-70 db) are transmitted to the final efferent neurons of the motor pathway, the motoneurons, in naive animals.
4. The potentials are greatest at the cortical areas that support production of the conditioned motor response by virtue of appropriate corticofugal projection.

Secondarily Produced Changes in Brain Potentials

One should distinguish the neural changes that produce conditioning from those produced secondarily by conditioning. Much the same can be said for the related gross potentials. At the least there should be correlations between the shifts in the potentials and the development of the CR. Also, the latencies of onset of potentials should be shown to precede the movement.

> The evoked potential changes described above in relation to conditioned eye blinking were abolished by KCl-induced cortical spreading depression at the same time that the ability to perform the conditioned eye-blink response was lost, and they returned later when the CR reappeared [1113]. This plus the fact that their onset preceded that of the CR by an appropriate latency suggest that they were directly involved in producing the CR rather than secondarily produced by the CR. The ability to perform the unconditioned response endured throughout.

Earlier reports of changes in EEG and evoked potential activity produced during the course of development of conditioning have been comprehensively

---

*This observation is of interest in view of reports of alterations in response latencies during conditioning mentioned earlier (e.g., Fig. 3.24). Evidently not all CRs are of such variable latency.

reviewed by John [462] and are excerpted here in Table 4.1. The reader is advised, however, that it is unclear in many of these studies which of the changes reflect neural events underlying the conditioning process and which reflect the production of changes secondary to other effects. For example, several of the studies described in Table 4.1 involve EEG conditioning. This is a complex phenomenon that requires detailed explanation for its significance to be understood.

Delivery of any stimulus that produces behavioral arousal can also block or desynchronize the rhythmic pattern of the EEG, given certain limitations of background stimulation and behavioral state. With EEG conditioning one can pick a US that produces EEG desynchronization as a UR. This stimulus is then paired with a CS that fails to produce desynchronized EEG activity. After pairing, the CS elicits EEG desynchronization as a CR [691,692]. Such effects can be demonstrated at almost any level of the nervous system at which alpha blocking can occur [cf. 309]. So can changes in gross potential activity brought about by conventional shaping procedures [843].

The problem is that these conditioned changes in EEG activity may be secondary to conditioning of a behavioral arousal response and not in any way a primary reflection of the brain processes supporting conditioning. EEG conditioning, may also result from sensitization-like effects wherein nonassociative pairing increases the effectiveness of a response to the CS [245]. Thus, the phenomenon of EEG "conditioning" is complex; use of the term in the context of conditioning may sometimes be misleading; and it may be virtually impossible to distinguish the electrical changes supporting the production of conditioning from those produced secondary to conditioning, arousal or sensitization.

Technical Limitations

Why should the gross potential correlates of learned behavior be inconsistent and the findings be viewed as inconclusive? There are several reasons. First, most studies have been concerned with gross potentials recorded at afferent levels of sensory reception in the cortex. These would be the regions most sensitive to disturbance by extraneous environmental noise. It has proved difficult to demonstrate a convincing relationship at this level between the evoked response and a particular neuronal population concerned specifically with conditioning (or habituation) as opposed simply to sensory reception. Second, changes in the amplitude of gross potentials may have nothing to do with conditioning per se, but may instead reflect changes in other associated experimental variables such as fear, vigilance, or sensitization. Third, complications in attempting to use gross potentials as an index of neural activity at a particular locus arise because the spread of current to the extracellular space is affected significantly by the pattern of dendritic branching [804] as described below. As a result, the generating afferent volleys and their associated electrical fields are often too complicated to provide information about single generator components [252].

Table 4.1. Some Findings of EEG Studies Relative to Conditioning Processes, Organized According to Functional Systems[a]

1. Cortical Regions

Early Phase of Conditioning - Generalized cortical desynchronization and widespread evoked potentials elicited by CS [32,329,463-465,496,593,824, 829,848,890,892,897,958,1044,1134]. Amplitude increase in all cortical layers [789]. During conditioned discrimination, transient increase in number of trials with reduced amplitude [165].

Late Phase of Conditioning - Appearance of cortical slow waves [329,496, 684,1137], or maintained desynchronization to CS [829,1137,1142]. Overtrained animals show localized arousal. Occurrence of driven rhythm decreases [593,958,1150] but in other studies becomes more prominent [165,463,465] or localized [640]. Changes marked in layer 4 of CS region and layer 5 of motor cortex [789,831].

Differentiation - Negative stimulus elicits generalized cortical depression or desynchronization [1044]. Cortical slow waves observed [329,354,831,890, 1044,1130,1137]. With stable differentiation, S⁻ most pronounced at layer 4 of CS area and in layer 5 of motor cortex [794]. S⁻ evokes S⁺ frequency pattern in sensory motor cortex [640].

II. Hypothalamus

Early Phase of Conditioning - Alimentary CS elicits evoked responses [465].

Late Phase of Conditioning - Frequency-specific CS represented in region where self-stimulation rate covaries with hunger [789].

III. Thalamic Structures

EEG arousal is present in animals with extensive lesion of rostral thalamus [167].

Early Phase of Conditioning - CS elicits generalized desynchronized fast activity [1137] and regularized rhythm in medial thalamus [897], and slow activity in CL (centralis lateralis) [890].

Late Phase of Conditioning - VA (ventralis anterior) response to the CS appears [463]. Initial desynchronization is replaced by 4 per sec slow waves [1135,1137]. Increased response in CL [1135]. Increase in evoked potentials during approach conditioning [465].

IV. Mesencephalic Reticular Formation (MRF)

Stimulation of points facilitating CRs elicits diffuse desynchronization [353].

Early Phase of Conditioning - During initial stages CS elicits (a) small-amplitude slow potentials [354,1137]; (b) enhanced evoked potentials [463, 1134] or regularized rhythm [897].

Late Phase of Conditioning - During state of well-established CR the CS elicits (a) slow waves [1132]; (b) diminution or disappearance of evoked responses [463,684] more marked in avoidance [463] than approach training [464, 465].

Differentiation - Negative stimulus elicits irregular slow waves [890].

V. Hippocampal System

Early Phase of Conditioning - Response to CS consists of rhythmic slow waves [6,352,354,1137]. More prominent in dorsal hippocampus while ventral hippocampus resembles neocortex [6,354]. CS elicits evoked potentials [311, 463,593,1134].

Late Phase of Conditioning - CS evokes desynchronized activity [352,354]. Previously observed evoked potentials are diminished or eliminated [593,684,

Table 4.1 (Cont'd)

1133]. This decrease in evoked potentials is differential, appearing in avoidance [463] but not in approach CRs [465]. Different parts of hippocampus show changes in phase angles from early to late training [6].

Differentiation - At early stages of differentiation, the S⁻ elicits rhythmic slow potentials. After elaboration of the differentiation, the S⁻ elicits desynchronization [352] and finally exerts no influence [354]. At the beginning of differentiation, S⁺ elicits hippocampal slow waves. This changes to hippocampal desynchronization and short-latency CRs [352]. Differential conditioning stabilizes frequency-specific response patterns [463].

a Modified from John [462] ; see that source for additional material not included herein.

This third difficulty in interpreting gross potentials is perhaps the most serious. There may be unavoidable limitations in separating out the contributions of various elements of brain tissue to the potentials measured [704, 1099,1123].

Let us consider the spread of current from cells within the cortex. To take one example, current flows along the entire vertical and circumferential axes of the dendrites of large pyramidal cells. The vertical processes arise in layer I (and in other layers) and project to somas located in layer V [141], a distance of 2 mm or more in some species. It is difficult to determine the source of a current generated millimeters away from the point of recording. Circumferentially, where the dendritic arborizations extend only a few hundreds of micrometers, it may take several millimeters for field potentials, generated by direct electrical stimulation of the cortex, to decrease to 10% of their original amplitude [113,1104]. Moreover, the unequal resistance of the extracellular space in different directions (anisotropicity) [298,713] makes this spread variable. It is then problematic to define the relationship of a particular potential field to the sinks and sources of current density of the generating loci.

Some gross potential data have been interpreted with the assumption that negativity reflects areas of current flow from the extracellular medium (sink) and positivity reflects the opposite (source). This has been shown to be problematic. Figure 4.8 illustrates the antithetic situation wherein negative extracellular potentials appear at the surface of the passive dendritic membrane that is acting as a current source [441,804].

Complications of analyzing current spread in a volume conductor can be reduced, but not eliminated, by considering only the areas of maximum voltage gradient. Examination of the model of Rall (Figs. 7 and 9 in [804]) discloses that the maximal voltage gradient consistently appears in close spatial relation to the soma membrane surface. If recordings are made in three dimensions over a broad volume of tissue (see Fig. 4.9), the focal region of maximal voltage gradient will indicate the proximity of the corresponding focal region of maximal current density. By focusing on the maximal voltage gradients, the spatial organization of at least some of the current generators to the extracellular space can be specified. This method will be less sensitive to violations of the assumption of constant conductivity in the surrounding

Current Flow From A Neuron Into the Extracellular Space

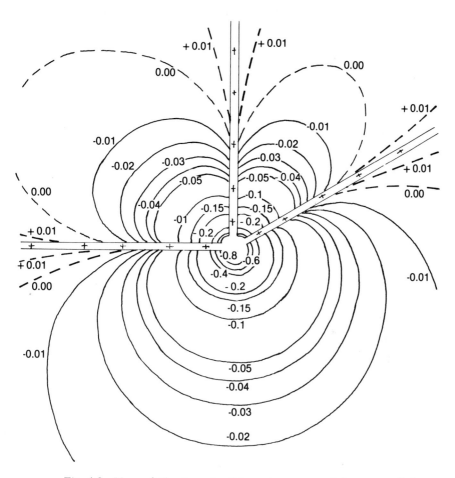

Fig. 4.8. Map of the isopotential contours caused by extracellular current spread obtained for seven theoretical dendrites by application of Rall's formulations. Negative extracellular potentials are found at the surface of the passive dendritic membrane for radial distances up to R = 8 from the soma. This contradicts the widely held belief that an electrode must record a positive potential (relative to a distant reference electrode) when it is placed near a portion of membrane from which current flows into the extracellular space. (From Rall [804].)

medium [298,713] than will that involving the use of second derivatives of voltage [441]. It will also be less sensitive to variation in the amplitude of the recorded potentials due to high noise variance or failure to correct for latency variation [1103].

Use of Laplacian approaches [430], in which potentials are measured over a three-dimensional electrode array, can distinguish crude differences in the

Three-dimensional Reconstruction of Complex Current Spread

A. Field Potentials

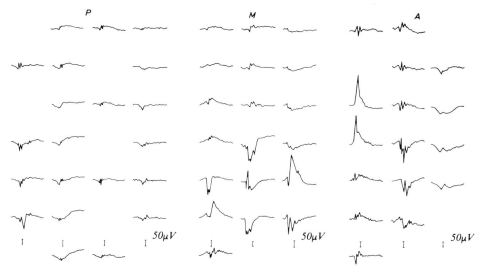

Fig. 4.9. Evoked potentials from the facial and trigeminal nucleus recon-structed over a three-dimensional space. A. Averaged potentials evoked by glabella tap recorded along tracts of electrode penetration of brain stem toward facial nucleus. Posterior (P), middle (M), and anterior (A) tract groups relative to the nucleus are shown; vertical arrangements correspond to relative anatomical positions from which recorded [see B. for precise locations]. Traces are 23 msec in duration; stimulus delivery 3 msec after start. B. Iso-potential plots of field spread of potentials shown in A. Electrode positions are shown below. Numbers correspond in vertical position to recording locus. One numerical unit represents 10 μV potential difference from initial baseline level (monopolar recording). Solid lines represent negative potential differ-ences with respect to ground; dotted lines positive differences. Latencies after tap delivery are as follows: I, 1.8 msec; II, 3.4 msec; III, 5 msec; IV, 6.6 msec; V, 8.2 msec; VI, 15.4 msec. (From Woody and Brožek [1112].)

sources and signal content of some field potentials [298,713,1112], and can sometimes show a relationship between the wave shape of the evoked potential and the poststimulus histogram of unit discharge from cells in the same area [252,292,298,1104,1125]. However, attempts to enhance the signal: noise ratios of gross potentials by advanced data processing techniques have failed to achieve enough improvement to make these potentials useful indicators of information transmitted during learning [1103,1123]. In fact, the results have instead emphasized the *un*likelihood of achieving sufficient improvement to do so, even if the theoretical limits of enhancement were reached [704]. The techniques, which involve averaging and matched filter analysis by means of cross-correlation, are described in Chapter 7 in relation to other applications.

B. Reconstruction

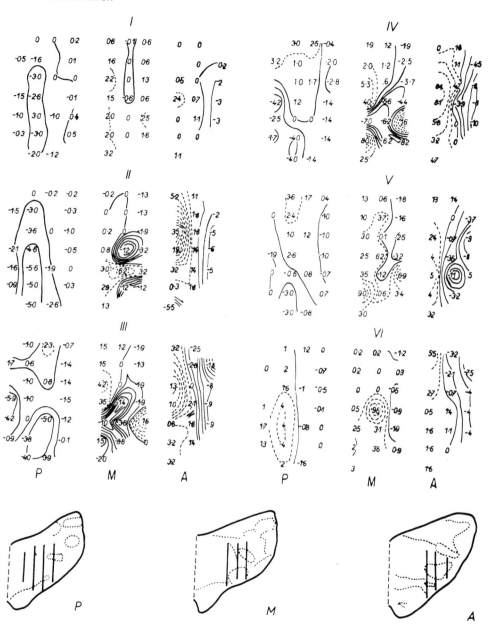

In summary, due to their technical limitations, gross potentials do not permit direct observations of cellular function. Since the first criterion of useful neural correlates of behavior stipulates that direct observations of cellular function be made, most investigators have turned away from gross potential measurements toward measurements of unit activity.

Unit Activity

Use of unit activity as an index of neuronal change avoids some of the physiologic ambiguities of gross potentials. Single unit recordings represent direct measurements of neuronal activity. Spike impulses may be measured either close to or inside the neuron by a properly positioned microelectrode (see, for example, Fig. 5.17). Since the spike activity is the binary, all-or-none output of the neuron, there is no doubt that the electrical activity unambiguously reflects message transmission at the recorded cell. Patterns of unit spike activity correlated with learned behavior were demonstrated in monkeys as early as 1959 [456]. The behavior included alerting, orienting, and habituation as well as conditioning of an instrumental avoidance task. These studies have been continued in a variety of preparations and at an increasingly detailed level, and now provide us with much of our current knowledge of the cellular physiology of mammalian learning and memory.

Conditioning

With mammalian conditioning, changes in single unit activity occur at most regions of the CNS (see Table 4.2) including cortex, mesencephalon, hypothalamus, thalamus, reticular formation, hippocampus, amygdala, and spinal cord [e.g., 57,58,64,66,122,222,223,307,456,477,515,728,729,738,739,742, 743,757,827,1105,1107,1136]. However, once again, establishment of a change in unit activity correlated with conditioning should not be taken as equivalent to identifying, electrophysiologically, a neuronal effect mediating production of the conditioned response. For the latter, it is suggested that at least the following findings are necessary:

1. The electrical event should precede the conditioned response by an interval appropriate for efferent conduction time.
2. Distinctive patterns of spike activity should be evoked selectively by the CS, particularly in areas of the nervous system in which the CR can be shown to have motor representation.
3. Patterns of spike activity should be closely correlated with performance of the behavioral response during conditioning, but not necessarily during extinction because of learning savings.

In addition, controls are needed to establish whether or not the changes in unit activity depend on the same associative features of stimulus pairing that are responsible for the conditioned behavior. One will want to determine the effects of reversing the order of CS-US presentation, of presenting the US alone, and of repeated CS presentation. It may also be necessary to distinguish secondary effects of altered vigilance or emotional state from primary conditioned activity, particularly when one of the CS-US pair is omitted, since this omission may induce a change in vigilance. Finally, inferences drawn from studies of unit activity must be shown to be valid over a group of animals, and the units sampled must either be identified or the sampling shown to be without bias with respect to the in situ population of cells. Although it may be difficult to obtain an adequate statistical sampling without inadvertent sample bias, this limitation has proved surmountable [862,1107].

Jasper and colleagues' pioneering experiments have shown us some typical cellular correlates of conditioning.

Jasper et al. [456] studied unit responses before and after shock avoidance conditioning of a hand movement. Light flash was used as the CS. Cells were studied in the prefrontal, parietal,* somatosensory, and motor cortex of monkeys. Changes in unit activity in response to the light CS (and to repetitive or habituating CS presentations) were found prior to conditioning in all cortical areas studied including the motor regions. Before conditioning, the CS usually evoked increases in spike activity in the motor and somatosensory regions and decreases in activity in the prefrontal and parietal cortex. Enhancement of the activity changes to the CS occurred in most cortical regions after conditioning, with the most significant enhancement seen in the motor cortex. In the parietal areas in which decreases in unit activity to the CS were typically observed, increases in firing were more likely to occur during conditioning than during the initial habituation trials.

Latencies of unit activation were not examined quantitatively in this study, but alterations in unit activity frequently outlasted performance of the response. Activity in the motor area appeared to be linked to performance of the motor response; activity in the parietal area appeared to be linked to reception of the CS; and activity in the somatosensory area may have reflected proprioceptive feedback from the production of the conditioned movement itself.

The firing pattern of cells in the precentral (motor) cortex varied greatly during performance of the conditioned motor response. Great variation in the activity between different units within adjacent cortical microareas was also found. About half the units sampled showed an increase in discharge rate in relation to the defensive movement. Much the same was found for units in the postcentral (somatosensory) cortex, except that activity was more closely related to muscle contraction, with discharges following rather than preceding hand movement.

In parietal areas other than the postcentral gyrus, unit discharge was correlated with characteristics of the CS. Some units could pattern their rates of discharge to the 5/sec rate of light flashes used as CS. Some units also showed discriminative responses to differential conditioning using light stimuli at different frequencies. Thus, patterns of unit discharge at the parietal cortex supported reception and discrimination of the CS.

The possibility of correlating changes in unit activity at the motor cortex in the monkey with performance of an operantly conditioned motor response was confirmed by Evarts [275]. His studies extended the investigations of Jasper and colleagues to encompass the problem of motor control of the learned movement. The movements were cleverly controlled so that they would involve primarily finger and wrist flexion. Increasingly quantitative relationships were sought between the latency and

---

*(Apart from the somatosensory area of the postcentral gyrus.)

Table 4.2. Some Areas[a] of the Vertebrate CNS Examined for Changes in Unit Activity with Conditioning

Isomorphic activity found	Isomorphic activity not found
Neocortex	Dorsal midbrain reticular formation
Pontine reticular formation	Tectum
Ventral tegmentum	(CA_1) Hippocampus
Posterior nuclei of thalamus	Medial septal area
Inferior colliculus	Mammillary bodies
Lateral nuclei of thalamus	
Medial geniculate bodies	
Hippocampus (especially hippocampal pyramidal neurons)	
Cingulate cortex	
Anterior nuclei of thalamus	
Entorhinal cortex	
Hypothalamus[b]	
Amygdala	

[a] partial listing; see ref. [1109] for additional material
[b] but not septal areas or mammillary bodies

duration of changes in unit activity and the production of the corresponding movements. In keeping with the observations cited above, some response latencies, particularly of units of the precentral gyrus, were thought to precede the movement; others, particularly of units of the postcentral gyrus, followed and outlasted the movements. It was concluded that the units were not only involved in initiating the movements but also in tracking and controlling them. The latter was accomplished by feedback circuits, some not requiring the movement itself. The circuits involved additional regions of the brain besides the motor cortex such as the pons, thalamus, basal ganglia, and cerebellum [204,278,643,869,1007,1008]. Some of these circuits were thought to be analogous to those supporting corollary discharge, wherein not only efferent but afferent systems are sent information to prepare them for incipient movement. The phenomenon of *corollary discharge* has been defined by Teuber with reference to a cortically mediated (intentional) eye movement "which transports contours across the retina . . . (but) leaves the spatial order of perception undisturbed, because the impulses to the eye muscles are accompanied by appropriate corollary discharges which preset the visual system for anticipated shifts in the spatial order of visual inputs. By contrast, when we push against our eyeball, moving it passively, the visual scene jumps" [1006].

Further studies [276,277,442] attempted to relate the patterns of unit activity to physical aspects of the movement, such as force, direction, and velocity. They indicated that control of such motor performance is physiologically complex and requires detailed analysis.

The early studies of unit correlates of conditioning in the motor cortex of monkeys did not establish a direct relationship between the investigated neurons and the target muscles performing the CR, other than that the neurons were pyramidal tract units. That was done later, first in the cat [1110] and then in monkey [284]. Neither did these early studies focus on differences in unit activity before and after extinction of the learned behavior. That was also accomplished in the cat as described below.

In cats, changes in unit activity with conditioning were found to be comparable to those found by Jasper in the monkey [273,1118,1122,1125]. In addition to conditioning, O'Brien and colleagues examined habituation, pseudoconditioning, and extinction of the activity of units in the sensorimotor cortex of cats [728-731]. The CS was a light flash, and the US was a shock. The response in this case was a change in unit activity rather than a behavioral response; thus, in these studies a specific relationship between the neural changes and particular behavioral alterations was not demonstrated. It was possible either to increase or decrease unit activity with associative procedures. The magnitude of the changes in unit activity increased with the amount of exposure to conditioning associations. The changes occurred rapidly, after 30-60 conditioning trials, and preferentially in units originally responsive to the CS [730]. The responses dissipated with extinction and returned, with savings, after additional conditioning trials. The last results were confirmed in subsequent studies in which behavioral conditioning was employed [273,1118,1125] (also see Fig. 4.14).

Analogous changes in unit activity with conditioning were observed in the reticular formation [1136] and in the thalamus [477,732]. However, many units in Yoshii and Ogura's study [1136] that responded to a few dozen associative pairings of CS (acoustic or visual) and US (nerve stimulation) responded transiently, the response being lost with continued training. The transient changes in unit activity may have represented effects secondary to conditioned arousal reactions that occurred in the early stages of classical aversion conditioning and gradually subsided later [128].

In summary, these studies lead to the following conclusions:

1. Neural pathways for mediating the CR exist prior to conditioning.
2. Preexisting neural responses to the CS are the rule rather than the exception [273,456,728,759,1113] (for another view see Kandel [480, 486]).
3. Overt startle or defensive motor responses, though commonly evoked by the initial presentations of a novel stimulus such as a CS, are rapidly lost prior to the development of conditioning.
4. Postconditioning changes in unit activity are found preferentially in cells which respond initially to the CS and, as later studies will confirm, in cells which project to the target musculature of the CR [111,467,651,724,1056, 1118,1122,1125].

Jasper additionally inferred that conditioning is "more than the establishment of connections between the cortical receiving area of the CS and the cells of the motor cortex involved in a particular response" [456]. He suggested that inhibition of irrelevant neuronal activity is as important as the facilitation of transmission over functionally connected pathways.

While this may be so [cf. 109],* the specificity of the motor CR and its restricted pattern of sensorimotor generalization may depend most directly on facilitatory adaptations established within the appropriate, functionally connected pathways. Some of these connections are formed by opening up latent transmission pathways by means of facilitatory adaptations.

Habituation

Unit correlates of habituation were first demonstrated in monkeys [456], and then in mollusks [119,998], cats [931-933], and crustacea [550].

Mammal. The tibialis anterior flexion-reflex was used to study habituation in the cat [931-933]. This reflex diminishes after elicitation by closely spaced, repetitive stimuli [782,886]. The habituated reflex can be restored by a strong additional stimulus. Decrement and restoration of this flexion reflex exhibit the nine features of habituation (see Chapter 2) described by Thompson and Spencer [1018]. Of these, dishabituation describes restoration of the reflex after habituation is established. Restoration of the response is believed to be due to an independent, superimposed facilitatory physiologic process [885,931-933]. Thus, dishabituation may involve a mechanism distinct from those supporting the other eight features of the habituatory process.

A carefully designed series of experiments led Spencer and colleagues [931-933] to the conclusion that interneurons within the spinal cord contained adaptations supporting the habituation response.

First, the spinal cord was transected to remove contributions from descending pathways. Then, the muscle spindle afferent pathways were disrupted pharmacologically with gallamine triethiodide (Flaxedil). The activity of the motoneurons was monitored during the period of muscle paralysis and the habituation was found to persist. By interrupting the muscle spindle inputs to the cord, it was shown that response decrement and restoration were caused by adaptive neuronal phenomena rather than by muscle fatigue and that inputs from these afferents were not required for these aspects of habituation. Thus it was shown that the cellular changes supporting these features of habituation were not located in the muscle spindle portion of the gamma efferent system.

Local synaptic depressions due to transmitter depletion could not be excluded from possible causes of the decrement, and neither could some other deterioration of the preparation over time be ruled out. These possibilities seemed unlikely since motoneuron EPSPs increased during dishabituation as well as decreased during habituation.

Although IPSPs also decreased in amplitude with repeated cutaneous stimulation, no significant persistent shifts in transmembrane potential were demonstrated. Thus, changes in the motoneuron were thought not to be responsible for this reflex habituation. The decrement in the flexion reflex also occurred after administration of picrotoxin, which is thought to

---

*And inhibition may even occur automatically, to a certain extent, because of recurrent (lateral) inhibition (see Fig. 6.7).

block presynaptic inhibition, and strychnine, which blocks some types of postsynaptic inhibition. On the basis of these results, changes in the efficacy of synaptic transmission were postulated to occur within interneurons mediating the flexion response rather than in the motoneurons [933].

Other loci of the mammalian CNS at which changes in unit activity have been correlated with habituation include the cortex, inferior colliculus, brainstem, spinal cord, and amygdala [56-58,122,129,456,867]. However, inconsistent or negative results have been obtained for effects of habituation in units of the reticular formation [1136] and of some of the cortical regions as well [730].

Crustacea. Correlations between habituation and unit activity have also been found in crustacea. Escape behavior in the crayfish is mediated by the tail flip reflex. The required reflex contraction is elicited, in part, through the lateral giant (LG) neuron (Fig. 4.10), which shows prolonged habituation for up to 48 hr after a few dozen elicitations. Two criteria of Thompson and Spencer's for habituation are not significantly involved with the process. One is dishabituation; the other is generalization of habituation to other stimuli.

The elucidation of various features of the neural substrate of this response has evolved from work of Wiersma [1088], Zucker et al. [1149], Krasne [485,550-552], Krasne and Bryan [553], and Kennedy and colleagues

Circuits Involved with Habitation of Crayfish Tail Flip Reflex

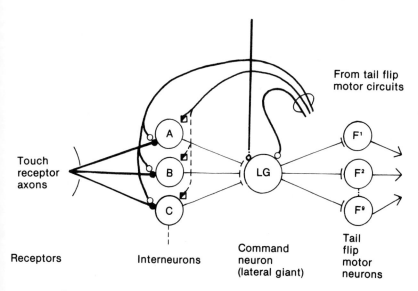

Fig. 4.10. Lateral giant reflex circuitry (thin lines) and some postulated modulatory loci (thick lines). (Krasne [485,551].)

[509]. Habituation of the tail flip reflex produces decreased firing in the lateral giant (LG) fibers that project to and command firing of the motoneurons that activate the tail flip muscles. One mechanism for this appears to be located at afferents to interneurons leading to the LG neuron because (1) "repetitive activation of sensory fibers results in cessation of interneuron firing, whereas direct activation of individual interneurons produces absolutely constant excitatory postsynaptic potentials (EPSPs) in the lateral giants" [552], the neurons to which they project, and (2) cutting the nerve cord to isolate this region from higher centers fails to prevent habituation [552]. It should be kept in mind that there are recurrent pathways to the interneurons in the abdominal ganglion that are not cut. They arise from both the LG neurons and the motoneurons to the tail flip muscles. These recurrent afferents participate in the normal habituation process. The lateral giant fiber can inhibit the interneurons directly via IPSP production. However, additional evidence indicates that the giant fiber can also prevent EPSP production in the interneurons by short-term presynaptic inhibition. Mechanisms for controlling transmission to the lateral giant command neuron include presynaptic inhibition, postsynaptic inhibition, and inhibition via polysynaptic excitatory-inhibitory recurrent pathways.

There is no indication that habituation is mediated through a postsynaptic effect on the interneurons of the disynaptic primary sensory pathway; it has been established that there are no persistent postsynaptic conductance changes in these cells related to habituation [552,1149]. However, the possibility that transmitter depletion at some synapses contributes to this repetitively induced habituation cannot be excluded.

The main adaptations supporting habituation appear to be manifested by presynaptic inhibition acting at the afferents terminating on the interneurons that project to the LG neuron (see Fig. 4.10). For example, Kennedy et al. [509] penetrated sensory fibers, showing primary afferent depolarization (PAD) of fibers activating interneurons. It is widely accepted that PAD reflects presynaptic inhibition in these fibers. The inhibitory effects of the PAD and those of central giant fiber inhibition were coincidental in time, except that the giant fiber inhibition outlasted the PAD by approximately 20 msec. One may infer that presynaptic mechanisms at the interneurons are directly involved in modulating the activity of the central giant fiber and are involved with some aspects of LG habituation.

It is even clearer that protection from or antagonism of the habituation can arise from a classical presynaptic inhibition of the primary afferent terminals themselves. That is, some of the axons from the sensory receptor neurons terminate on the afferents to the interneurons instead of the interneurons themselves. When repetitively activated, they produce an inhibition of the afferent terminals, thus inhibiting the habituatory effects supported by those terminals. Thus, more than one type and locus of adaptation is involved with various aspects of habituation in this preparation, and all forms of adaptation that are presently known to be involved are presynaptic according to the classification given in Chapter 5.

In other aquatic creatures, such as the goldfish, habituation and dishabituation of analogous motor responses [830] may involve the Mauthner cell. This neuron has interesting physiologic properties, the most notable among which is the presence of electrical as well as chemical synapses [303,305,541].

Mollusk. Habituation of postsynaptic potentials has been studied quite elegantly in the left pleural and abdominal ganglia of the gastropod mollusk *Aplysia* [119,480]. The studies were undertaken on the assumptions that:

1. More rapid progress at the cellular level could be made here than in a mammalian preparation
2. Cells located similarly within different ganglia would be unique and invariant in their adaptive characteristics
3. Results concerning phylogenetically remote systems and behaviors would ultimately be applicable to human behavior.

Several features of the habituation observed are similar to those seen in mammals [cf. 1018]: response decrement and restoration; sensitivity to stimulus intensity and interstimulus interval; dishabituation by rest or a novel stimulus; and habituation of dishabituation. In the molluscan preparation, decreases in EPSP amplitude follow repetitive nerve stimulation or repeated natural stimulation of the skin. The amplitude is restored by other natural (or artificial) stimulation and by rest. There is no associated change in the membrane resistance of the postsynaptic neuron. Therefore, it is inferred that this effect must be mediated by a change in the quanta of transmitter released at the synaptic terminal [119,480].

Neurons in *Aplysia* that send axons to the siphon, gill, or mantle shelf have been identified. Their activity is involved in controlling the digestive reflex movements of these organs [574]. Both short and long latency components of the movements can be distinguished [146]. *Behaviorally*, habituation of the gill-withdrawal reflex of *Aplysia* satisfies most of the nine features of habituation of Thompson and Spencer. Two that are not satisfied are (1) generalization of habituation, and (2) increasingly rapid decrement with repeated habituation and intervening rest periods [484].

Three different preparations have been used to study decrement and restoration of these digestive reflexes: (1) the intact preparation, (2) the semi-intact preparation with ganglion externalized, and (3) a preparation with a completely isolated ganglion. In various preparations the reflexes can undergo either short-term habituation lasting for a few hours or long-term habituation lasting for as long as three weeks [151]. The duration of these effects depends on the number of stimulus repetitions. Habituation of siphon withdrawal lasts less than a day after 10-15 stimulations of the siphon, but lasts for weeks after four repeated sessions of 10 stimulations each.

Short-term habituation apparently does not involve protein synthesis since it is not impaired by anisomycin, an agent that can block 95% of protein synthesis [877]. However, more recent indications [483] raise the question of whether protein synthesis might be involved in long-term habituation.

Kandel et al. [484] suggest that ... "the locus of the mechanism responsible for the change is presynaptic to the involved motoneurons."

During habituation there is a gradual decrease in the size of EPSPs in the motor neurons involved with gill withdrawal. The EPSP size recovers with dishabituation or with reflex recovery. The decrease in EPSP with habituation is not due to postsynaptic inhibition or to a postsynaptic change in input resistance [484].

Kandel and colleagues also suggest that restoration of the EPSP with a dishabituatory stimulus is due to presynaptic facilitation [cf. 119,488]. However, as Bures notes, in some reports only 15% of the neurons studied showed facilitation, while 80% of the neurons tested did not change. In a later review of studies of habituation with Castellucci, Kandel pointed out that a "decrease in the amplitude of the synaptic action potential [sic] with habituation was paralleled by a decrease in the number of chemical quanta released. In contrast, the size of the miniature postsynaptic potential did not change, indicating that there was no change in the sensitivity of the postsynaptic receptor" [483].

In this simple system involving digestive and other alimentary functions, it has clearly been possible to identify some of the neural elements involved in producing the decrement in unit activity. These include the presynaptic terminals of some sensory neurons that impinge upon a variety of motoneurons, including those serving the habituated movement. One of the adaptive mechanisms supporting short-term habituation has been shown to involve alterations in transmitter release at these terminals analogous to those demonstrated earlier with other repetitive stimuli. It is possible that cyclic AMP plays a role in modulating these effects [160]. Calcium surely does [499, 503]. As with mammalian conditioning, the end result would be to alter transmission along preexisting neural pathways rather than to produce new pathways by proliferative growth processes. Extensive reviews of these important contributions toward an understanding of molluscan habituation are available elsewhere [481-483].

One must not overlook the contribution of the peripheral nervous system to habituation of the gill-withdrawal reflex. Peripheral mechanisms completely apart from those in the central ganglion can mediate response decrement, restoration, and disinhibition. The results show that "the terminations of central motor neurons in the gill are sites of habituation, and the central nervous system exerts excitatory and inhibitory influences on the peripheral system." In these studies of the peripheral nervous system of *Aplysia with central ganglion removed*, "the reflex habituated to repeated stimulation with the same time course as the observed before removal. Gill stimulation caused dishabituation of the reflex" [763].

In *Aplysia*, then, both habituation and dishabituation can occur *without* the presence of the central neurons in which putative engrams are found [480, 763]. That is, other, peripheral neural pathways can support the same type of habituation. Evidently, multiple engrams are involved with digestive habituation in this species. How each is specifically linked to the overall process remains to be determined.

The same problem in identifying each component of adaptation that contributes to a change in unit activity in *Aplysia* occurs in the mammal as a result of redundantly stored information [578,1102]. There, strategies have been devised specifically to track as well as to localize engrams and to identify patterns of activity common to different units and relevant to particular behavioral functions, as described later in this chapter.

Sensory Preconditioning
Cellular correlates of behavioral paradigms other than conditioning and habituation have been established in mammals. Changes in unit activity in the visual cortex have been observed in cats with a paradigm much like that of sensory preconditioning [687]. Neurons in this region respond to tactile and acoustic stimuli as well as to visual stimuli. Thus, they are said to be polyreceptive.

In studies by Morrell and colleagues [687], associatively pairing either two visual stimuli or stimuli of visual and nonvisual sensory modalities changed the response to the original visual stimulus in over one quarter of the cells tested. The changes in unit activity persisted for 20-30 min (approximately 50 test trials) and then decayed. By repeating the stimulus associations it was possible to produce more persistent changes in activity.

Ben-Ari and colleagues used associative procedures to study modifications in unit activity in the amygdala of cats [57,58]. One stimulus (S_1) was visual or auditory and the other (S_2) was somatic (weak electrical stimulation of the paw). Extinction was carried out by presenting the S_1 alone, repeatedly. Only 15% of the cells showed associatively related changes in activity, and it was unclear whether these represented conditioning or sensory preconditioning. Most of the changes were transient; a few were persistent. Again, changes generally occurred in units which responded selectively to the S_1 stimulus. Some long-term changes in spontaneous activity were reported following habituation as well as after associative procedures.

Recent experiments have shown that the excitability of neurons in the motor cortex increases in the course of paired associations used explicitly for sensory preconditioning [120]. The neurons involved are those that respond to the paired stimuli. These findings are discussed later, in the section on unit excitability.

Extinction
While there is evidence of changes in unit activity corresponding to extinction [e.g., 728,729,731], there is as yet no indication of the locus of the principally involved adaptations. Unit activity evoked by a CS has been shown to decrease in the rostral cortex of cats with extinction of a behavioral CR [1125]. However, the enhanced postsynaptic excitability to injected current of neurons projecting polysynaptically to the target musculature of the CR persists [111] together with learning savings of the conditioned motor response.

In these motor projective units, activity evoked by the CS is not necessarily decreased, and the main mechanisms responsible for behavioral extinction and the decreased activity of the surrounding units are presumed to reside elsewhere.

Sensitization

Sensitization of a gill withdrawal reflex has been studied in *Aplysia* by Castellucci and colleagues [38,147,158,482]. They believe that this process is mediated by neurons that end on the presynaptic terminals of the moto-neurons involved with habituation. In this case the release of transmitter is enhanced and the motor response is facilitated. The same stimulation that leads to sensitization also leads to an increase in cyclic AMP in the entire ganglion. Thus, this agent may have a role in mediating sensitization as well as habituation. The possibility that cyclic AMP may affect vesicular neurotransmitter release by altering the concentration of calcium in the presynaptic terminal is discussed later in Chapter 5. An increased calcium conductance is thought to be responsible for this sensitization [392], but this could also depend on levels of transmembrane potential in the presynaptic terminal.

Additional mechanisms may be involved with sensitization in mammals as discussed later in this chapter.

Artificially Produced Changes in Unit Activity

Changes in the activity of single neurons can be produced artificially within the CNS by conditioning procedures. As noted earlier, the same procedures that serve to produce behavioral conditioning succeed in conditioning electrical events [cf. 456,728,729]. Whether control over the modification of the unit's activity is exercised directly or only secondarily (e.g., by unconditioned proprioceptive-like feedback from conditioned arousal) has not, as a rule, been established. Moreover, if one could directly modify the activity of some units by conditioning procedures, it would still be difficult to establish to what degree and with what selectivity control over such modifications might be exercised.

One can alter the activity of single neurons in the sensorimotor cortex as a consequence of repeated combinations of photic or acoustic CS with shock US at regular 30 sec intervals or following periodic presentation of a shock stimulus alone, the latter representing Pavlovian "temporal" conditioning [456,540]. Also, sensorimotor units that originally fail to respond to splanchnic nerve stimulation can be conditioned to do so when splanchnic stimulation serves as a CS [2]. However, the units must respond to another stimulus, such as sciatic nerve shock, as a US. By repetitive pairing of CS and US with an interstimulus interval of 20 msec and an intertrial interval of 5 sec, approximately one-fourth of units which respond to the US can be conditioned to respond to the CS. The response can be extinguished and retrained. In most units the response involves an increased rate of firing, but in others a decreased rate of firing can be produced.

Vassilevsky was able to modify cortical unit activity using peripheral stimuli as CS and US [1043]. Fetz showed that either increases or decreases in the activity of some cortical neurons could be conditioned by shaping procedures [283].

In other experiments neurons of the ventral medial and lateral areas of the hypothalamus were conditioned to respond to associative combinations of visual or auditory stimuli with somatosensory (shock) stimuli or intracarotid injections of glucose. More than 40% of hypothalamic glucoreceptive units changed their response upon pairing a tone of 400 Hz as CS overlapped in time with intracarotid glucose injection as US [549]. In these experiments the intertrial interval was 1½-2 min. Some pseudo-conditioning controls were also run.

These studies suggest that substantial changes in both the degree and direction of activity of cortical and hypothalamic neurons can be produced by conditioning; however, the same procedures fail when applied to more than half of the neurons of these areas. Some of the successful experiments could represent relatively direct and specific control of a single unit's activity. It would be difficult, however, to demonstrate this conclusively without coinciding evidence for control over some local, adaptive cellular change. Any demonstration of direct control over the development of local plastic cellular changes would probably require the introduction of artificial, associative stimuli locally and restrictively into the cells under study.

One can conclude that, while it is possible to produce artificial changes in neural activity experimentally by associative procedures, it has not proved easy to control the extent, duration, and specificity of the modifications.

The Tracking of Engrams

Early studies of conditioning in the mammal failed to establish specific functional relationships between changes in unit activity and the process of conditioning. Accordingly, later investigators increasingly concentrated on the problem of elucidating more direct relationships between changes in central unit activity and conditioning [111,222,273,728,729,738,739,767, 790,791,880,1110,1118,1125]. These studies confirmed Jasper and colleagues' observations that unit activity at many loci within the brain mirrored the acquisition of conditioned behavior. The import of this finding in the mammalian preparation should not be underestimated. It tends to confirm the view of redundant and diffuse representation of memory and learning functions at the level of single cells within the CNS.

One potential limitation of many of these experiments is that behavior is assumed to be characterizable in terms of statistical identities, linked with behavioral states common to different subjects. That is, effects of learning are studied by comparisons made between different samples of neuronal activity, excitability, etc., obtained from the same cortical regions of different naive and conditioned animals. However, this limitation has not proved overly restrictive. Repeatable data have been obtained by this means in different groups of animals [1108,1110] and requirements of statistical F tests sensitive to possible bias from single animals have been satisfied [111,1110, 1122]. Recently, the capability has been acquired to study and recover morphologically identified units at both cortical and subcortical levels [523, 861,862] and to follow the activity in specific units during the entire conditioning procedure [64,518,860,1055]. Remarkably, the sampling bias of the recording electrode for particular types of cells has proved to be small [862]. There is some predisposition toward penetration of and recording from units with the most extensive dendritic branchings; however, it seems possible to obtain recordings from cortical neurons of virtually every size and configuration [862]. Thus, what has been a potentially great limitation in working with the complex mammalian circuitry has apparently been overcome.

Three major strategies have been devised for establishing whether changes in unit activity at a particular locus are primarily or secondarily involved with the production of conditioned behavior. They are described next. In addition, attention has been directed to elucidating the cellular and molecular mechanisms underlying complex neural adaptations signaled by persistent changes in neural activity, as will shortly be seen.

System Isolation and Anatomical Definition

The first approach to tracking engrams is the most direct—simply that of isolating and identifying each of the main input, output, and transform elements involved in a single conditioned reflex. Cohen and colleagues' work [138-140, 174-176] exemplifies this approach. They would define, anatomically, the inputs and outputs involved in a cardiac conditioned reflex in the pigeon. In these experiments a light CS is paired with foot shock US. A change in heart rate is the conditioned response. The CS is carried by visual pathways ascending to the telencephalon. Cohen believes that the major plastic changes supporting this form of conditioning occur in or below the telencephalon and not at the retinal level. Changes in the output of the retina are not found as a function of conditioning.

The heart rate is influenced by two final common motor pathways: the right sympathetic cardiac nerve and the vagal nerves. The right sympathetic cardiac nerve originates in the sympathetic ganglia of the last three cervical segments. These fibers comprise the parasympathetic innervation. The changes supporting conditioning appear to occur prior to these pathways. Linkages between CS receptive pathways and motor pathways supporting performance of the CR have been found in many "cardioactive" regions similar to those described in the mammal [174,175]. One of the pathways can be followed "from the hypothalamus through the ventral medial brainstem at mesencephalic and rostral pontine levels; it then shifts to a ventrolateral position which is maintained through the medulla" [174]. This pathway is thought to be likely to undergo adaptation because conditioning is impaired when it is disrupted. Further evidence indicates that "the descending pathway for this conditioned response involves an amygdalar projection to the hypothalamus" [174]. Once the neural system regulating cardiac activity is completely defined, it should be possible to determine what physical changes occur in this system during cardiac conditioning as a consequence of associative paradigms and to investigate the molecular basis of these changes.

Progression in the Network

A second approach to determining the functional relationship between changes in unit activity and the process of conditioning is that identified with Olds, Disterhoft, and colleagues [222,223,544,738,739,742]. They aimed to distinguish the areas of the brain specifically involved with conditioned behavior by identifying areas with (1) the shortest latencies of unit activation in the course of performance of conditioned behavior or (2) the earliest times of development of activity changes during the course of conditioning. One advantage of this strategy is that activity is investigated in several different regions of the nervous system, many of which could potentially support different features of the learned behavior. Also, it might be possible to demonstrate a functional relationship between two or more loci along an involved pathway on the basis of latencies of unit activation, taking into account known conduction and synaptic delays.

> In one example typical of these experiments, chronic recordings of single unit activity were made in conditioned rats. Control experiments were performed to rule out pseudoconditioning and sensitization effects. In the early investigations [739], an auditory CS (tone) was reinforced with food if the animal did not move during the period of CS delivery. In later studies different auditory stimuli were presented as CS^+ or DS^- with food as reinforcer. Retrieval of food was the conditioned response. Rates of unit discharge changed with conditioning. Increases in activity were found at cortical and subcortical levels of the nervous system, but not at all points sampled within each level. These results were combined with those of other investigators in Table 4.2.
>
> The *shortest latency responses* were found in the posterior nucleus of the thalamus and in the pontine reticular areas. In the posterior thalamus, the responses were evoked nonspecifically. That is, many neurons showed similar responses to CS^+, DS^-, and other novel stimuli. In the frontal cortex and hippocampus, responses were more specific and did not generalize across auditory stimuli; however, only 5% of the sampled neurons responded.
>
> In the course of *development* of conditioning, the posterior part of the pons showed changes earliest. Then, changes appeared in the reticular and limbic activating systems, and thereafter in thalamus and cortex.

In retrospect, several limitations in the strategies underlying these experiments can be found. First, it is difficult to determine which response controls the "primacy" of activation when differences in response latencies are less than a few milliseconds. This is because of an unavoidable variance of 4-16 msec in estimating the activation latencies of units with irregular rates of discharge averaging less than 20 impulses/sec. Second, when differences in latencies are longer than a few milliseconds, it is not possible to determine if the response reflects a directly involved neural pathway; many conduction delays encountered in transmitting messages between neurons are long enough to permit activation via secondary feedback loops in addition to primary anatomical pathways. Because of such latency variations and possible feedback circuitry, the latency of activation cannot properly be used as the sole means for determining the locus of an engram directly involved in the production of conditioned behavior.

Another limitation concerns what inferences are permissible on the basis of the changes in neural activity that develop earliest in the course of conditioning. Assume that engrams are encoded at two separate neural areas, but that the manifestations are weak at these regions. A subliminal fringe might arise from projections of these altered neurons to CS-receptive neurons at another region. That, then, might be the region at which the earliest overt changes in unit activity would be recognized, and erroneous conclusions could thus be reached.

Useful inferences can still be drawn from the above experiments, provided these limitations are recognized. More serious drawbacks could arise, however, in investigating adaptations supported by multiple engrams occurring at different neural loci.

Informational Approach

A third approach has been devised for investigating primary relationships between single unit activity and conditioned behavior. It focuses on how information related to stimulus reception and motor performance is encoded within an ensemble of functionally related units. This is done by separating units according to those that respond selectively to the CS, those that respond to other stimuli such as the DS, and those that fail to respond to either stimulus. Then, the progression of response latencies is investigated along known neurotransmission pathways. Further separations are based on the units' motor projections, when they can be determined. In this way the function of the units can be analyzed in terms of sensory and motor labeling (see Chaps. 3 and 7). A simplified conditioned reflex with a short response latency, a high degree of motor specificity, and a selectivity in being evoked by a particular CS helps establish critically involved neural pathways and facilitates the analysis [1105,1113,1125]. The eye blink reflex meets these criteria.

It is possible in cats to condition three different short-latency facial movements (as shown in Fig. 4.11) by pairing click CS with an appropriate US. One movement is a mixed eye blink in which both orbicularis oculi and levator ori muscles are involved (*i*); the second is a pure eye blink (*ii*). The third movement is a conditioned nose twitch (*iii*) and requires a puff of ammoniated air to the nostrils as US instead of glabella tap.

After this type of conditioning, unit activity evoked by the CS is found to be increased selectively in areas of the motor cortex that project to the target musculature of the conditioned response [1107,1125]. Histograms

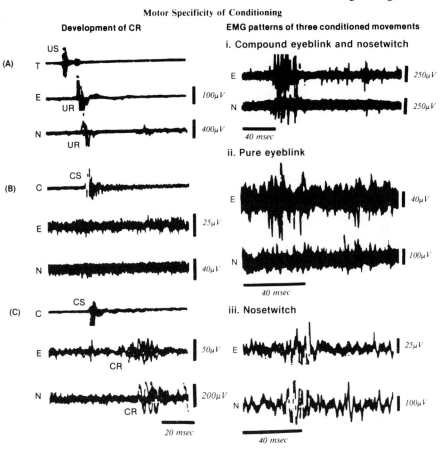

Fig. 4.11. Left: Myographic recordings of the response to glabella tap US and to click CS before and after conditioning. Stimulus deliveries tap T, and click, C are shown as amplified microphone recordings in the top traces. Right: Three different conditioned facial movements recorded myographically from orbicularis oculi (E) and levator ori (N) muscles. The compound eyeblink in i is similar to that produced by the pairings of CS and US shown on the left. (From Woody [1108].)

of this activity are shown in Fig. 4.12. The increase in activity is correlated with the type of motor pathway(s) needed to perform the conditioned response. Experimentally, the projections of the recorded loci are established by electrically stimulating the cortex (either microstimulation of unit areas [1118,1125] or stimulation of single units [1110]) and recording the response from the peripheral musculature. After extinction, enhancement of unit activity to the CS decreases back toward its original levels. Spontaneous rates of discharge of units of the motor cortex are not significantly changed by conditioning or extinction. (Voronin also finds changes in unit activity at motor regions; the changes are associated with production of a local conditioned startle reflex [1053,1054,1056]. The response latencies are as brief as those found with conditioned blinking.)

Conditioned Blink: Unit Activity at Motor Cortex

A. Detection of single unit discharges

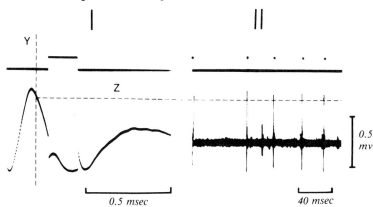

Fig. 4.12.A. Example of unit activity studied. I: Schmitt trigger discriminating unit discharges at time (Y) and threshold (Z) shown by dotted lines. Lower trace is electrode potential; upper trace discriminator output. Discriminator fires with inherent delay of 70 μsec when electrode potential exceeds and then falls below threshold. Positive up. II; successive spikes being discriminated. (Woody et al. [1125].) B. Patterns of activity evoked in motor cortex of cats trained to perform the movements illustrated in Fig. 4.11: upper graph, mixed eye blink; middle graph, pure eye blink; lower graph, nose twitch. Unit activity is divided according to the projection of the area from which it was recorded (N-to nose twitch musculature, E-to eyeblink musculature, B-to both types of musculature). The traces are the summations of recordings from many single units. (From Woody [1108].)

With conditioning of short latency facial reflexes, an increased level of unit response conveys information for discriminating the CS at sensory association regions of the cortex. At cortical motor regions, however, an increased number of responsive units as well as an enhanced level of response provides this information (Fig. 4.13). The changes in the motor cortex occur most frequently in units of target (CR) muscle projection, the pyramidal cells of layer V that project corticofugally via the pyramidal tract, hence facilitating production of the specific conditioned movement.

More caudally at sensory (association) cortical regions, the magnitude of stimulus-evoked unit discharge and rates of spontaneous neural activity are found to be exquisitely sensitive to both associative and nonassociative stimulus presentation [827,1122]. Rates of spontaneous unit activity increase above naive levels after conditioning and after nonassociative, "random" temporal presentation of conditioned and unconditioned stimuli. However, the magnitude of unit discharge evoked by the CS is increased to a greater degree (and more selectively) by associative presentations of the stimuli employed in conditioning than by nonassociative representations of

B. Histograms of spike activity

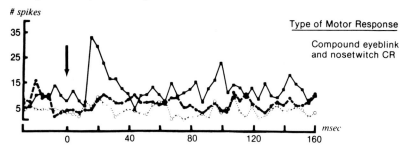

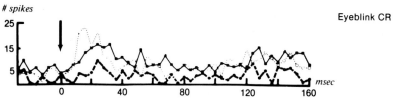

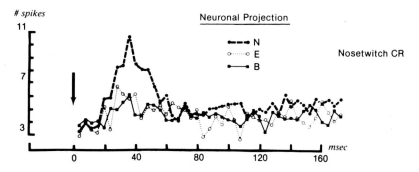

the same stimuli given randomly [1122]. Interestingly, some correspondence is found between the patterns of activity evoked by the click CS at the auditory association cortex and those evoked at the more rostral cortical motor regions (Fig. 4.14).

The following insights into coding processes mediating reception of the CS and performance of the CR are then suggested:

1. Patterns of unit activity evoked by auditory CSs are correlated with physical characteristics of the stimuli, such as amplitude and duration. This is so not only at the primary auditory cortex and the peripheral auditory receptive areas of the CNS, but at the auditory association cortex and the motor cortex as well.

2. The number of units encountered at the motor cortex that respond to the CS is increased after conditioning. So is the number of units that can be demonstrated, by electrical stimulation, to project polysynaptically to the target musculature of the CR. This reflects facilitation along reflex pathways needed to perform the CR. The number of units encountered at the auditory association cortex that respond to the CS does not increase after conditioning a short latency blink response.

Plasticity of Projections of Unit Areas

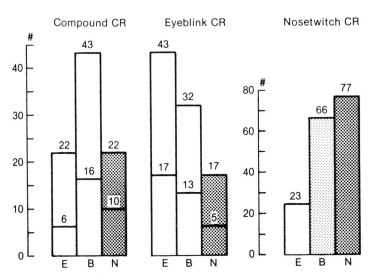

Fig. 4.13. Numbers of unit areas found to project from the motor cortex to the target musculature (E, B, and N as in Fig. 4.12) for the cats performing the three conditioned facial movements described earlier. The differences in numbers of projective areas with conditioning of different motor responses reflects an enhancement of conduction through specific polysynaptic motor pathways. (From Woody [1108].)

3. Another difference between the motor cortex and the auditory association cortex is that significant numbers of units at the latter areas respond to auditory stimuli with a *decreased* rather than increased rate of discharge. This finding in the cat supports the earlier results in the monkey by Jasper and colleagues [456].

4. Unit activity at both motor effector and sensory receptive cortical areas can be altered by either associative or nonassociative pairing. In the posterior "association" areas of the cortex, spontaneous activity may be increased as much by nonassociative presentations as by associative presentations of the same stimuli. However, *appropriate associative pairing of CS with US enhances the responses evoked by the CS selectively with respect to responses evoked by a DS.* The consequences of this may be manifest in the patterns of activity evoked by the CS at the motor cortex and in the numbers of units activated.

5. Sensory generalization gradients for performance of the CR occur, in part, because *many cells undergoing changes in activity with conditioning are of polysensory reception.* They respond to light, click, somatosensory stimuli, and activation of the reticular formation [56,273,1107]. Motor generalization of the conditioned response may occur for analogous reasons [456]. *Most neurons of the motor cortex that undergo changes with conditioning are of polymotor projection* [1110]. Thus, alterations in activity and in excitability will occur not only along neural pathways that directly

mediate the CR [1105] but also along pathways that can potentially mediate related movements.

6. At the motor cortex the increases in CS-evoked unit discharge after conditioning do not necessarily exceed levels of discharge found in response to different stimuli of comparable intensity. Thus, mean levels of evoked discharge per se do not provide a basis for discriminating the conditional stimulus from a discriminative stimulus at rostral, motor areas. Mean levels of evoked discharge *times* the numbers of units activated provide this basis. In contrast, at more caudal association areas, levels of activity evoked by the CS, after conditioning, *are* comparatively greater in responding units than are levels of activity evoked by equally loud but behaviorally neutral auditory stimuli.

The neocortex is not the only telencephalic region in which unit activity is closely correlated with a conditioned behavioral response and precedes it in latency of occurrence. Experiments by Thompson's group have related the activity of hippocampal units to conditioning of a long latency nictitating membrane response [64,65]. The strongest correlations are found in the hippocampal pyramidal cells as opposed to the other units of the hippocampus. Unit activity studied in the entorhinal cortex, cingulate cortex, thalamus lateral septal area, and abducens nucleus also shows positive correlations* with the conditioned behavioral response, while activity studied in the medial septal area and the mammillary bodies does not [66,172,1109,1140]. A particularly interesting feature of nictitating membrane conditioning is the rapidity with which the CR is acquired. Another is the tendency of the unit response to extinguish together with the conditioned behavior. A third is the observation that animals may learn this reflex with hippocampus removed bilaterally but not with unilateral lesion of the cerebellum.

Unit Excitability

The three approaches discussed above are concerned with unit activity as a significant correlate of learned behavior. However, *unit excitability* to locally injected current is as useful a correlate of learned behavior as is unit activity [1107]. In addition, it can provide an indication of local neuronal change. Excitability is measured by the amount of current required to produce unit discharge.

Motor Excitability
The excitability of the motor cortex to locally injected current increases as a function of conditioning [231,533,724,1030,1032]. This generalization holds true whether the test stimulus is delivered through large electordes placed extracellularly into the brain tissue or is delivered through microelectrodes placed inside single neurons [111,1104,1110,1125].

Direct stimulation of the motor cortex can be used as a US to produce movements that subsequently become a CR to an external stimulus [326,626]. Changes in the stimulation threshold of these and adjacent motor loci occur

*See ref. [1109] for further details of these and other recent studies.

Conditioned Eye Blink: Unit Activity

Average Response Histograms

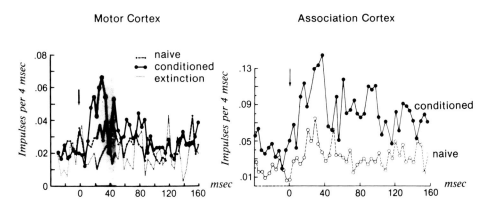

Fig. 4.14. Above: Averaged patterns of unit activity evoked in two different cortical regions by similar behavioral procedures. The arrow designates delivery of the click stimulus that was used as the CS. The recordings from the association cortex did not have 1-2 msec delay in response due to air conduction subtracted from the histogram latencies; the recordings from the motor cortex did. (From Woody [1108].) Following page: Study of a single unit through extinction and reconditioning of blink. A. 32-sweep raster display of unit activity evoked by click CS in conditioned animal and discriminated as shown in Fig. 4.12 (each dot equals one spike; each row equals one sweep-trial). B: activity after extinction. C: activity after reconditioning. Initial bars designate conditioned blink response on that sweep. Solid line corresponds to click presentation. Arrows show increased unit response. 40-msec time calibration is shown in C. D: number of impulses above spontaneous rate of discharge per 32 sweeps in 8- to 28-msec period after click, averaged and shown at real time intervals during extinction and reconditioning (above), and compared with corresponding percent conditioned response performance (following page). (From Woody et al. [1125].)

as the CR is established. Early in conditioning, the thresholds for eliciting movement may actually increase, but as conditioning proceeds, motor excitability increases and thresholds decrease. Nonassociative presentation of USs alone appears to decrease neural excitability to extracellularly injected nA current while increasing excitability to intracellularly injected current [109-111]. The intracellular excitability increases are smaller than those found after associative conditioning and are transient, lasting but weeks [111]. Analogous excitability increases to intracellularly injected current occur in facial motoneurons [467,651]. Both the changes in the motor cortex and in the facial nucleus can be made to persist when the US is paired associatively with a CS [111,651]. These changes are isomorphic with the persistence of the conditioned motor response. Learning savings of the latter persist through extinction (and may last for over a year). The excitability changes are thought

Single Unit Response

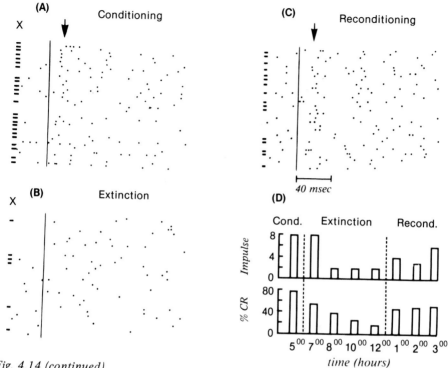

Fig. 4.14 (continued)

to reflect the presence of engrams responsible for the motor specificity of the conditioned response [111,651,1109,1110,1118,1125].

The possibility that the excitability of motor pathways is enhanced by conditioning was postulated many years ago by Giurgea [325] and by Doty and Rutledge [236]. Giurgea [325, cf. 232] noted that as a conditioned motor reflex (stepping) developed, an increase in the frequency of non-CS elicited, similar movement also occurred. This led to the inference that the excitability of the motor areas had increased. Doty and Rutledge also reached this conclusion on the basis of experiments in which—during the course of conditioning training, just prior to the appearance of any CRs,—touching a few hairs on the limb involved in performance of the CR during presentation of the CS would elicit CR performance. Touching this region between presentations of the CS did not elicit the reaction, nor did touching any other limb during CS presentation do so. Further studies have revealed cellular changes supporting this *latent facilitation* of motor performance.

The excitability of single cortical neurons projecting polysynaptically to the target muscles of conditioned facial movements has now been shown to be selectively enhanced after associative conditioning of the Pavlovian type [111,1110].

Initial studies [1104] showed that small areas of the motor cortex at which evoked potentials were augmented during conditioning of a blink reflex required the lowest injected currents for producing an eye blink movement. There was also a correlation between the least amount of current needed to excite and the greatest magnitude of increase in evoked response after conditioning.

Further studies [1125], illustrated in Fig. 4.15, used extracellular microstimulation of the sort developed by Asanuma and colleagues [31]. Small cortical areas of less than 100 μm radius were stimulated with currents in the microampere range. The results showed that areas projecting polysynaptically to the target muscle of the CR had selectively increased excitability after conditioning. The production of peripheral EMG activity by stimulation of these cortical areas required less current than did that by stimulating immediately adjacent areas projecting to different target musculature. Subsequent studies [1118] indicated that neural excitability changed as a function of the type of motor response that was learned. On conditioning of a nose twitch movement, the excitability was greatest at areas projecting to the nose twitch musculature. After reversal training to eye blink, the thresholds were lower at areas projecting to eye blink musculature.

The excitability changes were determined to occur postsynaptically in the cortical neurons that projected polysynaptically through brainstem motor nuclei to the involved facial musculature. This was demonstrated by intracellular recording and stimulation in conditioned animals [111,1110]. It took less current *intracellularly* to fire single neurons of target CR muscle projection than those that projected elsewhere [1110], and, although their spontaneous rates of discharge were not significantly increased, their excitability to intracellularly injected current was enhanced in comparison with that of comparable units in naive animals [111]. As will later be seen, the postsynaptic changes in the motor neurons need not result in increased rates of discharge since they appear to be mediated by decreases in the transmembrane conductance of ions with equilibrium potentials near the resting potential of the cell.

Selectively increased excitability in motor neurons of target muscle projection could give rise to the phenomenon of latent facilitation, e.g., the ability to elicit the not yet completely established CR by supplying slightly increased excitation to skin stimulation. Neural excitability increases in the motor cortex after presentations of the US alone, although as mentioned above the increases are of lesser degree than those produced associatively and are transient [111]. Although nonassociative presentation is not as effective as is associative pairing of CS and US in producing these changes in cortical neural excitability, the changes that occur by this means are readily measurable in units projecting to the target musculature of the UR [107,111]. Cells of this motor labeling may be transiently prepared for production of the specific CR by delivery of the US. *Persistent changes of excitability in neurons of specific motor projection occur contingent upon repeated association with a CS during the time when this labeling is being accomplished.*

The excitability of motoneurons of the facial nucleus is also found to be enhanced after blink conditioning when tested intracellularly [467,651].

Plasticity of Thresholds to Electrical Stimulation

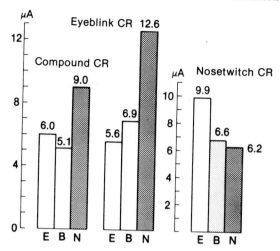

Fig. 4.15. *Changes in excitability to electrical stimulation of unit areas of the motor cortex with projection determined as described earlier. The excitability changes as a function of conditioning for the three facial responses shown here and in Figs. 4.11-4.14. Excitability is selectively increased (threshold lowest) for unit areas that project polysynaptically to the target muscles of the CR (E, B, N) as in Fig. 4.12. (From Woody [1108].)*

Changes in motoneurons could support the phenomenon of *reflex dominance* of Ukhtomsky [1030-1032] in which repetitive production of an extensor, spinal* motor response by a strong stimulus results in enhanced ability to produce the same response by other stimuli some of which do not previously do so. Some types of conditioning can also occur at the level of spinal motoneurons and their immediate reflex connections [122,246,280,819,898]. Persistent cellular changes supporting blink conditioning may occur within the motoneurons of the facial nucleus after associative stimulus presentation [467,651]. However, the normal, short-latency blink CR is not acquired after removal of the rostral cortex [1113,1128].

Clearly, increased excitabilities of neurons of *both* the motor cortex and subcortical motor nuclei play a role in supporting learned motor performance. Since still other neural adaptations support reception of the CS, one concludes that mammalian conditioning involves more than one type of neural adaptation.

*Ukhtomsky showed that in the spinal frog, the response to a stimulus which originally produced a flexion contraction could be altered to an extensor contraction following repetitive stimulation of portions of the receptive field that induced an extensor reflex. In separate experiments he also demonstrated a latent facilitation of response on repetitively stimulating the cortex.

Sensory Excitability

The excitability at the sensory association cortex of neurons receptive to the CS is increased after Pavlovian blink conditioning. The mechanism of this alteration appears to be different from that supporting the postsynaptic changes in excitability of the frontally located, cortical motor neurons since it is disclosed by extracellular nanoampere (nA) stimulation, but not by intracellular stimulation [1122]. Neural excitability is increased nonspecifically when CS, US, and DS are presented randomly, but when CS and US are presented together associatively, followed by a DS, excitability is increased selectively in the CS-responsive cells. This, then, seems to be a critical *associative* mechanism controlling the development of classical conditioning, the changes in excitability of neurons of the motor cortex and of motoneurons being necessary also, but *not* depending on associative presentations of CS and US for their inception. The enhanced excitability to extracellular current in CS-responsive neurons apparently reflects a neural adaptation that promotes selective reception of the CS and its discrimination from other stimuli. The changes in sensory excitability are of different functional significance than are changes in motor excitability and represent different cellular adaptations.

Levels of neural excitability to extracellular current are found to be altered in other behavioral states besides classical conditioning. For example, the excitability of sensory receptive units of the motor cortex is increased after sensory preconditioning [120]. Furthermore, after presenting a strong glabella tap (US) or after behavioral extinction by reversing the order of CS-US presentation, a decreased excitability to extracellular nA current of cortical neurons of all motor projections tested can be demonstrated [107,109]. The latter changes in motor excitability are less specific than those revealed by intracellular stimulation and imply the existence, after conditioning, US-CS extinction, H-adaptation, and other forms of US presentation, of inhibitory cellular adaptations in the motor cortex different from the facilitatory adaptations found by intracellular electrical stimulation.

Biophysical Approach

A separate, *biophysical approach*, such as that exemplified by the voltage clamp studies of Alkon in *Hermissenda* [12,1109], may be needed for specification and characterization of any engrams that are found by the above means. Further details can be found on pp. 177, 178.

Summary of Cellular Substrates of Simple Behavior

The preliminary findings of electrophysiologic studies of simple learning and memory processes may be summarized as follows. Habituation, as studied in mammals, crustacea, and mollusks, is supported by changes in the presynaptic terminals (presynaptic inhibition) on neurons along afferent and efferent pathways that support production of the habituated response. Sensitization involves opposite changes (presynaptic facilitation) at analogous terminations. Latent inhibition and habituatory adaptation appear to involve other changes, some occurring in cortical motor neurons, reflected by reduced excitability to weak (nA) extracellular stimulation. Reflex dominance, latent facilitation, and perhaps pseudoconditioning are supported by transient (but long-lasting) postsynaptic changes in cortical and subcortical motor neurons—the neurons along the efferent pathway leading to performance of the facilitated motor response. Conditioning involves these changes, made persistent by associative pairing of CS and US, plus other facilitatory changes in CS-receptive neurons that support discrimination of the CS from other stimuli. The latter changes are revealed by increases in excitability to weak extracellular currents and by increased rates of spontaneous discharge. Sensory preconditioning is supported by analogous increases in neural excitability to weak extracellular current occurring in cells of the motor cortex that are receptive to the paired sensory stimuli. Some of the studies supporting these conclusions are summarized briefly in Table 4.3 and represent but a preliminary, partial, and greatly oversimplified listing of the mechanisms involved in the above.

Neural Stimulation and Behavioral Changes

Direct electrical or chemical stimulation of the brain can be used to *produce* behavioral changes and to investigate generalization of behavioral effects to different reflex pathways within the brain. The effects on learned behavior of direct neural stimulation, used associatively, will be discussed first.

Table 4.3. Electrophysiologic Determination of Some Neural Mechanisms Thought to Support Simple Memory and Learning

Habituation[a]	- presynaptic inhibition [119,279,480-484, 488,509,553,998]
Sensitization	- presynaptic facilitation [38,147,158,392, 482]
Reflex dominance Latent facilitation (Pseudoconditioning)	- postsynaptic facilitation (transient) [111, 651,1109]
H-Adaptation (Latent inhibition)	- inhibition reflected by decreased neural excitability to weak (nA) extracellular current [107,109]
Conditioning[b] Motor specificity	- postsynaptic facilitation (persistent) [111, 651,1110]
Discriminative reception	- facilitation reflected by increased neural excitability to weak (nA) extracellular current [1122]
Sensory preconditioning[b]	- facilitation reflected by increased neural excitability to weak (nA) extracellular current [120]

[a]Habituation has 9 reflex outcomes, but, as yet, only one established physiologic mechanism. Similar considerations undoubtedly apply to the other processes listed herein.
[b]Changes found in *Hermissenda* apply, but as yet it is uncertain to which category.

Electrical Stimulation

Electrical CS

Loucks [626,627] was the first to use electrical stimulation of the cortex successfully as a CS for the production of a conventional CR. His observation that conditioned reflexes could be established by electrically stimulating the cortex was subsequently confirmed by Doty and colleagues [235]. They controlled for possible sensory effects of the stimuli on meninges and blood vessels by performing trigeminal neurotomies and using low levels of stimulus intensity.

In subsequent studies [1127], levels of stimulus intensity as low as 20 μA were used successfully for this type of conditioning (with 2 msec pulses delivered directly into the motor cortex as CS). When associated with glabella tap as US, the resulting conditioned response was a short latency eyeblink.

Electrical stimulation of almost any neocortical or subcortical locus can serve as an adequate CS [230], but subcortical stimulation is not as effective as cortical stimulation. Stimulation of deep cerebellar nuclei as well as the neocerebellar cortex is ineffective as a CS unless the stimulus intensity is increased to levels that produce gross movement instead of simply field potential activity [226,230]. Conditioned reflexes have also failed to be established to stimulation of Group I muscle proprioceptors as a CS even though field potentials are produced at the level of the sensorimotor cortex [978].

It has been suggested that these differences in effectiveness of electrical stimulation as a CS may be a matter of "perceptual" versus "motoric" thresholds [231].* A motoric threshold would be one at which some peripheral motor response could be observed. A perceptual threshold would presumably be one at which the stimulus delivery could be perceived by the recipient or the effective reception of the stimulus could be measured in some way other than peripherally. However, in view of recently demonstrated peripheral effects of stimulating single cortical neurons (such as the production of subliminal muscle contraction [1110]), this separation of terms may prove problematic. Effectiveness of a stimulus may instead be a matter of locus, intensity, frequency, density, and duration of application.

Electrical US

Direct electrical stimulation of central neural tissue can be used effectively as a US for conditioning [326,626]. Loucks used electrical stimulation of the motor cortex as a US in combination with a motivational reinforcer† to pro-

---

* "The first effect of a moderate current would produce a tingling sensation in the part which would contract when the strength of current was increased" (observations made during electrical stimulation of the human brain) [811].

† The term "motivational reinforcer" has been used to describe stimuli that have strong positive or negative reinforcing effects, such as those seen with septal stimulation. However, used in the context of associative conditioning, the term is physiologically imprecise. The stimuli may directly facilitate the formation of associatively induced adaptations arising from separate CS-US pairing (by neurochemical release that may or may not be equivalent to "motivational reinforcement") or may serve as extremely effective USs in their own right.

duce a conditioned motor response. The CS was a light in some experiments and a sound in others. Giurgea [325] and later Doty and Giurgea [233] showed that the motivational reinforcer was not necessary. It was possible to elaborate a conditioned reflex using direct electrical stimulation of the cortex as the US and stimulation of the visual cortex as the CS. The CR was comparable to the unconditioned movement produced by stimulation of the motor cortex.

The time required for the acquisition of conditioned reflexes can be greatly reduced by adding a "third" (electrical) stimulus to associative pairings of other CSs and USs [518,1053]. Voronin combined electrical stimulation of the motor cortex as US plus hypothalamic stimulation as a supplemental "motivational" stimulus with an auditory (click) or visual (light flash) stimulus as CS to produce conditioned startle reflexes. Conditioned changes in EMG and cortical unit activity were produced with as few as 15-30 associative stimulus pairings. The EMG responses were of extremely short latency, some as short as 12-16 msec following presentation of the CS. Most of the units in the motor cortex had activation latencies between 8 and 17 msec. The conditioned responses were extinguished by unpaired presentations of the CS, recovered spontaneously after extinction, showed long-term savings as indicated by rapid restoration a few days later, showed more rapid extinction after repairing, and showed limited afferent and efferent generalization. The responses thus demonstrated most of the critical parametric features of Pavlovian conditioning. Moreover, they did not develop with pseudoconditioning procedures or pairings in random temporal order [1052,1053]. In studies of these effects, the area of the brain stimulated electrically is the part of the hypothalamus that serves as a positive reinforcer in self-stimulation investigations. The addition of this electrical stimulus has been viewed by some in a specific "motivational" context [1053]. It might instead be considered as the physiologic effect of a different intertrial interval or different neurotransmitter activated by the additional stimulus. Also, there might be some other specific cellular attribute of the region or network stimulated during "motivational" reinforcement which might serve to make this stimulus simply an extremely effective US.

Several loci besides the motor cortex have been used to produce conditioning with electrical stimulation as a US.

Brogden and Gantt [105] used electrical stimulation of the cerebellum as a US, with auditory or visual CSs. After associative pairings, the CS evoked responses somewhat similar to those produced by cerebellar stimulation.

Segundo et al. [881] studied the effects of direct electrical stimulation of the mesencephalic reticular formation or centromedian nucleus used as US in combination with a previously habituated tone as CS. The unconditioned response to electrical stimulation could be conditioned. There was an absence of response to the CS until 10-30 pairings, after which the CS elicited orienting or startle responses. Subsequently, the CS evoked the response characteristic of central stimulation.

Black-Cleworth et al. [83,84] showed that antidromic stimulation of the facial nucleus was an adequate US for Pavlovian blink conditioning. O'Brien and colleagues then showed that electrical stimulation of the pyramidal tract was an adequate US for the development of conditioning [733]. Finally, activation of brainstem motor nuclei was shown to be effective in producing nictitating membrane conditioning [673].

Instrumental as well as classical conditioning can be produced by electrical means. Tarnecki and Konorski [991] as well as Loucks [627] conditioned movements to direct cortical stimulation using food as reinforcement; this could also be done by substituting reinforcing electrical stimulation for food [232,737,741]. As might be expected, stimulus cessation can also act as a reinforcer for this type of conditioning [462].

In summary, electrical stimulation of the CNS is satisfactory as a CS or US for the production of essentially all types of conditioned reflexes and, when applied to regions such as the hypothalamus, can even be used as an "extra" associative or reinforcing stimulus to speed the development of conditioned reflex formation. The studies demonstrate:

1. The diffuse distribution of anatomical pathways labeled for sensory reception and motor effectuation in ways discussed further in Chapters 6 and 7.
2. The accessibility of adaptive processes supporting conditioning via these pathways.
3. The greater accessibility to adaptive processes critical for conditioning by stimulating final efferent pathways at the level of the motor cortex than at the level of other, subcortical areas. The latter include the deep cerebellar nuclei but not the hypothalamus, within which stimulation can be extremely effective as noted above.

Electrical Generalization Gradients

Electrical stimulation can be used to investigate generalization gradients. This can be done, after conditioning, by applying electrical stimuli to different central or peripheral loci of the nervous system to see if a CR is elicited. Care must be taken lest elicitation of an unconditioned response be mistaken for elicitation of a conditioned response. Generalization gradients can also be evaluated by changing the frequency, intensity, or duration of the stimulus. When stimulating currents of microamps or greater are used, the results may be difficult to interpret because an indeterminate numbers of cells may be activated. The reason for this is the same as that complicating the interpretation of gross potential data. That is, the effectiveness of electrical stimulation in neuronal tissue with currents of microamps or greater will be a complex function of conductivity through the extracellular space—neuronal packing density, the patterns of dendritic arborization, tissue impedance, etc. Large currents will stimulate nonselectively due to their spread. With smaller currents there will be greater selectivity. (The electrode tip must be located at or very near the cell membrane for weak stimulation to be effective.)

Doty and Rutledge [236] trained animals to respond to microampere electrical stimulation of the cortex as a CS and then tested generalization to electrical stimulation of peripheral neural regions, the opposite cortex, or other regions of the ipsilateral cortex. The results of these and later studies were as follows:

1. Some generalization to electrical stimulation could be found in virtually every case in which extensive studies were carried out.
2. The greatest generalization occurred with stimulation of equivalent points of the opposite hemisphere after stimulating cortical area 17 unilaterally as the CS. Stimulation of other, distant regions of the same hemisphere produced generalization less frequently, and peripheral stimulation or stimulation of most other hemispheric areas fell in between.
3. Transhemispheric generalization depended on either the anterior commissure or the splenium of the corpus callosum being intact.
4. Generalization was almost completely absent when either ipsilateral or contralateral hippocampal areas were stimulated [230,232].

Stimulation of functionally and neuroanatomically related systems produced generalization more frequently than did stimulation of unrelated systems. However, instances of the latter did occur, and there was also generalization from electrical CSs delivered at the parietal cortex to "natural" visual or auditory CSs [326].

Determination of generalization gradients to electrical stimulation of the CNS may be complicated by ancillary effects of the stimulus on local neuronal excitability. For large currents of 0.5 mA or more, Doty [230] points out that "the threshold for CR elicitation by a cortical CS is lower for a minute to two following presentation of a moderately supramaximal CS than it is following subliminal or barely liminal stimuli. Similar results have been obtained in man." The phenomenon is thought to be the same as that studied by Graham-Brown and Sherrington*. Note further that:

The result of [repetitive, electrical] stimulation at the same central locus "may [also] vary depending upon environmental setting, satiation, hormonal level, simple repetition, or previous activity. Stimulation at some points yields a constant response throughout hundreds of repetitions. Repeating stimulation at [other] points leads to disappearance of the response." [232]

Stimulation of discrete cortical areas with lower ranges of microampere currents [1127] indicates that sites can be stimulated without eliciting the CR as little as 1.5 mm away from sites at which an 0.5 msec current pulse is

---

*See Proc. Roy. Soc. B 85:250-277, 1912 as well as the citation in ref. 231. A particularly insightful description of these and related phenomena can be found in a recent text by Bindman and Lippold on the *Neurophysiology of the Cerebral Cortex* (E. Arnold, publ., 1981).

an effective CS. While this is a typical observation in the motor cortex and appears to hold for the visual cortex as well [236], the generality of this observation has not yet been established at subcortical regions. There may also be species differences in tissue impedance or neural excitability to injected current. Threshold levels of electrical currents that will serve as a CS are reported to be lower in macaques than in cats [231].

In sum, these studies indicate that direct electrical stimulation of the brain can effectively induce associative adaptations and that the adaptations occur along pathways of sufficient specificity to produce coherent learned behavior. The specificity of the behavior conforms to that expected neuroanatomically; that is, if areas of the motor cortex projecting to the limb musculature are stimulated as US, limb movements become the resulting conditioned response. Studies of generalization of this form of conditioning also suggest that specific line labeled pathways are involved. Generalization is best when functionally related neuroanatomical connections are stimulated.

Repetitive Electrical Stimuli and Habituation
Repetitive presentations of electrical stimuli such as those used as a CS or US can result in habituation of the responses elicited by these stimuli. Included are arousal responses as well as unconditioned and conditioned motor behavior. Moreover, alterations of cellular activity, including spikes and PSPs evoked by a discrete stimulus, can be habituated in the same manner [230].

Habituation-like decrements of EPSP amplitude in spinal motoneurons can be produced by repetitive stimulation of the lateral columns of the frog's spinal cord at rates of one stimulus every 5 sec [279]. With the exception of response generalization, all the parametric features of habituation of Thompson and Spencer [1018] are observed.

Lack of generalization of this habituation effect to other stimuli reaching the same motoneuron pool suggests that a reduction in excitability does not occur in the motoneurons per se. Nor does there appear to be a depolarization of their presynaptic terminals as is found with other forms of presynaptic inhibition (see Figure 5.2), although presynaptic inhibition involving some adjacent interneurons cannot be ruled out. The response to antidromic stimulation of the motoneurons is normal. Farel [279] hypothesizes that changes in the number of transmitter quanta released at afferent terminals, changes in the amount of transmitter released, or changes in the chemosensitivity of the postsynaptic membrane to the transmitter substance are responsible for the habituation-like decrement of the EPSPs.

Habituation-like decrements as well as facilitatory increments of EPSP amplitude have been described in *Aplysia* by Kandel, Tauc, Bruner, and colleagues [119,487,488,998]. These studies have commonly used repetitive electrical stimuli to produce habituation analogous to that discussed earlier. Alterations in cellular properties resulting from direct electrical (presynaptic) stimulation are discussed separately later on. Long-term habituation in *Aplysia* can be acquired after as few as four, 10-trial training sessions with ½ hr intersession intervals and can be retained for more than 1 week [cf. 146]. A similar paradigm can be applied to produce comparable changes in the isolated abdominal ganglion. Behavioral habituation in that preparation is associated with a progressive decrease in EPSP amplitude. The latter lasts at least 24 hr.

As noted perspicaciously by Kandel and Spencer [486],

the fact that electrical stimulation of neural tissue can be used to produce the same forms of habituation and conditioning seen with natural stimuli supports the cellular basis of this type of learned behavior. Moreover, the cellular effects of the stimuli can constitute analogs of simple learning and memory that are available for direct investigation.

Chemical Stimulation

Certain chemical agents ranging from complex pheromones to compounds as simple as LiCl have properties that greatly facilitate the production of behavioral changes. The remarkable feature of these agents is that in many instances minute amounts or only one associative trial is required for behavioral modification or stable learning to occur [125,317]. Thus, a few molecules of a pheromone can induce mating and a single application of lithium chloride can be used as a stimulus to produce aversive alimentary conditioning. While the cellular mechanisms supporting these changes are as yet unknown, they must be highly specific and capable of selective operation since the effects are limited to certain receptor systems which vary from species to species.

Pharmacologists have long considered the neuronal effects of chemical agents to be as important as their gross behavioral effects. As Swartz points out [975], "early investigators noted that the EEG desynchronization produced by either arousal or stimulation of the mesencephalic reticular formation (MRF) could be blocked by atropine and that either cholinesterase or cholinomimetic (muscarinic) treatment could produce cortical desynchronization [93,396]. Kanai and Szerb [479] showed that stimulation of the reticular formation of rats, which produced EEG desynchronization, also produced a 5-6 fold increase in ACh (acetylcholine) output from the ipsilateral cortex . . . atropine nearly abolished the desynchronization but did not decrease ACh release." Investigators have also studied the effects of cholinergic agents on conditioning and other forms of learning, but most of these studies have failed to demonstrate any direct causal relationship between the drug effect and the cellular mechanisms of learning and memory. Suffice it to say that both facilitatory cholinergic effects on learning [77,152,153,471,493, 697,907] and disfacilitatory cholinergic effects [215,216,492,845,847, 955] have been found. It has, however, been demonstrated that conditioned behavior and other forms of learning can be *acquired* in curarized preparations where the *nicotinic* action of cholinergic agents is blocked [e.g., 860]. Conversely, scopolamine and atropine (both blockers of *muscarinic*, cholinergic neurotransmission) clearly *interfere* with the acquisition of conditioned behavior [238]. Further information concerning these types of studies is available elsewhere [186,975]. Other cellular effects of chemical stimulation that may trigger associative or repetitively induced adaptations will be considered further below.

Neural Stimulation and Cellular Changes

Changes in membrane conductance, transmitter release, and other fundamental neural properties can be produced as a direct consequence of electrical
or chemical stimulation. The changes are sensitive to parametric aspects of
stimulus presentation as well as to qualitative differences between stimuli.
The parametric effects have typically been investigated at the cellular level by
giving a "conditioning" or a repetitive stimulus followed at various intervals
by a test stimulus. Comparing the neural response to the test stimulus with
that to the original stimulus reveals changes in neural state. Usually the stimuli have been delivered electrically, extracellularly; rarely have they been
delivered chemically or intracellularly, even though the latter might be a more
precise means of stimulation.

Most changes disclosed by direct neural stimulation, as employed above,
are of brief duration and are relatable to simple or repetitively induced adaptation. Some changes of longer duration have been found in invertebrate
neurons [484,999]. However, those cells have much slower rates of spontaneous discharge than are observed in most neurons of mammalian species. Thus,
some long-lasting effects of repetitive stimulation may be more isomorphic
with this feature of invertebrate cells than with mammalian behavior. Other
long-lasting cellular effects arise from tetanic rates of stimulation (p. 168
ff.); however, these frequencies are not often realized in the natural state.

Still other effects of direct neural stimulation have been found that are
persistent and appear to represent cellular changes supporting conditioning
rather than unspecified alterations revealed by "conditioning-testing." Some
of the earliest changes in single neurons that can be attributed to direct unit
conditioning were produced in the mammalian CNS by Bures and Buresova
[128]. A further description of their studies is provided on p. 175. Other
mammalian experiments of potential behavioral significance were performed
by Voronin [1051,1053,1055], who measured the intracellular, conditioning-
like effects on cortical neurons of electrical stimuli introduced locally as CS
and US.

Electrical Stimulation
Conditioning-Testing
Most conditioning-testing experiments have employed electrical rather than
chemical stimuli. The stimuli produce elementary conductance changes*
within the neuron. The cellular consequences of their interactions may be
investigated by altering the timing of the applied stimuli. Although most
investigators have used conditioning-testing intervals of less than 100 msec (a
curious choice in view of the optimal interstimulus intervals for producing behavioral effects described in Chapter 3), a few have studied interactions over
intervals of 500 msec or longer.

---

*However, the conductance changes resulting from chemical transmitter release are not
separated from more direct effects of the current on transmembrane conductances.

The classical effects have been described in detail by Eccles [248,250]. Most of the early work was performed in motoneurons or at the muscle endplate. In the latter preparation miniature endplate potentials (minepps*) provide a useful indication of spontaneous transmitter release, and changes in minepp size and frequency are used as an index of adaptation. "To improve the quantitation", extracellular application of magnesium has been used to reduce the amount of transmitter produced by the conditioning stimulus, thereby avoiding transmitter depletion but incurring possible side effects of magnesium on membrane conductance. Curarization has also been employed to reduce the size of the endplate potential.

Minepp Enhancement and Depression. At the neuromuscular junction, the "conditioning" stimulus can produce either enhancement or depression of minepps evoked by a subsequent test stimulus. Whether the result is enhancement or depression depends on the frequency, interval, and number of conditioning stimulus presentations. A typical example of enhancement follows.

After 1-20 nerve impulses in the magnesium treated (rat diaphragm) preparation [431], there was a 33% increase in the probability of minepp occurrence lasting 100 msec (time constant). The amplitude of the minepps was also increased. The conditioning-testing stimuli used to obtain the data in Fig. 4.16 were delivered as pulses at rates of 200/sec and intervals of up to 200 msec. The enhancement was greater as more stimulus trials were presented. The highest rates of repetitive stimulation resulted in tetanic muscle contraction and sometimes long lasting potentiation (as discussed later). Here (Fig. 4.16), the potentiation lasted about 100 msec. It is not clear in either instance whether the responsible cellular adaptations are graded phenomena, augmented by higher rates of stimulus repetition, or are instead separate cellular mechanisms of adaptation that are induced selectively at the higher repetitive frequencies [250].

The potentiation is attributed to a transmitter mobilization which is facilitated when presynaptic impulses follow each other at high frequency. The mechanism of the facilitation is thought to involve an accumulation of calcium in the presynaptic terminal [499], the same mechanism postulated to be involved with sensitization at the presynaptic terminals on motor neurons (also see Chapter 5).

Postsynaptic Potential Enhancement and Depression. Effects similar to those seen at the neuromuscular junction occur in neurons. That is, either enhancement or depression can occur as a parametric feature of conditioning stimulus presentations. Use of repetitive conditioning stimuli to depress the amplitude of a monosynaptic EPSP[†] recorded from a motoneuron is shown in Fig. 4.17.

---

*Minepps are the elementary postsynaptic conductance changes produced by quantal release of neurotransmitter.
[†]Excitatory postsynaptic potential

Potentiation of End Plate Potential and Frequency of EPPs
After High Rates of Repetitive Stimulation

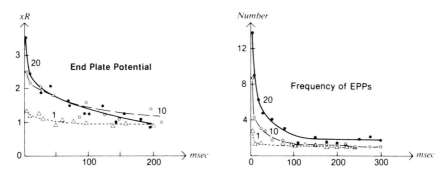

Fig. 4.16. The amplitude of diaphragmatic muscle end plate potential is shown to the left after 1, 10, and 20 repetitions at 200 Hz for durations up to 200 msec (note decay with prolonged repetition). R is ratio of amplitude to that determined in absence of stimulation. The frequency of miniature end plate potentials relative to spontaneous occurrence is shown to the right. (Hubbard [431] in Eccles [250].)

Depression of EPSP Amplitude by Repetitive Stimulation

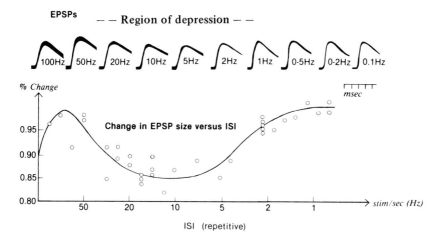

Fig. 4.17. The changes in size of the EPSPs after the indicated frequencies (Hz) of stimulation are shown above. Their magnitude of change relative to the mean size of EPSP obtained at 0.4 Hz is plotted below as a function of stimulus interval. (After Curtis and Eccles [199] in Eccles [250].)

In addition to alterations in the size of evoked PSPs, changes in PSP frequency and in the resting polarization and conductance of the neural element can be produced.

It has long been recognized that repetitive stimulation of motoneurons can cause depolarization and sodium inactivation which can last for over 100 msec [250]. The action potentials decrease in amplitude and finally drop out. The size of the recorded PSPs may change directly as a function of their voltage dependence. Their size may also change with alterations in cell input resistance as, for example, with changes in potassium conductances or when the conductance of sodium increases during normal spike production.

The dependence of neural adaptation on parametric features of stimulus presentation such as those shown in Figs. 4.16, 4.17, 5.13, and 5.16 demonstrates *an intrinsic mnemonic feature of neural tissue* sensitive to the same temporal parameters that influence associative, repetitive, and other nonassociative stimulus effects at the behavioral level.

Afterdischarge. Afterdischarges are secondary spike potentials that follow primary spike initiation as a consequence of molecular trace effects, either within the neuron or via extrinsic recurrent pathways. Such afterdischarges could play a significant role in mediating conditioning. For example, the afterdischarge could represent a trace effect of the first stimulus and could provide a contingency on which second stimuli would result in persistent cellular changes. Included among the mechanisms that might support afterdischarge within the neuron are (1) rebound excitation following inhibition, (2) alteration of pacemaker properties, and (3) persistence or augmentation of the effects of transmitter substances.

Kandel and Spencer [486] point out that in the eserinized sympathetic ganglion, an afterdischarge follows a preganglionic volley, presumably because of a persistence of acetylcholine that normally would be inactivated by cholinesterase. Prolonged afterdischarge also occurs in endogenously active (pacemaker) cells of *Aplysia* after brief, strong nerve stimulation and can be found in neurosecretory cells. Von Baumgarten [1046] was able to modify pacemaker activity in single *Aplysia* neurons directly by intracellular stimulation. Strumwasser and colleagues have elegantly demonstrated a role of peptides in initiating such afterdischarges and of cyclic nucleotide induced phosphorylation in their generation [164,400, 459,470].

Posttetanic Potentiation and Depression
As mentioned earlier, use of rapid, repetitive, tetanic conditioning volleys produces pronounced neural effects that persist through administration of a test stimulus and thus have a potential role in mnemonic processes.

Effects on Minepps. Posttetanic potentiation at the neuromuscular junction is associated with an increased frequency of minepps [604], particularly at the end plates of slow muscle fibers where the safety factor for spike initiation is low. The potentiation is attributed to an accumulation of calcium at the presynaptic terminals that results in an increase in the probability of transmitter release [499,844].

Posttetanic Neuronal Effects. The posttetanic response of motoneurons is one of potentiation at higher rates of tetanus and of depression at slightly lower rates of stimulation.

> At rapid, tetanic rates of conditioning-testing of 200 per sec or more, potentiation is seen over 1-2 seconds. At rates of 100 per sec or less, there is instead mild depression of monosynaptic EPSPs (see Fig. 4.17). There is no appreciable change in the size of the EPSPs until the frequency is in excess of 0.4 per sec. Then there is a progressive depression as the frequency is raised to 5-10 per sec. Then, with higher frequencies, the EPSP increases back towards the normal size with further depression above 50-100 per sec [250].

In posttetanic potentiation of spinal motoneurons produced by stimulating their monosynaptic afferent pathways, the amplitude of the EPSP is increased [101,199]. The potentiation is associated with hyperpolarization of the presynaptic terminals [613] and is thought to be due to an increase in transmitter release. Krnjević has snown that injections of calcium into spinal motoneurons produces a decrease in membrane resistance and, in about half the cells, a hyperpolarization [563]. Hyperpolarization of the soma, near the site of spike initiation, would result in a decrease in excitability. In the presynaptic terminals, however, hyperpolarization would be expected to produce a facilitation as shown in Fig. 5.2.* The conductance increase in spinal motoneurons is thought to be mediated primarily by potassium (see Chapter 5), in keeping with earlier observations of effects of injected calcium on *Aplysia* neurons [660].

The duration of posttetanic neuronal potentiation is sufficiently long to serve as a stimulus trace for signaling associative contingency.

> "Some types of motoneuron potentiation may last for several minutes [c.f. 199,256,613] or even for hours [cf. 73,74,934] if the tetanization is delivered for periods of 15 minutes or more. Once established, the potentiation is relatively resistant to disruption by high frequency stimulation" [934 also see 484]. Posttetanic potentiation can occur in spinal motoneurons at lower, physiologic rates of stimulation [199,347,928] or after tetanic stimulation of the cortex at rates of 10-20/sec [930].
>
> Orthodromic tetanization of preganglionic fibers to the stellate ganglion produces facilitation of the response, measured as action potentials evoked over a group of fibers, which lasts for 2 min or more [cf. 577]. Repetitive activation of this postsynaptic element by antidromic stimu-

---

*For another view see p. 191.

lation does not alter its response to synaptic activation. A comparable presynaptic facilitation lasting 2 min was found after tetanic stimulation of the monosynaptic spinal reflex in the cat [613]. This type of change may be termed a change in the efficacy of synaptic transmission since the locus of the adaptation is presynaptic and the excitability of the postsynaptic cell is not changed.

The effects of repetitive electrical stimulation have also been studied in cortical neurons [e.g., 89,635,1057].

Bliss and Lømo [89] have shown that the population response of granule cells of the dentate gyrus of the hippocampal formation is increased by repetitive stimulation of the perforant paths. There is enhancement of the EPSPs to the granule cells and augmentation of their rates of discharge. Conditioning trains at 10-20/sec for 10-15 sec or 100/sec for 3-4 sec produce potentiation for ½-10 hr. Some have reported effects lasting for days and even weeks [89,237,619]. Both an increased efficacy of transmission at the perforant path synapses and an increased excitability of the granule cell population may underlie this long-lasting posttetanic potentiation [89]. Recent studies by Lynch and colleagues indicate that the long-term potentiation depends on the presence of calcium and may be mediated via a calcium dependent phosphorylation of a 40,000 dalton protein [635].

Bliss and colleagues [88] were earlier able to alter the rates of discharge of cortical neurons* evoked by slow, repetitive stimulation of subcortical input pathways. They were, however, unable to predict the response to an individual stimulus with any degree of certainty. Alterations were produced by stimulation of transcortical as well as subcortical pathways.

Phenomena analogous to posttetanic potentiation have also been studied in invertebrates such as *Aplysia* [e.g., 870,1025,1100].

Posttetanic potentiation is not the only long-lasting effect produced by repetitive neuronal stimulation. Recently, repetitive stimulation of the pyramidal tract has been shown to affect the excitability of neurons of the motor cortex. With high frequency stimulation of 100 Hz there is an increased excitability in PT cells [78]. With low frequency stimulation (<10 Hz), the excitability is decreased [1028]. The changes appear to be postsynaptic in that they are not abolished by $MgCl_2$ [78], and some are supported by corresponding changes in cell membrane resistance [1028]. Cells of the motor cortex that are activated transsynaptically rather than antidromically often show changes in excitability of opposite direction [78,1028].

The changes after pyramidal tract stimulation differ from most of those postulated to occur after posttetanic potentiation in that they seem to be produced postsynaptically. In contrast, most of the effects of posttetanic potentiation are attributed to hyperpolarization of presynaptic terminals.

---

*In an isolated cortical slab from the forebrain of the cat.

Heterosynaptic Facilitation and Inhibition

When adaptation occurs because two or more *dissimilar* synapses are activated, the consequences may be termed heterosynaptic facilitation [cf. 251, 488] or inhibition [cf. 242,257,293] depending on the outcome. The dissimilarities may arise from activating a synapse on another presynaptic terminal while activating the terminal itself [999] or by activating two different presynaptic terminals on a single postsynaptic neuron.

Physiologically, "heterosynaptic" effects will not be distinct from repetitive or tetanic effects if the actions of the two synapses are similar. Thus, this term should be reserved for instances where the stimulated synapses can be shown to differ either pharmacologically or in some physiologically relevant way. Accordingly, whenever the activation of two synapses on a postsynaptic neuron simply produces differences in the space over which the resulting PSPs are represented rather than different neurotransmitters or second messenger effects, the terms pseudoheterosynaptic or homosynaptic should be used.

Heterosynaptic inhibition in *Aplysia* can last for several seconds or many minutes [998]. So can heterosynaptic facilitation in that species. Yet the duration of the adaptation cannot be reliably used to distinguish heterosynaptic from homosynaptic changes. Posttetanic potentiation of presynaptic terminals, evoked by stimulating a homosynaptic set of fibers, may produce equally long-lasting effects.

Investigation of the mechanisms of heterosynaptic facilitation in the giant cell of *Aplysia* [488] indicates that changes do not occur in the passive properties or spike generating mechanisms of the postjunctional membrane. According to Kandel and Spencer [486], the priming stimulus does not significantly alter membrane conductance, nor can a train of directly initiated spikes serve as a priming stimulus. In addition, the facilitation can occur after partial blockage of postsynaptic inhibition by curare or under conditions such as low temperature and lithium substitution for sodium, in which posttetanic potentiation has not been demonstrated. As with conditioning-testing and posttetanic effects, the quanta of transmitter molecules released at the presynaptic terminals are altered. Despite the apparent similarities in locus of adaptive change, the mechanism of heterosynaptically induced facilitation may, in *Aplysia*, be dissimilar to that of potentiation induced posttetanically and homosynaptically in other genera.

Conditioning of Neural Activity Changes

Extensive studies of the use of electrical stimulation of the brain to alter the activity of single neurons have been conducted by Voronin and colleagues. These studies complement those of Doty, described earlier, in which electrical stimulation of the brain was used to alter behavior. Alterations in EPSP or IPSP activity were found in Voronin's experiments, but these effects were not specifically induced by associative pairing in most cells. Instead, they were induced nonassociatively. How similar in this respect would be the other "artificially produced" changes in unit activity described earlier (p. 142) is not known. Voronin's changes were attributed either to pseudoconditioning or to a dominant focus type of effect analogous to the facilitation of response after electrical stimulation of the motor cortex described on p. 161 and possibly related to the reflex dominance of Ukhtomsky. Similarities were also noted between this process and that of posttetanic potentiation.

Voronin [1051,1053] used bipolar stimulation of the cortical surface near the recording microelectrode as a US and stimulation of a remote caudal cortical point as the CS. In these experiments the US produced alterations in the rate of spike discharge and also usually evoked a contralateral foreleg movement. Pairing CS and US with intertrial intervals of 1-5 sec produced a transient alteration in the unit response to the CS. With longer intertrial intervals the changes in spike responses and in EPSPs and IPSPs were reduced. Approximately one-third of the units tested showed long-lasting associative modifications which had some of the characteristics of behavioral CRs described on p. 159.

This ability to produce modifications of all-or-none unit activity by presenting paired electrical stimuli is also consistent with the results of other investigators [129,728,729,793,895,1043, and material cited below].

Rusinov's experiments [851-854], which were confirmed by Morrell [685], showed that neural activity could be altered by pairing a sensory CS with weak *anodal polarization* of the motor cortex as a US. Alterations in the rate of unit activity induced by such procedures persisted for minutes and were specific for the sensory modality used as a CS.

Rabinovitch and Kopytova [792] conducted experiments in alert rabbits in which an acoustic CS was paired with anodal polarization of the cortex as a US. The effect of these stimuli on unit activity was studied with the additional use of another neutral tone as a discriminative stimulus. Polarization changed the spontaneous activity of most units, reversibly. About half the cells were able to respond discriminatively to the CS with an alteration in activity following associative pairings. Differential responses persisted for up to 20-30 min in some neurons. Polarization has also been shown to influence synaptic transmission in the spinal cord [253] and at the neuromuscular junction [432].

Skrebitsky [911] showed that pairing an electrical CS delivered to the VB thalamus with weak, 300 msec polarization of neurons of motor cortex as US facilitated the response of the latter neurons to CS presentation. Baranyi and Feher [46] reported conditioning* of PT cells by pairing antidromic PT stimulation with stimulation of VL thalamus. As a result there was a facilitation of VL EPSP's in these cells. In non-PT cells the same procedures augmented the size of PSPs and increased rates of spontaneous discharge.

Shinkman et al. [894] report "the ability to influence segments of unit activity patterns by using electrical stimulation of the hypothalamus as a reinforcer. The single unit response patterns that were changed were in neurons of the visual cortex. Conditioned cells were located equally often in the posterolateral and suprasylvian gyri."

---

*But these changes may not have resulted from associations analogous to conditioning.

Corticocortical CRs, induced by using electrical stimulation of separate cortical loci as CS and US, were studied with extracellular recordings by Balashova [45], by Khananashvili et al. [514] in isolated cortical slabs, and by Kholodof [515], also in an isolated cortical slab. They were studied intracellularly by Voronin [1053]. Many changes in activity were similar to those expected as a consequence of posttetanic potentiation. Others differed in time course, rapidity of elaboration, or ease of extinction.

The activity of single cells may be followed through conditioning and extinction of a response. Either natural or electrical stimuli can be used as CS and US [320,738,899,1053,1055,1125]. Changes in patterns of evoked activity are of small degree. In Voronin's experiments [1053], changes in activity through electrical conditioning and extinction procedures were observed in 7 of 17 cells of cortical motor regions. Six of the seven cells showed increases in activity to click CS during acquisition of a conditioned startle reflex and decreases with extinction.

Chemical Stimulation

The earlier discussion of the effects of chemical stimulation on behavior (p. 163) must now be expanded. Stimulus effects at chemical synapses are mediated naturally by neurotransmitters which are synthesized, stored, and released in the synaptic region [52]. These chemicals can produce characteristic neuronal effects at the cellular or subcellular level [562,812,973]. Chemically induced changes in membrane conductance are likely to form the fundamental building blocks of adaptive changes supporting the associative and nonassociative processes described earlier in Chapter 3. As a result, chemical agents applied directly to single neurons may be more precise forms of experimental CSs or USs than are natural or electrical stimuli.

The chemical synapses which comprise the majority of synaptic contacts in the CNS consist of a presynaptic nerve ending and a juxtaposed postsynaptic site, separated by a synaptic gap that is about 200 Å wide. The presynaptic element is capable of synthesis, storage and release of the neurotransmitter. Influx of Ca^{2+} couples excitation of the presynaptic membrane and the release process. The release involves one (or more) neurotransmitters and may also involve other substances (e.g., ATP, dopamine β-hydroxylase) that are packed together with the neurotransmitter. It is assumed that the neurotransmitter diffuses across the synaptic gap and binds to specific recognition sites located on the postsynaptic membrane of a dendrite, soma, or axon. Binding of an agonist brings about changes in the membrane potential of the postsynaptic cell. These changes involve the opening of ion channels with concomitant changes in membrane permeability to various ions. Binding of neurotransmitters to specific receptor sites in the membrane of the receptive cell influences membrane permeability via reactions which are restricted to the synaptic membrane or via a cascade of reactions which involve intracellular second messengers [52].

Nonassociative Chemical Agents

Neurotransmitters. Certain naturally occurring chemicals may be thought of as producing nonassociative changes in neuronal membranes. The changes occur automatically after combination of the chemical with a receptor in the postsynaptic membrane and do not depend on any other stimulus induced contingencies. When these effects occur rapidly and naturally at specialized junctions (synapses) between two cells and meet certain other criteria,* they are referred to as neurotransmitter effects. There are, of course, some steps in this process where associative or contingent processes may intervene. First, transmitter release by exocytosis from vesicles located within the presynaptic terminals occurs as a consequence of voltage and calcium-dependent interactions [cf. 499,609,611]. Second, the postsynaptic changes may be influenced by a number of different variables described further in Chapter 5.

With respect to learning and memory, the more interesting of the neurotransmitter effects occur centrally. They have been reviewed by Krnjevic [cf. 562]. The agents acting on cortical neurons include acetylcholine, norepinephrine, dopamine, glutamate, and γ-aminobutyric acid (GABA). Peptides such as the enkephalins and endorphins also occur naturally in nervous tissue [449, 460,918,919] and are involved in some forms of neural adaptation [see 485]. They act like opiate drugs in producing analgesia and may inhibit the release of substance P. Substance P is thought to act as a neurotransmitter along pathways that support the response to noxious stimuli, including the substantia gelatinosa and portions of the reticular projections of the anterolateral system. The list of peptides and other chemicals that may potentially serve as neurotransmitters grows daily, but the list of chemicals that fulfill the criteria necessary for their effectiveness to be proved does not.

Messengers and Modulators. Classically, neurotransmitters act rapidly and their actions are transient. Recently, however, some slower effects have been identified. These effects are mediated, postsynaptically, by chemicals such as calcium and the cyclic nucleotides, which may be activated or released as a consequence of neurotransmission. The same chemicals may influence transmission at presynaptic terminals. Typically, the chemicals act as internal, postsynaptic mediators or second messengers of neurotransmission to produce conductance changes and other postsynaptic effects.

Empirically, identification of a second messenger system involving *cyclic nucleotides* requires that the following criteria be satisfied:

1. Application of the first messenger to the cell must lead to a rise in the intracellular concentration of the cyclic nucleotide in proportion to its biological effects as should stimulation of appropriate synaptic inputs.
2. Inhibitors of phosphodiesterase[†] must enhance the physiologic effects of submaximal concentrations of the first messenger.

*Local occurrence, release, and degradation; mimicry of neural effect by application of purified agent; etc.
[†]Phosphodiesterase splits the cyclic nucleotide (see Fig. 5.9).

3. Application of the cyclic nucleotide should mimic the physiologic effect of the first messenger.
4. First messenger-sensitive adenylate or guanylate cyclases should be identified in the plasma membrane fraction of the cell homogenate.
5. Pharmacologic antagonists to the above should act appropriately.

Without satisfying the above criteria, documentation of the existence of such processes is incomplete.

Cyclic AMP (cAMP) has been implicated as a second messenger for noradrenergic, dopaminergic neurotransmission and cyclic GMP (cGMP) for cholinergic, muscarinic neurotransmission [90,160,355-358,976,1124], though not in all types of neurons [566,1076]. Further details are given in Chapter 5 (see Table 5.2 for example). Norepinephrine acts, in vertebrates, to produce IPSPs, with conductance decreases in cerebellar Purkinje cells [903] and in spinal motoneurons [272]. Acetylcholine acts, in vertebrates, to decrease membrane conductance in neurons of the neocortex [568, 1124], the hippocampus [224], and the spinal cord [566,1148].

Extracellular application of cAMP and norepinephrine is reported to decrease the rate of discharge of cortical PT neurons [966], and intracellular application of cAMP decreases firing rate and membrane resistance [1121]. Extracellular application of acetylcholine and cGMP increases the discharge rates of such neurons [562,966]. Extracellular application of cAMP increases the resistance of Purkinje cells and produces hyperpolarization comparable to the effects of norepinephrine [903]. Locus coeruleus projections to Purkinje cells are thought to be noradrenergic [1101]. Stimulation of these afferents produces effects similar to application of norepinephrine and cAMP, including the potentiation of inhibitory transmitter effects of GABA. Intracellular application of cGMP produces transient increases in the membrane resistance of cortical neurons remarkably similar to those produced by extracellular iontophoresis of acetylcholine [976,1116,1117,1124]. This does not appear to be the case in spinal motoneurons [566], nor is it the major consequence found in the superior cervical ganglion [314]. Thus, the effect is not general, but is seen only in certain types of neurons.

The effects of acetylcholine on mammalian cortical neurons are blocked by atropine, but those of intracellularly applied cGMP are not [976]. Both effects can be demonstrated in the same cells—of which at least some are pyramidal neurons of layer V [1121]. The results suggest that cGMP mediates neurotransmission at cholinergic, muscarinic synapses of layer V pyramidal cells in the mammalian motor cortex.

The possibility must be considered that such mediators do not simply carry the message of neurotransmission. They may instead be involved in the regulation or modulation of other changes within the neuron. For example, regulation of the internal metabolic activity of the neuron may be controlled as a function of the amount of neurotransmitter activity seen by the cell (cf. internal state as a regulator of adaptation, Chapter 7). Pacemaker activity may also be regulated by transmitter-dependent postsynaptic chemicals as mentioned earlier [485].

Behaviorally, the possibility arises that messengers such as cyclic nucleotides constitute a temporal trace that can serve as a subcellular means for permitting associative linkages, over time, between CS and US. A trace chemical compound or its cellular effects would have to last several hundred msec or longer to serve as the basis of the 200-400 msec interstimulus interval required for optimal learning of many types of conditioning. Associative trace-dependent interactions of cyclic nucleotides, calcium and various neurotransmitters may last this long and could well control the development of persistent neuronal changes subserving memory and learning.

Chemical CS

Little is known about the effectiveness of acetylcholine or other putative neurotransmitters as one of an associative CS-US pair. In experiments mentioned earlier [46], postsynaptic potentials of neurons of the motor cortex were said to be increased by pairing VL thalamus stimulation and stimulation of the pyramidal tract. Stimulation of the thalamus could simply have resulted in the release of acetylcholine at the nerve terminals in the cortex. Acetylcholine is an adequate stimulus to produce transiently increased resistance in 50% of the cortical neurons to which it is applied [566,1116, 1124]. The increase in resistance would cause an increase in size of postsynaptic potentials such as was seen on stimulating the thalamus. When application of acetylcholine is associated with depolarizing current sufficient to produce repeated spike initiation, a persistent rather than transient increase in resistance results [1116,1124].

Chemical US

Two groups of investigators have produced changes in neural activity using chemicals as USs. Bureš and Burešova have successfully used glutamate as a US in conjunction with weak electrical current [128]. Although it is not entirely clear whether the unit responses that develop with this compound US result from chemical or from electrical attributes of the stimulus, these studies characterize typical responses of central neurons to discrete associative stimuli.

In Bureš and Burešova's studies, only a few conditioned responses could be established in neurons of the non-specific thalamus, reticular formation, hippocampus or neocortex by reinforcing an auditory tone with electrical or chemical stimuli (10-50 nA glutamate iontophoresis). Despite several hundred reinforcements, responses to the CS could be established in only 17 of 128 neurons (13%). Transient changes were found in an additional 34 cells. In further experiments in the inferior colliculus, habituatory changes to repetitive auditory stimuli could be produced in 37 of 64 units. These changes could be dishabituated by interrupting the stimulation. Reinforcing the habituated sound stimulus with polarizing current then produced conditioned changes in response to the auditory stimulus in 14 of 17 neurons (increased activity in six, decreased activity in five, and inversion of response in three).

Kotlyar successfully used glucose as a US for conditioning involving gluco-receptor neurons in the hypothalamus [549]. Also, he subsequently used acetylcholine as a US to alter the activity of units in the sensorimotor cortex of unanesthetized rates [548]. The possibility that acetylcholine acts as part of the US to produce the increases in excitability of units of the motor cortex described earlier seems likely [1109].

In Kotlyar's studies sound was paired associatively as a CS with acetyl-choline as a US in 44 units. The response to sound changed in 14 of 36 units (50%). Control studies with pseudoconditioning produced changes in the response to sound in 4 of 15 units (27%). In seven other units in which both pseudoconditioning and associative pairing were tested successively, four cells showed selective associative changes to the pairing and two showed changes both to pseudoconditioning and to associative pairing.

Summary

In summary, the cellular basis of learned behavior is experimentally sup-ported but incompletely understood. Correlates between simple forms of learning and measurable indices of neuronal function have been established in a variety of species. Throughout much of the nervous system, changes in acti-vity are found to subserve phenomena such as conditioning and habituation. activity are found to subserve phenomena such as conditioning and habituation. Field potentials have not provided correlates of comparable specificity or usefulness to those obtained from single unit studies. This is because the wave shapes of field potentials may reflect the spread of current as much as the messages transmitted. Changes in the excitability of single, mammalian cortical units have been correlated with conditioning, H-adaptation, latent facilitation, reflex dominance, and sensory preconditioning. Excitability is measured as the level of current required to produce neural activity. Current is delivered through micropipettes in or near the cell. That measured by intracellular nA current delivery reflects different adaptive mechanisms than that measured by extracellular nA current delivery.

Many cellular manifestations of *repetitively* induced adaptations appear to be small in magnitude and *transient*. Many cellular manifestations of *associatively* induced adaptations appear to be small in magnitude and *persistent*. The number of neurons responding, though circumscribed, may be quite large. The subtlety of this and the earlier described stochastic forms of information processing within the mammalian nervous system has eluded some and disap-pointed others—many being completely dissuaded from pursuing cellular studies in mammalian preparations. However, changes of small magnitude reflect a natural process characteristic of mammalian learning. Amplification and expression of enduring effects of learning, though of small magnitude per cell, will take place over a numerically large ensemble of functionally related units. This is a desirable form of information processing in mammals where central units are highly polysensory in reception and polymotor in projection.

(Too extreme a change in the transfer property of a single unit could lead to an abnormal outcome such as epilepsy.) Orderly change of many units rather than invariance appears to be a major requirement for the forms of learning and higher function seen in the more advanced species.

Model systems of simplified behavior provide the best chance of finding neural correlates that can lead to localization of engrams, the cellular changes responsible for learned behavior.* The search for an engram involves localization, specification, and characterization. Thus, the discovery of unit correlates of a learned behavior is commonly followed by lesion studies and then artificial reproduction of the phenomenon. The studies lead to localization of the neural populations in which changes responsible for the correlates have taken place. The specific neurons involved must be identified. Then, the specificity of their altered function in relation to the behavior in question must be determined. Finally, the changes must be characterized at the subcellular level according to their locus, mechanisms of action, and means of production.

As suggested herein and by the material that follows in Chapter 5, engrams supporting conditioning and habituation have been localized in mammals, crustacea, and mollusks. Some engrams for the performance of motor-specific conditioned behavior are localized postsynaptically in motor neurons that project either directly or polysynaptically to the target musculature of the CR. They are persistent and could support long-term memory. Analogous changes may support conditioning in invertebrates [12]. Some engrams for habituation are localized to the presynaptic terminals of sensory neurons and interneurons at or before the level of motoneurons involved with the habituated motor response. They are transient. Although engrams supporting habituation have been linked to specific neurons in the mollusk, these neurons have also been shown to be unnecessary for habituation to occur. Thus, specification of their role in habituation is incomplete. This complexity emphasizes the redundancy of engrams within the neural network. The principle of redundant information storage has long been recognized in mammalian mnemonic processes, as has the need for probabilistic considerations in relating processes in single cells to functions of the network as a whole.

Studies of habituation, though satisfying the criteria of localization and unit correlation, have not yet led to specification or characterization of an engram in any species. However, Alkon's studies of conditioning[†] have led to biophysical specification of an engram involved in associative conditioning of a light-cued rotational response in *Hermissenda* (a nudibranch mollusk). The response is mediated through a light-receptive neuron (a type B photoreceptor) in which a long lasting inactivation or decrease in a fast, 4-AP sensitive potassium conductance (see g K_{TEA} in Chapter 5) enhances the magni-

---

*Obviously those representing trace effects should be distinguished from those supporting persistent or permanent memory functions (see Chaps. 5-7).

[†] See refs. [12,1109] and Alkon, D. L., Lederhendler, I., and Shoukimas, J. Primary changes of membrane currents during retention of associative learning. *Science* (in press, 1982).

tude of depolarization arising from a slow, voltage dependent calcium conductance (g Ca_{sv} in Chapter 5). The increased depolarization mirrors effects of light and is thought to reduce the ability of *Hermissenda* to discriminate between light and dark, thus supporting the learned suppression of discriminative responses to light. The learned behavior is maintained for about five days. The neural changes are not yet characterized with respect to their CS specificity or their possible relation to sensory preconditioning. The characterization and specification of additional neural changes involved in this and other forms of conditioning remains to be established.

Cellular changes analogous to those accompanying simple learning can be produced by electrical or chemical stimuli. In fact, virtually all simple, associatively induced learned behavior can be reproduced by direct electrical or chemical stimulation of neural tissue. This further supports the cellular basis of learned behavior, as does the production of neural analogs of the behavior itself.

Associative and nonassociative effects of stimulus presentations may also be usefully elucidated by conditioning-testing studies, particularly where the chemical effects of the stimuli are specifically characterized. The dependence of these neurochemical effects on parameters of stimulus presentation can be readily investigated if the stimuli are sufficiently discrete. In addition, stimuli can be applied at different anatomical loci to test generalization of learned responses at the cellular level. A variety of approaches have thus proved useful for investigating the cellular basis of memory, learning, and higher function. How these mechanisms of neural adaptation might be represented and controlled at the subcellular level is the subject of the next chapter.

Chapter 5

Subcellular Substrates of Learning and Memory

The ways that nerve cells, dendrites and axons receive, evaluate, filter, sum and transmit signals are key processes in the function of the nervous system. It was thought at one time that neurons are simply all-or-none elements... real nervous systems employ graded signals of various kinds and have several forms of excitability besides the spike threshold. By the early fifties local potentials, generator potentials, excitatory postsynaptic potentials (EPSPs), inhibitory postsynaptic potentials (IPSPs), positive and negative after potentials, facilitation, spontaneity, and neurosecretion were somewhat appreciated. Still later there were added other complications such as presynaptic inhibition, pump potentials, calcium spikes, electrical transmission, electrotonic connections without impulse influence, hormonal effects upon neurons, neurophysins, identifiable neurons and a whole array of light microscopic and electron microscopic advances.

(Bullock, 1979)

As we have seen, a fundamental tenet of learning theory is that the proximity, in time, of certain stimuli profoundly influences brain function. Brain function, in turn, depends on processes at the cellular and subcellular levels. Simple, repetitive, and associative presentations of stimuli are thought to influence these processes relatively directly. This chapter is concerned with the possible effects of temporally associated stimuli on ionic conductances and other molecularly based functions that form the ultimate substrates of learning and memory.

The material is separated into five portions: the first concerns theories of cellular plasticity and adaptation; the second takes up membrane ionic conductances by which many cellular changes are mediated; the third and fourth consider the mechanisms by which these changes are controlled; and the fifth discusses the means for investigating these phenomena.

Theories of Cellular Plasticity

In general, theories of cellular plasticity concerned with learning and memory may be divided into two types: (1) *connectional theories* that postulate the growth of cell processes which form new connective paths; and (2) *elemental theories* that postulate alterations in the transmission of messages through preconnected, anatomically fixed elements.

Pavlov was an early proponent of the connectional hypothesis. He believed that new connections were formed between the sensory-receptive and motor-effective elements of the cortex during associative processes such as conditioning.

The alternative view, i.e., the elemental hypothesis, was supported by Hebb in his book, *The Organization of Behavior* [397]. As it has presently evolved, this hypothesis proposes. that transmission along preexisting, preconnected elements is altered by changing the efficacy of transmission through synaptic couplings [397,486] and by modifying the integrative properties of postsynaptic elements [805,1110]. Ramon y Cajal [141] had proposed earlier that some aspects of complex motor learning could be explained "by either a progressive thickening of the nervous pathways or the formation of new cell processes." Thus, Cajal recognized both alternatives.

Although the evidence is still far from complete, it favors the position that novel connectional changes between neurons occur primarily during developmental periods rather than during adulthood. Early in life modification of neural circuitry can proceed by eliminating as well as by adding connections. As a result, some neural pathways organized initially on the basis of genetically transmitted information may be replaced by pathways organized according to experiential factors. It is this redistribution of connections during the developmental period that optimizes the organization of the neural network upon which all, later processing of information will take place.

In adulthood, learning will depend primarily on elemental changes involving alterations in the weighting of transmission along neural pathways with fixed anatomical connections. There may also occur changes in the size or even the number of connections, but in general, the neurons connected will remain the same. These inferences follow if one assumes that preservation of specified pathways with line-labeled connections is necessary for efficient parallel processing of information to take place. This assumption is based on constraints of information processing described in Chapter 7. The major constraint is that whatever information processing occurs over new connections requires identification and specification of the new pathways in the context of the old. The formation of new connections would result in switching the flow of some messages into new channels. Not only encoding but decoding of messages would need to be accomplished through these channels. Once the period of developmental tuning of circuitry is past, decoding of messages will be based on an increasingly extensive volume of stored information. The stored information will be made accessible by preestablished motor- and sensory-labeled relationships along the pathways of information processing. It would be difficult to achieve this by a form of processing based on the continuous formation of novel connections. If novel connectional changes were the basis of such learning, each newly formed pathway would have to reestablish its relationship to each preexisting pathway of relevance and vice versa. On the other hand, if changes in elemental weighting were the rule, the line-labeled pathways might remain much the same and an orderly flow of messages could readily be maintained. The weighting of transmission and integration through these pathways would then change in accordance with the repetitive and associative laws of neural adaptation.

Connectional Theories

Connectional theories postulate that learning proceeds from the formation of novel connections between neurons. Workable connectional theories must then satisfy two constraints: (1) new cellular growth must occur and (2) connections must be formed between cells in some orderly and specific fashion that permits appropriate messages to be transmitted through the neurons involved in the changes. The latter is no trivial matter when one considers the need, noted above, for maintaining orderly information storage, processing, and retrieval through all neural pathways linked through these connections.

Growth

What evidence is there that new neuronal growth can actually occur? As will be described in further detail below, the nervous system exhibits *normal developmental growth* as well as *regenerative growth* after injury. Morphologic [799-802], biochemical [952,1089,1090], and electrophysiologic [435] studies agree that neuronal processes proliferate and can form new connections in infancy and early developmental periods.

New Growth of Neuronal Processes. Morphologically, new growth can be demonstrated by direct microscopic examination. Growth may involve elongation, extension, or proliferation. In the adult, most growth appears to be regenerative, occurring after injury or after the normal wear and tear of constant use in the process of aging. Proliferative regeneration occurs throughout the nervous sytem, but is decidedly more limited in central than in peripheral nervous tissue. Central axons do not usually regenerate when cut. Central "regrowth" consists mainly of sprouting and hypertrophy with the end effect being maintenance of existing connections rather than regeneration of injured ones. Occasionally, some disrupted connections may be reestablished, and even the formation of a few new connections may be seen as, for example, in the hippocampus [962,963]. Spike generation, which is lost during degenerative changes, is regained after successful regeneration. Other differences in regeneration that appear as a function of species, age, and locus of the process within the nervous system are reviewed by Bjorklund and Stenevi [80].

In the early period of life, growth occurs in both the central and peripheral nervous system [786]. Biochemically, there are molecularly coded pathways and surfaces that permit the completion of linkages between appropriate nerve elements. Electrophysiologically, the spike generating ability of neurons is maintained throughout most growth changes that occur during developmental periods, although in some species there is a change-over in the ionic basis of the spike from calcium to sodium [675]. Cultures of isolated neurons have also been studied during their development [219,710], but this type of growth is far from equatable with natural development. An example of normal developmental growth, in vivo, may be taken from the mammalian visual system. During its development the visual cortex becomes organized according to vertical columns of specific, functionally related units. The normal course of this process is a direct consequence of specific visual experience. In animals deprived of such experience, such changes either do not occur or fail to occur normally. These animals then have permanent defects in visual information processing.

Changes in neural structure may also be needed for new motor behavior to be performed in the adult. In moths, for example, motor neurons undergo reorganization during metamorphosis. and new dendritic branches develop that are unique to the adult [1027]. Evidence of this type leads to the conclusion that during developmental periods critical neuronal changes occur which can significantly affect learning, memory, and higher function throughout the remaining existence of the organism.

Note that biochemical, morphologic, and electrophysiologic correlates of *abnormal* growth changes can be found in addition to those supporting normal development [e.g., 17,454,784,785]. Some of these abnormalities may result in impaired learning ability. For example, Purpura [784] has found that "abnormally long, thin spines and the absence of short, thick, spines on dendrites of cortical neurons" are associated with profound mental retardation.

Effects of Experience and Sensory Stimulation. The reorganization of neural connections that occurs developmentally is sensitive to experience and to sensory stimulation. During development, "the dendrites of stellate cells of the visual cortex of rats . . . seem to change the orientation of their arborization" [801]. What happens when changes of this type fail to occur was mentioned just above. The changes are mediated through effects consequential to the pattern of afferent input to the cortex. Reorganization of the ocular dominance columns in monkey striate cortex [1089], presumably through the process of sprouting (discussed next) also may involve reorganization of local neural circuitry dependent on visual experience. This reorganization is confined to the developmental period [399,454].

Sprouting. Sprouting of nerve fibers can occur after transection and can lead to the reestablishment of long axonal tracts. This has been demonstrated by grafting and implant procedures in the spinal cord [490] and elsewhere [80,217]. Primary afferent fibers can sprout several weeks after severance of descending pathways by spinal hemisection. Still earlier sprouting can be observed after a circumscribed lesion of the cortex [644]. The collateral sprouts do not always make functionally useful connections. For example, in experiments by Goldberger [333], sprouting appears to be the "signal for the cell body to become chromatolytic and produce protein, and not the converse." Correspondingly, Kuypers has shown that little or no functional recovery occurs after disruption of neuroanatomical motor systems in the monkey. He points out that the apparent recovery that takes place in some cases may be the result of nonspecific testing, "which fails to show the loss of a specific function because the animal is allowed to employ different tactics in performing the task" [575]. It appears then that, while sprouting may give rise to useful new growth developmentally, it may not do so later in life.

Control of Connectional Specificity

During neuronal growth the specificity between newly formed connections is controlled at two levels. The first level may be thought of as ontogenetic, employing genetic coding to transmit information concerning which processes are to be appropriately matched, developmentally. Chemical templates are formed by means of which appropriate pre- and postsynaptic elements can be linked during the maturation process. The second level at which control between connections is exercised involves humoral factors that maintain appropriate functional connections in intact preparations and ensure their proper reconnection in regenerating preparations. This is also done by means of specific chemical labels on cell surfaces that, in turn, permit the formation of designated cell to cell contacts.

Complementary Matching. Complementary chemical matching between pre- and postsynaptic neural elements is thought to influence their connections [935,936,965].* The most striking example of this is the precision with which reconnection of optic nerve fibers is observed to take place in amphibians and fish. As described by Kuffler and Nicholls [571]:

> Stone, Sperry and colleagues showed that if the optic nerve was cut in a frog or salamander, fibers grow back to the appropriate region of the brain (the tectum). There they form synapses, and eventually the animal is able to see once again. This regrowth is orderly. Neurons reform their original connections with a high degree of precision. In Sperry's experiments, the optic nerve of a frog was cut and the eye rotated through 180 degrees. About three weeks later, the nerve had regenerated and the frog could see again, but it behaved as though its vision was inverted. Thus, all its movements directed toward objects, as when the frog struck at a fly, were 180 degrees out of phase.
>
> The simplest interpretation of this and other similar experiments is that the fiber had grown back from the inverted retina to the original destinations in the tectum. Attardi and Sperry [34] showed in the goldfish that regeneration of cut optic nerve fibers was specific to appropriate regions of the tectum, thus confirming the inferences above. That is, after quadrantic lesions, fibers regrew selectively to the matching quadrant of the optic tectum. This was also confirmed by Gaze [321] using physiological techniques.
>
> A further important observation is that the animal never learned to correct its mistakes; frogs with rotated eyes continued to strike down-

---

*There is surprisingly little direct evidence for how this is done and which chemicals do it (the most direct evidence is probably that of Black et al., *NRP Bull.* 14: 250, 1976).

wards at a fly held up in the air for as long as they lived after the operation. There was no evidence that neural connections could be reorganized through the negative reinforcement of behavioral errors. In this respect, the behavior of frogs appears to be different from that of higher animals; a man or a monkey can compensate for the effect of an inverting prism placed on the eyes . . . [571; cf. 534,968] .

However, if one turns to a different behavioral example, an analogous failure to correct mistakes can be observed in man. After unilateral parietal lobe or dorsal column lesions, human beings do not easily compensate for the resulting sensory neglect (see Chapter 6). One interpretation of these results is that compensatory learning arises within the context provided by the original, line-labeled pathways formed developmentally. When these are disrupted, so is this contextual background, and then when regrowth occurs, it may not be sufficiently specific or complete to permit this context to be regained. With prisms, the original connections remain intact and only the input is changed.

Still other chemicals support the proliferative aspects of growth. For example, a chemical nerve growth factor has been found that selectively influences the growth of sympathetic neurons [587,588]. The microtubule content of chick embryo sensory ganglia also increases after treatment with nerve growth factor [412]. Glia are thought to produce nerve growth factor [1041], but the natural action of this compound on central neural networks is as yet unknown.

Role of Glia in Ontogenetic Specificity. Ontogenetically, some information concerning the specificity of developing neural connections is also carried by glial tissue [799-802]. Glia form an organized lattice upon which neurons will grow in the proper direction, finally establishing specific connections as a consequence of terminal interactions between the neurons themselves. "Electron microscopic examination of migrating [nerve] cells suggests they find their way to the cortex by using radially orienting glial fibers as guides" [802].

An alternative view [864] suggests that central nervous tissue is organized as a pseudostratified epithelium. The cell nucleus moves within an elongated but fixed cytoplasmic, epithelial cylinder which alternately loses and then regrows its external processes in the course of nuclear translocation [801].

Other Factors

Other variables such as receptor expression and "trophic" factors can influence cell growth and the completion of functionally useful connections between pre- and postsynaptic nerve elements.

Receptor Expression. Postsynaptic elements contain considerable potential for receptor expression. Receptor expression refers to the ability of latent receptor complexes to be transformed into receptor complexes capable of supporting neurotransmission. The best evidence for such expression is found at the neuromuscular junction in studies of muscle hypersensitivity after denervation or blockage of neurotransmission or nerve metabolism. Denervated skeletal muscle fibers develop increased chemosensitivity to acetylcholine [36] attributable, at least in part, to increases in the density of specific acetylcholine receptors. However, these extrajunctional receptors do not necessarily function the same as normal receptors [380]. Development of new receptor complexes is a type of plasticity that may occur centrally as well as peripherally [545] when previously uninnervated portions of nerve membranes demonstrate the capacity to receive new synaptic connections. This may occur as part of the normal developmental process. For example, Cragg has found changes in the numbers of synapses observed a few hours after rats, reared in darkness, are given their first exposure to light [192,194]. In the adult, however, it is not clear if such connections continue to arise normally or occur only in the presence of injury.

Other Trophic Factors. Connected neural elements exert reciprocal chemical influences transmitted through the surrounding medium. These chemical, trophic factors influence the specificity of new connections as well as the specific functional role that the reconnected elements play. For example, at the neuromuscular junction, both the size of the chemosensitive region of the postsynaptic membrane and the contractile properties of the muscle fiber itself are influenced by chemical factors available from the presynaptic membrane. These influences are sustained and sometimes enhanced after cell contact is disrupted by artificial lesion or disease.

The changes in chemosensitivity include those of receptor expression seen with hypersensitivity. They appear after denervation or blockade of neurotransmitter release by botulinus toxin, and are influenced by acetylcholine [663] and by additional non-transmitter trophic effects [620,664]. They can also be produced by disuse.

The changes in muscle contractility depend, in part, on the muscle end plate. The type of end plate in a muscle is controlled by trophic factors related to the type of nerve that innervates it [144,372,420,833-835]:

Cross-innervating red and white muscles, i.e., slow and fast muscles, results in a conversion of many of the physiological, biochemical, and anatomical properties that are specific to these muscles. After cross innervation, fast muscles are transformed to slow ones, although not vice versa. Most muscles are not homogeneous, being composed of both fast and slow muscle types [833]. After cross innervation, reinnervation of the slow and fast muscles by their original nerve results in a return of the characteristic speed of the muscles as well as their metabolic redifferentiation [833-835]. These processes are age-dependent. Gutmann has reported that the speed of contraction of slow or fast muscles after a cross reinnervation operation changes in young chickens, but not in adults [420]. Correlations are also found between glycolytic and oxidative biochemical characteristics of muscle tissue and the speed of contraction and neurotransmission.

Elemental (Weighting) Theories

Elemental theories of neural plasticity postulate changes in the *weighting* of transmission through anatomically fixed nerve elements. This can be accomplished through changes in neuronal properties in the plasma membrane (and elsewhere) resulting in:

1. Altered efficacy of transmission between pre- and postsynaptic terminals.
2. Changes in integrative processes that affect postsynaptic potential (PSP) summation and lead to the generation of the postsynaptic action potential.

Much has been learned about the physiology and pharmacology of nerve cells over the past 50 years, and some knowledge of the Nernst and Goldman equations [335] as well as of theories of neurotransmission is assumed in the exposition that follows. Excellent reviews of the pre-assumed material can be found elsewhere [9,497,562].

The subcellular processes governing elemental adaptation may be divided according to their locus of operation within the neuron (Fig. 5.1). There are *presynaptic, intrasynaptic,* and *postsynaptic* mechanisms that influence the integration and transmission of information from one cell to the next.

Presynaptic Plasticity

Changes in the presynaptic terminals that could alter the efficacy of synaptic transmission have been among the first predicted, the most often implicated, and the least clarified by direct experimental evidence. All presently known changes in the efficacy of synaptic transmission appear to be transient rather than persistent. As one learns more about their potential means of operation, one recognizes how complex are the molecular processes involved in these changes and how difficult it is to pinpoint their interactions in the laboratory.

Four types of *presynaptic changes* can be readily identified. They are: (1) potential-dependent presynaptic facilitation and inhibition; (2) calcium-dependent changes in transmitter release from synaptic vesicles; (3) alterations in synthesis or storage-cycling of neurotransmitter; and (4) accumulation of potassium at the presynaptic terminal.

Potential-Dependent Presynaptic Facilitation and Inhibition. As shown in Fig. 5.2, steady polarization across the membrane of the presynaptic terminal can result in alterations in the size of the action potential as it invades this region. Spike generation at the presynaptic terminal depends critically on the relation of the resting transmembrane potential to the firing threshold as well as on a large spike actively invading the axonal branches leading to each terminal. Hyperpolarization of the terminal will result in a larger potential shift as the action potential actively invades. There is a substantial safety factor for active propagation along axons, and this may be assumed to hold for propagation into or near the presynaptic terminal. In other words the potential change associated with the invading action potential is large enough to overcome much hyperpolarization and still reach firing threshold. Thus, considerable hyperpolarization can occur before spike invasion is blocked. The hyperpolarization and the larger size of action potentials invading the terminal are relatable to an augmentation of PSPs produced in the postsynaptic cell. This facilitation of synaptic transmission is referred to as *presynaptic facilitation.*

The converse can also occur. That is, the resting potential of the presynaptic terminal can be depolarized toward, but not completely to, the

Some Subcellular Regions and Processes That May Support Neural Adaptation

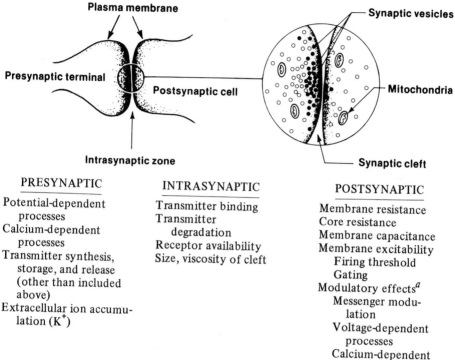

PRESYNAPTIC	INTRASYNAPTIC	POSTSYNAPTIC
Potential-dependent processes	Transmitter binding	Membrane resistance
Calcium-dependent processes	Transmitter degradation	Core resistance
Transmitter synthesis, storage, and release (other than included above)	Receptor availability	Membrane capacitance
	Size, viscosity of cleft	Membrane excitability
Extracellular ion accumulation (K⁺)		Firing threshold
		Gating
		Modulatory effects[a]
		Messenger modulation
		Voltage-dependent processes
		Calcium-dependent processes

[a] can also occur presynaptically

Fig. 5.1. Diagrammatic representation of a synapse, the region where neurons communicate, illustrating pre- and postsynaptic elements and the intrasynaptic zone. A portion is expanded to the right. The vesicular hypothesis postulates that on arrival of an action potential, transmitter is released by exocytosis (Figs. 5.15 and 5.20), diffuses across the intrasynaptic zone (the synaptic cleft), and is received by the receptors on the outside of the postsynaptic membrane.

critical firing threshold. Under these circumstances, an invading action potential will produce a relatively smaller potential shift (see Fig. 5.2c). Associated with the smaller change in potential is a decrement in the size of PSPs produced in the postsynaptic cell. This process is termed *presynaptic inhibition*. Postsynaptically, depolarization facilitates spike generation by making it easier for summated PSPs to reach critical firing threshold (the transmembrane potential at which sodium spikes are initiated). Presynaptically, depolarization has at least four different effects: (1) if small, it reduces the size of propagated action potentials as shown in Fig. 5.2, (2) it may further reduce the size of propagated action potentials by enhancing sodium inactivation (and shortening the top of the spike), (3) if moderate, it will activate calcium conductance at the presynaptic terminal (see Fig. 5.3 and ref. 610), and (4) if

The Resting Potential May Affect the Amplitude of Spikes
Invading the Presynaptic Terminal

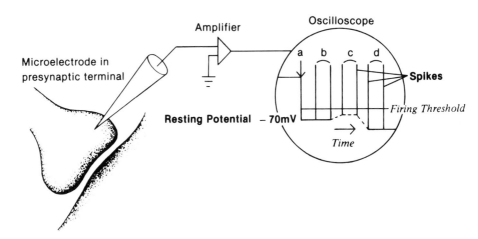

Fig. 5.2. Hypothetical oscilloscope display of amplified recording obtained from a microelectrode in a presynaptic terminal. (a) Penetration of the terminal causes a shift of about −70 mV in the baseline voltage. An arriving action potential exceeds the critical firing threshold (the transmembrane potential at which sodium spikes are initiated), and the action potentials of normal amplitude shown in (b) result. (c) Partial depolarization of the presynaptic terminal results in smaller-sized action potential shifts. Hyperpolarization (d) results in larger-sized action potential shifts.

extreme, it can lead to de novo spike generation and can also inactivate calcium conductance via an accumulation of calcium, intracellularly. Presumably, depolarization is brought about by the action of other chemical synapses on the presynaptic terminal itself. There are several mechanisms by which the depolarization could be prolonged internally, for example, through cyclic nucleotide- or calcium-dependent conductance changes as well as by extracellular accumulation of potassium. Over the years, a great deal of evidence has been amassed to support depolarization of the presynaptic terminal as the basis of presynaptic inhibition [e.g. 250,252-254,257], but as yet not even the critical firing threshold of the presynaptic terminal is known with certainty.* These complexities greatly complicate our understanding of the exact mechanisms supporting presynaptic facilitation and inhibition. Further discussion follows the section on calcium dependent release of neurotransmitter.

*The critical firing threshold for the production of the IS (initial segment) spike in the initial segment of some axons is thought to be about −60 mV with an associated resting potential of about −70 mV. That in the soma of some neurons is −45 mV with an associated resting potential of about −50 mV (see Fig. 5.17). The problem of maintaining a gradient in resting potential within the cell has not been given much consideration, but will be in the future, particularly as evidence for still more positive resting potentials in some distal dendritic regions accumulates.

Calcium-Dependent Vesicular Release of Neurotransmitter. Calcium ions are obligatory for normal neurotransmission [203,499]. Transmitter release at the presynaptic terminal of the squid giant synapse is insensitive to blockers of sodium conductance such as tetrodotoxin (TTX) and partial blockers of potassium conductance such as tetraethylammonium (TEA), but is inhibited by calcium blockers such as magnesium and manganese ions [40,504]. At the presynaptic terminal *decreases in intracellular free calcium ion concentration decrease the efficacy of transmission.* The decreases in $[Ca]_i$ may result either from reducing calcium conductance or from increasing the uptake of free calcium within the cell [15,40,676,1042]. *Increases in intracellular free calcium concentration* produce changes that *facilitate transmission* [15,503].

Transmitter release following tetanic stimulation also varies as a function of *extracellular* calcium concentration [844,1078]. In the absence of extracellular calcium, nerve impulses can propagate into the presynaptic terminal, but they will fail to cause an increase in the probability of transmitter release [498]. Usually, however, control of transmitter release is thought to be more a function of intracellular than of extracellular calcium ions. Residual calcium ions left internally after repetitive invasion of the nerve terminal by the action potential undoubtedly contribute to alterations in the efficacy of transmission at the presynaptic terminal [503,641,797,798,1141].

Katz and Miledi [503] advanced the hypothesis that residual calcium is responsible for short-term facilitation at the neuromuscular junction* following delivery of conditioning stimuli. By increasing the calcium concentration directly, a comparable facilitation is produced. Much the same occurs upon introducing a short pulse of depolarization. (This is opposite to the Ca^{2+}-dependent effects of prolonged depolarization, which will be described later.) The effect continues in the TTX-treated preparation. Katz and Miledi [500-502] had found earlier that "the release of acetylcholine by brief depolarizing pulses increases more than in a linear proportion when the duration of the pulse is lengthened." Curtailing the falling phase of the action potential in the nerve terminal has also been shown to suppress transmitter release. Younkin [1141] points out that "the process facilitating transmitter release at the neuromuscular junction following a single impulse or brief train of impulses has two components." Katz and Miledi [499,503] proposed that the first component of facilitation was due to calcium, and Miledi and Thies [665] proposed that both components of facilitation could be accounted for by an effect of calcium. The first component of facilitation is maximal immediately after the impulse and decays exponentially with a time constant of about 35 msec [641]. The second component peaks 120 msec after the impulse and decays exponentially with a time constant of about 250 msec. The second com-

*It is important that these presynaptic effects of Katz and Miledi and of Llinas and colleagues not be confused with the effect of calcium when injected into the postsynaptic cell. In that case the effects reported by Meech and Strumwasser [660] and Krnjevic and Lisiewicz [563] are seen: (1) decreased excitability, (2) decreased membrane resistance, and (3) increased potassium conductance (g K). Also, as seen here and discussed later, calcium conductance is itself complexly voltage dependent.

ponent is sensitive to the amount of calcium present during tetanization. Younkin found that the quantitated behavior of the facilitation accompanying tetanization versus the frequencies and durations of stimulation was consistent with the residual calcium hypothesis.

Llinas has directly demonstrated in the synaptic terminal of the giant fiber of the squid that calcium interacts with the synaptic membrane in such a way as to promote transmitter release and directly influence the efficacy of PSP production in the postsynaptic cell. Llinas and colleagues [611] voltage clamped the presynaptic terminals of the stellate ganglion of the squid. Calcium current in this preparation is dependent on the presynaptic membrane potential. Postsynaptic potentials resulting from synaptic transmission depend closely on the calcium current entering the presynaptic terminal* (Fig. 5.3). In the voltage clamped squid axon, sodium current was blocked with TTX, and potassium conductance was reduced with 3-aminopyridine (3-AP). A model was advanced for potential-dependent calcium conductance changes in the cell membrane of this preparation. Earlier experimental results implied "that the binding of a single calcium ion suffices for a discharge of 1 quantum of transmitter" [40]. Llinas and colleagues have suggested that fifth-order kinetics are involved in the process.

As the reader has probably recognized, depolarization of the presynaptic terminals can have several distinctly opposing effects on the efficacy of synaptic transmission. (The basic effects of different levels of depolarization were mentioned earlier on p. 187.) As will be discussed in the section on state depiction, the opposing effects may be desirable for controlling both adaptation and neurotransmission. The consequences of depolarization depend on the magnitude and duration of depolarization. Most would agree that the shift in potential resulting from invasion of a spike potential into the synaptic terminal produces an increase in calcium current and an increase in intracellular calcium concentration that rapidly [611] leads to vesicular release of neurotransmitter [408,409,969]. Quantal analysis can be used to study the process [505,604,960,961]. The more calcium, the more transmitter released; the more transmitter released, the greater the size of the postsynaptic potential (PSP).

Small changes in the resting potential of the presynaptic terminal would be expected to alter the size of invading spikes as described earlier and produce changes in the amount of transmitter release according to the magnitude of the potential shift produced by spike invasion. This view is generally accepted [9,250] and fits available evidence for vesicular transmission at the synaptic terminals of mammals and squid. An additional modulatory effect on neurotransmission of residual calcium in the presynaptic terminal [503], described above, is also generally accepted. Note that this will have an opposing effect (facilitation) from that of small, steady depolarization of the terminals (inhibition).

*Cf. footnote p. 189.

Some recent attempts to voltage clamp the synaptic terminals of *Aplysia* neurons by introducing electrodes rather far away from these regions have focused on a relationship between larger magnitude depolarization and facilitation of PSPs much like that in the *Squid* (Fig. 5.3). The question arises whether presynaptic facilitation is mediated by a small hyperpolarization, as above, or by a larger depolarization. (Analogous considerations may be raised for presynaptic inhibition.) Given the degree of depolarization ($\geqslant +20$ mV above resting level) required for calcium activation (see Figs. 5.3, 5.7 and ref. 611), one wonders if depolarization of this magnitude could occur under normal circumstances without exceeding critical firing threshold and producing tetanic discharge and/or sodium inactivation. The latter (as well as the tendency of g Ca to inactivate with prolonged depolarization and accumulation of intracellular calcium) further complicates interpretation of these matters. As will shortly be seen, it is likely that these complications arise, in part, from the existence of a complex control system within the cell designed to permit orderly adaptations while maintaining the overall system state. Since these issues are of fundamental importance to our understanding of learning and memory, they will be pursued, experimentally, over the years to come and resolved as improved techniques afford more direct measurement of neuronal function.

Presynaptic Depolarization, Presynaptic Calcium Current and Size of Postsynaptic Potential

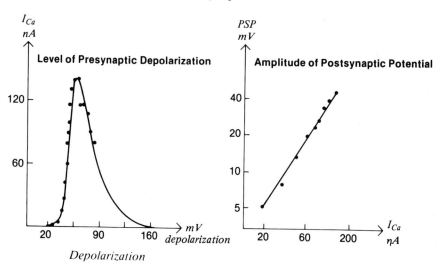

Fig. 5.3. *"Evidence suggesting linear relationship between calcium current and transmitter release. Left: The relationship between depolarization and [calcium] current, I_{Ca}, at the presynaptic terminal of the squid giant axon.* ●, *data points; solid line is the numerical solution for I_{Ca} determined from Llinas and Walton's hypothesis of membrane channel effect assuming fifth-order kinetics. Right: The peak presynaptic current, I_{Ca}, versus the amplitude of the postsynaptic potential, plotted on double log coordinates."* (Llinas [610].)

Nonvesicular Functional Neurotransmitter Pools. Still other mechanisms for controlling neurotransmitter action exist in the presynaptic terminal [457, 1000]. Changes in *synthesis, release-uptake,* and *pooling-storage* of transmitter between vesicles and the cytosol can each potentially influence the efficacy of transmission. Synthesis of neurotransmitter is required to replenish the store of used transmitter chemical. Some synthesis may occur centrally in the cell soma, with the product transported along the neural filaments (a slow process relative to the 0.3-0.5 msec required for synaptic transmission). More synthesis may occur locally in the presynaptic terminal itself. Evidence for this possibility arises from the specific activities of choline acetyltransferase and tyrosine hydroxylase (two enzymes affecting transmitter synthesis) being three- to four-fold higher in synaptosomes (the isolated components of nerve terminals) than in nerve tissue. Appreciable amounts of transmitter may also be recovered by re-uptake from the synaptic cleft after the transmitter is released at the synaptic junction. It is therefore unclear how much of the transmitter present in the terminals is synthesized locally, how much is transported from the soma, and how much is recovered through the re-uptake process.

Storage of the neurotransmitter at the terminal may be accomplished by several different means. Some involve storage in synaptic vesicles (see 5.20); others involve nonvesicular storage. Although some of the nonvesicular storage pools are inaccessible to voltage-dependent events, such as the arrival of an action potential, others are voltage-dependent and contribute directly to the process of neurotransmission [1000]. Changes in the polarization of the synaptic terminals that are known to influence vesicular synaptic transmission may therefore further influence transmission by voltage dependent, nonvesicular storage effects.

Potassium Accumulation. Another means for modifying the efficacy of transmission through the presynaptic terminal involves the *accumulation of potassium* outside the terminal [201,561,832,1040]. With repeated neural activity, potassium flux across the cell membrane may cause local increases in external potassium ion concentration. The accumulation of this ion will influence the polarization across the cell membrane and, by the means described earlier (Fig. 5.2), decrement PSP production.*

Repetitive antidromic stimulation of the giant axon of the squid results in a reduction of presynaptic transmitter release and may reflect an alteration in local potassium concentration [1072]. Increasing the concentration of potassium ions extracellularly reduces the excitatory postsynaptic potential (EPSP) and decreases the amplitude of the presynaptic spike after-hyperpolarization. Weight and Erulkar [1072] postulate, like Decima [201], that accumulation of extracellular potassium ions modulates synaptic transmission and suggest that this is a possible mechanism of plasticity in the nervous system.

---

*$\uparrow$ $[K]_o \rightarrow$ depolarization; see Nernst equation in Table 5.1.

Although there is evidence that sufficient potassium accumulates in the extracellular space to warrant its uptake by glia [367,923] and that an excess of potassium in the extracellular space can influence neural activity [1040], it has not been possible to measure the accumulation of potassium directly at the synaptic terminal itself during modifications of the above types. The failure may be due (1) to technical complications preventing insertion of a potassium-sensitive microelectrode (tip) into the appropriate paraterminal region, (2) to very active uptake of potassium from the extracellular space, or (3) to the rapid diffusion of potassium away from the terminal membrane [561,1060]. Or it may be that one of the other mechanisms is responsible for the modulatory effects attributed to an accumulation of potassium at the presynaptic terminal.

Consequences of Presynaptic Changes. The presynaptic mechanisms of neural adaptation support the neural effects of conditioning-testing, posttetanic potentiation, and heterosynaptic facilitation discussed earlier. Following repetitive stimulation it may be assumed that the efficacy of neurotransmission will be altered by residual calcium in the presynaptic terminals with a single repetition tending to facilitate, and multiple repetitions tending to inhibit. Tetanic repetition may either facilitate or inhibit, depending on the rate of repetition (see Chapter 4). Heterosynaptic stimulation may facilitate transmission by producing hyperpolarization of the synaptic terminals (postsynaptic changes have been excluded as the basis of this phenomenon in mollusks, though not in other species [486,488,1091]). Hyperpolarization of the presynaptic terminals has also been demonstrated after posttetanic potentiation of spinal cord afferents [308,613].

The presynaptic facilitatory and inhibitory mechanisms also play a significant role in modifying transmission in ascending neural pathways by which sensory information gains access centrally from the periphery. These modifications are transient, often lasting only a matter of seconds. Control of the changes appears to be exercised through descending neural pathways that synapse on the presynaptic terminals of the ascending pathways. It is likely that presynaptic adaptive mechanisms exist at all levels of the nervous system and permit regulatory control over most incoming information. The behavioral consequences of facilitatory presynaptic neural changes appear to include sensitization and alerting, those of inhibitory changes including habituation as discussed in Chapter 4.

According to Castellucci and Kandel [158,483], sensitization is an elementary form of nonassociative learning, related to behavioral arousal. Their evidence supports the view that short-term sensitization of the gill withdrawal reflex in the isolated abdominal ganglion of *Aplysia* is due to presynaptic facilitation. This facilitation results in an increase of transmitter release onto the motoneuron. Serotonin enhances synaptic transmission at this junction [118]. Cyclic AMP (adenosine $3'$, $5'$-monophosphate) injected intracellularly or dibutryl cyclic AMP applied extracellularly enhances the synaptic action of sensory neurons. It is suggested that cyclic AMP (cAMP) mediates serotonin effects as well as the presynaptic facilitation associated with sensitization of the gill withdrawal reflex [573].

Cedar and Schwartz [160] report that serotonin and dopamine stimulate the formation of cAMP in cells of *Aplysia*. The concentrations of cAMP are found to be increased in the regions of the presynaptic terminals after stimulation. Elevating magnesium concentration blocks the stimulation of cAMP caused by synaptic activity but does not prevent the elaboration of cAMP to serotonin. (This is possible since there are both Ca-activated and 5-HT-activated adenylate cyclases.)

Intrasynaptic Mechanisms

Apart from changes in the number of transmitter quanta or amount of transmitter per quantum released at the presynaptic terminal, there are other, *intrasynaptic mechanisms* that may influence the efficacy of neurotransmission. The three most prominent of these are (1) alterations in the binding or complexing of neurotransmitter molecules by receptors on the postsynaptic membrane; (2) alterations in the recovery or the breakdown of neurotransmitter once released, for example, by presynaptic membrane events or by differences in the concentration of local cholinesterase at cholinergic synapses; and (3) alterations in diffusion of the neurotransmitter across the synaptic cleft, resulting from differences in the size of the cleft or the viscosity of the extracellular medium within the space itself. Changes in the densities of receptors on the postsynaptic membrane and changes in receptor kinetics may produce effects similar to these and need not be considered separately at this time.

Some evidence exists that the first two mechanisms actually cause plastic changes, but as yet none of these changes has been related to learning.

That repetitive synaptic transmission may be potentiated by inhibition of acetylcholinesterase is suggested by experiments of Hartzell and colleagues [390]. They showed that doubling the amount of acetylcholine (ACh) released at the neuromuscular junction resulted in a synergistic, more-than-doubling increase in the size of the postsynaptic EPSP. This was attributed to an interaction of multiple quanta of ACh at receptor sites on the postsynaptic membrane, as when acetylcholinesterase is inhibited.

Disease processes such as myasthenia gravis as well as some of the muscular dystrophies are attributed to altered reception of transmitter. Myasthenia is thought to arise from an autoimmune disease where antibodies are formed to nicotinic receptors and block the reception of acetylcholine [239]. Myasthenia can be treated by cholinomimetics or anticholinesterases. Clinical research is also being directed toward finding ways to improve transmitter reception by dystrophic muscle.

The third intrasynaptic mechanism, alterations in the size of the cleft itself, or viscosity changes in the cleft medium, remains speculative at present.

Postsynaptic Mechanisms

Three types of plastic changes *might* occur postsynaptically to alter neuronal information transmission: (1) alterations in critical firing threshold, (2) changes in the membrane conductance of the neuron or its electrically coupled surrounding glia, and (3) changes in neuronal core or coupling resistance. The first, a change in the critical firing threshold, could alter the efficacy of synaptic transmission directly by augmenting or reducing the PSP input required for spike discharge. However, there is as yet no convincing evidence to indicate that the critical firing threshold, per se, changes in a way to support cellular plasticity. Changes in membrane properties leading to accommodation or to sodium inactivation may make it appear that changes in critical firing threshold occur,* but careful examination of the electrophysiologic data [535,992] suggests that the alterations in neural excitability instead reflect changes in voltage-dependent conductance across the membrane that influence the amount of current reaching the site of spike initiation. Given the changes in integrative properties of the postsynaptic cell that do occur, it is not surprising that some constancy of firing threshold is maintained. This should enable local plastic changes at selected synapses to act with reference to some stable threshold for the system's operation. Were the threshold to change, that stability (the potential at which the action potential is generated) would be lost and disorderly processing of information could ensue.

There *is* considerable evidence suggesting that changes in neuronal conductance may support cellular plasticity involved with learning, and these are discussed next.

Changes in the Integrative Properties of the Postsynaptic Element. Following hypotheses advanced by Rall in 1970 [805] and Woody and Black-Cleworth in 1973 [1110], interest has focussed on changes in neuronal resistance that might alter the integrative properties of the postsynaptic element so as to support adaptive behavior. In general, all such changes may be said to influence λ, the space constant over which current will spread passively within the cell [cf. 9,451,806]. Changes in λ will alter the weighting of PSPs transmitted between passive dendrites and the locus of spike initiation in the soma. Changes in the resistance of dendritic processes could selectively enhance CS reception if they occurred near synapses responsible for CS-evoked EPSPs. Otherwise, they would simply alter performance of the motor responses served by the projections of the cells.

Two properties of the cell relate directly to λ. These are the membrane resistance, R_m, and the internal core resistance, R_i, λ being proportional to $(R_m/R_i)^{1/2}$. Accumulated evidence suggests that membrane resistance can change in ways that can result in the augmentation or decrement of PSP spread within the neuron [12,651,1110,1124,1129]. Such changes may be involved in mediating neuronal adaptations supporting the acquisition of specific learned motor behavior. With respect to simple conditioned movements, it has been shown in mammals that the *postsynaptic excitability* of

---

*After the sodium gates have been opened, sodium activation may proceed at a different voltage threshold than was required for gating, but the critical firing threshold for gating itself does not appear to be changed.

neurons in the motor cortex and the facial nucleus increases after conditioning in such a way as to facilitate performance of the specific learned motor response [111,651,1110]. This effect is attributable to an increase in neuronal membrane resistance. Increases in input resistance can be produced in vivo in neurons of the motor cortex by pairing extracellular administration of acetylcholine or intracellular administration of cyclic GMP (guanosine 3′, 5′-monophosphate) with depolarizing currents sufficient to repetitively discharge the cell (Fig. 5.4). Such changes persist for as long as the cell can be studied, which is as long as 1 or 2 hr with present intracellular techniques [1116,1117,1124]. Changes in neural excitability supporting conditioning have been demonstrated to persist for weeks and longer [111], and would have to persist for months or years in association with savings of the conditioned reflex to support this form of learning.

How would increases in resistance be produced at the membrane level? A likely means would involve conductance decreases* associated with EPSP

Changes in Resistance in Mammalian Cortical Neurons Induced By Acetylcholine and Cyclic GMP

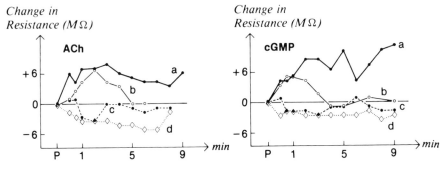

Fig. 5.4. Average changes in input resistance (R_m) in different groups of cortical neurons following extracellular iontophoresis of acetylcholine (ACh), intracellular iontophoresis of cyclic GMP (cGMP), and control iontophoretic procedures performed in awake cats. Left: (a) in neurons responding to ACh plus current-induced discharge with increased R_m, (b) in neurons responding to ACh alone with increased R_m, (c) in neurons given current-induced discharge without iontophoresis of ACh, and (d) in neurons which failed to respond to ACh with an increased R_m. Half of the cells in (c) were given control iontophoresis of saline. Right: (a) in neurons responding to cGMP plus current-induced discharge with increased R_m, (b) in neurons responding to cGMP alone with increased R_m, (c) in neurons given 5′-GMP, and (d) in neurons which failed to respond to cGMP with increased R_m. (Woody et al. [1124].) Potentiated evoked activity to click CS was seen in comparable cortical neurons after conditioning (see Figs. 4.7 and 4.12). These cells support performance of the conditioned blink movement by virtue of their increased excitability (Fig. 4.15) and their projection, polysynaptically, to the target musculature of the CR (Fig. 4.13).

*Conductance is electrically the inverse of resistance.

production, such as have been described by Krnjevic and colleagues in central neurons [330,568], by Weight and coworkers in the superior cervical (sympathetic) ganglion [1077], and by Dudel and Kuffler at the neuromuscular junction [242]. In the sympathetic ganglion, it is unclear if passive changes in ionic conductances across the cell membrane are solely responsible for the slow PSPs seen in this preparation [599,875] or if active ionic pumping mechanisms also contribute [597]. This will be discussed further, below.

Neuronal resistance changes are linked to learning in invertebrates as well as in vertebrates. Woolacott and Hoyle [1129] have reported changes in membrane conductance in locust neurons during conditioning. The resistance may increase or decrease depending on the aspect of behavior that is reinforced. TEA eliminates undershoot of the action potentials in this preparation, which suggests that there is a voltage dependent potassium conductance in these cells. The investigators postulate that "the increase in resistance is mediated by a decrease in potassium conductance and the decrease in resistance by an increase in potassium conductance" [1129]. In *Hermissenda*, a nudibranch mollusk, Alkon and colleagues have elegantly demonstrated changes in membrane conductance that are related to conditioning of a light-cued avoidance reflex in this preparation. Changes in *both* potassium and calcium conductance appear to be involved (see [12] and p. 177). In another mollusk, *Aplysia*, postsynaptic integration is enhanced by an increased resistance associated with a decreased conductance EPSP produced by one of the stimuli that leads to inking behavior. In addition to depolarization, this subthreshold EPSP produces an increase in input resistance that facilitates the ability of other, conductance *increase* EPSPs to summate and spread in such a way as to excite [148-150]. The changes in this preparation last from seconds to minutes; those in *Hermissenda* last for days.

Other Mechanisms

Still other mechanisms exist by which the transmission of messages between cells can be affected. Increased and decreased conductances can result from changes in electrical coupling between cells by means discussed below. The junctional resistance between coupled cells may change during EPSP and IPSP activity since it may be voltage as well as pH and calcium dependent. It may be difficult to prove that these changes occur in the junctional membrane of the neurons and not in the nonjunctional plasma membranes of these cells or in the surrounding glia where there may be additional electrical coupling between the glia and the neurons so ensheathed.

Conduction at Electrical Synapses. Changes in the electrical coupling between cells involve changes in resistance across gap or close junctions and require specialized membrane contacts between cells [60-63,302-304]. These junctions usually pass electrical current bidirectionally and may even permit the transport of certain chemical substances (see Table 5.5). Some junctions favor unidirectional electrical conduction and are thus rectifying junctions [62]. Loewenstein [616-618] describes electrical coupling between epithelial cells at analogous junctions at which the membrane permeability can be increased.

The permeability depends on calcium, increases in "intracellular" calcium concentration leading to uncoupling, and on pH.* The rise in cytoplasmic calcium concentration is accompanied by depolarization, but depolarization is not necessary for this uncoupling to occur.

In *Navanax*, a carnivorous sea slug, Spira and colleagues [943] suggest that an anomalous, reciprocal adaptation is mediated by electrical coupling. Motor neurons which control the pharyngeal muscles show typical electrical coupling wherein depolarization of one cell leads to depolarization of the other. However, with involvement of another, inhibitory synapse, hyperpolarization of the first cell does not result in hyperpolarization of its electrically coupled neighbor. Instead, depolarization is seen. It is hypothesized that this phenomenon occurs via a third, coupled neuron. That is, the hyperpolarization in cell A depolarizes cell B by removing inhibition coming from a third cell C, or group of cells. The circuitry for this is illustrated in their report [943].

Adaptive neural mechanisms related to coupling effects have also been described by Waziri [1069] in *Aplysia*. In the L 10 cholinergic interneuron of the abdominal ganglion, both chemical and electrical synaptic transmission can be demonstrated. The amplitude of the postsynaptic potential produced across the electrically coupled synapse is voltage sensitive, increasing with depolarization and decreasing with hyperpolarization. These changes are presumably a result of voltage-dependent changes in an electrically coupled presynaptic element, and are akin to the effects of presynaptic inhibition and facilitation. The possibility exists in some preparations that recurrent chemical synaptic influences from the postsynaptic element can also influence these effects.

In sum, conductances within coupled cells can be influenced either by altering the permeability of the coupling membrane or by altering the conductance of the plasma membrane separating either cell from the extracellular space.

Alterations in Active Spike Invasion. Another mechanism of neural plasticity depends on the possibility that active invasion of axonal and dendritic processes by spike impulses may be subject to adaptive control. In the dendrites or cell processes, work by Spencer and Kandel [929], Llinas et al. [611], and by Dudek and Blankenship [241] has been interpreted as consistent with this possibility. Prepotential or partial spike activity is reported not only in hippocampal neurons but also in bag cells of *Aplysia*. The latter show differences in excitability [241] that have been attributed to potentiation as a function of movement of the site of spike blockade, but electrical coupling between adjacent membranes of two different neurons could also explain these findings. Coupling of this type is thought to occur in cerebellar Purkinje cells [703,823] and to account for what has sometimes been attributed to dendritic calcium spikes. In axons, work by several different investigators [156,750,752,753, 944] suggests that shifts in spike transmission may occur as a consequence of

---

*also see Spray *et al* (*Science* 211: 712-714, 1981) for effects of pH on neuronal junctions.

conduction block, resulting in a failure of spike propagation within certain axonal branches. Other work by Kocsis and colleagues [532] has provided a convincing demonstration of *super*normality in central axons wherein both excitability and conduction velocity may be increased. Conduction block appears to be sensitive to spike frequency, being found after repetitive stimulation. Whether conduction block at points of low safety factor is a useful mechanism of information transfer in mammalian systems in which high safety factor is normal remains to be seen, but evidence that this may be so in the lobster seems convincing [752].

Synaptic Gating. A third type of synaptic contact changes in the course of several behavioral processes so as to alter cellular excitability, but evidence for the cellular mechanism underlying this type of adaptation is scant and largely indirect. Thresholds for neural excitation by weak, nanoampere extracellular currents are altered by associative procedures such as conditioning and sensory preconditioning as well as by repetitive stimulus presentation [107,109,120, 1122]. These effects appear to be supported by synaptic mechanisms apart from electrical coupling or previously described forms of chemical neurotransmission. This is inferred from (1) the absence of corresponding postsynaptic changes in neural excitability when the same cells are tested with intracellularly injected current [1122] and (2) further physiologic studies which indicate that the extracellularly applied nanoampere current fails to excite by postsynaptic depolarization or conventional presynaptic chemical release [1119]. Synaptic contacts at which electrical spike activity facilitates postsynaptic sodium gating by charge mediated effects might help explain such observations.

Another possible explanation might be found in studies of the Mauthner cell in goldfish. There, specialized endings surround the axon hillock and initial segment. Activation of these endings leads to a positive, extracellular potential which is associated with hyperpolarization of the axons of the Mauthner neurons. The mechanism for this action is unclear, but it seems to involve electrical as well as chemical neurotransmission [541,542].

Ionic Conductance Mechanisms Mediating Neuronal Changes

Several conductance changes in the plasma membrane can be identified that could potentially support many of the simple, repetitive and associatively induced neural adaptations described earlier. Most would agree that these changes can best be described in the context of the Nernst-Goldman equations (for tenable opposing views, see Tasaki [993,994]). Changes in macromolecules within the plasma membrane, discussed further below and in Chapter 7, control these conductance changes. The mechanisms primarily involve changes in the permeability of the membrane that affect the conductance of sodium, potassium, chloride, and calcium ions. Metabolic pumps are also involved. Apart from their role in the resistive or integrative properties of the passive membrane, changes in conductance will directly alter E, the resting transmembrane potential. There will be hyperpolarization or depolarization of the cell with respect to the critical firing threshold required for spike initiation. Extreme depolarization will lead to entrained discharges with spikes arising within the relative refractory or partial sodium inactivation period of others.

It will be useful to classify conductance changes according to their time course and persistence: those that might mediate fast, brief informational events and those that might serve as slower and longer trace mediators or as engrams. One very preliminary classification is offered in Table 5.1.

Fast, Brief "Event" Mediators

This class of conductance changes can itself be subdivided into two groups: first, the mediators of regenerative potential changes that support the propagation of action potentials, and second, those conductance changes that support the production of fast EPSP and IPSPs. All these changes appear to be voltage dependent.*

Mediators of Regenerative Potentials
There are three different types of membranes supporting regenerative action potentials:

1. Sodium-dependent membranes
2. Calcium-dependent membranes
3. Sodium- and-calcium-dependent membranes

Thus, the ionic mechanisms in the cell membrane responsible for the initiation of action potentials are the sodium and calcium channels [377].

In the squid [43], the primary sodium channel, which normally produces action potentials, is also permeable to calcium[†], and is sensitive to TTX. So far, no action potentials that depend on the calcium permeability of the calcium channel and are *not* blocked by TTX have been found in this preparation. This suggests that in some preparations, the TTX-insensitive calcium channel may be used primarily for passive rather than for regenerative conductance changes. Nonetheless, according to Baker [40], experiments with aequorin[‡] suggest that there can be entry of calcium during the action potential and that this entry can occur in two phases in the squid: "1) an early phase blocked by TTX, reflecting calcium entering through the sodium channel and 2) a late phase which is insensitive to TTX and TEA but inhibited by calcium-blocking agents and by maintained depolarization." Thus, there is a fast calcium conductance, g Ca_f, which is TTX-insensitive and can potentially be involved in some regenerative processes.

---

*The flux of ions across the cell membrane is dependent upon concentration and potential according to the Nernst-Goldman formulation [334]. But not all permeability changes need be voltage sensitive.
†whether *any* sodium channels fail to pass some calcium and are really calcium independent is not completely resolved at this time, but it will be assumed that some are for the present discussion.
‡As later discussed, the use of aequorin is not without limitations.

TTX-insensitive action potentials in which the inward current may be carried by calcium ions have, in fact, been described in a number of different tissues [377]. Baker [40] believes that sodium as well as calcium ions can pass through the calcium channel supporting g Ca$_f$. He points out that this action potential (1) is not blocked by TTX or TEA in the absence of external sodium, (2) is blocked by external cobalt and manganese ions, and that (3) the rising phase of the action potential is rather slow. Lanthanum also blocks calcium-dependent action potentials at low concentrations.

Fast, Passive Mediators

In addition to the rapid, depolarizing conductance changes of sodium and calcium identified above that support regenerative spike activity* , other passive (nonregenerative) conductance changes can be identified that have a time course fast enough to support rapidly rising PSPs. They involve potassium and chloride ions. The increases in potassium conductance support outward currents (given resting potential, $V_m > E_k$, the equilibrium potential of potassium). Some changes in potassium conductance are TEA (and 4-AP) sensitive, i.e., g K$_{TEA}$. They mediate the repolarization of the membrane after spike depolarization. Some of these channels[†] are thought to be responsible for the delayed rectification seen at this time. The TEA-sensitive potassium channels may also mediate slower "trace" events as described below.

The chloride conductances, g Cl, produce fast outward currents when increased (given $V_m > E_{Cl}$) and support inhibitory postsynaptic potential changes in the hyperpolarizing direction [312,424,983]. They appear to be activated by depolarization, at least in some species [368].

Slow, Passive "Trace" Mediators

The slowly changing or maintained, passive permeabilities of cell membranes last longer than the few milliseconds required for spike generation and depend largely on potassium and calcium conductances, either separately or in combination. Some changes in conductance across neuronal plasma membranes may be maintained long enough to support long-term memory storage. However, the distinctions made presently between "fast" and "slow" conductances are likely to require some future revision. The actual times needed for activation and the periods over which activation is maintained are just now being defined using voltage clamp techniques.

Calcium

Two types of slowly changing calcium conductances can be identified (Table 5.1). One reflects a slow calcium channel, g Ca$_{sV}$; it is voltage dependent. The other reflects a pump[‡], Ca/Na^P, that metabolically exchanges calcium for

---

*and in some membranes also support rapid, nonregenerative conductance changes resulting in an inward flow of current, typically with a depolarizing effect.
†These are sometimes referred to as "A" currents and the other TEA-sensitive conductances as "K" currents [1019], but, herein, both will be called g K$_{TEA}$. The "A" currents are faster and more sensitive to 4-AP than to TEA [182].
‡Strictly speaking it may be improper to term this a conductance, but see [92] and below.

Table 5.1. **Ionic and Metabolic Conductances**

	1. **Sodium conductance** (inward current when increased)[a]
g Na$_{TTX}$	a. TTX sensitive, voltage dependent, ?Ca^{2+} dependent [377]
Ca/Na^P (pump)	b. TTX insensitive, Ca^{2+} dependent [40,43], ouabain insensitive, K$^+$ dependent, voltage insensitive [813]
Na/K^P (pump)	c. TTX insensitive, Ca^{2+} insensitive [40,43], ouabain sensitive

	2. **Calcium conductance** (inward current when increased)[a]
g Ca$_f$	a. Fast Ca^{2+} (through Ca^{2+} channels—voltage dependent; blocked by Mg^{2+}, Co^{2+}, Mn^{2+}; not blocked by TTX; probably mediates transmitter release at presynaptic terminal [611]; may support calcium spiking [377].
g Ca$_{(Na)}$	b. Fast Ca^{2+} (through Na$^+$ channels)—blocked by TTX, Mg^{2+}, Co^{2+}, Mn^{2+} [40,377]; may support calcium spiking.
Ca/Na^P (pump)	c. Slow Ca^{2+}- see description above
g Ca$_{sV}$	d. Slow Ca^{2+}- voltage dependent [43,262,377,410,411]; TEA* and TTX insensitive

　　　　1) Voltage dependency (in *Helix*)
　　　　　　a) Hyperpolarization before test pulse ↓ g Ca$^†_{sV}$
　　　　　　b) Depolarization before test pulse ↑ g Ca$_{sV}$
　　　　2) Frequency dependency (in *Helix*)
　　　　　　　　Depolarization with:
　　　　　　a) Short interstimulus interval (20 msec) - inactivates
　　　　　　b) Medium interstimulus interval (400 msec) - facilitates
　　　　　　c) Long interstimulus interval (700 msec) - defacilitates

	3. **Potassium conductance** (outward current when increased)[a] [cf. 182,410,411,658-660,1019]
g K$_{TEA}$[‡]	a. Fast K$^+$- calcium insensitive (supports delayed rectification/spike repolarization), TEA sensitive

　　　　1) Voltage dependency (*Helix*)
　　　　　　a) Depolarization ↑ I$_K$, then inactivates with further, sustained depolarization
　　　　　　b) Repeated depolarization with short pulses produces less inactivation than does sustained depolarization¶
　　　　　　c) Repolarization removes inactivation
　　　　　　d) Inactivation is not due to accumulation of K$^+$ extracellularly—(K$^+$ efflux is decreased)

[a] at normal resting potential
*TEA slows *onset* of g Ca$_{sV}$ but does not block it.
[†]Eckert and colleagues find that depolarization before a test pulse *defacilitates* g Ca$_{sV}$ (see text and frequency dependency immediately below).
[‡]The fast 4-AP sensitive component of this conductance is particularly important in *Hermissenda* (see p. 177).
¶"When stimulation with ten, 100 msec pulses is used, the depression . . . is less than that produced by 1000 msec continuous depolarization and the depression decreases as a function of increasing interstimulus interval" [410].

2) Frequency dependency (*Helix*)
   a) I_K smaller in test pulses preceded by depolarization
   b) I_K larger in test pulses preceded by hyperpolarization

b. Slow K^+- calcium dependent (activation depends on $\uparrow g\,Ca_{sV}$; inactivation depends on $\uparrow [Ca]_i$), TEA resistant, voltage dependent (g Ca_{sV} is voltage dependent)
   1) Calcium dependency (primary)–(*Helix*)
      a) $\uparrow$ g Ca_{sV} activates g K_{Ca} by increasing $[Ca^{2+}]$ at inner surface of membrane.
      b) $\uparrow\uparrow [Ca]_i$ inactivates g K_{Ca} (i.e. $\downarrow\downarrow$ g K_{Ca}, $\uparrow$ Rm)
      c) $\uparrow\uparrow$ g Ca_{sV} leads to $\uparrow\uparrow [Ca]_i$
      d) Calcium plus repetitive depolarization depresses the activated $I_{K(Ca)}$ for seconds.
   2) Voltage dependency (secondary)–(*Helix*)
      a) Depolarization tends to $\uparrow$ g K_{Ca} by $\uparrow$ g Ca_{sV}
      b) Sustained moderate depolarization does not inactivate g K_{Ca} because g Ca_{sV} is not completely inactivated, nor is $[Ca]_i \uparrow\uparrow$.
      c) Large depolarization inactivates g K_{Ca} whether or not it is sustained, because it $\downarrow\downarrow$ g Ca_{sV} (if the depolarization is large, but fails to inactivate g Ca_{sV} because it doesn't reach the negative resistance region*, $[Ca]_i$ will $\uparrow\uparrow$, and inactivation will then occur for this reason).
   3) Frequency dependency–(*Helix*)
      Small - moderate depolarization:
      a) Does not inactivate with sustained, steady depolarization
      b) Repetitive depolarization at intermediate (400 msec) intervals facilitates g Ca_{sV} which $\uparrow$ I_{in} and thereby $\downarrow$ net I_{out}. As g $Ca_{sV} \uparrow$, $[Ca]_i \uparrow$. Ultimately, $\uparrow\uparrow [Ca]_i$ leads to $\downarrow$ g K_{Ca}.
      c) $I_{out} \uparrow$ with short interval repolarizing pulse because $I_{in} \downarrow$ due to $\downarrow$ g Ca_{sV}.

4. Chloride conductance
(Little is presently known, in part, because chloride ions equilibrate so rapidly across the cell membrane.)

(continued)

---

*"A considerable part of the K^+ current that appears during a moderate depolarization can be instantaneously switched off by stepping the membrane potential into the negative resistance region. Increasing intracellular free calcium enhances this phenomenon" [633].

Goldman Equation

$$E = \frac{RT}{FZ} \log_e \frac{P_K [K]_o + P_{Na} [Na]_o + P_{Cl} [Cl]_i}{P_K [K]_i + P_{Na} [Na]_i + P_{Cl}[Cl]_o}$$

where E = resting transmembrane potential, R = gas constant, T = absolute temperature, F = Faraday, Z = charge and is 1 for monovalent ions and 2 for divalent ions such as Ca^{2+}, when the latter is included, and P = permeability (E_{Na} = +55 mV, E_K = −75 mV, E_{Cl} = −65 mV).

Schematized Nerve Terminal

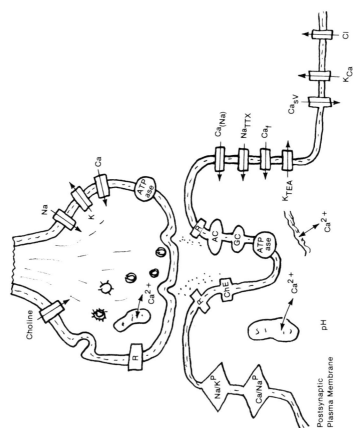

Schematic representation of a nerve terminal showing conductances, transport, and other processes in the pre- and postsynaptic membranes (modified from Standaert and Dretchen [954]). Adenylate cyclase (AC), guanylate cyclase (GC), Ca^{2+} transport in mitochondria and endoplasmic reticulum, and pH effects are considered in the text. The added conductances and pumps could appear presynaptically as well as postsynaptically. R = receptor, Ch E = cholinesterase.

Legend to Table 5.1. (Summary of Ionic and Metabolic Conductances)

FAST CONDUCTANCES

	CURRENT*	BLOCKED BY†
	Supporting regenerative and nonregenerative changes	
g Na$_{TTX}$	I_{Na} - inward (Vm $< E_{Na}$)	TTX
g Ca(Na)	$I_{Ca(Na)}$ - inward (Vm $< E_{Ca}$)	TTX
g Ca$_f$	$I_{Ca(f)}$ - inward (Vm $< E_{Ca}$)	Cobalt, Lanthanum
	Supporting nonregenerative changes - e.g., PSPs, generator potentials	
‡ g K$_{TEA}$	$I_{K(TEA)}$ - outward (Vm $> E_K$)	TEA, 4-AP
g Cl	I_{Cl} - outward (Vm $> E_{Cl}$)	bicuculline

SLOW CONDUCTANCES

	CURRENT*	BLOCKED BY†
	Supporting nonregenerative changes	
g Ca$_s$V	$I_{Ca(sV)}$ - inward (Vm $< E_{Ca}$)	Cobalt
g K$_{Ca}$	$I_{K(Ca)}$ - outward (Vm $> E_K$)	Cobalt
(‡ g K$_{TEA}$)	(see above)	(see above)
PUMPS		
Ca/Na^P	Pumps: 1 Ca^{2+} out for 3 Na$^+$ in	- - -
Na/K^P	Pumps: 3 Na$^+$ out for 2 K$^+$ in	Ouabain, DNP, Cyanide, Azide

*Currents sum algebraically; Vm = resting transmembrane potential; E = equilibrium potential

†TTX = tetrodotoxin, TEA = tetraethyl ammonium, 4-AP = 4-amino pyridine, DNP = dinitrophenol

‡turn on rapidly enough to support fast changes; last long enough to support slow changes; the fast current contains a very fast 4-AP sensitive component

¶may either exchange (at low energy cost) or transport metabolically (at high energy cost) against concentration gradient sodium. It may operate independently of voltage [813]. The slow, voltage-dependent calcium channel, g Ca_{sV}, has been described by Hagiwara, Baker, Eckert, Lux, and Heyer [43,262,377,410,411]. It is blocked by cobalt, magnesium, manganese, iproveritril, and D-600. It is also inactivated by main-tained depolarization. Baker suggests that calcium entering in the course of a depolarization leads to the depolarization produced inactivation. So do Eckert and colleagues. The exact relation between this channel and those supporting g Ca_f and g Ca_{Na} is still unclear.

Potassium

At least three mechanisms* can mediate long-lasting changes in potassium con-ductance (see Table 5.1). One is by the calcium-independent, TEA sensitive channel, g K_{TEA}, mentioned above. The second is by a calcium-dependent, TEA resistant channel, g K_{Ca}.[†] The third is by a pump that metabolically exchanges K for Na, Na/K^P. All these conductance changes involving K^+ (and Ca^{2+}) appear to be voltage-dependent, with the exception of Ca/Na^P which is said to be voltage-insensitive [812], and represents a metabolic contribution to ionic concentration rather than a direct conductance effect.** All poten-tially may serve as direct mediators of long-lasting "trace" events within the neuron.

The Metablic Ion-Exchanging Pumps

In contrast to the passive ionic conductance changes which vary according to E (the transmembrane potential), g (the permeability or conductance of the membrane to a particular ion), and $[X]_i/[X]_o$ (the concentrations of the ion across the membrane) (see Table 5.1), there are conductance components that arise from active pumping of ions across the membrane. The result of this pumping is to change $[X]_i/[X]_o$ and, thereby, E. These active pump transport processes must be incorporated with classical Nernst equilibrium potentials, ion currents, and ionic resistances to form a complete description of the basis of the transmembrane potential. Boulpaep and Sakin describe equivalent circuits for the cell membrane in the context of this amendment to classical electrochemical formulations [92], and the reader is referred to those descriptions for further information on this topic.

For active pumping to exist, there must be some energy source apart from concentration or potential. This source of energy is metabolic. Generally, for efficient operation, the metabolic energy transfer supports an exchange of ions across the membrane. Hence, of the two best known metabolic pumps, one exchanges sodium for potassium, and the other exchanges sodium for calcium [41,42,421]. Either could conceivably mediate slow traces or fast, brief events. Other metabolic pumps are also recognized. For example, Helman has described a Na/K pump that extrudes potassium when the intra-cellular sodium concentration falls below certain levels [401].

---

*more, actually, if one counts "A" currents, leakage currents, etc.
[†]sometimes called the "C" current.
[‡]Recent experiments by Hotson and colleagues [428] suggest that g Ca/Na may help mediate anomalous rectification in hippocampal neurons either as a direct conductance or as a voltage sensitive Ca/Na^P operating in the hyperpolarizing region beyond –50 mV.

Na/K Pump. The Na/K exchange pump (Na/K^P) transports 3 sodium ions outward, across the membrane for every 2 potassium ions transported inward. The result is an increase in $[K]_i$ and a decrease in $[Na]_i$. Since $g K > g Na$, this tends to support outward current flow via I_K. Hence, with respect to the typical inward current associated with g Na (Table 5.1), this pump produces an inverse current effect.

The Na/K pump involves activation of Na/K ATPase, an enzyme that catalyzes the breakdown of ATP (adenosine triphosphate). Ouabain inhibits the ATPase enzyme activity. ATP is the substrate that provides the metabolic energy for the pump transfer operation, and the pump operation is retarded by blockers of ATP formation such as dinitrophenol (DNP), cyanide and other azides.

Ca/Na Pump. The Ca/Na pump (Ca/Na^P) transports 1 calcium ion outward for every 3 sodium ions transported inward. However, since $[Ca^{2+}]_i$ is exceedingly small (10^{-6} *M*), and since the conductance of sodium is small at rest compared with that of potassium, this pump contributes little to E, the *resting* transmembrane potential. Instead, it seems to serve as a means for regulating the intracellular concentration of calcium, $[Ca^{2+}]_i$. At present, little is known about the metabolic energy source for the operation of this pump in neurons. The reader is again referred to the summary of the presently recognized membrane conductances and metabolic pumps in Table 5.1. The actual numbers and distributions of pumps and channels along different portions of the nerve membranes remain to be determined.

Critical Variables Controlling Changes in Membrane Conductance

The main variables controlling *changes* in cell membrane conductance are:

1. The level of polarization within the cell (V) and the rate, frequency, and duration of its change
2. The concentration of calcium within the cell, $[Ca^{2+}]_i$
3. The levels of cyclic nucleotides: cAMP and cGMP
4. pH

Level of Polarization and Its Rate of Change

The level of polarization and its rate of change have been shown to influence Na^+, Ca^{2+}, and K^+ conductance across the cell membrane.

Sodium Conductance

A regenerative change in sodium conductance is activated by depolarization beyond the critical firing threshold. With further depolarization, sodium inactivation occurs, i.e., the sodium conductance is turned off or reduced. In some cells, when the rate of depolarization is slow, depolarization beyond critical firing threshold appears to be required for spike activation.* This phenomenon is called accommodation. It may be moderate ("ceiling") or extreme ("minimal gradient") and is found in cortical as well as spinal motor neurons [535,536]. Extreme accommodation may reflect shunting of current across the cell membrane due to gross physical disruption.

Calcium Conductance

The slow, voltage-dependent calcium conductance, g Ca_{sV}, has been shown in Helix to depend on both the magnitude, polarity, and frequency of change in the transmembrane potential [410] (Figs. 5.5, 5.6).

Application of intracellular hyperpolarizing current before a test pulse decreases the amount of the induced calcium conductance; application of depolarization before the test pulse does just the opposite. Eckert et al., (Fed. Proc. 1981, in press) suggest that some measurements of these effects may be obscured by a facilitation of aequorin signals rather than an increase in g Ca. They find that with depolarization of ≤ 20 mV, g Ca is reduced. However, they also point out that the inactivation becomes weaker at stronger test pulse depolarizations. Calcium entry is involved in mediating the inactivation. Differences in calcium entry may contribute to the differences in inactivation of g Ca produced by strong versus weak depolarization.

The frequency-dependent aspect of the passive calcium conductance in Helix is revealed with repetitive depolarizing stimuli [410]. With short interstimulus intervals of 20 msec, there is inactivation of the calcium conductance; a medium interstimulus interval (400 msec) facilitates it, and a long interstimulus interval (700 msec) defacilitates the conductance (cf. Table 5.1).

Potassium Conductance

Comparable dependencies also exist for potassium conductances. Again in Helix, the slow potassium conductance which is calcium independent and TEA sensitive, g K_{TEA}, is sensitive to the polarization (Fig. 5.7 trace A minus trace B plus consideration of Fig. 5.5B) and frequency (Figs. 5.13, 5.14) of applied potentials. Application of intracellular depolarizing current increases potassium conductance and, if sustained, leads to inactivation. Repolarization then removes this inactivation. The time dependency of these effects is complex since potassium conductance is actually smaller when test pulses are preceded by depolarization and larger when test pulses are preceded by hyperpolarization.

The slow potassium channel, g K_{Ca}, which is calcium dependent and TEA and 3,4-amino pyridine resistant is also voltage-dependent (Figs. 5.7 and 5.14). However, part of this voltage dependency is thought to be similar to that influencing calcium entry and to be manifest secondarily to the calcium-

---

*As alluded to earlier, it is not demonstrated that the critical firing threshold is exceeded (as opposed to met) at the actual point of spike initiation or that the threshold for sodium gating has changed, but the potential recorded within the cell is beyond the normal threshold value and/or more current than usual is required to produce discharge.

K^+ and Ca^2 Membrane Currents in *Helix* Neurons

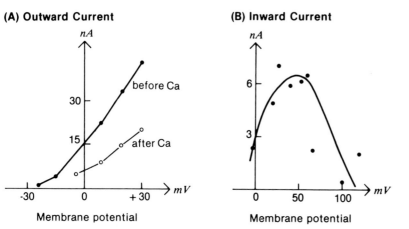

(A) Outward Current

nA

before Ca

after Ca

Membrane potential

(B) Inward Current

nA

Membrane potential

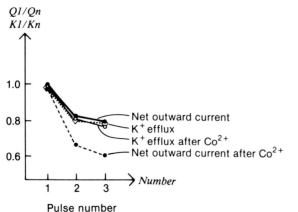

(C) Outward Current and Potassium Efflux

$Q1/Qn$
$K1/Kn$

Net outward current
K^+ efflux
K^+ efflux after Co^{2+}
Net outward current after Co^{2+}

Number

Pulse number

Fig. 5.5. (A) Voltage dependence and calcium dependence of the total net outward current (measured after 100 msec of depolarization) before (●) and after (○) intracellular injection of Ca by electrophoresis under voltage clamp. The outward current after Ca injection is about 50% of control values at all potentials. The total net outward current is decreased despite an increase in the instantaneous conductance [411]. (B) Voltage dependence of the inward current (Ca not injected). (C) Decreased outward current and K^+ efflux with repetitive stimulation before and after cobalt blocking of g Ca_{sV} and g K_{Ca}. Normalized values for the net outward current (Q_1/Q_n, circles) and K efflux (K_1/K_n, squares) for the first, second, and third pulses in the series before and after cobalt application (Heyer and Lux [410].)

Ca Current Depends on Frequency of Stimulation

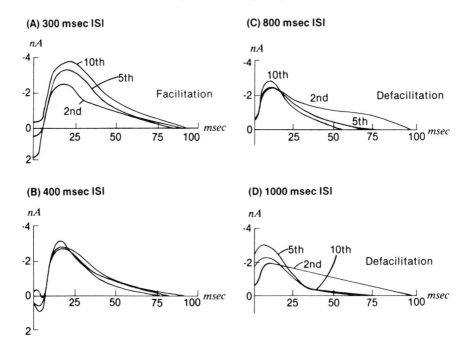

Fig. 5.6. *Frequency dependence of Ca current: facilitation and defacilitation shown during series of repetitive stimulations at different ISIs (A-D) for a single* Helix *neuron. Current deficits calculated by subtracting current trajectories of 1st pulse from normalized trajectories of 2nd, 5th, and 10th pulses. Results as shown—all pulses 100 msec. Note facilitation at 300 msec ISI and defacilitation at 800 and 1000 msec ISIs (Heyer and Lux [410].) A summary of the net charge transfer deficit as a function of the ISI was shown earlier in Fig. 2.3.*

dependency of this potassium channel. The accumulation of Ca^{2+} at the inner surface of the membrane or, perhaps, the increase in the concentration of calcium inside the cell reduces $g\ K_{Ca}$.* Like $g\ Ca_{sV}$ this slow, calcium dependent, potassium channel also does not completely inactivate with sustained depolarization of moderate degree but its conductance is depressed. The total outward current is decreased with repetitive depolarization at intermediate (400 msec) intervals and increased with short-interval repolarizing pulses. Since calcium is involved interdependently (via Ca^{2+} entry), the changes in outward current are a complex function of $g\ K$, $[Ca]_i$, and the increased inward current of $g\ Ca$. Finally, according to Lux [633], "a considerable part of the potassium current that appears during a moderate depolarization can be instantaneously switched off by stepping the membrane

---

*But see, again, Eckert and Tillotson [266] as well as Lux and Heyer [634], Eckert and Lux [263], and Meech and Standen [659].

Voltage Dependency of gCa_{sV}, gK_{TEA}, and gK_{Ca} in *Helix*

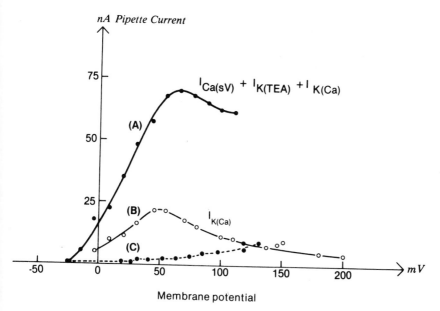

Fig. 5.7. Trace (A) shows the magnitude of $I_{Ca(sV)} + I_{K(TEA)} + I_{K(Ca)}$ as a function of membrane potential in a Helix neuron. Trace (B) shows the magnitude of $I_{K(Ca)}$ as a function of membrane potential. $I_{K(Ca)}$ was calculated as the difference between the net outward currents at 100 msec before and after substitution with Co^{2+} in the Ringer for a typical fast burster (different neuron from A and C). $I_{K(TEA)}$ represents the difference between trace A and B, less $g Ca_{(sV)}$. Trace (C) shows the outward currents (measured at 100 msec) of a fast burster neuron injected with TEA and bathed in Co^{2+}-Ringer as functions of membrane potential (with pulses from a -50 mV holding potential). Simultaneous intracellular TEA and extracellular Co^{2+} virtually abolish the voltage and time-dependent net outward current. (Heyer and Lux [411].)

potential into the negative resistance region (i.e., with extreme depolarization beyond the supposed Ca^{2+} equilibrium potential). Increasing intracellular free calcium enhances this phenomenon" [also see 634]. Repetitive depolarization in the presence of calcium can depress the activated potassium conductance for seconds [263,411]. The reduction in $I_{K(Ca)}$ is proportional to the reduction in Ca^{2+} entry and accumulation during that period.

Some of the voltage-dependent properties of potassium conductances across cell membranes that were mentioned earlier have been described in terms of anomalous and delayed rectification. In heart muscle, there is a potassium conductance that falls immediately on depolarization (anomalous rectification). As a result, the outward movement of K^+ is restricted. The reason for the term "anomalous rectification" is that the Goldman constant field equation (see Table 5.1) would predict rectification in the opposite direction from that seen as a function of voltage dependency. Hotson and colleagues' experiments suggest that anomalous rectification is also supported by changes in $g\,Ca_{(Na)}$ [428], but the voltage dependence of this conductance and its channels need further clarification. The conductance of the outwardly conducting potassium channel, $g\,K_{TEA}$, has been conclusively shown to be voltage dependent, rising slowly with depolarization (delayed rectification). Delayed rectification reflects the expected conductance changes associated with a depolarization-dependent increase in the permeability of the membrane to potassium ions.

Concentration of Calcium within the Cell

Calcium ions affect (1) the initiation of the action potential and (2) its conduction [295], as well as (3) neurotransmitter release [203,502,503], (4) the reaction of the neurotransmitter with the postsynaptic membrane [708,982], and (5) the potassium permeability of the membrane including particularly the resting passive membrane conductance.

The concentration of free calcium within the cell, $[Ca^{2+}]_i$, depends on the rate of inflow and outflow of Ca^{2+} across the cell plasma membrane and on the buffering or binding of intracellular calcium. Apart from the specific calcium conductances, $g\,Ca_{(Na)}$, $g\,Ca_f$ and $g\,Ca_{sV}$ described earlier, the following means exist for regulating $[Ca]_i$ within neurons:

1. Calcium buffering by cytoplasmic protein [cf. 11,162,836].
2. Mitochondrial* uptake of calcium [cf. 15,585,676].
3. Nonmitochondrial, ATP dependent sequestration of calcium [508].
4. Transmembrane Ca^{2+}-Na^+ exchange via the metabolic pump described earlier [86]. (See [85,87] for further information.)

According to Baker [40], the bulk of calcium in the squid axoplasm is neither diffusable nor ionized. Much of this calcium is sequestered by an energy dependent process in intracellular organelles, probably mitochondria. Changes in the redox state of the mitochondria may regulate the release of calcium from this organelle [585]. The diffusible but un-ionized calcium is thought to be associated with ATP, citrate, and glutamate, all of which are present in axoplasm. These buffers seem to have a large capacity and to equilibrate very rapidly with ionized calcium entering the cell. However, it is not clear whether a similar pattern exists in mammalian nerve. Mitochondrial uptake in nerve is likely to be small. DiPolo et al. [221] found a $[Ca^{2+}]_i$ in squid axon of 10^{-8} M. The $[Ca^{2+}]_i$ of mammalian neurons is generally assumed to be 10^{-6} M; the $[Ca^{2+}]$ outside is 10^{-3} M. Estimates of a $[Ca^{2+}]$ of 10^{-3} M in mitochondria of nonneural tissue are somewhat higher than measurements in squid axon of $10^{-4} - 10^{-6}$ M [40,99,814]. Thus, mitochondrial calcium concentration may differ between neural and nonneural tissue.

*and endoplasmic reticulum [402,403].

Increases in intracellular ionized calcium can be produced by (1) a rise in external calcium, (2) a reduction in external sodium, (3) a rise in internal sodium, and (4) anything reducing the effectiveness of the intracellular buffers (cf. Figs. 5.8, 5.9, 5.12). The effects of sodium are thought to be manifest via the dependence of the Ca/Na pump on the gradient of sodium concentration across the cell membrane. The additional, direct contribution of g Ca has already been treated. Decreases in intracellular calcium could be produced by these same mechanisms acting in an opposite direction. Cyclic nucleotides will influence $[Ca^{2+}]_i$ by means of intracellular buffers and possibly by changes in g Ca as described below.

Levels of Cyclic Nucleotides

Mechanisms of Action

Theories advanced by Robison et al. [828], Goldberg and Singer [331], and Greengard [355], suggest that adrenergic neurotransmission causes the activation of adenylate cyclase when the transmitter combines with the receptor (Fig. 5.8). Adenylate cyclase then acts within the plasma membrane of the postsynaptic cell to increase the formation of cyclic AMP from ATP. Cyclic AMP activates a protein kinase which leads to a conductance change in the membrane through a series of calcium dependent phosphorylations or dephosphorylations. The kinase itself is independent of calcium. Some of these effects may change $[Ca^{2+}]_i$, but there is some evidence against this occurring directly [865]. In muscarinic cholinergic systems, it has been proposed that an analogous transmitter-receptor coupling leads to the activation of a guanylate cyclase with subsequent elaboration of cGMP and, again, a kinase-dependent, phosphorylation-induced conductance change [332,357]. These effects are also summarized in Fig. 5.9 and their dependence on calcium is indicated. Excerpts from a more detailed analysis (Bartfai [52]) are given in Fig. 5.9 B and below.

Cyclic nucleotides are among the better understood intracellular second messengers of neurotransmission. Synthesis of cAMP is carried out by a single membrane-bound enzyme, adenylate cyclase. Activation of Ca^{2+}-sensitive adenylate cyclase requires the presence of a protein component, the calcium-dependent regulator (CDR or calmodulin) [114,115,162]. This protein is identical to the Ca^{2+} binding protein which is required for activation of the $3',5'$-cyclic nucleotide phosphodiesterase. Increased cytosolic Ca^{2+} will (1) inhibit some adenylate cyclases, (2) activate cGMP synthesis, (3) after combination with CDR activate additional adenylate cyclases, (4) in Ca^{2+}-CDR complex form activate a membrane bound protein kinase, and (5) in Ca^{2+}-CDR, complex form activate some $3',5'$-cyclic nucleotide phosphodiesterases. The increase in cAMP and cGMP levels is potentiated by phosphodiesterase inhibitors. H_2-histamine receptors have been shown to mediate increases in cAMP levels in the brain. H_1-histamine receptors have been shown to mediate increases in cGMP levels in blocks of sympathetic ganglia and in N1E 115 neuroblastoma cells. Not all cyclic nucleotide

Theories of Adrenergic and Muscarinic Cholinergic Neurotransmission with Postsynaptic Formation of Cyclic AMP and Cyclic GMP

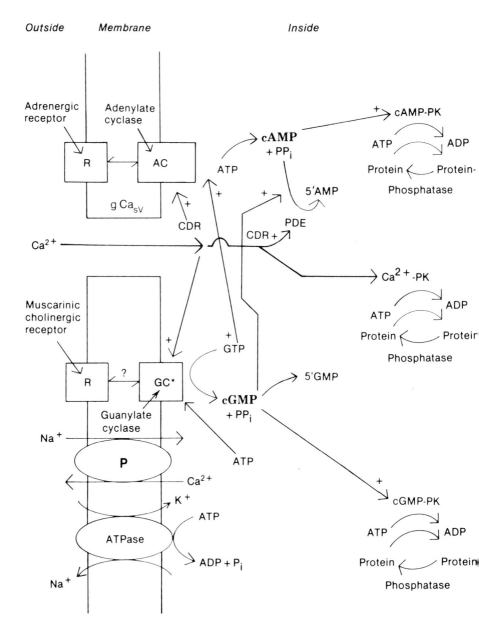

*(may not be present in the plasma membrane)

synthesizing and degrading capacity in the brain is associated with neuronal elements; glia cells possess hormone- or neurotransmitter-sensitive adenylate cyclases.

It is assumed [by many] that in animal cells all effects of cyclic nucleotides are exercised through activation of the corresponding protein kinases. The majority of cAMP-binding proteins in all tissues including nervous tissues are identical to a subunit of cAMP-dependent protein kinases. Similarly, most of the cGMP-binding sites appear to be identical to the cGMP-dependent protein kinase. Brain contains both type I and type II cAMP-dependent protein kinases. These both consist of $R_2 C_2$ subunits and bind 2-4 moles of cAMP with K_d values in the submicromolar range (0.01-0.05 μM). The cAMP-dependent protein kinases are classified on the basis of their ion exchange chromatographic properties and on the basis of differences in the ability to autophosphorylate their regulatory subunit. It appears that both isoenzymes of the cAMP-dependent protein kinase, type I and type II, occur in all regions of the rat, guinea pig, and bovine brain.

Phosphoproteins assume a central role in the regulatory cascade shown in Fig. 5.9B by representing the interconvertible unit of the cascade. Distribution of these proteins between phospho- and dephospho- states reflects the nonlinear sum of several enzyme activities at a given time. Phosphorylation of the target protein (substrate) of the protein kinase plays a central role in the cascade since this target protein is the only covalently labeled, interconvertible unit in the cascade. Part III of Fig. 5.9B involves the only reaction which is reversed by another enzyme (protein phosphatase) just like important phosphorylation steps in intermediary metabolism that are catalyzed by different enzymes in forward and backward directions (e.g., hexokinase and glucose-6-phosphatase).

cAMP regulates phosphorylation of several proteins in the synaptic membranes. The best characterized substrate protein in synaptic fraction is Protein I [52,357], which is phosphorylated and dephosphorylated by endogenous enzymes that are also localized in the same membranes. The phosphorylation of this collagen-like protein is also carried out by a protein kinase that is activated by Ca^{2+} in complex with the calcium dependent regulator protein. Depolarizing agents cause phosphorylation of Protein I both in vivo and in vitro, probably by a Ca^{2+}-dependent mecha-

---

Fig. 5.8. Schema of postsynaptic formation of cAMP and cGMP. AC, adenylate cyclase, fully membrane bound; GC, guanylate cyclase, mostly soluble, some membrane bound; cAMP-PK, cGMP-PK, Ca^{2+}-PK stand for cAMP-, cGMP-, and Ca^{2+}-dependent protein kinases, the first two of which occur both in soluble and membrane-bound form;, the last has been reported as a membrane-bound protein. CDR stands for Ca^{2+}-dependent regulator, e.g., calmodulin (see Cheung [162]), and PDE for phosphodiesterase, a splitter of cyclic nucleotides. The protein substrates and phosphoprotein phosphatases are soluble and membrane-bound proteins. The nucleotides serve as substrates in the form of divalent metal-nucleotide complexes. Mg^{2+} is thought to be the natural divalent cation. Ca^{2+} and Na^+ concentrations are regulated by the Na^+ and K^+ ATPase, the Ca^{2+}-Na^+ exchange pump (P), and by the opening of g Ca_{sV} channels in the membrane of the postsynaptic cell. (Modified slightly from Bartfai [51].)

Calcium Dependence of Release of Cyclic AMP and Cyclic GMP

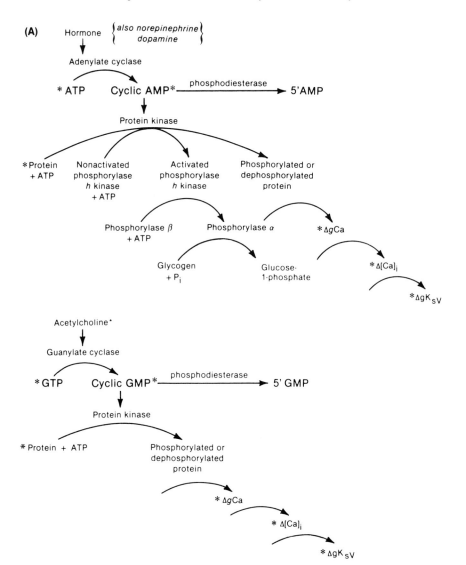

* Can be regulated by calcium

Fig. 5.9. (A) Calcium dependence of mechanisms of generation of cAMP and cGMP and their subsequent, putative intracellular effects. Reaction sequences in the breakdown of tissue glycogen, as described by Robison et al. [828] are included. ATP, adenosine triphosphate; AMP, adenosine monophosphate; P_i, inorganic phosphate; GTP, guanosine triphosphate; GMP, guanosine monophosphate. Calcium dependencies of these effects are also shown as are some possible but unconfirmed effects on neuronal conductance. (B) The reaction cascade that may take place in a neuron upon agonist binding. R, neurotrans-

and Their Subsequent Putative Intracellular Effects

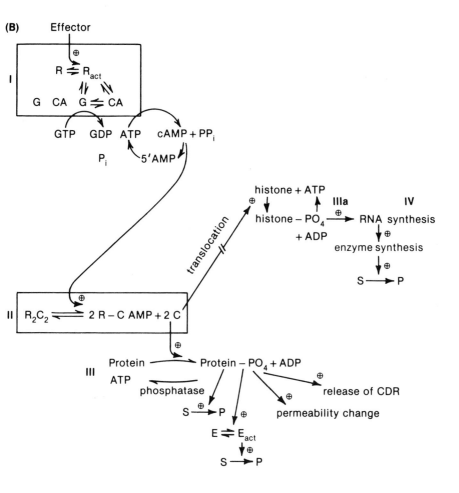

mitter or hormone receptor in monomeric or oligomeric form; G, GTP-binding subunit and the GTPase (which may not be identical); CA, catalytic subunit of the adenylate cyclase; R_2C_2, cAMP-dependent protein kinase (type I and type II), R is its regulatory subunit; C, active catalytic subunit of the protein kinase; Protein, target protein of phosphorylation that can be dephosphorylated by a protein phosphatase. It is assumed that protein-PO4 is a modified form of an enzyme that catalyzes formation of product (P) from substrate (S), or release of CDR, or controls the permeability for an ion, or regulates an additional enzyme, E, which in its activated form catalyzes formation of P from S. The active catalytic unit of protein kinase may translocate into the nucleus and via histone phosphorylation control RNA synthesis and finally synthesis of a protein which will catalyze the reaction S → P. The + sign indicates activation by the effector indicated. Blocks I and II indicate that within this "reaction" a number of regulatory interactions take place which are omitted from the figure for simplicity. (B from Bartfai [52].)

nism. Another protein that shows strong incorporation of $[^{32}P]$ phosphate in synaptic membranes has been identified as the regulatory subunit of the type II cAMP-dependent protein kinase that undergoes autophosphorylation. Tyrosine hydroxylase, the key enzyme for catecholamine synthesis, represents another substrate for cAMP-dependent phosphorylation in the synaptic region. Thermodynamically, phosphoproteins are well suited for storage of regulatory information since the protein-phosphate (serine-phosphate) represents a medium high energy bond (7 kcal/mole) that is formed and hydrolyzed by separate enzymes that are under separate controls [52].

Superior Cervical Ganglion

The role of cyclic nucleotides in controlling conductance changes governing PSP production has been extensively investigated in sympathetic ganglia. In the superior cervical ganglion, a fast EPSP of 5 msec duration, a slow IPSP reaching a maximum at 500 msec, and a slow EPSP lasting up to 2 min can be seen upon stimulating the synaptic inputs to the ganglion [594,595]. The potentials are illustrated in Fig. 5.10. Production of the fast EPSP is attributed to a nicotinic, cholinergic activation of g Na. Production of the slow PSPs appears to be controlled by interdependent actions of calcium, cyclic nucleotides, and voltage. Active metabolic pumps also appear to be involved.

**Three Conductance Changes (Fast-EPSP; Slow-IPSP; Slow-EPSP)
In the Superior Cervical Ganglion**

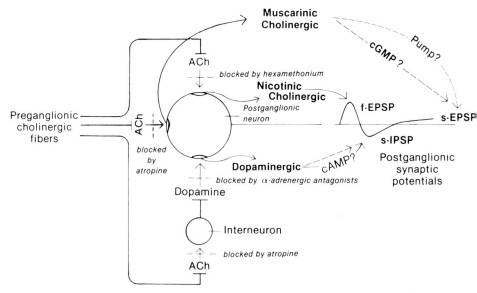

Fig. 5.10. Schema of neurotransmission and second messenger effects in the superior cervical (sympathetic) ganglion: f-EPSP = fast EPSP; s-IPSP = slow IPSP; s-EPSP = slow EPSP. ACh = acetylcholine (modified slightly from Greengard [358] in Tower [1024].)

At present, there is still too little information to specify exactly how these interdependencies are played out. However, levels of cAMP are known to be increased at the time of production of the slow, dopaminergically induced, hyperpolarizing IPSP [cf. 358,506,653]. An increase in conductance ($\downarrow R_m$) accompanies the change in potential. Excitation of small, intensely fluorescent (SIF) interneurons [274] within the ganglion produces similar effects. These chromaffin cells are themselves excited by a muscarinic cholinergic synaptic input, and they provide an adrenergic input (dopamine) to the postsynaptic ganglion cell [259,595]. Nicotine may alter the response [1022].

The postganglionic IPSP could result from (1) a kinase-dependent, phosphorylation-induced conductance change [355], (2) a small increase in $[Ca^{2+}]_i$ produced by cAMP with an $\uparrow g K_{Ca}$ [653, cf. 1073], or (3) activation of Na/K^P [597]. However, it is still questionable whether cAMP is the direct intermediary of any of these mechanisms in the superior cervical ganglion. This is because application of cAMP directly to the ganglion, either intra or extracellularly, fails to produce hyperpolarization. Instead, either depolarization is seen [313,314] or no significant potential shift occurs [135,529,1075]. The effects of cAMP on membrane conductance are also unresolved. Both decreases in resistance and an absence of significant change in R_m have been found to follow application of cAMP [135, 313,314,391,1075].

It seems most likely that the slow, hyperpolarizing IPSP is produced by an increased potassium conductance triggered by the entry of calcium ions, with or without the help of cAMP. McAfee and Yarowsky [653] have shown that the increase in g K is calcium dependent and that neurons of sympathetic ganglia have both a calcium and potassium conductance. The former is suggested by the presence of regenerative spikes that are TTX insensitive. Norepinephrine antagonizes production of the slow IPSP as well as the regenerative calcium action potential. Because this action is antagonized by the α-adrenergic antagonist phentolamine, but not by MJ 1999, a β-adrenergic antagonist, norepinephrine is thought to act through an α-adrenergic receptor to inhibit g Ca. However, the effects of dopamine on cAMP are also blocked by β-antagonists [475]. (Some agonists and antagonists of cAMP and cGMP are shown in Table 5.2.) Attributing the slow IPSP (or EPSP) simply to changes in g K may be an oversimplification, since several physiologically distinct K^+ channels have been described in mollusks [1019], and, at other muscarinic synapses, acetylcholine is thought to act directly on Ca^{2+} channels [446,569]. Meech found earlier that an analogous change in g K triggered by Ca^{2+} could occur in different neurons in *Aplysia* [658], and Jansen and Nicholls [455] found this in leech neurons as well. The delayed hyperpolarization of Parnas and Strumwasser [754] may depend on a similar mechanism involving an increase in potassium conductance. Long-lasting hyperpolarizing PSPs analogous to those described above are thought to be due to activation of an electrogenic pump by the entry of sodium ions during repetitive action potentials [754].

The role of cGMP in the production of the slow EPSP is equally unclear. The level of cGMP in the superior cervical ganglion is increased during the production of the slow, depolarizing EPSP [1074] shown in Fig. 5.10. Stimulation of cholinergic, preganglionic fibers in bullfrog sympathetic

Table 5.2. Agonists and Antagonists of cAMP and cGMP[a]

Neurotransmitter agonists	Antagonists
Associated with cAMP system	
Dopamine	Chlorpromazine
Serotonin	LSD
Norepinephrine (β)	Propranolol
Histamine (H$_2$)	Metiamide
Octopamine	Phentolamine
Associated with cGMP system	
Acetylcholine	
(muscarinic)	Atropine
Histamine (H$_1$)	Diphenhydramine
Norepinephrine (α)	Phentolamine
Glutamate	
GABA[b]	

[a] Compiled from Greengard [356].
[b] Added by this author.

ganglia produces an increase in firing as well as in postganglionic concentrations of cGMP [1074]. Blocking the release of synaptic transmitters with high magnesium-low calcium prevents the increase in cGMP. The increase is also blocked by atropine*, a muscarinic, cholinergic blocker. The slow EPSP is accompanied by a conductance decrease ($\uparrow R_m$), probably mediated by $\downarrow g$ K [1077]. Interestingly, with cells hyperpolarized beyond -60 mV, no conductance changes are found to accompany either the slow EPSP or IPSP [598].

Elsewhere, in certain vertebrate and invertebrate photoreceptor cells, there are rod-shaped outer segments that appear to signal photon absorption by a decrease in g Na. In the dark, it is hypothesized [cf. 433] that the sodium channel is kept open "by a cGMP dependent phosphorylation. Light activates the enzymatic degradation of cGMP, protein is dephosphorylated, and sodium channels close."

It is doubtful that a cGMP mediated ionic conductance change is the specific intermediary for the slow EPSP in the superior cervical ganglion. Instead, cGMP may activate an electrogenic pump leading to metabolically altered potassium concentrations [597]. Consistent with a postulated pump mechanism, investigators find that the alterations are sensitive to disruption of oxidative metabolism [391,530,595]. When cGMP is applied directly, either intra- or extracellularly, it reportedly produces a $\downarrow$ in R_m [314,391] or no significant change in R_m [135,530,720]. Some have reported a depolarization of resting potential to accompany the intracellular iontophoresis of large amounts of cGMP [313]; others have reported no effect[†]; and Freschi and Shain report a depolarization plus an *increased* resistance obtained from cultures of ganglion cells [301]. Further studies

*see Kebabian et al. *J. Pharm. exp. Ther.* 193:474-488, 1975.
[†] Weight—comments at Symposium on Iontophoresis and Neurotransmitters, Cambridge, 1977.

indicate that the changes in resistance are both dosage and voltage dependent [391]. Low extracellular concentrations (25-100 μM) of cGMP result in a large, early decrease in R_m that is somewhat dissociated from the accompanying depolarization [391]. The decrease in R_m is abolished by returning the membrane potential to the normal resting level with hyperpolarizing current. At higher concentrations of cGMP (500-1000 μM), the depolarization is greater and the decrease in R_m is larger, but the change in R_m is not abolished by hyperpolarization. At lower, more physiologic dose levels of cGMP in the superior cervical ganglion, a small late increase in resistance was found 5 to 10 min after application, comparable to that reported in cortical neurons [391,1109,1124]. When the membrane was repolarized to normal level during the slow EPSP, "a definite but small increase in membrane resistance (about 20%) above resting level was usually visible" [391]. cGMP may mediate this effect.

Interestingly, the slow EPSP in the superior cervical ganglion is enhanced by cAMP or dopamine and by conditioning stimulation of the SIF interneuron. This enhancement is reduced by application of cGMP. A further discussion of this plasticity follows later.

pH

pH also affects ionic conductances across cell membranes [102,218,591,682, 1013,1014]. Examples of the dependence of g Na, g K and g Cl on pH are shown in Fig. 5.11 for epithelial cells of the gall bladder. In neurons and in muscle there is also a dependency between [H^+], [Na^+] and [Cl^-]. On recovery from acidification, Thomas [1013,1014] reports a fall in intracellular concentrations of sodium and chloride. There are also indications that decreases in pH can lead to increases in the resistance of gap junctions with a resulting uncoupling of electrical conductivity between cells.

Control of Neuronal Adaptation

A central theme of this book asserts that adaptations in neural networks underlie complex behavioral phenomena such as learning, memory, and higher function. Another is that parallels can be drawn between parametric features controlling reflex behavior and those controlling adaptive neural changes. As we have just seen, the variables active in the support of neural adaptation are complex and can be viewed as operating at several different levels ranging from conductance mechanisms located along different portions of the nerve cell to control variables such as calcium concentration or voltage across the cell membrane. Some of these variables are summarized in Table 5.3. They will function to support the simple, repetitive and associative adaptations described in detail in Chapters 2 and 3. Simple adaptations involve the summation of graded PSPs along networks of neurons with all-or-none action potentials. Nonassociative and nonrepetitive stimulus events suffice to induce this form of adaptation. The next level of adaptation is induced by repetitive events. These adaptations underlie the production of

Dependence of gNa and gCl on pH

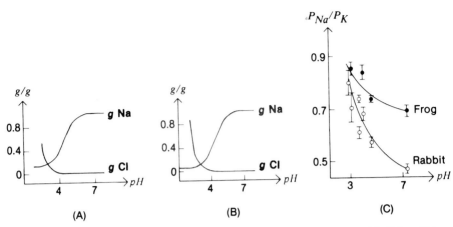

Fig. 5.11. pH dependence of g Na and g Cl in rabbit (A) and bullfrog (B) gall-bladders. All values referred to g Na at pH 7.5 as per ordinate scale. (C) pH dependence of Na/K permeability ratios: upper curve, bullfrog; lower, rabbit. (Moreno and Diamond [682] in Diamond [218].)

habituation, presynaptic inhibition, and the like. These and still more complex adaptations such as those induced associatively are supported by subcellular mechanisms local to pre-, and postsynaptic regions and perhaps to intrasynaptic regions as well. All neuronal adaptations except those at primary sensory receptors begin with simple neurotransmission, but depend critically on additional features such as (1) trace mechanisms supporting time delay, (2) contingent cellular events, and (3) cellular feedback reflecting earlier as well as present system states. Currently, we have but glimpses of these latter processes.

As will be seen in Chapter 7, one can think of information processing and message transmission through an element such as a nerve cell in terms of input, summation, threshold detection, and output. When the element is adaptive, further consideration must be given to the algorithm or contingencies re-

Table 5.3. Substrates of Learning

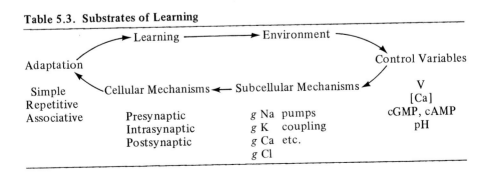

quired for adaptation, including representation of the state of the element following past adaptations and regulation of other functions of the element that could be affected by adaptation.

Surprisingly much has been learned in the last decade about intracellular processes supporting learning and involving the above operations. A number of interdependencies between molecular substrates involved in adaptations have been described in detail (Fig. 5.12). In years to come, further research will be devoted to describing the operation of these molecular substrates in the context of integration, threshold detection, maintenance of chemical traces over time, control of adaptation, and regulation of interrelated cellular processes. Further considerations might begin with the description of open- versus closed-loop processes suggested by Rasmussen.

Closed Loop versus Open Loop Control

Rasmussen [812] has emphasized the distinction between closed-loop and open-loop control of effects at the cellular level. When simple or compound stimuli act on a particular cell to produce a physiologic response independent of the previous state of the cell, this is classified as open-loop control of cellular function [526]. As discussed later (p. 384), an open-loop system receives no feedback information regarding the state of the adaptive part of the system. Control is exercised entirely by predetermined adaptations. Note the parallel between this type of control and that exerted by nonassociative processes. Even some potentially associative processes such as heterosynaptic facilitation may be analogous since they do not require feedback from the target neuron.

In contrast, "closed-loop" cellular responses depend on the past state of the cell. The loop provides information concerning the effects of prior adaptations. The cellular response is not only a function of input stimuli but of the organization of the receptive cell and its particular environment. As Rasmussen points out, cellular responses to hormonal stimuli operate not as open- but as closed-loop systems. In an open-loop system, the response depends on the stimulus, but the converse is not true. In a closed-loop system, the response influences the reception of the stimulus by its effect on system adaptation. Feedback also allows modification of adaptations consequential to the original stimulus.

Subcellular processes controlling most associatively induced neural adaptations are likely to involve loop systems with interdependencies between control process and the process controlled. Any complete analysis must specify the role of feedback through the loops in terms of control and systems theory. Because of the complexity of the involved molecular processes (Fig. 5.12), it will be difficult to describe these adaptive operations at the subcellular level. Nonetheless, some preliminary descriptions of significant components of adaptive operations can be offered, though with the understanding that they are severely limited by the extent of our present knowledge. For example, neuronal mechanisms can be specified such as gating that

Two Views of Chemical Control of Adaptation in Nerve Cells

(A) How Ca^{2+} Is Regulated

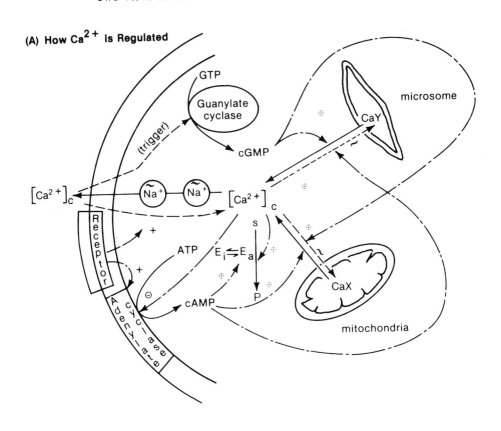

(B) What Ca^{2+} Does

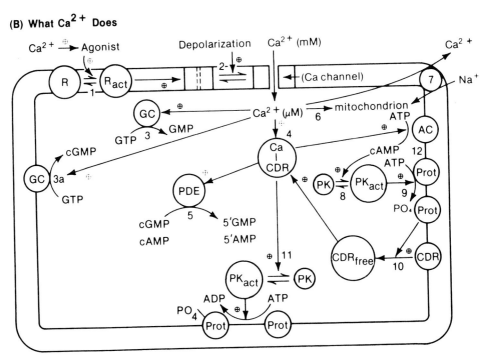

will serve for threshold detection within the cell. Other mechanisms such as calcium-dependent changes in potassium conductance may mediate or activate traces for the storage of information over time. Still other mechanisms can provide indexes of the system state and can support complex regulatory processes.

Gating: A Means for Threshold Detection

Channel gating is the initial step required for alteration of the permeability of the sodium conductance channel*; it arises from a voltage-induced change in the charge across the membrane, represents detection of voltage exceeding critical firing threshold, and leads to generation of an all-or-none spike output. Within the cell membrane, there is an electric field. Hille [415] notes that three sources contribute to this field:

1. The transmembrane potential based upon differences in internal and external ion concentrations
2. The local field from fixed negative surface charges
3. The local field from excess counter ions at the surface.

Quantitative properties of such a system are well-known in surface chemistry and are described by the Gouy-Chapman-Stern theory of ionic double layers. In the Hodgkin-Huxley model, the sequence of depolarization

---

Fig. 5.12. (A) Generalized model of Rasmussen integrating the relationship between calcium and cyclic nucleotides in an idealized cell. Active transport of Ca^{2+} is represented by $\sim$ or $\widetilde{Na}^+$, energy for the latter provided by the Na^+ gradient across the membrane. Passive movements of Ca^{2+} are shown by dashed arrows. CaX and CaY are nonionic pools of calcium in mitochondria and microsomes, respectively. A broken arrow with dots represents a control signal; and $\oplus$ and $\ominus$, indicating the particular control chemical, either enhances or inhibits the particular process. $[Ca^{2+}]_c$ is the concentration of calcium in the cytosol. S and P are the substrate and product of an enzyme, E_a, which is the phosphorylated form of E_i. The phosphorylation is controlled by a cAMP-dependent protein kinase. (From Rasmussen [814].) (B) Generalized model of Bartfai [52] summarizing some important interactions between Ca^{2+}-dependent and cAMP- and cGMP-dependent processes in nervous tissue: (1) Activation of a receptor, R, which controls opening of a Ca channel; (2) The same or other Ca channels may also be opened by direct depolarization; (3-3a) Ca^{2+} activates the membrane bound and soluble guanylate cyclases, GC; (4) Ca^{2+} forms complex with the calcium-dependent regulator (CDR) which activates phosphodiesterases, PDE (5); (12) CDR activates adenylate cyclases, AC; (11) CDR activates protein kinases, PK; (8,9) cAMP-dependent phosphorylation releases (10) some membrane bound CDR; (6) Ca^{2+} is removed by mitochondrial uptake; (7) Ca^{2+} is removed by Na^+-Ca^{2+} exchange. $\oplus$ = activation by the effector indicated. (From Bartfai [52].)

---

*Presently, only the Na^+ channel.

which opens and closes sodium channels is explained by the simultaneous and independent relaxation of an activation and an inactivation process, both of which must be in a permissive state for the channel to be open. The permissive state, m3, of the activating process rises with a sigmoid time course and, simultaneously, the permissive state, h, of the inactivation process falls with an exponential time course during a maintained depolarization. More recent evidence suggests that the inactivation processes may not be completely independent of the activation processes [295,415].

The actual molecular basis of voltage-sensing and gating by the membrane is poorly understood. Hille asks, "is the sensory gate mechanism entirely built into the channel and associated parts of the membrane, or are soluble cofactors such as ions or small molecules essential participants?" "Can individual channels open in a partial or graded way, or is each opening in an all or none process?" Calcium ions appear to be involved in these phenomena, not as a sensor or as a gate, but rather as a counterion to surface charges. During sodium gating, charge is transferred. The gating current is reversibly reduced about one-third by 1% Procaine, and abolished by 10 mM zinc chloride [75, 512]. The gating current is the same whether or not TTX is present.

Once gating has occurred the opportunity arises for other classes of events to take place, such as the regenerative spike potential changes seen in some types of burst discharge neurons. Bullock points out the behavioral significance of such a process in his discussion of Russell and Hartline's [855] regenerative plateau potentials which switch in and out "like a bistable flip-flop" [124].

In cells of the stomatogastric ganglion of lobsters two kinds of input are necessary to release the regenerative plateau potentials (RPPs). There must be both (a) a background, or predisposing input from the central nervous system that induces a triggerable state, and (b) an adequate, depolarizing, trigger input, which can be a pulse we inject intracellularly . . . or e.p.s.p.'s from other cells or spontaneous, slow pacemaker depolarizations. Without the c.n.s. background, triggering input in the ganglion causes synaptic potentials. Without the trigger input, these elicit a simple response, for example an e.p.s.p. and the cells are either silent or exhibit pacemaker activity as isolated spikes. The predisposing effect of the c.n.s. input that allows RPPs in response to trigger input lasts for many seconds after even a brief c.n.s. burst. Once into the plateau the regenerative repolarization can be triggered by a hyperpolarizing pulse, or by an i.p.s.p. or by spontaneous processes. During the plateau the cell fires at high frequency, that is, the degree of depolarization at plateau height is not so much as to cause a block; rather it excites rapid pacemaker activity [124].

Still other phenomena occur at the membrane in the course of generation of the action potential. Tasaki and Warashina [996,1066] describe "changes in light absorption, emission and energy transfer produced by electrical stimulation of nerves labelled with a fluorescent probe" and also give evidence for "rotation of dye molecules and membrane macromolecules associated with excitation."

"Trace" Mediators

Trace mediators maintain the signal of inputs (old and new) within the neuron. They permit contingent adaptation to occur by holding information over time within the cell. When they maintain old inputs over long time periods, they may be viewed as a type of engram.

Changes in potassium conductance could serve as a trace mediator for either old or new inputs since the changes appear rapidly, need not drastically alter the resting potential of the cell, are long-lasting, and can be altered as a function of input frequency and duration (Fig. 5.13). The delayed outward current resulting from $g\,K_{TEA} + g\,K_{Ca}$ is depressed with repeated depolarization. The depression can last for hundreds of milliseconds, and is greatest for 100 msec depolarizing pulses repeated every 200-400 msec. The abrupt reduction in $g\,K_{Ca}$ by stepping the membrane potential into the negative resistance region [633] could serve as a basis for controlling persistent cellular adaptation [764].

Potassium flux across the membrane is highly calcium dependent. Large increases in $[Ca^{2+}]_i$ lead to inactivation of $g\,K_{Ca}$. Small increases in $[Ca^{2+}]_i$ lead to increases in potassium permeability [50,266,563,660]. Decreases in the potassium concentration gradient across the membrane can activate sodium-potassium ATPase and hence lead to a fall in sodium within the cell, thus causing an increase in calcium efflux by sodium-calcium exchange. The latter constitutes a negative feedback loop controlling the rise of intracellular calcium ion concentration [813].

Plots of these effects are shown in Figs. 5.5, 5.6, and 5.13. Their sensitivity to repetitive contingencies parallels that of the processes in Figs. 3.8, 3.10, 3.11, 4.16, and 4.17.

The above effects differ among different types of cells, even within *Helix*. The effects of Co and TEA on g Ca, $g\,K_{TEA}$ and $g\,K_{Ca}$ are shown for two different types of cells in Fig. 5.14.

Voltage changes (the PSPs arising from conductance changes) generally signal the arrival of new inputs into the neuron. This may result either from primary neurotransmitter effects (the first messengers) or from their secondary consequences (the second messengers). The summation of groups of PSPs beyond critical firing threshold follows well known laws of current spread and integration within a passive cable [451] and represents a trace effect over the period of summation. This type of trace mediation may be short indeed. Thus, many PSPs must be viewed as stimulus traces rather than as engrams, and some stimulus traces may be primarily involved with immediate message transmission.

For certain PSPs the distinction between stimulus trace and engram is again blurred because of the time course of second messenger chemical effects. As we have seen, the first messengers in the transmission of informa-

Trace Mediation by gK

Equivalence between outward current (left) and K$^+$ efflux (right)

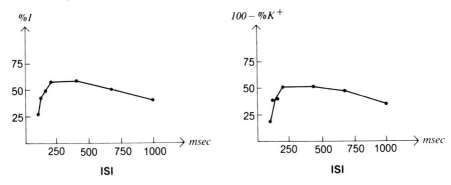

Effects of ISI (left) versus stimulus duration (right)

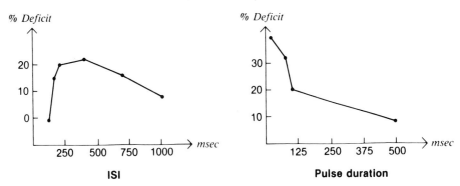

Fig. 5.13. Top: Net outward current (left) and K$^+$ efflux (right) versus fre-
quencies of stimulation (100 msec clamp depolarizations). Current is % total
current for the sum of ten 100 msec pulses relative to that during a single
1000 msec depolarization. K$^+$ efflux is 100 minus the ratio of efflux from ten
100 msec pulses to that from a single 1000 msec pulse. (Heyer and Lux
[411].) Bottom: Net charge transfer deficit (the sum of net outward current
and K$^+$ efflux relative to sum during a sustained 1000-msec pulse of the same
magnitude) for (right): a total of 1000 msec in voltage clamp depolarizations
presented as forty 25-msec, twenty 50-msec, ten 100-msec, or two 500-msec
pulses with repolarization intervals of 300-500 msec; (left): ten 100 msec
pulses; versus pulse duration (right) or ISI (left). Partial inactivation can be
seen on the right with prolonged depolarization. Note peaking of deficit at
400 msec ISI on left. (Heyer and Lux [410].)

tion from cell to cell are the chemicals released at the presynaptic membrane
of the synapse. They diffuse across the synaptic cleft and complex with
postsynaptic receptors. Subsequently, a conductance change is produced in
the postsynaptic membrane. Except for the action of acetylcholine at the

Differences in *g*K (and *g*Ca) Between Cells

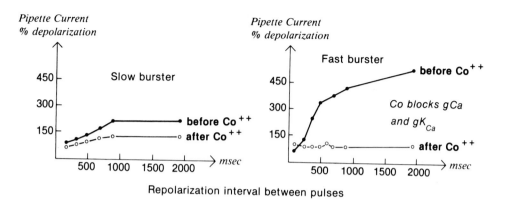

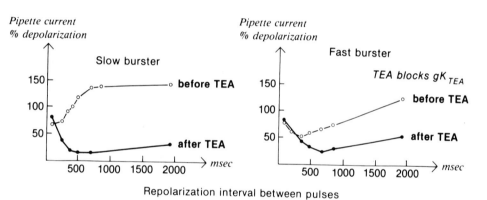

Repolarization interval between pulses

Fig. 5.14. (A) Depression of net outward current after ten 100 msec pulses for two types of cells: left, slow burster; right, fast burster. 100% indicates equal depression with interrupted and sustained depolarization; higher values reflect increasing depression of outward current. After cobalt, there is a relative decrease in the amount of depression produced as ISI increases. (Heyer and Lux [411].) (B) Depression of net outward current of slow (left) and fast (right) burster, before and after TEA. (Heyer and Lux [411].)

nicotinic receptor, it is unlikely that simple binding of a neurotransmitter molecule at a receptor leads directly to the production of a postsynaptic conductance change. Instead, this occurs through some intervening chemical mediator—the "second messenger." These chemicals, then, carry the message of transmission postsynaptically, prior to production of the actual conductance change within the postsynaptic cell. Obviously, this further complicates attempts to distinguish stimulus traces from engrams.

To take a specific example, much previous attention has focused on cyclic nucleotides as possible second messengers; however, the nature of the message transmitted is still unclear. These agents perform several different operations. If one defines a second messenger as "a chemical signal generated by an interaction of an external stimulus with a cell surface receptor, which passes into one or more subcellular compartments and therein initiative the appropriate cellular response" [813], the message carried may be one of immediate neurotransmission, i.e., the elemental conductance change underlying production of the EPSP or IPSP. Or, instead, the message could signal a contingency required for controlling the production of a cellular change involved with engram formation. A third possibility is that the message involves a regulatory input needed for the control of some other cellular function unrelated, directly, to either PSP production or engram formation.

Rasmussen points out that the second messenger model may be inadequate to explain all of the effects of cyclic nucleotides without due consideration of the role of calcium. This may occur when the concept of a coupling factor is confused with that of a second messenger. Rasmussen would use the term "coupling factor" to describe the critical regulator of the major response within the cell, as apart from the context of other (e.g., behavioral) information transmission. Sometimes when calcium serves as the eventual coupling factor between excitation and response, it is released by the action of another second messenger. Then, in the hierarchy of information transfer, the calcium ion plays the role of a third messenger. However, in systems in which an increase in calcium uptake by the cell must precede the formation intracellularly of cyclic nucleotides, calcium will function more directly as a second messenger rather than as a coupling factor or third messenger. To complicate matters further these substrates may also function as state depictors.

State Depictors

State depictors signal the state of the adaptive system. Information about the consequences of adaptive processes on the system state within the neuron may be needed for orderly adaptation to occur (see Chap. 7, p. 347). Some information of this type (state depiction) is furnished by the resting transmembrane potential and by voltage and concentration dependent calcium flux. In *Helix*, moderate depolarization leads to increased $g\,Ca_{sV}$ and an increased $[Ca^{2+}]_i$. Strong depolarization leads to an inactivation of $g\,Ca_{sV}$ and a reduction of calcium influx as the membrane potential approaches the calcium equilibrium potential [410]. At the presynaptic terminal of the squid axon, there is a linear relationship between calcium current, $I\,Ca_{(f)}$, and transmitter release (Fig. 5.3). Depolarization of 25-60 mV results in an increase in neurotransmitter release in proportion to the level of depolarization, yet steady depolarization of lesser magnitude results in a *decrease* in neurotransmitter release. Evidently, voltage and calcium concentration inside the cell depict the state of facilitation or inhibition at the presynaptic terminal *and* also control transmitter release. Cyclic AMP could significantly modulate these effects by an action on $[Ca^{2+}]_i$ at the presynaptic terminal [160,480, 483], but there is no conclusive evidence for this as yet, and in fact, some evidence against [865].

The possible significance of state depiction for controlling the operation of adaptive systems may be better appreciated by considering the following:

Artificial adaptive systems commonly function at more than one level: i.e., to transmit messages and to adapt in such a way as to alter the outcome of message transmission. Examples may be found in Figs. 5.31, 6.9, 7.1, 7.6, etc. In order to perform both functions successfully careful attention must be paid to maintaining the system state within its proper operating range (normalization). That is, the system must not be allowed to adapt so much that it cannot operate. In some of the better understood artificial adaptive systems such as the informon (p. 346), this is done by introducing negative feedback of information concerning the system state.

At the presynaptic terminals of neurons, there are two operations that must be performed. One is chemical neurotransmission, i.e., the exocytosis of transmitter molecules on receipt of a spike potential (Figs. 5.15, 5.20). The other is adaptive alteration in the efficacy of this transmission process.

Maintaining the system in a state suitable for these operations to be performed appears to be done though calcium. Calcium concentration changes over time as a function of synaptic activation [cf. 118,502,503] and reflects the state of the adaptive system. In addition, calcium acts directly to promote fusion of vesicles containing neurotransmitter within the membrane of the synaptic cleft, followed by exocytosis—discharge of the vesicle contents into the intrasynaptic space [610,611]. Calcium may then be said to depict the state of three different, hypothetical levels of the system's operation:

(1) *the "normal" level*, at which small changes in polarization control the amount of transmitter released per spike arrival. Here, for example, repeated spikes will cause additional depolarization and inhibition of transmission.

(2) *the "supranormal" level*, at which fast (e.g. tetanic) rates of spiking have led (a) to a build up of intracellular calcium that will potentiate transmission and (b) to a degree of depolarization perhaps sufficient to potentiate transmission by further increasing calcium flux into the terminal.

(3) *the "inactivation" level*, at which too great a depolarization and too high an internal calcium concentration will inactivate calcium flux into the terminal and will also inactivate sodium conductance, thereby resulting in a suppression of neurotransmission.

Note that in case (1) feedback resulting from small increases in calcium concentration opposes the inhibition and tends to return the system to a neutral state. In case (2) calcium eventually accumulates sufficiently to produce inactivation as in case (3); this will then oppose the potentiation of transmission and return the system to a neutral state. As a result of these complex negative feedback mechanisms, the system will be normalized, and its proper range of functioning will be maintained.

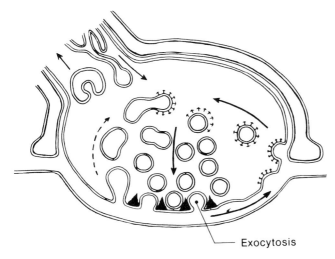

Fig. 5.15. Exocytosis of synaptic vesicles with recycling as schematized by Heuser and Reese [From 408]. (Also see Fig. 5.20.)

Regulatory Modulators

Regulatory modulators, including calcium, control cellular processes including and apart from the primary adaptations serving learning. One of the nicest examples is that of the reversal of ciliary beating controlling movement in *Paramecium* [261,264,265,638]. In neural systems of more complex organisms, Goldberg et al. [332] have advanced the Yin-Yang hypothesis by which cGMP and cAMP impose contrasting or opposing regulatory influences on the neuron (cf. Table 5.2). Type A cellular processes are activated by cAMP and inhibited by cGMP. Type B cellular processes are activated by cGMP and inhibited by cAMP. As we have seen, most of these effects depend on the presence of calcium for their occurrence, and calcium may also act separately to affect other fundamental molecular properties within the cell. Thus, interdependent ionic conductances, cyclic nucleotides, calcium, voltage, and pH may all influence fundamental molecular processes within the cell in the manners described earlier (Fig. 5.12). Improved understanding of how the interactions among such complex, interdependent processes are regulated may provide better insight into neuroregulatory control of adaptive processes serving learning.

In some systems, cyclic nucleotides may function as single coupling factors. Cyclic nucleotides can act as part of a fixed pathway controlling the activation of further calcium release. Subsequent increases in intracellular calcium can then inhibit the activity of cAMP phosphodiesterase and thereby cause a rise in cAMP [812,813]. The latter will act as a negative feedback regulator of intracellular calcium by stimulating re-uptake of calcium by the internal membranes.

Another example of a cyclic nucleotide regulatory effect is that reported by Byus and Russell [137] in the adrenal gland in which increases in cAMP within 30 min after administration of aminophylline are associated with later increases in the activity of ornithine-decarboxylase. Presumably, the synthesis of the latter enzyme is controlled by levels of cAMP. Drugs that block protein synthesis prevent the synthesis of ornithine decarboxylase without affecting the earlier increase in cyclic AMP. It is thought that cAMP may control new enzyme synthesis, perhaps by means of a protein kinase that controls gene transcription.

The *result* of the above enzyme effects could be the induction of an adaptive change or, instead, maintenance of the status quo of cell function. One could also consider this example from the point of view of a 30 min "trace" effect. Which of the above is (are) correct depends on an understanding of how the adrenal cell functions relative to a specified assembly of other cells (see again Figs. 6.9, 7.1, 7.22, and the frontispiece) or, in the case of a neuron, how the neuron functions within a specific reflex network. The next chapter is devoted to consideration of the function of different reflex networks. It is admittedly difficult to distinguish trace mediation from state depiction and regulatory modulation (and no claims are made for success in doing so above). Nonetheless, it is worthwhile to attempt this in preparation for the analytic approaches to learning advanced in Chapter 7. The alternative is to map subcellular molecular effects on the simple, repetitive, and associative adaptations described earlier—a useful but interim approach to an understanding of cellular mechanisms of complex behavior.

"Simple," "Repetitive," and "Associatively" Induced Neuronal Changes

The identification of subcellular processes that require single versus repetitive stimuli for their induction supports the distinction between simple and repetitive adaptations made earlier in Chapter 2. Conditioning-testing studies reveal that facilitation of neural transmission is generally observed after a single stimulation. Repetitive stimulation generally results in inhibitory effects. This is particularly apparent at frequencies of repetition near those found to produce habituation. Many of these changes appear to be presynaptic and require numbers of repetitions, $n > 1$ and $<$ tetanus, for their induction. As repetitive stimulation approaches a single event (tetanus), facilitation rather than inhibition may be seen.

Physiologically, this is still something of an oversimplification. First, there are the exceptions to the above (for example, the inhibitory effects of tetanus in some systems—Chapter 4). Second, repetitively induced phenomena such as habituation have several features and more than one underlying mechanism. A proper physiologic explanation of these effects requires a detailed analysis of facilitatory and inhibitory synaptic events at each neuron along the pathways linking repeated presentations of the stimulus with the nine features of the habituated response (see Chapter 2). Nonetheless, one must not overlook the general correspondence between Pavlov's observations of reflex outcomes and physiologists' observations of neural effects of stimulus presentation. Examination of the frequency dependencies of the long-lasting conductance changes shown in Figs. 5.6 and 5.14 reveals similarities between these and the frequency dependencies of associative behavioral processes (Fig. 2.3). Though presently but correlates of repetitively and associatively induced events, their continued study may ultimately produce causal demonstrations of learning mechanisms.

What of the mechanisms that might serve to support associative learning or the types of changes contingent on trace effects described in Chapter 3? A few studies have uncovered mechanisms that might mediate some aspects of associative adaptations. The first example involves a potentiation of the slow EPSP of the superior cervical ganglion to either acetylcholine (ACh) or the muscarinic agonist, acetyl-β-methylcholine (MCh). Studies by Libet and colleagues [599] have shown that the size of this EPSP is increased if ACh or MCh is given after administration of dopamine (DA), (Fig. 5.16). Dopamine itself produces an IPSP in this ganglion. It has been suggested that this IPSP is mediated by cAMP (Figs. 5.10 and 5.16), but the studies described earlier make this possibility questionable. Cyclic AMP does, however, appear to be involved in potentiating the EPSP to ACh or MCh. Further studies [529] have reproduced the EPSP enhancement by iontophoresing cAMP directly into the single ganglion cells. Interestingly, in view of the Yin-Yang hypothesis, administration of cGMP aborts the dopamine-induced facilitatory effect (Fig. 5.16). If the administration of cGMP is delayed 10-15 min after DA, the potentiation remains unaffected [599]. The enhancement of PSP amplitude can last for as long as the in vitro ganglion preparation can be maintained, i.e., for more than 3 hr. cAMP may also potentiate muscle contraction [954] and inhibit transmitter release in other cells [see 52,573].

In the context of Libet's experiment, adaptation contingent on two or more variables would be possible. However, since cAMP may be released by the action of a single neurotransmitter, it may not serve to mediate associatively learned behavioral processes at all but instead may support sensitization or even repetitively induced behavior.

The second example is that of the modulation of circadian bursting in a pacemaker neuron of *Aplysia*. Parnas et al. [751] describe "long-lasting synaptically induced modulation of the spontaneous activity of an identified neuron in the parietal visceral ganglion of *Aplysia*. The R15 (parabolic burster) neurons show a (circadian) rhythm of impulse activity which can be entrained in the intact animal to different light-dark cycles." This report describes three axons innervating the cell. One is excitatory; the other two evoke biphasic PSPs with hyperpolarization predominating. Activating the excitatory input for 3 min leads to an increase in the number and frequencies of spikes per burst that persists for hours. Bursting is normal in this cell. Hyperpolarizing the cell to block spiking for several minutes reverses the effect back to the prestimulation level. The long-lasting excitatory effect is not produced by directly inducing unit activity by applying intracellular depolarizing current postsynaptically. Thus, synaptic activation is necessary to produce the effect. Stimulating one of the other inputs can block bursting for nearly 1 hr.

Nucleotide-Induced Adaptation

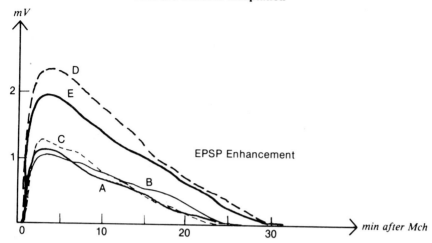

Fig. 5.16. Modulatory effect of dopamine (DA) on EPSPs produced by acetyl-β-methylcholine (MCh) in the superior cervical ganglion can be disrupted by cGMP. (A,B) control responses to MCh; (D) enhanced response to MCh 35 min after DA; (C) response to MCh after DA + cGMP (enhancement disrupted); (E) enhanced response to MCh 85 min after DA. cAMP appears to mediate the DA modulatory action [529,597]. (Libet et al. [599].)

Bursting neurons (L2-L6) of the abdominal ganglia of *Aplysia* also exhibit a complex IPSP which is thought to be mediated through a monosynaptic input from a cholinergic cell (L10). The complex IPSP may last for as long as several seconds and has both a short phase, which is thought to be mediated by g Cl, and a long phase. The long phase may in part be mediated by (1) an electrogenic pump which is sensitive to temperature and ouabain [769] and by (2) inactivation of a calcium conductance which underlies the regenerative bursting discharge [1092]. The prolonged IPSP is insensitive to changes in extracellular potassium.

The third example is that, cited earlier, of increased input resistance (R_m) and excitability to intracellularly injected current in neurons of the mammalian motor cortex [1124]. The persistence of this effect is contingent on the cell being simultaneously discharged with depolarizing current [1124]. However, the *associative* dependence of this change has not been investigated, and its time course differs from the motor learning that is induced nonassociatively by a US and made persistent by CS-US pairing [111].

The fourth and only convincing example of an associatively induced cellular modulation occurs in the invertebrate, *Hermissenda*. As described earlier (p. 177), it involves an alteration in the "A" current component of $g K_{TEA}$ that modulates $g Ca_{sV}$. Its role in learning awaits clarification.

For a conclusive demonstration of the neural basis of even the simplest form of learning, the following minimal criteria are suggested:

1. An acceptable system should be studied behaviorally* and described in terms of sensory and motor labeled reflex outcomes dependent on simple, repetitive *and* associatively induced adaptation.
2. The neuronal circuitry supporting the above should be elucidated. Activities and latencies of transmission through this circuitry should be such that the elements studied may be viewed as contributory to the above reflex outcomes. Sensitivity of these outcomes to disruption of this circuitry is desirable.
3. The loci and mechanisms of neural changes within the circuitry should be clearly demonstrated as should the changes in transmission or integration at these loci.
4. It should be possible to induce neural changes similar to those in part 3 by appropriate single, repetitive or associative stimulus presentation.

As this set of criteria has yet to be satisfied, one must conclude that the cellular basis of learning and higher function awaits elucidation at the membrane level.

Apart from the behavioral requirements of part 1, such demonstrations may more easily be made in simple invertebrate systems and in in vitro preparations, but with such demonstrations, the burden of proof remains that mechanisms of invertebrates are applicable to vertebrates, and those, ultimately to humans. Also, in culture and slice preparations just as in intact preparations, the mechanisms studied must be shown to be undisturbed by injury processes.

Selected Techniques for Studying Cellular Plasticity

Many insights into the cellular substrates of learning and memory await new or improved technologies for investigating cellular operations. Thus, before concluding this chapter, a brief survey of current technologies will be made. Exclusive of purely biochemical approaches, the present methods for studying cellular plasticity may be divided into four categories:

1. Electrophysiologic approaches
2. Anatomical approaches, including the use of fluorescent and immunohistochemical techniques to improve anatomical definitions
3. Pharmacologic approaches
4. Analytical approaches

In addition, improved methodologies for tissue culture of single cells and tissue slices permit the use of greatly simplified, if presumptively abnormal, preparations.

---

*with appropriate behavioral controls, otherwise the demonstration might pertain to an adaptation supporting a cellular analog of learning.

Electrophysiologic Approaches

Electrophysiologic approaches include techniques of voltage and current recording, electrical stimulation, and measurement of intracellular and extracellular ion concentrations.

Voltage and Current Recording Techniques

Voltage recording (Chapter 4) measures potential differences extrinsically or intrinsically to single neurons. Among the extrinsic potential measurements are those of gross potential activity and extracellular unit activity. The limitations of the gross potential technique as applied to studies of cellular plasticity have already been discussed. Significant advances in this area will require the development of new means for improving signal to noise ratios as well as the ability to localize current-generator sources. Techniques for recording single unit activity extracellularly in relation to behavioral events were significantly advanced by Jasper *et al.* [824] and Hubel and Wiesel [434,436]. Jasper's holder, designed around metal screws implanted in the cranium, enables the investigator to record semichronically from a stable, awake preparation without causing the animal undue discomfort. Hubel and Wiesel's tungsten microelectrodes insulated with epoxy lacquer have given way to glass-coated, platinum-iridium or stainless steel electrodes [1094] which have lower coefficients of friction that permit more stable recording. Of greater advantage still are fine glass micropipettes filled with a conducting solution. It is possible to introduce such electrodes into virtually any region of the brain by using a guide tube [467,1110]. In addition to their improved stability, such electrodes permit discrete stimulation with minute currents while the recording is in progress.

Intracellular recording and stimulation techniques can be used to measure cell resistances and EPSPs and IPSPs as well as active spike discharges. Fine-tipped (0.5-1.0 μm) glass micropipettes are led to high-impedance amplifiers with capacitance compensation. The theoretical considerations that form the basis of such measurements are summarized in Aidley and others' neurophysiologic texts [9,179]. Applications of these techniques in mammals were pioneered by Eccles and colleagues [248,250].

Still more specialized recording techniques include the use of voltage and current clamping to evaluate conductance changes across the membrane. The patch clamp [294] *, achieved by placing a polished glass electrode tip directly against a section of the cell membrane, permits measurement of current flow across a locally clamped membrane region. A separate, intracellular electrode is used for current injection. Clamp techniques have their own limitations: (1) insufficient speed of clamping, (2) cross talk between the voltage-recording electrode and the current-injecting electrode, and (3) nonuniform current leakage across different portions of the cell membrane, leading to nonuniform clamping. These limitations have been reviewed elsewhere, in detail, by Cole [179] and Tasaki [993]. The only alternative at present to this most direct approach to measurement of specific conductance changes is to couple measures of change in resistance with use of neuropharmacologic conductance probes discussed later.

*Also see Hamill et al. *Pflügers Arch* 391:85-100, 1981.

Stimulation

Electrical stimulation suitable for studying cellular and behavioral plasticity employs constant amplitude pulsed currents ranging from nanoamps to milliamps. Such currents can be delivered at specifiable frequencies and durations via electrodes that have tip sizes ranging from 0.1 μm to 1 mm. Apart from physiologic difficulties in achieving a reproducible functional effect from a particular pattern of stimulation, three potential drawbacks have emerged in the use of this technique. The first is toxicity due to metal deposition or direct effects of the current. This problem can be overcome, or at least greatly reduced, by using nonmetal electrodes and passing low currents for short periods of time. Nonetheless, caution is advised since even currents in the microampere range have the capacity to induce epileptic foci when delivered cortically.

The second drawback is the nonhomogeneous spread of current in the extracellular space, which makes it difficult to control the amount of current reaching a particular neural locus. Further discussion of this and related problems may be found elsewhere [807,967].

The third drawback is in determining the locus of cell excitation. Given the possibility of separate mechanisms of cellular plasticity at pre-, intra-, and postsynaptic loci, it would be advisable to know how, where, and which neural elements are excited. Means for accomplishing this are just beginning to be developed [e.g., 1097,1119]. In part they involve penetrating an identifiable neuron and recording spike initiation while simultaneously stimulating through an adjacent (or otherwise appropriately located) electrode. In addition, they may require use of pharmacologic conductance probes, membrane marking agents, and other techniques described below.

Ion-Sensitive Electrodes

Ion-sensitive electrodes can be used to determine local concentrations of potassium, sodium, calcium, and pH, as well as larger molecules such as enzymes and cyclic nucleotides [510,591,1062,1065,1147]. They consist of glass pipettes filled with a chemical that changes its electrical properties as a function of a particular ion concentration. An example of their use to measure potassium efflux was given earlier (Fig. 5.13). Membrane electrodes may be used to measure antibody-haptene interactions [466], and oxygen may be measured by multi-wire platinum electrodes [511]. The biggest problems lie in making the electrode both sensitive and small enough to record the desired cellular event. The selectivity of the inserted compound in detecting the desired material must also be considered.

A number of advances in this technology have permitted recordings of intracellular as well as extracellular ion concentrations in a variety of species, including awake mammals (Fig. 5.17). Further information may be found in the following sources: Kessler et al. [510], Lux [633], Nicholson et al. [714], Vyskočil and Kříz [1062], Wong and Woody [1097], and Zeuthen [1147].

Other approaches to measuring shifts in potential or ion concentrations across the cell membrane include the use of dyes or bioluminescent agents whose light absorption or emission properties change as a function of potential or local ionic flux. For example, aequorin, a compound obtained from sea urchins, has light-emitting properties that allow it to be used to determine free calcium concentrations. At concentrations above 10^{-8} M, the light emission properties of this bioluminescent protein depend directly upon calcium concentration. At lower concentrations, however, light emission appears to be independent of calcium concentration [13]. According to Baker [40] purified aequorin can be injected into large cells without ill effect. The preparation and purification of aequorin has been described elsewhere by Shimomura and Johnson [893]. The detection of calcium by aequorin is compared in Table 5.4 with that by another calcium-photosensitive agent, arsenazo, and by use of ion sensitive electrodes. The sensitivity of the calcium exchanger used for the ion sensitive approach has recently been improved to $10^{-6}-10^{-7}M$ [28].

Examples of the use of aequorin to measure $[Ca]_i$ in single neurons of invertebrates are shown in Figs. 5.18 and 5.19. In both *Helix* and *Anisodorus*, the calcium current, I_{Ca}, and internal concentration of calcium, $[Ca]_i$, are found to be positively correlated. Use of aequorin as a measure of this current can be hazardous, as mentioned earlier, and the forms of some of the current-frequency plots shown for *Helix*, etc. may ultimately require some revision.

Arsenazo III undergoes an absorbance change on forming a complex with calcium. Thomas and Gorman [1012] injected this dye intracellularly and then used a fiber optic probe to pass a tungsten light through the cell to a photodiode. In this way, it was possible to measure free calcium ion concentration intracellularly.

Fiber optics allow noninvasive measurement of the luminescence of intracellular compounds. Compounds can be administered such as dipentyloxacarbocyanine (CC5), whose luminescence-emission properties depend on potential dependent changes in potassium or sodium concentration. These techniques can be used to estimate changes in transmembrane potential as fast as those associated with spike activity [85,177,178,1063,1066]. However, the specificity and power of resolution of these agents is still quite limited.

Anatomical Techniques

Light microscopy (including that in the fluorescent spectra), electron microscopy, and nuclear magnetic resonance spectroscopy can be used to study the fine morphology of cell structure. The present discussion will be confined to those techniques that have emerged relatively recently and may not be found in the more general reference books.

Scanning Techniques

Electron probe X-ray analysis and nuclear magnetic resonance spectroscopy can be used to detect local concentrations of selected ions, radioactive tracers, or metabolites within single cells [cf. 134,371,603,896]. Dick et al. [220] describe electron probe analyses in which different concentrations of P, S, Cl, and K were measured in cell nuclei and cytoplasm. The studies were performed on 10-μm freeze-dried sections. A drawback of this technique is that it is restricted to inorganic and elemental analysis. A new technique, using a laser beam to excite within the micro-Raman spectrum, permits spectroscopic identification of organic compounds [1]. However, the specimen must not be highly absorbing at the exciting wavelength.

The fluidity of biomembranes can be measured accurately by electron paramagnetic resonance techniques utilizing fatty acid spin labeling [163]. The label aligns itself with the fatty acid chain of phospholipids in the mem-

Specialized Electrodes Used to Record Simultaneous Intracellular and Extracellular Unit Activity and to Record Potassium Concentration

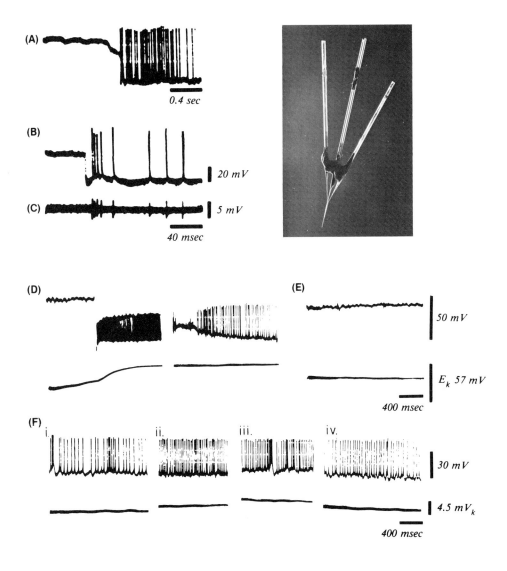

brane bilayer. The magnetic resonance spectrum is affected by its motion, i.e., by the fluidity of its environment. Electron spin resonance (ESR) techniques are not sensitive to the diffusion of radicals in viscous liquids, liquid crystals, polymers, or bilayers [71]. Hence, the technique is useful primarily in low viscosity liquids. This poses severe limitations for biological applications where low viscosity is infeasible. In contrast, nuclear magnetic resonance measurements depending upon paramagnetic relaxation enhancement appear to be feasible over the entire biological viscosity range.

Marking Agents

Several agents have been used to mark neurons. One of the most successful is a foreign protein, horseradish peroxidase (HRP). HRP can be injected intracellularly or administered extracellularly for uptake or binding by the membrane [523,524,861,862,916]. "It is taken up by nerve endings and carried into the axon and the cell body. The exogenous enzyme is incorporated into vesicles in the terminal which deliver it to the agranular endoplasmic reticulum via which it is transported retrogradely up the axon to the Golgi apparatus" [85]. When injected near the dendrites and cell body, there may be anterograde transport as well. Eventually, HRP is deposited in lysosomes and ultimately destroyed. The result of reacting cells containing HRP with H_2O_2 and diaminobenzidine (Figs. 5.21 and 5.23) is an enhanced ability to see certain portions of the cell, much as in the classical Golgi marking technique (Fig. 5.22), or to study transport across the membrane or through the neurofilaments. (Further discussion of intracellular transport is available elsewhere [189-191].)

One can study the fine detail of injected cells by means of electron microscopy (Figs. 5.20 and 5.21). Ferritin and thorotrast may eventually prove better than HRP in these regards. Tritium and ^{14}C-labeled compounds [557,

----

Fig. 5.17. Simultaneous intracellular and extracellular recording from a single unit of the cortex of an awake cat. (A) Penetration of the unit (intracellular recording). (B) An expanded portion of the record in (A). (C) A simultaneous extracellular recording obtained through a second microelectrode with tip adjacent to and recessed about 25 μm from that of the electrode used to record intracellularly. (Woody, unpublished). An example of the compound microelectrode is shown to the right. The central barrels are used for iontophoretic application of pharmacologic agents. The lateral barrels (pulled from theta capillaries) are used for extracellular and intracellular recording, and for recording $[K^+]$ when one side of the capillary has been filled at the tip with Corning 477317 potassium exchanger [1097]. The results (below) show (D) penetration of a cell with voltage record (upper trace) and potassium record (lower trace), (E) withdrawal from the cell at the end of the experiment, (F) a period in between (D) and (E) when extracellular iontophoresis of acetylcholine for 30 sec led to a transient increase in firing rate and in intracellular $[K^+]$: (i) onset of iontophoresis, (ii) 25 sec during iontophoresis, (iii) 10 sec after end of iontophoresis, (iv) 1/2 min after end of iontophoresis. (Woody and Wong [1126]).

Table 5.4. Comparison of Methods Used for Detection of Calcium[a]

	Calcium ion sensitive electrode	Arsenazo dye	Photoprotein (aequorin)
Does technique have to complex calcium in order to work?	No	Yes	Yes
Ratio of selectivity for calcium with respect to magnesium*	10^5	10^2	10^3
Selectivity of calcium versus pH	?	Low (arsenazo is pH sensitive)	High (aequorin unaffected by pH)
Scale of response	Log	Linear	Sigmoid/Log
Speed of response	$\leqslant 3$ sec	$\geqslant 2$ msec	$\leqslant 10$ msec
Sampling of calcium (how detected)	Film at electrode tip	Average of free calcium conc.	Weighted average of free calcium conc.

[a] After Brinley [98].
*May change with different compositions of these agents.

**Comparisons of Membrane Current and Aequorin Current
Versus Membrane Potential**

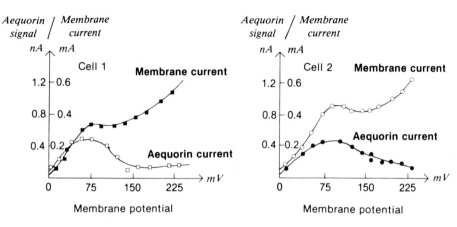

Fig. 5.18. *I-V plots from two fast-burster pacemaker neurons (left and right)
of* Helix. *The upper I-V plots measure membrane current by the usual means;
the lower plots measure light emitted by aequorin, in part as a function of
calcium concentration. (Lux and Heyer [634].)*

**Comparisons of Membrane Current and Aequorin Current
plus g Ca and g K_{Ca} Versus Membrane Potential**

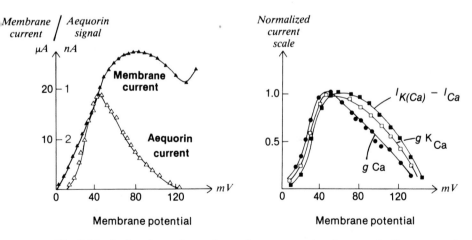

Fig. 5.19. *Left: plots of membrane (upper trace) and aequorin (lower trace)
currents versus voltage in voltage clamped neuron of* Anisodorus nobilis, *a sea
slug. Right: calculations of g Ca and g K_{Ca}, derived from $[Ca]_i$ and the net
hump current $(I_{K(Ca)} - I_{Ca})$. g K_{Ca} is proportional to $[Ca]_i$ and $I_{K(Ca)} = g
K_{Ca} (V_m - E_k)$ when $E_k = -70\ mV$ and V_m = membrane potential. $I_{K(Ca)}$ is
assumed to equal 3 I_{Ca} at 50 mV. (Eckert and Tillotson [266].)*

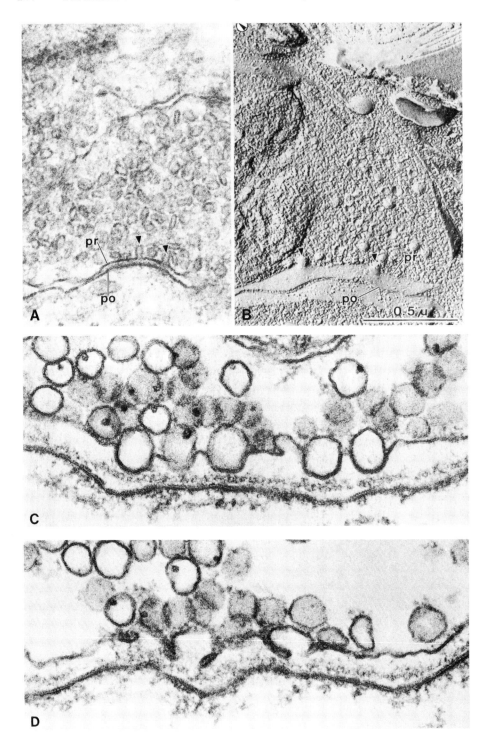

Fig. 5.20.

558,873,874] (Fig. 5.24), dyes such as Procion (Fig. 5.23) with special light emission properties [see 495], or antibodies to selected cellular components [183,370,796] are also used effectively as marking agents. Some of these agents can even be used to study highly active membrane processes. For example, Weinstein et al. [1079] describe a method to monitor the uptake of vesicles containing the fluorescent dye, 6-carboxyfluorescein (6-CF), into the cell membranes. When a detergent such as Triton X-100 is added, the 6-CF is released. Since the vesiculated dye undergoes self-quenching, which prevents most of the fluorescence, it can be distinguished from that which has been released from the vesicles, i.e., by detergent, and fluoresces normally. This dye uptake method purportedly permits morphological studies of the incorporation of vesicles into the membrane. It can also be used to monitor transfer of calcium buffers from vesicles to retinal rods [376].

The above methodologies can also be used for tracing the synaptic connections of neurons. For example, autoradiography can be performed after local instillation of tritiated amino acids such as glycine or leucine, or of other, appropriate, radioactively labeled compounds. Some of these radioactive compounds can be used to selectively mark the terminal endings of the injected cells. Their potential for ultrastructural analysis is only just beginning to be exploited [191].

Another method for tracing synaptic connections involves the use of specialized junctional labelers. Much of our knowledge concerning electrical coupling between cells with specialized junctional membranes (Fig. 5.25) arises from the use of fluorescent dyes which pass through junctional but not through nonjunctional (e.g., ionic conductance) channels. Channels that will pass a dye should be expected to pass electrical current. Presently used junctional labelers include Procion yellow, Dansel *DL*-aspartate, Dansel *L*-glutamate, and Lucifer yellow. Fluorescent polymers of glucose and glycine as well as fluorescent polypeptides have also been used [618,905]. A list of tracer molecules used in probing junctional permeability is provided in Table 5.5.

The incorporation of radioactively labeled compounds [e.g. 1144] can also be studied with respect to the actions of transmitters, messengers, and their catalytic agents such as phosphodiesterases, cholinesterases, etc. Correspondingly, immunocytochemical techniques permit the demonstration of cyclic nucleotides such as cAMP and cGMP within single cells. This can be

---

Fig. 5.20. Electron micrographs of exocytosis. (A-B): At synapses of ventral horn neurons from the spinal cord of the rat: (A) thin-section technique, Pr = presynaptic terminal; sv = synaptic vesicles. (B) freeze-etched technique, Po = postsynaptic membrane, from Streit et al. [969] in [610]. (C-D): at synapses of Torpedo electric organ, from Heuser [610]. The fusion of cytoplasmic vesicles with the plasma membrane (exocytosis) is thought to be catalyzed by calcium. Changes in the resting potential and baseline level of calcium in the presynaptic terminal may modulate the amount of transmitter released. Adaptations at presynaptic loci such as these appear to support behavioral phenomena such as sensitization and habituation.

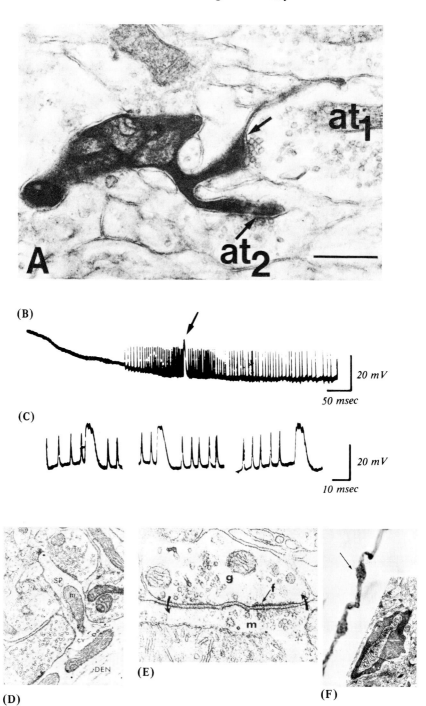

Fig. 5.21.

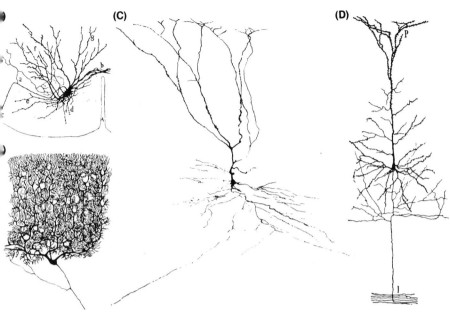

Fig. 5.22. Neurons of different morphologies found by Golgi staining techniques in the CNS. (A). Spinal motoneuron (cat foetus) (B). Cerebellar
Purkinje cell (human) (D). Cortical pyramidal cell (rabbit). (From Ramon y
Cajal [141] in [9]) (C). A cortical pyramidal cell (cat) injected with horseradish peroxidase is shown for comparison. (Pretorius and Woody, unpublished). Increases in the membrane resistance of pyramidal cells of the motor
cortex are thought to support the specificity of conditioned facial movements
in cats [111,1110,1118]. These and complementary increases in the resistance of the motoneurons to which they project also support a latent facilitation of subsequently learned motor behavior [111,651].

Fig. 5.21. (A). Electron micrograph from a horseradish peroxidase (HRP) injected cerebellar Purkinje cell (Ribak et al. [823]). (B,C): recordings made
from cell in (A) showing climbing fiber response (arrow) (From Ribak et al.
[823]). (D). Electron micrograph of a dendritic spine (SP) of a neuron in the
oculomotor nucleus of the cat − m = mitochondrion (From Pappas and
Waxman in [749]). (E). Dendrodendritic synapse of mitral-granule (m,g) cell
junction in olfactory bulb (From Rall et al. [810]). (F). Dendritic bead from
motor cortex of cat. (Ribak and Woody, unpublished). Many neurons have
specialized dendritic branches, called spines, that receive synapses from other
neurons. Rall points out that the resistance of the spine stems is ideally
matched to that of the remainder of the postsynaptic cell, thus optimizing
effects of changes in spine stem resistance on integration of postsynaptic potentials [806]. As yet the function of dendritic beads is unknown, but some
appear to contain mitochondria, as shown in the electron micrograph inserted
at the lower right of (F).

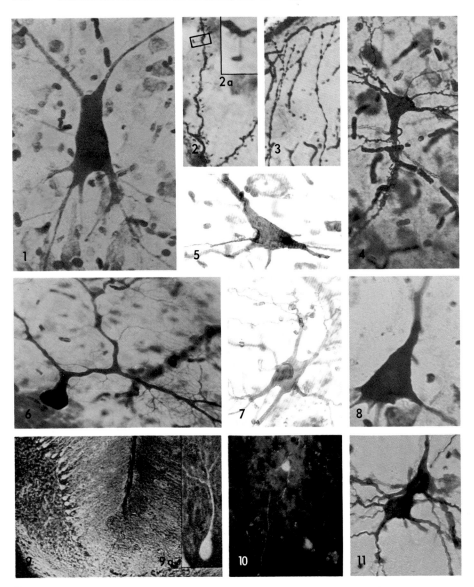

Fig. 5.23.

done by injecting a fluorescent antibody to the nucleotide [747,1070]. The specific location of the bound fluorescent antibody within the tissue is then determined by microspectroscopic techniques. The use of marking agents such as fluorescein or HRP conjugated to specific antibodies for the material to be marked is an exceedingly promising technique [see 959].

Pharmacologic Methods

"Classical" Pharmacologic Techniques
"Classical" pharmacologic techniques employing agents that block transmitter release (Mg^{2+}), alter transmitter degradation (cholinesterase), or block binding at the receptor (α-bungarotoxin) have provided an effective means for studying neuronal plasticity. Such techniques as the blockade of muscarinic cholinergic neurotransmission with atropine and nicotinic transmission with curare have been used for several decades and need not be described here. However, the strategy employed in their application, namely, the use of a specific agonist or antagonist to reveal a more primary cellular effect (e.g., a neurotransmitter action), has now been expanded to probe conductance mechanisms.

Pharmacologic Conductance Probes
Narahashi and others [cf. 159,377,707,716,717,760,825] have used pharmacologic probes to evaluate the contribution of various conductance channels to intracellular events. The effects of these probes on conductance properties of the membrane are summarized in Table 5.6. A more detailed description of the probes for g Na and for sodium gating is provided in Fig. 5.26.

Other, less specific agents are also available. They include Procaine, ouabain, and the barbiturates. According to Hagiwara [377], "Procaine reduces sodium conductance and eliminates sodium dependent action potentials. Calcium permeability is not affected by Procaine at low concentrations. Procaine also suppresses the current of the potassium channel. The net result is enhancement of the calcium dependent action potential. However, when the concentration of Procaine is increased, the calcium channel is affected." Ouabain may act in a somewhat comparable manner by blocking active Na-K

Fig. 5.23 (color insert). Neurons marked with intracellularly injected horseradish peroxidase and Procion yellow (cells 9 and 9a showing axonal uptake of Procion from Llinas [608]; remainder from Woody and colleagues). 1. Betz cell; 2. Dendritic spines with detail (2a); 3. Dendritic beads; 4. Inverted pyramidal cell layer VI; 5, 8, 10, 11. Pyramidal cells layer V; 7. Martinotti cell layer III (all from motor cortex of cat); 6, 9 Purkinje cells of cerebellum (for purposes of comparison. Differences in the morphologies of some pyramidal cells may result from new connections formed early in life rather than in adulthood. These dendrites and their synaptic inputs constitute microcircuits of different labeling through which information processing necessary for some types of learning takes place.

Table 5.5. Fluorescent Molecules Used to Probe Junctional Permeability and
the Permeance of a Few Other Molecules

Molecule	Molecular Weight	Cell-Cell Passage
K^+	39	+
Co^{2+}	59	+
Amino Acids	75-131	+
TEA	130	+
Uridine	244	+
DANS(SO$_3$H)	251	+
Fluorescein	332	+
cAMP	347	+
6-Carboxyfluorescein	376	+
DANS(Glu)OH	380	+
FITC(Gly)OH	464	+
FITC(Glu)OH	536	+
LRB(SO$_3$H)	559	+
DANS(Gly)$_6$OH	593	+
Procion yellow	630	+
DANS(Glu)$_3$OH	640	+
FITC(Glu)$_2$OH	665	+
LRB(Glu)OH	688	+
FITC maltose	725	+
FITC(Gly)$_6$OH	749	+
FITC(Glu)$_3$OH	794	+
LRB(Glu)$_2$OH	817	+
DANS(Leu)$_3$(Glu)$_2$OH	849	+
FITC(Glu-Try-Glu)OH	851	+/-
LRB(Gly)$_6$OH	901	+
LRB(Glu)$_3$OH	946	+/-
LRB(Glu-Tyr-Glu)OH	980	+
FITC(Leu)$_3$(Glu)$_2$OH	1,005	+/-
FITC(Lys)$_5$OH	1,048	+
LRB(Leu)$_3$(Glu)$_2$OH	1,158	+/-
LRB(Lys)$_2$OH	1,200	+
FITC Angiotensin II	1,444	+
FITC(Pro-Pro-Gly)$_5$OH	1,664	+/-
FITC Fibrinopeptide 'A'	1,926	−
FITC Microperoxidase	2,268	−
FITC Insulin 'A' chain	2,921	−
DANS Insulin 'A' chain	3,232	−
FITC Insulin 'B' chain	3,897	−
LRB Insulin 'A' chain	4,158	−
Proteins		−
RNA, DNA		−

(Glu)OH = glutamic acid; (Gly)OH = glycine; (Leu)OH = leucine; (Tyr)OH =
tyrosine; (Lys)OH = lysine; (Try)OH = tryptophan; (Pro)OH = proline; FITC
= fluorescein isothiocianate; DANS = dansyl; LRB = lissainine rhodamine.

Modified from Loewenstein et al. [618], Flagg-Newton et al. [289], and
Bennett [63].

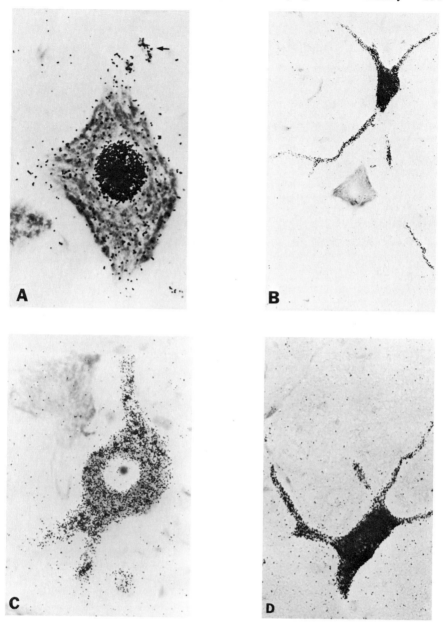

Fig. 5.24. Autoradiography of single neurons injected intracellularly with ^{3}H-adenosine (A), ^{3}H-glycine (B), ^{3}H-fucose (C), and ^{3}H-lysine (D). (From Schubert and Kreutzberg (A) [874]; Kreutzberg (B) [557]; and Kreutzberg et al. (C,D) [558]). The development of improved techniques for marking changes within neuronal membranes may help us visualize the engrams that support learned behavior.

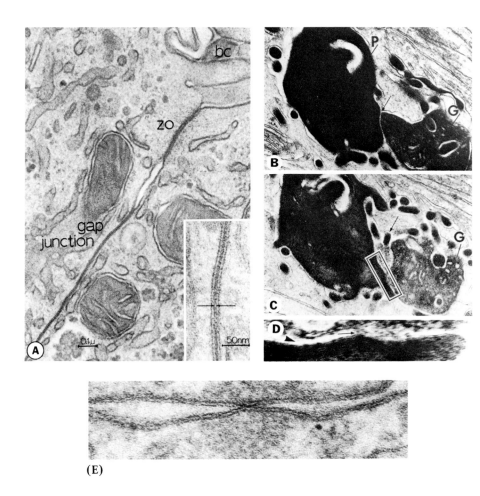

Fig. 5.25. Gap junction between mouse hepatocytes (A), from Goodenough in [63]; junction between Golgi (G) and Purkinje (P) cells in cerebellum – serial sections showing lamina adherens (B) and the junction (C,D), from Ribak et al. [823]; close junction (E) between a retinal cone fine and a rod, from Fain et al. ([63]). Direct communication between nerve cells may be mediated electrically through junctions such as these, the resistance of which is sensitive to calcium and to pH.

exchange and decreasing g K. Cesium is said to block g K because it will not pass through potassium channels. TEA blocks g K$_{TEA}$ at 100 mM concentrations extracellularly. Both TEA and EGTA alter pH. Theophylline is not as good a phosphodiesterase inhibitor as might be thought since it releases calcium. Calcium and cyanide can decrease the input resistance of cells by increasing g K. Meves [662] suggests that zinc and glutaraldehyde may block sodium activation and sodium gating. Barbiturates appear to alter chloride conductance; however, the specificity of this effect has not been clearly demonstrated.

Methods for Analyzing Neuroelectric Data

Improvements in mathematical analysis have led to significant advances in our ability to interpret the data obtained by the above technologies. Among the useful analytic techniques are statistical averaging, time series analysis or filtering, adaptive filtering, linear systems analysis, quantal analysis, and finally simulations of various cellular processes. Detailed descriptions of the statistical considerations underlying these processes are provided in Chapter 7, and their implementation through the use of digital computers has also been recently reviewed [556]. Some of their applications are discussed here by way of introduction.

Table 5.6. Some Commonly Used Pharmacologic Conductance Probes

Channel	Agent
Na$^+$	TTX—*blocks closed Na$^+$ channel* Pancuronium—*blocks open Na$^+$ channel*
Na$^+$ gate	Pronase (internally)—*blocks Na$^+$ inactivation by destroying gate* Grayanotoxin—*freezes gated Na$^+$ channel* Batrachotoxin—*blocks Na$^+$ inactivation* Veratridine—*blocks Na$^+$ inactivation*
K$^+$	4-AP—*blocks closed K$^+$ channel* TEA—*blocks open K$^+$ channel*
Ca^{2+}	Co^{2+}, Mn^{2+}, Mg^{2+}, EDTA, EGTA, Verapamil, Veratridine, D-600—*block* *Ca^{2+} channel or complex (chelate) free Ca^{2+}*
Cl$^-$	Barbiturates, Bicuculline, Picrotoxin, Pentylenetetrazol
(Phosphodiesterase inhibitors)	SQ 20009, SQ 20006, IBMX

Pharmacologic Analysis of the Na Channel

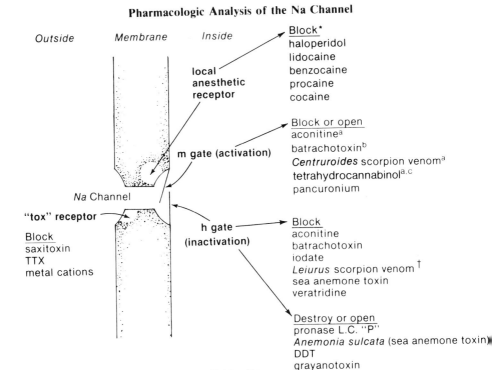

Outside   *Membrane*   *Inside*

local anesthetic receptor

Block*
haloperidol
lidocaine
benzocaine
procaine
cocaine

m gate (activation)

Block or open
aconitine[a]
batrachotoxin[b]
Centruroides scorpion venom[a]
tetrahydrocannabinol[a,c]
pancuronium

Na Channel

"tox" receptor

Block
saxitoxin
TTX
metal cations

h gate (inactivation)

Block
aconitine
batrachotoxin
iodate
Leiurus scorpion venom [†]
sea anemone toxin
veratridine

Destroy or open
pronase L.C. "P"
Anemonia sulcata (sea anemone toxin)
DDT
grayanotoxin

[a]Blocks by shifting membrane potential for Na activation in the hyperpolarizing direction

[b]Opens

[c]Blocks by slowing opening

*The agents must first cross the membrane (in lipid soluble form) before they can act

[†]also markedly affects *g*K

Fig. 5.26. Pharmacologic probes of the sodium channel. The receptor locations are different. The local anesthetic receptor is blocked by drugs applied inside the membrane and not outside. The "tox" receptor is blocked by separate drugs, applied externally. (After Ritchie [825]).

Averaging

How can one distinguish a neural signal from its noisy background activity? Without this background (Fig. 5.27, A), the relevance of the signal may be obvious and its identification a trivial matter. With the noisy background present, both the identification and the establishment of relevance become matters for statistical analysis [582,677,900]. The detection of signals that are time invariant with respect to an initial stimulus and their separation from accompanying background noise can be accomplished by means of averaging techniques. The underlying principle is intuitively simple. It is based on

Analysis of Neuroelectric Signals in Noise

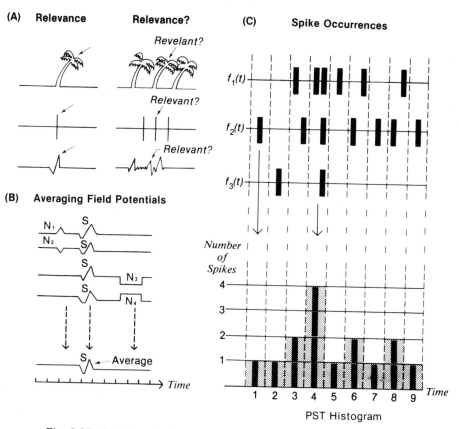

Fig. 5.27. (A) Signal relevance (left) and possible relevance (right) as a function of background noise. (B,C) Averaging of continuous time functions such as field potentials (left) or discrete spike trains (right) can be performed as indicated herein and in Fig. 5.28. In (B), the upper four traces are averaged to remove noise (N) distributed randomly about the baseline and retain the signal (S) evoked by the click stimulus as shown in the single trace below. In (C), three spike trains $f_1(t)$, $f_2(t)$, and $f_3(t)$ are summed to form the histogram shown below. Normalization may be performed by dividing the result by the number of traces sampled, as was done to obtain the average in (B).

the fact that noise is randomly distributed, positively and negatively, about the signal mean. The signal is a *non*randomly occurring event with respect to the initiating stimulus. By averaging repeated measurements taken at the time of signal appearance following stimulus delivery, noise is reduced in proportion to its variance about the nonrandom signal mean. However, even random noise has a variance. This should not be forgotten!

Examples: A group of time functions such as the field potentials and spike trains shown in Fig. 5.27 can be averaged by:

1. Partitioning each function into an orderly series of time slots (t_1, t_2, t_3, etc.).
2. Summing amplitude values of each time function, $f_n(t)$, at each time slot.
3. Dividing the result by the number of time functions (i.e. normalization, as shown in Fig. 5.28).

In each of the above examples, the stimulus is delivered at time t_1. Averaging enhances the time invariant response, i.e., the signal evoked by the stimulus, while reducing random background noise (Fig. 5.28).

The nervous system appears to use averaging as a means of information processing. The "integrative properties" of the nervous system mean just that. Both temporal and spatial summation involve averaging! In the case of spatial summation, the process resembles an *ensemble average*. Consider, for example, the information obtained by flipping one coin many times versus that obtained by flipping many coins one time. The same average probability of flipping a head is obtained in either case, given a statistically stable (stationary and ergodic) process, but by the latter procedure an ensemble average has been determined. The ensemble average is derived mathematically in Table 5.7.

Time Series Analysis–Filtering

Other signals can be detected by filtering. Filters can be constructed that will pass or reject a selected frequency range as shown in Figs. 5.29 and 5.30. A group of time functions can be filtered when the signal information is re-

---

Table 5.7. Derivation of Ensemble Average[a]

i. Let a random variable, X (such as spinning a roulette wheel), assume any of several values: E_i, E_{ii}, ..., E_n (e.g., *1, 2, ... n*).

ii. The probability of occurrence of a value, k, is:

$$P(X = E_k) = \lim_{N \to \infty} \frac{n_k}{N}$$

where n_k = the number of k occurrences per N spins.

iii. There will exist a probability distribution of the sample functions with $P(X = E_k)$ for all ks.

iv. The average height of these sample functions will equal:

$$\frac{E_1 n_1}{N} + \frac{E_2 n_2}{N} + \ldots + \frac{E_m n_m}{N}$$

v. The ensemble average of the sample functions is then:

$$E[X] = \sum_{k=1}^{m} E_k P(X = E_k)$$

---

[a] After Siebert [900].

Step-by-Step Guide to Averaging

(A) Digitization of a waveform

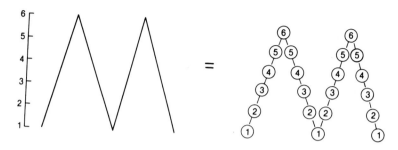

(B) Adding digitized waveforms reduces noise

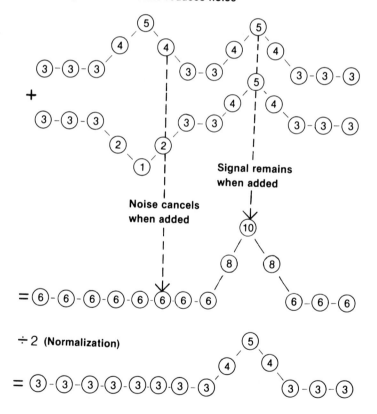

Fig. 5.28. (A) A continuous waveform is digitized by being assigned numeric values at different points in time. (B) Two digitized waveforms are added, numerically, to form the sum shown below. Note how noise, distributed randomly +/- about the signal mean, is reduced upon summation. Normalization is performed by dividing the sum by the number of traces sampled.

stricted to a relatively narrow range of frequency (Fig. 5.29 left), for example, 1-3 Hz delta range EEG activity, $\leqslant$ 30 Hz, fast epileptic spikes, or even repetitive PSPs of a characteristic frequency-amplitude profile.

Some neurons in sensory systems have "tuning curves" similar to those of the electronic filters described above (see Fig. 5.30). Thus, it appears that the neural components of some sensory systems also act as finely tuned filters by which increasingly fine distinctions between incoming stimuli can be discriminated. As will shortly be seen, properties of single elements within a network such as averaging and filtering, when combined with the ability to adapt, lead to some surprising capabilities in the area of information processing—both in automata (Chapter 7) and in nervous systems (Chapter 6).

The mathematics of Fourier series (p. 354) and their transforms (p. 355ff.) define the means for separating waveforms into their characteristic frequency components [200,582,1084], as does engineering theory based on resistance-inductance-capacitance circuitry [200]. Extension of the theory admits:

1. The construction of filters that will pass a selected frequency range through the filter (Fig. 5.29).
2. A means for comparing two separate waveforms with respect to the degree of similarity in their characteristic frequency components (matched filtering—Figs. 7.13 and Lee [582]).
3. An extremely powerful description of transfer function operations within a linear system.

Further details will be described together with other means of signal analysis in Chapter 7.

Simulation

Simulation allows a synthesis of proposed functional relationships (and an examination of their interactions) as an analytic means for studying cellular events. Fitzhugh [287,288] simulated action potential generation many years ago. More recently, Dodge and Cooley [225] have been able to reproduce both graded and all-or-none intracellular events in simulations of single neurons. Another approach [589,1115] has studied the dependence of transfer properties of single neurons on alterations in the efficacy of synaptic transmission and in the integrative properties of the postsynaptic cell. Simulations were made of the effects on rates of neuronal discharge of combined changes in the levels of presynaptic inputs and in the postsynaptic spread of current. Some cellular biophysical operations were simplified to permit iterative processing. The results are shown in Fig. 5.31. The outcome suggests that concurrent pre- and postsynaptic adaptations can change a neuron from a linear modulator of sensory input to an all or none transmitter of a binary, yes or no output deciding whether or not a particular input has been received.

In sum, advances in instrumentational techniques are allowing us increasingly to determine the molecular mechanisms within the cell that control neuronal adaptation. In turn, advances in mathematical techniques are per-

Filtering

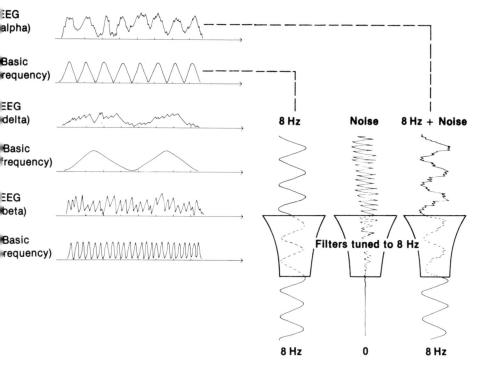

Fig. 5.29. Left: examples of three EEG records with different characteristic underlying frequencies: alpha–8 Hz; delta–2 Hz; beta–16 Hz. Right: filtering retains a selected frequency and rejects unwanted frequencies; left: a 8-Hz signal passes undiminished through a 8-Hz (pass) filter; middle: a 60-Hz signal is reduced by a 8-Hz filter; right: the signal: noise ratio of a 8-Hz EEG signal distorted by 60-Hz noise is improved by passage through a 8-Hz filter.

mitting us to view these mechanisms in the context of information transfer. How these operations tie in with the reflex circuitry, how the operations are specified analytically, and how behavior as complex as "higher function" might be a reasonable extension of these operations are the subjects of the next two chapters.

(continued)

A Comparison of Neuronal (Receptor) Filtering With Electronic Filtering

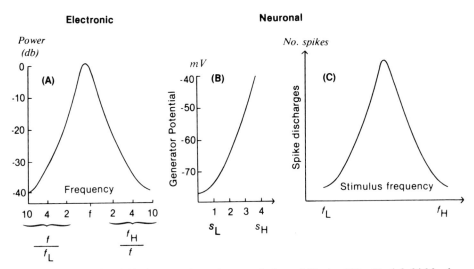

Fig. 5.30. (A) Attenuation characteristics of Krohn-Hite Model 3100 electronic filter. f is the passed frequency. f_H and f_L are the high and low cut-off frequencies, respectively. (B) Low cut-off filtering at the Pacinian corpuscle, a vibration-sensitive somatosensory receptor [693]. S_H and S_L are the high and low stimulus frequencies. A generator potential positive to −60 mV is thought to be required for spike initiation. (C) A "tuning curve" of rate of spike discharge versus frequency of steadily applied tone for a typical auditory receptive neuron of the CNS.

Simulation of Neural Adaptation

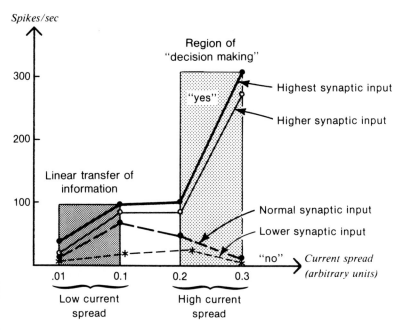

Fig. 5.31. Diagram of effects on rate of unit discharge of changing presynap-tic input and *rate of proximal and distal current spread in the postsynaptic cell. Determined from simulations of changes in threshold versus changes in current spread. Changing threshold was found to be equivalent to changing the presynaptic input. Note graded unit response to graded synaptic inputs in the darkly shaded region, as opposed to "decisional" response in the lightly shaded region. (After Woody et al. [1115].)*

Chapter 6

Reflex Circuitry Supporting Higher Functions

The verbal, grammatical and semantic disorders of speech can ultimately be approached in terms of physiological analysis of disturbance of speech function of increasing degrees of complexity, as can disorders of perception.

(D. Denny-Brown, 1963)

Introduction to Higher Functions

The forms of learning that support higher functions emerge as the sums of properties of neuronal systems at the subcellular, cellular, and network levels. We have already seen how the cellular and subcellular properties influence neural adaptation and thereby the operations of neural networks that support learned behavior. But what of the reflex circuitry? How does the architecture of the reflex circuitry influence memory, learning, and higher function? In engineering, the design of electrical circuitry is important since each design has its own consequences on information processing. Some logic circuits, for example, may be distinguished by whether they operate serially or in parallel. Two all-or-none elements (a and b) placed in series have the logical effect on message transmission of "if *both* a and b are true, then . . .", whereas the same two elements placed in parallel have the effect of "if *either* a or b is true, then . . ." (see Fig. 7.4). Parallel circuits may be more redundant and less than serial circuits, but may also be more resistant to disruption (see Fig. 7.5) and may invite use by multiple, differently labeled lines.

Most people think of a circuit as a specialized network that accomplishes one particular function: a logical *and*, a logical *or*, habituation, etc. This view may be erroneous. Most neural circuits have not one, but multiple functions.*

---

*although some circuits may have one (transfer function, mathematically; see p. 367).

Even highly specialized circuits designed for quite specific biologic applications may be shown to serve multiple functions. For example, a difference detection circuit designed by Horn [425] to support habituation can also transmit the messages necessary to perform secondary responses contingent on stimulus omission. In fact, the number of functions or characteristic actions that pertain to a circuit's operation is constrained by the number of possible inputs and their outcomes as a consequence of the circuit's transfer function(s).

In a recent book*, Hofstadter points out that canons of Bach, drawings of Escher, and mathematics of Euclid and Kantor (taken in the context of Gödel's theorem), have curious and important multiple meanings in which the original can be interpreted to be part of more than one set. So it is with circuit functions. Because of this, it would be improper or at least incomplete to say that one particular circuit does one particular thing. Instead, each basic circuit consisting of nodes and transmittances (p. 369) should be treated in terms of a set of input-output functions. One can then say that a particular circuit has associated with its operation a set of functions (under certain specialized conditions perhaps served by one characteristic transfer operation) and those functions a set of meanings. The set of meanings may be treated as a set of messages in the context of communication theory. Analysis of circuits and their functions may then be done in the manner of Hofstadter by analogy and allegory, *or* descriptively as herein (Chapter 6), *or* mathematically as in Chapter 7.

None of these analytic approaches is entirely satisfactory on its own. However, as we better understand the functions of neural circuits, we begin to see each circuit not in terms of a single output function (e.g., limb flexion) but in terms of its control or transfer function (control of stretch-length, twitch-tension, etc.). Nowhere is this more apparent than in the analysis of the gamma efferent system (cf. Houk [429]). If we apply this observation to our present task (a survey of circuitry relevant to higher functions), we see how misleading the descriptive view of this subject taken of necessity in this chapter must be, and we aspire to a more suitable treatment, at some future date, in the context of the control and systems theories of Chapter 7.

Evaluating the Functions of Reflex Circuits

In neuroscience, the functions of reflex circuits have been evaluated using three different approaches. The first approach has been to correlate disturbances of function (and residual, undisturbed functions) with lesions of the nervous system and, from accumulated evidence, draw reductive inferences concerning the functions of various portions of the neural circuitry. That is

---

*Hofstadter, D. R. *Gödel, Escher, Bach: an Eternal Golden Braid* New York: Vintage Books, 1980.

the main approach taken in this chapter. Our examination is confined to areas of special relevance to memory, learning, and higher functions, and is directed to the argument that even the most complex of human functions can be examined by physiologic means.

A second approach to evaluating the functions of reflex circuits examines the relationships between inputs and outputs through a restricted portion of the nervous system:

(a) by addressing known inputs and examining known outputs in the intact preparation,

(b) by doing so after removing other regions to isolate the local system, and

(c) by removing the region in question and studying it in vitro.

Method a is relatively easy to accomplish with simple, accessible, peripheral systems (e.g., the gamma efferent system) and much harder to accomplish with less accessible, more complex central systems. Method b merges at some point with the first approach described above. Method c assumes that the in vitro preparation is normal, which may not at all be the case.

A third approach is that of constructing a model based on known anatomical and physiologic features of a neural circuit and then studying the response of the model in simulation experiments. However, in the absence of detailed knowledge, it is difficult to construct models with circuits and elements that will correspond exactly with those of the nervous system.

In general, each of the above approaches has proved valuable; but, each has had its limitations as well as its successes. Reductive examination of the brain has led to the identification of different neuranatomical systems such as the thalamus, the hypothalamus, the basal ganglia, the reticular formation, and so forth; however, our understanding of their circuitries and functions remains incomplete. As a result, a detailed analysis herein of a particular neuroanatomical circuit supporting a specific higher function remains infeasible given the present state of knowledge. Even the basic anatomical unit of many regions is still unknown. For example, the reticular formation is not a uniform cellular region but is composed of at least ninety-eight different nuclei [744], each presumably with different functions. On the other hand, the reductive approach to brain function has sometimes led to success. One well know example is the analysis of the visual system. The major pathways between retina and visual cortex are known, and the primary types of processing done by units in these areas have been investigated and will be reviewed later in this chapter.

Analysis of the input-output functions of known circuits (the second approach) has also led to a few analytic breakthroughs. Again, the most conspicuous of these concerns the spinal control of movement, exemplified by the material in Fig. 2.1 and elsewhere. However, in more complex systems such as the cerebellum, even where much of the circuitry has been worked out [255,607], the relationship between circuitry and functions remains obscure, the major revelation in the cerebellum being the curious predisposition of its circuitry to inhibitory regulation.

One conclusion that might be drawn from the outcome of the above approaches is that instead of asking how the circuit architecture influences memory and higher function, the question should be more precisely formulated to ask what is the transfer function of the circuit in question and which labeled lines are affected by the circuit's operations. The ground rules for this approach are described in Chapter 7. Meanwhile, one can obtain useful preliminary information at the descriptive level about possible influences of the circuit architecture on brain functions by considering the evidence summarized in this chapter, brief abstracts of which now follow.

Higher Function

Higher function appears to be a set of functions that has as its commonality an extra level of circuit construction that operates on the level immediately below. Higher function, in man, is characterized by conceptualization. The difference between higher and lower function is quite analogous to the difference between an operation in Fortran language versus machine language in a modern digital computer. There, the same operation may be performed at either a complex or a more basic level of programmed circuit function. The difference in performed operations is that in one case the operation appears to be conceptualized, and can be handled as such in higher level statements.* In the other it does not. An example would be a "greater than" operation programmed by a Fortran statement instead of by subtracting one variable from the other and seeing if the difference is positive. An example of an analogous phenomenon in man might be going through the motions of drinking from an imaginary glass as opposed to actually drinking from a filled glass. A person with a lesion of the dominant parietal cortex might be unable to do the former but be quite able to do the latter.

Conceptualized functions can potentially be linked to other conceptualized functions through conceptual isomorphisms. These linkages or perceptions of isomorphisms may be said to create meaning [cf. Hofstadter]. An alternative view is simply that the circuitry creates the isomorphism and the illusion of meaning. Readily identified higher functions include speech, writing, reading, navigational skills, and the ability to construct and compose. The functions show considerable variability, and it is this diversity that makes them difficult to characterize. They are not static from species to species, nor are they unique to man. Thus, while man has developed language to the level of an art, far surpassing the ability found in apes, apes can nonetheless use syntax constructively [779] (though some say not to create new meanings [1005]) and apes can also measure quantitative differences quite accurately. Maze skills in rats and navigational skills in birds may even surpass comparable skills in man [53,416,1021].

Memory and the Mnemonic Process

Memory appears to be a fundamental property of adaptive components in which information is retained over time. The mnemonic process is more complex, reflecting adaptive components functioning within an organized

---

*See generalization of conditioning to higher level conceptualizations, p. 308.

circuit. The mnemonic process involves the reception, encoding-storage, and decoding-retrieval* of information. Highly faithful functioning of each aspect of the process can lead to the phenomenon of total recall. Disorders of decoding-retrieval may lead to the expressive aphasias or to the apraxias described later in this chapter. Rarely, if ever, can a global disorder of memory or of the mnemonic process be identified. This is because so many functions of the nervous system depend on pure memory that total disruption would lead to total breakdown—perhaps even to unconsciousness or coma. Nowhere is the confusion so apparent between circuit function and *sets* of functions as in consideration of circuits related to "memory function". Sometimes these considerations have even failed to distinguish between aspects of the mnemonic process related to encoding-storage and those related to decoding-retrieval. These issues will be discussed further later.

"Simple" Control Systems

The simpler the control system or the better it is understood, the more its "function" tends to be described in terms of a control *feature,* i.e., a mathematical transfer function as opposed to a particular outcome. Analysis of such features in one of the relatively simpler reflex control systems, the gamma efferent system, has already been mentioned [429]. Another control system is that of recurrent or lateral inhibition (see p. 292). This type of inhibition is found to be widespread throughout the nervous system. Recurrent inhibition appears to provide negative feedback which damps subsequent transmission through the activated nerve channel. This tends to heighten or sharpen contrasts between incoming messages, as can be seen in Figure 6.7. An analogous electrical control mechanism is used to sharpen the sound of many hi-fi systems. The possibly analogous role of negative feedback in theoretical (generalized) control systems is discussed in detail in Chapter 7.

"Complex" Control Systems

The limbic system is more complex. The "BAHHST" portion of the limbic system (see p. 280 and Fig. 6.4) provides a revealing example of how sets of basic circuit functions make up the more complex conceptualized functions that we think of and tend to use descriptively. When one stimulates different portions of the BAHHST system, one elicits the physiologic microeffects noted in Table 6.1. One sees changes in gastric motility, cardiovascular effects, changes in attention, sniffing, etc., *not* the more conceptualized macrofunctions (fighting, fleeing, feeding or mating) described on p. 282. Inspection of Table 6.1 indicates that these physiologic microeffects are in fact the building blocks from which the conceptualized macrofunctions of fighting, fleeing, etc., are composed. Feeding *involves* sniffing, licking, chewing, changes in gastric motility, etc. It would be imprecise to describe the function of the circuits of the BAHHST system in terms of the four

---

*including expression or appropriately directed transmission.

Table 6.1. Effects of Stimulation and Lesion of the Amygdala and Cingulate Cortex

Amygdala	
Stimulation	Lesion (bilateral)
1. *"Visceral changes"*: respiration, cardiovascular, GI motility and secretion, defecation 2. *Autonomic effects*: piloerection, salivation, pupillary changes, micturition 3. *Endocrine hormone release*: gonadotropic hormones, ACTH, ADH 4. *Behavioral changes*: fear, rage, changes in attention 5. *Movements*: *Stereotyped* - sniffing, licking, lip movements, chewing, swallowing *Nonstereotyped* - change in head, eye, neck, jaws	(The same functions are affected by lesion as by stimulation—the direction of change in function may differ, since some frequencies of stimulation may inhibit rather than facilitate transmission through the affected neural network.)

Cingulate Cortex[a]	
Stimulation	Lesion
1. *Visceral changes*: blood pressure, peristalsis, respiration 2. *Autonomic effects*: pupillary dilation, salivation, micturition 3. *Movements*: *Stereotyped* - chewing, licking, swallowing *Nonstereotyped* - general inhibition: head and eyes (opposite) 4. *Behavioral changes*: arrest of sexual reactions, grooming	1. Vivid daydreaming (man) 2. *Some frontal lobe symptoms*: loss of social conscience, perseveration, apathy, reduced anxiety, indifference to pain 3. *Movements*: akinesia, mutism

[a]Note that cingulate and other cortical areas project directly or indirectly to the entorhinal cortex and other parts of the BAHHST system.

macrofunctions. Rather they should be described in terms of *control* of the microeffects that lead to the realization of the many different forms or meanings of the highly conceptualized macrofunctions. This is because the macrofunctions are really composed of different probabilistic sequences of the microeffects listed in Table 6.1. When the circuits are briefly activated by electrical stimulation or circuits supporting the longer sequences are disrupted by lesion, the microfunctions emerge. If the reader will reflect a bit upon this, it may be easier to understand and accept the earlier statements that circuits have multiple functions, that the functions have multiple meanings, and that the meanings may be treated as sets of messages in the context of information and communication theory. What analysis based on those theories will attempt to do is not to find the law for the exact outcome or message produced by a circuit at one particular time, but instead to find a mathematical description of the rules by which possible outcomes can arise. Much the same sort of rules or laws apply to the behavior of gas molecules in a partitioned chamber. In this view, while the macrofunctions represent the isomorphisms or meanings, the microfunctions represent what is really going on.

Hierarchies or Partitioned Levels of Operations
Visual cortex. Information processing in the visual cortex appears to be performed through hierarchical assemblies of cells. At one level, a particular type of image processing predominates; at another, a different (or more complex) type is seen, as described later in this chapter. Similar hierarchies of information processing may be found in the circuits of man-made image recognizers such as those shown later in Figure 7.5.

Unilateral Representation of Speech, Linguistic Conceptualization, and Other Conceptualization. As will be seen, linguistic and other conceptual functions appear to be mediated by the circuitry of one side of the brain. Following review of this topic, the conclusion is drawn that this unilateral representation reflects an extended level of processing arising from a hierarchically organized circuit.

Image Perception
Some evidence indicates that the process of image "perception" is not as complicated as might be thought. That is, while there may be specialized circuits developed for the purpose of recognizing very specialized features of certain images, the perceptual process itself emerges relatively directly from serial and parallel processing of line labeled sensory information. Essentially similar disturbances of body image recognition can arise from dorsal column lesions, i.e., from loss of ascending sensory inputs, as from lesions of the cortical region at which image recognition is said to take place (the parietal lobe). Evidently, the critical organization of message lines on which this type of image recognition is based occurs subcortically.

Tracking
The remarkable ability of neural circuitry to track external events is manifest in the appearance of tropisms, echolalia, and the emergence of a grasp reflex after lesions of certain telencephalic structures. What is remarkable is that these seem to be normal functions of the brain that are performed when the overlying cortical control circuitry is intact but obscured when this control makes their outcome appear more purposive. Detailed examples are provided later in this chapter.

Inertial Processing

Another feature of brain circuitry that appears after lesions is the (normal) tendency of the circuits to promote inertial message processing—the continued processing of the same message to ensure its expression at the output of the network. This property is reflected by the perseveration that appears when overlying control circuits are lost. The inertial operation also hinges on the ability of the circuitry to reject or "neglect" certain inputs in favor of other inputs during the course of normal processing operations.

Other Functions

There are functions that we assume we can perform normally but sometimes, surprisingly, we cannot. For example, Minsky and Papert assume (as do most of us) that image recognizers should be able to compute connectedness between lines and objects. The reader may wish to test his or her ability to compute connectedness between the lines or objects of Fig. 6.6 C. As mentioned above, there are also functions in humans that are thought to be *abnormal,* e.g., the tropisms or aspects of inertial processing such as neglect, but instead appear to be features of *normally* working nerve circuits that are uncovered when other control circuits are absent. This inability to perceive ourselves as we actually are makes accurate discussion of the material within this chapter particularly difficult.

Questions About Higher Functions and Their Underlying Circuitry

In continuing our considerations of higher functions and their underlying circuitry, the major questions that we would ask are:

1. What are the functions of the different regions of the cortex and other brain areas that support conceptually directed behavior?
2. What are the higher functions and how may they best be characterized?
3. Are there any obvious adaptive reflex networks supporting the higher functions?
4. Does it make any difference how the building blocks of adaptation are assembled and the reflexes organized when conceptual functions are served?
5. Should we be concerned with the subtleties of neural circuit design as the key to opening new doors to our knowledge and to our capability to design clever machines?

These are difficult questions, and although it may not be possible to provide completely satisfactory answers, this chapter may provide some information upon which satisfactory answers would have to be based.

Use of Lesions to Study Deranged Function

The anatomical and physiologic organization of neural reflex pathways results in circuits that transform specified inputs into characteristic outputs. It may be possible to make useful characterizations of the circuits involved with higher functions by comparing observations of higher functions in intact circuit systems with observations made after portions of the system have been disrupted. The form and degree of the derangement reveal information about the process that is disrupted as well as the process that remains. Thus, insights into the mnemonic process may be gained by comparing the absent mindedness of senility with simple forgetting, insights into learning by comparing idiocy with dullness, and insights into higher functions by comparing aphasia with slips of the tongue. What is clear from such comparisons is that different parts of the brain preferentially support different functions.

The obvious adaptive reflex networks supporting higher functions include those of the frontal, parietal, temporal, occipital, and limbic lobes. While these regions do not necessarily function uniquely as centers performing operations that no other area can perform, they do function selectively, as regions wherein the organization of the reflex network facilitates specific performance. This is inferred because the same functions are repeatedly (though not invariably) impaired when these regions are damaged. It does, then, make a difference how the building blocks of memory are assembled and how the adaptive reflex pathways are constructed. The different forms of learning and higher function are reflections of these constructions. The question is frequently raised that if a function arises from a circuit, why isn't the function lost when the circuit is disrupted. The answer may be that parallel, redundant circuitry serves the function (and other functions) in a manner resistant to local disruption (see Fig. 7.5).

Investigators have used both artificial and natural lesions to study deranged function experimentally. Though useful, the approach has a few limitations that it would be well to recognize. (1) One cannot directly relate the derangement produced to the aggregate of tissue removed. Different cells within the destroyed tissue may be more or less concerned with the function in question. (2) There may be unrecognized damage to portions of tissue left behind. This damage may arise from vascular insufficiency, toxins, or pressure from posttraumatic edema. (3) Even though a characteristic symptomatology may appear following lesions of an area, the capacity for performing particular functions is rarely confined to one specific neuroanatomical region or center. Cellular operations supporting a given function take place diffusely and redundantly over broad areas of the CNS, the densities of the involved neural elements being high in certain regions and low in others. Disturbances of function produced by circumscribed lesions are correlated with these densities.

The Mnemonic Process and Amnesia

What happens when the mnemonic process is impaired? The answer, of course, depends on the type of impairment. Since the mnemonic process involves the reception, encoding-storage, and decoding-retrieval of information peculiar to a variety of different circuits within the brain several different kinds of memory disturbances can be observed clinically. The most common disturbances of memory are those that occur normally. They include slips of the tongue and simple forgetting. Slips of the tongue, or parapraxis, are thought to reflect simple errors in the memory retrieval process. This may be inferred when the word intended to be spoken as "acrobat" appears as "acroback" (see the appendix to this chapter), or when a concept emerges accurately but in a different form than intended (a Freudian slip). The ability to pronounce the word or articulate the concept correctly later suggests that the defect is in retrieval. The error may lie in picking the correct engrams from storage, or it may reflect a difficulty in transmitting a particular message in an error-free way. Simple forgetting may involve either a disturbance of retrieval (e.g., from distraction or other interference) or the physical decay of engrams. The former represents a "normal" impairment of the mnemonic process; the latter a frank loss of memory.

Categorical forgetting of names, places, and events (*categorical amnesia*) is a rare occurrence, and usually has a hysterical overlay. Forgetting of the "lost weekend" or gap type is more typical, particularly after having alcohol or anesthetics. That type of disturbance is called a *posttraumatic amnesia*, being similar in form to that found after concussion and other types of acute brain injury. The defect may involve disturbances in encoding-storage as well as in retrieval. With that type of memory disturbance, there has usually been a specific period of time during which storage was impaired. Retrieval may have been affected during the same period. Subsequently, retrieval of the defectively stored information is difficult or impossible. The line labeling of the stored information may be so uncharacteristic as to preclude access by output mechanisms that depend on more characteristically labeled (coded) operations (cf. Chap. 3 and Fig. 7.5). Or the input may not have been stored at all. The ability to retrieve part of this information under hypnosis or with prompting [818,947,951] suggests, however, that at least some is usually stored. Thus, residual islands of memory may persist in relation to some dramatic event that occurred at the time of the trauma. The intensity and salience of such events seem to facilitate their retention.

A more common type of forgetting is absent-mindedness. It can either be mild (normal) or severe (abnormal) in degree. The normal or mild type of absent mindedness may arise from overstocking adaptive elements with multiple information, as in professors. Normal absent-mindedness then represents an interference effect rather than a true memory loss. Severe absent-mindedness appears to arise from loss of cellular elements, as in senility. The senile type of absent-mindedness then represents a true loss of memory. It is sometimes combined with inattentiveness.

The most severe disturbances of memory are those that occur abnormally. They include posttraumatic amnesia, Korsakoff's syndrome, and disturbances of a wide variety of higher functions that depend on memory. Thus, when speech, writing, fine motor control, or perception of visual, auditory, or tactile sensation is disrupted, so may be memories on which these functions depend. Physiologically, the functions and the memories are intertwined. In considering disorders of higher function and memory, it should be kept in mind that remembering requires a perceptual operation involving both retrieval and transmission of previously stored information. Thus, disorders of the mnemonic process are likely to involve disorders of perception as well as disorders of recollection.

Korsakoff's Syndrome

Korsakoff's syndrome is a phenomenon involving impaired recollection of recent events that occurs in chronic alcoholics with thiamine nutritional deficiency. People with Korsakoff's syndrome have trouble recalling the date, what they had for breakfast, where they were the previous day, and the like. The defect is not confined to one class of events or experiences. Careful examination usually discloses additional problems with recollection of names, places, and events from the remote past. Interestingly, events from the immediate past can be recalled perfectly (e.g., a telephone number just looked up or the Wechsler-Bellevue Digit Span). Thus, recent and remote recall are impaired, while immediate recall is generally intact.

What circuits in the brain support the functions impaired in Korsakoff's syndrome? For many years, the hippocampus was viewed as the center of memory function because this region of the brain was thought to be selectively impaired in people with this syndrome. Also, surgical removal of portions of the temporal lobes, including the hippocampal regions [see 762, 878], bilaterally, frequently produced much the same symptomatology.* Nonetheless, viewing the hippocampus as the center of memory function is problematic for two reasons. First, lesions anywhere along Papez' circuit (Fig. 6.1) and the periventricular areas can be correlated with the appearance of Korsakoff's syndrome. Second, Korsakoff's syndrome may involve a disorder of cognitive-spatial mapping as opposed to a disorder of memory per se.

Korsakoff's syndrome occurs not only in humans with lesions of the hippocampal region, but also in those with lesions of the fornix, mammillary bodies, mammillothalamic tract, thalamus (especially anterior MD region), cingulate gyrus, cingulum, third ventricle (e.g., colloid cyst), and the periventricular gray matter [1045,1102]. More problematically, bilateral lesions of any of these structures, including the hippocampus, can occur without resulting in Korsakoff's syndrome [1102].

---

*For further partitioning see Squire and Moore [948] for a description of the DM thalamus syndrome, Milner [669,671] and Corsi [185] for the unilateral hippocampal syndrome, and Mishkin [674] for the amygdala-fornix-hippocampal syndrome.

Papez' Circuit

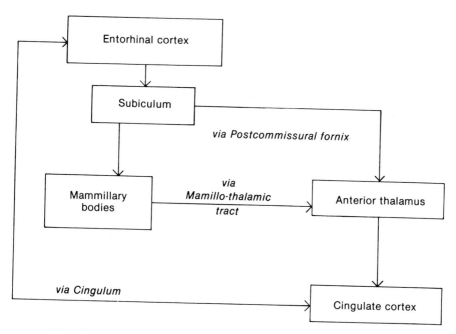

Fig. 6.1. Diagram of Papez' circuit.

Although impairment of "recent" recall appears to be the primary disturbance in Korsakoff's syndrome, the defect in recall is interspersed throughout the time continuum, simply being more evident for recent than for remote events.* Defects in the perception of time or of temporally based events occasionally appear, but Talland has shown that these are not basic to the disorder [986]. Confabulation (fibbing, or the insertion of erroneous verbal material into a conversation) is frequently a concomitant symptom. It is felt that confabulation is "not a manifestation of a desire to evade, but rather an attempt to impose order on speech by relating to the examiner whatever memories can be mustered" [985]. Although patients frequently lack awareness of or insight into their defective recall, their other cognitive functions are generally spared. Higher abilities, such as the ability to calculate or play chess, are preserved.

Detailed psychological testing reveals other defects such as impaired ability to solve maze puzzles that depend on cognitive mapping for solution (e.g., always choose the door 135 degrees to the right of the last successful door), and impaired ability to complete Wechsler-Bellevue Picture Arrangement Tests (e.g., ability to detect a car moving past a house in four pictures).

*With discrete lesions of the hippocampus or of the MD thalamus, the impairment of remote recall is less, being limited to the period surrounding the time the lesion was sustained and thereafter [947,948,950]. Nonetheless, retrograde defects extending one or two years before the time of the lesion are found even here.

Psychological testing also reveals some surprisingly preserved abilities in Korsakoff patients: (1) the ability to learn conditioned reflexes, although with faster rates of extinction; (2) the ability to recollect later, without further training, things that could not be recollected earlier; (3) the ability to remember speech, intelligence, and habits (e.g., toothbrushing); and (4) the ability to identify accurately all portions of the Poppelreuter Figure Test (see Fig. 6.2). In addition, defective recall can be improved by prompting or presenting multiple choices, one of which is the "unremembered" item.

Lesions in animals other than man, when restricted to the hippocampus so as not to produce the Kluver-Bucy syndrome (p. 283), produce a defect in cognitive-spatial mapping. They do not produce a global amnesia. Nor do they impair acquisition or retention of many types of conditioned responses. In the cat, for example, Grastyan [354] and Hunt and Diamond [443] found that bilateral hippocampal lesions had no effects on the acquisition of a conditioned response [cited in 462]. A thorough review of this literature has been provided by O'Keefe and Nadel [735].

Poppelreuter Figure

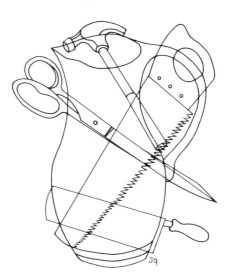

Fig. 6.2. The Poppelreuter test with superimposed figures of a scissors, hammer, cleaver, saw, and pitcher. With certain cortical derangements, only some portions of the figure may be recognized. "The patient with a right parietal lesion, for example, recognizes the saw, the cleaver, and perhaps the pitcher, but is unaware of the hammer and scissors until the diagram is inverted and objects previously in the left field appear on the right" [615]. (After Poppelreuter [775] in Locke [615].)

Penfield, Milner, Scoville, and "Loss of Memory"

The strongest support for the view, now believed to be erroneous, that the hippocampus is the seat of memory comes from surgical observations in humans. In 1958, Penfield and Milner gave the following interpretation to the results of human hippocampectomy: "The man who has lost the bilateral hippocampal mechanisms cannot form a new record of his current experience." They also maintained that "memory for the distant past is not lost" [762].

This interpretation is not entirely consistent with their data. After the operation, one patient learned that Eisenhower was President, although he believed that Dempsey was still the heavyweight champion. Two hours after supper, he could still remember most of what he had eaten. Thus, these patients could form *some* records of their current experience. Also, the recollection of *some* events from the distant past was impaired. (As noted earlier, recall of remote events may be less impaired in those with restricted hippocampal or thalamic lesions than in those with Korsakoff's syndrome induced by thiamine deficiency [947,948,950]. However, some retrograde impairment is found regardless of etiology.)

One of Penfield's patients believed that his memory had deteriorated because of the increasing frequency of his seizures. In fact, most of the patients had had surgery because of severe epilepsy, and many had also had prolonged series of electric shock treatments. Since both epilepsy and electric shock can affect memory, it is possible that these effects and those of hippocampectomy were at times confused.

The studies did demonstrate that the hippocampectomized patients achieved lower than average scores on the McGill Picture Assembly Series and the Wechsler Picture Arrangement Subtest, both of which require the comprehension of abstract spatial relationships between different pictorial material. Their impaired performance on these tests provided the first indication that the underlying problem might be perceptual rather than mnemonic and involve impairment of the ability to perform certain kinds of cognitive spatial mapping.

Talland and Disturbed Perception

In 1965, after a lengthy series of psychological studies conducted in chronic alcoholic Korsakoff patients, Talland [990] concluded that their primary defect was in recall of information rather than in storage or encoding, and that the defect might be perceptual rather than strictly mnemonic. He also showed that the disturbance in recall could not be attributed to interference by new sensory impressions. He further established that there was no corresponding loss of attention, concentration, or reasoning ability for previously acquired skills in these patients [987]. The more significant results of the tests that led to these conclusions are summarized in his book, *Deranged Memory* [990]. Talland's findings can be summarized as follows.

The Korsakoff patients that Talland studied all knew their own name. They had memories of their premorbid life; however, some recollections were poorer in quality and content than normal. Although they were fairly well oriented in time, they had usually lost count of the years. They condensed long spans of time and tended to telescope repeated occurrences of similar events into one or two occasions. Testing of immediate memory span did not show a deficit; however, if the material was unfamiliar, perceived as "meaningless", or involved the transposition from one sense modality to another, the Korsakoff patients' immediate recall was abnormally low. Their rate of forgetting or inability to recall was steeper than normal for all types of material. (Note that much the same observations apply to their abilities in the area of conditioning [315,605], with most patients showing normal acquisition of conditioned reflexes, but extinguishing very rapidly.)

Some of the Korsakoff patients at times showed genuine concern about their forgetfulness; others, when asked how it happened that they had forgotten simple things, pleaded lack of interest or too deep involvement in other concerns. As far as attention was concerned, in the sense of sticking to a task, Korsakoff patients could attend to repetitive jobs as well as anybody. They could listen to and follow instructions and were especially impervious to distraction by noise or incidents occurring in their surroundings. However, in tasks demanding divided attention, they performed poorly [988]. When their attention had to be constantly shifted, as when they listened to a story, they soon lost the thread and made no attempt to pick it up again.

Impairment of performance on tests of perception and concept formation was greatest when the subject was required to alter his set or maintain more than a single set at a time, to scan a range, to prepare figures, or to change criteria of classification. There were also deficiencies in integration of sequential information with failure to resume uncompleted tasks. In tests of reproducing continua at intervals of time ranging from 2 to 30 sec, the Korsakoff patients showed somewhat greater inaccuracies than did control groups [986]. There was, however, no consistent tendency toward over- or underestimation of time. They were fairly accurate in assessing the time spent in an interviewing or experimental session (30-90 min). Rates of motor activity and reaction time also did not appear to be disturbed.

Talland's observations confirmed that some new learning could take place despite other disabilities. Korsakoff patients were able to establish new associations as long as they were simple and were presented in small doses. On the basis of these and other results, Talland concluded that neither decay, retroactive interference, nor inhibition [989] could account in any major way for the deranged functions seen in Korsakoff patients, and that the defect was not in memory but rather in perceptual processes involved with recall. Nonetheless, the view that Korsakoff's syndrome represented a primary disorder of memory tended to persist. For example, in 1971, Victor and colleagues stated, "Korsakoff's psychosis is characterized by ... loss of past memories, invariably coupled with inability to form new memories or to learn" [1045].

O'Keefe and Nadel and Disorders of Cognitive Mapping

O'Keefe and Nadel [699,735] have now advanced the hypothesis that "the hippocampus subserves the function of a cognitive mapping system." The cognitive mapping involves establishment of a framework within which spatial relationships can be developed and maintained. Although they hold that an absolute rather than a relational perceptual construct of space is involved, they view the Korsakoff defect primarily as perceptual or constructional rather than mnemonic.

Evidence by Olton and colleagues [745,746] purports to refute the cognitive mapping hypothesis on the following basis. Animals are trained to perform two types of tasks: One (said to involve "working memory") requires evolving learning with both remembering and forgetting necessary for correct performance. The other (said to involve "reference memory") does not require knowledge of the previous choice for proper solution and permits only one strategy to be learned, ever more thoroughly, for success. The former type of learning is selectively impaired after hippocampal lesions irrespective of whether further experimental context, designed to test spatial mapping, is employed or not.

The outcome of these experiments does not necessarily refute the hypothesis that the hippocampus is involved in cognitive-spatial mapping but instead may simply corroborate Linskii's observation that extinction is more rapid in those with Korsakoff's syndrome than in normals [605]. Rapid extinction could explain selective loss of the evolving task since there would never be time to learn it well (the task would be changed and savings would vanish too rapidly). With the fixed strategy, even reduced learning savings could build up over time and facilitate the task's solution.

Stable versus Dynamic Memory Storage

Memory storage involving the encoding of engrams via adaptive neural changes may be characterized as either stable or dynamic. It is retrieval of the stable type of stored information that appears to be impaired in the Korsakoff defect. The implication is that the perceptual process used for cognitive-spatial mapping is also needed for retrieval of much stably stored information. The dynamic, short-term memory of the telephone number recall type is spared. Stable storage may be expected to involve durable molecular changes that persistently influence neural transmission or integration. Memories that survive anesthesia and anoxia provide evidence for such stable storage, since they must be encoded in some chemical structural change that persists despite the lack of sustained neural activity. In contrast, short-term memories may be stored dynamically as patterns of neural activity cycling about closed neural loops.

When associations of stimuli lead to adaptive changes in neural elements, both dynamic and stable engrams will be formed. Recollection will provide a further source of associative stimuli, which will lead to further adaptations. The stable engrams will be built up, over time, in a pyramidal cascade. The older and more frequently used associations (e.g., mother, food) will have the greater numbers of corresponding, often redundant, engrams represented diffusely through the nervous system. Recent or unique associations will have fewer engrams. The numeric differences in representation of "old" and "new" memories may, in part, account for the temporally graded retrograde defects reported with Korsakoff's syndrome [947-951]. In addition, engrams derived from recollection and formed after the onset of the disorder in stable engram retrieval will be subject to progressive error or distortion.

Given a disorder of cognitive-spatial mapping needed for stable engram retrieval: the greatest apparent functional derangement will then be in recalling recent information represented by fewer and more distorted engrams. This is precisely the symptomatology seen in the Korsakoff patient.

Mnemonic Features Revealed by Electrical Stimulation of the Brain

Electrical stimulation of the human brain provides direct insights into the mnemonic process by evoking what appear to be memories. In doing so the interdependence of memory and perception is again revealed. Repetitive stimulation at a single locus sometimes evokes identical "engrammatic" responses, but more often it evokes perceptually related responses (Figure 6.3). The relationships between responses are closer the more closely they are evoked in time or sequence and the nearer the loci of brain stimulated, though with occasional exceptions (Fig. 6.3).

The effects of brain stimulation suggest that:

1. Commonly line labeled pathways, such as those shown in Fig. 7.22, extend broadly over the space of the brain. This, rather than similarity between neural elements, may give rise to hypotheses of equipotentiality such as that of Lashley [53,578-580].

2. Functionally related (commonly line labeled) neural elements tend to be located close together rather than far apart. One can think of function in terms of a probability density of commonly labeled elements distributed over the space of the brain. Where their density is high, stimulation is more likely to evoke that function than another. However, activation of a single pathway can sometimes result in activation of a disproportionately large number of connected neural elements.

3. Responses are probabilistic rather than fixed processes. They evolve with time, further adaptation, and changes in behavioral state and background activity. Therefore, if one stimulates the same place the same way but at a different time, one may not get the same effect, although the probability of doing so is likely to be higher than if different locations are stimulated.

4. The fact that memories, sensory events, and motor responses are easily (and often repeatedly) elicited by stimulating the brain with brief electrical

Sequential Responses to Repeated Electrical Stimulation

5   Patient did not reply
5   "Something"
5   Patient did not reply
5   "Something"
5   "Peoples voices talking" (could not tell what they were
    saying, seemed to be far away)
5   "Now I hear them" (a little like in a dream)
5   "People's voices" Relatives, my mother (when asked if
    it was over, he said "I do not know")
5   "I am trying"
    Later after electrode removed. "It seemed as if my niece
    and nephew were visiting. My mother was talking to them.
    I could not see them clearly or hear them clearly"

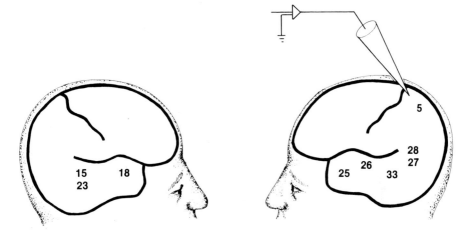

15	Singing	26	Hear talking, murmuring or something
15	White Xmas	25	Talking or murmuring
15	White Xmas	27	Heard the voices
18	White Xmas	28	I hear something A man buzzing or murmuring
23	Singing	27	A man talking
		33	Man talking

Fig. 6.3. Sequential responses to repeated stimulation of the numbered loci [761].

pulses and that such stimulation can be successfully applied to many different brain regions (Fig. 6.3) suggests that the underlying circuitry is represented diffusely as in a parallel processor. Since successful (and repeatable) transmissions are frequently obtained from introducing one or two stimulus pulses, it appears that relatively uncomplicated pulse codes may suffice to transmit meaningful messages along the nerve channels within these cortical areas. At the channels stimulated, the coded representation of complex information may not even be as elaborate a temporal sequence as that found in Morse telegraphic code, but may instead be a spatially referenced code which is converted downstream to a more lengthy temporal sequence.

Interconnected Adaptive Networks of Functional Significance

The evidence presented thus far indicates that there is no single memory center, but, instead, that memory function is parceled out along complex reflex pathways and is irrevocably wedded to the functions supported by those pathways. In general, different sets of neural networks support many different functions arising, as said earlier, from local circuit microeffects. As examples, we shall consider the functions of those networks comprising the limbic, frontal, temporal, occipital, and parietal cortex. The descriptions of these systems that follow are oversimplified for the sake of brevity.

The Limbic System

The limbic lobes form the medial borders of each cortical hemisphere and consist of the subcallosal, cingulate, and parahippocampal gyri, as well as the hippocampal formation and dentate gyri [1026]. The term limbic system is anatomically and physiologically imprecise since it includes not only the limbic lobes but also "associated" subcortical structures, which vary according to who is defining what constitutes a key association. The term is nonetheless of some use since two primitive, anatomically distinct yet occasionally overlapping circuits can indeed be identified within these regions of the brain. The first shall be called the BAHHST system (for applied mnemonic purposes); the other is Papez' circuit. The BAHHST system seems to be particularly involved in visceral-emotional function; Papez' circuit is concerned with cognitive spatial mapping. Both functions are interdependent, and both depend on memory for their operation.

Anatomy of Limbic Circuits
The BAHHST system is composed of:

1. Basolateral amygdala
2. Hippocampus (and entorhinal cortex)
3. Hypothalamus
4. Septal area
5. Thalamus (MD—mediodorsal)

Specific connecting pathways (e.g., ventral amygdalo-fugal, precommissural fornix) and substructures (e.g., hypothalamic nuclei) are shown in Fig. 6.4.
    Papez' circuit consists of:

1. Entorhinal cortex
2. Subiculum
3. Fornix
4. Mammillary bodies

The Bahhst System

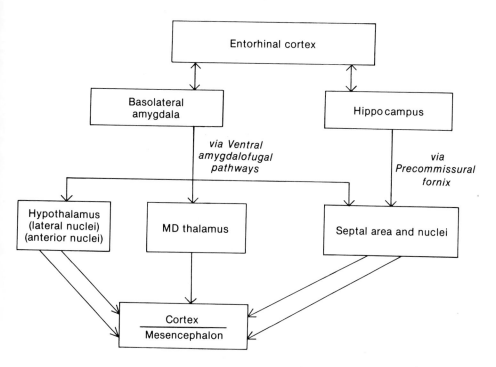

Fig. 6.4. Diagram of the BAHHST system.

5. Mammillothalamic tract
6. Anterior thalamus
7. Cingulate cortex
8. Cingulum
9. Entorhinal cortex

as shown in Fig. 6.1.

Systems that are functionally important may be expected to have extensive inputs and outputs. The extensive inputs and outputs of both Papez' circuit and the BAHHST system are as follows. First, the thalamus, septal areas, and cingulate cortex project to essentially the entire cortex. Second, the septal areas and hypothalamus project to (and probably receive projections from) the reticular formation and adjacent regions of the mesencephalon via the (1) medial forebrain bundle, (2) mammillotegmental tract, and (3) stria medullaris and habenulointerpeduncular tract. Third, all areas of the cortex project to the basolateral amygdala and to the entorhinal cortex, most of the projections being polysynaptic.

Since these structures are quite old phylogenetically, it is likely that the functions mediated by the BAHHST system and Papez' circuit are primitive and basic to the survival of the organism. A primordial hippocampus is recognized in cyclostomes, and a more distinct structure appears in selachians, ganoids, and teleosts. A more circumscribed archipallial area, with fiber connections comparable to those found in higher forms, occurs in amphibians, with differentiation in some reptiles into pars dorsalis and pars dorsomedialis. The pars dorsalis is analogous to Ammon's horn [27] and is thought to subserve some function other than olfaction such as integration and correlation of higher nervous processes. The pars dorsomedialis is thought to be more directly related to olfaction. Further discussion can be found in refs. 27 and 197.

Functional Correlates of the BAHHST System

What are the functions supported by the BAHHST system? The effects of stimulation and lesion of the amygdala and the cingulate cortex* shown in Table 6.1 provide some clues. As mentioned earlier these microeffects form the building blocks of which the macrofunctions of the BAHHST system are comprised. The principal functions macrofunctions of this system appear to be

1. Fighting
2. Fleeing
3. Feeding
4. Mating

Functional Correlates of Papez' Circuit

The functional correlates of Papez' circuit are the functions that are impaired in Korsakoff's syndrome. In effect, Papez' circuit appears to support cognitive-spatial mapping and the retrieval of related, permanently stored information. The BAHHST system and Papez' circuit overlap anatomically as well as functionally.[†] Fighting, fleeing, feeding, and mating are all done in the context of some kind of cognitive-spatial map. The anatomical overlap supports these necessary interactions.

The Temporal Lobes

The temporal lobes support higher functions that also depend on memory but differ somewhat from those supported by the BAHHST system and Papez' circuit. The temporal lobes receive auditory inputs to Heschl's gyrus (Fig. 6.8) from the cochlea via subcortical relay nuclei, but, as shall shortly be seen, simple auditory reception is not the sole or even necessarily the principal function of this region of the cortex. The limbic system overlaps portions

---

*Since the cingulate gyrus and other cortical areas project either directly or indirectly to the entorhinal cortex and thence to the hippocampus and other parts of the BAHHST system, it is not surprising that the effects in Table 6.1 are representative of those found from stimulation and lesion of all portions of the BAHHST system. (Note that stimulation can inhibit as well as excite.)

[†] Recently, it has been shown that ablation of amygdala and hippocampus together impairs learning of visual recognition tasks more than lesions of hippocampus alone [674].

of the temporal lobes both anatomically and functionally [1026]. This overlap is doubtless responsible for components of the syndrome seen by Kluver and Bucy in Rhesus monkeys following ablation of the temporal lobes bilaterally [527,528]. The syndrome includes (1) hypersexuality, (2) various changes in emotional behavior, (3) rage, and (4) changes in dietary habits. Leaving aside features attributable to destruction of portions of the limbic system mentioned above, the Kluver-Bucy syndrome of intrinsic temporal lobe dysfunction consists of the following manifestations:

1. *Visual agnosia*—the animals exhibited no gross defects in their ability to discriminate visually, but appeared to have lost the ability to recognize and detect the meaning of animate and inanimate objects on the basis of visual criteria alone.
2. *Oral tendencies*—the animals tended to examine all objects by mouth and used their teeth rather than their hands to grasp initially.
3. *Hypermetamorphosis*—there was a tendency to notice and attend to every unusual object and to examine every object in sight (note the obvious relationship to visual agnosia).
4. *Changes in emotional behavior and dietary habits*—the animals were placid and did not respond emotionally to many situations that would normally elicit an emotional response. For example, the monkeys would approach live snakes as though they had lost their capacity for fear or anger. After this type of surgery, monkeys that were normally vegetarians would eat meat.

These changes occurred only after bilateral ablation. Humans with unilateral, nondominant temporal lobe resections do tend to have deficits in facial recognition and other image mediated learning, while patients with dominant temporal lobe resection have associated disorders of linguistic based learning [185,669,671]. Some of the defects ascribed to dominant hippocampal function may result from damage to surrounding temporal-parietal areas or to fibers en passage. A quadrantanopsic visual defect can result from unilateral interruption of Meyer's loop in man and in animals that have similar visual pathways within the temporal lobe. In man, symptomatologies consisting of deranged linguistic ability or impairment of other "higher" skills can also occur after unilateral lesions of the dominant temporal hemisphere. These and other aspects of temporal lobe function related to linguistics, communication, and perception are discussed on p. 295 ff., and it is these complex functions that are thought to be the principal higher functions of the temporal lobes in man.

The Occipital Lobes

The occipital lobes receive visual input from the retina via the lateral geniculate bodies. This system is interesting because the types of primary processing of visual information that it performs have been extensively investigated. At the retina, photons of light are detected by the 10^7 cones and 10^8 rods therein. Next, the retinal ganglion cells transmit processed messages from the retina to relay neurons in the lateral geniculate bodies. As Eccles notes:

> The retinal ganglion cells . . . respond particularly to spatial and temporal changes of luminosity of the retinal image by two neuronal subsystems signalling brightness and darkness, respectively. One type of ganglion cell is excited by a spot of light applied to the retina over it and is inhibited by light on the surrounding retina. The other type gives the reverse response, inhibition by light shone into the centre and excitation by the surround. The combined responses . . . result in a contoured abstraction of the retinal image . . . what the eye tells the brain is an abstraction of brightness and colour contrasts. [776]

Further processing of visual information takes place at the visual cortex, where three processing levels of increasing complexity are recognized. The first (simple cells) is observed in the striate cortex in area 17–the primary visual cortex. Here, "a bright line in the visual field is coded as a linear arrangement of excited neurons that project onto the stellate cells in lamina IV . . . These neurones . . . respond to a bright line in the retinal image and are selective to the orientation of this line. Moving bright lines are particularly effective" [776].

The second level of processing (complex and hypercomplex cells) is observed in areas 18 and 19 as well as in area 17. Here, neurons detect length, thickness, orientation, and intersections of bright and dark lines.

The third level of processing is observed in cells receptive to the output of neurons of the visual cortex, e.g., in cells of the inferotemporal cortex (areas 20, 21) of the monkey. Those cells have the property of feature detectors in that they recognize specific features of visual inputs.

> Neurones may be fired by rectangles in the visual field and not by discs, or by stars and not by circles . . . it can be envisaged that this specific response to geometrical forms, such as squares, rectangles, triangles, stars, is dependent on the ordered projection onto those feature-detection neurones from complex and hypercomplex neurones sensitive to bright or dark lines or edges of a particular orientation and length and meeting at particular angles . . . The feature detection of a triangle would be the property of a neurone receiving inputs from neurones in the extra-striate visual cortex that have angles and orientations for composing the triangle. [776]

This hierarchically organized form of information processing is characteristic not only of the visual system but also of other sensory systems. It reflects an aspect of circuit design that may be of considerable significance to complex forms of information processing that lead to the generation of "higher" functions (see Figs. 6.9 and 7.5).

The Frontal Lobes

The frontal lobes support a variety of motor functions, and, since they are large, the types of defects found after either unilateral or bilateral damage depend very much on the locus and extent of the injury. Gross defects of motor function range from impairment of fine movements and diminished skeletal motor control to disturbances of gait, eye movement, blinking, and speech, and even to paralysis itself. As might be expected, electrical stimulation of the frontal lobes evokes a variety of movements (see [206] for a detailed discussion). Maps of the somatotopic representation of various motor functions can be drawn on the basis of the type of movement evoked by the lowest stimulus currents applied to a particular cortical region. The more discrete the stimulus, the more apparent it becomes that neurons of a variety of motor projections are scattered throughout these regions. While the greatest densities consist of neuronal aggregates with motor projections corresponding to the somatotopic maps, neurons of quite different motor projection are interspersed immediately adjacently. Surprisingly, in view of the commonly accepted somatotopy, most single neurons are found to have multiple motor projections [1110].

Complex, memory-dependent functions arise from the frontal lobes just as they do from other regions of the cortex. No better description of these complex functions of the frontal lobes has appeared than that by Denny-Brown [206], portions of which are abstracted here:

> The frontal lobes and prefrontal areas are involved in a broad variety of complex functions including reactions of expectancy or orientation, mnemonic functions such as recollecting where food was placed (in dogs [418]), and the release of grasping automatisms. Autonomic, visceral, and emotional disturbances such as those listed in Table 6.1 frequently accompany lesions of portions of the frontal lobes adjacent (and sometimes projecting) to the limbic regions.

Still more subtle behavioral changes can be found after frontal lesions. These include perseveration, the inability to shift response to meet changing environmental situations; forgetfulness involving absent-mindedness and impaired attention; indifference to neurosis and lack of concern for the feelings of others; sexual impropriety; loss of sense of responsibility; and apathy. In addition, Bianchi [76] has described defects in perceptive power, memory for recent and long-term acquisitions, associative power, and emotional and sentimental manifestations, as well as incoherent conduct. In monkeys, Hitsig [418,419] noted a loss of habits that had been recently acquired. After frontal lesions, alterations in conditioned behavior occur with sufficient frequency that the results are said to be consistent with quantitative impairment of widespread representation of the effector site of a conditioning mechanism [76,1105,1107 1128]. This conclusion is supported by the electrophysiologic studies described earlier [111,456,1105]. Nielson [718] also suggests that the prefrontal regions contain engrams for motor acts and that these engrams involve pathways that can be trained by repeated use. Head's considerations of apraxia and similar disorders support this view [394]. He asserts that motor acts involve more than simple effector functions. In particular, some involve the verbal consequences of comprehension of particular kinds of situations (i.e., blowing out a match—as the comprehension of the act of extinguishing a fire). Comprehension may or may not be performed at the same level of processing as conceptualization; see later descriptions of kinetic apraxia, echolalia, and echolexographia.

Denny-Brown notes that disturbances produced experimentally by bilateral temporal lobe lesions have much in common with those produced by lesions of the frontal lobes, including the same perseverative tendency to examine all small objects, disturbances along the aggression-fear axis, hyperreaction to certain stimuli, disturbances in sexual behavior, and a variety of curious tics and mannerisms. Animals with frontal or temporal lobectomy have enhanced sensitivity to tactile and proprioceptive stimuli. An unexpected touch or sudden passive movement induces a startle. "It is so violent in recently operated animals as to be a myoclonic paroxysm. In association with this response, there appears a great facility in exploration with the hands and lips. This is the basis of the instinctive grasping and sucking responses" [206].

In man, euphoria and defects in attention were found by Feuchtwanger [285] to be the most common symptoms of frontal lobe lesions. In addition, there occur well-known disorders of emissive speech (Broca's aphasia), as well as disturbances in the ability to produce vocal music, to play a musical instrument, and to write. Damage to the frontal lobes can also result in alterations in personality including indifference, inappropriateness, tactlessness, cruelty, indecency, and other asocial or amoral behavior. Associated defects in intelligence are also seen, although the nature of the cognitive defect resulting from frontal lobe lesions is not well understood. Most emotional disturbances said to result from frontal lobe lesions can be interpreted as secondary phenomena resulting from intellectual disturbances [206].

Denny-Brown suggests that a striking feature of frontal lobe defects in both animals and man is the failure of reaction to a predictable (neurophysiologic) event. "The function of the cerebral cortex in general is concerned with projected sense data. The failure in reaction following frontal lobe lesion appears to be the absence (of reception or response to) a normally predictably affective stimulus, the propeties of which should ultimately be accurately definable" [206]. Two phenomena accompanying such lesions may be directly related to the defect in effectuation of motor performance. The first is the inability to act on the projected consequence of a motor act. This destruction of effectuation may also disrupt mnemonic-based perceptions related to projections of effectuations. As a patient of Freeman and Watts [297] said after leucotomy, "Now that I have done it, I can see that it was not the thing to do, but beforehand, I couldn't say whether or not it would be right." The other aspect of disrupted effectuation involves the lack of response to emotional events such as pain, specifically the absence of expected contextual motor reactions. The painful stimulus is perceived. Primary affective reactions may occur and be intense. However, more complex responses such as fear or retaliation are no longer possible, and the experience itself is remembered as a colorless event.

Tropismic motor activity, that is, activity involving exaggerated or abnormal involuntary orienting, following, or tracking movements with stereotyped action patterns, can be released after frontal lobe lesions. Denny-Brown recognizes two physiologic components accompanying such release. The first is spasticity; the second is hyperactivity of opposing cortical reactions resulting from a disequilibrium between the different parts of the cortical effector mechanism. The appearance of instinctive grasping or sucking is one example. Tactile, proprioceptive, or even visual stimuli directed toward the hand or mouth can cause the compulsive performance of a grasping or sucking response. Other types of compulsive behavior may be the psychic accompaniments of this phenomenon. Anyone who doubts the significance of feedback, not only in cellular events but also in complex motor behavior, need only consider tropismic behavior such as forced grasping, acaudate following, and other more severe or extensive compulsions to be convinced of the importance of closed loop environment-organism interactions.

The Parietal Lobes

The parietal lobes receive somatosensory inputs that arise from receptors in the skin and are transmitted via the dorsal columns and thalamus. Inputs from the anterolateral and reticular systems supporting somatosensation are also received, but less directly. As might be expected, these areas perform functions other than simple somatosensory reception. Disturbances of motor function such as constructional apraxia, apraxia of dressing, and ideational apraxia can follow lesions of the parietal lobes. These disturbances are complex and represent more than just a deficit in effectuation per se [212]. Conceptual behavior is involved.

Basic Parietal Functions

Basic functions of the parietal lobe include the reception of highly specific somatosensory information, particularly at the region of the postcentral gyrus, and the integration* of information from the somatosensory, visual, and auditory spheres.

Conspicuous sensory deficits can result from parietal lesions. The simpler deficits include astereognosis (inability to recognize the shape of objects by palpation), decreased ability to discriminate two points or localize the region stimulated, and impaired position sense. They reflect disturbances in the relatively simpler processing of sensory input transmitted through the dorsal columns of the spinal cord to the parietal cortex.

Complex Sensory Disturbances

Other, more complex sensory disturbances are found with parietal lobe lesions. They include:

1. *Sensory extinction.* This disturbance is exemplified by a failure to recognize one of two stimuli when both are delivered simultaneously to dif-

---

*Comparable integration goes on in the temporal, limbic, and other areas, but derangement of this function is particularly apparent with lesions of the parietal lobe in man.

ferent loci, for example, touching each arm at the same time or presenting two objects to different sides of the visual fields. In many instances, the undistinguished, neglected stimulus is recognized when its intensity is increased. Though called sensory extinction, it is not known if there are parallels, physiologically, between the failure in stimulus recognition here and the loss of response to a CS in behavioral extinction.

2. *Neglectful inattention to parts of body and parts of ideational space.* The person neglects or fails to distinguish parts of his body (amorphosynthesis)* or ideational space. This disturbance may be, in part, a consequence of the same process (i.e., perceptual rivalry)† that gives rise to sensory extinction, but it is a more profound disorder and is most difficult to overcome. The term ideational is a significant qualifier since the space neglected may be a perceived extracorporeal space, highly abstract, such as the left portion of a clock face. It is as though the person were unaware of that region or had difficulty in perceiving it. When objects are drawn, they may appear as shown in Fig. 6.5. That some perception of these stimuli is still possible is indicated by the preserved ability to react to a visual threat delivered from the left side, or to a painful stimulus applied to the neglected part of the body.

3. *Gerstmann's syndrome.* This tetrad of symptoms includes acalculia, agraphia, impaired right-left discrimination, and finger agnosia. All may be seen after lesions near the angular gyrus of the dominant hemisphere in man.

4. *Alexia.* This is an impairment of the ability to read. It, too, is seen with lesions of the dominant hemisphere in man, particularly those involving the angular gyrus.

Tropismic Behavior

Parietal lesions of either hemisphere may result in tropismic behavior, which involves aspects of motor performance that can be released by abnormalities in sensory reception. This behavior has commonalities with the tropismic behavior seen after frontal lesions. For example, exaggerated avoidance of tactile and visual simuli may be seen after parietal lobe lesions, both in man and in experimental animals. The most typical of the avoidance reactions in man is dorsiflexion of the hand and fanning of the fingers upon stroking the ventral surface. Presumably this is the counterpart of the exaggerated approach behavior seen with lesions of the frontal lobe or the caudate nucleus: grasping, sucking, following, circling, and the like.

It has been suggested that the tropisms reveal instinctive behavior reflecting the genetically stereotyped organization of certain circuits within the nervous system [207]. The circuits appear to be designed to process certain sensory inputs expressly through specific motor labeled pathways in such a

---

*Modified somewhat from Denny-Brown's definition (see [210]).
† As shall shortly be seen, perceptual rivalry is an attribute of the operation of undamaged portions of complex nerve networks. Sensory extinction and amorphosynthesis are manifestations of the uncovering or exaggeration of these operations when other, superimposed control mechanisms are lost.

Reflections of a Right Parietal Lobe Disorder

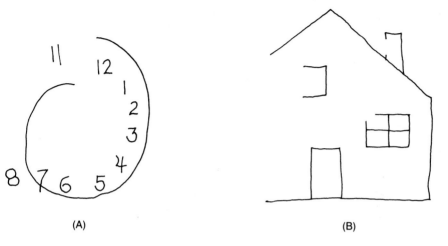

(A)   (B)

Fig. 6.5. A person with a right parietal lobe lesion may fail to draw in the left side of a clock face (as in A) or a house (as in B). When asked to go back and complete A, he may be able to put in the number "11," as shown.

manner as to cause a tight coupling between motor performance and selected environmental features. Apparently, the circuits operate normally in everyday functioning, but with superimposed controls. When these controls are removed, the operation is exposed. Examples of normal tropismic behavior can also be found in organisms with intact control mechanisms. For instance, complex, innate tropismic behavior is well recognized in birds (homing, imprinted following), fish (schooling), and other species [416,625,1021].

Complexities of Sensory Reception and Motor Synthesis Revealed by Lesions and by Exceptional Stimuli

Some other complexities of *normal* sensory reception and motor synthesis are revealed by what are commonly viewed as *abnormal* disturbances of these processes. Consider the following clinical example:

> A patient with a right parietal lesion is unable to perceive that his left hand is his own. When asked, "Whose hand is this?" he replies, "I don't know— it's not mine; it must be yours." When shown that his hand is attached to his forearm and that to his upper arm and that to his chest (which he perceives as his own as his attention is drawn to the midline), he can then deduce that his hand is, in fact, his own. When asked whose hand it is, he then replies, "It is mine." However, when asked the same question a few seconds later, he gives the original reply: "I don't know; it's someone else's."

The patient's sanity and intelligence can be demonstrated in other perceptual and mnemonic areas, as well as by his ability to make the correct perception* deductively, though transiently. What, then, is the explanation for his curious behavior? Clearly, at the moment he denies that his hand is his, the assertion must seem valid to him.

Remarkably enough, analogous misperceptions, termed optical illusions, occur normally in people who are completely healthy. These "normal" perceptual disturbances have features comparable to those seen with misperceptions following cortical lesions. One of these features is the inability to correct the misperception. That is, the misperception recurs time and time again. Examples of the distortions of information processing that occur normally with optical illusions are shown in Fig. 6.6.

The illusion in Fig. 6.6A is detectable. The interjections of dark areas between the corners of the squares occur intermittently and are transient. They are recognized as an illusion. However, they recur, and although the locus of their recurrence can be varied by shifting the fixation of gaze, their recurrence cannot be prevented. This, then, is a detectable illusion that is transient, but cannot be totally corrected. The misperception is attributed to an effect of lateral inhibition occurring at the level of the visual receptor organ, the retina. The physiologic basis of this misperception can be explained by the organization of the interconnections between neighboring cells in the retinal network (see Fig. 6.7). In this instance *the network organization is responsible, at least in part, for misperception or illusion as well as for perception itself.*

The illusions in Fig. 6.6B and C are not transient.[†] For most people, they recur continually and cannot be corrected. The straight lines in B continue to be perceived as curved; the figure in C appears to have three distinct exten-

Detection of the illusion itself is a problem in Figs. 6.6B and C. (Are you certain that the contiguity of the middle extension in C is really an illusion?) The fact that many illusions are misperceived again and again in normal people, even after logical deduction has momentarily resolved the illusion, makes the behavior of the patient with a parietal lesion who denies the existence of his arm more comprehensible. He, too, cannot correct the misperception (in his case arising from a defective input). And apparently he cannot detect the misperception with sufficient certainty to avoid it.

What then are the functions that are revealed by optical illusions and by parietal lesions?

Perceptual Rivalry

Perceptual rivalry, the competition between different stimuli for processing by the network, is one feature of neural networks that is revealed both by lesions and by optical illusions. Competitive selection of certain inputs for

---

*Further definition of this term can be found on p. 309 ff. (and in Chap. 1).
[†] and, as will be seen, a different feature of the nerve network may be responsible.

Three "Normal" Illusions

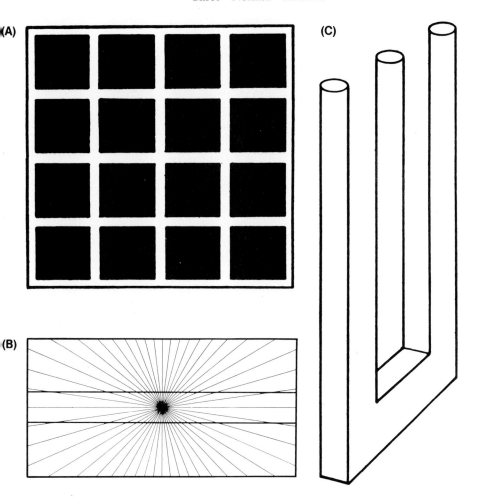

Fig. 6.6. Three optical illusions. The first illusion (A) is attributed to lateral inhibition occurring at the level of the retina.

further processing allows sensory discrimination wherein one input is disregarded in favor of another. When this disregard is exaggerated, it becomes neglectful misperception. With optical illusions arising from exceptional visual inputs based on unique lineal arrangements, there occur (1) acceptance of "erroneous" (distorted or exceptional) inputs, i.e., misperception, and (2) rejection of other "correct" inputs, i.e., neglect. This is just the opposite of the usual occurrence, wherein erroneous or distorted inputs are rejected. Once a distorted sensory input fails to be rejected, distortion is accepted as the "reality" and other, possibly less distorted inputs become candidates for rejection. It is as though further processing occurred inertially on the premise

Lateral Inhibition

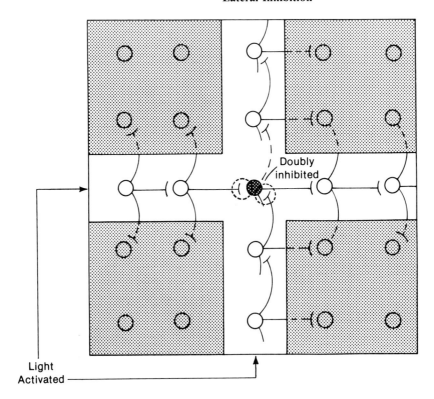

Fig. 6.7. Lateral inhibition [388,389] between neural elements activated by light results in disproportionately large (2x) inhibition of the center element, as well as reduced inhibition of the neighbors to which it projects. As a result the central area is misperceived as being darker than the adjacent light areas.

of acceptance of the distorted input and along the reflex pathways labeled by that input. As a result, in the example in Fig. 6.6C, the "real" orientation of the lines is repeatedly rejected in favor of the "illusory" orientation, and the illusory misperception is maintained again and again. Support for this view of neglect arising from a normal competition between stimuli for subsequent, discriminative processing (i.e., perceptual rivalry) comes from the ability to overcome neglect by inserting a stronger stimulus. The parietal patient who fails to recognize one of two hands held up simultaneously, does so when it is waved. The stronger stimulus presumably tips the balance enough to permit processing along new, sensory-labeled pathways, and the new input pattern is then accepted and recognized.

By considering the competitive, discriminative aspects of sensory reception, the logic in the "illogical" aspects of amorphosynthesis and denial is revealed. Amorphosynthesis may reasonably arise from acceptance of distorted inputs in preference to normal inputs if the distorted inputs are competitively stronger or if the normal inputs are reduced in strength or effectiveness due to lesion.

Amorphosynthesis occurs after high dorsal column lesions as well as after damage to the parietal lobe [324,576]. This suggests that it is the weakening (or distortion) of sensory input that is caused by the lesion that is responsible for the induction of amorphosynthesis, not the disturbance of a central image processor as some would believe. The central image is not "made" by a processor, just as an image is not "made" by a mirror. Instead, the image is a reflection of the input. In the brain, it is an input that is increasingly modified during each stage of transmission.

Although the sensory processing system can recognize frank loss of sensory input as anesthesia, it cannot distinguish certain degraded inputs from those normally received. Subsequent "normal" processing along pathways labeled according to the "distorted" sensory inputs then leads to misperception and rejection of other sensory inputs. Given these circumstances, plus an inertial form of information processing, distortion becomes reality; hence, amorphosynthesis. Neglect then becomes denial, wherein the very existence of the organ from which sensation normally emanates is denied, except perhaps as an experience of the past.

Because of the inertia of perceptual processing that results from the normal organization of the brain reflex circuitry, many illusions of awareness are sustained without awareness of the disability. Although behavioral disorders may eventually draw the patient's attention to a particular problem caused by the illness, there is ordinarily no generalized insight into the disorder, nor is there a subjective sense of altered perception. (The latter may easily be substantiated by examination of Fig. 6.6B.) Thus, with disorders of higher function, there may be denial of visual loss [24] or of motor hemiplegia, failure to comprehend a linguistic disorder as in Wernicke's aphasia, unawareness of disturbances in dressing and toilet, ignorance of avoiding reactions, and perhaps also "asymbolia for pain" [212,398].

Perseveration

Perseveration is the continuation of motor behavior beyond its usual termination. For example, an elderly patient with bifrontal lesions may get up to perform the same task (going to the bathroom, turning off the furnace) over and over again. Sometimes (particularly in the hospital) the inappropriateness of the behavior is easily recognized (e.g., turning off the furnace). The repeated interjection of isolated reflex patterns in an inappropriate context is readily seen to be a basic manifestation of perseveration. Simpler reflex patterns also occur, such as picking repeatedly at a tie, pajamas, or the bedding. The complex patterns of interjected motor activity differ from those of epilepsy in that they appear to be purposeful and are found in the absence of ictal spike discharge. They are more reminiscent of movements seen with chorea or athetosis (abrupt hemiballismal swinging or slower, snakelike writhing appearing with damage to the basal ganglia—especially the caudate and putamen). Tropisms, such as circling, also have a distinct perseverative aspect.

Perseveration is found in the conceptual and linguistic as well as in the perceptual domain. It occurs in aphasia. After parietal or temporal lesions of the dominant hemisphere, identical or nearly-similar-but-irrelevant words, syllables, or phrases are interjected into speech. Extreme perseveration conceivably contributes to hallucinatory or compulsive behavior, depending on whether the interjections are toward the afferent or efferent side of central neural processing. The aphasic type of perseveration is also found in the absence of lesions. With stuttering, the interjected reflex patterns are organized into syllables or parts of syllables. With slips of the tongue, words or phrases embodying concepts are interjected. Thus, perseveration may be entirely normal, even in a conceptual context.

The motor patterns that are interjected with perseveration appear purposeful regardless of whether they represent conceptualized behavior.* The patterns of motor activity are often stereotyped, and the sequences of interjected activity are frequently related, suggesting commonalities of motor labeling along the neural pathways that synthesize them. An inertial information processing along these pathways is suggested by the tendency of the system to fill in or make up for any lack of completeness and to pursue a given pathway with an outcome approaching continuity. Confabulation may also be a manifestation of this tendency.

The flow of information transmission from one labeled pathway to another appears to require some additional control or redirection for complete continuity to be achieved. Without inhibitory control of certain outputs, there emerges a stream of perseverative information processing not unlike that of Molly Bloom:

> ... Molly darling he called me what was his name Jack Joe Harry Mulvey was it yet I think a lieutenant he was rather fair he had a laughing kind of a voice so I went around to the whatyoucallit everything was whatyoucallit moustache had he he said hed come back Lord its just like yesterday to me and if I was married hed do it to me and I promised him yes faithfully Id let him block me now flying perhaps hes dead or killed or a Captain or admiral its nearly 20 years ... [468].

Inertial perseveration and redirective control, then, are normal aspects of information processing that must interact before the stage of overt motor performance. Perseveration arises from impaired rejection of inappropriate motor activity and reveals uncontrolled inertial processing. Without redirective control, the patient with frontal damage tends to repeat earlier motor acts.

The same type of perseverative processing that leads to repetitive, theme-fixed motor performance may result in a fixation on distorted sensory inputs in patients with parietal damage. As a consequence of this fixation, the inability to detect subsequent misperception is increased and denial of the defect in perception is reinforced.

---

*Probably because they have been "shaped" in a purposeful way.

Agnosia, Apraxia, and Aphasia

Most would agree that the highest behavioral functions are those concerned with language and similarly abstract conceptualizations. They depend on memory and learning and tend to be best developed in man. The possibility that these functions require some specialized reflex circuitry is raised by the observation that they are characteristically deranged by unilateral lesions. Other, perceptual functions may be deranged by lesions of either hemisphere, but functions such as speech are typically disrupted by lesions of one hemisphere—the dominant one. This indicates that some circuitry critical for the generation (or control) of abstract conceptualization is represented selectively, unilaterally. Analogous functions may be mediated selectively by the nondominant hemisphere. For example, abstract spatial conceptualizations are said to be mediated by comparable nondominant circuitry [469]. Musical abilities are also said to be nondominant functions; amusia typically results from lesions of the nondominant hemisphere. Spatial conceptualization is required for the performance of such visual constructive tasks as recognizing two-dimensional sketches of three-dimensional figures or perceiving the direction of lines or movements, tasks that are disrupted by lesions of the right hemisphere, the nondominant hemisphere in right handed persons and in most left handed persons as well. Since it is nonlinguistic, spatial conceptualization is difficult to assess. Moreover, its impairment may easily be confused with spatial misperception arising from damage to either parietal hemisphere or to the dorsal columns, as described earlier.

As described next, the agnosias, apraxias, and aphasias represent the classic disorders of linguistic or conceptualized information processing arising from lesions of the dominant cortex in man. They may be separated into sensory labeled receptive functions and motor labeled effectuative or synthetic functions (e.g., Table 6.2). A hierarchically organized neural network with key features of the circuitry contained within a single hemisphere appears to underlie these linguistic and conceptual functions.

Agnosia

Agnosia involves a disturbance of conceptualized sensory information processing exemplified by a failure of recognition. Most agnosias arise from dominant hemisphere lesions. Those that do not are pseudo-agnosias representing perceptual disorders misclassified as conceptual disorders. This is recognized by Brain in his description of tactile agnosia:

> Confusion will be avoided if, as already suggested, the term astereognosis is used to describe disorders of the tactile recognition of objects caused by sensory loss, and the term tactile agnosia reserved for the failure to recognize objects when the ability to distinguish their size, shape and texture is preserved . . . . Tactile agnosia thus defined is associated with a lesion of the opposite parietal lobe, perhaps especially the supramarginal gyrus, but there is evidence that in right-handed persons bilateral tactile agnosia may

be produced by a lesion in this situation in the left cerebral hemisphere, in which case it may be associated with visual object-agnosia . . . . Thus it would appear that the left cerebral hemisphere may be the dominant one for tactile recognition. [94]

Analogous conceptual functions mediated selectively by the nondominant hemisphere could, when disrupted, produce a true agnosia.

Agnosias can involve any sensory modality, but the two sensory modalities most greatly used for abstract conceptualization, vision and audition, are the ones most obviously affected.

With a visual agnosia, the patient may have a lack of visual comprehension equivalent to an aperceptive blindness. With an auditory agnosia, the lack of auditory comprehension is equivalent to an aperceptive deafness; the patient is unable to comprehend his own speech as well as the words of others. The ability to comprehend other, preserved sensory modalities is retained. Hence, with visual agnosia, the patient may recognize an object by touch which he does not recognize visually. That some crude visual input processing can still be performed is indicated by the ability to flinch from visual threat. The appearance of the object seems to be distorted [606] in a manner analogous to, but exceeding that of, the illusion shown in Fig. 6.6B, wherein the distortion itself is difficult to perceive! With agnosia, the distortion involves an abstract concept that is difficult to perceive.

Just where misperception, as in amorphosynthesis, ends and misconceptualization, as in agnosia, begins is difficult to say, and if said, is inevitably controversial. An attempt to clarify the usage is made on p. 307 ff. after further discussion of the phenomena. That amorphosynthesis is not a disturbance of higher level conceptualization is supported by the following finding of Denny-Brown [209]: "If a patient makes a drawing of a house or a daisy from which the left side is missing, it does not follow that his concept of the house is defective. Shown a real daisy with half the petals removed, the patient can tell you what is the matter with it. When his attention is drawn to his left arm by the shoulder, etc., he can deduce where his arm is, and have knowledge of his own left arm and that he should have only one left arm."

Higher levels of conceptualization are possible in the patient with amorphosynthesis and can be used to overcome the disturbance, temporarily. It appears, therefore, that the derangement is perceptual rather than conceptual. The perceptual disorders, including amorphosynthesis, can be seen with lesions of either hemisphere. They are more easily observed when the agnosias are not superimposed, i.e., after lesions of the nondominant hemisphere [211]. After bilateral parietal lesions in man, difficulties arise in perceiving the geometric features or interrelationships of objects [cf. 915]. More often, says Denny-Brown [212], the defect is apparent only in the perception of symbolic features such as the shape of numerals, letters, objects (as in the Poppelreuter test), or the sequence of word sounds.

Apraxia

Apraxia is defined as an incapacity for purposive motor performance with conservation of the power of movement [602]. It is as though there was a disturbance of the ability to resynthesize partially processed neuronal messages according to appropriately labeled motor channels, with a resulting impairment of motor effectuation. One form of apraxia involves a failure in processing abstract, conceptualized motor information. This type of deficit always appears after lesion of the dominant hemisphere. Other forms of apraxia involve failures in motor performance reflecting release of perseverative or tropismic behavior. This type of deficit is closer to a perceptual than to a conceptual disorder and is seen after lesions of either hemisphere.

Conceptual or Ideational Apraxia

Ideational apraxia is the inability to perform conceptualized motor acts. The patient cannot go through the motions of drinking from a imaginary glass or even an empty glass, yet he can drink from a full one. As pointed out by Denny-Brown [209], "the defect in motor performance appears in the context of the propositional nature of the task." It is not the movement that is lost, but the ability to perform it as an imagined proposition. This disorder is seen with lesions of the dominant parietal lobe.

The remaining apraxias are nonideational, showing motor incapacities of the kinetic, adexterous, or constructional types.

Kinetic Apraxia

Kinetic apraxia is manifested by difficulty in performing a volitionally initiated motor act. For example, when asked to blow out a match, the subject may attempt to do so, and may even purse his lips, but will fail to produce a coordinated, directed puff. Paradoxically, the same person when threatened by a lit match a few moments later may immediately blow it out. Denny-Brown suggests that kinetic apraxia is produced by a bias of the cortical reactions resulting from overactivity of either the exploratory or the repellent set of cortical tropisms [209]. The slowness in initiating movement seen with kinetic apraxia parallels that seen with the perseverative effects of frontal lesions such as Brun's frontal ataxia or Gegenhalter's syndrome. These disorders appear with lesions of either hemisphere.

Adexterous Apraxia

Adexterous apraxia involves a loss of dexterity in acquired motor performance. Like kinetic apraxia, it also results from damage to either hemisphere. Although both kinetic and adexterous apraxias may involve disturbances in writing or drawing, they may basically be aconceptual disorders involving disturbances at other than conceptual levels of processing. That behavior such as the ability to purse the lips or to make a fist is separable from ideational behavior using the same movements is demonstrated by echolalia and echolexographia—disturbances in which there is a conceptual deficit despite preservation of the motor abilities of speaking or writing (see p. 300 and Table 6.3).

Constructional Apraxia

Constructional apraxia is a complicated disorder in which geometric forms, such as triangles or squares, may not be copied correctly. Attempts to copy diagrams may be more successful, though the spatial relationships may be drawn incorrectly. The constructional apraxias are seen after lesions of the angular gyrus of either hemisphere or bilaterally [196]; however, it is not clear whether the constructional apraxias are entirely aconceptual. It appears that unilaterally mediated conceptual messages may be transmitted to either hemisphere to elicit appropriate motor outcomes. There are also instances of agraphia in the right hand related to left hemisphere lesions in left-handed patients, although they are few. In these cases the main difficulty appears to be in re-visualization of letters, a special type of constructional apraxia. The patient is unable ideationally to form the desired pattern; he brings his construct closer and closer to the model, but still cannot copy it. Denny-Brown terms this type of disorder an imperceptive apraxia.

Aphasia

Aphasia involves disturbances of abstract communication and results from unilateral lesions of the dominant hemisphere. Receptive and expressive linguistic skills are impaired. In the visual sphere, reading is impaired (alexia); in the auditory sphere, there is a disorder of listening. On the motor side, there are disturbances of writing (agraphia) or speaking.

Some would confine aphasia to impairments of speech alone, arbitrarily excluding the alexias and the agraphias. However, it would seem more reasonable to define aphasia as an agnosia or apraxia of linguistic communication. A receptive aphasia would then be an agnosia of communication involving disturbances in the processing of sensory-labeled linguistic information. An expressive aphasia would be an apraxia of communication involving disturbances in the synthesis of motor-labeled linguistic information. Interestingly, insight or awareness of the degree of the disorder is commonly lacking in people with receptive aphasias, but not necessarily in those with expressive aphasias.

Classifying aphasias according to receptive and expressive symptomatology is attractive because such classifications correspond more to the underlying physiologic operations than to a subjective concept of linguistics. Some may object to any attempt to categorize aphasia on the grounds that the aphasias, (as well as the apraxias and agnosias) are only occasionally "pure" or confined to a particular category of functional impairment. This objection confuses complexity with inseparability. Two dissimilar line labeled operations may be carried out, physiologically, within the same neural element. To argue otherwise would be to ignore the capacities of the neuronal operations described in Chapters 3-5 and amplified in Figs. 3.42, 7.1, and 7.22. Analytically, it is perfectly proper to separate the operations according to their respective inputs and outputs and their more fundamental levels of operation (Fig. 7.20). It is also reasonable to ascribe an order, direction, or hierarchy to a particular set of processing operations, even though it may be difficult to trace the hierarchy through a redundant neural network.

A particularly lucid attempt to categorize the aphasias is that of Sir Russell Brain [94]. His outline, shown in Table 6.2, is the guide for the definitions that follow, many of which have been abstracted from those of Brain and Denny-Brown. The reader may wish to compare this analysis of the symptomatology of aphasia with the raw clinical observations cited in the appendix to this chapter (p. 317). The appendix is a typescript of a conversation with a patient who was recovering from aphasia. Again, note that in any given aphasic disorder, one may expect to find multiple aphasic symptomatologies as well as some variability in the site of the lesion(s).

Receptive Aphasia

Cortical deafness represents a profound auditory agnosia in which the patient cannot recognize speech as speech and might be thought deaf except for the ability to respond to certain sounds with a startle or orienting response.

Cortical blindness is the visual analogue of this disorder. These disorders are found after widespread damage to the respective cortical receptive areas or their immediate inputs.

Word deafness occurs with lesions of the middle part of the first temporal convolution of the left hemisphere adjacent to Heschl's gyrus. The patient can hear and respond to the sound of the spoken voice, but does not recognize the words. Sounds come, but words do not separate. It is like hearing a foreign language.

Word blindness, ranging from the inability to recognize any letters to verbal alexia, occurs with lesions of the left angular gyrus that interrupt neural impulses derived from the visual cortex of both occipital lobes. While the patient cannot recognize letters visually, he can still describe them verbal-

---

Table 6.2. A Hierarchy of Agnosia—Aphasia[a]

A. Receptive
   (1) *Cortical deafness*—total (except for possible startle by loud sounds).
   (2) *Auditory agnosia*—can't recognize speech as speech
   (3) *Word deafness*—can't recognize (auditory) spoken word (even own correct speech!); sounds like foreign language. (Heschl's gyrus)
   (4) *Central (Wernicke's) aphasia*—can't recognize words—speech (spoken or written—auditory or visual).
   (5) *Amnesic aphasia*—can't recognize names.
B. Expressive
   (1) *Jargon aphasia—paragrammatism—paraphasia*—difficulty with initial steps of resynthesis into words, grammar, sentences; thoughts.
   (2) *Amnesic aphasia*—again, but here the inability to synthesize names.
   (3) *Broca's expressive aphasia*—inability to express the synthesized words, sentences, thoughts, etc.
   (4) *Subcortical motor aphasia—anarthria*—loss of spoken speech with preservation of inner speech and writing.

[a]From Brain [94].

ly. Moreover, he may be able to recognize letters by tracing them with his forefinger, thus substituting kinesthetic sensory impulses to get around the visual defect. Right homonymous hemianopia usually accompanies word blindness.

In both word deafness and word blindness, there is an interruption of the pathways leading out of the respective primary receptive cortex and to the areas of the dominant hemisphere at which the next stage of processing occurs. Brain suggests that in these disorders words fail to arouse the word-schemas necessary for their recognition [94].

(Mixed) Receptive and Expressive Aphasia

Central aphasia is characterized by both receptive and expressive disturbances and is seen with lesions of the posterior part of the superior temporal convolution of the left side, which may extend to the adjacent portion of the parietal lobe. On the receptive side, the patient has difficulty in understanding the meaning of what he hears, ranging from isolated words to complex sentences. There is variable disability from patient to patient and even within the same patient from time to time. The expressive defect frequently takes the form of choosing the wrong word (paraphasia) and/or grammatical confusions (paragrammatism). The basis for errors in the choice of words is often similarity in structure or vowel sounds, or similar class as the word or object for which it is substituted.

Semantic aphasia [394] represents an equally complex disorder of conceptual function seen typically with lesions of the dominant parietal and parietal-occipital regions. Linguistic disturbances of the verbal, nominal, and syntactic types occur.

Amnesic or nominal aphasia is found with lesions of the dominant temporal-parietal region, ordinarily between the site of the lesion responsible for central aphasia and that responsible for visual asymbolia. Patients can say many words but cannot use them precisely. Moreover, their verbal form may suffer as they attempt to discover the correct name. Internal speech is severely affected and there is often difficulty in understanding or performing oral or printed commands. The patient cannot understand what he reads to himself. Spontaneous writing may also be affected. A full-blown Gerstmann syndrome (p. 288) may be associated with amnesic aphasia. When offered a series of names including the right one for an object he has just misnamed, the patient will often recognize his mistake. Yet he may immediately repeat it without realizing he is again using the incorrect word. For example, one patient when shown a pair of scissors, called it a nail file. When given the word "scissors," he subsequently said, "yes, that's it. Of course it's not a nail file, it's a nail file." He did not recognize that he had repeated his mistake; the wrong word, "nail file," had for the time being acquired the symbolic value for the patient of the right word, "scissors" [94].

Transcortical aphasia and *echolalia* are characterized by the relative preservation of the power of repetition. The symptomatology resembles that of central aphasia but the receptive and expressive deficits are more profound. Despite the degree of impaired recognition of speech and disturbance of internal speech and volitional utterance, the ability to repeat words and phrases is preserved. The echolalic patient resembles an infant learning to speak. He repeats words but does not understand their meaning. Thus, a typical "conversation" would be: Q. "How are you?" A. "How are you?" Q. "What day is it?" A. "What day is it?" Q. "What is your name?" A. "What is your name?" More detailed examples are given in Table 6.3.

Transcortical central aphasia is frequently associated with lesions of the left first temporal convolution. Echolalia seems to be the result of a lesion in the temporal and the neighboring part of the parietal lobe. Both kinds of dis-

Table 6.3. Two Examples of Echolalic Speech from Patients With Dominant Hemisphere Lesions[a]

Question	Answer
I.	
What is your name?	"what is your name?"
Is your name Mary?	"is your name Mary?"
What is this place?	"what is this place?"
Mary, what is the matter with you?	"Mary, what is the matter with you?"
How are you?	"how are you?"
Can you whistle?	"can you whistle?"
Whistle like this (whistle)	(pouted her lips but did not blow)
Come on, try to whistle	"try whistle"
Can you sing a song?	"can you sing?"
(Examiner sings Jingle Bells)	"jingle bells—away" (in sing-song voice)
	"come on, come on" (spontaneously)
Are you Mary?	"are you Mary?"
(Was shown a glass of water)	"come on, I said" (spontaneously)
	"drink of water please"
Is this what you wanted?	"is this what you wanted?"
Mary, can you read what it says here?	"Mary, can you read what it says here?" (showed no inclination to read)
II.	
How are you;	"how are you?"
What day is this?	"what day is this?"
What is your name?	"what is your name?"
Is your name Katherine?	"Katherine S---s" (correct)
How old are you?	"how old are you?"
Try not to say what I say, do you understand?	"understand"
Today is Tuesday	"Tuesday today"
Do you know what hospital this is?	"what hospital this is"
Tell me where you were born?	"where you born"
Sprechen sie Deutsch?	"Sprak zee doytch"
La, la, la, la	"la, la, la"
Do, de, do	"do, de, do"

[a] From Denny-Brown [210].

turbances require the integrity of the neural pathways concerned with repetition in the face of disruption of pathways handling messages conceptually. The right cerebral hemisphere has been thought to play a part in this. Echolalia differs from the transcortical aphasias in that there is no intention to repeat.

Denny-Brown points out that the phenomena of automatic reading and automatic, echolalic repetition demonstrate beyond doubt that "the recognition of words by vision and sound can reach a high degree of effective performance in terms of their reproduction, without any propositional activity" [209]. In addition to echolalic mimicry of speech, there is also echolexographic mimicry of writing. Some completely aphasic patients can copy print, although they cannot express themselves [1001]. Thus, there must be cerebral sensory-motor mechanisms for letter copying as well as for speech, reading, and writing.

Mirror-writing is the term applied to script that runs from right to left, the letters being reversed and forming mirror images of normal script. Brain says, "Normal individuals can frequently carry out mirror-writing with the left hand, either when writing with the left hand alone or when writing simultaneously" [94]. With echolalia, there is mimetic utterance of received information. With mirror-writing, there is mimetic writing of the mirror image of the correct construct. In both cases, there is lack of insight into the error and the mimicry has tropismic, perseverative aspects.

Expressive Aphasia

In expressive aphasia, the patient has difficulty in speaking or writing, but it can be inferred that the physiologic defect is not in the cortical motor cells of the pyramidal system, which project di- or trisynaptically to the muscles of articulation, since this system can function satisfactorily in performing other acts involving the same musculature. Broca's aphasia and the other forms of expressive aphasia described below are, however, frequently accompanied by varying degrees of dysarthria. *Dysarthria* is slurring of articulation without any difficulty in word finding. It is commonly produced by subcortical lesions involving the lenticular nuclei or the external capsule. When severe, the defect is termed an anarthria.

Although *anarthria* is commonly classified as a subcortical motor aphasia, it may instead involve extensive lesions of the frontal speech area, particularly in the lower area of the precentral convolution. The patient may be totally unable to speak spontaneously or repeat words that he hears or reads aloud. He can on occasion indicate, by tapping, the number of syllables in a word that he cannot utter. Writing is normal, as are all other linguistic functions.

Broca's aphasia involves difficulties in expressive speech. There are two types of difficulties: inability to begin a word and difficulty in producing a second or third syllable. Words are seldom pronounced the same way in two successive utterances. Such difficulties in speaking (or writing) appear without any associated propositional disturbance. This type of deficit must be discriminated from subcortical dysarthria. In right-handed people Broca's aphasia is produced only by left hemisphere lesions. The left, third frontal convolution is typically involved. Denny-Brown believes that "the essential lesion in Broca's aphasia [for speaking] must lie in the audito-motor connections of the cortical areas controlling movements of the lips and tongue" [209]. The third frontal convolution is shown as area 44 in Fig. 6.8. Written speech is usually affected almost as severely as articulation and may show similar defects. It is clearly an apraxia of speech, and is most obvious in relation to propositional tasks. With analogous lesions of nearby regions, it may be impossible, as a requested act, to wave the hand as in saying good-bye, yet possible to do so in actual farewell.

Broca's aphasia may represent a relatively selective impairment of the means for motor labeled linguistic information processing that is preserved in echolalia and echolexographia. However, it may also involve aspects of kinetic apraxias complicated by disorders of rhythm, including rhythmic perseverations of syllables. In this disorder, the functional significance of serial order, noted by Lashley [580], is apparent. Learned, serially ordered information is particularly critical for motor performance at high speed. Denny-Brown points out that just as the patient who is beginning to suffer from

Brodmann's Areas of the Human Cortex

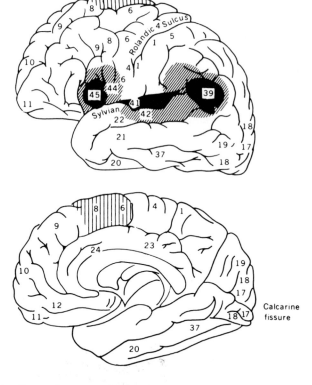

Fig. 6.8. Cortical areas numbered according to the scheme of Brodmann. Areas 44, 45 = Broca's area; area 41 = Heschl's gyrus; area 39 = Wernicke's area. (From Harrison et al. [387].)

frontal apraxia of gait has great difficulty in initiating the first step and shuffles a few times before walking naturally, the aphasic hesitates and stammers, using abnormal phonemes, in trying to speak. This searching activity seems to reflect a fundamental feature of the physiologic processes underlying data sorting and retrieval through networks of adaptive elements.

Jargon or paraphasic aphasia is characterized by rambling, nonsensical speech. The patient speaks at appropriate moments in the course of a conversation, but his speech is filled with incoherent, repetitive hybridizations of proper words or phrases. The appropriateness of initiation indicates preservation of some receptive processing permitting this type of linguistic recognition. Interestingly, although the patient may not recognize many of his own mistakes, he can usually be taught to do so. In paraphasia a similar difficulty in initiating phrases or sentences occurs, resulting in agrammatism (syntactical errors). The problem is compounded when the patient attempts to say alliterative words or phrases, such as "baby hippopotamus."

Commissural and Transcallosal Control of Information Processing in Split-Brain Experiments

The role of the corpus callosum is to transmit information between the two cerebral hemispheres. Anatomically, this structure consists of all-or-none axons linking neurons on one side of the cortex to those of opposite, homologous regions. The callosal pathways may serve as linkages between different hierarchies of processing within the cortex. Without the callosum, information presented to the nondominant hemisphere cannot be verbalized via the necessary circuitry available only within the dominant hemisphere. Callosal pathways, together with those of the anterior commissure, promote the storage of duplicate information bilaterally and permit more adept performance of movements requiring bilateral coordination.

The role of the corpus callosum in information processing in the brain has been studied by interrupting the corpus callosum and other commissures supporting communication between the cerebral hemispheres.

Split-Brain Studies

The effects of cutting the corpus callosum and related commissural structures (the optic chiasm and anterior commissure most particularly) have been investigated in man as well as in experimental animals [cf. 126,322,937,938]. The split-brain human with callosum and anterior commissure transected can use either hemisphere to receive information and perform complex motor tasks. The central nervous system is in effect divided into two symmetrical halves with comparable inputs, outputs, and processing faculties, except for the dominant lobe (or unilaterally mediated) functions. Motor performance is controlled competitively by either hemisphere, the brain effectively competing with itself for control at any particular moment.

Testing of IQ and associated mnemonic and motor skills fails to disclose any deficit in split-brain patients unless information is presented through lateralized sensory pathways that fail to reach the dominant hemisphere. Then, linguistic communication concerning that information is interrupted. The deficit has the characteristics of an agnosia or a severe receptive aphasia, with a conceptual failure comparable to that resulting from lesions of the dominant hemisphere. The patient can verbalize concerning information presented to sensory pathways that reach the dominant hemisphere but cannot easily verbalize about information that does not.

The following excerpt exemplifies the "deficit" in information processing characteristic of split-brain patients:

> Left and right halves of two different faces joined in the sagittal plane were presented to split-brain patients [590]. When one half of the face was flashed to one hemisphere, it was perceived as a bilaterally symmetrical whole image. When the point of visual fixation was at the mid-line, both hemispheres were simultaneously exposed to the two half faces, and then the subject was asked either to pick the complete face from a group of pictures or to describe it verbally. The face picked was usually that presented to the left visual field (i.e., the right hemisphere); that described or named was usually the face seen by the left hemisphere. When asked to name the face first and point at it, the subjects referred verbally to the right field face, but picked out the left field face. [125]

An example of the more overt competition between hemispheres for control of the organism's performance, coupled with an agnosia, is shown in Sperry's report [939] of a patient who was instructed to perform different tasks on a single object with each hand controlled separately by either hemisphere.

> In this case, control of motor performance passed from time to time from one hemisphere to the other. As this occurred *one hand would begin to interfere in the task performed by the other.* As might be expected, there was commonly neglect or denial of the interference posed by the opposite extremity. That is, there was loss of insight into the nature of the competition with lack of recognition that the interference arose from the same entity that was trying to accomplish the task unilaterally. Control of performance at each particular moment appeared to be exercised by the hemisphere most suitable for the task, with the dominant hemisphere* usually predominating. Transfer of control back and forth from time to time appeared to be spontaneous. Environmental stimuli and transmissions within the neural network controlled the operations performed including the choice of operator.

This observation supports the view taken in Chapter 1 that higher functions can be described as characteristics of neural reflexes since it indicates that

---

*see glossary, esp. definition 2.

control of these functions is divisible "hemispherically" and can switch back and forth insightlessly on the basis of which reflex operation happens to be performed at a particular moment in each hemisphere. The *competition between hemispheres* suggests that "volition" can be partitioned hemispherically; the *spontaneous transfer of control* favors the involvement of so-called "involuntary" reflex functions; and the juxtaposition may constitute an antimony (see p. 401).

In summary, the split-brain studies confirm that the performance of linguistic, conceptualized function is controlled by the dominant hemisphere. They also indicate that control passes from one hemisphere to the other in the course of normal information processing and motor performance. The nondominant hemisphere may have the ability to perform certain nonlinguistic conceptual functions, but because they are *non*linguistic, these are difficult to define. Either hemisphere may have the ability to acquire conceptual as well as perceptual functions, particularly in infancy and early childhood, but once acquired by one hemisphere, some functions may never be acquired by the other.

Reversible Split-Brain Experiments

Bureš and Burešova [126] found that the functions of one hemisphere could be blocked, selectively and reversibly in experimental animals, by inducing spreading depression unilaterally and then allowing recovery. In such preparations, certain conditioned reflexes could be acquired unilaterally, while one hemisphere was temporarily depressed. After recovery, there was often no spontaneous transfer to the other hemisphere until after one or two "priming" conditioning trials were given. This preparation permits other-than-lateralized inputs to be used to test unilateral functions *in a reversible "split-brain" preparation* and offers unique experimental opportunities to study the transfer of learned information between hemispheres.

Engram Formation and Memory Transfer between Hemispheres

Doty and colleagues investigated the functional role of the anterior commissure and the splenium (caudal portion) of the corpus callosum in the transfer of learned information from one hemisphere to the other [234]. They concluded that the anterior commissure reads engrams into a storage area in the opposite hemisphere and that the splenium of the corpus callosum reads stored engrams out from the opposite hemisphere. They also found that tetanization of the anterior commissure disrupted the storage-retrieval process.

In their experiments monkeys were trained to press a lever for a food reward after being cued by unilateral electrical stimulation of the striate cortex. During training with corpus callosum and anterior commissure intact, the animals responded to the electrical CS delivered to either the trained hemisphere or the opposite, "untrained" hemisphere. If, however, the splenium was then cut, the animals failed thereafter to respond to the contralaterally delivered CS. This suggested that the engram was read out from the trained hemisphere via the commissural connections.

If either the anterior commissure or splenium of the corpus callosum was left intact during training and testing, a response could be performed to contralateral application of the CS. The response was elicited selectively; it was not performed if the CS was delivered rostrally to other cortical areas. Animals with both commissures cut after training could still respond to the electrical cue stimulus with appropriate arm movements, controlled primarily by the contralateral hemisphere. However, if both commissures were cut prior to training, there was no response to stimulation of the "untrained" hemisphere. As a result of these studies, the researchers postulated that the anterior commissure was useful in reading in information necessary for formation of the learning trace in the opposite hemisphere. It was also possible that the callosal system acted to suppress the formation of engrams in the hemisphere contralateral to that receiving significant sensory input, since generalization of the CS from sighted (normal) striate cortex to contralateral blind side cortex (optic tracts cut) occurred when the callosum was cut and the anterior commissure was intact, but did not occur when both callosum and anterior commissure were intact. Tetanic stimulation of the anterior commissure or its radiation, prevented both acquisition and performance of the conditioned response. [234]

Doty and Overman hypothesized that the engram for interpreting the significance of the CS remains unilateral when the splenial system alone is present during training, but is bilateral if the anterior commissure is intact. They also concluded that the engram for organization of the CR passes from one hemisphere to the other when forebrain commissures are completely absent.

Evidence for the Separation of Perceptual and Conceptual Functions

Functions mediated selectively by one hemisphere differ from those mediated by either hemisphere. Linguistic functions such as speech, reading, writing, calculating, and distinguishing right from left are mediated selectively by the dominant cortex. For want of a better term, I have called these functions conceptual. Nonlinguistic conceptual functions (putting two sticks together to reach a high object) are also mediated selectively unilaterally, but by the nondominant hemisphere.* Thus, a split-brain patient shown a picture of a pen selectively to the nondominant hemisphere, though unable to name the object seen, can still pick it out from a set of objects or even pick its name from a set of names.

Further support for the separation of perceptual from conceptual functions is furnished by the existence of isolated aconceptual or apropositional be-

*(which is actually the dominant hemisphere for those tasks)

havior, and by the ability of certain conditioned reflexes to generalize across purely conceptual contexts.

Aconceptual, Apropositional Action

Aconceptual, apropositional action occurs with echolalic and echolexographic mimicry in which the conceptual counterparts of certain spoken or written behaviors are lost. These disorders occur following dominant lobe lesions. Denny-Brown describes a patient of Bramwell who could echo speech and write to dictation without any understanding until she had read her own writing. Her disorder, he says, represents a restricted auditory agnosia. Word sounds were perceived correctly and could be transposed into written language as a learned auditory-visual-motor performance, without being conceptually understood. What was missing, says Denny-Brown, was the ability to relate auditory perception to a propositional context. It is this propositional or conceptual context that may arise from functions served by a dominant hemisphere.

Generalization of Conditioned Reflexes across Conceptual Lines (Linguistic Generalization and the Second-Signal System)

Other evidence supporting separation of conceptual and perceptual disorders arises from the ability of reflex processes to generalize in terms of concepts. Pavlov viewed words as second-order signals of first-order signals generated by direct sensory stimuli [132]. His colleagues observed generalization gradients between relatively direct, uncomplicated sensory stimuli and their linguistic, abstracted secondary representations.

> In a recent review of work by Kapustnik [491], Ivanov-Smolensky [448], and Krasnogorsky [554,555], Burešova points out that after a conditioned reflex had been established in humans to the sound of a bell as CS, the same CR was evoked by the spoken word "bell" [132]. The same results were obtained with central-autonomic as with peripheral conditioned motor responses, and could be demonstrated for suppressive as well as for facilitatory responses. In other experiments, Krasnogorsky taught children the names of six birds and then reinforced one of these names with candy. The remaining five names on the list also elicited positive CRs although they were never directly reinforced. The names of other birds or animals, however, were ineffective. Finally, the word "bird" itself elicited the conditioned response immediately.
>
> Burešova asserts that the conditioned response to verbal stimuli is decisively influenced by the abstract meaning of the word and that this is relatively independent of acoustic similarity or dissimilarity. There appears to be a perfect transfer between synonyms from one language to another, and between arithmetic expressions of the same values, such as five; two plus three; or ten divided by two.

The combined evidence indicates that generalization can occur on the basis of abstract concepts and suggests that there is a reflex circuitry in the dominant hemisphere of man that mediates conceptual processes and has access to related, aconceptual information stored elsewhere in the brain.

Perception and Primary Image Construction

Both perception and conceptualization arise from physiologic operations of the neural network but are distinguished by different organizational features in that network. It seems that perception involves primary image construction and arises from uncomplicated processing of sensory-coded information. Conceptualization and linguistics appear to involve extended, secondary image construction.

What is a primary image? An image is defined herein as an aggregate of sensory-coded information distributed among a commonly line labeled set of neurons (see Fig. 7.22). Parts of more than one image may be represented within a particular neural element, provided there is more than one labeling contained by that element. A primary image simply reflects characteristic activation or suppression of a particular set of neurons, recruited on the basis of this common sensory line labeling. Perception follows activation of such a set.

Clinically, echolalia and echolexographia reflect a preservation of the primary sensori-motor imagery of linguistics in face of a loss of conceptualized communication. It appears that the primary perceptual images are not recognized (i.e. remain aconceptual) unless extended, secondary receptive processing takes place as described below. However, motor effectuation may still occur and behavior may still be performed on the basis of the primary images. Echolalia without insightful speech, echolexographia without insightful writing, mirror-writing without awareness of the transposition, and the tropisms and other "unconscious" reflex behaviors reflect operations of this type.

Conceptualization, Linguistics, and Extended Image Formation

What is an extended image? The term, which was developed by Bergson [69, cf. 67], implies some inference drawn from perception. It is an image of an image. The construction itself may or may not correspond to physical reality. It is a conceptualization that seems to depend on isomorphisms having been detected between primary images. According to Kant, the world causes only the matter of sensation [489]; it is our own mental apparatus, that is, the CNS, that orders this matter in space and time and supplies the concepts by means of which we understand experience. It does this by extended imagery (cf. Fig. 6.9).

Conceptualized or extended images appear to depend on being represented selectively within a single hemisphere of the brain. The more apparent representations are those related to linguistics. These functions are unique in that they require unilateral processing within the dominant hemisphere. Considering the competition for control found in the split-brain human and in perseverative disorders, it seems likely that the conceptual functions are kept unilateral and dominant in order to avoid confusion between duplicate representations during motor performance. Perhaps one must sit back and look at things selectively from a distance before conceptualizations or secondary images can be assembled and effectuated.

Can One Have Abstract Conceptualization Without Linguistics?

Some contend that abstract thinking cannot be carried out without words or comparable (e.g., mathematical) symbols and that all conceptualization depends on linguistics, but this may not be entirely correct. Brain says that although linguistics clearly influence our ways of thinking, this does not necessarily mean that we think entirely in words. He cites Helen Keller: "Ideas derived from material objects appear to me first in ideas similar to those of touch. Instantly, they pass into intellectual meanings. Afterwards, the meaning finds expression in what is called inner speech" [94]. Presumably, linguistic, conceptualized functions of one modality can be mirrored by those of other modalities including those used by skilled dancers, musical composers, artists, builders, and the like. Thus, though linguistics usually are visual or auditory, a congenitally blind person who has used Braille all his life could show a somesthetic "aperceptive blindness" from lesions of portions of the dominant parietal lobe supporting this type of somesthetic function. The same might occur in the congenitally blind whose visual impressions were formed by a prosthesis that transduced light waves (the substrate of visual imagery) into tactile stimuli.

What Is Perceptual Function Physiologically?

The act of perceiving appears to be equivalent to the operation of the physiologic substrates relating sensory reception to motor effectuation. No extended imagery need be involved. Thus, perception is a simpler process than might be imagined. One may analyze this process as consisting of several parts, one due to the primary physical stimulus, the others due to the apparatus of the CNS and its mnemonic influence, which lends an unavoidable complexity to the process as discussed earlier (p. 2). The primary physical stimulus exists as a physical entity, i.e., matter or radiation with certain spatiotemporal characteristics or power-spectral densities. In the course of reception and sensory processing through the central nervous system, substantial changes occur. Frequencies, amplitudes, and phase characteristics may be transformed or distorted. Similarity between the set of stimuli and the set of percepts is necessary only in the sense that there must be relatable transforms between the two. What is preserved from the point of view of the organism is the line labeled representation of the stimulus. It is this line labeled information that, when aggregated, constitutes a particular image.

What Is Conceptual Function Physiologically?

Can conceptual functions be understood physiologically? As indicated at the beginning of this chapter, Denny-Brown believes that verbal, grammatic, and semantic disorders of speech (linguistic conceptual function) can best be understood in terms of physiologic analysis. I agree. An example of one kind of analysis is provided by Denny-Brown. He states, "If speech is provided by a low level automatic cortical automatism and disintegration of phonemes is related to damage to this automatism, it appears likely that the conceptual elaboration of this function is not concerned with such phonemes, but with complete speech units (semantemes). It appears that certain stock phrases become first conditioned to appropriate situations, certain nouns become identified with their usual meaning, and finally some causality becomes attached in the form of verbs" [209].

Another example of analysis pertains to the kind of operation performed and the organization of the underlying circuitry. Herein, conceptualization is attributed to a class of operations that generates extended images by forming secondary perceptions derived from isomorphisms between images arising from primary perceptions of sensory labeled aggregates of information.

In a sense, the separability of reflex circuitries supporting conceptualization from those supporting perception may resemble the separation between forms of address or levels of organization used in computer programming. In the example shown in Fig. 6.9, three levels of programming can be distinguished. One, the command level, controls overall flow of the program. Another, the "interim control" level, controls interim flow of the program within subroutines. A third level, that of listing or machine language, simply represents the fundamental, rote processing of the basic computer circuitry, performed sequentially without any superimposed organization or logic. Separation between these levels* must be maintained within the program though not necessarily within the elements performing its operation in order for the flow of information processing to proceed coherently. For conceptualized functions to be realized, there must always be the opportunity to move from one level to another, particularly from the lowest, most basic list mode to the highest, most abstract "command" level. This movement is illustrated in Fig. 6.9.

There are differences in the probability of getting a particular outcome with processing done by the brain and that done by a digital computer. Within a biological system of information processing such as the brain, the outcome of processing involving competitive selection between stimulus inputs will be somewhat uncertain, i.e. a stochastic process (see Fig. 6.6A,C). The same word or percept or memory may not be generated by the same neural network each time it is used. The probability of a similar outcome,

---

*An analogous separation of levels will be familiar to those who have performed complex, multi-user computer system generations.

Higher Function

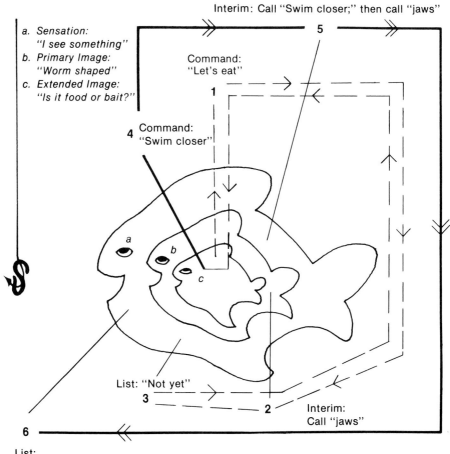

Interim: Call "Swim closer;" then call "jaws"

a. Sensation:
   "I see something"
b. Primary Image:
   "Worm shaped"
c. Extended Image:
   "Is it food or bait?"

Command:
"Let's eat"

Command:
"Swim closer"

List: "Not yet"

Interim:
Call "jaws"

List:
"OK" (1) Set dorsal fin, (2) . . .

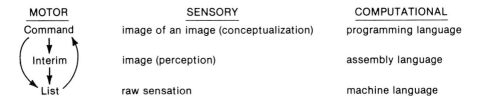

MOTOR	SENSORY	COMPUTATIONAL
Command	image of an image (conceptualization)	programming language
Interim	image (perception)	assembly language
List	raw sensation	machine language

Fig. 6.9. Different levels of information transfer in organism and machine.

given a particular input, is high, but not near unity as in most modern digital computers. The stochastic process of response assembly is particularly apparent in disorders of speech. Consider the initiation of syllables in the patient with a lesion of Broca's area (Table 6.4A) and the paraphasia of the patient with a parietal lesion (Table 6.4B). Once again we see variable outcomes

Table 6.4. (A) Speech of a Patient with a Lesion of Broca's Area; (B) Speech of a Patient with a Dominant Parietal Lobe Lesion

(A) Broca's Area

What is your name?	"Wil-il–wil-il–orl-or"
Wilfred?	"Wilfred"
Where do you live?	"War-yu-on-at–ert–so-wap-wel woy-- on–try"
	"Walton--street"
Is it Waltham Street?	"yeah---woolarm--street"
	"Walltharm-steet"
What is this? (a pencil)	"a–pen–pen–a penchil"
(a pocket book)	"a–pat–pato-bal––ubal"
	"a pak-i-pok- a pokot book"
(a safety pin)	"a pay-ne-shay--pen–a pay"
	"wait--a shay--pin"
	"shay-pet-i-pin"
(keys)	"ker–put–keys"
(ruler)	"woo-wool--wooler"
(a dollar bill)	"willo–rul—wall-woller"
What is this? (a pencil)	"a pencher–pul--chow--cho-a-che- ch--hipol–penchul–a chowl–a penshule"
Say "be, be, be, be, be, be"	"be--be–be–bip--bip--ruler"
"la, la, la, la, la, la"	"la--la--la--la--thig--da--la-- --cher--dattal--tut"
"la-di-da"	"ch-ch-cha"

(B) Parietal Lobe

How long have you been here?	"I have been here twice in hospital and as long since expected did not come it came and it was at last and what I have is long time–This is the last time and the house is expected to go again and I go expected to go again and I go expected as in hospital to go."
Read what it says here (Boston City Hospital)	"poto-total-ospital--Boston City Hospital-Billi-Billi-ospital."
Say "Baby Hippopotamus"	"Baby hipput-hippitopotamo-baby hippopotamus-nine for my hipate-tanus-baby-nine years a baby hip pat an otamus."
What is your name?	"Babee-my name-one babee-one my name-my pale pit a motamus my alien-pit-ann-broke-baby pipanota-mus-my-name is Ann."
How old are you?	"I'm fifty two name pame pit an otamus."
Do you have difficulty speaking?	"Yes, I have but it reams a same a spear a bale a sikaway mile fits baby pit an otamus pitee ann three nine two your which ever pita nota-mus that is the number."

[a] From Denny-Brown [210].

reflecting exaggerations of normal operations due to the removal of selected control processes. A comparison of these examples of defective speech with any accurate transcription of "normal" conversation will reveal analogous phenomena. This type of information processing is quite different from that in most digital computers, even though some aspects of the control of information flow and processing may be the same. Given this physiologic variability, one would expect to find comparable variabilities in higher functions, and indeed they can be found. The same words are used by different people with different thoughts in mind. (How stands *your* ideational horse—head on? aside? a-rear?) The underlying neural operations are probabilistic operations involving aggregates of coded information represented over sets of neurons, labeled in the ways previously described. Order, reproducibility, and similarity must arise stochastically through the operations of adaptive reflexes with common sensory and motor labelings. The adaptations may support error correction. Further understandings of these operations may be gained by inspecting the forms of normal processing revealed by the aphasic symptomatology in the Aphasia Interview (appendix to Chapter 6). The aphasia may seem severe from the transcript, but played back on videotape, the response of the first paragraph cannot be easily distinguished from that of a normal person.

Higher Function and the Organization of the Neural Network

We now return to the questions posed at the beginning of this chapter. In response to "What are the higher functions?", one suspects that they are operations linking image processing with motor performance wherein the processing commonly involves secondary or extended images.

Higher functions are supported by a number of obvious regional reflex networks. The most conspicuous of these are the frontal, parietal, temporal, occipital, and limbic regions of the cortex. A number of other network systems within the brain, such as the cerebellum, basal ganglia, thalamus, and reticular systems, play significant roles in these and other complex functions such as sleep, arousal, postural control, movement, and sensation, not to mention regulation of respiration, blood pressure, heart rate, and neuroendocrinologic functions. They have not been discussed here. Some of these systems are critical for the initiation of the cortical activity that has been discussed, and all contribute to the generation of higher functions.

It *does* make a difference how neural networks are organized since lesions of different areas commonly give rise to different symptomatologies. Failure of the organization to be completed in the developmental period results in a variety of deficits of higher functions. Obvious impairments of intellectual function are found with failures of network development as in anencephaly, in which cortical structures are lacking or malformed. Comparable defects of intelligence accompany more selective deficiencies in genetically transmitted network features, as with mongolism. Biochemical abnormalities give rise to the deficits seen with Tay-Sachs disease and phenylketonuria [952]. As developmental changes in the network take place postnatally, increasingly higher functions are acquired.

If the organization of the neural network is critical for higher function, what are the critical features of this organization? Several features have already been described, including differences in local circuitries, transmitters, labeling, adaptive properties, and mechanisms of adaptation. The differences between simple, repetitive, and associatively induced adaptations are also thought to be significant as indicated in Chapters 2 and 3. In addition, two other important features of the overall system can be identified. One is the error-correcting property of the system. The other appears to be hierarchical processing through cascaded circuitries.

Error Correction

The brain-damaged organism can cope, using what adaptive processes remain, with many defects, whether they arise developmentally or from later damage to the system. This implies that the nervous system is capable of error correction. Gazzaniga [322] reports a patient with agenesis of the corpus callosum who at age 11 seemed to show "a remarkable ability to cross-integrate information presented in one hemisphere with information presented to the other. Information flashed exclusively to the right hemisphere could ... be named and described. ... [He] could easily verbally describe objects placed in either hand out of view." Further testing revealed the development of "spinal [sic] cross-cueing strategies" that compensated remarkably for the deficit of information transfer due to callosal agenesis. However, when these strategies were eliminated, Gazzaniga's patient with callosal agenesis resembled a split-brain adult.

> The subject's hand was placed under a partition, and out of view. The test first required the patient to localize, with the thumb of one hand, a point lightly stimulated on that hand. Thus, over a series of trials, several points on each finger were stimulated. In the second phase of testing, the patient was required to locate the corresponding point of stimulation on the opposite hand. If, for example, the patient was stimulated on the right index finger, the test would be to find the left index finger with the left thumb.
>
> In previous testing of the brain-bisected adults, it had been unequivocally shown that this test could be carried out so long as stimulus and response were kept to the same side. As long as the right thumb was responding to stimulation of points on the right hand, there was no difficulty; and likewise, for the left hand responding to left hand stimulation. Correct performance broke down in the brain-bisected patients, however, when cross-integration of information was required. Thus, the left thumb was unable to find a corresponding point of stimulation on the right hand. The same was true the other way around. [322]

The above findings were obtained consistently through six years of testing the brain-bisected patients. Testing the one agenesis patient (with error correcting strategies eliminated) gave the same results.

After brain damage, it appears that the remaining network makes use of its adaptive properties to compensate for defects that would otherwise impair information processing. Some of these defects can be well compensated by means of the general processing abilities that remain. This is demonstrated by the patient with agenesis who compensates for deficient interhemispheric integration by cross-cueing strategies, and by the patient with aphasia (see appendix) who "thinks" around her auditory speech problem by using another sensory modality. In the latter instance compensation is possible because: (1) linguistic, conceptualized functions of one modality can be mimicked by those of other modalities (e.g., p. 321); (2) there is closed loop control of adaptation in an error-correcting manner between the organism and its environment (e.g., p. 319, l. 31-40).

There are, however, some defects that cannot be corrected. With callosal agenesis, there remains a basic defect in cross-integration. Just as the frog with optic nerve rotation may never learn to strike upwards (instead of downwards) at a fly [454,935], so may the patient with callosal agenesis never learn the thumb-hand integration task. With aphasia, impaired linguistic communication may never be compensated completely. Thus, although error correcting, closed loop circuitries exist between the organism and the environment, not all errors can be corrected by such means, and not all closed loop circuitries readily admit adaptation.

The degree of closed loop control of reflex function is remarkable. Tropisms such as grasping, avoiding, circling, and following are highly visible examples of such control. They connote tight feedback between the organism and the environment. Stereotyped, patterned behaviors such as courtship and mating progress only if the proper contingencies are fed back into the reflex system. Perhaps the most compelling example of extrinsic, closed loop interaction with intrinsic reflex operations is echolalia. One can only be amazed by whatever organization exists within the neural network that permits an aphasic patient who is conceptually speechless to utter perfect mimicry!

Hierarchical Organization

If significant aspects of higher function emerge simply as a consequence of hierarchical processing, what are the key features of the hierarchy? One feature could be an innate structural dissimilarity between hemispheres. Unilateral engrams would arise because only one hemisphere had the structural mechanisms required for their formation. Thus, to understand speech, one would have to explore the structural organization of the dominant hemisphere and determine how it differed uniquely from its nondominant counterpart. A postulate of innate structural differences between hemispheres seems untenable because linguistic engrams can be formed in either hemisphere in humans with agenesis of the corpus callosum [322]. Therefore, the major structural differences must be acquired rather than innate.

Another feature could be the operation of interhemispheric transfer to provide "unilateral" engrams, selectively, to a particular hemisphere. In this way, a transferred engram might become an extended version of an original engram. Although this may at times be the case, it seems unlikely that callosal transfer per se leads to the genesis of dominant function—"dominant" abilities are found in both hemispheres of patients with callosal agenesis. On the other hand, Doty and Overman found that information could be passed from hemisphere to hemisphere when the forebrain commissures were absent. Thus, other means than callosal transfer may lead to the formation of "unilateral" engrams.

A third possibility is that "unilateral" operations arise de facto from two distinct levels of processing. If a hierarchy in processing leads to an extended or secondary transfer, a representation of that processed information may be formed unilaterally. If, as these operations occur, mnemonic cellular adaptations predispose toward unilateral representation of similarly line-labeled information, then speech may indeed tend to be represented dominantly and spatial analysis nondominantly. This possibility suggests that there is a hierarchical level of information processing that can take place in either hemisphere, but once begun in one hemisphere, it takes place more and more selectively in that hemisphere and thus promotes a highly specialized function.

In summary, higher functions depend on the form of the organization of the neural network as well as on the kinds of adaptive elements therein. Aspects of the organization as simple as a second-order hierarchical level of operation may suffice, at least hypothetically, to support and distinguish operations involving conceptualization, linguistics, and the like from those involving simpler, noninsightful perception. Physiologic analysis of higher function then requires an analysis of the network organization as well as its adaptive properties. A reductionist cellular approach may succeed in defining some characteristic adaptive properties of network elements, but may miss critical features of the network organization. The next chapter concerns means by which these features might be distinguished, partitioned, and treated mathematically.

Appendix

Aphasia Interview

The following is a typescript of an interview with a patient who had partially recovered from a severe "aphasia." Clinically, the most important part of this interview is the rare expression of insight by the patient concerning how to treat her abnormalities! Physiologically, the content of the italicized material provides an insightful view of normal as well as deranged higher functions. The capitalized words indicate perseverative repetition of single words, phrases or "concepts".

Q. Would you tell the doctors a little bit about the problem which you have and how it began?

A. Well it's gotten so much better . . . it needs to be . . . every week I get . . . if I go, IF I GO slow you can understand me . . . if I, IF I talk too fast, uh, uh, *I get all the words in the wrong place.* I might have the right words but

I'll have them in the wrong place as I go. Uhm, now I'm just joining this speech therapy I'm doing uh, memory work he calls it because if someone gives me a series of numbers, uh, or a series of words and I'm to repeat, REPEAT it I find uhm my, MY, *I can't listen very good.* I, I know what the concept is, I know what the concept of the sentence is, *or I can read something and get the concept but the words, I can't get 'em.* I have to substitute, in, IN my every day life, which is main conversation, just regular conversation uhm, *I have to substitute all the time* and I have to stutter to, TO, sub - substitute.

Q. O.K. Do you think that this problem has gotten better since your hospitalization?

A. Oh, much better. Just a month ago it was much worse. But now I can, I CAN I CAN rattle off whole concepts of my own, you know, MY OWN thinking that, it seems like I talk automatically if I'm not, IF I'M NOT trying too hard, IF I'M TRYING TOO HARD to talk, uh, it gets all all confused. *I can do it pretty good automatically.*

Q. How about your reading and your writing, has that suffered in any way?

A. Uh, it depends again on - if I'm calm, if I take it slow I can uh, I CAN read almost, ALMOST exactly what's written, but I usually have to, I get the concept and just stick with that that's the only, with writing I've, *I'VE written small notes for my children at school or something like that, and then I find after I read it, uh, that t-h-e doesn't belong there,* that o-f doesn't belong there, this one doesn't belong, *they're in the wrong place, small words are.*

Q. Do you have any trouble with comprehension, do you understand everything that's said to you?

A. *If it's too fast,* uh, if I watch the news it, I'm, it goes right through me, I, *I don't understand anything* if I watch the news, things like that, or fast, FAST talking.

Q. Even if Walter Cronkite is . . . ?

A. No, even real heavy things when Nixon's on . . . gone.

A. (re: question concerning hospital admission) Apparently I was talking in numbers and I don't have any recollec . . . rec . . . I, I can't recall at all for three weeks, uh, and when I . . . *what was the question?*

Q. I was just asking you about the headaches. You say that you do not in fact have any recollection of your hospitalization?

A. Not for the first three weeks. No, not at all.

Q. How about now, how about your memory now? Do you think . . . ?

A. Very bad, uh, I, I, AT FIRST I figured it was something psychologically, maybe it was such a, SUCH A bad time for me I just don't even wanna remember, but I really can't, I, people that I met here, even from the nurses and everything, I just don't even remember 'em, their names or what . . . how come they know me, you know . . .

Q. How about during your activities of daily living, do you have trouble remembering things that are placed around the house—telephone numbers . . .

A. Right, uh, telephone numbers are ridiculous, I have to have them written down. In order to even dial it I have to have it written down. Uhm, yeah, *it's my memory. Actually it's not too bad though.*

Q. How about when you go out to do some marketing, do you have trouble with counting?

A. I go with my husband always, because I get so confused when I get in there, and *sometimes it's like looking at a foreign language in written*, when I'm confused, if I'm in a supermark, market, uh, I, I, I just don't want to deal with it at this time.

Q. What is it that gives you the most difficulty when you say you get confused? Is it calculating how much it's gonna cost or just to find where the food is?

A. Yeh, it's, it's like e . . . even finding something very sim, FAMIL, FAMILIAR, FAMILIAR, I think that's the word, *when something's very familiar, uh, I have trouble deciding whether or not this is it*, that I'm looking for, you know, things like that, I get confused like that.

Q. Do you find that the problem of your speech is aggravated when you become upset in any way?

A. Right, it's worse, uh, then I, THEN I talk uh where it doesn't even make some sense sometimes, where it's so crooked, just really crooked, the words, I can't even talk the words. If, in fact when I get upset I just shut up, other times when I'm very calm or I have an idea of what I'm trying to get across, sometimes *I just rattle through very automatically* and, AND I, AND *I seem to even use the words I like, you know, rather than the ones I have to use.*

Q. And, can you tell me what the name of this place is?

A. UCLA

Q. O.K.

A. Neuropsy, neurops, I can't do that . . . neuropsycho, no . . .

Q. You're going in the right direction, you said the most important part first.

A. Right, neuro.

Q. I'm going to spell a word and I want you to tell me what word it is, O.K.? c-o-m-b-a-t.

A. I haven't any idea, you went too fast, go slower.

Q. c..o..m..b..a..t

A. Comeback.

Q. Say it a little bit . . .

A. COMEBACK? What is it, C-O-M-E? No, c-o . . . combat . . . combat.

Q. Very good.

A. Combat, c-o-m-b-a-t.

Q. Very, very good.

I'm sure you may be aware there are several meanings to one word. How many meanings can you give me for the word fire?

A. Well, it could, it, what do yo, fire . . . uh, first fire, the nom, NUN, NON, the name of fire. Uh, fire somebody from a job, fire from a cannon . . .

Q. Very good. I'd like to tell you a little story and what I want you to do is try and remember it as best you can and when I'm finished, just tell the story back to me in your own words, but try and stick to the content of the story as best you're able. There once was a king who was very sick and his doctors were unable to cure him, so he sent for his wisemen who told him he would get well if he wore the shirt of a truly happy man. So he sent his messengers out all over the kingdom looking for a truly happy man and they finally found one, but he didn't have a shirt.

A. Uhm, O.K. There once was a, THERE ONCE WAS A very sick king, uh, he . . . HE went to some wisemen, HE WENT TO SOME WISEMEN and the wise men told him that he would get better if he found, IF HE WOULD WEAR uh, the shirt of a truly happy man. And so they went, uh EVERY-BODY IN THE KINGDOM WENT looking for a very happy person, and they finally found one but he didn't have a shirt.

Q. Very good, your memory isn't that bad at all. I'd like to have you repeat something for me. I'm going to say a sentence and you repeat it as best you can. Say - it is a nice day outside but the forecast is for rain.

A. It's a nice day, IT'S A, IT'S A, *I know what the concept is*, what the words are, uh, it's a nice day, even though the forecast is uh rain.

Q. O.K. That was very good. Would you try and write that on the board for us?

A. *What was it?*

Q. It is a nice day outside, why don't you just write that much.

A. *Say it again . . .*

Q. It is a nice day outside. O.K. You left out, there's one more word, re-member what it was?

A. Rain?

Q. Could you write that now in script?
Let's see how you do with naming some things. Right in, what about right in here . . . what will we call that (lapel)

A. Lap, LAP, LAPER, PEAR, LA, LA, LA, LAPEAR, PAR, PAPAY, LA-PLAY, I DON'T KNOW. LAPAY, PLAY, LA, I DON'T KNOW. LA, LA, LA . . .

Q. Remember this?

A. Lapel.

Q. How do you know if and when you make a mistake?

A. I hear it, I know when I'm talking really wrong because I can, I, I try to, *I have to stop* almost immediately, immedi, immediately to uh, con, *correct* that's the only way, I, I can figure out how to talk anything, is uh, *listen to myself*. If I'm not listening, if I'm just going fast uh, then I understand that *I get pretty bad, if I don't listen.*

Q. How does it feel when you're having difficulty with the words, when the words won't come?

A. *It's in my head but to use my mouth to, to say the white, the right words, uh, I, I know I'm wrong and I have an idea, I have special ways* to, that other, other than speech therapy, and I've only gone to speech, SPEECH they twice and that's men it's mainly to be for memory work, but I find

if I, *if I can't find a work I'll read it in my head, I'll visualate it*, VIZ, I'LL
ENVIZUL IT, INVIZULATE IT, I'll have it on the side of my head and
I'll read it to myself, right, that's that's what I do with words. Or I'll
substitute, sometimes if I can't substitute then I have to just try and remember how I read it before, like that.

*I find that after I learned lapel AND I, AND I learn these words, uh, I can,
I CAN use them almost perfectly.*

Chapter 7

Cybernetics: A Means for Analysis of Neural Networks

> *The development of the statistical theory of communication is a landmark in the history of communication theory. Our primary concern in a communication or control problem is the flow of messages. Since the central idea in the statistical theory is that messages and noise should be considered as random phenomena, the theory incorporates probability theory and generalized harmonic analysis in its foundation.*

> (Y. W. Lee, 1960)

Commonsense approaches to an understanding of "higher function" are useful but, as we have seen, are basically introspective. Such approaches could be ill advised if used analytically because of their intrinsic susceptibility to errors, particularly those of the type illustrated in Fig. 6.6. Other, more objective means must be found to analyze the complex integrative functions of neural networks. As our knowledge of anatomically and physiologically based memory and learning advances, so must our expression of this knowledge. The form of this improved expression is likely to be mathematical and as specific as expression of our modern knowledge of genetics and the genetic codes. The purpose of this chapter is to explore some of the forms that are likely to serve for expression of our knowledge of memory and learning.

Analysis of large populations of neurons can, in principle, be approached from the same standpoint as analysis of numerically small reflex networks. The analysis requires application of systems approaches from engineering disciplines plus consideration of the limiting physiologic constraints that apply to each system analyzed. In addition, since large populations of neurons deal substantially with the processing of information, their overall analysis requires concepts from information theory.

This concluding chapter examines possible means for analyzing complex systems using mathematics, engineering, and physics. The approach is called systems analysis, but when applied to adaptive systems, it is more properly termed cybernetics, the analytic science that deals with the control of information processing in man and machine. By using the techniques described herein, a rigorous analysis can be made of *linear* information processing systems and, perhaps, of some nonlinear systems as well [582,583,1086]. Some reflexes within the brain can be assumed to behave as a linear system and can be investigated by linear systems analysis [429,1123]. Such an analysis, though properly applicable only to theoretical systems meeting strict statistical criteria, still provides the most useful beginning toward a rigorous analysis of complex nerve networks. It simplifies the complexities of the networks, leads to formulations of the transforms of given inputs into particular outputs, and generates more precise transforms than those presently existing.

A few suitable *models* of information transfer in the brain have been developed that are amenable to mathematical analysis [cf. 18-22,366,838-841, 883,1033-1038]. The most elegant of these deals with image recognition, i.e. the transmission and processing of sensory labeled messages arising at the receptors. Minsky and Papert [672] have transformed certain problems of image recognition into problems of geometry—a transformation that elegantly simplifies many problems of analysis. Then, they have devised a theorem, the Group Invariance Theorem, that provides a general analytic solution for one set of the geometry. In application, the Group Invariance Theorem (p. 388) adequately describes the geometry of sensory reception for the components of two specific models of elements of an image recognition network, the perceptron and the informon. In these models, as in the brain itself, line labeling appears to be the key to following the flow of information through its complex transformation from sensory input into motor output. Flowgraphs and linear systems analysis are also helpful in this regard.

Each of these analytic approaches properly begins by considering known constraints on the system to be analyzed. Therefore, before discussing the models and their analysis, some constraints on information processing that any useful model of brain function should satisfy will be considered.

Constraints

Time Constants of Neural Information Flow

How rapidly can information be transmitted and processed within the CNS?

Conduction Time and Transmission Delay

As noted earlier in Chapter 2, the rate of nerve conduction is a function of fiber size, with large axons conducting more rapidly than small axons. Transmission of an electrically propagated impulse along a neuron may proceed as rapidly as 160 m/sec in the dorsal spinocerebellar tract of the cat [369] or as slowly as 0.5 m/sec in the finest, unmyelinated axons of the spinothalamic system [693]. Thus, while it could take as little as 2 msec for proprioceptive information concerning hindleg position to reach the cerebellum of the cat (a distance of about 320 mm), it could take as long as 640 msec for information concerning the burning quality of a painful stimulus applied at that region to reach the cortex. Conduction time will constrain aspects of learning ranging from effects of interstimulus interval on associatively induced neural adaptations to effects of temporal dispersion on information transmitted through networks of neurons. For example, by comparison with the spinal afferent systems discussed above, conduction across fibers of the corpus callosum occurs within a relatively narrow range of 1 to 16 m/sec [581], thereby significantly reducing the temporal dispersion of information transmitted through that system.

Transmissions between interconnected neurons are slow in comparison with transmissions through most electrical circuits. Transmission across a chemical synapse takes of the order of 0.3-0.5 msec per synapse. The minimum time between independent impulse transmissions (*absolute refractory time*) along a peripheral neuron of the all-or-none type is about 0.5 msec, with a more typical refractory period being 1.4 msec. It takes between 3 and 15 msec (*relative refractory period*) for a neuron to return to its original resting potential. This factor contributes as significantly to the slowing of transmissions as does the actual time involved in summing PSPs in central neurons with membrane time constants of similar duration.

Reaction Time

Many neural circuits that control the flow of information between sensory receptors and motor effectors require between 100 and 200 msec for their operation. Reaction time for reception of an auditory or visual stimulus and effectuation of a simple motor response is usually between 100 and 200 msec in monkeys as in humans [668]. Spontaneously switching the control of performance of one movement to that of another takes the nervous system about the same amount of time. A shift in attention of auditory reception from one ear to the other also takes about 166 msec in the human [100]. Much of this time is spent simply in transmitting the signal as opposed to being used up by processing delays. This can be seen on examining the transmission times required for the different reflex segments that make up a typical mammalian auditory-motor reaction time of 100 msec. *It takes from 6 to 35 msec for sound-information to arrive at the auditory cortex,* depending on the character of the auditory stimulus and the pathway by which it is transmitted. The variability reflects (1) differences in conduction velocities over different neural pathways, (2) different numbers of synaptic inputs required to excite different reflex pathways along which the auditory information is transmitted, and (3) prolongation of the initial response due to recurrent reflex pathways admitting recursive information with time delay. The arrival of visual stimuli at the visual cortex takes about 20 msec longer than does the arrival of auditory information [1104]. Much of this appears to represent a delay of transmission within the retina. *The motor component (from cortex to peripheral musculature) of the reaction to either auditory or visual stimuli takes from 25 to 50 msec to be initiated.* Much of this represents simple conduction velocity along di- or trisynaptic pathways running between the motor cortex and the peripheral muscles, such as those of the hand. On the basis of the above values, the time spent for integration of auditory reception and organization of the appropriate motor output within the CNS can be estimated as ranging between 15 and 69 msec. Therefore, one can conclude that in performing 100 msec responses involving "higher" functions much of the total reaction time is devoted to axonal transmission rather than to somatodendritic integration. Under such circumstances, circuit layout may be as important to information processing as mechanisms of integration at each circuit component.

Still shorter "reaction" times were noted earlier for polysynaptic enactment of discriminatively conditioned responses such as an eyeblink to a sound CS. In the cat, auditory information reached the auditory cortex 6-7 msec after presentation of the stimulus and arrived at the motor cortex 2-5 msec later. It took only 8 msec more for the message to flow from the cortex through the facial motor nucleus to the orbicularis oculi muscles—a total of 16-20 msec for the conditioned response to be initiated. Other subcortical pathways enable motor responses to some stimuli to be performed even more rapidly than those described above. For example, *unconditioned* eyeblink responses follow the occurrence of loud sounds by as little as 12 msec [1113] and blink responses to tapping of the bridge of the nose (glabella) are performed with latencies of 7-8 msec [1112]. Even less time is required for the performance of simpler functions over shorter pathways. It takes but 3.9 msec for a muscle stretch stimulus to evoke a motor reaction in the cat via a spinal, monosynaptic reflex [258]. Obviously, much longer times than these may be required for more complex motor responses generated over longer pathways within the nervous system, particularly those requiring cyclical feedback processing or careful thought, as in chess, with repeated generation and rejection of subliminal responses.

Capacity for Transmission of Information

How much information* may be transmitted within the CNS at certain peak periods? It is estimated that the *potential information inflow* into the CNS via a single sensory modality such as vision is as much as $10^7 - 10^8$ bits/sec [271,363]. The transmission *capacity* of the optic nerve is estimated at 4×10^8 bits/sec by Griffith [363]. In his calculation each of the 1,000,000 fibers in the nerve was assigned a transmission capacity of 400 bits/sec. A bit is defined as the information contained in one binary choice (not in making it, but rather in expressing the number of alternative outcomes in binary form as a logarithm to the base 2, where $\log_2$ of 2 outcomes = one bit). Quantification of information transfer within the CNS in bits does not require that it actually be coded in binary form. Nonetheless, much information is, in fact, transmitted within the CNS by all-or-none, binary impulse functions.

Although a great deal of information may potentially enter the CNS, far less is actually processed and expressed as a motor response. Quastel measured rates of information processing in humans many years ago by giving them

---

*See pp. 379-381 and glossary for important distinctions between information in the analytic as opposed to the generic sense. When the term information is used in any quantitative sense, it must conform to its highly restrictive analytic meaning, a meaning quite different from its generic definition.

tasks of quantifiable information content to perform [787]. He reported peak processing rates of 20-25 bits/sec regardless of whether the task was piano playing, reading random sequences of words, or performing mathematical calculations. This is not far from "record" performance such as that of one telegrapher who was said to recognize transmissions at a rate of 50 bits/sec. As can be seen, information may be presented to the visual receptors of humans at much higher rates (e.g., television transmission) but will still encounter limiting rates of "cognitive" processing following its reception. It appears then that normal and even peak rates of information processing by the CNS are considerably lower than the capacity of nerve channels for transmitting information.

When estimates of nerve transmission capacities are made, as above, by assuming binary coded impulse transmission, the transmission *capacity,* in bits, will be equivalent to the maximum possible rate of spiking if the probability of spike generation is taken as 50%. A maximum transmission rate of about 700 spikes/sec is found in many axons. However, actual peak rates of information transmission through most neurons are less because (1) the probability of spiking versus the absence of a spike is much less than 50% (that of a spike occurring in the next millisecond after another spike being near zero), and (2) most somas generate spikes at maximum rates of less than 300 impulses/sec. If the probability of spike generation is not 50%, then the information per spike must be recalculated from

$$-(p_1 \log_2 p_1 + p_2 \log_2 p_2 + \ldots + p_n \log_2 p_n)$$

the average information per symbol, where $1 \ldots n$ equals the number of different representations of information transmitted through the channel and p represents their probabilities of occurrence [822,906].*

If one considers only the *mean* rate of discharge of most neurons of 10 impulses/sec, then an average of less than 10 bits/sec is transmitted by most neurons.[†] The distinctions between maximal transmission capacity, peak rates of transmission, and mean rates of transmission are then significant. Peak and mean rates of transmission must actually be measured in order to be accurate, whereas the transmission capacity can be calculated given the maximum frequency that the channel can transmit and assuming signal transmissions of determinable probabilities in Gaussian noise. The basis for making a theoretical estimate of channel transmission capacity is described below.

Channel Coding Capacity

Any channel through which information can be transmitted has a coding capacity that may be specified irrespective of whether it is of neural or non-neural composition. The code represents the transmission of the information content of a signal by the transmission channel or by a network of channels. Shannon has shown that the maximum information capacity for transmission

---

*the negative sign making information content the reciprocal of the probability of occurrence.

[†]See MacKay and McCulloch, *Bull. Math. Biophys.* 14:127-135, 1952; 15:107 for a more detailed analysis.

over a channel (the channel coding capacity, C) is a function of channel noise as well as frequency, i.e.,

$$C = K\omega \ln (1 + P_s/P_n),$$ (7.1)

where K = constant*, ω = width of frequency band possible over channel, P_s = signal power, P_n = noise power [884].

In neurons where binary spiking is assumed with a 50% probability of spike occurrence, the signal power may approach that of the noise without loss in transmission. Hence, $P_s/P_n = 1$ and $C = \omega$.

In cortical neurons with possible input rates of 10 discharge-elicited PSPs per 10^4-10^5 synapses, the limiting transmission frequency is the rate of spike production after integration of PSP inputs has occurred.

Multiplexing

Multiplexing is a form of message transmission in which signals of different identities or labelings are mixed during transmission. Subsequently, they are separated and reconstituted as the original signals. Because every transmission channel has a maximum capacity and a maximum speed of transmission, each channel may transmit more than one signal if the information content of each signal is much less than the capacity of the channel. Single telephone cables used to carry a single conversation at a time, but when it was recognized that one conversation could be understood by the human ear when sampled for a hundredth of a second, ten times per second, it was an easy matter to carry 10 multiplexed phone conversations along a single wire. An illustration of how the first two conversations were encoded is provided in Fig. 7.1.

Transmission of ten conversations was accomplished by encoding each second of transmission as follows: the first 0-9 msec carried the first sample of the first conversation, the 10th-19th msec carried the first sample of the second phone conversation, the 20th-29th msec carried the first sample of the third, and soon until the first sample of the tenth phone conversation appeared in the 90th-99th msec. Then the 100th-109th msec carried the second sample of the first conversation, the 110th-119th msec carried the second sample of the second phone conversation and so on until all ten phone conversations were represented by ten, 10-msec samples per each second along the transmission line. Since the order of samples was known, the messages could be separated and regrouped into the original conversations at the other end of the line. In this manner, the full channel capacity was more effectively utilized, and signal transmission was increased tenfold. The important variables here were the lowest sampling rate at which sense could be made of the conversation, the faithfulness of signal reproduction along the channel, and the designation of a specific, unvarying code which could be encoded at one end and decoded at the other.
This is an example of time-division multiplexing. One can also think of spatial multiplexing in which the identities of mixed messages are preserved by designating specific line labeled junctions within the network at which

*As Brillouin has pointed out [96], K is usually taken as $\log_2 e$ by information theorists to get capacity in bits, but K may be taken as Boltzmann's constant to get capacity in entropy units (see p. 379).

Multiplexing

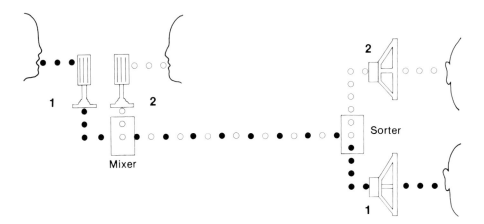

Fig. 7.1. Multiplexing of two conversations. The conversation of the first speaker (● ● ●) is regularly interspersed (○ ● ○ ●) with that of the second speaker (○ ○ ○). Upon reception at the receiver, the conversations are easily separated by alternate switching and can then be reconstituted.

the desired transmissions will co-occur (see Fig. 7.5 III). Most multiplexing codes require the maintenance of precise timings during message transmission to allow subsequent decoding (Fig. 7.5 II). Some systems may fail to have sufficiently precise transmission or clocking mechanisms for this to be accomplished.

Multiplexing offers three advantages for message transmission systems:

1. It allows more efficient utilization of channel transmission capacity as indicated above.
2. Given the proper circuitry, it can permit reliable transmission to arise from networks of relatively unreliable elements. (Von Neumann showed that majority logic could be used to improve the performance of a network of elements each with a probability of up to 0.16 transmission error [1048]. His idea was that by arranging the elements into parallel, redundant channels, one could accept the decision of the majority of channels during processing and thereby reduce the error of the network.) Multiplexing allows majority logic to be performed efficiently in numerically small networks by eliminating the need for astronomically large numbers of separate input lines [906].
3. The error from noise arising from sources immediately outside the channel may also be reduced by distributing the signal redundantly over different transmission channels.

Noise
Noise is whatever enters the transmission system that is not signal. As implied by Eq. 7.1, avoidance of error in the process of information handling will depend on preservation of an adequate signal to noise level throughout the infor-

mation processing system, be it mechanical or biological. In the CNS a major source of mnemonic noise is distortion or decay of physically stored signals over time due to constant molecular turnover. There is also direct interference during transmission from noisy environmental phenomena such as alterations in blood pressure, temperature and metabolism (including pH and electrolytes), respiration, cardiac contraction and other bioelectric signals of movement, as well as effects of trauma. Coding must be stable or at least invariant enough to permit decoding from time to time. The problem that arises from biochemical storage of memory is not only decay of the original information with time but distortion by subsequent information transmissions, particularly those that induce further lasting changes.

Several methods are known for preserving the integrity of a signal in background noise. They include:

1. Redundancy—the creation of many representations of the signal so that a few representations may become lost or distorted without serious detriment to overall processing (the same principle can apply here as with parallel processed majority logic).
2. Insulation of the transmission channel from the noise of other, nearby operating elements (e.g., by myelinization).
3. Filtering to reduce noise extraneous to the frequency of neurally coded information with selective reamplification of the signal to preserve its initial strength (the latter occurs with spike generation, the former with PSP summation).

Redundancy can significantly reduce errors in encoding, retrieval, and transmission, the total output signal to noise ratio being improved by a factor equivalent to the square root of the number of independent channels added [704]. When dependency between duplicated channels is large, the noise is more difficult to eliminate by redundant addition of channels. Thus, while the risk of error will be significantly reduced by small increases in the numbers of channels [704], continued redundant duplication does not always continue to reduce the risk of error. With multiplexed storage or transmission, the mixed signals can themselves become a source of in-channel noise, with similarity or amplification for one particular signal or labeling becoming dissimilarity or degradation for another signal.

Codes that are particularly resistant to noise of constant electrical amplitude are those that are based on some numerical system such as frequency modulation. The coded signal is given a frequency spectrum quite different from that of the surrounding noise. Within a narrow range, the frequency is changed as a function of signal magnitude per unit time. The resistance of signals thus encoded to distortion by noise can be appreciated by comparing the reception of an FM radio with that of an AM radio.

Sensitivity of the Nervous System to Reception of Information

How sensitive is the nervous system to the reception of information? The human retina is thought to be capable of responding to currents of 6×10^{-12}

amps per rod or about one photon of light [871]. Cortical neurons are excited by 0.2×10^{-9} amps delivered at the plasma membrane [1122]. The aquatic species, *Gymnarchus*, is capable of responding behaviorally to $0.15 \; \mu V/cm$ in aquarium water (resistivity,[†] 2 kohmCM) environment [476]. This is a current of about $0.1 \; nA/cm^2$ or 10^{-14} amps/receptor, a detection capability of about 35 electrons/cell.

The level of sensitivity at the sensory receptors must be sufficient for detection of incoming information; however, the same level of sensitivity may not be required (or desirable) for subsequent processing. The squid axon is triggered by currents of 10^{-6} amps/cm in seawater (resistivity, 15-20 ohm·cm), as are many axons of mammalian tissue. This is a current density of about 50 nA/cm^2. Faithful transmission along axons requires that the nerve fiber be insensitive to or shielded from significant outside interference.

Capacity for Storage of Information

How much information might be stored within the CNS over a lifetime? Von Neumann [1050] estimated that as much as 2.8×10^{20} bits of information might be stored during such a period within the human CNS. He based this estimate on a storage rate of 14 bits/sec per each of 10^{10} cells over a lifetime of 2×10^9 sec. Griffith [363] estimates storage on the basis of "encyclopaedic knowledge" of 10^{11} bits stored some 10^3 times redundantly over a lifetime. Thus, there is a sizable difference in the estimates depending on the basis of the estimation, i.e., what is received versus what is received, stored, and accessible. Given the additional factor of internally generated inputs the larger estimate of storage capacity is to be favored.

Forms of Storage of Information

How is information actually stored within the CNS? Although the exact neurochemical forms of long-term information storage used within the CNS are still not known, one can surmise that mechanisms controlling the ionic conductances of neurons are likely to be involved (see Chapter 5). The chemical forms that are theoretically available for controlling engram formation are submolecules, molecules, macromolecules, and molecular aggregates. The forms actually used must have the properties of stability, rapid establishment, rapid access time, sufficient configurations to satisfy information requirements of the storage system, and possibly the ability to be further modified while still supporting earlier storage. Their abilities to meet these constraints allow us to infer which of these forms or their combinations are most likely involved with direct engram formation at the level of the nerve membrane.

[†]Specific resistance along one unit length of a 1-cm cube.

Subionic Particles

Wiener states that substances with high resonance or quantum degeneracy have a high capacity for information storage [1085]. This is because they are numerically large and may be organized into a variety of states. Quantum energy within the orbital rings of an atom would provide a storage form capable of satisfying large capacity requirements. However, this system lacks stability and ease of access to stored information due to rapid change and spatial lability. It is therefore too noisy to represent engram formation directly.

Ions and Molecules

Ions and molecules provide sufficient capacity to store information due to large numeric availability. The stability of ions and molecules is, however, problematic. Thus, while neurotransmitters and neural modulators may trigger engrammatic changes in ionic conductances, macromolecules may be required for their long-term mediation [e.g., 23,871]. Some extraneuronal systems for the storage and transport of biological information have already been identified at the molecular and macromolecular levels. They include immunologic, genetic, and hormonal systems. Generally, the time constants of information transport via these systems are slow. Although there are noteworthy exceptions involving more rapid processes, antibody levels may take days to rise, genetic information may be expressed over weeks or months, and hormonal reactions generally occur over periods of several seconds or minutes. Nonetheless, although expression and transport may be slow, the actual transfer of a single quantum of information within a particular system may be quite rapid. An antigen-antibody reaction can occur almost as rapidly as the process of generation of macromolecules which, in the case of RNA-DNA synthesis, may proceed at a rate of 300 nucleotides/sec.

Macromolecules

Macromolecules are molecular complexes such as those consisting of proteins and nucleic acids that store genetic information. There, the information is encoded in different sequences of nucleotides and amino acids. The capacity for storage by this means is quite large; it has been estimated that 330,000 bits of information could be stored per protein molecule (see Table 7.4). Sufficient structural stability is possible to make access to a specific quantum of information, stored in a specific structural and biochemical locus within a gene, a relatively easy matter during genetic transcription [1068]. Of course, this represents genetically rather than neurally coded information. There is no evidence that neurally coded information is stored in neurons by its transcription into lengthy combinatorial sequences. Instead, it is likely that changes in a small number of species of selected macromolecules support local changes in ionic conductance across nerve membranes and that these changes influence neurotransmission either transiently or persistently as described in Chapter 5. Bluntly speaking, engrams for the word "mother" are likely to be represented as locally altered conductances across networks of many, *many* different cells, the labeled connections between sets of cells being as crucial to the generation of different representations of the word "mother" as the locations and types of altered conductances within each cell. The macromolecules mediating these conductance changes and their codes are likely to be different from those mediating the genetic code in which information is represented by different combinations among transcribed molecules. Nonetheless, the contributions of genetic transcription and molecular coding to the organization and maintenance of nerve networks are extensive. Moreover, they are presently better understood than most forms of neuronal information storage and retrieval.

Complex Molecular Aggregates

Complex molecular aggregates* are frequently suggested as possible sites for information storage within the CNS. The synapse with its presynaptic terminal and postsynaptic receptor is an example of one such aggregate that was discussed earlier. If information were stored as only one engram per synapse, the capacity of the nervous system would be limited to 10^5 synapses $\times 10^{10}$ number of cells.† Were a greater capacity needed, graded control of pre- and postsynaptic adaptation supported by each engram would be required to furnish the necessary additional degrees of freedom here and along other portions of the cell's cable space. Presumably, the graded control would be exercised through macromolecules controlling ionic conductances, the alternative described above.

In summary then, four possible general forms of information storage in the CNS can be identified: subionic particles, ions and molecules, macromolecules, and complex molecular aggregates. For reasons given above and in Chapter 5, macromolecules controlling graded ionic conductances within pre- and postsynaptic nerve membranes appear most likely to satisfy both capacity and stability requirements needed for long-term memory store, not counting that supported by developmental growth.

Efficiency of Storage

Another constraint of any mnemonic process is that it be able to handle the problems of reception and encoding of information efficiently. Information must first be transferred into some storage form, then maintained as a recognizable coded signal within the background noise, and finally, decoded or retrieved later, when needed. For efficient operation:

1. The coded signal must be capable of being created and deposited at a rapid enough rate to keep up with information flow in the system.
2. The capacity of coding and storage in a stable form must be equivalent to that needed by the information processing system.
3. Access and retrieval of coded signals should be of comparable speed to the output requirements of the system.

---

*beyond the less complex aggregates such as the macromolecules [cf. 8,327,397,655].
†And of the cortex to 10^{13}-10^{14} synapses, totally, as calculated from data of Cragg and Parkenberg by Griffith [363] —but, actually, less due to cell death.

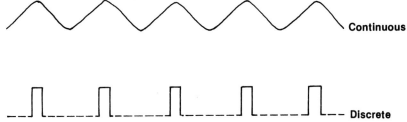

Fig. 7.2. Examples of continuous and discrete signals.

4. Coding may be either discrete or continuous, e.g., impulse functions versus harmonic coding (Fig. 7.2). Information transmitted as a frequency modulated impulse function is highly resistant to distortion by ambient noise, as indicated earlier on p. 329. It is not surprising then that pulse trains are used by engineers as well as nervous systems to transmit messages rapidly over long distances. It is important, however, to recognize the difference between the frequency modulated code of many afferent systems wherein rate of spike discharge is proportional to stimulus intensity and the spatially modulated transmission of many motor systems.* There, the frequencies of spike transmission are low since too high a frequency will produce an undesired motor response such as tetanic muscle contraction. Successful transmission may depend on the coincidental arrival of many different PSP inputs at a single motoneuron as well as on the temporal pattern of discharge.

5. The signal to noise ratio must be preserved either by (a) insulation, (b) filtering, (c) special coding schemes, (d) redundancy, or (e) selective amplification.

Different Systems for Short-Term and Long-Term Memory Storage

It is questionable whether one single storage system within the brain could meet input speed requirements and storage capacity for all the information handled by the nervous system. The evidence indicates that, at the least, one separate short-term storage system buffers information not yet accessible through the long-term storage systems.

It was noted in Chapter 6 that in those suffering from Korsakoff's syndrome, immediate, short-term memory storage (e.g., digit span) was preserved, whereas the recall of longer-term, 'stably' stored material was impaired. Broadbent studied the phenomenon of interference with short-term memory storage in normal humans by presenting extraneous material in the course of a short-term learning task (e.g., trying to remember a newly learned phone number while someone else was interrupting one's train of thought). He concluded that there was a selective interference with short-term storage (his results also supporting the separation of short-term from long-term memory storage).

The selectivity of impairment of short-term storage with anesthesia and drug effects also points to a separation between long- and short-term

*The converse may sometimes occur, as in the visuo-oculomotor system.

storage processes. (An interesting exception to the usual findings with anesthesia and drugs is their relative lack of effect on the consolidation of memory required for learning conditioned taste aversion. Provided the animal receives the CS (taste stimulus) satisfactorily, conditioning is *resistant* to disruption by drugs, shock, etc., given before or during presentation of the US (LiCl) [130,131,133]. It seems likely that the CS traces and the immediate associatively induced adaptations produced by this type of CS-US pairing are mediated by chemicals such as hormones, rather than by active neural processes.)

It has been postulated that most short-term memory is mediated by a neural net in which the information is constantly recycled. Lorente de No [622,623] described short, closed neural loops comprised largely of recurrent collaterals which might serve as such a net, though with an exceedingly brief cycle time. It would be expected that a neural network that constantly recycled information would be disrupted by factors such as shock, freezing, and pharmacologic agents which are known to have a disorganizing effect on neural activity. Exactly those features selectively disrupt short-term memory storage.

Some features of short- versus long-term memory processes are compared in Table 7.1. A system comprised of closed neural loops would be particularly suitable for handling short-term memory due to the rapidity of storage and access to storage of such a system. However, this system would not be suitable for long-term store because of its lability to disruptive forces and the relatively large energy demands for its operation during the period of recycling. Comparatively, the long-term storage system would be energy efficient, stable, and would have a larger overall storage capacity.

Order and Timing in Encoding-Retrieval

Every signal* entering a transmission network is transformed into a coded message. When more than one signal is transmitted, the order and timing of signal entries becomes an important part of the message (e.g., UCLA beats anything). If order or temporal relation is to be specified between two signals entering a network, either the relationship must be preserved physically by stacking procedures in transmission and storage, or else the relationship must be defined in an extra, order generating or timing code added to the code representing the signal information itself. Alternatively, order and timing may be deduced, reconstructively, from the context[†] in which the information that is being transmitted is embedded. However, since the deductive process is cumbersome and the deduction itself may be incorrect, this method is rarely used in successful information transmission networks.

---

*See glossary for definition of terms.
[†]for example, in the case of two cars parked bumper to bumper in a single driveway to a garage, the order of entry of the cars may be deduced. The context and the deductive process may be considered to be a rather complex error-correcting code.

Table 7.1. A Comparison of the Operating Features of Short-Term and Long-Term Memory Storage

Advantages or Features	Disadvantages or Constraints
I. Short-term memory: reverberating circuit (dynamic storage)	
1. Speedy access	1. Lability-physical interruption (shock, freezing) causes loss of stored elements
2. Large immediate capacity	2. Small overall capacity
3. Storage arises from the time delay of the circuit	3. Regenerative looping is metabolically expensive and requires means for preserving signal:noise ratio
4. Easy access, with coupling between storage and processing	4. High energy requirements (the human brain dissipates an estimated 10 watts [1050])
II. Long-term memory: static storage	
1. Stability	1. Processing more complicated, requires extra state transformations
2. Low energy requirements	2. Access more difficult and slower
3. Large storage capacity	3. Time coupling between storage and processing problematic
	4. Storage subject to slow gradual deterioration of signal by noise
	5. May need macromolecular representation which can be additively modified in its stably stored form

In most coding schemes it is further necessary to keep track of time or to know how the coding itself varies with time in order to properly decode the signal. Thus, in addition to the signal code and the code for the order and timing between different signals, some representation of the order-timing features of the codes themselves may be required.

In the earlier example of multiplexing, it was necessary to encode the conversations at fixed intervals of time, to keep these time intervals constant while the code was transmitted, and to know the exact time when decoding so as to separate the messages properly. This timing requirement could have been avoided by attaching a specific identifying label like a check register to each component of the coded message. The label would have specified the order (or timing) and could have been discriminated during retrieval. This would have taken additional space along the transmission channel and thereby decreased the effective channel capacity, the total capacity being fixed.

How temporal and spatial order might be preserved in parallel processing systems within the brain is a most difficult question to answer, and yet is a constraint that must be satisfied. The signals impinging on the receptor organs have both temporal and spatial attributes (Fig. 7.3). When a message is transformed by the neural network into a coded message, the code itself has temporal and spatial dependencies (Fig. 7.3 III) and will be influenced significantly by temporal and spatial features of the network (Fig. 7.3 II).

As indicated earlier, one way of processing orderly temporal information (or any information coded in temporal fashion) is by stacking or maintaining roughly the same sequence during processing. Neurons that fire with fixed latencies after the onset of different stimuli exemplify this type of coding. However, further information (as by supplemental circuits) will ordinarily be needed to decode or sort this sequential data appropriately (Fig. 7.5). Spatial relationships may also have to be maintained during processing. Networks of neurons such as those in the initial parts of the visual system (that maintain the visual fields) exemplify one form of spatial coding. Clearly, it would not be easy to maintain the serial order and geometric relation of information in strict physical, temporal-spatial equivalence simply by sequences of order-related material assigned to specific locations within the brain. For one thing, the sequences would have to be within the time constants of temporal summation or related properties of neural integration and transmission. For another, it would be difficult to maintain order or temporal relationship between signals transmitted through separate, independently labeled channels.

A different means of maintaining temporal and spatial order between messages transmitted through the brain could involve long-term, piecewise error correction by means of adaptive neural properties within the network channels. For example, the organism's behavior could be shaped by feedback from the environment, resulting from actions by the organism itself. In this way the timing between two messages transmitted through separate network channels would be adjusted by error correction, provided one or both channels were capable of such adaptation. This could take some time to accomplish (as in learning to hit a golf ball), and could lead to the generation of additional errors in the course of the correction process (the slice mentioned earlier).

A third possibility for processing information of this type would involve reconstitution of order or timing from contextual integration of two separately stored segments of data as mentioned above. This would presumably be done in a portion of the neural network "downstream" of the separately stored or coded representations. At that level, where both coded representations came together, it would be possible for contextual integration to occur. Cross-correlation (iterative, two variable multiplication and summation; see Eq. 7.13) provides a means by which the temporal or spatial relationship between two variables might be detected and specified through components such as neurons.

Whatever the forms used for encoding information within the neural networks of the brain, the codes themselves must be stable (or systematically variable) and have suitable capacities if the coded messages are to be satisfactorily decoded. One way of examining the codes that are actually used

Temporal and Spatial Features of Signals

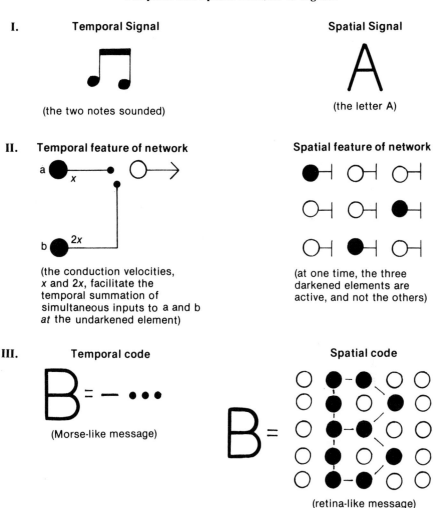

I.

Temporal Signal

(the two notes sounded)

Spatial Signal

(the letter A)

II. **Temporal feature of network**

a

x

b

2x

(the conduction velocities,
x and 2x, facilitate the
temporal summation of
simultaneous inputs to a and b
at the undarkened element)

Spatial feature of network

(at one time, the three
darkened elements are
active, and not the others)

III.   **Temporal code**

B = — •••

(Morse-like message)

Spatial code

B =

(retina-like message)

Fig. 7.3. Temporal and spatial features of signals, networks, and codes.

during neuronal transmission has been to compare histograms of unit activity taken from different locations of the brain but evoked by the same stimulus (Fig. 4.14). Preliminary analysis of such histograms indicates that there is the expected temporal flow from sensory receptive areas through appropriate motor regions but that the form of the code is primarily spatial [1105,1107, 1125]. The form of coding involves patterns of unit discharge quite different from and not necessarily of temporal equivalence to the sequences representing the original signals (cf. Fig. 7.4).

Processing of Information by Automata

Further constraints on how information may be encoded, stored and retrieved arise from observation of successful and unsuccessful processing of information by automata. Automata are artificial, self-organizing adaptive systems, i.e., learning machines. Their operations may be performed by means of a digital computer or other mechanical device. Some elementary logical operations can be performed by binary circuitry as can mathematics (Fig. 7.4). As in most digital computers, serial operations may be used in a stepwise manner to handle information transfer, and the logic or algorithm for any adaptation may be programmed a step at a time. When logical operations are programmed, the specific means of coding, storage, or retrieval are of less interest (they are established) than the program itself since it is on the basis of the latter that the operation of the automata will succeed or fail. Nonetheless, the efficiency of the operation depends on how coding, storage, retrieval, and processing are handled. Thus, one might ask if there is an advantage in machines or networks that use spatial instead of temporal coding or parallel instead of serial processing? Let us approach this question by first examining some simple examples of each type of coding and message processing and then considering the adaptive properties that support selected automata.

Temporal versus Spatial Coding

Temporal Coding
Temporal coding makes use of temporal order or sequence physically, as shown in Fig. 7.4D. Here, the insertion of a spike into the pattern of impulses reflects the occurrence of stimulus "A"; the suppression of an impulse reflects the occurrence of stimulus "B". On the basis of the different temporal patterns of spike discharge, different codes representing A, AB, BA, etc., are generated.

Fig. 7.4. (A) Examples of circuitry used to perform some simple logical operations. (B) Binary versus decimal coding of numbers. The binary numerics can be expressed in circuitry with series of open or closed switches. (C) Comparison of the mathematical operations of addition and multiplication performed by binary versus decimal operations. (D) Temporal coding of the order of presenting stimulus A and stimulus B. Activation of + synapses promotes impulse generation; activation of – synapses promotes impulse suppression. One "+" input neuron is an A detector. The "–" input neuron is a B detector. The other "+" input neuron is a pacemaker. Timing of A – B presentations is reflected directly in the timing of the altered firing of the output neuron. If A and B detectors are reversed (A detecting B and vice versa), the sequence of coding would be changed, but could still provide a satisfactory representation of the original signals. (E) Different coding of the order of engram A and engram B; t = conduction delay. If the output neuron only fired upon receiving two simultaneous inputs, its firing would represent detection of stimulus A and stimulus B presented in the order, BA.

Binary Codes and Switching Circuits

(A)

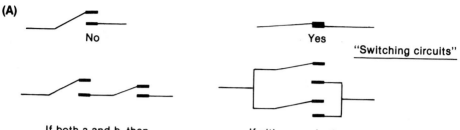

No   Yes

"Switching circuits"

If both a and b, then   If either a or b, then

(B)   Coding

Binary		Decimal
000	=	0
001	=	1
010	=	2
011	=	3
100	=	4
101	=	5
110	=	6
111	=	7
1000	=	8
1001	=	9
1010	=	10
1011	=	11
1100	=	12
1101	=	13
1110	=	14
1111	=	15

(C)   Mathematics

Binary	Decimal
001 =	1
+010 =	2
011 =	3

010 =	2
+010 =	2
100 =	4

Binary	Decimal
011 =	3
× 100 =	4
1100 =	12

101 =	5
× 010 =	2
1010 =	10

101 =	5
× 011 =	3
101	
+ 101	
1111 =	15

Codes Generated by the Timing of Signal and Network

(D)

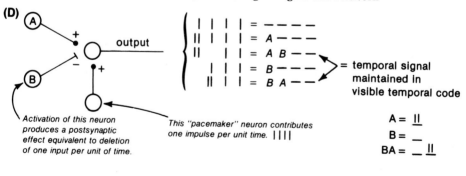

output

$$
\begin{aligned}
| \ | \ | \ | &= - \ - \ - \ - \\
|| \ | \ | \ | &= A \ - \ - \ - \\
|| \quad\ | \ | \ | &= A \ B \ - \ - \\
| \ | \ | \ | &= B \ - \ - \ - \\
|| \ | \ | \ | &= B \ A \ - \ -
\end{aligned}
$$

= temporal signal maintained in visible temporal code

Activation of this neuron produces a postsynaptic effect equivalent to deletion of one input per unit of time.

This "pacemaker" neuron contributes one impulse per unit time. ||||

A = ‖
B = _
BA = _ ‖

(E)

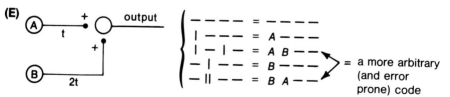

output

$$
\begin{aligned}
- \ - \ - \ - &= - \ - \ - \ - \\
| \ - \ - \ - &= A \ - \ - \ - \\
| \ - \ | \ - &= A \ B \ - \ - \\
- \ | \ - \ - &= B \ - \ - \ - \\
- \ || \ - \ - &= B \ A \ - \ -
\end{aligned}
$$

= a more arbitrary (and error prone) code

As mentioned above, strict temporal coding requires clock mechanisms sufficiently precise to decode the temporal sequences. In the CNS this precision would have to be of the order of milliseconds. Evidence for the existence of slow, biological clock mechanisms governing diurnal behavior has been available in many species for many years [770]. Analogous, "pacemaker" activity is well documented at the level of single neurons [971] with typical periodicities of *seconds*. However, this is still too slow to serve for precise decoding of *msec* events. As Wiener [1085] has pointed out, a more precise timing mechanism exists as the alpha rhythm of the brain, with a periodicity of 100-200 msec. The precision arises from the tendency of generators of slightly different frequencies, when linked together, to drive at one fixed, common frequency. Whether this would be sufficiently precise or reliable (consider *de*synchronizing, arousal effects: Chapter 4) to serve as a clock for millisecond neural coding remains to be seen. In general, present evidence weighs against strict temporal coding using a biological clock for much of the information processing done by the CNS . On the other hand, adaptation in the CNS appears to depend on relatively strict temporal relationships and on the maintenance of particular timings during transmission.

Spatial Coding
Spatial coding employs differences in coding distributed over space to represent a signal. An example is shown in Fig. 7.5 III. The spatially distributed code enables the signal "A", "B", or "D" to be detected, depending on the message transmitted to the end element, d.

Spatial Representation of Temporal Signals; Temporal Representation of Spatial Signals
In Fig. 7.4D, a temporal signal is maintained in temporal code; in Fig. 7.4E, it is transformed into a more arbitrary code in which the temporal representation of the signal is not so easily recognized; in Fig. 7.5 III, the spatial aspects of the code predominate. Nonetheless, in each case the code depends on (1) the timing of the signal, (2) the space (or number) of the network receptors activated by the signal, (3) the timing of transmission through the network, and (4) the spatial arrangement of the network. In coded form (as in uncoded form), space and time are interdependent and may be interchangeable or transferable within the code.

Temporal and Spatial Processing in the CNS
As Sherrington recognized [887], temporal and spatial processing involve *summation* and related consequences of coincidental arrival of separately generated transmissions at a single downstream element. (Sequential arrivals have their own consequences as noted in Chaps. 2 and 3.) Temporal and spatial summation permit transmissions depending on engrams contained in a group of widely dispersed neural elements to influence activity at a common downstream locus. The outcomes of this type of processing take on the form of an ensemble average (p. 258). Let us see just how this occurs.

Within the brain an aggregate of information may be stored within a set of engrams distributed across a field of similarly line labeled neurons much as shown in Figs. 3.42, 7.5 III, and 7.22. Another aggregate may be stored within a different set and field. Some neurons may be included in more than one field, and some engrams may appear in more than one set. Each aggregate, set, and field will have a characteristic identity analogous, for example, to the sides with one spot in groups of multi-sided playing dice. These identities will be isomorphic* with certain possible outcomes of the operations of the ensemble (the overall network). Different probabilistic outcomes within the network can also be used to represent order and sequence, if order and sequence are responsible for their generation. The probability of a particular outcome or response to a given stimulus (such as a limb flexion or a limb extension) will be much like that of a "1" or a "2" in Table 5.7, except that the outcome will also be strongly biased by the initiating stimulus itself.

One can imagine what will happen as new inputs enter the network. New engrams will be formed, and old engrams will influence subsequent information processing and message transmission. If enough commonly labeled engrams are addressed by a particular input, their contributions may supersede those of more randomly addressed engrams and control (or influence) downstream transmission and processing through the network.

As can be seen with reference to Figs. 7.5 III and 7.22, each stimulus input will access a restricted set of possible (response) outcomes by virtue of its labeling during transmission through the network. This feature of the network, together with the property of adaptation, will bias stimulus inputs toward transmission and processing along channels that contain potentially relevant engrams.

Several features of information processing in a network such as this can be identified:

1. Inputs and outputs will be linked by labeled transmission (cf. Fig. 3.42).
2. Inputs and engrams will also be linked by labeled transmission (cf. Fig. 7.22).
3. Engrams may be "recruited" by coactivation leading to summation downstream. The result (as described above) will be much like the operation of Von Neumann's majority logic organ [1048,1050] or the averaging described in Chapter 5.

Serial versus Parallel Processing

Serial processing is normally performed by sequential operations through serial circuitry, frequently using a discontinuous, binary code. Figure 7.5, II, shows a complex network incorporating serial processing and a time-delay code to distinguish between letters.

---

*strictly speaking, probabilistically related to or will probabilistically predispose toward certain outcomes, but nonetheless, the identities will be isomorphic in the sense that they can be mapped on the outcomes and vice versa.

Automata Design

I. Receptors

II. Spatial signal-serial processor-temporal code

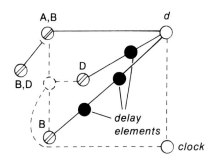

$$\text{at } d: \begin{cases} | \; - \; - \; = (A) \\ - \; | \; - \; = (D) \\ - \; - \; | \; = (B) \end{cases}$$

$$\overbrace{}^{B} \; \overbrace{}^{D} \; \overbrace{}^{D}$$

but then: $-- \underset{D}{|} - \underset{A}{|} -- | -$

III. Spatial signal-parallel processor-Spatial code

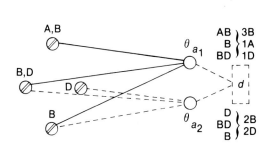

$\theta_{a_1} = 3; \theta_{a_2} = 3$:

Discriminates B, but not A, D

$\theta_{a_1} = 2; \theta_{a_2} = 2$:

Discriminates A, B, D and survives ablation of any 1 of 3 inputs to a_1

$\theta_{a_1} = 2; \theta_{a_2} = 1$:

Discriminates A, B, D and survives ablation of any 1 of 3 inputs to a_1 and/or a_2

Fig. 7.5. Examples of the components of different automata. I. Receptor elements common to each example. The uppermost of the four elements is receptive to (and intersected by) the letters A and B but not D. The lowest element is receptive to B only. The receptivity of the remaining two elements is as indicated. II-IV. Automata with different network architectures: II, serial time dependent, III, parallel perceptron, IV, parallel pandemonium. In II three

IV. Feature weighting and analysis plus feedback control

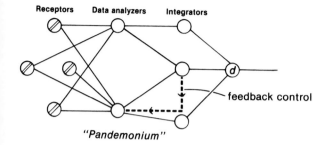

Receptors   Data analyzers   Integrators

feedback control

"Pandemonium"

V. Feature detection and evolution

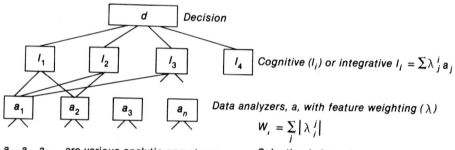

d Decision

I_1 I_2 I_3 I_4 Cognitive (I_i) or integrative $I_i = \sum \lambda_j^i a_j$

a_1 a_2 a_3 a_n Data analyzers, a, with feature weighting (λ)

$$W_i = \sum_j |\lambda_i^j|$$

$a_1, a_2, a_3,...$ are various analytic operators: e.g., template matching, summing, differentiating, etc.

Selection is based on the sum W_i of the weightings λ_i of the a_j individual features analyzed

different coded outputs of the decisional element, d, are shown to the right. Below, the ambiguity of this coding is illustrated when its beginning in time is uncertain. In III changing θ, the number of inputs required to fire the second order elements, changes the discriminative property of the network as discussed in the text and summarized in the diagram to the right. In IV a variation on III introduces feature detection (e.g., summation, filtering, etc.) as well as feedback control (heavy dashed line) into the circuit. A version of IV is shown below (V) in which details have been inserted after Selfridge's pandemonium [883]. Selection of evaluation of the individual demons for permutation is based on W_i, the sum of the weightings, λ_i, of the individual feature detectors, a_j.

The filled circles represent serial time delay elements. The elements comprised by dashed lines represent a clocking mechanism that keeps track of time following presentation of the stimulus pattern at the receptors. Depending on which receptor is activated, a time coded signal 1--, -1-, or --1 will be generated at the decision-making element, d. Note that if track is not kept of time (see Fig. 7.5, II, lower right), the code becomes ambiguous. Though the example is oversimplified, it is quite representative of the type of processing that is widely used in digital computers.

The term parallel processing was originally used to designate performance of the same processing operation by more than one channel at a time. The purpose was to support majority logic and redundant signal processing as discussed earlier. *Multiplexed,* parallel processing resembles much of the processing done by the brain. In the example shown in Fig. 7.5, III, the second-order elements receive redundant messages and parallel processing is used to generate a "decisional" output at element "d". As can be seen, this type of processing has remarkable sorting or discriminative properties when adaptation is introduced.

If each of the second order elements in Fig. 7.5 III is set to fire when three inputs are received (3/3), the network will distinguish B, but not A from D, i.e., a_1 (fires) = B. If the "threshold" is reduced to discharge upon reception of two inputs (2/2), the network will then discriminate A, B, and D. An A will be designated by no discharge, a B by discharge of both elements, and a D by discharge of the lower element, i.e., $\overline{a}_1 \overline{a}_2$ = A (or nothing presented), $a_1 a_2$ = B, $\overline{a}_1 a_2$ = D. Moreover, the network will continue to function despite destruction of any one of the three input lines to the upper element.

Although one must beware of making exact transpositions between mechanical and physiologic models, many of the same, general theoretical considerations concerning learning, memory, and even higher function apply to machines as to physiologic systems. The machines give us a physical model which is more accessible to analysis and is more easily studied. Three machine automata stand out from the others in providing insightful models of learning operations, component interactions, and the constraints thereof. They are the perceptron, pandemonium, and the informon.

Perceptron

The perceptron represents an early attempt by Rosenblatt and colleagues to develop a learning automaton based on their conceptions of brain organization [838-841]. In this device, the components consist simply of modifiable elements and their interconnections. As shown in Fig. 7.26, ψ is the sum of the components $\varphi_{(\chi)}$, each weighted by α_φ. When the weightings are modified ($\Delta \alpha$), the system can adapt to distinguish a particular input, identified when ψ is $\geqslant$ some predetermined value, θ.

$$\psi = \Sigma \, \alpha_\varphi \varphi(\chi) \geqslant \theta, \tag{7.2}$$

where $\Delta \alpha$ reflects adaptation.

The example of parallel processing (Fig. 7.5, III) can be viewed as a perceptron by making d = Σ and considering a_1 and a_2 as having weighted inputs depending on the threshold settings, θ_a.

In such systems, the performance of pattern recognition can be adaptively improved with relatively simple algorithms of element modification as illustrated in Fig. 7.5 (additional algorithms are listed on p. 395). Although this can be done among elements with randomly organized connections, as the original perceptron demonstrated, a more efficient operation will be provided by a nonrandomly organized network. Thus, the organization of the adaptive network may become a critical variable in the learning operations that are performed by such a system.

Pandemonium

An example of a nonrandomly organized automaton is *pandemonium* of Oliver Selfridge [883]. Its organization is hierarchical, being characterized by multiple layers supporting different operations as shown in Fig. 7.5, IV and V. The initial layer again consists of simple receptor or data collecting elements, termed data demons by Selfridge. The second layer consists of specialized analyzers or computational demons. They process incoming data by stereotyped procedures such as matched filtering, summation, or differentiation. The third layer consists of integrators or cognitive demons. They integrate weighted inputs from various computational demons. Finally, a decision maker or "decision demon" selects the loudest or most active cognitive demon(s) and by its (their) identity gives priority to a selected set of receptors.

Within this hierarchy, adaptation occurs according to rules of reinforcement specified in terms of the effectiveness of each element in performing the selected recognition task. Elements which are more contributory to successful image recognition are positively reinforced by increasing their weighting. Elements which are less contributory are eliminated. Permutations of the analytic algorithms of successful elements are generated to replace those of unsuccessful elements. Hill-climbing techniques are used to secure continued improvements of the adaptations with extensive attention paid to the problem of avoiding false peaks.

Several insights into adaptive information processing are provided by pandemonium. Pandemonium is characterized as a chaotic operation with demons, subdemons, and sub-subdemons shrieking their outputs, adapting, deciding, and sometimes evolving. However, the chaos turns out to be more orderly than expected. All the analytic functions are particularized and are, to a significant degree, predetermined. Despite the great degree of adaptability within the hierarchy, the hierarchy is relatively fixed. The reason for this is that, although the adaptability permits evolution, it is along a predictable pathway, and occurs within a particular hierarchy. (This feature appears to have led this particular automata to a particularly tenacious pursuit of false peaks during hill-climbing adaptive operations.) Differences in the design of the hierarchy selected for Pandemonium versus that shown in Fig. 3.42 may therefore be of some consequence. The ability to switch between elements may need to be matched by an ability to switch between hierarchies.

Informon

The *informon* model of Uttley [1033-1038] takes a somewhat different approach to the design of an automaton, concentrating on improving the construction of the fundamental adaptive element itself. The basic informon consists of a single element with multiple inputs $F(x_n)$ and an output (Fig. 7.6). The inputs have variable weightings, α. One of the inputs is defined as a reinforcing input $F(z)$ with a fixed negative weighting, $-k$. There is also provision for negative feedback of information concerning the operational state of the element, $F(Y)$. The negative feedback is required for stability of the adaptive process. $F(Y)$ is some function of the output of the element prior to the state of binary, spike discharge. There is finally a threshold device, θ, at or just before the output, which can be used to discriminate between different sets of inputs.

Several additional variables (or constraints) are required for the informon to discriminate successfully one particular input $F(x_i)$ from another, $F(x_{ii})$. These are:

1. The algorithm by which α_i is altered ($\Delta \alpha$).
2. The need for a reinforcing input, $F(z)$, to distinguish or identify which input signal is the particular signal to be discriminated.
3. The need to achieve some system normalization through negative (not positive) feedback of information regarding the current system state, $F(Y)$.

Note also that by picking the adaptive algorithm correctly (e.g., log of the mutual information between inputs), one can greatly facilitate both normalization and input discrimination.

Algorithm for $\Delta \alpha$
The trick here is to choose an algorithm that will produce S-shaped adaptive operations such as are found with conditioning or other simple forms of learning. It will also be useful to have a decay or extinction phase of adaptation. Adaptation is performed by changing the weighting, α, of an input.

Simple Informon

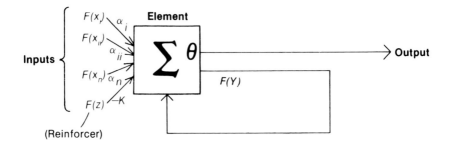

Fig. 7.6. The basic informon element. See text for further details. (After Uttley [1038].)

Figure 7.7 shows such an operation graphically and enables us to see how a particular choice of algorithm may or may not produce a stable change in weighting.

Uttley points out that analysis in the phase plane between change in α(i.e., $\Delta\alpha$) and α itself reveals the limitations of certain algorithms, notably those proposed by Hebb [397] and by Brindley [97] and Marr [646]. This is shown in Fig. 7.8.

> Hebb's postulate that an input causes an increased output simply indicates that if α is positive so must be $\Delta\alpha$. This postulate places the algorithm for acquisition within the right upper quadrant (++) of Fig. 7.8, but fails to specify a relationship or slope between variables $\Delta\alpha$ and α. Brindley [97] and Marr [646], in effect, consider a pathway with two states, one initial and one final, in which $\Delta\alpha$ and α increase together. With limiting values this reduces to an all-or-none, two state process. Without limiting values this represents an unstable system with positive feedback which will lead to regenerative explosion (line "a" in Fig. 7.8).* Uttley picks an algorithm which allows the values of $\Delta\alpha$ and α to fluctuate in the manner shown by lines "b" and "c" of Fig. 7.8 [1036].

System Normalization by Feedback of System State

Uttley points out that regenerative explosion may be avoided by introducing a normalization process, such as that of Malsburg [1047]. However, Malsburg's type of normalization shows an overly restrictive range of successful

Adaptation in an Informon

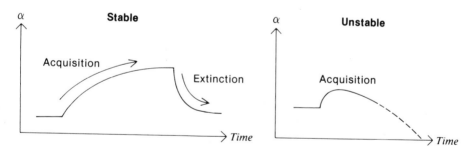

Fig. 7.7. *Adaptation in an informon involves changes in* α, *the weightings of input, over time. In the example to the left an increase in* α *occurs during acquisition or input facilitation and a decrease occurs during its extinction or defacilitation. The parallel between this and conditioned behavior is deliberate. In the example to the right acquisition is an unstable process with* α *declining unintentionally past a certain transition point. This may occur because of failure to regulate the system state appropriately during the adaptive process. See text for further details about regulating the system state (After Uttley [1036].)*

---

*This problem is avoided in some nonlinear systems that change state as levels reach certain limits.

Phase Plane Between $\Delta\alpha$ **and** α

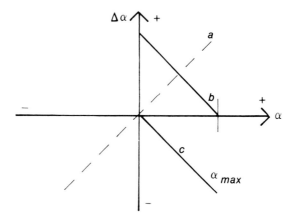

Fig. 7.8. *Phase plane of α versus change in α (i.e., $\Delta\alpha$). State changes along "a" such as those proposed by Marr [646] and Brindley [97] are unstable, while those along "b" or "c" are not. b mirrors the state change during acquisition in Fig. 7.7; "c" mirrors the state change during extinction. (After Uttley [1036].)*

operation when applied to a system with positive feedback. To avoid this, Uttley turns to negative feedback as shown in Eq. 7.3b. Thus, the adaptation of his element, and probably some neuronal elements as well, depends critically on *negative feedback of information concerning the system state, $F(Y)$.* Normalization results in part from the negative feedback of information concerning the system state (Fig. 7.9) and in part from the choice of adaptive algorithms described below (Eqs. 7.3a, 7.3b, and 7.5).

$$\Delta\alpha_i = -kF(x_i)F(Y), \tag{7.3a}$$

where $F(Y) = \Sigma\ F(x_i)\alpha_i$ and k is a positive constant.

However, this is still not enough to permit successful input discrimination, which depends additionally upon introduction of a reinforcing input.

Reinforcing Input
Reinforcement, or identification of the particular input $F(x_i)$ to be discriminated or enhanced by increasing α_i, is done by introducing a separate, labeling input $F(z)$ with α_z fixed and negative (Eq. 7.3b).

$$\Delta\alpha_i = -kF(x_i)\ [\Sigma_i F(x_i)\ \alpha_i + F(z)\ \alpha_z] \tag{7.3b}$$

Given an input $F(x_i)$, α_i will increase if $F(z)$ is present and will decrease if $F(z)$ is absent. With repeated reinforcement, α_i assumes the function of the acquisition curve shown in Fig. 7.7 (left) with $\Delta\alpha_i = \alpha_{max} - \alpha_i$ (line "b" of

Significance of Locus of Negative Feedback of Information Concerning System State Relative to Level at which the System State Becomes a Binary, All-or-None Output

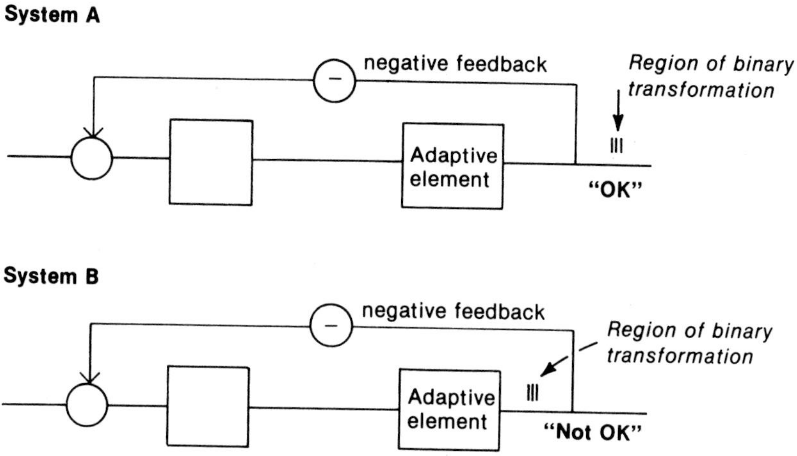

System A

System B

Fig. 7.9. By changing the locus of negative feedback so that instead of sampling the internal state of the adaptive element, as in (A), one samples only the binary output of the adaptive element, as in (B), one loses information required for normalization and an unsatisfactory adaptive process may ensue. The location of the binary encoder is shown by ‖‖. *(Cf. Uttley [1033].)*

Fig. 7.8). Without reinforcement, α_i assumes the function of the extinction curve in Fig. 7.7 (left), with $\Delta\alpha_i = \alpha_i$ (line "c" of Fig. 7.8). Without a reinforcer, $F(z)$, a curve such as that shown in Fig. 7.7 (right) would be obtained.

The transfer properties of Uttley's adaptive element are designed then to simulate the S-shaped acquisition curve of conditioning plus its decrement during extinction. Considerable attention is also paid to controlling and limiting elemental adaptation by closed loop, negative feedback of the element's internal state. This variable provides a significant constraint on the operation of the adaptive element and may constitute a general requirement of successful self-organizing adaptive operations.

Mutual Information Constraint

Uttley imposes one further constraint on the operation of an informon, namely, that α be a modification of Shannon's mutual information function*:

$$\log\frac{P(x_i \text{ and } Y)}{P(x_i)\,P(Y)} = I(x_i:Y)$$

*see p. 381

This constraint can be applied to the operation specified in Eq. 7.3b. As a result:

$$\alpha_i = K[\ln F(x_i) + \ln F(Y) - \ln F(x_i)F(Y)] * \qquad (7.4)$$

or to simplify

$$\alpha_i = -KI(x_i:Y) \qquad (7.5)$$

Thus, an increase in $F(x_i)$ will result in an increase in α_i; an increase in $F(Y)$ will also increase α_i, but an increase in $F(x_i) F(Y)$ will decrease α_i.[†]

In summary, parallel processing systems with adaptive elements appear to handle discrimination tasks quite easily. Hierarchically organized networks, such as pandemonium, with non-uniform elements and specialized adaptive properties can handle some forms of learning with particular ease, but may cling tenaciously to errors in discrimination arising from their particular design. (This erroneous "behavior" is not unlike that of perseveration and neglect described in Chapter 6.) Other automata, such as the informon, may rely on optimized properties of more uniform adaptive elements. As Uttley has shown [1036-1038], the adaptive weightings must change in ways that are nonexplosive. Introduction of negative feedback of information concerning the state of the controlled system can contribute to a normalization process which, in turn, can reduce the possibility of explosive change. Other features such as relaxation of increased weighting and discriminative control of the weighting changes of certain inputs require additional features. These may include particularized dependencies between inputs such as the mutual information feature of Uttley's model or labeled reinforcing inputs such as $F(z)$ of Uttley's model.[‡]

By slightly redefining Uttley's circuits (Fig. 7.10), it is possible to form closed loop, positive feedback pathways that might support motor labeling in classical, associative conditioning (see Chapter 3). Positive feedback would augment a particular message of motor significance transmitted within a specific, closed loop circuit. The augmented message would facilitate the formation of adaptations along the pathway. Another mechanism (e.g. inactivation) would be required to avoid explosive change.

Further support for a possible role of positive feedback in neural control systems is furnished by Freeman's model of olfactory bulb circuitry [299]. In that model, the effect of the stimulus is to increase feedback gain in an ensemble of neurons that are receptive to the stimulus. "If a local ensemble containing sensitized subsets that are mutually excitatory is excited, the basis exists for a regenerative increase in activity in response to an adequate stimulus" [299]. The model has five main features:

---

*a simplification; properly, the equation incorporates the ensemble average of the frequencies of signal occurrence. See Uttley [1036].
† Further material concerning these equations can be found on pp. 381,382.
‡For further particularizations of interest, see Uttley, A. M. *Information Transmission in the Nervous System.* London: Academic Press, 1979.

Feedback of Motor Labeled Information

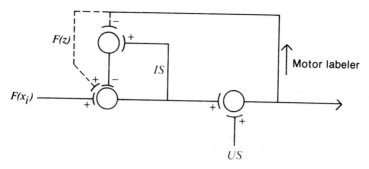

Fig. 7.10. Schema for motor (M) labeled reinforcements derived from Uttley's informon model. The US activates neurons which act directly (or indirectly) as the F(z) input. Selective labeling of the "upstream" neurons which project, selectively, to the activated units is potentiated because of positive feedback within the circuitry. For this schema to operate successfully, some feature such as local recurrent inhibition would be required to monitor the system state and prevent explosive buildup from the positive feedback. IS=feedback of information concerning internal system state.

1. A nonlinear signal range that is near linear about the origin.
2. Bilateral saturation with gain approaching zero at both extremes of wave amplitude (this feature provides stability).
3. A 2:1 asymmetry of the asymptotes of the circuit transfer function (arising from the features of the olfactory bulb and cortical electrophysiology on which the system is modeled).
4. A gain that increases with positive (excitatory) input.
5. A gain that is modifiable in a pattern that depends on background or steady state activity, which in turn is presumed to be under centrifugal control.

The positive feedback should satisfy three constraints for stability: (1) the regenerative effect should not be unduly perturbed by noise, (2) it should be self-limiting in maximal amplitude, and (3) it should be rapidly self-terminating to permit additional inputs to pass [299].

Analysis

Analysis of the organization of systems as complex as the brain need not be considered impossible when systems involving complex communication (television), learning (computer automata), elaborate control mechanisms (guided missiles), and even uncertainty (the atom) have proved amenable to analysis. It is possible, in principle, to analyze a complex system if it is finite, obeys the laws of physics, and meets the constraints of the analytic method.* This

---

*One should never underestimate the importance of this latter consideration (see pp. 322-401 and Epilogue).

is so irrespective of whether the system is biological or mechanical. Means exist, such as linear systems analysis (p. 366), for partitioning many complex systems into relevant suboperations that are easier to analyze, and some neural systems are amenable to this form of partitioning [429,1103,1123]. Other means such as flow graph techniques (p. 368) can be used to analyze neural network operations on a cell to cell basis despite complex interrelationships including feedback between receptor and effector functions. Finally, means can be found, as by computer simulations, to reassemble and test the analyzed component functions with reference to the overall organization of the network.

Apart from complexity, another objection that is frequently raised to analyzing brain function is that general physical theories comparable to those found in chemistry or other basic disciplines are lacking. While it is true that theories of information handling are not so advanced as those in other fields, the existing theories have been found applicable to predictive treatment of information handling by real systems. The usefulness of Shannon's information coding theories in the communications industry is well established and has been complemented by the emergence of additional theories in the areas of systems control. The challenge for neuroscientists is to develop extensions of the above theories that are applicable to treatment of specific neural information processing systems. The basic purpose of the material that follows is less ambitious, being simply to outline some of the potentially relevant analytic methodologies.

Signal Analysis

The fundamental idea of Wiener and Lee's approach to analysis of communications systems is that messages, signals, and noise should be considered statistically and described in terms of probability theory [582]. Messages are information carrying functions, i.e. member functions in an ensemble, or numerically large aggregate, of signals (relevant information) *and* noise (irrelevant information) and their combination. Communication theory has led to analysis of linear message-transmission systems using convolution as the basic analytic device. Given a linear system (p. 396) and consideration of signals and noise as random processes [582], signal analysis can be performed by time series analysis utilizing (1) Fourier series, (2) power spectral density, (3) correlation, and (4) convolution (Table 7.2).

Most signals to be analyzed within the CNS are changes in voltage or current as a function of time. To determine the structure of a signal, it is analyzed in terms of its frequency components (c.f. Figs. 5.30, 7.11, 7.12, and 7.14). The signal may be described in terms of its *major* frequency components (Figs. 7.11, 7.12) or, more precisely, in terms of the power consumed across a 1 ohm resistor by passage of the different frequency components of the signal (including harmonics). The latter is called the power spectral density (Fig. 7.14). Some information, that concerning the phase of one frequency component

Table 7.2. A Summary of Methods for Time Series and Linear Systems Analysis

---

1. *Fourier Series*

$$f(t) = \frac{a_0}{2} + (a_1 \cos \omega t + b_1 \sin \omega t) + (a_2 \cos 2\omega t + b_2 \sin 2\omega t)$$

$$+ \ldots + (a_n \cos n\omega t + b_n \sin n\omega t)$$

$$= \frac{a_0}{2} + \sum_{n=1}^{\infty} (a_n \cos n\omega t + b_n \sin n\omega t),$$

where $\omega = 2\pi/T$ (radians per sec) $= 2\pi f$ (Hz)

$$= \sum_{n=-\infty}^{\infty} a_n^* e^{jn\omega t}.$$

since by Euler's identity $e^{iz} = \cos z + i \sin z$.

$$\cos n\omega t = \tfrac{1}{2}(e^{jn\omega t} + e^{-jn\omega t})$$

$$\sin n\omega t = \tfrac{1}{2}j(e^{jn\omega t} - e^{-jn\omega t})$$

2. *Power Spectral Density* $S(f)$

$$S(f) = \sum_{n=-\infty}^{\infty} |a_n|^2 \, \delta(f - nf_0)$$

where $f_0 = 1/T$ (T = period in seconds and δ is a delta, unit-step function)

$$a_n = \frac{1}{T} \int_0^T f(t) \, e^{-jn\omega t} \, dt$$

Note that $\displaystyle\int_{-\infty}^{\infty} |a_n|^2 \, \delta f = \int_{-\infty}^{\infty} |f(t)|^2 \, dt$; i.e., $\psi(t)$ the autocorrelation

function is the inverse Fourier transform of the power spectral density.

3. *Correlation* $\psi(t)$

$$\psi(t) = \frac{1}{T} \int_0^T f(t) \cdot f'(t - \Delta\tau) \, dt.$$

4. *Convolution–Linear Systems Analysis*

$$h(t) = \frac{1}{2T} \int_{-T}^{T} g(t) \, f(\tau - t) \, dt$$

(The convolution integral, $h(t)$, is the Fourier transform of $\psi(t)$.)

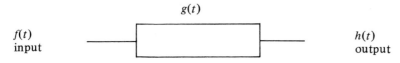

$$g(t)$$

$f(t)$ input $h(t)$ output

*if imaginary terms are excluded; if not, then should be $\tfrac{1}{2}(a_n \pm jbn)$ with $e^{\pm jn\omega t}$, respectively.

Fourier Components of a Waveform

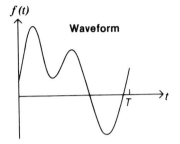

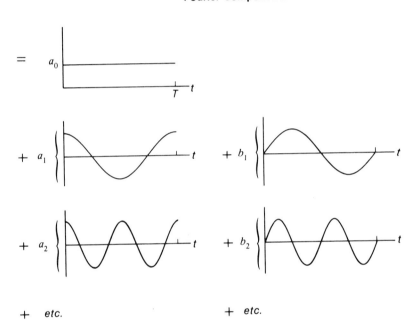

Fig. 7.11. Fourier frequency components of a waveform. (See definition of Fourier series in Table 7.2 and discussion in text.)

versus another, is lost in determining either the power spectral density of the signal or its Fourier transform, the autocorrelation function. Mathematically, the variation of any periodic, aperiodic, or "random" signal over time whose autocorrelation function exists for every value of τ (see p. 359) is characterizable using Fourier series. Let us examine how these analyses are accomplished.

Waveform   **Frequency Spectrum**

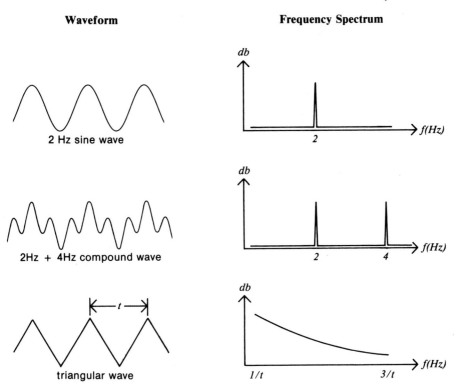

Fig. 7.12. Examples of signal waveforms and their frequency spectra. The power spectral densities may differ (see Fig. 7.14).

Fourier Series
Just as a signal can be broken up into its basic frequency components or Fourier series (Fig. 7.11), it can be reapproximated* from a series of sine and cosine functions of different amplitudes and phases as indicated in Table 7.2 and Fig. 7.13. The analysis of the energies of the frequencies (power spectral density) is equivalent to the analysis of the uniform signal power over time, i.e., the autocorrelation function (Fig. 7.14).

In fact, the power spectral density and the autocorrelation function are Fourier transforms of each other (see Table 7.2).

If $f(t)$ is a function of time, the Fourier transform F of $f(t)$ is a function of another variable, s, defined in the frequency domain as $F(s)$.

$$F(s) = \int_{-\infty}^{\infty} f(t)\, e^{-i2\pi st}\, dt.$$

$$(7.6)$$

*If it is periodic (and most time functions, even if aperiodic).

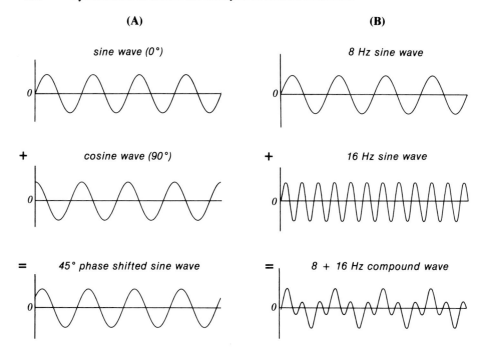

Fig. 7.13. (A) Adding a sine and cosine shifts the phase of the summated waveform. (B) Adding sine waves of different frequencies forms a waveform of complex periodic frequency (also see Fig. 7.11 and Table 7.2).

The connection with Fourier series becomes more apparent when one considers the inverse relation in the time domain:

$$f(t) = \int_{-\infty}^{\infty} F(s)\, e^{i2\pi ts}\, ds. \qquad (7.7)$$

Thus, $f(t)$ represents a function of time and $F(s)$ a function of frequency, and $e^{i2\pi ts} = \cos 2\pi st + i \sin 2\pi st$ is a "sinusoidal" function of frequency s if measured in appropriate units. $F(s)$ is the height of the s-frequency component in the spectrum for $f(t)$.

Power Spectral Density S(f)
Further appreciation may be gained of the significance of the power spectral density and its relation to Fourier series and the autocorrelation function by considering the derivation from Davenport and Root [200] given below.

If $x(t)$ is a real or complex valued function of a real variable such as time, and $x(t)$ is absolutely integrable over a period T, then $x(t)$ has associated with it a Fourier series:

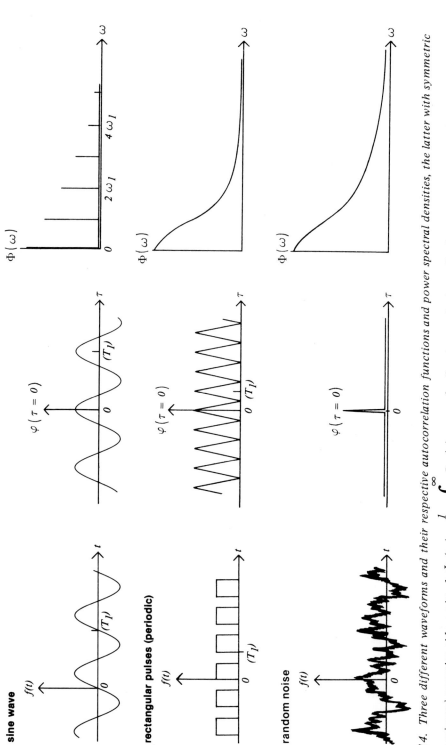

Fig. 7.14. Three different waveforms and their respective autocorrelation functions and power spectral densities, the latter with symmetric (and imaginary) negative side omitted. $\Phi\left(\omega\right) = \frac{1}{2\pi} \int_{-\infty}^{\infty} R_f\left(\tau\right) \cos \omega\tau d\tau$. Random noise has a flat frequency spectrum; the power spectral density of random noise is as shown. $\Phi = power$ (volts² ÷ radians per sec); $t = time$; $\tau = time\ interval$.

$$\hat{x}(t) = \sum_{n=-\infty}^{\infty} a_n \exp(jn\omega_0 t), \tag{7.8}$$

where a_n is the nth Fourier coefficient and

$$a_n = \frac{1}{T} \int_0^T x(t) \exp(-jn\omega_0 t) \, dt. \tag{7.9}$$

If $x(t)$ is of integrable square for $0 \leqslant t \leqslant T$, then Parseval's theorem holds, i.e.:

$$\sum_{-\infty}^{\infty} (a_n)^2 = \frac{1}{T} \int_0^T |x^2(t)| \, dt. \tag{7.10}$$

The power spectral density is then defined as:

$$S(f) = \sum_{n=-\infty}^{\infty} (a_n)^2 \, \delta(f-nf_0) \tag{7.11}$$

where $f_0 = 1/T$.

And the integrated power spectrum $G(f)$ of $x(t)$ is:

$$G(f) = \int_{-\infty}^{f} S(f) \, df. \tag{7.12}$$

Now the Fourier transform of the correlation function $R_x(\tau)$ is

$$\int_{-\infty}^{\infty} R_x(\tau) \exp(-j\omega_0 \tau) \, d\tau.$$

Substituting Eq. 7.17 this becomes:

$$\int_{-\infty}^{\infty} \sum_{-\infty}^{\infty} (a_n)^2 \, \exp(jn\omega_0 \tau) \exp(-jn\omega_0 \tau) \, d\tau.$$

For a random process this reduces to:

$$\sum_{n=-\infty}^{\infty} (a_n)^2 \, \delta \,(f\!-\!nf_0)$$

which is identical with Eq. 7.11.

Correlation
The process of correlation is performed according to the following formulation of Wiener:

$$R_f(\tau) = \lim_{T\to\infty} \frac{1}{2T} \int_{-T}^{T} f(t)\,f'(t\!-\!\Delta\tau)\, dt. \tag{7.13}$$

The two waveforms, $f(t)$ and $f'(t)$, are cross multiplied with $f'(t)$ shifted in time with respect to $f(t)$ by an amount $\Delta\tau$ over a finite period, T. The result is a correlation coefficient of the two waveforms (Fig. 7.15). *Autocorrelation* compares one waveform with itself by means of the above process; *cross correlation* compares two different waveforms. T refers to the durations of each of the waveforms. The integral sign means that the sum of the cross multiplicands is computed, and the right side of the equation computes the single value which represents the correlation coefficient, R_f, for the $\Delta\tau$ specified. $\varphi(t)$, the autocorrelation function, is the waveform or correlogram resulting from plotting all values of $R_f(\tau)$ for fixed increments of τ, e.g., Fig. 7.15, lower right.

If a random process is stationary and ergodic (see p. 362), the time autocorrelation function of a sample function of the process is equal to the statistical autocorrelation function of that process, i.e., the autocorrelation function of the ensemble average. This applies to any arbitrary function of time so long as the indicated time limit exists.

When autocorrelation is performed for every shift of τ, the correlogram obtained is equivalent to a power spectral analysis of the frequency components of the waveform. Then, for the case of a complex periodic function of time $x(t)$ such that its Fourier series converges [200]:

$$x(t) = \sum_{n=-\infty}^{\infty} \alpha(jn\omega_0)\,\exp(jn\omega_0 t), \tag{7.14}$$

where n is an integer representing number of coefficients, ω_0 is the fundamental angular frequency of $f(t)$ as expressed in $2\pi f_0$ radians, and the coefficient $\alpha(jn\omega_0)$ are the complex constants given by

$$\alpha(jn\omega_0) = \frac{\omega_0}{2\pi} \int_{0}^{2\pi/\omega_0} x(t)\,\exp(-jn\omega_0 t)\, dt \tag{7.15}$$

Computation of Correlation

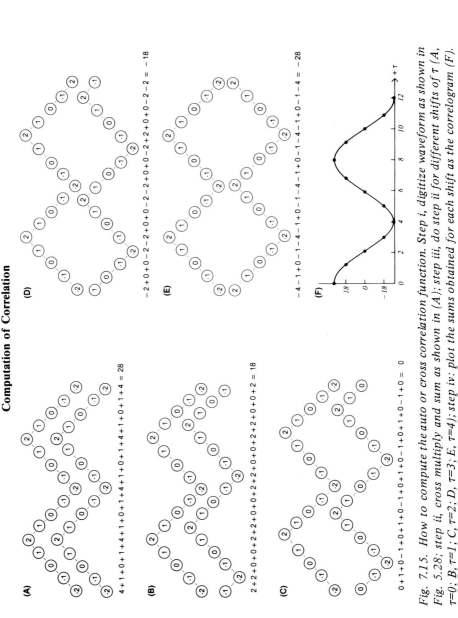

Fig. 7.15. How to compute the auto or cross correlation function. Step i, digitize waveform as shown in Fig. 5.28; step ii, cross multiply and sum as shown in (A); step iii, do step ii for different shifts of τ (A, τ=0; B, τ=1; C, τ=2; D, τ=3; E, τ=4); step iv: plot the sums obtained for each shift as the correlogram (F).

with $j = \sqrt{-1}$. Then:

$$\varphi(t) = \lim_{T \to \infty} \frac{1}{2T} \int_{-T}^{T} \left[\sum_{n=-\infty}^{\infty} \alpha^*(jn\omega_0) \exp(-jn\omega_0 t) \right] \cdot \qquad (7.16)$$

$$\left[\sum_{m=-\infty}^{\infty} \alpha(jm\omega_0) \exp(jm\omega_0 (t+\tau)) \right] dt$$

when values of α are orthogonal integers. When integers n are not equal and are orthogonal integers, the equation reduces to:

$$\varphi(t) = \sum_{n=-\infty}^{\infty} |\alpha(jn\omega_0)|^2 \; \exp(+jn\omega_0\tau) \qquad (7.17)$$

Which when $f(t)$ is a real function of time becomes:

$$\varphi(t) = \alpha^2(0) + 2\sum_{n=1}^{\infty} |\alpha(jn\omega_0)|^2 \; \cos(n\omega_0\tau) \qquad (7.18)$$

which is periodic, but in which phase information is lost. Finally, Eq. 7.17 may be expressed generally as:

$$\varphi(t) = \sum_{n=-\infty}^{\infty} (a_n)^2 \; \exp(jn\omega_0\tau) \qquad (7.19)$$

for any complex periodic function of time $f(t)$ whose Fourier series is stationary, converges and whose sample functions are ergodic [200,583]. This is the Fourier equivalent to Eq. 7.11 (the one being a function of time, the other of frequency). Thus:

$$S(f) = \varphi(t) \qquad (7.20)$$

Signal Detection

When two waveforms are cross multiplied, it can be shown that maximum values of $R_f(\tau)$ tend to occur for those values of (or shifts in) time, $\Delta\tau$, at which the two waveforms most closely resemble one another in frequency (e.g., Fig. 7.15). Further, any noise or unwanted information which is randomly distributed about the waveforms tends to cancel out to a weightless

---

*denotes complex conjugate

value when $R_f(\tau)$ is computed. This may be shown by deriving the autocorrelation function for a random process on the basis of ensemble averages (as opposed to time averages which have been described here).

The maximum value of $R_f(\tau)$ in the correlogram series designates that point in time at which the two waveforms most closely resemble each other. The value $R_f(\tau)$ may then be used to detect an input of similar appearance to that designated as $f(t)$ (e.g., Fig. 7.16).

It should be noted that identity between ensemble averages and time averages is very close when T approaches infinity. Although this can never be the case in neuroelectric data processing applications, the rule is not so strict that finite values of T necessarily invalidate the hypothesis that random components will tend to cancel out. Two other stipulations are made if the hypothesis is to be statistically valid. The waveforms must be stationary and ergodic with regard to the sample values used in the computation. Again, these conditions can only be met approximately in neuroelectric applications, and again it is assumed that the approximations are close enough so that the hypothesis of canceling random waveform components is not invalidated. Properly, *stationarity* means that a process is such, statistically, that it can be sampled at any point of time with homologous results. Here, it translates as there being no gross unidirectional shifts in the waveform, such as a pronounced shift in the DC level, during the time sampled. *Ergodicity* refers to the statistical comparability of the samples taken. If a property of the process generating the waveform, it implies the absence of such discontinuities in sampling as to disallow comparison of samples of one waveform with those of another. An ergodic process implies stationarity.

Convolution

A final theorem introduces a concept of great importance: convolution. If f and g are two functions of time, their convolution is defined as

$$(f * g)t = \int_{-\infty}^{\infty} f(t)\, g(\tau - t)\, dt \tag{7.21}$$

($*$ means convolved with).

Convolution is intimately related to Fourier transforms by the relations

$$\overline{fg(t)} = f(s) * g(s), \tag{7.22}$$

$$\overline{f * g(t)} = f(s)\, g(s). \tag{7.23}$$

In general, the Fourier transform of the Fourier transform of $f(t)$ is $f(-t)$; $f(-t)$ is $f(t)$ *flipped in time*. Flipping of a function is shown on p. 365.

Detection of a Neuroelectric Signal

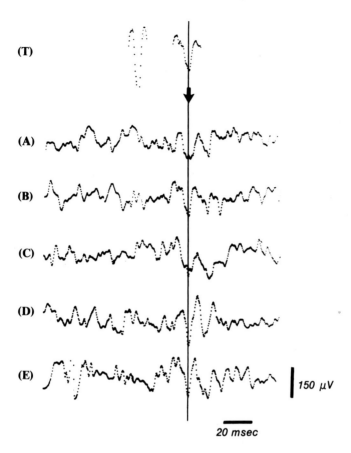

Fig. 7.16. Detection of an evoked potential using correlation with template matching. Data samples (A-E) are the electrocorticogram recorded from the surface of the motor cortex of a cat trained to twitch its nose in response to a hiss-CS. Each data sample contains an evoked cortical response immediately preceding a conditioned nose twitch movement. Each response was success-fully detected (vertical line) by matched filter analysis. The signal template used for matching is shown on the left side of the upper line (T). It was con-structed by filtering the response shown above the arrow to reduce noise. Additional responses immediately to the right of the vertical line occurred during the period of nose twitch movement and were identified, in (A), (C), (D), and (E), as responses by the template matching operation. (From Woody and Nahvi [1123].)

Convolution is performed in the following manner:

$$h(t) = x(t) * y(t)$$

$$= \int_{-\infty}^{\infty} x(t)\, y(\tau - t)\, dt \tag{7.24}$$

The trick is to get $y(t)$ into the form $y(\tau - t)$.

Let $x(t) =$

(1)

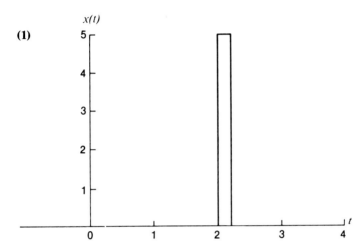

Let $y(t) =$

(2)

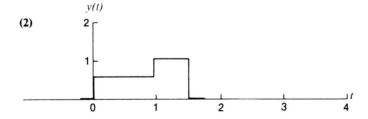

To get $y(t) \rightarrow y(-t)$

flip the function:

(3)

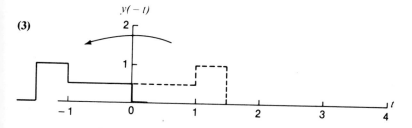

To get $y(-t) \rightarrow y(-t+\tau) = y(\tau-t)$,

shift the function by τ:

(4)

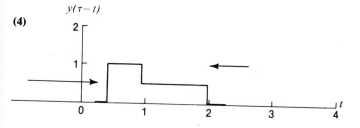

To get $x(t) \cdot y(\tau-t)$,

cross multiply for each τ along t:

(5)

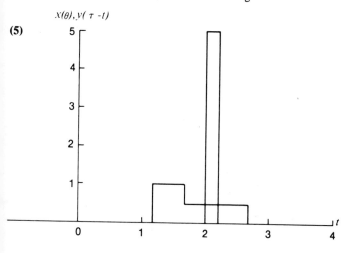

To get $\displaystyle\int_{-\infty}^{\infty} x(t)\, y\,(\tau-t)\, dt,$

sum the cross products for each value of τ.*

(6)

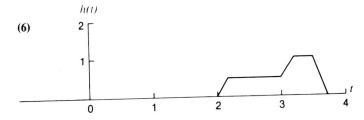

Use of Fourier series, power spectral densities, correlation, and convolution provides an objective means for evaluating the signal content of data recorded from different portions of a transmission network. As will be recalled, signal is definable in terms of random process statistics [582]. Reproducible spectral energies constitute a useful definition of a signal. The reproducibility may be evaluated by cross correlation against a template of the signal as a function of time, as shown in Fig. 7.16. This definition of a signal can be applied to the analysis of data from some neural systems with sufficient success to be predictive of the generation of incipient movements (Fig. 7.16 and [1123]). Nonetheless, the reader is again cautioned about the limitations of these techniques, both physiologically and mathematically. Properly, they apply only to linear systems and to other systems that can be satisfactorily approximated by use of the convolution integral.

Linear Systems
What is a linear system? A system is a set of objects with relationships. The relationships may be between the objects or their attributes, such as the coded representation of sensory or motor labeled information. A system is said to be linear if certain constraints on the transform of input into output are satisfied. The transforms of the original input must be commutative, associative, distributive, and linearly superimposable. These constraints are specified, in more detail, on p. 396.

The convolution relations hold for any linear system. Thus, if any two of (1) the input, (2) the transfer function, or (3) the output are known, the third can be determined. Moreover, if one can measure the output of the system, one can determine its *transfer function* (see *g(t)*, bottom of Table 7.2) by putting a known input such as a pulse or step function into the system.

By breaking the complex system into its subcomponent systems, a thorough analysis of the transfer functions of the components can be performed. Thus, systems analysis can define a particular relationship between a labeled input,

*Above graphs after Drake [240].

a manipulation of the input (the operator or transfer function), and a labeled output (the transform of the original input).

A limitation of the linear system analytic technique arises in attempting to apply it too specifically to characterization of the mechanisms underlying the transfer functions. This is because more than one mechanism may support a particular input-output transformation. If so, the error lies not in performing a single analysis of the multiple operations (together, the operations will in fact perform the compound transfer function as specified), but instead in assuming that only one underlying mechanism was represented physically.

White Noise Analysis

The transfer function of a linear system can also be determined by exciting the system with white noise (see Fig. 7.17). White noise is random and is evenly distributed throughout the frequency spectrum.

The input-output cross correlation of a linear system that has been excited by white noise is proportional to the system's unit-impulse response [582]. Thus, where $R_f(\tau)$ is the output of the correlator:

$$R_f(\tau) = \int_{-\infty}^{\infty} h(t)^* f'(\tau - t)\, dt + \text{constant.} \tag{7.25}$$

If the white noise excitation is independent of the input, the system's unit-response is, theoretically

$$R_f(\tau) = 2\pi K h(\tau) + \text{constant.} \tag{7.26}$$

This can be determined as shown in Fig. 7.17.

The spectral density of the output of a stable linear system in response to a stationary input random process is shown by Lee [583] to be "equal to the square of the magnitude of the system function times the spectral density of the system input." Since the power density spectrum, $G(f)$, of white noise is theoretically the same value, K, for all frequencies, the autocorrelation of the noise, R_{fi}, is $2\pi K$.

Therefore, when the system is excited by white noise, Eq. 7.25 becomes

$$R_f(\tau) = \int_{-\infty}^{\infty} h(t)\, 2\pi K h(\tau - t)\, dt \tag{7.27}$$

$$= 2\pi K h(\tau) + \text{constant,}$$

i.e., the input-output cross correlation, $R_f(\tau)$, is proportional by $2\pi K$ to the unit-impulse response, $h(\tau)$, of the linear system excited by the white noise.

*Here, $h(t)$ is used in place of $g(t)$ as the transfer function.

White Noise Analysis

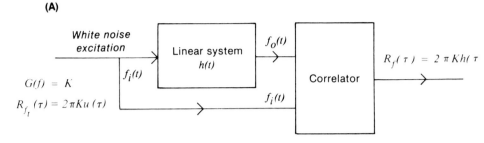

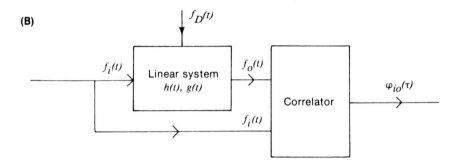

Fig. 7.17. (A) Determination of the unit-impulse response of a linear system by cross correlation using white noise excitation. (B) The above determination under a disturbance, $f_D(t)$. Slightly modified (from Lee [582].)

As shown in Fig. 7.17b and above, if any input to the system $f_D(t)$ is independent of the excitation by white noise, the equation $R_f(\tau)$ differs only by a constant from its value without that input. Moreover, if any of the variables $f_i(t)$, $f_D(t)$ or the transfer function for $f_D(t)$ is zero, the constant becomes zero. This means then that the determination of the unit-impulse response of a linear system by the cross correlation technique is independent of external or internal disturbances so long as they are independent of the white noise excitation (which is random by definition). As a result, *this technique can be used to analyze the transfer functions of linear systems that have a variety of inputs.*

Flowgraphs

Flowgraphs [621,650,884,1081] provide a means for depicting, graphically, the relationships between sets of interconnected elements. This method provides a visible systems analysis in terms of linear algebraic equations. It is ideally suited to analysis of information processing in the nervous system since the result is equivalent to an analysis of sensory and motor labeled information flow within a complex network.

Simple Network Analysis

The key feature of flowgraphs is to break down circuitry into *nodes* and the *transmittances* between them (see Fig. 7.18). The transmittance may be viewed as the conductance between nodes or, more generally, as the relationship between the node variables. A node will have at least one input and one output. As more inputs and outputs are added, two fundamental types of nodes may be distinguished: a contributive node and a distributive node.

A *contributive node* (Fig. 7.19A) is a node at which at least two transmittances terminate and at most one transmittance originates [1081]. It can represent an aggregate of sensory-labeled information with multiple sensory inputs and their transform via a single, motor-labeled output. The motor-labeled output can then be treated as a sensory-labeled input to a second-order system (for example, a distributive node) as will be apparent shortly.

A *distributive node* (Fig. 7.19B) is a node at which no more than one transmittance terminates and at least two transmittances originate [1081]. It can represent a single sensory-labeled input, a transfer function, and a distributed, motor-labeled output.

Complex nodes with multiple inputs and outputs can be broken down into fundamental nodes (Fig. 7.20). In this way, ambiguity over input-output terminologies may be avoided since each part of Fig. 7.20B can be labeled unambiguously.

Note that flowgraphing imposes a directionality upon transmission within the network. Thus, in Fig. 7.20B, the relationship between nodes M_1 and S_2 and their transmittance, $T_{M_1 S_2}$, is expressed as:

$$M_1 = S_2 \cdot T_{M_1 S_2}, \tag{7.28}$$

where the value of a node is equal to the sum of all incoming transmittances (see Fig. 7.18) multiplied by the values of their respective nodes of origin. Note also that the above equation can be readily convolved, and is subject to linear systems analysis provided the appropriate linear constraints (p. 366) are met.

If flow were in the opposite direction (a path inversion), the relationship would be that shown by Eq. 7.29 on the next page.

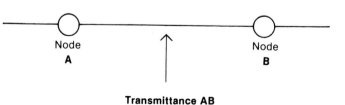

Node
A

Node
B

Transmittance AB

Fig. 7.18. A flowgraph of the transmittance (AB) between two nodes, A and B. (Whitehouse [1081].)

Contributive Node   **Distributive Node**

Fig. 7.19. Examples of a contributive node (left) and a distributive node (right). (Whitehouse [1081].)

$$M_1 = S_2 \cdot \frac{1}{T_{M_1 S_2}}. \tag{7.29}$$

Further mathematical analysis of Fig. 7.20B indicates that:

$$M_1 = [S_{1a} \cdot T_{M_1 S_{1a}}] + [S_{1b} \cdot T_{M_1 S_{1b}}]. \tag{7.30}$$

Flowgraphs can also deal with parallel channel transmission, Fig. 7.21, where:

$$M_1 = S_1 \cdot [T_{M_1 S_1} + T_{M_1 S_1}]. \tag{7.31}$$

$$\text{(a)} \qquad \text{(b)}$$

Complex Network Analysis
Complex networks are analyzed by breaking them down into fundamental nodes assembled in paths and loops [1081]:

(A) Complex Node   **(B) Two Fundamental Nodes:**
                                         one contributive, one distributive

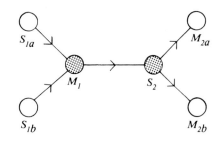

Fig. 7.20. Equatability between complex (A) and fundamental (B) nodes with sensory (S) and motor (M) labelings as indicated. Fundamental nodes consist of one contributive and one distributive node. (Whitehouse [1081].)

(A)   Parallel Circuit

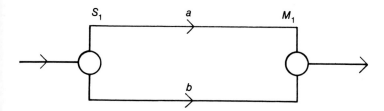

(B)   Six Second-Order Loops

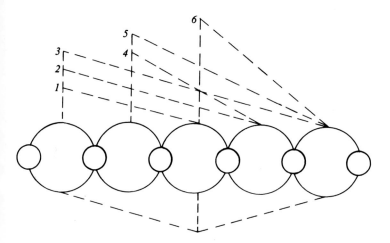

One Third-Order Loop

*Fig. 7.21. (A) Parallel channel (*a,b) transmission between two nodes. (B) Analysis of complex networks. (After Whitehouse [1081].)*

Complex Network

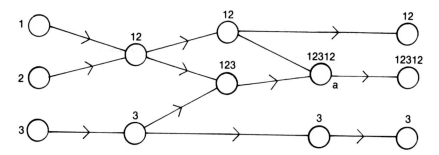

Fig. 7.22. A network with redundantly labeled lines (pathways) and some interdependent (multiply labeled) elements.

A *path* is a set of transmittances between nodes joined by those transmittances. Different paths may have common nodes. No path may have a recurrent path within, since a recurrent path is redefined as a loop and treated separately.

A *loop* is a recurrent path of any number of nodes or transmittances. A *first-order loop* is any path (made up of any number of transmittances between nodes) recurring upon a single node. A *second-order loop* is any pair of first order loops without nodes in common (Fig. 7.21B). A *third-order loop* is any triplet of first order loops without nodes in common, and so forth.

Closed flowgraphs, i.e., flowgraphs consisting only of loops, can be described (solved) as an entire network, *N*, where:

N = 1 − (sum of transmittances of all first-order loops) + (sum of transmittances of all second order loops) − (sum of transmittances of all third order loops) +...

N will always equal zero in a closed flowgraph. Open loop flowgraphs can be transformed into closed loop flowgraphs by arbitrarily linking the the terminal nodes with a transmittance, $1/T$. Open flowgraphs can be analyzed either by applying this principle or a variation of it, Mason's rule, which states that the transmittance,

$$T = \frac{[\Sigma \, (\text{path} \times \Sigma \, \text{nontouching loops})]}{\Sigma \, \text{loops}} \qquad (7.32)$$

Further details concerning this and other established means for reducing complex flowgraphs to simple forms can be found in the comprehensive review of this subject by Whitehouse [1081].

Treatment of System Dependency

One of the troublesome issues that should be considered in attempting to analyze the transmission of information through elements with as many as 10^5 different inputs is that of dependency within the system. Dependency arises when one input (or element operation) can influence another. Analytically, what should be done about dependency between signal inputs and noise inputs in single elements? And what should be done about dependency between signals in noise common to different elements?

Examination of Fig. 7.22 shows redundant convergence of inputs 1, 2, and 3 upon element *a*. Does the redundancy improve the signal: noise ratio of signals 1 and 2 within that element? Is signal 3 degraded by the addition? What happens if the separate transmittances of signals 1 and 2 have different noise levels such that the noise with respect to signal 3 in element *a* has both different and independent components?

The answers to the above questions can be deduced from existing knowledge concerning multiple channel signal detection. Intuitively, it can be seen that if the signal (*s*) and noise (*n*) of a second channel are identical to the signal and noise of a first channel, no improvement in $s{:}n$ ratio can be gained by means of the second channel. From this, one can infer that signals in correlated noise may be less discernible than signals in uncorrelated random noise. This is, in fact, the case.

Theorem. *The signal:noise ratio of the analog sum of the output of K matched filters with signals in correlated noise decreases as the dependency between noise of channels increases [704].*

At a single element the summed signal:noise ratios of several inputs will be decreased by correlated noise between inputs. And, similarly for analysis of multiple element outputs, their summed signal:noise ratios will also decrease as their noise correlation increases.

Fortunately, these relationships between signal and noise dependency can be described mathematically, given the assumption that linear systems analysis is applicable.

For signals in random, uncorrelated noise:

When a signal, $S_0(t)$, of known shape and of finite duration, T, is embedded in stationary additive noise, $n_0(t)$, with zero mean the signal can be separated best by means of a linear matched filter [1085]. The filter is matched to the signal such that its impulse response, $h(t)$ is equal to $S_0(T-t)$.

The output of the filter at the end of signal duration, i.e., at t=T, is Y_0 = S_0^2 = m_0 where S_0^2 is the total energy of the signal and m_0 is the filtered noise output [200]. At this moment ($t{=}T$), the signal to noise ratio, d, at the output of the filter is maximum and may be computed from signal and noise characteristics (see Nahvi [701]).

The effect of incorporating the signals and noise from K independent data channels, by combining the analog outputs of the respective matched filters may be described as follows [704]:

$$y = \sum_{i=1}^{k} y_i = \sum_{i=1}^{k} S_i^2 + \sum_{i=1}^{k} m_i = S^2 + m, \qquad (7.33)$$

where y is the combined filter output. S_i^2 is signal energy in the ith data channel. S^2 is the total energy of all signals, m_i is the noise output of the ith matched filter and m is the sum of all noise outputs. If we assume noise of each channel to be independent from that of the other channels, then the noise power, σ^2, in the combined filter output is:

$$E[m^2] = \sigma^2 = \sum_{i=1}^{k} E[m_i^2] = \sum_{i=1}^{k} \sigma_i^2 \qquad (7.34)$$

and the maximum signal-to-noise ratio in y is:

$$d = \frac{\sum\limits_{i=1}^{k} S_i^2}{\left[\sum\limits_{i=1}^{k} \sigma_i^2\right]^{1/2}}. \tag{7.35}$$

If each channel has the same signal-to-noise ratio,

$$d_1 = d_0 \text{ for all } i,$$

normalization can be performed to achieve:

$$\sigma_i^2 = \sigma_0^2 \text{ for all } i.$$

Then:

$$\sigma^2 = \sum_{i=1}^{k} \sigma_i^2 = K\sigma_i^2 \tag{7.36}$$

and

$$d = \frac{\sum\limits_{i=1}^{k} S_i^2}{\sqrt{K}\ \sigma_i} = \frac{1}{\sqrt{K}}\sum_{i=1}^{k} d_i, \tag{7.37}$$

where

$$d_i = \frac{S_i^2}{\sigma_0}$$

The case where each channel has a different signal-to-noise ratio can also be described by Eq. 7.37 after finding that combination of channels which, when added, will maximize d.

Let all data channels be assumed to have similar probability of signal detection, P_d, (versus missed signal) and similar probability of false alarm, P_f, (versus signal absence) at some optimum threshold setting such as has been described for the single channel case [1123]. Such an assumption facilitates the analysis, but does not limit application of the outcome, the latter being easily extendible to the case where channels have unequal P_d and unequal P_f under the assumption:

$$d = \sqrt{K}\ d_0,$$

and, thus, the total output signal-to-noise ratio of the combined channels is improved only by a factor of $\sqrt{K}$, K being the number of channels aggregated.

Adding channels in order of their highest signal-to-noise ratios, it is seen that to achieve $d_{(max)}$, the signal-to-noise ratio of each added data channel should be no less than the signal-to-noise ratio of the aggregate divided by $\sqrt{K}$.

$$d = d_k [\max] = \frac{1}{\sqrt{K}} \sum_{j=1}^{k} d_j > \sqrt{K} d_{k-1} [\max]$$

(7.38)

Consider the following example of addition of two channels with signal-to-noise ratios d_1 and d_2, respectively.

$$d = \frac{d_1 + d_2}{\sqrt{2}} .$$

Assuming $d_1 > d_2$, we need $d_2 > (\sqrt{2} - 1) d_1$ if addition of d_2 is to result in improvement in the signal-to-noise ratio of the aggregate (d) over that of d_1.

Table 7.3 shows values of d for combination of two data channels for which, respectively, $d_1 = 10$ and d_2 varies from 1 to 30. It is observed that only for $5 \leqslant d_2 < 25$ does the combination of the two channels improve the output signal-to-noise ratio.

We now consider the case when the noise in K data channels is not independent, i.e.,

$$E[m_i m_j] = \rho_{ij} \sigma_i \sigma_j \quad 0 \leqslant |\rho_{ij}| \leqslant 1 ,$$

where ρ_{ij} is the correlation coefficient between channel noise m_i and m_j. In this case, the output noise power, σ^2, of the aggregate is:

$$E[m^2] = E[\Sigma \Sigma m_i m_j] = \sigma^2 .$$

(7.39)

If, for simplicity of computation, we assume: (1) that all signals have the same energy, S_0^2; (2) that noise at the output of each filter has the same noise power, σ_0^2; and (3) that the correlation coefficient is the same between all noise outputs, i.e., $p_i = p_j$ for all i, j, then:

$$E[m^2] = \sigma_0^2 K[1 + \rho(K - 1)] = \sigma^2$$

(7.40)

and the aggregate output signal-to-noise ratio, d, is

$$d = \frac{S^2}{\sigma} = \frac{K S_0^2}{\sigma_0 \sqrt{K[1 + \rho(K - 1)]}} = \sqrt{\frac{K}{1 + \rho(K - 1)}} d_0 .$$

(7.41)

Table 7.3. Values of d for Analog Combination of Two Data Channels

d_1	d_2	$d = \dfrac{d_1 + d_2}{\sqrt{2}}$
10	1	7.7
10	2	8.4
10	3	9.1
10	4	9.8
10	5	10.5
10	6	11.2
10	7	11.9
10	8	12.6
10	9	13.3
10	10	14.0
10	15	17.7
10	20	21.2
10	25	24.8
10	30	28.2

[a] From Nahvi et al. [704].

In Fig. 7.23 the improvement in signal-to-noise ratio, i.e., d/d_0, obtained from Eq. 7.41 is plotted versus K, the number of channels incorporated, for different values of ρ. All curves fall below the curve for $\rho=0$, and except for $\rho=0$, all curves approach an asymptotic value, i.e.,

$$\lim_{k \to \infty} \frac{d}{d_0} = \sqrt{\frac{1}{\rho}} . \tag{7.42}$$

This indicates that (1) the signal-to-noise ratio of the analog sum decreases as the dependency between noise of channels increases; and (2) except for $\rho=0$, one cannot, in the presence of correlated channel noise, arbitrarily increase d/d_0 to any desired level, simply by increasing the number of channels, even if $K \to \infty$ [704]. As a result, *the operation of a nerve network cannot be indefinitely improved simply by adding redundant elements and parallel transmission lines. Nor can detection of a signal transmitted through the network be indefinitely improved simply by adding more of the same monitoring devices.*

General Theories of Information Handling

Several general theories have arisen concerning information handling. The best known of these is information theory. Other theories concern control of adaptive operations, with or without feedback. Still other mathematical formulations are directed toward description of the stochastics of stationary random processes and of complex field arrays [cf. 300,537,583]. All the theories have been found applicable in the predictive sense to real systems. We should consider them because they may apply to information handling by neural systems. As pointed out by Lee [583], the purpose is not to find the law for the exact outcome or message produced by the system, but rather to

Values of *d* for Analog Combination of Two or More Data Channels

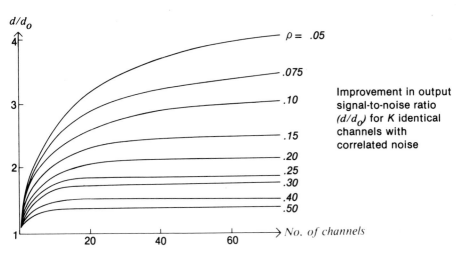

Fig. 7.23. *Improvement in output signal-to-noise ratio* (d/d$_0$) *for K identical channels with correlated noise; the cross-correlation coefficient, ρ, is an index of noise dependency between channels. Note rapid asymptotes as K increases (Nahvi et al. [704]).*

find a mathematical description of the rules by which possible outcomes or messages arise. Using Boltzmann's thermodynamics one cannot determine which gas molecule will pass from one compartment to another, but one can accurately predict what the overall statistical outcome of the passage of many molecules will be. Analogously, using systems analysis, random process statistics, and information theory, one will not be able to determine which message the system will generate next, but knowing the system's functions, one may be able to assign probabilities of occurrence to different possible outcomes, much like those assigned to throwing dice or playing poker.

Information Theory

Entropy

Any physical system, including any information processing system, may be characterized by the interactions of the components with themselves and their environment. In the realm of chemical interactions, Boltzmann was able to formulate a mathematical description of the exchange between a physical-chemical system and its surroundings in terms of the entropy, that is, the order or disorder of the involved variables. Thus (Table 7.4), the entropy, S, of a number of gas molecules in a box is proportional to a constant, k (the Boltzmann constant), and the natural logarithm of C, a thermodynamic probability* relatable to the number of possible configurations of mole-

---

*$-\ln C$ = thermodynamic probability; ln C = the natural logarithm of the number of possible configurations or quantum states.

Table 7.4. Relationships between Entropy, the Boltzmann Equation, and Information Theory

ENTROPY (HEAT*)	BOLTZMANN
1) $dS = \delta q/T$ dS - rate of change of entropy δq - rate of heat absorption (lost) in reversible expansion T - temperature at which loss occurs	1) $S = k \ln C$ S - entropy k - Boltzmann constant C - # of possible configu- rations[†]
2) $\Delta S = \displaystyle\int_{T_1}^{T_2} \frac{\delta q}{T}\, dT = S_2 - S_1$ ΔS - change in entropy over a range, i.e., from one state to another (B = before or state 1; A=after or state 2)	2) $\Delta S = k \ln C_B - k \ln C_A$ $= k \ln (C_B/C_A)$ $= k \ln (P_B/P_A)$

*2nd Law of Thermodynamics:
It is impossible by a cyclic process to take heat from a hot reservoir and convert it into work without at the same time transferring some of this heat from the hot to a cold reservoir.
  or
  A machine with an efficiency equal to unity cannot be possible.
†The thermodynamic probability is taken as the ratio of the probability of the actual state to that in which there is complete order or the number of possible quantum states of the system corresponding to approximately the same energy [328].

cules or "quantum states of the system corresponding to approximately the same energy" [328].

As any physical chemist knows, these configurations, concentrations, or probabilistic states can be related to measurable energy lost in a cyclic process by which heat is taken from a hot reservoir and converted into work (Table 7.4). That is, dS, the rate of change of entropy, is proportional to δq, the rate of heat absorption or heat lost in reversible expansion, divided by the absolute temperature, T, at which the loss occurs. In other words, heat cannot be converted into an equivalent amount of work without leaving changes in some parts of the system. This change is the change in entropy.

The increase in entropy, dS, is equal to the amount of heat absorbed, δq (if the process were carried out in a reversible manner), with respect to the absolute temperature, T.

$$dS = \frac{\delta q}{T}. \tag{7.43}$$

For a finite increase, the equation must be integrated over a range, ΔS, giving:

$$\Delta S = \int_{T_1}^{T_2} \frac{\delta q}{T}\, dt. \tag{7.44}$$

Coupled with the law of conservation of energy (first law of thermodynamics), this means that any chemical reaction initiated at a particular ab-

Table 7.4. (Continued)

INFORMATION THEORY

1) $I=k \ln P$
   I - information
   k - base constant
   P - # of possible, equally probable
     outcomes (result—pure number)*

2) For answer in bits:
   Substitute:
     2^n for P
   $n = n$ different independent selec-
     tions, each corresponding to bi-
     nary (hence base 2) choice: 0 or 1
   Make:
     $k=1/\ln 2$
   So:
     $I=k \ \ln 2^n$
     $I=kn \ln 2$
      $=n \ (\ln 2/\ln 2)$
     $I=n$
  For picking 1 from 32 cards
     $P=32=2^5$
     $\therefore I=5$ bits

3) For words:
   n - # of binary bits/word length

4) For protein storage capacity:
   Assume 10 different amino acids
   (equal probability of occurrence) †
   repeated N times on a single protein chain
   P is 10^N

$$N = \frac{\text{protein mol. wt.}}{\text{average amino acid mol. wt.}}$$
$$= \frac{10,000,000}{100} = 100,000$$

   $k=1/\ln 2$
   $I =k \ln P$
     $=kN \ln 10$
     $[(\log_2 10) (\ln 2) = (\ln 10)]$
     $=N \log_2 10$
     $=N (3.3)$
     $=330,000$ bits per protein
     molecule

*Note that $\ln P = -\ln \frac{1}{P}$, where $\frac{1}{P}$ = the probability, p, of the outcome (see p. 326).

†hypothetical; the actual numbers and probabilities will, of course, differ.

solute temperature (T) can be expressed in terms of its free energy (F), heat content (H), and entropy (S):

$$\Delta F = \Delta H - T\Delta S \tag{7.45}$$

e.g., for $6C(s) + 3H_2(g) = C_6H_6(l)$ (s = solid, g = gas, l = liquid),

$$\Delta H = 12.3 \text{ Kcal.-mole}^{-1}$$

$$\Delta S = -60.1 \text{ cal. deg.}^{-1} \text{ mole}^{-1},$$

at $25°C$ ($298.2°K$), $\Delta F = 30,200$ cal. mole^{-1},

i.e., the free energy of formation of benzene from graphite and hydrogen gas at $25°C$ is 30.2 Kcal. per mole [328].

    Spontaneous processes are characteristically associated with a decrease in the organization of the system. For example, given heated gas molecules on one side of a partitioned box, there is a kind of ordered aggregation of the high energy molecules in one area, the low energy molecules in another. As the high energy molecules pass to the other side of the box, by diffusion, a less orderly state occurs. The same treatment may be applicable for different ionic concentrations or different gas molecules as well as for gas expansion. (For a solid, C in the Boltzmann equation equals 1 and $S = 0$).

Expression of the second law of thermodynamics is equivalent to saying that no machine has an efficiency of unity. When heat or any other form of energy is converted into work, a certain amount of energy is dissipated in the process of transfer. This energy loss is equivalent to the change in entropy of the system.

Since "a knowledge of the standard entropy change in conjunction with the change of heat content and reaction permits the evaluation of the standard free energy change of the process," it is possible to determine the equilibrium constant of a reaction from purely thermal measurements [328]. Boltzmann's linkage of the thermodynamic entropy of a system with probability is useful since it permits probabilistic descriptions of relationships between kinetic energy, free energy, chemical equilibrium, and Maxwell's kinetic theory of gases. The last asserts that the mean kinetic energies of the molecules of all gases are the same at constant temperature.

To summarize the above more simply, physical chemical interactions can either be described in terms of their energetics or in terms of the probabilistic states of the involved molecular components themselves. Two further conclusions may be drawn upon this observation. First, the equatability between probability and energy provides a new insight into processes that are more conventionally thought of in terms of the energetics alone. Second, the possibility arises that probabilistic considerations in the realm of information theory may have some equivalence with those in chemistry and physics.

Information Theory and Entropy

To explore the possible relationship between information theory and entropy, let us consider the seeming paradox of the Maxwell "demon."

Suppose there is some gas in a box divided by a partition into two sides. The individual molecules of the gas have a random motion—some fast, some slow at any given time. If a "demon" could sit on the partition and open a gate whenever a "fast" molecule approached, but close the gate whenever a "slow" one approached, there would eventually accumulate a preponderance of fast molecules on one side and slow molecules on the other—thereby decreasing the entropy or disorder of the system. Given that the "demon" required no further energy in its operation other than a gating energy equal to that provided by the change in molecular concentrations, the second law of thermodynamics (i.e., efficiency less than one) would be violated.

One sees, on closer inspection, that the "demon" must also have information as to which molecules are fast and which are slow in order to function appropriately [980]. This information makes up for the difference in entropy missing in the above formulation and may be considered as entropy.

Were information equatable with entropy, then it could be related to physically measurable variables such as those covered by the laws of thermodynamics.

Information Theory and Probability

Irrespective of any direct relationship to physics, information theory affords a precise description of systems interactions in terms of the number of possible, equally probable outcomes of the system's operations. Information (I) is taken as equivalent to a constant (k) times $\ln(P)$, the number of possible outcomes. Note from Table 7.4 that by substituting the number of independent binary choices, 2^n, for P and defining k as $1/\ln 2$, I is quantified in terms of binary bits, the latter being useful computationally. Again, *note that the "meaning" of the information is completely irrelevant to the above considerations. I simply represents different possible states or outcomes, without any attempt at particularizing their content.*

Some examples of informational descriptions of everyday occurrences are as follows:

Example 1: Five binary bits of information correspond to the possible outcomes in picking one out of 32 cards (2^5 possible outcomes = 5 bits; see Table 7.4).

Example 2: An informational description can be made of the storage capacity of certain protein molecules. If one assumes 10 different amino acids (with equal probability of occurrence) repeated n times on a single protein chain, the number of possible, molecularly coded outcomes is 10^n. n may be determined by dividing the molecular weight of the protein molecule by the average amino acid molecular weight and, as shown in Table 7.4, is approximately 100,000. Substituting in the Shannon formula, one finds that 330,000 bits of information can be stored per protein molecule.

Note that these informational descriptions are mathematically the inverse of probabilistic descriptions, i.e. 32 possible outcomes versus the probability of picking 1 out of 32 cards.

Mutual or Common Information Content of Two Sets of Random Variables

The mutual information content or information* that is common to two sets of random variables can be computed as follows:

Let there be two sets of random variables, set A and set B. Let $I(A)$ be the log to the base 2 of the number of possible outcomes of the random variable A. Let $I(B)$ be the log to the base 2 of the number of possible outcomes of random variable B. (The number of possible outcomes, it will be recalled, is equatable with the information content.) The information content of the cross product of these variables will be $I(A \cdot B)$.

$$I(A \cdot B) = I(A) + I(B/A) = I(B) + I(A/B) \qquad (7.46)$$

If: $I(A)$ and $I(B)$ are independent, $I(A \cdot B) \leqslant I(A) + I(B)$

The sum $I(A) + I(B)$ will be larger than $I(A \cdot B)$ if the two random variables are dependent, because they have some common information. That component of common information will be called $M(A,B)$ and

*defined analytically, not generically

$$M(A,B) = I(A) + I(B) - I(A \cdot B),\qquad(7.47)$$

then,

$$M(A,B) = I(B) - I(B/A) = I(A) - I(A/B).\qquad(7.48)$$

The above may be applied to the outcomes of tossing one die:

Set A						Set B	
1	2	3	4	5	6	odd	even
1/6	1/6	1/6	1/6	1/6	1/6	1/2	1/2

Then:

$I(A)$ = $\log_2$ (number of possible outcomes of Set A)
= $\log_2 6$
= 1.8 bits.

$I(B)$ = $\log_2$ (number of possible outcomes of Set B)
= $\log_2 2$
= 1 bit.

$I(A/B)$ = $\log_2$ (number of possible outcomes of Set A, given knowledge of whether Set B odd or even)*
= $\log_2 3$
= 0.8 bit.

$I(B/A)$ = $\log_2$ (number of possible outcomes of Set B, given knowledge of whether Set A 1,2,. . ., or 6)
= $\log_2 1$
= 0 bits.

And:

$M(A,B)$ = $\log_2 6 + \log_2 2 - \log_2 6$
= $\log_2 2$
= 1 bit.

In summary:

$I(A)$ = $\log_2 6 = 1.8$ bit
$I(A/B)$ = $\log_2 3 = 0.8$ bit
$I(A \cdot B)$ = $\log_2 6 + (0) = \log_2 2 + \log_2 3 = 1.8$ bit
$M(A,B)$ = $\log_2 6 + \log_2 2 - \log_2 6 = \log_2 2 = 1$ bit
$I(B)$ = $\log_2 2 = 1$ bit
$I(B/A)$ = $\log_2 1 = 0$

One expects that formulations such as these will prove useful in describing possible motor outcomes of neural networks. Further discussion of this possibility can be found on p. 396. Let us next consider analytic theories of *adaptive* systems, i.e., control theories.

---

*See discussion of conditional probability, p. 397

Control of Adaptive Systems

Linear systems analysis admits a general theory of adaptive control provided that the system is linear and the usual constraints are satisfied. One constraint is that the result of adaptation depend on the entire past history of adaptation within the system. Another is (usually) that the transfer function of the system be time invariant.

When using this theory, adaptation is introduced as a controller function, $g(t)$, as in Fig. 7.24. It operates *by adding an additional input to the system* much like $F(Y)$, the negative feedback of the system state, in Uttley's informon. It does not directly modify the original system transfer function, $H(t)$. To do the latter would lead to a time-variant or self-organizing adaptive system which could easily be nonlinear and, therefore, not amenable to analysis by this theory.

For a linear system with the feedback circuit shown in Fig. 7.24(A), the output, $Y(t)$ is a function of the input, $X(t)$, the system transfer function, $H(t)$ and the controller function, $g(t)$. If the LaPlace transform, $F(s)$, of each function is taken,

$$\text{e.g.,}\quad \text{Output } F(y) = \mathcal{L}\, Y(t) = \int_0^\infty Y(t) e^{-\mathcal{L}t} dt, \qquad (7.49)$$

(note relationship to Fourier transform, Eq. 7.6), then, for a linear system,

$$\text{where}\qquad f_1 * f_2 = F_1(s) F_2(s), \qquad (7.50)$$

i.e., in the absence of a control loop,

$$F(y) = F(x) F(h). \qquad (7.51)$$

The output of the linear system with *negative* feedback (Fig. 7.24A) may therefore be expressed as

$$F(y) = \frac{F(h) F(x)}{1 + F(h) F(g)} \qquad (7.52)$$

For the feedforward circuit shown in Fig. 7.24(B),

$$F(y) = \left[1 + F(g)\right] F(x) F(h) \qquad (7.53)$$

assuming *positive* feedforward.

One may wish to consider the linear control circuits of Fig. 7.24, the designs of automata shown in Fig. 7.5, and the algorithms of adaptation listed on p. 395 in relation to the descriptions of control systems that follow.

Control Systems

Several types of control systems are recognized, each with its own critical feature(s). For example, there are:

Control systems:
1. With or without memory.
2. With or without set point variance.
3. With or without self-organizing adaptation.
4. With open or closed loop control.
5. With feedforward or feedback control.

The list is by no means complete or (in considering how to classify different types of switches, flywheel governors, thermostats, and innate or learned behaviors) are all of the differences unique or mutually exclusive.

Adaptations involved in control may reach some maximum or minimum value, or may proceed at some steady state level with or without range bounding as was described earlier (Figs. 7.7, 7.8).

Open Loop Adaptive Control Systems

An open loop control system receives no feedback information regarding the state of the adaptive system. There may be indirect feedback of information (e.g., from the environment and changes therein caused by the system's operation) to support the predetermined system operation, but not to cause the controller to adapt. Control is exercised entirely by predetermined adaptations based on the detection of predefined contingencies. Thus, in a thermostat adaptation occurs on the basis of temperature detection plus a prespecified contingency (if the temperature is low, turn on the heat; if high, turn it off). There is no feedback to alter the rules of adaptation based on past performance. There is instead an input of ambient temperature and a fixed course of adaptation contingent on its level. Neuronally, open loop adaptation may be contingent on two different synaptic inputs occurring together, as with heterosynaptic facilitation and inhibition.

Open loop control systems will typically have great stability since their adaptive features are entirely predetermined. However, it may be difficult to achieve a control operation of high sensitivity with an open loop system. This is because the accuracy of control depends on the system's initial calibration and on the precision of the involved components. The operation of open loop control systems will be vulnerable to component breakdown or interference from outside noise that was unanticipated in their original control design. Driftage away from the initial component set point is uncorrectable with an open loop control system. There is also no possibility for self-organizing adaptation, since there is no regard for the present or past system state.

Closed Loop, Feedback Control Systems

A closed loop control system normally uses feedback concerning the value of a controlled variable or the state of the adaptive control system, as a means to control further adaptation. In a closed loop, self-organizing control system, the response of the modified element should have a direct effect on the control action (Fig. 7.24A). This circuit may be compared with that of a feed-forward control system (Fig. 7.24B) in which information from the input modifies the controller without regard to the system state.

Either feedback or feedforward circuitry can be used to reduce the error or improve the response time of linear control operations, such as described earlier, and the circuitries may be either positive or negative. Because of the closed loop operation, feedback may have self-potentiating effects when it operates either as a supplemental control input to the system or as a self-organizing modifier of the system's original transfer function. Positive (re-generative) feedback is distinguished from negative (degenerative) feedback in that the former augments the gain of the loop system and can lead to explo-sive buildup. *Positive feedback* returns an output to the input so as to add another, positive input. This will permit rapid change or increased sensitivity of the system by which transforms between input and output are performed; however, it also tends to unstabilize the system and increase distortion of the signal input. *Negative feedback* returns the output to the input in such a way as to add another; negative input. Negative feedback then decreases the gain of the loop system and can lead to damping or a cut off of signal transmission. This tends to stabilize the transfer between input and output and reduce distor-tion, although the sensitivity and rapidity of the transfer operation may be reduced.

Negative feedback control systems have a system response that is relatively insensitive to brief external disturbances and to internal variations in para-meters of the operations controlled. This is because the output, e.g., $F(y)$ in Eq. 7.52, approaches $F(x) \div F(g)$ if $F(h) F(g) \gg 1$. Thus, small deviations in component operations or even the original control parameters may not overly disturb the control system, provided that their manifestations are accessible to the control loop. This permits relatively noisy components to be used for the system operation. Note, however, that when a closed loop system is

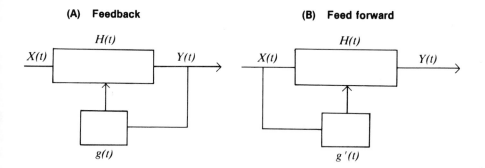

Fig. 7.24. *Linear systems with feedback control (A) and feedforward control (B). The systems have input X (t), transfer function H (t) and output Y (t). g (t) and g' (t) are the controller functions. Differences between applying the output of the controller function as an "extra" (additive) system input versus applying it to direct adaptation of the system transfer function are discussed in the text.*

carrying a range of frequencies over the feedback path, the frequency characteristics of the network may become an important source of error. At one frequency the phase of the signal fed back may be such as to produce negative feedback, but at another frequency the phase relationships may be such as to cause positive feedback, and oscillations may occur. Stability of control can therefore be a problem with closed loop control operations, since with closed loop adaptive control, there may be oscillating errors of overcorrection leading to explosive instability or drift in an undesired direction. The latter feature, taken in a converse manner, lends itself to self-organizing adaptive control, provided that some means be found to avoid maladaptation.

Some typical characteristics of closed loop systems which may be of interest with regard to their possible use in the design of self-organizing systems are as follows:

1. Some stable closed loop systems tend to have a transient response performance which can be predicted from the steady-state, closed loop plot of magnitude versus frequency (e.g., Nyquist plot).
2. A system designed for optimal steady-state operation may have unstable transient characteristics.
3. Self-organizing adaptive systems, i.e., control systems that incorporate time-variance based on system operation into the adaptive scheme, must have some means of evaluating how well the control operations are being performed. This index of performance must be reliable and unambiguous with respect to the optimal range of operation.
4. It should be possible to obtain a performance index without disturbing the operation of the system and in a form which is amenable to insertion into that part of the system in which control of adaptation is accomplished.
5. If hill-climbing techniques are used to control steady-state adaptation [e.g., 883], false peaks must be defined and avoided.

Other Mathematical Techniques

The two theories that follow are introduced because of their promise for advancing our ability to analyze complex adaptive networks. Their mention is abbreviated because of their novelty and because so little is known at present about their proper application.

Ergodic Theory

Ergodic theory "is concerned with the average behavior of large collections of molecules that move randomly for indefinite periods of time . . . Ergodic theorists commonly deal with measure and probability spaces and have developed powerful theorems involving ramification of these ideas [537]." The reader is referred to Kolata [537] for further discussion of ergodic theory.

Field Theory

"Field theory, as elaborated by Weiss, Wolpert, and others," indicates that a field "can be defined operationally as a domain within which changes in the presumptive fates of cells can occur" [300]. Cells may be assigned positional values according to their physical locations in the coordinate system of a particular field. In terms of positional information theory, the field can be defined as a set of cells which have their positions specified with respect to the same coordinate system. Further information is available elsewhere [300].

Specific Theories of Line Labeled Information Handling

A Geometry of Perception–Processing of Sensory Labeled Information

Minsky and Papert [672] have uncovered the beginnings of a powerful mathematical theory concerning a geometry of perception pertaining to the processing of sensory labeled information. The theory also deals with adaptive features of the processing. The topologic transformation of problems of image recognition and perception into problems of line labeled geometry is insightful and potentially more useful than these authors may have imagined originally.

As shown in Fig. 7.25, image processing involves sets of receptive elements that receive and process aggregates of sensory labeled information. Each unique, sensory labeled set independently processes its sensory aggregate according to some function, φ_i. The results of processing by each set are combined by means of a function Ω to obtain the value, ψ. The problems to be resolved are:

1. How can arrays of this sort be organized to permit a particular $\psi(X)$ to be a useful designator of a particular input, X, at the receptor elements?
2. Can a geometry be devised that will describe this process precisely and define some reasonably optimal approach to this problem?

Minsky and Papert begin their solution of these problems by pointing out that some meaningful restrictions must be placed on the function Ω and the set Φ of functions $\varphi_1, \varphi_2, \ldots, \varphi_n$ if the geometry is to be useful. And they point out that previous treatments of this type have been more anecdotal than mathematical.

It is also desirable to introduce variable weighting or some other potential means of adaptation, into the analysis. As shown in Fig. 7.26, weightings $\alpha_1, \alpha_2, \ldots, \alpha_n$ may be assigned each function $\varphi_1, \varphi_2, \ldots, \varphi_n$.

In addition, Ω may be replaced by a summation or integration function, Σ, and a threshold detector, θ, may be added to designate a particular value or region of ψ. When α is variable, this constitutes a simple perceptron, named after the automata of this general type that were designed by Rosenblatt [838-841]. It is noted by Minsky and Papert that in such automata α tends to grow faster than Ω in adaptive processing operations requiring memory storage.

The more complex perceptron admits multiple, redundant inputs as shown in Fig. 7.27. This type of processing of sensory labeled information corresponds closely to that carried out by the nervous system and is amenable to analysis by means of the Group Invariance Theorem.

A Simple Image-Processing Automaton

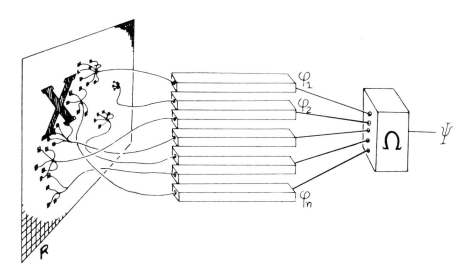

Fig. 7.25. An example of simple, multiple channel, image processing. See text for further details (From Minsky and Papert [672].)

Group Invariance Theorem

The Group Invariance Theorem of Minsky and Papert permits analysis of perceptron operations (i.e., the geometry of sensory image processing) by algebra instead of statistics. This theorem examines the relationship between all possible receptor activations (all sets of sensory labels, $r_1, r_2, \ldots, r_n$) and their representation across a theoretical space of $\alpha_\varphi \varphi(X)$ for $\varphi \epsilon \Phi$.

A Perceptron

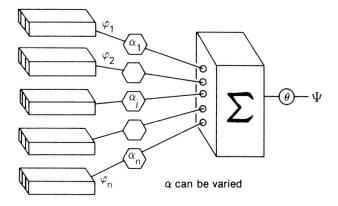

Fig. 7.26. Elementary perceptron (α can be varied). (From Minsky and Papert [672].)

Equivalence Between Parallel Processing and Group Invariance Theorem

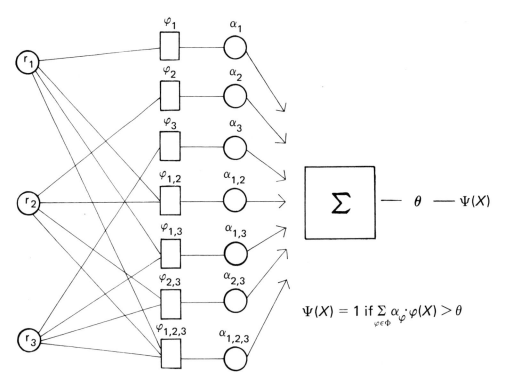

Fig. 7.27. A perceptron reduced to Group Invariance Theorem coefficients. (From Minsky and Papert [672].)

In effect, the Group Invariance Theorem permits an algebraic analysis of all geometries of rearrangements (or representations) of the original set of possible receptor labeled activations. It allows determination of which aggregates of $\alpha_\varphi \varphi(X)$ (or values of ψ) reflect a unique transformation of the group of possible transformations of the space of the receptor labelings, $r_1, r_2, \ldots, r_n$, upon the predicates, $\varphi_1, \varphi_2, \ldots, \varphi_n$.

Given any predicate φ and group element g,* Minsky and Papert define φg to be the predicate that, for each X, has the value $\varphi(X)$. Thus, one will always have $\varphi g(X) = \varphi(gX)$. Φ will be said to be closed under G if for every φ in Φ and g in G the predicate φg is also in Φ. If a perceptron predicate is invariant under a group, G, then its coefficients need depend only on the G-equivalence classes of their φ's [672].

The Group Invariance Theorem states that if:

(i) G is a finite group of transformations of a finite space, R;

---

*Given a group G, two figures, M and N, are G-equivalent if there is a member g of G for which $M = gN$.

(ii) Φ is a set of predicates on that space closed under G;

(iii) ψ is in L (Φ) and invariant under G. Then, there exists a linear representation of

$$\psi = [\sum_{\varphi \in \Phi} \beta_\varphi \varphi > 0]$$

for which the coefficients β_φ depend only on the G-equivalence class of φ, that is if $\varphi \underset{G}{\equiv} \varphi'$ then $\beta_\varphi \equiv \beta_\varphi'$.

L Φ is the set of all predicates for which ψ is a linear threshold function with respect to Φ, and a predicate is a function that has two possible values, i.e., a binary function. ψ is a linear threshold function with respect to Φ, (φ is in $L(\Phi)$, if there exists a number θ, and a set of numbers, α_φ one for each φ in Φ, such that:

$$\psi(X) = [\sum_{\psi \in \Phi} \alpha_\varphi \varphi(X) > \theta] . \tag{7.54}$$

Restrictions on Perceptron Operations and Limitations in Geometric Patterns That Can Be Recognized

Perceptrons are not without restrictions in the types of operations that can be performed and the geometric patterns that can be recognized.

Restrictions of Geometry. The perceptron operations discussed by Minsky and Papert have a receptor geometry restricted as follows:

1. The number of points (or receptive elements) is limited. Hence, the predicates of the points are of limited order.

2. The distances between points are restricted. Hence, their predicates are diameter-limited.

Order has to do with the number of characteristic variables needed to represent a set of particular functions. For example, the order of ψ is the smallest number, K, for which a set Φ of predicates can be found satisfying:

$$|S(\varphi)| \leqslant K \quad \text{for all} \quad \varphi \text{ in } \Phi, \quad \psi \epsilon L(\Phi)$$

where $S(\varphi)$ is that subset of receptors, $r_1, r_2, \ldots, r_n$, upon which $\psi(X)$ (the set of functions required for recognizing X) really depends, and $L(\Phi)$ is the linear threshold function of Φ, the set of all predicates that can be defined by Eq. 7.54.

Linear threshold function perceptron operations are of order 1. So are all the Boolean functions of two variables except for:

i. Exclusive-or $(XY' + X'Y > 0)$ and

ii. Its complement identity, $X \equiv Y$ $(XY + X'Y' > 0)$

which are of order 2.

Type of Processing Operations. Perceptrons are particularly good at doing processing operations of the types called "local" or "conjunctively local" by Minsky and Papert [672]. By local is meant that all tests (analytic or logical) can be done independently and the final decision can be made by a logically simple procedure such as unanimity of all tests.

A predicate, ψ, is conjunctively local of order K if it can be computed by a set Φ of predicates φ such that:

i. Each φ depends on no more than K points of the space R;

ii. $\psi(X) = \begin{cases} 1 & \text{if } \varphi(X) = 1 \text{ for every } \varphi \text{ in } \Phi \\ 0 & \text{otherwise.} \end{cases}$

Such processing will enable a perceptron to distinguish convex from non-convex figures at the receptors by the test that if there exist three receptor points, p, q, and r, such that q is in the line segment joining p and r, and

$$p \text{ is in } X,$$
$$q \text{ is not in } X,$$
$$r \text{ is in } X, t$$

then the set X is not convex (Fig. 7.28). Thus, $\psi_{\text{convex}}(X)$ is conjunctively local of order 3 by application of this three-point rule [672].

Interestingly, the determination of connectedness between points can be shown not to be conjunctively local of any order in a diameter-limited perceptron processing operation. Hence, perceptrons of this type cannot compute connectedness of geometric figures whereas they can compute convexity. However, as inspection of Fig. 6.6C will indicate, we, too, have our difficulties in determining connectedness.

Types of Perceptrons

Given that "a Perceptron is a device capable of computing all predicates which are linear in some given set Φ of partial predicates" [672], five different types of perceptrons can be distinguished. They are:

1. *Diameter-limited Perceptrons*—the set of points upon which each φ depends (for each φ in some given set Φ) is restricted not to exceed a certain fixed diameter in the plane.

2. *Order-restricted Perceptrons*—a perceptron has order $\leqslant n$ if no member of Φ depends on more than n points.

3. *Gamba Perceptrons*—each member of Φ may depend on all the points but must be a linear threshold function, with each member of Φ itself being computed by a perceptron of order 1. Thus,

$$\varphi_i = [\sum_j \beta_{ij} r_j > \theta_i]$$

(each φ_i is a threshold perceptron of order 1) and

Determination of Convexity by Three-Point Rule

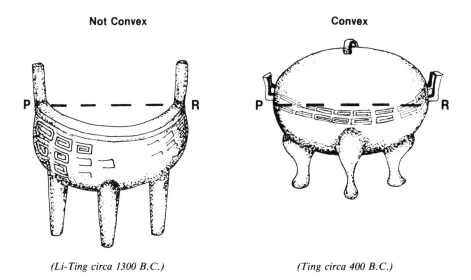

Not Convex   **Convex**

(Li-Ting circa 1300 B.C.)   *(Ting circa 400 B.C.)*

Fig. 7.28. Determination of convexity by three-point rule [672]. Draw a straight line connecting surface points such as P and R. If a third point, taken anywhere along this line, is inside the space of the object, the surface is convex.

$$\psi_{\text{gamba}} = [\sum_i \alpha_i [\sum_j \beta_{ij} r_j > \theta_i] > \theta] \qquad (7.55)$$

The Gamba perceptron is thus a two-layered perceptron. Note, however, that no improvement is afforded by any multi-layered system, without loops, in which there is an order restriction at each layer wherein only predicates of finite order are computed.

4. *Random Perceptrons*—the φ's are random Boolean functions. They are order-restricted and Φ is generated by a stochastic process according to an assigned distribution function (cf. Rosenblatt [838-841]).

5. *Bounded Perceptrons*—Φ contains an infinite number of φ's, but all the α_φ lie in a finite set of numbers [672].

Size, Speed, and Layer-Hierarchy Considerations in Perceptron Operations
Given application of the group invariance theorem to analysis of perceptrons of the above types, several observations may be drawn concerning effects of size, speed, and layer or hierarchy of operation.

First, using more "memory" does not seem to advance the kinds or efficiencies of linear threshold operations that are performed. This is interesting because many believe that adding memory will greatly improve the types of operations that can be performed. Minsky and Papert would suggest that design is more important than size.*

Second, it should be possible to specify connection-matrices between elements that will optimize the efficiency of processing vis-à-vis the number of elements involved. Examples of different connection matrices are shown in Fig. 7.29.

Multilayer Perceptrons with Loops

According to Minsky and Papert, the group invariance theorem cannot be applied to multilayered perceptrons with loops.[†] The addition of loops thus reopens analytic questions. It remains to be seen how the addition of loops limits general theories of sensory information processing by perceptron-like automata.[‡] Some analytic questions can be answered a priori. For example, the use of loops in processing will not improve the speed of computation afforded by loop-free serial processing. Other questions cannot. Thus, it is unclear whether or not loops afford the possibility of more complex analytic operations. Given finite order processing, a prerequisite for mathematical analysis, it is questionable whether loops afford any order-improvement beyond that possible with a hierarchical multilayered construction.

What loops do offer is the possibility of using the simple feedback principle for "training" or error correction. Minsky and Papert believe that the perceptron convergence theorem provides analytic proof that where such "learning, adaptation or self organization does occur, its occurrence can be thoroughly elucidated (mathematically)" [672].

A Geometry of Sorting—Treatment of Motor Labeled Effectuation, Synthesis, and Decision Making

Comparison of Fig. 7.30 with Fig. 3.42 will disclose how motor-labeled effectuation or decision making is implicit in the design of perceptrons.

What has not been treated explicitly in the course of analysis of perceptron operations is the geometry of sorting, i.e., an algebraic analysis of motor labeled effectuation comparable to that for sensory reception presented earlier. Three positions are possible. One is that this geometry is completely implicit in the classification algorithms described by Minsky and Papert (perhaps as a substructure of predicates). The second is that significant extensions of their algorithms and theory need to be made—perhaps by an expanded treatment of conditional probabilities and Markov processes.[¶] The third position, that such

---

*It is not yet clear if artificial intelligence performed by a large, specifically designed computer (capable of "logical" operation) can adequately simulate intelligence based on *unincorporated* design features. Logic may be used to approximate the needed features, but the results may be unsatisfactory and the errors difficult to detect, as in some of the phenomena illustrated in Chapter 6.

[†]Although it will be recalled that closed flowgraphs, consisting of loop circuits, *can* be solved.

[‡]Also, some loops can be eliminated by use of flowgraphs.

[¶]Another class of algorithm that can compute connectedness may be required—Turing machines can compute connectedness; perceptrons cannot.

Connection-Matrices

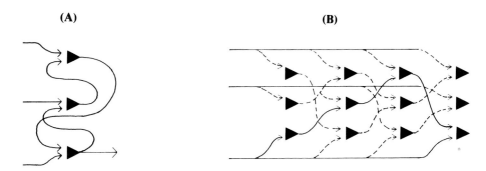

Fig. 7.29. *Different connection matrices. Are those in (A) equivalent to those darkened in (B)? (There is feedback in A.) Are some elements and connections in B superfluous? (Even if different transfer functions of several elements could be combined, the connections would allow unique dependencies between inputs, elements, and outputs). (Sketches after Minsky and Papert [672].)*

A Learning Machine

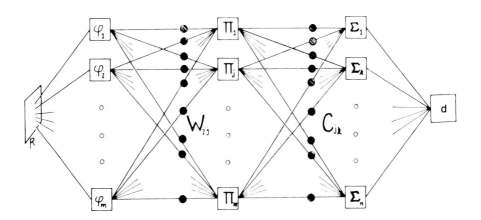

Fig. 7.30. *A multilayer perceptron capable of making decisions (d). (From Minsky and Papert [672].) The adaptations controlling Δw_{ij} and Δc_{jk} might benefit from feedback of information concerning the system state.*

a geometry and analysis is unrealizable, may be dismissed if one accepts Minsky and Papert's view that workable systems are subject to analysis and this author's assertion that such systems are visible within the reflex pathways of the nervous system.

Classification Algorithms

The following classification algorithms for separating different sensory labeled aggregates at d in Fig. 7.30 have been suggested by Minsky and Papert [672].

1. *Perceptron convergence theorem.* Let F be a set of unit-length vectors. Let $A \cdot \Phi$ be the vector notation of $\Sigma \, \alpha_\varphi \, \varphi(X)$. If there exists a unit vector A^* and a number $\delta > 0$ such that $A^* \cdot \Phi > \delta$ for all Φ in F, then a simple program (see Minsky and Papert [672], p. 167) can be devised that will converge in a finite number of iterations on a separation of all $\Phi \in F$. A variation of this program (see [672]) will separate more than two classes of input figures: $F_1, F_2, \ldots, F_n$.

A limitation of this classification algorithm is that only linear separations are performed optimally by this method.

2. *Bayes' linear statistical procedure.* Again, let F be a set of unit-length vectors, with one vector, A_i^* such that $A_i \cdot \Phi > \delta$ for all Φ in F. If $A_j = (\theta_j \, \omega_{1j}, \omega_{2j}, \ldots)$,

$$\text{where } \omega_{ij} = \text{Log} \left(\frac{P_{ij}}{1 - P_{ij}} \right)$$

and P is the probability that $\varphi_i = 1$, given that Φ is in F_j, then $\Phi \in F$ will be separated with the lowest possible error rate, given that the φ's are statistically independent. (This is, remarkably, a linear formula that can perform non-linear separation.)

3. *Best planes procedure*—This is essentially an error-minimizing tracking procedure whereby the set of A's is used for which choice of the largest $A_i \cdot \Phi$ gives the fewest errors. The presence of false peaks in hillclimbing searches by this method may limit its applicability.

4. *Cluster analysis*—Techniques are used to minimize the least square distance between different points in the receptor array (R) reflected by the different $A_i \cdot \Phi$. In effect, separation is performed on the basis of spatial clustering of each sensory aggregate. A more complete description of this approach and a cluster-analysis convergence theorem, with proof, can be found in Minsky and Papert's book [672].

5. *Exact matching or best matching*—This approach requires a large memory and is cumbersome. Each Φ that has ever been encountered, together with the identity of its associated F-class, is stored. New inputs are "recognized" on the basis of match against the store contents. With exact matching, a tedious search results in a solution with no errors. With

*denotes unit vector

"best" matching, a completely different type of procedure (e.g., algorithms such as those incorporating matched filtering—see Woody [1103]) is used to optimize signal detection, minimize errors, and reduce search time (see [672,704,1123]).

Probability as a Descriptor of Motor Effectuation: The Conditional Probability of Sorting, An Algebra of Events

Just as entropy is relatable to the uncertainty of configurations of gas molecules in a dimensional space, and provides some measure thereof, so does probability provide a measure or index of the likelihood of events. As we have seen from the work of Boltzmann and of Shannon, the events may be physical-chemical or they may be informational-probabilistic.

Just as chemical events may be described as occupying a space [328], so may other probabilistic events be described in terms of the space they occupy. The space of probabilistic events is described by set theory and Venn diagrams thereof. The sample space (Fig. 7.31) represents the number of possible different arrangements of sample points or outcomes, and each event or specific outcome in the sample space can be assigned a probability of occurrence.

Set theory is described by a set of axioms that fully define the algebra of events [cf. 240]. With respect to Fig. 7.31, they are:

1. $A + B = B + A$ (commutative law); also for multiplication, $AB = BA$
2. $A + (B + C) = (A+B) + C$ (associative law); also for multiplication, $A(BY) = (AB)Y$
3. $A(B + C) = AB + AC$ (distributive law)
4. $(A')' = A$ (' = "not" or the complement of whatever it follows)
5. $(AB) = A' + B'$
6. $AA' = \Phi$ (Φ = complement of U)
7. $AU = A$ (U = union of two events—the collection of all points in either or both event spaces)

This set of axioms is also the set of constraints by which linear systems are bound and defined.

Simple Probability. Could probability be used to describe motor effectuation, i.e., the motor events (or decisional space) possible as outcomes of a particular network? If so, could some general formulation be derived, comparable to the group invariance theorem to permit a general algebraic treatment of the geometry of sorting or motor effectuation? The answer to the first question is yes; the answer to the second, perhaps. The sample space, S, of possible motor outcomes is made up of a number of points, $E_1, E_2, \ldots, E_n$. Each point, E_k, has an expected probability of occurrence $P(E_k)$.*

The probability of occurrence of event A, $P(A)$, is the sum of the probabilities of all points within it. The sum of the probabilities of occurrence of all points equals 1, which is equal to the probability of the entire sample space. Thus, $P(A)$ must be between 0 and 1.

*Event A may be mapped from sets of $P(E_k)$.

Sample Space

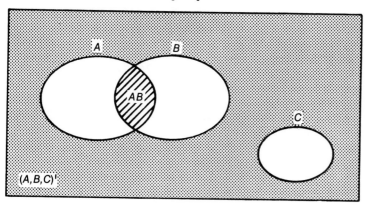

Fig. 7.31. The sample space of A, B, C *and* (A,B,C)'.

Conditional Probability. Conditional probability deals with the probability of an event A occurring given that some other event B has just occurred. If the events are completely independent, the probability of event A occurring will be equal to the general probability of occurrence of event A, $P(A)$. If there is some dependency, the probability of event A occurring, once B has occurred, may be different from the general probability of occurrence of event A. Bayes has systematized this relationship. If one thinks of B as the causal event and A as the affected event, the probability that A occurs given that B has occurred, $P(A/B)$, is equal to the general probability of occurrence of A, $P(A)$, times the probability of the effect B given that the phenomenon A has occurred, $P(B/A)$, divided by the probability of event B, $P(B)$. Thus:

$$P(A/B) = \frac{P(A)\,P(B/A)}{P(B)} \, . \qquad (7.56)$$

Interestingly, this theorem may be generalized to encompass the relationship of a set of events A_1, A_2, ..., A_n. This is because $P(B)$ will equal $P[(A_1 + A_2 + \ldots A_n)B]$ or $\Sigma P(A_i B)$.

Thus,

$$P(B) = \sum_{i=1}^{N} P(A_i B). \qquad (7.57)$$

It can be shown that:

$$\sum_{i=1}^{N} P(A_i B) = \sum_{i=1}^{N} P(A_i)\,P(B/A_i). \qquad (7.58)$$

Therefore, for a particular event A_i:

$$P(A_i B) = \frac{P(A_i) P(B/A_i)}{\displaystyle\sum_{i=1}^{N} P(A_i) P(B/A_i)} \qquad (7.59)$$

The following example has been adapted from that of Feller [282] for purposes of illustration:

Let us consider a group of color-blind males and females.

Let $P(c)$ equal the probability of a color-blind person. $P(c)$ will thus be equal to the number of color-blind people (n_c) over the total population, N.

$$P(c) = \frac{n_c}{N} . \qquad (7.60)$$

The probability of a female will be $P(f)$ and will equal the number of females, n_f, over the total population, N.

$$P(f) = \frac{n_f}{N} . \qquad (7.61)$$

Now, the probability of the person being color-blind, given that a female has been chosen, i.e., $P(c/f)$, = the number of color-blind females (n_{cf}) over the number of females (n_f), and is also equal to the probability of being color-blind and female, $P(cf)$, over the probability of being female, $P(f)$.

$$P(c/f) = \frac{n_{cf}}{n_f} = \frac{P(cf)}{P(f)} . \qquad (7.62)$$

Bayes theorem says that the probability of being female given that a color-blind person is selected, i.e., $P(f/c)$, is equal to the probability of being female and color-blind (P_{cf}) over the probability of being color-blind, $P(c)$.

$$P(f/c) = \frac{P(cf)}{P(c)} . \qquad (7.63)$$

If one substitutes the formulation obtained from Eq. 7.62 for $P(cf)$, one obtains:

$$P(f/c) = \frac{P(c/f) P(f)}{P(c)} . \qquad (7.64)$$

That is, the probability of being female, given that a color-blind person is selected, is equal to the probability of being color-blind, given a female person, times the probability of being female, divided by the probability of being color-blind.

Still one further extension is possible. Consider that the probability of being color-blind, $P(c)$, is equal to the number of color-blind people (n_c) over the total population (N). This would be equal to the sum of color-blind females plus color-blind males over the total population (N).

$$P(c) = \frac{n_{cf} + n_{cm}}{N}, \tag{7.65}$$

since

$$n_{cf} = P(c/f) \cdot n_f,$$
$$n_{cm} = P(c/m) \cdot n_m,$$
$$P(c) = \frac{P(c/f) \cdot n_f + P(c/m) \cdot n_m}{N}$$

since

$$n_f = P(f) \cdot N,$$
$$n_m = P(m) \cdot N,$$
$$P(c) = \frac{P(c/f) \cdot P(f) \cdot N + P(c/m) \cdot P(m) \cdot N}{N},$$
$$P(c) = P(c/f) \cdot P(f) + P(c/m) \cdot P(m).$$

Substituting in Eq. 7.64,

$$P(f/c) = \frac{P(c/f) P(f)}{P(c/f) \cdot P(f) + P(c/m) \cdot P(m)}. \tag{7.66}$$

Here the denominator is generalized to the sum of the probability of being color-blind given all classes of other possibilities times the probability of all other classes.

Markov Processes. A Markov process is a system with probabilistic events whose outcome is influenced by or conditional upon the immediately preceding system state or outcome of events.* No earlier outcomes except those immediately preceding the event will influence the probability of that event. Thus, given a temporal order of processes: X_1 goes to X_2 goes to X_3, the probability X_3, given $X_1 X_2$ equals the probability X_3, given X_2 only.

*A Markovian process is, therefore, *not* a linear system, cf. Lee [582] and p. 383.

This type of analysis, when applied to an algebra of sorting motor outcomes, admits the effects of all adaptations up to the moment at which the probability of a particular motor outcome is calculated, but assumes no further inertial effects of past adaptations. Flowgraphing permits assignment of properly identified conditional probabilities within a context of sensory and motor labeling. Transmittances between nodel elements can be described in terms of adaptations and their weightings relative to inputs and outputs. The adaptations and labeled interconnections of the network would control the sorting of motor operations. Transfer functions between inputs and outputs would also be influenced by the integrative properties of the cell cables and by feedback in the manners described earlier.

Given these assumptions and their limitations, one could conceivably use conditional probability and Markov processes to characterize an algebra of motor events based on flowgraphed operations arising from a network of *adaptive* elements.

Evaluation of the Merit of the Analysis

One would like to evaluate the merit of these and other analyses of network function. There appear to be three ways that this can be done, objectively.

Parsimony

The first is by applying the principle of parsimony, i.e., Occam's razor. Given a complex system, analytic worth lies in a parsimonious, optimized, and preferably unique description.

Just as models of automata incorporate cost effectiveness into their design to reduce error (cf. Fig. 7.30)*, so might analyses of such systems be evaluated on their own efficiencies and selectivities. Mathematical means exist for doing so [cf. 672,704]. Most, but not all, involve the use of random process statistics.

Detection and Avoidance of Error

The second means for objectively evaluating the merit of analyses of network function lies in the detection of error. This may be done in several ways. One is by simply noting obvious mathematical, logical, or factual inconsistencies. Another is by formal consideration of error itself. For example, a theorem of probabilistic outcomes of sorting is likely to be more worthwhile if it considers sorting errors as well as successes [704]. Still another, less objective means relies primarily on the perception of agreement or disagreement. For example, it is said that the best test of error is surprise. Kant elaborated on

---

*Minimizing $\sum_j C_{jk} \cdot B_j \cdot \prod_j (P_{ij}/q_{ij}) \varphi_i$, where C_{jk} is the cost of guessing F_k when it is really F_j that has occurred, $B_j = \prod q_{ij}$, and p and q are probabilities of a correct guess and an error, respectively [672].

this by constructing a view of fallacies in which antinomies* would signal possible errors in perception as they are being made [489,856]. This idea that the generation of fallacies or antinomies may provide an indication of improperly drawn relationships is interesting. An example of an antinomy is the following. Thesis: The world has a beginning in time and is limited in space. Antithesis: The world has no beginning in time and no limits in space. The fact that both statements sound reasonable but are antithetic, suggests that their construction is in error.

The Scientific Method

The third means for evaluating the merit of analysis is often described as the scientific method. Here, analyses lead to testable hypotheses. If the predictions made by a hypothesis fail to be validated experimentally, the hypothesis is rejected. If validated, the hypothesis is supported and eventually (upon further validation) becomes a theory which is accepted until disproved by other evidence.

Relatively few neurobiologic applications have been made of the analytic approaches advanced herein, largely because the underlying theories are relatively new and the hypotheses to which these analyses may be applied still rather crudely formed. However, the results of the few studies already performed are promising. As mentioned earlier, some neurophysiologic systems, or restricted aspects thereof, have proved amenable to linear systems analysis [429], and, in at least one instance [1123], the analysis has been of predictive value, though in a limited and ultimately pessimistic way. In addition, simulations by models such as the informon have affirmed the merit of control features such as negative feedback of messages concerning the system state for the regulation of adaptive systems. Further tests and hypotheses of relevant features of the circuitry and the adaptive elements therein are needed if the field of cybernetics applying to memory, learning and higher function is to be advanced. It is a young science, one presently at the stage of outgrowing some of the terminologies of Chapters 2 and 3 and of accumulating biochemical, anatomical, physiological, and neuropsychological data to add further substance to the material in Chapters 4 and 5. Only in this matter may it be possible to determine if the graphs to the left and right of Fig. 2.3 are other than fancifully related. If so, application of those results to the problems described in Chapter 6 may ultimately be attempted using, perhaps, the approaches described within the present chapter.

*alias strange loops, *c.f. Gödel, Escher, Bach.*

Epilogue

It is dangerous to identify the real . . . world with the models which are constructed to explain it. The problem of understanding the animal nervous action is far deeper than the problem of understanding the mechanism of a computing machine. Even plausible explanations of nervous reaction should be taken with a very large grain of salt.

(Von Neumann, 1956)

The frontispiece was selected with much the same thoughts in mind.

REFERENCES

1. Abraham JL, Etz ES (1979) Molecular microanalysis of pathological specimens in situ with a Laser-Raman microprobe. Science 206:716-718
2. Adam G, Adey WR, Porter RW (1966) Interoceptive conditional response in cortical neurones. Nature 209:920-921
3. Adams DJ, Smith SJ, Thompson SH (1980) Ionic currents in molluscan soma. Annu Rev Neurosci 3:141-167
4. Adams RD (1958) The clinical signs of focal cerebral disease and the syndrome of dementia. In: Harrison TR et al. (eds) Principles of internal medicine, 3rd edn. McGraw-Hill, New York, pp 336-347
5. Adams RD (1958) Affectations of speech. In: Harrison TR et al. (eds) Principles of internal medicine, 3rd edn. McGraw-Hill, New York, pp 366-376
6. Adey WR, Dunlop CW, Hendrix CE (1960) Hippocampal slow waves: Distribution and phase relationships in the course of approach learning. AMA Arch Neurol 3:74-90
7. Adrian ED (1936) The spread of activity in the cerebral cortex. J Physiol (Lond) 88:127-161
8. Agranoff BW, Davis RE, Brink JJ (1966) Chemical studies on memory fixation in goldfish. Brain Res 1:303-309
9. Aidley DJ (1971) The physiology of excitable cells. Cambridge University Press, London and New York
10. Aleksanyan ZA, Skvařil J, Bureš J (1972) Stability of firing pattern of hypothalamic neurons subjected to direct electrical or chemical stimulation. Exp Brain Res 15:29-38
11. Alema S, Calissano P, Rusca G, Guiditta A (1973) Identification of a calcium-binding, brain-specific protein in the axoplasm of squid giant axons. J Neurochem 20:681-689
12. Alkon DL (1979) Voltage-dependent calcium and potassium ion conductances: A contingency mechanism for an associative learning model. Science 205:810-816; also see Biol Bull 159: 505-560, 1980
13. Allen DG, Blinks JR, Prendergast FG (1977) Aequorin luminescence: Relation of light emission to calcium concentration—a calcium-independent component. Science 195:996-998
14. Allen WF (1940) Effect of ablating the frontal lobes, hippocampi, and occipito-parieto-temporal (excepting pyriform areas) lobes on positive and negative olfactory conditioned reflexes. Am J Physiol 128:754-771; also see idem 132:81-92 (1941)
15. Alnaes E, Rahamimoff R (1975) On the role of mitochondria in transmitter release from motor nerve terminals. J Physiol (Lond) 248:285-306
16. Altman JA (1975) Neurophysiological mechanisms in auditory localization. Woody CD (ed) Soviet research reports, Vol. I. Brain Information Service, University of California, Los Angeles, pp 1-36
17. Altman, JL (1975) Effects of interference with cerebellar maturation on the development of locomotion. An experimental model of neurobehavioral retardation. UCLA Forum Med Sci 18:41-91
18. Amari S (1977) Mathematical approach to neural systems. In: Metzler J (ed) Systems neuroscience. Academic Press, New York, pp 67-117

19. Amari S (1977) Neural theory of association and concept-formation. Biol Cyber 26:175-185

20. Amari S, Arbib MA (1977) Competition and cooperation in neural nets. In: Metzler J (ed) Systems neuroscience. Academic Press, New York, pp 119-165

21. Amari S, Kishimoto K (1978) Dynamics of excitation patterns in lateral-inhibitory neural fields (in Japanese). Proc Jp Tsushingakkai 61-A: 625-632; also see: (1977) Biol Cyber 27:77-87, (1979) J Math Biol 7:303-318

22. Amari S, Takeuchi A (1978) Mathematical theory on formation of category detecting nerve cells. Biol Cybern 29:127-136

23. Anderson CM, Zucker FH, Steitz TA (1979) Space-filling models of kinase clefts and conformation changes. Science 204:375-380

24. Anton G (1899) Ueber die Selbstwahrnehmung der Herderkrankungen des Gehirns durch den Kranken bei Rindenblindheit und Rindentaubheit. Arch Psychiat Nervenkr 32:36-127

25. Araki T, Otani T (1955) Response of single motoneurons to direct stimulation in toad's spinal cord. J Neurophysiol 18:472-485

26. Arbib MA (1964) Brains, machines and mathematics. McGraw-Hill, New York

27. Ariens-Kappers CU, Huber GC, Crosby EC (1936) The comparative anatomy of the nervous system of vertebrates, including man. (2 vols.) Macmillan, New York (cf ref 197)

28. Armstrong WMcD, O'Doherty J, Stark RJ, Youmans SJ (1980) Ca^{++}-Selective microelectrodes for intracellular studies. Proc Int Union Physiol Sci 14:303

29. Artemyev VV, Bezladnova NI (1952) Electrical reaction of the auditory area of the cortex of the cerebral hemispheres during the formation of a conditioned defense reflex. Tr Inst Fiziol Akad Nauk SSSR 1:228-236

30. Asanuma H, Rosen I (1973) Spread of mono- and polysynaptic connections within cat's motor cortex. Exp Brain Res 16:507-520

31. Asanuma H, Stoney SD, Jr, Abzug C (1968) Relationship between afferent input and motor outflow in cat motorsensory cortex. J Neurophysiol 31:670-681

32. Asratyan EA (1958) Switching in conditioned reflex activity: Some new observations. Zh Vyssh Nerv Deiat 8:289-295

33. Asratyan EA (ed) (1970-1971) Physiology of higher nervous activity, Vols. I and II (in Russian). Nauka, Moscow

34. Attardi G, Sperry RW (1963) Preferential selection of central pathways by regenerating optic fibers. Exp Neurol 7:46-64

35. Avery DD, Moss DE, Hendrick SA (1976) Food deprivation at weaning and adult behavior elicited by hypothalamic stimulation in the rat. Behav Biol 16:155-160

36. Axelsson J, Thesleff S (1959) A study of supersensitivity in denervated mammalian skeletal muscle. J Physiol (Lond) 147:178-193

37. Bahrick HP (1952) Latent learning as a function of the strength of unrewarded need states. J Comp Physiol Psychol 45:192-197

38. Bailey CH, Thompson EB, Chen M, Hawkins R (1978) Insights into the morphological basis of presynaptic faciliation in the gill–withdrawal reflex of Aplysia: Analysis of the fine structure of a modulatory synapse. Soc Neurosci Symp 4:187

39. Baker AG, Mackintosh NJ (1979) Preexposure to the CS alone, or CS and US uncorrelated: Latent inhibition, blocking by context or learned irrelevance? Learn Motiv 10:278-294

40. Baker PF (1972) Transport and metabolism of calcium ions in nerve. Prog Biophys Mol Biol 24:177-223

41. Baker PF, Blaustein MP, Hodgkin AL, Steinhardt RA (1969) The influence of calcium on sodium efflux in squid axons. J Physiol (Lond) 200:431-458

42. Baker PF, Blaustein MP, Keynes RD, Manil J, Shaw TI, Steinhardt RA (1969) The ouabain-sensitive fluxes of sodium and potassium in squid giant axon. J Physiol (Lond) 200:459-496

43. Baker PF, Hodgkin AL, Ridgway EB (1971) Depolarization and calcium entry in squid giant axons. J Physiol (Lond) 218:709-755

44. Baker PF, Schlaepfer W (1975) Calcium uptake by axoplasm extruded from giant axons of Loligo. J Physiol (Lond) 249:37P-38P

45. Balashova RN (1970) On the influence of electrical stimulation of the rabbit cerebral cortex on spatial synchronization of biopotentials. Zh Vyssh Nerv Deiat 20:1189-1197

46. Baranyi A, Feher O (1978) Conditioned changes of synaptic transmission in the motor cortex of the cat. Exp Brain Res 33:283-298

47. Barker JL (1976) Peptides: Roles in neuronal excitability. Physiol Rev 56:435-452

48. Barlow JA (1956) Secondary motivation through classical conditioning: A reconsideration of the nature of backward conditioning. Psychol Rev 63:406-408

49. Barondes SH, Cohen HD (1966) Puromycin effect on successive phases of memory storage. Science 151:594-595

50. Barrett EF, Barrett JN (1976) Separation of two voltage-sensitive potassium currents and demonstration of a tetrodotoxin-resistant calcium current in frog motoneurones. J Physiol 255:737-774

51. Bartfai T (1978) Cyclic nucleotides in the central nervous system. Trends Biochem Sci 3:121-124

52. Bartfai T (1980) Cyclic nucleotides in the central nervous system. Curr Top Cell Regul 16:226-263

53. Beach FA, Hebb DO, Morgan CT, Nissen, HW (eds) (1960) The neuropsychology of Lashley—Selected papers of K.S. Lashley. McGraw-Hill, New York

54. Beck EC, Doty RW (1957) Conditioned flexion reflexes acquired during combined catalepsy and de-efferentation. J Comp Physiol Psychol 50:211-216

55. Belenkov NYu (1965) Conditioned reflex and subcortical structures (in Russian). Meditsina, Moscow

56. Bell C, Sierra G, Buendia N, Segundo JP (1964) Sensory properties of neurons in the mesencephalic reticular formation. J Neurophysiol 27:961-987

57. Ben-Ari Y (1972) Plasticity at unitary level. I. An experimental design. Electroencephalogr Clin Neurophysiol 32:655-665

58. Ben-Ari Y, LaSalle GLG (1972) Plasticity at unitary level. II. Modifications during sensory-sensory association procedures. Electroencephalogr Clin Neurophysiol 32:667-679

59. Bennett MVL (1964) Nervous function at the cellular level. Annu Rev Physiol 26:289-340

60. Bennett MVL (1973) Function of electrotonic junctions in embryonic and adult tissues. Fed Proc 32:65-75

61. Bennett MVL (1973) Permeability and structure of electrotonic junctions and intercellular movements of tracers. In: Kater SD, Nicholson C (eds) Intracellular staining in neurobiology. Springer-Verlag, New York, pp 113-133

62. Bennett MVL (1974) Cellular interactions mediated by gap junctions. In: Woody CD, Brown KA, Crow TJ, Jr, Knispel JD (eds) Cellular mechanisms subserving changes in neuronal activity. Brain Information Service, University of California, Los Angeles, pp 119-131

63. Bennett MVL, Goodenough DA (1978) Gap junctions, electrotonic coupling, and intercellular communication. Neurosci Res Program Bull 16:373-486

64. Berger WT, Thompson RF (1978) Identification of pyramidal cells as the critical elements in hippocampal neuronal plasticity during learning. Proc Natl Acad Sci USA 75:1572-1576

65. Berger WT, Thompson RF (1978) Neuronal plasticity in the limbic system during classical conditioning of the rabbit nictitating membrane response. I. The hippocampus. Brain Res 145:323-346

66. Berger WT, Thompson RF (1978) Neuronal plasticity in the limbic system during classical conditioning of the rabbit nictitating membrane response. II. Septum and mammillary bodies. Brain Res 156:293-314

67. Bergson, H (1908) Matiere et memoire. F. Alkan, Paris

68. Bergson HL (1913) Creative evolution (authorized translation by Arthur Mitchell). Macmillan, New York

69. Bergson H (1971) Time and free will. Muirhead Library of Philosophy Humanities, Atlantic Highlands, NJ

70. Berman AL (1961) Interaction of cortical responses to somatic and auditory stimuli in anterior ectosylvian gyrus of cat. J Neurophysiol 24:608-620

71. Berner B (1978) Spin-label magnetic resonance studies of membranes and simpler model systems. PhD thesis, University of California, Los Angeles

72. Berridge MJ (1975) The interaction of cyclic nucleotides and calcium in the control of cellular activity. Adv Cyclic Nucleotide Res 6:1-98

73. Beswick FB, Conroy RTWL (1964) Maximal heteronymous monosynaptic reflex discharges. J Physiol (Lond) 172:62P

74. Beswick FB, Conroy RTWL (1965) Optimal tetanic conditioning of heteronymous monosynaptic reflexes. J Physiol (Lond) 180:134-146

75. Bezanilla F, Armstrong CM (1974) Gating currents of the sodium channels: Three ways to block them. Science 183:753-754

76. Bianchi L (1922) The mechanism of the brain and the function of the frontal lobe (translation by J.H. MacDonald). Wood, New York

77. Biederman GB (1973-1974) The search for the chemistry of memory: Recent trends and the logic of investigation in the role of cholinergic and adrenergic transmitters. Prog Neurobiol 2:291-307

78. Bindman LJ, Lippold CJ, Milne AR (1979) Prolonged changes in excitability of pyramidal tract neurones in the cat: A post-synaptic mechanism. J Physiol (Lond) 286:457-477

79. Bitterman ME, Reed PC, Kubala AL (1953) The strength of sensory preconditioning. J Exp Psychol 46:178-182

80. Bjorklund A, Stenevi U (1979) Regeneration of monoaminergic and cholinergic neurons in the mammalian central nervous system. Physiol Rev 59:62-100

81. Black AH (1968) Operant conditioning of autonomic responses. Cond Reflex 3:130

82. Black RW (1968) Shifts in magnitude of reward and contrast effects in instrumental and selective learning. Psychol Rev 75:114-126

83. Black-Cleworth P (1974) Conditioned blink acquired by pairing click and electrical stimulation of the facial nerve. In: Woody CD, Brown RA, Crow TJ, Jr, Knispel JD (eds) Cellular mechanisms subserving changes in neuronal activity, Brain Information Service, University of California, Los Angeles, pp 111-118

84. Black-Cleworth PA, Woody CD, Niemann J (1975) A conditioned eyeblink obtained by using electrical stimulation of the facial nerve as the unconditioned stimulus. Brain Res 90:45-56

85. Blaustein MP (1977) The regulation of intracellular calcium in nerve terminals: Lessons from the synaptosome. Neurosci Res Program Bull 15:582-590

86. Blaustein MP, Ector AC (1976) Carrier-mediated sodium-dependent and calcium-dependent calcium efflux from pinched-off presynaptic nerve terminals (synaptosomes) in vitro. Biochim Biophys Acta 419: 295-308

87. Blaustein MP, Ratzlaff RW, Schweitzer ES (1980) Control of intracellular calcium in presynaptic nerve terminals. Fed Proc 39:2790-2795

88. Bliss TVP, Burns BD, Uttley AM (1968) Factors affecting the conductivity of pathways in the cerebral cortex. J Physiol (Lond) 193: 339-367

89. Bliss TVP, Lømo T (1973) Long-lasting potentiation of synaptic transmission in the dentate area of the anaesthetized rabbit following stimulation of the perforant path. J Physiol (Lond) 232:331-356

90. Bloom FE (1979) Cyclic nucleotides in central synaptic function. Fed Proc 38:2203-2207

91. Boneau CA (1958) The interstimulus interval and the latency of the conditioned eyelid response. J Exp Psychol 56:464-472

92. Boulpaep EL, Sackin H (1979) Equivalent electrical circuit analysis and rheogenic pumps in epithelia. Fed Proc 38:2030-2036

93. Bovet D, Longo VG (1956) Pharmacologie de la substance reticulee du tronc cerebral. Abstr Rev 20th Int Physiol Conf, St. Catherine Press, Bruges, p 306

94. Brain R (1955) Aphasia, apraxia and agnosia. In: Wilson SAK, Bruce AN (eds) (Vol 3). Baltimore, Williams and Wilkins, pp. 1413-1483

95. Brauth SE, Olds J (1977) Midbrain unit activity during classical conditioning. Brain Res 134:73-82

96. Brillouin L (1962) Science and information theory. Academic Press, New York

97. Brindley GS (1969) Nerve net models of plausible size that perform many simple learning tasks. Proc R Soc Lond [Biol] 174:173-191

98. Brinley FJ, Jr (1978) Comment on the relation between calcium entry and change in ionized calcium. Ann NY Acad Sci 307:424-426 (and after further material presented by Dr. Brinley at this and other meetings on calcium transport and cell function).

99. Brinley FJ, Jr (1980) Regulation of intracellular calcium in squid axons. Fed Proc 39:2778-2782

100. Broadbent DE (1958) Perception and communication. Pergamon, Oxford
101. Brock LG, Coombs JS, Eccles JC (1952) The recording of potentials from motoneurones with an intracellular electrode. J Physiol (Lond) 117:431-460
102. Brodwick MS, Eaton DC (1978) Sodium channel inactivation in squid axon is removed by high internal pH or tyrosine-specific reagents. Science 200:1494-1496
103. Brogden WJ (1939) The effect of frequency of reinforcement upon the level of conditioning. J Exp Psychol 24:419-431
104. Brogden WJ (1947) Sensory preconditioning of human subjects. J Exp Psychol 37:527-539
105. Brogden WJ, Gantt WH (1942) Intraneural conditioning. Cerebellar conditioned reflexes. AMA Arch Neurol Psychiatry 48:437-455
106. Bronk DW (1939) Synaptic mechanisms in sympathetic ganglia. J Neurophysiol 2:380-401
107. Brons J (1979) Differences in excitability and activity in cortical neurons after Pavlovian conditioning, extinction, and prevention of the US alone. PhD thesis, University of California, Los Angeles
108. Brons J, Woody CD (1979) Changes in responsiveness to glabella tap among neurons in the sensorimotor cortex of awake cats. Soc Neurosci Abstr 5:314
109. Brons J, Woody CD (1977) Decreases in cortical neuronal excitability to injected current with extinction of a conditioned blink reflex in cats. Fed Proc 36:1923
110. Brons J, Buchhalter J, Woody CD (1978) Increases in excitability of cortical neurons to injected intracellular current after eyeblink conditioning, extinction, and presentation of US alone. Fed Proc 37:252
111. Brons J, Woody CD (1980) Long-term changes in excitability of cortical neurons after Pavlovian conditioning and extinction. J Neurophysiol 44:605-615
112. Brookhart JM, Fadiga E (1960) Potential fields initiated during monosynaptic activation of frog motoneurones. J Physiol (Lond) 150:633-655
113. Brooks VB, Enger PS (1959) Spread of directly evoked responses in the cat's cerebral cortex. J Gen Physiol 42:761-777
114. Brostrom CO, Brostrom MA, Wolff DJ (1977) Calcium-dependent adenylate cyclase from rat cerebral cortex. J Biol Chem 252:5677-5685
115. Brostrom CO, Huang Y-C, Breckenridge BMcL, Wolff DJ (1975) Identification of a calcium-binding protein as a calcium-dependent regulator of brain adenylate cyclase. Proc Nat Acad Sci USA 72:64-68
116. Brownell P, Mayeri E (1979) Prolonged inhibition of neurons by neuroendocrine cells in Aplysia. Science 204:417-420
117. Browning M, Dunwiddie T, Bennett W, Gispen W, Lynch G (1979) Synaptic phosphoproteins: Specific changes after repetitive stimulation of the hippocampal slice. Science 203:60-62
118. Brunelli M, Castellucci VF, Kandel ER (1976) Synaptic facilitation and behavioral sensitization in Aplysia: Possible role of serotonin and cyclic AMP. Science 194:1178-1180
119. Bruner J, Tauc L (1964) Les modifications de l'activité synaptique au cours de l'habituation chez l'Aplysie. J Physiol (Paris) 56:306-307

120. Buchhalter J, Brons J, Woody CD (1978) Changes in cortical neuronal excitability after presentations of a compound auditory stimulus. Brain Res 156:162-167

121. Buchwald JS, Brown KA (1973) Subcortical mechanisms of behavioral plasticity. In: Maser JD (ed) Efferent organization and the integration of behavior. Academic Press, New York, pp 99-136

122. Buchwald JS, Halas ES, Schramm S (1965) Progressive changes in efferent unit responses to repeated cutaneous stimulation in spinal cats. J Neurophysiol 28:200-215

123. Bullock TH, Horridge GA (1965) Structure and function in the nervous systems of invertebrates, Vol 1. Freeman, San Francisco, p 274ff

124. Bullock TH (1979) Parameters of neuronal integration. Grass Instrument Co, Grass Calendar, Quincy, Massachusetts

125. Bureš J (1977) Physiological basis of learning. In: Zeier H (ed) Pawlow und die Folgen, Psychologie des 20 Jahrhunderts. Kindler Verlag, Zürich, pp 476-524

126. Bureš J, Burešova O (1960) The use of Leâo's spreading depression in the study of interhemispheric transfer of memory traces. J Comp Physiol Psychol 53:558-563

127. Bureš J, Burešova O (1965) Relationship between spontaneous and evoked unit activity in the inferior colliculus of rats. J Neurophysiol 28:641-654

128. Bureš J, Burešova O (1967) Plastic changes of unit activity based on reinforcing properties of extracellular stimulation of single neurons. J Neurophysiol 30:98-113

129. Bureš J, Burešova O (1970) Plasticity in single neurons and neural populations. In: Horn G, Hinde RA (eds) Short-term changes in neural activity and behavior. Cambridge University Press, London and New York, pp 363-403

130. Bureš J, Burešova O (1979) Neurophysiological analysis of conditioned taste aversion. In: Brazier MAB (ed) Brain mechanisms in memory and learning. Raven Press, New York, pp 127-138

131. Bureš J, Burešova O (1980) Elementary learning phenomena in food selection. Proc Int Union Physiol Sci 14:13-14

132. Burešova O (1977) Post-Pavlovian investigations of higher nervous activity in the USSR. In: Zeier H (ed) Pawlow und die Folgen, Psychologie des 20 Jahrhunderts. Kindler Verlag, Zürich, pp 57-82

133. Burešova O, Bureš J (1979) The anterograde effect of ECS on the acquisition, retrieval and extinction of conditioned taste aversion. Physiol Behav 22:641-645

134. Burt CT, Glonek T, Barany M (1977) Analysis of living tissue to phosphorus-31 magnetic resonance. Science 195:145-149

135. Busis NA, Weight FF, Smith PA (1978) Synaptic potentials in sympathetic ganglia: Are they mediated by cyclic nucleotides? Science 200:1079-1081

136. Butters N, Cermak LS (1975) Some analyses of amnesic syndromes in brain-damaged patients. In: Isaacson RL, Pribam K (eds) The hippocampus, Vol 2. Plenum Press, New York, pp 377-409

137. Byus CV, Russell DH (1975) Ornithine decarboxylase activity. Control by cyclic nucleotides. Science 187:650-652

138. Cabot JB, Cohen DH (1977) Avian sympathetic cardiac fibers and their cells of origin: Anatomical and electrophysiological characteristics. Brain Res 131:73-87

139. Cabot JB, Cohen DH (1977) Anatomical and physiological characterization of Avian sympathetic cardiac afferents. Brain Res 131:89-101

140. Cabot JB, Wild JM, Cohen DH (1979) Raphe inhibition of sympathetic preganglionic neurons. Science 203:184-186

141. Cajal S Ramon y (1909) Histologie du système nerveux de l'homme et des vertébrés système, Vols. I and II. Maloine, Paris

142. Cajal S Ramon y (1937) Recollections of my life, MIT Press, Cambridge, Massachusetts

143. Campbell BA, Misanin JR, White BC, Lytle LD (1974) Species differences in ontogeny of memory: Direct support for neural maturation as a determinant of forgetting. J Comp Physiol Psychol 87:193-202

144. Cangiano A, Lutzemberger L (1977) Partial denervation affects both denervated and innervated fibers in the mammalian skeletal muscle. Science 196:542-544

145. Carew TJ, Castellucci VF, Kandel ER (1979) Sensitization in Aplysia: Restoration of transmission in synapses inactivated by long-term habituation. Science 205:417-419

146. Carew TJ, Kandel ER (1973) Acquisition and retention of long-term habituation in Aplysia: Correlation of behavioral and cellular processes. Science 182:1158-1160

147. Carew TJ, Kandel ER (1976) Two functional effects of decreased conductance EPSP's: Synaptic augmentation and increased electrotonic coupling. Science 192:150-153

148. Carew TJ, Kandel ER (1977) Inking in Aplysia californica. I. Neural circuit of an all-or-none behavioral response. J Neurophysiol 40:692-707

149. Carew TJ, Kandel ER (1977) Inking in Aplysia californica. II. Central program for inking. J Neurophysiol 40:708-720

150. Carew TJ, Kandel ER (1977) Inking in Aplysia californica. III. Two different synaptic conductance mechanisms for triggering central program inking. J Neurophysiol 40:721-734

151. Carew TJ, Pinsker HM, Kandel ER (1972) Long-term habituation of a defensive withdrawal reflex in Aplysia. Science 175:451-454

152. Carlton PL (1968) Cholinergic mechanisms in the control of behavior. In: Efron DH (ed) Psychopharmacology—A review of progress 1957-1967, PHS Publ No 836. US Government Printing Office, Washington, DC, pp 125-135

153. Carlton PL, Markiewicz B (1971) Behavioral effects of atropine and scopolamine. In: Furchtgott E (ed) Pharmacological and biophysiological agents and behavior. Academic Press, New York, pp 345-373

154. Carnay LD, Tasaki I (1971) Ion exchange properties and excitability of the squid giant axon. In: Adelman WJ (ed) Biophysics and physiology of excitable membranes, Van-Nostrand-Reinhold, Princeton, New Jersey, pp 379-442

155. Carpenter DO, Rudomin P (1973) The organization of primary afferent depolarization in the isolated spinal cord of the frog. J Physiol (Lond) 229:471-493

156. Castel M, Spira MW, Parnas I, Yarom Y (1976) Ultrastructure of region of a low safety factor in inhomogeneous giant axon of the cockroach. J Neurophysiol 39:900-908

157. Castellucci VF, Carew TJ, Kandel ER (1978) Cellular analysis of long-term habituation of the gill-withdrawal reflex of Aplysia californica. Science 202:1306-1308

158. Castellucci VF, Kandel ER (1976) Presynaptic facilitation as a mechanism for behavioral sensitization in Aplysia. Science 194:1176-1178

159. Catterall WA, Ray R, Morrow CS (1976) Membrane potential dependent binding of scorpion toxin to action potential Na^+ ionophore. Proc Natl Acad Sci USA 73:8:2682-2686

160. Cedar H, Schwartz JH (1972) Cyclic adenosine monophosphate in the nervous system of Aplysia californica. II. Effect of serotonin and dopamine. J Gen Physiol 60:570-587

161. Chernikoff R, Brogden WJ (1949) The effect of instructions upon sensory preconditioning of human subjects. J Exp Psychol 39:200-207

162. Cheung WY (1980) Calmodulin plays a pivotal role in cellular regulation. Science 207:19-27

163. Chin JH, Goldstein DB (1977) Drug tolerance in biomembranes; a spin label study of the effects of ethanol. Science 196:684-685

164. Chiu AY, Hunkapiller M, Strumwasser F (1979) The neuropeptide, egg laying hormone of Aplysia: Purification, amino acid sequence and antibodies. Soc Neurosci Abstr 5:243

165. Chow KL (1960) Brain waves and visual discrimination learning in monkey. In: Wortis J (ed) Recent advances in biological psychiatry. Grune & Stratton, New York, pp 149-157

166. Chow KL (1961) Changes of brain electropotentials during visual discrimination learning in monkey. J Neurophysiol 24:377-390

167. Chow KL, Dement WC, Mitchell SA (1959) Effects of lesions of the rostral thalamus on brain waves and behavior in cats. Electroencephalogr Clin Neurophysiol 11:107-120

168. Chung SH, Raymond SA, Lettvin JY (1970) Multiple meaning in single visual units. Brain Behav Evol 3:72-101

169. Church RM, Black AH (1958) Latency of the conditioned heart rate as a function of the CS-UCS interval. J Comp Physiol Psychol 51:478-487

170. Ciment G, De Vellis S (1978) Cellular interactions uncouple β-adrenergic receptors from adenylate cyclase. Science 202:765-768

171. Claparede E (1911) Recognition et moite. Arch Psychol (Geneve) 11:79-90

172. Clark GA, Berger TW, Thompson RF (1978) The role of entorhinal cortex during classical conditioning: Evidence for entorhinal-dentate facilitation. Soc Neurosci Abstr 4:673

173. Clusin WT, Bennett MVL (1977) Calcium-activated conductance in skate electroreceptors, J Gen Physiol 69:121-182

174. Cohen DH (1982) A vertebrate model system for long-term associative learning: an extended case study. In: McGaugh J, Thompson RD (ed) The neurobiology of learning and memory. Plenum Press, New York, (in press)

175. Cohen DH, Macdonald RL (1971) Some variables affecting orienting and conditioned heart rate responses in the pigeon. J Comp Physiol Psychol 74:123-133

176. Cohen DH, Pitts LH (1968) Vagal and sympathetic components of conditioned cardioacceleration in the pigeon. Brain Res 9:14-31

177. Cohen LB, Salzburg BM (1978) Optical measurement of membrane potential. Rev Physiol Biochem Pharmacol 83:35-88

178. Cohen LB, Salzberg BM, Davila HV, Ross WN, Landowne D, Waggoner AS, Wang CH (1974) Changes in axon fluorescence during activity: Molecular probes of membrane potential. J Membr Biol 19:1-36

179. Cole KS (1968) Membranes, ions and impulses. University of California Press, Berkeley

180. Coleman SR, Gormezano I (1971) Classical conditioning of the rabbit's (Oryctolanus cuniculis) nictitating membrane response under symmetrical CS-US interval shifts. J Comp Physiol Psychol 77:447-455

181. Collewijin H, van Harreveld A (1966) Membrane potential of cerebral cortical cells during spreading depression and asphyxia. Exp Neurol 15:425-436

182. Connor JA, Stevens CF (1971) Inward and delayed outward membrane currents in isolated neural somata under voltage clamp. J Physiol (Lond) 213:1-19

183. Coons AH, Kaplan MH (1950) Localization of antigens in tissue cells. II. Improvement in a method for the detection of antigens by means of fluorescent antibody. J Exp Med 91:1-13

184. Coppock WJ (1958) Pre-extinction in sensory preconditioning. J Exp Psychol 55:213-219

185. Corsi PM (1972) Human memory and the medial temporal regions of the brain. PhD thesis, McGill University, Montreal

186. Cotman C, McGaugh J (1979) Behavioral neuroscience: An introduction. Academic Press, New York

187. Couteaux R, Pécot-Dechavassine M (1970) Vésicules synaptiques et poches au niveau des "zones actives" de la jonction neuromusculaire. CR Acad Sci [D] (Paris) 271:2346-2349

188. Couteaux R, Pécot-Dechavassine M (1973) Données ultrastructurales et cytochimiques sur le mécanisme de liberation de l'acétylcholine dans la transmission synaptique. Arch Ital Biol 111:231-262

189. Cowan WM (1975) Recent advances in neuroanatomical methodology. In: Tower DB (ed) The nervous system, Vol 1 Raven Press, New York, pp 59-70

190. Cowan WM, Cuenod M (eds) (1975) The use of axonal transport for studies of neuronal connectivity. Elsevier, New York

191. Cowan WM, Gottlieb DJ, Hendrickson AE, Price JL, Woolsey TA (1972) The autoradiographic demonstration of axonal connections in the central nervous system. Brain Res 37:21-51

192. Cragg BG (1967) Changes in visual cortex on first exposure of rats to light. Nature 215:251-253

193. Cragg BG (1967) The density of synapses and neurons in the motor and visual areas of the cerebral cortex. J Anat 101:639-654

194. Cragg BG (1968) Are there structural alterations in synapses related to functioning? Proc R Soc Lond [Biol] 171:319-323

195. Crawford JM, Curtis DR (1966) Pharmacological studies on feline Betz cells. J Physiol (Lond) 186:121-138

196. Critchley M (1953) The parietal lobes. Arnold, London

197. Crosby EC, Humphrey T, Lauer EW (1962) Correlative anatomy of the nervous system. Macmillan, New York (cf Ariens-Kappers et al, 27)

198. Crow TJ, Woody CD (1973) Acquisition of a conditioned eyeblink response during reversible denervation of orbicularis oculi muscles in the cat. Brain Res 64:414-418
199. Curtis DR, Eccles JC (1960) Synaptic action during and after repetitive stimulation. J Physiol (Lond) 150:374-398
200. Davenport WB, Jr, Root WL (1958) An introduction to the theory of random signals and noise. McGraw-Hill, New York
201. Decima EE (1974) Plastic synaptic changes induced by orthodromic-antidromic pairing. In: Mechanisms of Synaptic Action, Proc Int 26th Congr Physiol Sci, Jerusalem Satellite Symposium Abstracts, p 14
202. DeJong RN (1967) The neurologic examination. Harper & Row, New York
203. Del Castillo J, Stark L (1952) Local responses in single medullated nerve fibers. J Physiol (Lond) 118:207-215
204. DeLong MR, Strick PL (1971) Relation of basal ganglia, cerebellum, and motor cortex to ramp and ballistic movement. Brain Res 71:327-335
205. De Luco JV (1971) A study of memory in insects. In: Kao FF, Koizumi K, Vassalle M (eds) Research in physiology. Aulo Gaggi, Bologna, pp 591-595
206. Denny-Brown D (1951) Frontal lobes and their functions. In: Feiling A (ed) Modern trends in neurology. Harper (Hoeber), New York, pp 13-89
207. Denny-Brown D (1956) Positive and negative aspects of cerebral cortical functions. NC Med J 17:7:295-303
208. Denny-Brown D (1958) The nature of apraxia. J Nerv Ment Dis 126: 9-32
209. Denny-Brown D (1963) The physiological basis of perception and speech. In: Halpern L (ed) Problems of dynamic neurology, Studies on the higher functions of the human nervous system. Department of Nervous Diseases of the Rothschild Hadassah University Hospital and the Hebrew University Hadassah Medical School, Jerusalem, Israel, pp 30-62
210. Denny-Brown D (1965) Physiological aspects of disturbances of speech. Aust J Exp Biol Med Sci 43:455-463
211. Denny-Brown D, Banker B (1954) Amorphosynthesis from left parietal lesion. Arch Neurol Psychiatry 71:302-313
212. Denny-Brown D, Chambers RA (1958) The parietal lobe and behavior. Brain Hum Behav 36: 35-117
213. Descartes R (1662) De Homine. Leiden
214. Descartes R (1952) Philosophical writings (selected and translated by Norman Kemp Smith). Macmillan, New York
215. Deutsch JA (1971) The cholinergic synapse and the site of memory. Science 174:788-794
216. Deutsch JA, Hamburg MD, Dahl H (1966) Anticholinesterase-induced amnesia and its temporal aspects. Science 151:221-222
217. Diamond J, Cooper E, Turner C, MacIntyre L (1976) Trophic regulation of nerve sprouting. Science 193:371-377
218. Diamond JM (1978) Channels in epithelial cell membranes and junctions. Fed Proc 37:2639-2644
219. Dichter MA (1975) Physiological properties of vertebrate nerve cells in tissue culture. UCLA Forum Med Sci 18:101-114

220. Dick DAT (1977) Distribution of Na, K and C in toad oocytes measured by electron microprobe analysis. Proc Int Union Physiol Sci 13: 184

221. Di Polo R, Requena J, Brundley FJ, Mullins LJ, Scarpa A, Tiffert T (1976) Ionized calcium concentrations in squid axons. J Gen Physiol 67:433-463

222. Disterhoft JF, Olds J (1972) Differential development of conditioned unit changes in thalamus and cortex of rat. J Neurophysiol 35:665-679

223. Disterhoft JF, Stuart DK (1976) Trial sequence of changed unit activity in auditory system of alert rat during conditioned response acquisition and extinction. J Neurophysiol 39:266-281

224. Dodd J, Dingledine R, Kelly JS (1978) Intracellular recording from CA3 pyramidal neurones of hippocampus slices and the action of iontophoretic acetylcholine. In: Ryall RW, Kelly JS (eds) Iontophoresis and transmitter mechanisms in the mammalian central nervous system. Elsevier/North Holland Biomedical Press, New York, pp 182-184

225. Dodge FA, Jr, Cooley JW (1973) Action potential of the motoneuron. IBM J Res Dev 17:219-229

226. Donhoffer H (1966) The role of the cerebellum in the instrumental conditioned reflex. Acta Physiol Acad Sci Hung 29:247-251

227. Dostálek C (1976) Časové a silové vztahy podnětu při tvorbě podmíněneho spoje (in Czech). Academia, Praha

228. Dostálek C, Krasa H (1972) Backward conditioning: One session vs. ten-session experiment. Act Nerv Super 14:58-59

229. Dostálek C, Krasa H (1973) The role of unconditional stimulus intensity in backward conditioning. Act Nerv Super 15:239-240

230. Doty RW (1961) Conditioned reflexes formed and evoked by brain stimulation. In: Scheer DE (ed) Electrical stimulation of the brain. Univ. Texas Press, Austin, pp 397-412

231. Doty RW (1965) Conditioned reflexes elicited by electrical stimulation of the brain in macaques. J Neurophysiol 28:623-640

232. Doty RW (1969) Electrical stimulation of the brain in behavioral context. Annu Rev Psychol 20:289-320

233. Doty RW, Giurgea C (1961) Conditioned reflex established by coupling electrical excitability of two cortical areas. In: Delafresnaye J, Fessard A, Gerard RW, Konorski J (eds) Brain mechanisms and learning. Blackwell, Oxford, pp 133-151

234. Doty RW, Overman WH, Jr (1977) The mnemonic role of forebrain commissures in Macaques. In: Harnad S, Doty RW, Goldstein L, Jaynes J, Krauthamer G (eds) Lateralization in the nervous system. Academic Press, New York, pp 75-88

235. Doty RW, Rutledge LT, Jr, Larsen RM (1956) Conditioned reflexes established to electrical stimulation of cat cerebral cortex. J Neurophysiol 19:401-415

236. Doty RW, Rutledge LT (1959) Generalization between cortically and peripherally applied stimuli eliciting conditioned reflexes. J Neurophysiol 22:428-435

237. Douglas RM, Goddard GV (1975) Long-term potentiation of the perforant path-granule cell synapse in the rat hippocampus. Brain Res 86:205-215

238. Downs D, Cardozo C, Schneiderman N, Yehle AL, Vandercar DH, Zwilling G (1972) Central effects of atropine upon aversive classical conditioning in rabbits. Psychopharmacology (Berlin) 23:319-333

239. Drachman DB (1979) Immunopathology of myasthenia gravis. Fed Proc 38:2613-2615

240. Drake AW (1967) Fundamentals of applied probability theory. McGraw-Hill, New York

241. Dudek FE, Blankenship JE (1976) Neuroendocrine (bag) cells of Aplysia: Spike blockade and a mechanism for potentiation. Science 192:1009-1010

242. Dudel JR, Kuffler SW (1960) Excitation at the crayfish neuromuscular junction with decreased membrane conductance. Nature 187:246-247

243. Dudel JR, Kuffler SW (1961) Presynaptic inhibition at the crayfish neuromuscular junction. J Physiol (Lond) 155:543-562

244. Dunn AJ (1976) The chemistry of learning and the formation of memory. In: Gispen WH (ed) Molecular and functional neurobiology. Elsevier, Amsterdam, pp 347-387

245. Durup G, Fessard A (1956) L'electroencephalogramme de l'homme. CR Soc Biol (Paris) 122:756-758

246. Dykman RA, Shurrager PS (1956) Successive and maintained conditioning in spinal carnivores. J Comp Physiol Psychol 49:27-35

247. Ebashi S, Lipmann F (1962) Adenosine triphosphate-linked contraction of calcium ions in a particulate fraction of rabbit muscle. J Cell Biol 14:389-400

248. Eccles JC (1957) The physiology of nerve cells. Johns Hopkins Press, Baltimore, Maryland

249. Eccles JC (1959) Progress in neurobiology. Williams & Wilkins, Baltimore, Maryland

250. Eccles JC (1964) The physiology of synapses. Springer-Verlag, Berlin

251. Eccles JC (1965) Possible ways in which synaptic mechanisms participate in learning, remembering and forgetting. In: Kimble DP (ed) The anatomy of memory. Science and Behavior Books, Inc, Palo Alto, California, pp 12-87

252. Eccles JC, Fatt P, Landgren S, Winsbury GJ (1954) Spinal cord potentials generated by volleys in the large muscle afferents. J Physiol (Lond) 125:590-606

253. Eccles JC, Kostyuk PG, Schmidt RF (1962) The effect of electric polarization of the spinal cord on central efferent fibres and their excitatory synaptic action. J Physiol (Lond) 162:138-150

254. Eccles JC, Krnjevic K (1959) Potential changes recorded inside primary afferent fibres within the spinal cord. J Physiol (Lond) 149:250-273

255. Eccles JC, Ito M, Szentagothai J (1967) The cerebellum as a neuronal machine. Springer-Verlag, Berlin

256. Eccles JC, Rall W (1951) Effects induced in a monosynaptic reflex path by its activation. J Neurophysiol 14:353-376

257. Eccles JC, Schmidt RF, Willis WD (1962) Presynaptic inhibition of the spinal monosynaptic reflex pathway. J Physiol (Lond) 161:282-297

258. Eccles JC, Sherrington CS (1931) Studies on the flexor reflex.—I. Latent period. Proc R Soc Lond [Biol] 107:511-534

259. Eccles RM, Libet B (1961) Origin and blockade of the synaptic responses of curarized sympathetic ganglia. J Physiol (Lond) 157:484-503

260. Eck KO, Noel RC, Thomas DR (1969) Discrimination learning as a function of prior discrimination and nondifferential training. J Exp Psychol 82:156-162

261. Eckert R (1972) Bioelectric control of ciliary activity. Science 176:473-481

262. Eckert R, Lux HD (1976) A voltage-sensitive persistent calcium conductance in neuronal somata of Helix. J Physiol (Lond) 254:129-151

263. Eckert R, Lux HD (1977) Calcium-dependent depression of a late outward current in snail neurons. Science 197:472-475

264. Eckert R, Machemer H (1975) Regulation of ciliary beating frequency by the surface membrane. In: Inoue S, Stephens RG (eds) Molecules and cell movement. Raven Press, New York, pp 151-164

265. Eckert R, Naitoh Y, Friedman K (1972) Sensory mechanisms in Paramecium. J Exp Biol 56:683-694

266. Eckert R, Tilotson D (1978) Potassium activation associated with intraneuronal free calcium. Science 200:437-439

267. Eckert R, Tillotson D, Ridgway EB (1977) Voltage-dependent facilitation of Ca^{2+} entry in voltage-clamped, aequorin-injected molluscan neurons. Proc Natl Acad Sci USA 74:1748-1752

268. Edelman GM, Mountcastle VB (1978) The mindful brain: Cortical organization and the group-selective theory of higher brain function. MIT Press, Cambridge, Massachusetts

269. Egger GI (1974) Escape learning: Acquisition and extinction rates as a function of age in rats. Dev Psychobiol 7:281-288

270. Ellison GD (1964) Differential salivary conditioning to traces. J Comp Physiol Psychol 57:373-380

271. Elsasser WM (1958) The physical foundation of biology: An analytical study. Pergamon Press, Oxford

272. Engberg I, Marshall KC (1971) Mechanism of noradrenaline hyperpolarization in spinal cord motoneurones of the cat. Acta Physiol Scand 83:142-144

273. Engel J, Jr, Woody CD (1972) Effects of character and significance of stimulus on unit activity at coronal-pericruciate cortex of cat during performance of conditioned motor response. J Neurophysiol 35:220-229

274. Eränkö O, Härkönen M (1965) Monoamine-containing small cells in the superior cervical ganglion of the rat and an organ composed of them. Acta Physiol Scand 63:511-512

275. Evarts EV (1966) Pyramidal tract activity associated with a conditioned hand movement in the monkey. J Neurophysiol 29:1011-1027

276. Evarts EV (1968) Relation of pyramidal tract activity to force exerted during voluntary movement. J Neurophysiol 31:14-27

277. Evarts EV (1969) Activity of pyramidal tract neurons during postural fixation. J Neurophysiol 32:375-385

278. Evarts EV, Bizzi E, Burke RE, DeLong M, Thatch WT, Jr (1971) Central control of movement. Neurosci Res Program Bull 9:1-170

279. Farel PB (1974) Habituation and persistent PTP of a monosynaptic response. In: Woody CD, Brown KA, Crow TJ, Jr, Knispel JD (eds) Cellular mechanisms subserving changes in neuronal activity. Brain Information Service, University of California, Los Angeles, 3:45-56

280. Farel PB, Buerger AA (1972) Instrumental conditioning of leg position in chronic spinal frog: Before and after sciatic section. Brain Res 47:345-351

281. Farthing GW (1972) Overshadowing in the discrimination of successive compound stimuli. Psychon Sci 28:29-32

282. Feller W (1950) An introduction to probability theory and its application, Vol 1, Wiley, New York

283. Fetz EE (1969) Operant conditioning of cortical unit activity. Science 163:955-957

284. Fetz EE, Finocchio DV (1979) Correlations between activity of motor cortex cells and arm muscles during operantly conditioned response patterns. Exp Brain Res 23:217-240

285. Feuchtwanger E (1923) Die Funktionen des Stirnhirns. Monogr Neurol Psychiat 38:1-194

286. Fine RE, Parsegian VA (1977) The forces for and against contact: Stage 1: Vesicle and plasma membrane contact. Neurosci Res Program Bull 15:623-628

287. Fitzhugh R (1961) Impulses and physiological states in theoretical models of nerve membrane. Biophys J 1:6:445-466

288. Fitzhugh R (1962) Computation of impulse initiation and saltatory conductance in a myelinated nerve fiber. Biophys J 2:11-21

289. Flagg-Newton J, Simpson I, Loewenstein WR (1979) Permeability of the cell-to-cell membrane channels in mammalian cell junction. Science 205:404-407

290. Fleming DE (1967) Amplitude relationships between evoked potential components during trace conditioning. Electroencephalogr Clin Neurophysiol 23:449-455

291. Fomin SV, Sokolov EN, Vaetkiavichou GG (1979) Artificial sensory organs: Problems in modeling sensory systems, Nauka (Science Press), Moscow

292. Fox SS, O'Brien JH (1965) Duplication of evoked potential waveform by curve of probability of firing of a single cell. Science 147:888-890

293. Frank K, Fuortes MGF (1957) Presynaptic and postsynaptic inhibition of monosynaptic reflexes. Fed Proc 16:39-40

294. Frank K, Tauc L (1964) Voltage clamp studies of molluscan neuron membrane properties. In: Hoffman J (ed) The cellular function of membrane transport. Prentice-Hall, Englewood Cliffs, New Jersey, pp 113-135

295. Frankenhaeuser B, Hodgkin AL (1956) The after-effects of impulses in the giant nerve fibres of Loligo. J Physiol (Lond) 131:341-376

296. Frazier WT, Waziri R, Kandel ER (1965) Alterations in the frequency of spontaneous activity in Aplysia neurons with contingent and noncontingent nerve stimulation. Fed Proc 24:522

297. Freeman W, Watts JW (1942) Psychosurgery. Thomas, Springfield, Illinois

298. Freeman WJ (1968) Relations between unit activity and evoked potentials in pre-pyriform cortex of cats. J Neurophysiol 31:337-348

299. Freeman WJ (1979) Nonlinear gain mediating cortical stimulus-response relations. Biol Cyber 33: 237-247
300. French V, Bryant PJ, Bryant SV (1976) Pattern regulation in epimorphic fields. Science 193:969-980
301. Freschi JE, Shain WG (1979) Iontophoresis of acetylcholine evokes a slow muscarinic depolarization in neurons of dissociated rat superior cervical ganglion. Soc Neurosci Abstr 5:741
302. Furshpan EJ (1964) "Electrical transmission" at an excitatory synapse in a vertebrate brain. Science 144:878-880
303. Furshpan EJ, Furukawa T (1962) Intracellular and extracellular responses of the several regions of the Mauthner cell of the goldfish. J Neurophysiol 25:732-771
304. Furshpan EJ, Potter DD (1959) Transmission at the giant motor synapses of the crayfish. J Physiol (Lond) 145:289-325
305. Furukawa T, Furshpan EJ (1963) Two inhibitory mechanisms in the Mauthner neurons of goldfish. J Neurophysiol 26:140-176
306. Gabriel M, Foster K, Orona E (1980) Interaction of laminae of the cingulate cortex with the anteroventral thalamus during behavioral learning. Science 208:1050-1052
307. Gabriel M, Miller JD, Saltwick SE (1977) Unit activity in cingulate cortex and anteroventral thalamus of the rabbit during differential conditioning and reversal. J Comp Physiol Psychol 91:423-433
308. Gage PW, Hubbard JI (1966) The origin of the post-tetanic hyperpolarization of mammalian motor nerve terminals. J Physiol (Lond) 184:335-352
309. Galambos R, Morgan CT (1960) The neural basis of learning. In: Field J (ed) Handbook of physiology, Sect I, Vol III. Williams & Wilkins, Baltimore, Maryland, pp 1471-1499
310. Galambos R, Sheatz GC (1962) An electroencephalograph study of classical conditioning. Am J Physiol 203:173-184
311. Galambos R, Sheatz G, Vernier VG (1956) Electrophysiological correlates of a conditioned response in cats. Science 123:376-377
312. Gallagher JP, Higashi H, Nishi S (1978) Characterization and ionic basis of GABA-induced depolarizations recorded in vitro from cat primary afferent neurones. J Physiol (Lond) 275:263-282
313. Gallagher JP, Shinnick-Gallagher P (1977) Cyclic nucleotides injected intracellularly into rat superior cervical ganglion cells. Science 198:851-852
314. Gallagher JP, Shinnick-Gallagher P (1978) Electrophysiological effects of nucleotides injected intracellularly into rat sympathetic ganglion cells. In: Ryall RW, Kelly JS (eds) Iontophoresis and transmitter mechanisms in the mammalian central nervous system. Elsevier, Amsterdam, pp 152-154
315. Gantt WH, Muncie W (1942) Analysis of the mental defect in chronic Korsakov's psychosis by means of the conditioned reflex method. Bull Johns Hopkins Hosp 70:467-487
316. Garcia J, Hankins WG, Rusiniak KW (1974) Behavioral regulation of the milieu interne in man and rat. Science 185:824-831
317. Garcia J, McGowan BK, Ervin FR, Koelling RA (1968) Cues: Their relative effectiveness as a function of the reinforcer. Science 160:794-795

318. Garcia J, McGowan BK, Green KF (1972) Biological constraints on conditioning. In: Black AH, Prokasy WF (eds) Classical conditioning. II. Current research and theory. Appleton-Century-Crofts, New York pp 3-27

319. Garcia J, Palmerino CC, Rusiniak KW, Kiefer SW (1982) Taste aversions and the nurture of instinct. In: McGaugh JL, Thompson RF (eds) The neurobiology of learning and memory, Plenum Press, New York, (in press)

320. Gasanov UG (1972) Correlation between unit activity of the auditory cortex and the conditioned blink reflex in cats. Zh Vyssh Nerv Deiat 22:273-278

321. Gaze RM (1970) The formation of nerve connections. Academic Press, New York

322. Gazzaniga MS (1970) The bisected brain. Appleton-Century-Crofts, New York

323. Gerkin GM, Neff WD (1963) Experimental procedures affecting evoked responses recorded from the auditory cortex. Electroencephalogr Clin Neurophysiol 15:947-957

324. Gilman S, Denny-Brown D (1966) Disorders of movement and behavior following dorsal column lesions. Brain 89:397-418

325. Giurgea C (1953) Elaboration of conditioned reflexes by direct excitation of cerebral cortex (in Romanian). Acad Repub Pop Romine, Bucuresti

326. Giurgea C, Raiciulesco N (1959) Etude électroencéphalographique du réflexe conditionnel a l'excitation éectrique corticale directe. Proc 1st Int Cong Neurol Sci Vol III:156-176

327. Glassman E (1969) The biochemistry of learning: An evaluation of the role of RNA and protein. Annu Rev Biochem 38:605-646

328. Glasstone S (1946) The elements of physical chemistry. Van Nostrand & Reinhold, Princeton, New Jersey

329. Gluck H, Rowland V (1959) Defensive conditioning of electrographic arousal with delayed and differentiated auditory stimuli. Electroencephalogr Clin Neurophysiol 11:485-496

330. Godfraind JM, Krnjević K, Pumain R (1970) Unexpected features of the action of dinitrophenol on cortical neurones. Nature 228:562-564

331. Goldberg AL, Singer JJ (1969) Evidence for a role of cyclic AMP in neuromuscular transmission. Proc Natl Acad Sci USA 64:134-141

332. Goldberg ND, Haddox NK, Nicol SE, Glass DM, Sanford CH, Kuehl FA, Jr, Estensen R (1975) Biological regulation through opposing influences of cyclic GMP and cyclic AMP: The Yin-Yang hypothesis. Adv Cyclic Nucleotide Res 5:307-330

333. Goldberger ME (1974) Recovery of function and collateral sprouting in cat spinal cord. Neurosci Res Program Bull 12:235-239

334. Goldman DE (1943) Potential, impedance and rectification in membranes. J Gen Physiol 27:37-60

335. Goldman S (1953) Information theory. Dover, New York

336. Gonshor A, Jones GM (1976) Short-term adaptive change in the human vestibulo-ocular reflex arc. J Physiol (Lond) 256:361-379

337. Gonshor A, Jones GM (1976) Extreme vestibulo-ocular adaptation induced by prolonged optical reversal of vision. J Physiol (Lond) 256: 381-414

338. Goodrich KP, Ross LE, Wagner AR (1957) Performance in eyelid conditioning following interpolated presentations of the UCS. J Exp Psychol 53:214-217

339. Goodson FE, Brownstein A (1955) Secondary reinforcing and motivating properties of stimuli contiguous with shock onset and termination. J Comp Physiol Psychol 48:381-386

340. Gormezano I (1966) Classical conditioning. In: Sidowski JB (ed) Experimental methods and instrumentation in psychology. McGraw-Hill, New York, pp 385-428

341. Gormezano I (1972) Investigations of defense and reward conditioning in the rabbit. In: Black AH, Prokasy WF (eds) Classical conditioning. II. Current research and theory. Appleton-Century-Crofts, New York, pp 151-181

342. Gormezano I (1974) The interstimulus interval and mechanisms for CS-CR functions in classical conditioning. In: Woody CD, Brown KA, Crow TJ, Jr, Knispel JD (eds) Cellular mechanisms subserving changes in neuronal activity. Brain Information Service, University of California, Los Angeles, pp 97-110

343. Gormezano I, Coleman SR (1973) The law of effect and CR contingent modification of the UCS. Cond Reflex 8:41-56

344. Gormezano I, Coleman SR (1975) Effects of partial reinforcement on conditioning, conditional probabilities, asymptotic performance, and extinction of the rabbit's nictitating membrane response. Pavlovian J Biol Sci 10:1:13-22

345. Gormezano I, Moore JW (1969) Classical conditioning. In: Marx MH (ed) Learning: Processes, Part III. Macmillan, New York, pp 120-203

346. Gormezano I, Tait RW (1976) The Pavlovian analysis of instrumental conditioning. Pavlovian J Biol Sci 11:37-55

347. Granit R (1956) Reflex rebound by post-tetanic potentiation. Temporal summation-spasticity. J Physiol (Lond) 131:32-51

348. Grant DA (1943) Sensitization and association in eyelid conditioning. J Exp Psychol 32:201-212

349. Grant DA, Adams JK (1944) 'Alpha' conditioning in the eyelid. J Exp Psychol 34:136-142

350. Grant DA, Dittmer DG (1940) An experimental investigation of Pavlov's cortical irradiation hypothesis. J Exp Psychol 26:299-310

351. Grant DA, Norris EB (1947) Eyelid conditioning as influenced by the presence of sensitized beta-responses. J Exp Psychol 37:423-433

352. Grastyan E (1959) The hippocampus and higher nervous activity. In: Brazier MAB (ed) The central nervous system and behavior, Vol 2. Josiah Macy Jr, Found, New York, pp 119-205

353. Grastyan E, Lissak K, Kakesi F (1956) Facilitation and inhibition of conditioned alimentary and defensive reflexes by stimulation of the hypothalamus and reticular formation. Acta Physiol Acad Sci Hung 9:133-151

354. Grastyan EK, Lissak K, Madarasz I, Donhoffer H (1959) Hippocampal electrical activity during the development of conditioned reflexes. Electroencephalogr Clin Neurophysiol 11:409-430

355. Greengard P (1975) Cyclic nucleotides, protein phosphorylation, and neuronal function. Adv Cyclic Nucleotide Res 5:585-601

356. Greengard P (1978) Cyclic nucleotides, phosphorylated proteins, and neuronal function. Raven Press, New York

357. Greengard P (1979) Cyclic nucleotides, phosphorylated proteins, and the nervous system. Fed Proc 38:2208-2217

358. Greengard P, Kebabian JW (1974) Role of cyclic AMP in synaptic transmission in the mammalian peripheral nervous system. Fed Proc 33:1059-1067

359. Grether WF (1938) Pseudo-conditioning without paired stimulation encountered in attempted backward conditioning. J Comp Psychol 25:91-96

360. Grice GR, Davis JD (1958) Mediated stimulus equivalence and distinctiveness in human conditioning. J Exp Psychol 55:565-571

361. Grice GR, Hunter JJ (1964) Stimulus intensity effects depend upon the type of experimental design. Psychol Rev 71:247-256

362. Griffin DR (1976) The question of animal awareness. Rockefeller University Press, New York

363. Griffith JS (1970) The transition from short-to-long term memory. In: Horn G, Hinde RA (eds) Short-term changes in neural activity and behavior. Cambridge University Press, London and New York, pp 499-516

364. Griffith VV (1963) A model of the plastic neuron. IEEE Trans Mil Electron Mil-7:243-253

365. Grodins FS (1963) Control theory and biological behavior. Columbia University Press, New York

366. Grossberg S (1974) Classical and instrumental learning by neural networks. Prog Theor Biol 3:51-141

367. Grossman RG, Seregin A (1977) Glial-neural interaction demonstrated by the injection of Na^+ and Li^+ into cortical glia. Science 195:196-198

368. Grundfest H (1975) Excitable membranes. In: Tower DB (ed) The nervous system, Vol. 1: The basic neurosciences, Raven Press, New York, pp 153-164

369. Grundfest H, Campbell B (1942) Origin, conduction and termination of impulses in the dorsal spino-cerebellar tract of cats. J Neurophysiol 5:275-294

370. Guillemin R (1978) Peptides in the brain: The new endocrinology of the neuron. Science 202:390-402

371. Gupta B, Hall TA (1979) Quantitative electron probe x-ray microanalysis of electrolyte elements within epithelial tissue compartments. Fed Proc 38:144-153

372. Guth L (1969) "Trophic" effects of vertebrate neurons. Neurosci Res Program Bull 7:1-73

373. Gutmann W, Brožek G, Bureš J (1972) Cortical representation of conditioned eyeblink in the rabbit studied by a functional ablation technique. Brain Res 40:203-213

374. Guttman N, Kalish HI (1956) Discriminability and stimulus generalization. J Exp Psychol 51:79-88

375. Haber A, Kalish HI (1963) Prediction of discrimination from generalization. Science 142:412-413

376. Hagins WA, Yoshikami S (1977) Intracellular transmission of visual excitation in photoreceptors: Electrical effects of chelating agents introduced into rods by vesicle fusion. In: Barlow HB, Fatt P (eds) Vertebrate photoreception. Academic Press, New York, pp 97-139

377. Hagiwara S (1975) Ca-dependent action potential. In: Eisenman G (ed) Membranes and ionic conductors, Vol. 3, Dekker, New York, pp 359-381

378. Hall RD (1963) Habituation of evoked potentials in the rat under conditions of behavioral control. Electroencephalogr Clin Neurophysiol 24:155-165

379. Hall RD, Mark RG (1967) Fear and the modification of acoustically evoked potentials during conditioning. J Neurophysiol 30:893-910

380. Hall Z, Hildebrand JG, Kravitz EA (1974) Chemistry of synaptic transmission. Chiron Press, Newton, Massachusetts

381. Halpern L (ed) (1963) Problems of dynamic neurology. Studies on the Higher Functions of the Human Nervous System. Department of Nervous Diseases of the Rothschild Hadassah, University Hospital and Hebrew University Hadassah, Medical School, Jerusalem, Israel

382. Hanson HM (1959) Effects of discrimination training on stimulus generalization. J Exp Psychol 58:321-334

383. Harlow HF (1939) Forward conditioning, backward conditioning and pseudoconditioning in the goldfish. J Gen Psychol 55:49-58

384. Harlow HF, Toltzein F (1940) Formation of pseudo-conditioned responses in the cat. J Gen Psychol 23:367-375

385. Haroutunian V, Campbell BA (1979) Emergence of interoceptive and exteroceptive control of behavior in rats. Science 205:927-929

386. Harris JD (1941) Forward conditioning, backward conditioning, pseudo-conditioning, and adaptation to the conditioned stimulus. J Exp Psychol 28:491-502

387. Harrison TR, Adams RD, Bennett IL, Jr, Resnik WH, Thorn, GW, Wintrobe MM (eds) (1958) Principles of internal medicine. McGraw-Hill, New York

388. Hartline HK, Ratliff F, Miller WH (1961) Inhibitory interaction in the retina and its significance in vision. In: Florey E (ed) Nervous inhibition. Pergamon, Oxford, pp 241-284

389. Hartline HK, Wagner HG, Ratliff F (1956) Inhibition in the eye of Limulus. J Gen Physiol 39:651-673

390. Hartzell HC, Kuffler SW, Yoshikami D (1975) Postsynaptic potentiation: Interaction between quanta of acetylcholine at the skeletal neuromuscular synapse. J Physiol (Lond) 251:427-463

391. Hashiguchi T, Ushiyama N, Kobayashi H, Libet B (1978) Does cyclic GMP mediate the slow excitatory synaptic potential in sympathetic ganglia? Nature 271:267-268

392. Hawkins R, Klein M, Kandel ER (1978) Single identified neurons produce presynaptic facilitation of the gill-withdrawal reflex by increasing Ca^{++} conductance in sensory neurons of Aplysia. Soc Neurosci Abstr 4:196

393. Haymaker W (1969) Bing's local diagnosis in neurological diseases. Mosby, St Louis, Missouri

394. Head H (1926) Aphasia and kindred disorders of speech. Cambridge University Press, London and New York
395. Hearst E, Beer B, Sheatz G, Galambos R (1960) Some electrophysiological correlates of conditioning in the monkey. Electroencephalogr Clin Neurophysiol 12:137-152
396. Hebb CO, Krnjevic K (1962) The physiological significance of acetylcholine. In: Elliott KAC et al (eds) Neurochemistry, 2nd ed. Thomas, Springfield, Illinois, pp 452-521
397. Hebb DO (1949) The organization of behavior: A neuropsychological theory. Wiley, New York
398. Hécaen H, De Ajuriaguerra J (1950) Asymbolie a la douleur. Étude anatomoclinique ses rapports avec l'hémiagnosie douloureuse. Sem Hop Paris 26:4660-4664
399. Held R, Bauer JA, Jr (1967) Visually guided reaching in infant monkeys after restricted rearing. Science 155:718-720
400. Heller E, Kaczmarek LK, Hunkapiller M, Strumwasser F (1979) After discharge in bag cell neurons is initiated by peptides from the atrial gland of Aplysia. Soc Neurosci Abstr 5:248
401. Helman SI (1979) Electrochemical potentials in frog skin: Inferences for electrical and mechanistic models. Fed Proc 38:2743-2750
402. Henkart M (1980) Identification and function of intracellular calcium stores in axons and cell bodies of neurons. Fed Proc 39:2783-2789
403. Henkart MP, Reese TS, Brinley FJ, Jr (1978) Endoplasmic reticulum sequesters calcium in the squid giant axon. Science 202:1300-1303
404. Hernandez-Peon R, Jouvet M, Scherrer H (1957) Auditory potentials at cochlear nucleus during acoustic habituation. Acta Neurol Latinoam 3:144-157
405. Herrick CJ (1956) The evolution of human nature. University of Texas Press, Austin
406. Herrnstein RJ, Boring EG (eds) (1965) A source book in the history of psychology. Harvard University Press, Cambridge, Massachusetts
407. Herz A, Creutzfeldt O, Fuster J (1964) Statistische Eigenschaften der Neuronaktivität in ascendierenden visuellen System. Kybernetik 2: 61-71
408. Heuser JE, Reese TS (1974) Morphology of synaptic vesicle discharge and reformation at the frog neuromuscular junction. In: Bennett MVL (ed) Synaptic transmission and neuronal interaction, Raven Press, New York, pp 59-77
409. Heuser JE, Reese TS (1973) Evidence for recycling of synaptic vesicle membrane during transmitter release at the frog neuromuscular junction. J Cell Biol 57:315-344
410. Heyer CB, Lux HD (1976) Properties of a facilitating calcium current in pace-maker neurones of the snail, Helix pomatia. J Physiol (Lond) 262:319-348
411. Heyer CB, Lux HD (1976) Control of the delayed outward potassium currents in bursting pace-maker neurones of the snail, Helix pomatia. J Physiol (Lond) 262:349-382
412. Hier DB, Arnason BGW, Young M (1972) Studies on the mechanism of action of nerve growth factor. Proc Natl Acad Sci USA 69:2268-2272
413. Hilgard ER, Bowers GH (1975) Theories of learning. Prentice-Hall, Englewood Cliffs, New Jersey

414. Hilgard ER, Humphries LG (1938) The effect of supporting and anatagonistic voluntary instructions on conditioned discrimination. J Exp Psychol 22:291-304

415. Hille B (1976) Gating in sodium channels of nerve. Annu Rev Physiol 33:139-152

416. Hinde RA (1970) Animal behavior: A synthesis of ethology and comparative psychology. McGraw-Hill, New York

417. Hinde RA, Stevenson-Hinde J (eds) 1973) Constraints on learning: Limitations and predispositions. Academic Press, New York

418. Hitzig JE (1884) Zur Physiologie des Grosshirns. Arch Psychiat Nervenkr 15:270-275

419. Hitzig JE (1904) Physiologische und klinische Untersuchungen uber das Gehirn, Gesammelte Abhandlungen. Hirschwald, Berlin

420. Hnik P, Jirmanova I, Vyklicky L, Zelena J (1967) Fast and slow muscles of the chick after nerve cross union. J Physiol (Lond) 193: 309-325

421. Hodgkin AL, Keynes RD (1955) Active transport of cations in giant axons from Sepia and Loligo. J Physiol (Lond) 128:28-60

422. Hoffeld DR, Thompson RF, Brogden WJ (1958) Effect of stimuli-time relations during preconditioning training upon the magnitude of sensory preconditioning. J Exp Psychol 56:437-442

423. Holmes JD, Gormezano I (1970) Classical appetitive conditioning of the rabbit's jaw movement response under partial and continuous reinforcement schedules. Learn Motiv 1:110-120

424. Homma S, Rovainen CM (1978) Conductance increases produced by glycine and γ-aminobutyric acid in lamprey interneurones. J Physiol (Lond) 279:231-252

425. Horn G (1967) Neuronal mechanisms of habituation. Nature 215:707-711

426. Horn G, Rose SPR, Bateson PPG (1973) Experience and plasticity in the central nervous system. Science 181:506-514

427. Horn JP, McAfee DA (1979) Norepinephrine inhibits calcium-dependent potentials in rat sympathetic neurons. Science 204:1233-1234

428. Hotson JR, Prince DA, Schwartzkroin PA (1979) Anomalous inward rectification in hippocampal neurons. J Neurophysiol 42:899-895

429. Houk JC (1980) Principles of system theory as applied to physiology. In: Mountcastle VB (ed) Medical Physiology, 14th edn, Vol 1. Mosby, St Louis, Missouri, pp 225-267

430. Howland B, Lettvin JY, McCullogh WS, Pitts W, Wall PD (1955) Reflex inhibition by dorsal root interaction. J Neurophysiol 18:1-17

431. Hubbard JI (1963) An electrophysiological investigation of mammalian motor nerve terminals. J Physiol (Lond) 166:145-167

432. Hubbard JI, Willis WD (1962) Mobilization of transmitter by hyperpolarization. Nature 193:174-175

433. Hubbell WL, Bounds MD (1979) Visual transduction in vertebrate photoreceptors, Annu Rev Neurosci 2:17-34

434. Hubel DH, Wiesel TN (1962) Receptive fields, binocular interaction and functional architecture in the cat's visual cortex. J Physiol (Lond) 160:106-154

435. Hubel DH, Wiesel TN (1965) Binocular interaction in striate cortex of kittens reared with artificial squint. J Neurophysiol 28:1041-1059

436. Hubel DH, Wiesel TN (1968) Receptive fields and functional architecture of monkey striate cortex. J Physiol (Lond) 195:213-243

437. Hughes GM, Tauc L (1963) An electrophysiological study of the anatomical relations of two giant nerve cells in Aplysia depilens. J Exp Biol 40:469-486

438. Hughes JR, Evarts EV, Marshall WH (1958) Post-tetanic potentiation in the visual system of cats. Am J Physiol 186:483-486

439. Hull CL (1943) Principles of behavior. Appleton-Century-Crofts, New York

440. Hume D (1911) Treatise of human nature, Vol 1. Dutton, New York

441. Humphrey DR (1968) Re-analysis of the antidromic cortical response. II. On the contribution of cell discharge and PSP's to the evoked potentials. Electroencephalogr Clin Neurophysiol 25:421-422

442. Humphrey DR, Schmidt EM, Thompson WD (1970 Predicting measures of motor performance from multiple cortical spike trains. Science 170:758-762

443. Hunt HF, Diamond II (1961) Some effects of hippocampal lesions on conditioned avoidance behavior in the cat. Annu Rev Physiol 23:451-484

444. Huston JP, Borbely AA (1974) The thalamic rat: General behavior, operant learning with rewarding hypothalamic stimulation and effects of amphetamine. Physiol Behav 12:433-448

445. Huxley AF (1971) The activation of striated muscle and its mechanical response. Proc R Soc Lond [Biol] 178:1-27

446. Inui J, Imamura H (1977) Effects of acetylcholine on calcium-dependent electrical and mechanical responses in the guinea-pig papillary muscle partially depolarized by potassium. Naunyn Schmiedebergs Arch Pharmacol 299:1-7

447. Irwin LN (1974) Glycolipids and glycoproteins in brain function. Rev Neurosci 1:137-179

448. Ivanov-Smolensky AG (1933) Fundamental problems of the pathophysiology of higher nervous activity in man (in Russian). Moscow-Leningrad

449. Iversen LL, Nicoll RA, Vale WW (1978) Neurobiology of peptides. Neurosci Res Program Bull 16:211-370

450. Jack JJB, Miller S, Porter R, Redman SJ (1971) The time course of minimal excitatory post-synaptic potentials evoked in spinal motoneurones by group la afferent fibres. J Physiol (Lond) 215:353-380

451. Jack JJB, Noble D, Tsien RW (1975) Electric current flow in excitable cells. University Press (Clarendon), London and New York

452. Jack JJB, Redman SJ (1971) The propagation of transient potentials in some linear cable structures. J Physiol (Lond) 215:283-320

453. Jack JJB, Redman SJ (1971) An electrical description of the motoneurone and its application to the analysis of synaptic potentials. J Physiol (Lond) 215:321-352

454. Jacobson M (1970) Developmental neurobiology. Holt, New York

455. Jansen JKS, Nicholls JG (1973) Conductance changes, an electrogenic pump and the hyperpolarization of leech neurones following impulses. J Physiol (Lond) 229:635-655

456. Jasper H, Ricci G, Doane B (1960) Microelectrode analysis of cortical cell discharge during avoidance conditioning in the monkey. Electroencephalogr Clin Neurophysiol [Suppl] 13:137-155

457. Jenden DJ (1978) Estimation of acetylcholine and the dynamics of its metabolism. In: Jenden DJ (ed) Cholinergic mechanisms and psychopharmacology, Plenum Press, New York, pp 139-162

458. Jenkins HM, Harrison RH (1960) Effect of discrimination training on auditory generalization. J Exp Psychol 59:246-253

459. Jennings KR, Kaczmarek LK, Strumwasser F (1979) Protein phosphorylation during afterdischarge of the neuroendocrine bag cells in Aplysia. Soc Neurosci Abstr 5:249

460. Jessell TM, Iversen LL (1977) Opiate analgesics inhibit substance P release from rat trigeminal nucleus. Nature 268:549-551

461. Johansen IB, Hall WG (1979) Appetitive learning in 1-day-old rat pups. Science 205:419-421

462. John ER (1961) High nervous functions: Brain functions and learning. Annu Rev Physiol 23:451-484

463. John ER, Killam KF (1959) Electrophysiological correlates of avoidance conditioning in the cat. J Pharmacol Exp Ther 125:252-274

464. John ER, Killam KF (1960) Electrophysiological correlates of differential approach-avoidance conditioning in cats. J Nerv Ment Dis 131: 183-201

465. John ER, Killam KF (1960) Studies of electrical activity of brain durdifferential conditioning in cats. In: Wortis J (ed) Recent advances in biological psychiatry. Grune & Stratton, New York, pp 138-148

466. Johnson AL, Howards SS (1977) Antibody binding measurements with Hapten-selective membrane electrodes. Science 195:494-495

467. Jordan SE, Jordan J, Brozek G, Woody CD (1976) Intracellular recordings of antidromically identified facial motoneurons and unidentified brain stem interneurons of awake, blink conditioned cats. Physiologist 19:245

468. Joyce J (1922) Ulysses. Shakespeare & Co, Paris

469. Joynt RJ, Goldstein MN (1975) Minor cerebral hemisphere. Adv Neurol 7:147-183

470. Kaczmarek LK, Jennings KR, Strumwasser F (1979) Cyclic AMP analog generates afterdischarge in Aplysia bag cell neurons (abstr) Soc Neurosci Symp 5:249

471. Kakkinidis L, Anisman H (1976) Interaction between cholinergic and catecholaminergic agents in a spontaneous alteration task. Psychopharmacologia 48:261-270

472. Kalish HI (1958) The relationship between discriminability and generalization: a re-evaluation. J Exp Psychol 55:637-644

473. Kalish HI (1969) Stimulus generalization. In: Marx MH (ed) Learning: Processes, Vol. 1, Part IV. Macmillan, New York, pp 205-297

474. Kalish HI, Haber A (1963) Generalization: I. Generalization gradients from single and multiple stimulus points. II. Generalization of inhibition. J Exp Psychol 65:176-181

475. Kalix P, McAfee D, Schorderet M, Greengard P (1974) Pharmacological analysis of synaptically mediated increase in cyclic adenosine monophosphate in rabbit superior cervical ganglion. J Pharmacol Exp Ther 188:676-687

476. Kalmijn AJ (1974) The detection of electric fields from inanimate and animate sources other than electric organs. In: Fessard A (ed), Handbook of sensory physiology, Vol 3. Springer-Verlag, Berlin, pp 147-200

477. Kamikawa K, McIlwain JT, Adey WR (1964) Response patterns of thalamic neurons during classical conditioning. Electroencephalogr Clin Neurophysiol 17:485-496

478. Kamin LJ (1957) The retention of an incompletely learned avoidance response. J Comp Psychol 50:457-460

479. Kanai T, Szerb J (1965) The mesencephalic reticular activating system and cortical acetylcholine output. Nature 205:80-82

480. Kandel ER (1976) Cellular basis of behavior. Freeman, San Francisco

481. Kandel ER (1977) Neuronal plasticity and the modification of behavior. In: Brookhart JM, Mountcastle VB (eds) Handbook of physiology, Sect 1, Vol I (ed by Kandel ER). Williams & Wilkins, Baltimore, Maryland, pp 1137-1182

482. Kandel ER (1979) Cellular insights into behavior and learning. Harvey Lect 73:29-92

483. Kandel ER (1979) Small systems of neurons. Sci Am 241:66-76

484. Kandel ER, Castellucci V, Pinsker H, Kupferman I (1970) The role of synaptic plasticity in the short-term modification of behavior. In: Horn G, Hinde RA (eds) Short-term changes in neural activity and behavior. Cambridge University Press, London and New York, pp 281-322

485. Kandel ER, Krasne FB, Strumwasser F, Truman JW (eds) (1979) Cellular mechanisms in the selection and modulation of behavior. Neurosci Res Program Bull 17:523-710

486. Kandel ER, Spencer WA (1968) Cellular neurophysiological approaches in the study of learning. Physiol Rev 48:65-134

487. Kandel ER, Tauc L (1963) Augmentation prologée de l'efficacité d'une voie afférente d'un ganglion isolé après l'activation couplée d'une voie plus efficace. J Physiol (Paris) 55:271-272

488. Kandel ER, Tauc L (1965) Heterosynaptic facilitation in neurones of the abdominal ganglion of Aplysia depilans. J Physiol (Lond) 181:1-27

489. Kant I (1781) The critique of pure reason. Smith NK (ed). St. Martin, New York

490. Kao CC, Chang LW, Bloodworth JMB, Jr (1977) The mechanism of spinal cord cavitation following spinal cord transection. Part 3: Delayed grafting with and without spinal cord retransection. J Neurosurg 46: 757-766

491. Kapustnik OP (1927) Cited according to MM Koltsova and NI Kasatkin in: Asratyan EA (ed) Physiology of higher nervous activity (in Russian), Part I. Nauka, Moscow, 1970, pp 540-570

492. Karczmar AG (1969) Is the central cholinergic nervous system overexploited? Fed Proc 28:147-159

493. Karczmar AG (1977) Exploitable aspects of central cholinergic functions, particularly with respect to the EEG, motor, analgesic and mental functions. In: Jenden DJ (ed) Cholinergic mechanisms and psychopharmacology. Plenum Press, New York, pp 679-709

494. Karn HW (1947) Sensory preconditioning and incidental learning in human subjects. J Exp Psychol 37:540-544

495. Kater SB, Nicholson C (eds) (1973) Intracellular staining in neurobiology. Springer-Verlag, New York

496. Kats K (1958) Electroencephalographic study of reflex activity in man. Zh Vyssh Nerv Deiat 8:466-474
497. Katz B (1966) Nerve, muscle and synapse. McGraw-Hill, New York
498. Katz B (1969) The release of neural transmitter substances. Liverpool University Press, Liverpool
499. Katz B, Miledi R (1965) The effect of calcium on acetylcholine release from motor nerve terminals. Proc R Soc Lond [Biol] 161:495-503
500. Katz B, Miledi R (1967) Modification of transmitter release by electrical interference with motor nerve endings. Proc R Soc Lond [Biol] 167:1-7
501. Katz B, Miledi R (1967) Tetrodotoxin and neuromuscular transmission. Proc R Soc Lond [Biol] 167:8-22
502. Katz B, Miledi R (1967) The release of acetylcholine from nerve endings by graded electric pulses. Proc R Soc Lond [Biol] 167:23-38
503. Katz B, Miledi R (1968) The role of calcium in neuromuscular facilitation. J Physiol (Lond) 195:481-492
504. Katz B, Miledi R (1969) Tetrodotoxin-resistant electric activity in presynaptic terminals. J Physiol (Lond) 203:459-487
505. Katz B, Miledi R (1972) The statistical nature of the acetylcholine potential and its molecular components. J Physiol (Lond) 224:665-699
506. Kebabian JW, Greengard P (1971) Dopamine-sensitive adenylcyclase: Possible role in synaptic transmission. Science 174:1346-1349
507. Kelly JP, Van Essen DC (1974) Cell structure and function in the visual cortex of the cat. J Physiol (Lond) 238:515-547
508. Kendrick NC, Blaustein MP, Fried RC, Ratzlaff RW (1977) ATP-dependent calcium storage in presynaptic nerve terminals. Nature 265: 246-248
509. Kennedy D, Calabrese RL, Wine JJ (1974) Presynaptic inhibition: primary afferent depolarization in crayfish neurons. Science 186:451-454
510. Kessler M, Clark LC, Jr, Lubbers DW, Silver IA, Simon W (eds) (1976) Ion and enzyme electrodes in biology and medicine. University Park Press, Baltimore, Maryland
511. Kessler M, Grunewald W (1969) Possibilities of measuring oxygen pressure fields in tissue by multiwire platinum electrodes. Prog Resp Res 3:147-152
512. Keynes RD, Rojas E (1974) Kinetics and steady-state properties of the charged system controlling sodium conductance in the squid giant axon. J Physiol (Lond) 239:393-434
513. Khachaturian ZS, Gluck H (1969) The effects of arousal on the amplitude of evoked potentials. Brain Res 14:589-606
514. Khananashvili MM, Zarkeshev AG, Silakov VL (1971) Conditioning of single unit activity by intracortical electric stimulation of neuronal isolated cortex. Fiziol Zh SSSR 56:490-495
515. Kholodov IuA (1972) Creation of a model of the conditional reflex in neuronally isolated slab of the cerebral cortex. In: Adrianov OS (ed) Problems of higher nervous activity (23rd Conf.), Part II, Gorki, p 81
516. Kidokoro Y (1975) Developmental changes of membrane electrical properties in a rat skeletal muscle cell line. J Physiol (Lond) 244:129-143
517. Kim HJ (1978) Histochemical fluorescence study of the substantia nigra and role of the nigroneostriatal dopaminergic system in memory and motor functions. PhD thesis, Northwestern University

518. Kim HJ, Woody CD (1979) Facilitation of eye-blink conditioning by hypothalamic stimulation. Soc Neurosci Abstr 5:319

519. Kimble GA (1961) Hilgard and Marquis' conditioning and learning, 2nd edn. Appleton-Century-Crofts, New York

520. Kimble GA, Dufort RH (1956) The associative factor in eyelid conditioning. J Exp Psychol 52:386-391

521. Kimble GA, Mann LI, Dufort RH (1955) Classical and instrumental eyelid conditioning. J Exp Psychol 49:407-417

522. Kimble GA, Ost JWP (1961) A conditioned inhibitory process in eyelid conditioning. J Exp Psychol 61:150-156

523. Kitai S, Kocsis JD, Preston RJ, Sugimori M (1976) Monosynaptic inputs to caudate neurons identified by intracellular injection of horseradish peroxidase. Brain Res 109:601-605

524. Kitai ST, McCrea RA, Preston RJ, Bishop GA (1977) Electrophysiological and horseradish peroxidase studies of precerebellar afferents to the nucleus interpositus anterior. I. Climbing fiber system. Brain Res 122:197-214

525. Klein M, Kandel ER (1978) Presynaptic modulation of voltage-dependent Ca^{2+} current: Mechanism for behavioral sensitization in Aplysia californica. Proc Natl Acad Sci (USA) 75:3512-3516

526. Klopf AH (1972) Brain function and adaptive systems—a heterostatic theory. Air Force Camb Res Labs Special Rept No 133 (AFCRL-72-0164), LG Hanscom Field, Bedford, Mass (DDC Rept AD 742259)

527. Klüver H (1958) "The temporal lobe syndrome" produced by bilateral ablations. Ciba Found Symp Neurol Basis Behav pp 175-186

528. Klüver H, Bucy P (1939) Preliminary analysis of functions of the temporal lobes in monkeys. Arch Neurol Psychiatry 42:979-1000

529. Kobayashi H, Hashiguchi T, Ushiyama NS (1978) Postsynaptic modulation of excitatory process in sympathetic ganglia by cyclic AMP. Nature 271:268-270

530. Kobayashi H, Libet B (1968) Generation of slow postsynaptic potentials without increase in ionic conductance. Proc Natl Acad Sci USA 60:1304-1311

531. Kobayashi H, Libet B (1970) Actions of noradrenaline and acetylcholine on sympathetic ganglion cells. J Physiol (Lond) 208:353-372

532. Kocsis JD, Vander Maelen CP (1979) A supernormal period in central axons following single cell stimulation. Exp Brain Res 36:381-386

533. Kogan AB (1960) The manifestations of processes of higher nervous activity in the electrical potentials of the cortex during free behavior of animals. Electroencephalogr Clin Neurophysiol [Suppl] 13:51-64

534. Kohler I (1956) Der Brillenversuch in der Wahrnehumungspsychologie mit Bemerkungen zur Lehre von der Adaptation. Z Exp Angew Psychol 3:381-417

535. Koike H, Okada Y, Oshima T, Takahashi K (1968) Accommodative behavior of cat pyramidal tract cell investigated with intracellular injection of currents. Exp Brain Res 5:173-188

536. Koike H, Okada Y, Oshima T (1968) Accommodative properties of fast and slow pyramidal tract cells and their modification by different levels of their membrane potential. Exp Brain Res 5:189-201

537. Kolata GB (1977) Structure in large sets: Two proofs where there were none. Science 195:767-768

538. Konorski J (1948) Conditioned reflexes and neuron organization. Cambridge University Press, London and New York
539. Konorski J, Miller S (1936) Conditioned reflexes of the motor analyzer. Tr Fiziol Lab (English summary) 6:119-278
540. Kopytova FV, Rabinovitch MY (1967) Microelectrode investigations of conditioned reflexes to time. Zh Vyssh Nerv Deiat 17:1023-1033
541. Korn H, Faber DS (1976) Vertebrate central nervous system: Same neurons mediate both electrical and chemical inhibitions. Science 194:1166-1169
542. Korn H, Faber DS (1978) The M-cell as a model for multidisciplinary research in neurobiology. In: Faber DS, Korn H (eds) Neurobiology of the Mauthner cell. Raven Press, New York, pp 271-279 (also see pp 47-131)
543. Korn H, Sotelo C, Bennett MVL (1977) The lateral vestibular nucleus of the toadfish Opsanustau: Ultrastructural and electrophysiological observations with special reference to electronic transmission. Neuroscience 2:829-884
544. Kornblith C, Olds J (1973) Unit activity in brainstem reticular formation of the rat during learning. J Neurophysiol 36:489-501
545. Kostyuk PG (1960) Electrophysiological characteristics of individual spinal cord neurons. Sechenov Physiol J USSR 46:10-22
546. Kotlyar BI (1969) Activity of nerve cells given the formation of temporary connections. Nauchr Dokl Vyssh Shk Biol Nauki 12:20-38
547. Kotlyar B (1970) Microelectrode studies of conditioned reflex reactions. In: Sokolov EH (ed) Neuronal mechanisms of learning (in Russian). MGU, Moscow, pp 25-46
548. Kotlyar BI, Ovtcharenko YS (1976) Plasticity reactions of the sensory motor cortex to sound combined with electrophoretic application of acetylcholine. Zh Vyssh Nerv Deiat 26:971-977
549. Kotlyar BI, Yeroshenko T (1971) Hypothalmic glucoreceptors: The phenomenon of plasticity. Physiol Behav 7:609-615, also see Zh Vyssh Nerv Deiat 21:1287-1297 (1971)
550. Krasne FB (1969) Excitation and habituation of the crayfish escape reflex: The depolarizing response in lateral giant fibers of the isolated abdomen. J Exp Biol 50:29-46
551. Krasne FB (1974) Aspects of plasticity in the crayfish central nervous system. In: Woody CD, Brown KA, Crow T, Knispel FD (eds) Cellular mechanisms subserving changes in neuronal activity. Brain Information Service, University of California, Los Angeles, pp 63-77
552. Krasne FB (1976) Invertebrate systems as a means of gaining insight into the nature of learning and memory. In: Rosenzweig MR, Bennett EL (eds) Neural mechanisms of learning and memory. MIT Press, Cambridge, Massachusetts, pp 404-405
553. Krasne FB, Bryan JS (1973) Habituation: Regulation through presynaptic inhibition. Science 182:590-592
554. Krasnogorsky NI (1939) Contributions to the theory of the physiological activity of brain in children (in Russian). Leningrad
555. Krasnogorsky NI (1948) Trudy Sess Akad Nauk SSSR Akad Med Nauk SSSR, posv. 10-Letyu so dnya smerti IP Pavlova, Moscow-Leningrad
556. Krekule I, Bureš J, Brožek G (to be published) Practical guide to computer application in neurosciences. Wiley, New York

557. Kreutzberg GW (ed) (1975) Physiology and pathology of dendrites (Adv Neurol, Vol 12). Raven Press, New York
558. Kreutzberg GW, Schubert P, Toth L, Rieske E (1973) Intradendritic transport to postsynaptic sites. Brain Res 62:399-404
559. Křivanek J (1979) Brain cyclic adenosine 3', 5'-monophosphate during depolarization of the cerebral cortical cells in vivo. Brain Res 120: 493-505
560. Křivanek J (1979) Monocular pattern discrimination learning and amino acid incorporation into protein of occipital cortex in rats. Behav Neurobiol 27:385-397
561. Kříž N, Syková E, Vyklický L (1975) Extracellular potassium changes in the spinal cord of the cat and their relation to slow potentials, active transport and impulse transmission. J Physiol (Lond) 249:167-182
562. Krnjevic K (1974) Chemical nature of synaptic transmission in vertebrates. Physiol Rev 54:418-540
563. Krnjevic K, Lisiewicz A (1972) Injections of calcium ions into spinal motoneurones. J Physiol (Lond) 225:363-390
564. Krnjevic K, Phillis JW (1963) Acetylcholine-sensitive cells in the cerebral cortex. J Physiol (Lond) 166:296-327
565. Krnjevic K, Phillis JW (1963) Pharmacological properties of acetylcholine-sensitive cells in the cerebral cortex. J Physiol (Lond) 166: 328-350
566. Krnjevic K, Puil E, Werman R (1976) Is cyclic guanosine monophosphate the internal "second messenger" for cholinergic actions on central neurons? Can J Physiol Pharmacol 54:172-176
567. Krnjevic K, Pumain R, Renaud L (1971) Effects of Ba^{2+} and tetraethyl ammonium on cortical neurones. J Physiol (Lond) 215:223-245
568. Krnjevic K, Pumain R, Renaud L (1971) The mechanism of excitation by acetylcholine in the cerebral cortex. J Physiol (Lond) 215:247-268
569. Kuba K, Koketsu K (1977) Postsynaptic potentiation of the slow muscarinic excitatory response by tetraethylammonium chloride in the bullfrog sympathetic ganglion cells. Brain Res 137:381-386
570. Kuffler SW, Nicholls JG (1966) The physiology of neuroglial cells. Ergeb Physiol Biol Chem Exp Pharmakol 57:1-90
571. Kuffler SW, Nicholls JG (1976) From neuron to brain: A cellular approach to the function of the nervous system. Sinauer Assoc, Sunderland, Massachusetts
572. Kupalov PS (1957) On the mechanisms of the arisal of the internal inhibition. Zh Vyssh Nerv Deiat 7:3-12
573. Kupfermann I, Cohen JL, Mandelbaum DE, Schonberg M, Susswein AJ, Weiss KR (1979) Functional role of serotonergic neuromodulation in Aplysia. Fed Proc 38:2095-2102
574. Kupfermann I, Kandel ER, Coggeshall RE (1966) Synchronized activity in a neurosecretory cell cluster in Aplysia. Physiologist 9:233
575. Kuypers HGJM (1974) Recovery of motor function in rhesus monkeys. Neurosci Res Program Bull 12:240-244
576. Langworthy OR (1970) The sensory control of posture and movement - A review of the studies of Derek Denny-Brown. Williams & Wilkins, Baltimore, Maryland
577. Larrabee MG, Bronk DW (1947) Prolonged facilitation of synaptic excitation in sympathetic ganglia. J Neurophysiol 10:139-154

578. Lashley KS (1929) Brain mechanisms and intelligence: A quantitative study of injuries to the brain. Chicago University Press, Chicago

579. Lashley KS (1950) In search of the engram. Symp Soc Exp Biol 4: 454-482

580. Lashley KS (1951) The problem of serial order in behavior. In: The Cerebral mechanisms in behavior; The Hixon Symposium, Jeffress LA (ed). Wiley, New York, pp. 112-136

581. Latimer CN, Kennedy TT (1961) Cortical unit activity following transcallosal volleys. J Neurophysiol 24:66-79

582. Lee YW (1960) Statistical theory of communication. Wiley, New York

583. Lee YW, Schetzen M (1965) Measurement of the Wiener kernels of a non-linear system by cross-correlation. Intl J Control 2:237-254

584. Lee-Teng E, Sherman SM (1956) Memory consolidation of one-trial learning in chicks. Proc Natl Acad Sci USA 56:926-931

585. Lehninger AL, Verusi A, Bababunmi EA (1978) Regulation of Ca^{2+} release from mitochondria by the oxidation-reduction state of pyridine nucleotides. Proc Natl Acad Sci USA 75:1690-1694

586. Leung LS (1978) Hippocampal CA^{-1} region—demonstration of antidromic dendritic spike and dendritic inhibition. Brain Res 158:219-222

587. Levi-Montalcini R (1964) Growth-control of nerve cells by a protein factor and its antiserum. Science 143:105-110

588. Levi-Montalcini R, Angeletti PU (1968) Nerve growth factor. Physiol Rev 48:534-569

589. Levine DS, Woody CD (1978) Effects of active versus passive dendritic membranes on the transfer properties of a simulated neuron. Biol Cybern 31:63-70

590. Levy J, Trevarthen CB, Sperry RW (1972) Perception of bilateral chimeric figures following hemispheric deconnexion. Brain 95:61-78

591. Lewis S, Wills NK (1979) Intracellular ion activities and their relationship to membrane properties of tight epithelia. Fed Proc 38:2739-2742

592. Leyton ASF, Sherrington CS (1917) Observations on the excitable cortex of the chimpanzee, orang-utan, and gorilla. Q J Exp Physiol 11:135-122

593. Liberson WT, Ellen P (1960) Conditioning of the driven brain wave rhythm in the cortex and the hippocampus of the rat. In: Wortis J (ed) Recent advances in biological psychiatry. Grune & Stratton, New York, pp 158-171

594. Libet B (1962) Slow synaptic responses in sympathetic ganglia. Fed Proc 21:345

595. Libet B (1970) Generation of slow inhibitory and excitatory postsynaptic potentials. Fed Proc 29:1945-1956

596. Libet B (1979) Dopaminergic synaptic processes in the superior cervical ganglion: Models for synaptic actions. In: Horn A, Korf J, Westerink BHC (eds) The neurobiology of dopamine. Academic Press, New York, pp 453-474

597. Libet B (1979) Which postsynaptic action of dopamine is mediated by cyclic AMP? Life Sci 24:1043-1058

598. Libet B (1979) Slow postsynaptic actions in ganglionic functions. In: Brooks C et al (eds) Integrative functions of the autonomic nervous system. Elsevier/North-Holland Biomedical Press, Amsterdam, pp 197-222

599. Libet B, Kobayashi H, Tanaka T (1975) Synaptic coupling into the production and storage of a neuronal memory trace. Nature 258:155-157

600. Lichtman JW (1977) The reorganization of synaptic connexions in the rat submandibular ganglion during post-natal development. J Physiol (Lond) 273:155-177

601. Liddell EGT, Sherrington CS (1925) Further observations on myotatic reflexes. Proc R Soc Lond [Biol] 97:267-283

602. Liepmann H (1900) Das Kransheitsbild der Apraxie (motorische Asymbolie) auf Grund eines Falles yon einseitiger Apraxie. Monatsschr Psychiatr Neurol 8:15-44, 102-132, 182-197

603. Ligon WV, Jr (1979) Molecular analysis by mass spectrometry. Science 205:151-159

604. Liley AW (1956) The quantal components of the mammalian end-plate potential. J Physiol (Lond) 133:571-587

605. Linskii VP (1954) On the formation of conditioned reflexes in patients exhibiting Korsakoff's syndrome. Zh Vyssh Nerv Deiat 4:791-798; also see Psychol Abstr 30:128 (1956)

606. Lissauer H (1890) Ein Fall von Seelenblindheit nebst einem Beitrage zur Theorie derselben. Arch Psychiat Nervenkr 21:222-270

607. Llinas R (1969) Neurobiology of cerebellar evolution and development. American Medical Association, Chicago

608. Llinas R (1973) Procion yellow and cobalt as tools for the study of structure-function relationships in vertebrate central nervous systems. In: Kater SB, Nicholson C (eds) Intracellular staining in neurobiology. Springer-Verlag, New York, pp 211-225

609. Llinas RR (1977) Calcium and transmitter release in squid synapse. In: Cowan WM, Ferrendelli JA (eds) Soc Neurosci Symposia, Vol. II. Approaches to the cell biology of neurons. Society for Neuroscience, Bethesda, MD, pp 139-160

610. Llinas RR, Heuser JE (eds) (1977) Depolarization-release coupling systems in neurons. Neurosci Res Program Bull 15:555-687

611. Llinas R, Steinberg IZ, Walton K (1976) Presynaptic calcium currents and their relation to synaptic transmission: Voltage clamp study in squid giant synapse and theoretical model for the calcium gate. Proc Natl Acad Sci USA 73:2918-2922

612. Lloyd DPC (1943) Reflex action in relation to pattern and peripheral source of afferent stimulation. J Neurophysiol 6:111-120

613. Lloyd DPC (1949) Post-tetanic potentiation of response in monosynaptic reflex pathways of the spinal cord. J Gen Physiol 33:147-170

614. Lloyd DPC, Wilson VJ (1957) Reflex suppression in rhythmically active monosynaptic reflex pathways. J Gen Physiol 40:409-426

615. Locke S (1966) Neurology. Little, Brown, Boston, Massachusetts

616. Loewenstein WR (1973) Membrane junctions in growth and differentiation. Fed Proc 32:60-64

617. Loewenstein WR (1975) Permeable junctions. Cold Spring Harbor Symp Quant Biol 40:49-63

618. Loewenstein WR, Kanno Y, Socolar SJ (1978) The cell-to-cell channel. Fed Proc 37:2645-2650

619. Lømo T (1971) Potentiation of monosynaptic EPSP's in the perforant path-dentate granule cell synapse. Exp Brain Res 12:46-63

620. Lømo T, Westgaard RH (1975) Further studies on the control of ACh sensitivity by muscle activity in the rat. J Physiol (Lond) 252:602-626
621. Lorens CS (1964) Flowgraphs for the modeling and analysis of linear systems. McGraw-Hill, New York
622. Lorente de Nó R (1933) Studies in the structure of the cerebral cortex. J Psychol Neurol 45:381-438
623. Lorente de Nó R (1934) Studies on the structure of the cerebral cortex. II. Continuation of the study of the ammonic system. J Psychol Neurol 46:113-177
624. Lorente de Nó R (1938) Analysis of the activity of the chains of internuncial neurons J Neurophysiol 1:207-244
625. Lorenz KZ (1961) King Solomon's ring. T.Y. Crowell (Apollo paperback), New York
626. Loucks RB (1933) Preliminary report of a technique for stimulation or destruction of tissues beneath the integument and the establishing of a conditioned reaction with faradization of the cerebral cortex. J Comp Psychol 16:439-444
627. Loucks RB (1935) The experimental delimitation of neural structures essential for learning: The attempt to condition striped muscle responses with faradization of the sigmoid gyri. J Psychol 1:5-44
628. Lowry OH, Rosenbrough NR, Farr AL, Randall RJ (1951) Protein measurement with the Folin phenol reagent. J Biol Chem 193:265-275
629. Lubow RE (1973) Latent inhibition. Psychol Bull 79:398-407
630. Lubow RE, Moore AU (1959) Latent inhibition. The effect of non-reinforced pre-exposure to the conditioned stimulus. J Comp Physiol Psychol 52:415-419
631. Lumsdaine AA (1939) Conditioned eyelid responses as mediating generalized conditioned finger reactions. Psychol Bull Abstr 36:650
632. Lundberg A (1969) Reflex control of stepping. The Nansen Memorial Lecture V. Universitetsforlaget, Oslo, pp 1-42
633. Lux HD (1976) Change of potassium activity associated with membrane current flow. Fed Proc 35:1248-1253
634. Lux HD, Heyer CB (1977) An aequorin study of a facilitating calcium current in bursting pacemaker neurons of Helix. Neurosci 2:585-592
635. Lynch G, Browning M, Bennett WF (1979) Biochemical and physiological studies of long-term synaptic plasticity. Fed Proc 38:2117-2122
636. Lynch G, Gall C, Cotman CW (1977) Temporal parameters of axon sprouting in the adult brain. Exp Neurol 54:179-183
637. MacDonald A (1945) The effect of adaptation to the unconditioned stimulus upon formation of conditioned avoidance responses. J Exp Psychol 36:1-12
638. Machemer H, Eckert R (1973) Electrophysiological control of reversed ciliary beating in Paramecium. J Gen Physiol 61:572-587
639. MacIntosh NJ (1975) From classical conditioning to discrimination learning. In: Estes WK (ed) Handbook of learning and cognitive processes, Vol I. Erlbaum Associates, Hillsdale, New Jersey, pp 151-189
640. Majkowski J (1958) Badania nad obrazen EEG I Eng Róznicowania odruchów warunkowych. Acta Physiol Pol 9:565-581
641. Mallart A, Martin AR (1967) An analysis of facilitation of transmitter release at the neuromuscular junction of the frog. J Physiol (Lond) 193:679-694

642. Mandler G (1964) Traditional free recall method: A waste of time? Psychon Sci 1:13-14

643. Mano N-I, Yamamoto K-I (1980) Simple-spike activity of cerebellar purkinje cells related to visually guided wrist tracking movement in the monkey. J Neurophysiol 43:713-728

644. Mark RG, Hall RD (1967) Acoustically evoked potentials in the rat during conditioning. J Neurophysiol 30:875-892

645. Marks AF (1973) Recovery of structure in injured mammalian brain. Abstr Soc Neurosci (3rd annu mtng) p. 111.

646. Marr D (1970) A theory for cerebral neocortex. Proc R Soc Lond [Biol] 176:161-234

647. Marshall WH (1959) Spreading cortical depression of Leao. Physiol Rev 39:239-279

648. Martin RF, Haber LH, Willis WD (1979) Primary afferent depolarization of identified cutaneous fibers following stimulation in medial brain stem. J Neurophysiol 42:779-790

649. Martlatt GA, Lilie D, Selvidge BD, Sipes MD, Gormezano I (1966) Cross-modal generalization to tone and light in human eyelid conditioning. Psychon Sci 5:2:59-60

650. Mason SJ (1953) Feedback theory—Some properties of signal flowgraphs. Proc IRE 41:1144-1156

651. Matsumura M, Woody CD (1980) Excitability increases in facial motoneurones of the cat after serial presentation of glabella tap. Soc Neurosci Abstr 6:787

652. Mayeri E (1979) Local hormonal modulation of neural activity in Aplysia. Fed Proc 38:2103-2108

653. McAfee DA, Yarowsky PJ (1979) Calcium-dependent potentials in the mammalian sympathetic neurone. J Physiol (Lond) 290:507-523

654. McBurney RN, Crawford AC (1979) Amino acid synergism at synapses. Fed Proc 38:2080-2083

655. McGaugh JL, Herz MJ (1972) Memory consolidation. Albion, San Francisco

656. McGaugh JL (1972) The chemistry of mood, motivation and memory. Plenum Press, New York

657. McGeer PL, Eccles JC, McGeer EG (1978) Molecular neurobiology of the mammalian brain. Plenum Press, New York

658. Meech RW (1972) Intracellular calcium injection causes increased potassium conductance in Aplysia nerve cells. Comp Biochem Phsyiol [A] 42:493-499

659. Meech RW, Standen NB (1975) Potassium activation in Helix aspersa under voltage clamp: A component mediated by calcium influx. J Physiol (Lond) 249:211-239

660. Meech RW, Strumwasser F (1970) Intracellular calcium injection activates potassium conductance in Aplysia nerve cells. Fed Proc 29:834

661. Mering TA (1975) Investigations of the role of the auditory system in the closure of conditioned reflexes. In: Woody CD (ed) Soviet research reports, Vol 3. Brain Information Service, University of California, Los Angeles pp 1-55

662. Meves H (1977) Inactivation of the "gating current" in squid giant axons. Proc Int Union Physiol Sci 12:196

663. Miledi R (1960) The acetylcholine sensitivity of frog muscle fibres after complete or partial denervation. J Physiol (Lond) 151:1-23

664. Miledi R, Slater CD (1970) On the degeneration of rat neuromuscular junctions after nerve section. J Physiol (Lond) 207:504-528

665. Miledi R, Thies R (1971) Tetanic and post-tetanic rise in frequency of miniature end-plate potentials in low calcium solutions. J Physiol (Lond) 212:245-257

666. Millenson JR, Kehoe EJ, Gormezano I (1977) Classical conditioning of the rabbit's nictitating membrane response under fixed and mixed CS-US intervals. Learn Motiv 8:351-366

667. Miller J (1939) The effect of facilitatory and inhibitory attitudes on eyelid conditioning. PhD dissertation, Yale University; also see Psychol Bull 36:577-578

668. Miller JM, Glickstein M (1967) Neural circuits involved in visuomotor reaction time in monkeys. J Neurophysiol 30:399-414

669. Milner B (1968) Visual recognition and recall after right temporal-lobe excision in man. Neuropsychologia 6:191-209

670. Milner B (1970) Memory and the medial temporal regions of the brain. In: Pribram KH, Broadbent DE (eds) Biology of memory, Academic Press, New York, pp 29-50

671. Milner B (1972) Disorders of learning and memory after temporal lobe lesions in man. Clin Neurosurg 19:421-446

672. Minsky M, Papert S (1969) Perceptrons. An introduction to computational geometry. MIT Press, Cambridge, Massachusetts

673. Mis SW, Gormezano I, Harvey JA (1979) Stimulation of abducens nucleus supports classical conditioning of the nictitating membrane response. Science 206:473-475

674. Mishkin M (1978) Memory in monkeys severely impaired by combined but not by separate removal of amygdala and hippocampus. Nature 273:297-298

675. Miyazaki S, Takahashi K, Tsuda K (1972) Calcium and sodium contributions to regenerative responses in the embryonic excitable cell membrane. Science 176:1441-1443

676. Moore CL (1971) Specific inhibition of mitochondrial Ca^{++} transport by Ruthenium red. Biochem Biophys Res Commun 42:298-305

677. Moore GP, Purkel DH, Segundo JP (1961) Statistical analysis and functional interpretation of neuronal spike data. Annu Rev Physiol 28:493-522

678. Moore JW (1972) Stimulus control: Studies of auditory generalization in rabbits. In: Black AH, Prokasy WF (eds) Classical conditioning. II. Current research and theory. Appleton-Century-Crofts, New York, pp 206-230

679. Moore JW (1979) Brain processes and conditioning. In: Dickinson A, Boakes RA (eds) Associative mechanisms in conditioning. Erlbaum Associates, Hillsdale, New Jersey, pp 111-142

680. Moore JW, Goodell NA, Solomon PR (1976) Central cholinergic blockade by scopolamine and habituation, classical conditioning, and latent inhibition of the rabbit's nictitating membrane response. Physiol Psychol 4:395-399

681. Moore RY (1976) Synaptogenesis and the morphology of learning and memory. In: Rosenzweig MR, Bennett EL (eds) Neural mechanisms of

learning and memory. MIT Press, Cambridge, Massachusetts, pp 340-347

682. Moreno J, Diamond JM (1978) Discrimination of monovalent inorganic cations by "tight" junctions of gallbladder epithelium. Fed Proc 37:2639-2644

683. Morgan CT (1965) Physiological psychology. McGraw-Hill, New York

684. Morrell F (1960) Microelectrode and steady potential studies suggesting a dendritic locus of closure. Electroencephalogr Clin Neurophysiol [Suppl] 13:65-79

685. Morrell F (1961) Effect of anodal polarization on the firing pattern of single cortical cells. Ann NY Acad Sci 92:860-876

686. Morrell F (1961) Electrophysiological contributions to the neural basis of learning. Physiol Rev 41:443-494

687. Morrell F, Engel JP, Jr, Bouris W (1967) The effect of experience on the firing pattern of visual cortical neurons. Electroencephalogr Clin Neurophysiol 23:89

688. Morse DE, Hooker N, Duncan H, Jensen L (1979) γ-Aminobutyric acid, a neurotransmitter, induces planktonic abalone larvae to settle and begin metamorphosis. Science 204:407-410

689. Moruzzi G (1960) Synchronizing influences of the brainstem and the inhibitory mechanisms underlying the production of sleep by sensory stimulation. Electroencephalogr Clin Neurophysiol [suppl] 13:231-256

690. Moruzzi G, Magoun HW (1949) Brain stem reticular formation and activation of the EEG. Electroencephalogr Clin Neurophysiol 1:455-473

691. Motokowa K (1949) Electroencephalograms of man in the generalization and differentiation of conditioned reflexes. Tohoku J Exp Med 50:225-234

692. Motokowa K, Huzimori B (1949) Electroencephalograms and conditioned reflexes. Tohoku J Exp Med 50:215-223

693. Mountcastle VB (ed) (1974) Medical physiology, 13th edn, Vol 1. Mosby, St Louis, Missouri

694. Mountcastle VB, Lynch JC, Georgopoulos A, Sakata H, Acuna C (1975) Posterior parietal association cortex of the monkey: Command functions for operations within extrapersonal space. J Neurophysiol 38:871-908

695. Mowrer OH, Aiken EG (1954) Contiguity vs. drive-reduction in conditioned fear: Temporal variations in conditioned and unconditioned stimulus. Am J Psychol 67:26-38

696. Müller GE, Pilzecker A (1900) Experimentelle beiträge zur lehre vom gedachtniss. Z Psychol 1:1-288

697. Myers RD (1974) Handbook of drug and chemical stimulation of the brain: Behavioral pharmacological and physiological aspects, Van Nostrand-Reinhold, Princeton, New Jersey

698. Mysliveček J (1976) Vývoj pameti v ontogenesi. Česk Fysiol 25:115-123

699. Nadel L, O'Keefe J (1974) The hippocampus in pieces and patches. In: Bellairs R, Gray EG (eds) Essays on the nervous system. Oxford University Press (Clarendon), London and New York, pp 367-390

700. Nagy ZM, Sandman M (1973) Development of learning and memory of T-maze training in neonatal mice. J Comp Physiol Psychol 83:19-26

701. Nahvi MJ (1974) Reliability of human visual signal detection in the presence of noise. IEEE Trans Reliab 23:326-331
702. Nahvi MJ (1974) Modelling control systems in rapid motor tasks. Tech Rept No 6, Biocybern Syst Lab, Arya Mehr Univ, Tehran
703. Nahvi MJ, Woody CD, Tzebelikos E, Ribak CE (1980) Electrophysiologic characterization of morphologically identified neurons in the cerebellar cortex of awake cats. Exp Neurol 67:368-376
704. Nahvi MJ, Woody CD, Ungar R, Sharafat AR (1975) Detection of neuroelectric signals from multiple data channels by optimum linear filter method. Electroencephalogr Clin Neurophysiol 38:191-198
705. Naitoh Y, Eckert R, Freidman K (1972) A regenerative calcium response in Paramecium. J Exp Biol 56:667-681
706. Naitoh Y, Eckert R (1973) II. Ionic basis of hyperpolarizing mechanoreceptor potential. Sensory mechanisms in Paramecium, J Exp Biol 59:53-65
707. Narahashi T (1974) Chemicals as tools in the study of excitable membranes. Physiol Rev 54:813-889
708. Nastuk W, Liu JH (1966) Muscle postjunctional membrane: Changes in chemosensitivity produced by calcium. Science 154:266-267
709. Nauta WJH (1971) The problem of the frontal lobe: A reinterpretation. J Psychiatr Res 8:167-187
710. Nelson PG (1975) Central nervous system synapses in cell culture. Cold Spring Harbor Symp Quant Biol 40:359-371
711. Nernst W (1888) Zur Kinetik der in Lösung befindlichen Körper. I. Theorie der Diffusion. Z Phys Chem 2:613-637
712. Nicholls J, Wallace BG (1978) Modulation of transmission at an inhibitory synapse in the central nervous system of the leech. J Physiol (Lond) 281:157-170
713. Nicholson C, Llinas R (1971) Field potentials in the alligator cerebellum and theory of their relationship to Purkinje cell dendritic spikes. J Neurophysiol 34:509-531
714. Nicholson C, Ten Bruggencate G, Steinberg R, Stockle H (1977) Calcium modulation in brain extracellular microenvironment demonstrated with ion-selective micropipette. Proc Natl Acad Sci USA 74: 1287-1290
715. Nicoll RA (1978) Neurophysiological studies. Neurosci Res Program Bull 16:272-285
716. Nicoll RA (1978) Pentobarbital: Differential postsynaptic actions on sympathetic ganglion cells. Science 199:451-452
717. Nicoll RA, Iwamoto ET (1978) Action of pentobarbital on sympathetic ganglion cells. J Neurophysiol 41:977-987
718. Nielsen JM (1946) Agnosia, apraxia, aphasia: Their value in cerebral localization. Harper (Hoeber), New York
719. Nishi S, Koketsu K (1968) Early and late after-discharges of amphibian sympathetic ganglion cells. J Neurophysiol 31:109-121
720. Nishi S, Soeda H, Koketsu K (1969) Unusual nature of ganglionic slow EPSP studied by a voltage-clamp method. Life Sci 8:33-42
721. Norman RJ, Buchwald JS, Villablanca JR (1977) Classical conditioning with auditory discrimination of the eyeblink in decerebrate cats. Science 196:551-553

722. Norman RJ, Villablanca JR, Brown KA, Schwafel JA, Buchwald JS (1974) Classical eyeblink conditioning in the bilateral hemispherectomized cat. Exp Neurol 44:363-380

723. Norris EB, Grant DA (1948) Eyelid conditioning as affected by verbally induced inhibitory set and counter reënforcement. Am J Psychol 61:37-49

724. Novikova LA, Rusinov VS, Semiokhina AF (1952) Electrophysiological analysis of the function of temporary connection in the cerebral cortex of the rabbit in the presence of a dominant focus. Zh Vyssh Nerv Deiat 2:844-861

725. Oakley DA (1979) Neocortex and learning. Trends Neurosci 2:149-152

726. Oakley DA, Russell IS (1977) Subcortical storage of Pavlovian conditioning in the rabbit. Physiol Behav 18:931-937

727. Oakley DA, Russell IS (1979) Instrumental learning on fixed ratio and GO/NOGO schedules in neodecorticate rats. Brain Res 161:356-360

728. O'Brien JH, Fox SS (1969) Single-cell activity in cat motor cortex. I. Modifications during classical conditioning procedures. J Neurophysiol 32:267-284

729. O'Brien JH, Fox SS (1969) Single-cell activity in cat motor cortex. II. Functional characteristics of the cell related to conditioning changes. J Neurophysiol 32:285-296

730. O'Brien JH, Packham SC (1974) Habituation of cell activity in cat postcruciate cortex. J Comp Physiol Psychol 87:781-786

731. O'Brien JH, Packham SC, Brunnhoelzl WW (1973) Features of spike train related to learning. J Neurophysiol 36:1051-1061

732. O'Brien JH, Rosenblum SM (1974) Contribution of the nonspecific thalamus to sensory evoked activity in cat postcruciate cortex. J Neurophysiol 37:430-442

733. O'Brien JH, Wilder MB, Stevens CD (1977) Conditioning of cortical neurons in cat with antidromic activation as the unconditioned stimulus. J Comp Physiol Psychol 91:918-929

734. Ojemann G, Mateer C (1979) Human language cortex: Localization of memory, syntax, and sequential motor-phoneme identification systems. Science 205:1401-1403

735. O'Keefe J, Nadel L (1978) The hippocampus as a cognitive map. Oxford: Clarendon Press, London and New York

736. Olds J (1959) Untitled comments on limbic system. In: Brazier MAB (ed) The central nervous system and behavior. Josiah Macy Jr, Found, New York, pp 62-75

737. Olds J (1962) Hypothalamic substrates of reward. Physiol Rev 42:554-604

738. Olds J, Disterhoft JF, Segal M, Kornblith CL, Hirsh R (1972) Learning centers of the rat brain mapped by measuring latencies of conditioned unit responses. J Neurophysiol 35:202-219

739. Olds J, Hirano T (1969) Conditioned responses of hippocampal and other neurons. Electroencephalogr Clin Neurophysiol 26:159-166

740. Olds J, Liddell HS, Sperry RW (1958) Post-Pavlovian development in conditional reflexes. In: Brazier MAB (ed) The central nervous system and behavior. Josiah Macy, Jr, Found, New York, pp 211-231

741. Olds J, Milner P (1954) Positive reinforcement produced by electrical stimulation of septal area and other regions of rat brain. J Comp Physiol Psychol 47:419-427

742. Olds J, Nienhaus R, Olds ME (1978) Patterns of conditioned unit responses in the auditory system of the rat. Exp Neurol 59:209-228

743. Oleson TD, Ashe JH, Weinberger NM (1975) Modification of auditory and somatosensory system activity during pupillary conditioning in the paralyzed cat. J Neurophysiol 38:1114-1139

744. Olszewski J (1954) Cytoarchitecture of the human reticular formation. In: Delafresnaye JF (ed) Brain mechanisms and consciousness. Blackwell, Oxford, pp 54-80

745. Olton DS (1977) Spatial memory. Sci Am 236:6:82-98

746. Olton DS, Becker JT, Handelmann GE (1979) Hippocampus, space and memory. Behav Brain Sci 2:313-365

747. Ong SH, Steiner AL (1977) Localization of cyclic GMP and cyclic AMP in cardiac and skeletal muscle: Immunocytochemical demonstration. Science 195:183-185

748. Palmerino CC, Rusiniak KW, Garcia J (1980) Flavor-illness aversions: The peculiar roles of odor and taste in memory for poison. Science 208:753-755

749. Pappas GD, Purpura DP (1972) Structure and function of synapses. Raven Press, New York

750. Parnas I (1972) Differential block at high frequency of branches of a single axon innervating two muscles. J Neurophysiol 35:903-914

751. Parnas I, Armstrong D, Strumwasser F (1974) Prolonged excitatory and inhibitory synaptic modulation of a bursting pacemaker neuron. J Neurophysiol 37:594-608

752. Parnas I, Hochstein S, Parnas H (1976) Theoretical analysis of parameters leading to frequency modulation along an inhomogeneous axon. J Neurophysiol 39:909-923

753. Parnas I, Spira ME, Werman R, Bergmann F (1969) Non-homogeneous conduction in giant axons of the nerve cord of Periplaneta americana. J Exp Biol 50:635-649

754. Parnas I, Strumwasser F (1974) Mechanisms of long-lasting inhibition of a bursting pacemaker neuron. J Neurophysiol 37:609-620

755. Parsons PJ, Fagan T, Spear NE (1973) Short-term retention of habituation in the rat: A development study from infancy to old age. J Comp Physiol Psychol 84:545-553

756. Patterson MM (1970) The effects of intracranial CS and conditioned rabbit nictitating membrane response. Dis Abstr Int 30:3412-3413

757. Patterson MM, Berger TW, Thompson RF (1979) Neuronal plasticity recorded from cat hippocampus during classical conditioning. Brain Res 163:339-343

758. Pavlov IP (1910) Work of the digestive glands (translated by WH Thompson). Griffin, London

759. Pavlov IP (1927) Conditioned reflexes (GV Anrep, translator and ed). Oxford University Press, London

760. Pellmar TC, Wilson WA (1977) Synaptic mechanism of pentylene tetrazole: Selectivity for chloride conductance. Science 197:912-914

761. Penfield W, Jasper H (1954) Epilepsy and the functional anatomy of the human brain. Little, Brown, Boston, Massachusetts

762. Penfield W, Milner B (1958) Memory deficit produced by bilateral lesions in the hippocampal zone. AMA Arch Neurol Psychiatry 79: 475-497

763. Peretz B, Jacklet JW, Lukowiak K (1976) Habituation of reflexes in Aplysia; contribution of the peripheral and central nervous systems. Science 191:396-399

764. Pestka S (1971) Protein biosyntheses: Mechanisms, requirements and potassium-dependency. In: Bittar EE (ed) Membranes and ion transport, Vol 3. Wiley (Interscience), New York, pp 279-296

765. Peterson N (1962) Effect of monochromatic rearing on the control of responding by wavelength. Science 136:774-775

766. Phillips CS, Porter G (1977) Corticospinal neurons: Their role in movement. Academic Press, New York

767. Phillips MI, Olds J (1969) Unit activity: Motivation-dependent responses from midbrain neurons. Science 165:1269-1271

768. Pickenhain L, Klingberg F (1965) Behavioural and electrophysiological changes during avoidance conditioning to light flashes in the rat. Electroencephalogr Clin Neurophysiol 18:464-476

769. Pinsker H, Kandel ER (1969) Synaptic activation of an electrogenic sodium pump. Science 163:931-935

770. Pittendrigh CS, 2nd (1976) Circadian oscillations and organization in nervous systems. MIT Press, Cambridge, Massachusetts

771. Pollen DA (1964) Intracellular studies of cortical neurons during thalamic induced wave and spike. Electroencephalogr Clin Neurophysiol 17:398-404

772. Pollen DA, Reid KH, Perot P (1964) Micro-electrode studies of experimental 3 sec wave and spike in the cat. Electroencephalogr Clin Neurophysiol 17:57-67

773. Polytrev SS, Zeliony GP (1930) Grosshirnrinde und Assoziations-Funktion. Z Biol 90:157-160

774. Poppel E, Held R, Dowling JE (1977) Neuronal mechanisms in visual perception. Neurosci Res Program Bull 15:315-553

775. Poppelreuter W (1917) Die psychischen schadigungen durch kopfschuss, Leipzig

776. Popper HR, Eccles JC (1977) The self and its brain. An argument for interactionism. Springer, Heidelberg

777. Poulos CX, Gormezano I (1974) Effects of partial and continuous reinforcement on acquisition and extinction in classical appetitive conditioning. Bull Psychon Soc 4(3):197-198

778. Poulos CX, Sheafor PJ, Gormezano I (1971) Classical appetitive conditioning of the rabbit's (Oryctolagus Cuniculus) jaw-movement response with a single-alternation schedule. J Comp Physiol Psychol 75: 2:231-238

779. Premack D (1976) Intelligence in ape and man. Erlbaum Associates, Hillsdale, New Jersey; also see Science 202:903-905, 1978

780. Pribram KH, Spinelli DN (1967) Average evoked response and learning. Science 158:394-395

781. Prochaska G (1784) Adnotationum Academicarum; Fasc. tertius, Sect I. Prague, Gerle, pp 1-164

782. Prosser CL, Hunter WS (1936) The extinction of startle responses and spinal reflexes in the white rat. Am J Physiol 117:609-618

783. Purpura DP (1961) Morphophysiological basis of elementary evoked response patterns in the neocortex of the newborn cat. Ann NY Acad Sci 92:840-859

784. Purpura DP (1974) Dendritic spine "dysgenesis" and mental retardation. Science 186:1126-1128

785. Purpura DP (1975) Development of LCN's in the hippocampus and in perinatal trauma. Neurosci Res Program Bull 13:411-414

786. Purpura DP (1975) Normal and aberrant neuronal development in the cerebral cortex of human fetus and young infant. UCLA Forum Med Sci 18:141-167

787. Quastler H (1956) Studies of human channel capacity. In: Cherry C (ed) Information theory: Third London symposium. Butterworths, London, pp 361-371

788. Quastler H (ed) (1956) Information theory in psychology: Problems and methods. Free Press, Glencoe, Illinois

789. Rabinovich MYa (1958) The electrical activity in different layers of the cortex of the motor and acoustic analysers during the elaboration of conditioned defensive reflexes. Zh Vyssh Nerv Deiat 8:507-518

790. Rabinovich MYa (1970) Microelectrode study of neuronal mechanisms of the conditioned reflex. Zh Vyssh Nerv Deiat 20:303-316

791. Rabinovich MYa (1971) Neuronal mechanisms of conditioned reflexes (in Russian). In: Asratyan EA (ed) Physiology of higher nervous activity, Vol II. Nauka, Moscow, pp 3-33

792. Rabinovich MYa, Kopytova FV (1969) Combined effects of polarization of the motor cortex in acoustic stimulation. Zh Vyssh Nerv Deiat 19:768-777

793. Rabinovich MYa, Polonskaya EL (1973) Conditioned activity of cortical motor neurons. Acta Neurobiol Exp 33:575-595

794. Rabinovich MYa, Trofimov LG (1957) The dominant focus of excitation in the development of a conditioned reflex. Bull Exp Biol Medits 43:2:3-8

795. Rachlin H (1976) Behavior and learning. Freeman, San Francisco

796. Raff MC, Fields KL, Hakomori S-I, Mirsky R, Pruss RM, Winter J (1979) Cell-type-specific markers for distinguishing and studying neurons and the major classes of glial cells in culture. Brain Res 174:283-308

797. Rahamimoff R (1968) A dual effect of calcium ions on neuromuscular facilitation. J Physiol (Lond) 195:471-480

798. Rahamimoff R, Erulkar SD, Alnaes E, Meiri H, Rotshenker S, Rahamimoff H (1975) Modulation of transmitter release by calcium ions and nerve impulses. Cold Spring Harbor Symp Quant Biol 40:107-116

799. Rakic P (1971) Guidance of neurons migrating to the fetal monkey neocortex. Brain Res 33:471-478

800. Rakic P (1972) Mode of cell migration to the superficial layers of fetal monkey neocortex. J Comp Neurol 145:61-84

801. Rakic P (1975) Local circuit neurons. Neurosci Res Program Bull 13:291-446

802. Rakic P (1975) Timing of major ontogenetic events in the visual cortex of the rhesus monkey. UCLA Forum Med Sci 18:3-40

803. Rall TW, Gilman AG (1970) The role of cyclic AMP in the nervous system. Neurosci Res Program Bull 8:221-323

804. Rall W (1962) Electrophysiology of a dendritic neuron model. Biophys J 2:145-167
805. Rall W (1970) Cable properties of dendrites and effects of synaptic location. In: Andersen P, Jensen JKS (eds) Excitatory synaptic mechanisms. Universitats Forlaget, Oslo, pp 175-187
806. Rall W (1974) Dendritic spines, synaptic potency and neuronal plasticity. In: Woody CD, Brown KA, Crow TJ, Jr, Knispel JD (eds) Cellular mechanisms subserving changes in neuronal activity. Brain Information Service, University of California, Los Angeles, pp 13-21
807. Rall W, Burke RE, Smith TG, Nelson PG, Frank K (1967) Dendritic location of synapses and possible mechanisms for the monosynaptic EPSP in motoneurons. J Neurophysiol 30:1072-1193
808. Rall W, Rinzel J (1973) Branch input resistance and steady attenuation for input to one branch of a dendritic neuron model. Biophys J 13:648-688
809. Rall W, Shepherd GM (1968) Theoretical reconstruction of field potentials and dendrodendritic synaptic interactions in olfactory bulb. J Neurophysiol 31:884-915
810. Rall W, Shepherd GM, Reese TS, Brightman MW (1966) Dendrodendritic synaptic pathway for inhibition in the olfactory bulb. Exp Neurol 14:44-56
811. Ransom SW (1939) Somnolence caused by hypothalamic lesions in the monkey. AMA Arch Neurol Psychiatry 41:1-23
812. Rasmussen H (1970) Cell communication, calcium ion, and cyclic adenosine monophosphate. Science 170:404-412
813. Rasmussen H, Goodman DBP (1977) Relationships between calcium and cyclic nucleotides in cell activation. Physiol Rev 57:421-509
814. Rasmussen H, Jensen P, Lake W, Friedmann J, Goodman DBP (1975) Cyclic nucleotides and cellular calcium metabolism. Adv Cyclic Nucleotide Res 5:375-394
815. Raymond SA, Lettvin JY (1978) After-effects of activity in peripheral axons as a clue to nervous coding. In: Waxman SG (ed) Physiology and pathobiology of axons. Raven Press, New York, pp 203-225
816. Razran G (1949) Stimulus generalization of conditioned responses. Psychol Bull 46:337-365
817. Reese TS, Shepherd GM (1972) Dendro-dendritic synapses in the central nervous system. In: Pappas GD, Purpura DP (eds) Structure and function of synapses. Raven Press, New York, pp 121-136
818. Reiff R, Scheerer M (1959) Memory and hypnotic age regression. International Universities Press, New York
819. Rench B, Franzisket L (1954) Lang andauernde bedingte Reflexe bei Rückenmarksfroschen. Z Vergl Physiol 36:318
820. Rescorla RA (1969) Pavlovian conditioned inhibition. Psychol Bull 72:77-94
821. Reynolds GS (1961) Relativity of response rate and reinforcement frequency in the multiple schedule. J Exp Anal Behav 4:179-184
822. Reza FM (1961) An introduction to information theory. McGraw-Hill, New York
823. Ribak C, Woody C, Nahvi M, Tzebelikos E (1980) Ultrastructural identification of physiologically recorded neurons in the cat cerebellum. Exp Neurol 67:377-390

824. Ricci G, Doane B, Jasper H (1957) Microelectrode studies of conditioning: Technique and preliminary results. Int Cong Neurol Sci [Reun Plen] 1:401-417

825. Ritchie JM (1979) A pharmacological approach to the structure of sodium channels in myelinated axons. Ann Rev Neurosci 2:341-362

826. Rizley RC, Rescorla RA (1972) Associations in second-order conditioning and sensory preconditioning. J Comp Physiol Psychol 81:1-11

827. Robertson RT, Mayers KS, Teyler TJ, Bettinger LA, Birch H, Davis JL, Phillips DS, Thompson RF (1975) Unit activity in posterior association cortex of cat. J Neurophysiol 38:780-794

828. Robison AG, Butcher RW, Sutherland EW (1971) Cyclic AMP. Academic Press, New York

829. Roger A, Voronin LG, Sokolov EN (1958) Electroencephalographic study of temporary connection in cases of extinction of the orienting reflex in man. Zh Vyssh Nerv Deiat 8:1-16

830. Rogers WL, Melzack R (1963) "Tail flip response" in goldfish. J Comp Psychol 56:917-923

831. Roitbak AI (1958) Concerning the mechanism of extinction of orientation and conditioned reflexes. Physiol Bohemoslov 7:125-134

832. Roitbak AI (1960) Electrical phenomena in the cerebral cortex during the extinction of orientation and conditioned reflexes. Electroencephalogr Clin Neurophysiol [Suppl] 13:91-100

833. Romanul FCA (1964) Enzymes in mucles. I. Histochemical studies of enzymes in individual muscle fibers. Arch Neurol 11:355-368

834. Romanul FCA, Van Der Meulen JP (1966) Reversal of the enzyme profiles of muscle fibers in fast and slow muscles by cross-innervation. Nature 212:1269-1370

835. Romanul FCA, Van Der Meulen JP (1967) Slow and fast muscles after cross-innervation: Enzymatic and physiological changes. Arch Neurol 17:387-402

836. Rose B, Lowenstein WR (1975) Calcium ion distribution in cytoplasm visualized by aequorin: Diffusion in cytosol restricted by energized sequestering. Science 190:1204-1206

837. Rose JE, Malis LI, Kruger L, Bawer CP (1960) Effects of heavy ionizing monoenergetic particles on the cerebral cortex. II. Histological appearance of nerve fibers after laminar destruction. J Comp Neurol 115:243-296

838. Rosenblatt F (1958) The perceptron. Rep UG-1196-G-1, Cornell University, Cornell Aeronautical Lab, Ithaca, New York

839. Rosenblatt F (1958) The perceptron: A probabilistic model for information storage and organization in the brain. Psychol Rev 65:386-408

840. Rosenblatt F (1960) Perceptron simulation experiments. Proc IRE 48:301-309

841. Rosenblatt F (1961) Principles of neurodynamics. Spartan Books, Washington, DC

842. Rosene DL, Van Hoesen GW (1977) Hippocampal efferents reach widespread areas of cerebral cortex and amygdala in the rhesus monkey. Science 198:315-317

843. Rosenfeld JP, Rudell AP, Fox SS (1969) Operant control of neural events in humans. Science 165:821-823

844. Rosenthal J (1969) Post-tetanic potentiation at the neuromuscular junction of the frog. J Physiol (Lond) 203:121-133

845. Rosenzweig MR (1966) Evidence for anatomical and chemical changes in the brain during primary learning. Proc 18th Int Congr Psychol (part 20), pp 5-17

846. Rosenzweig MR, Bennett EL (eds) (1976) Neural mechanisms of learning and memory. MIT Press, Cambridge, Massachusetts

847. Rosenzweig MR, Krech D, Bennett EL (1960) A search for relations between brain chemistry and behavior. Psychol Bull 57:476-492

848. Rowland V (1957) Differential electroencephalographic response to conditioned auditory stimuli in arousal from sleep. Electroencephalogr Clin Neurophysiol 9:585-594

849. Ruch TC, Patton HD, Woodbury JW, Towe AL (1966) Neurophysiology. Saunders, Philadelphia

850. Rudenko LP (1965) Peculiarities of food conditioned reflexes to the cessation of stimuli. Zh Vyssh Nerv Deiat 15:647-663

851. Rusinov VS (1953) An electrophysiological analysis of the connecting function in the cerebral cortex in the presence of a dominant region area. Proc Int Congr Physiol Sci, 19th, pp 719-720

852. Rusinov VS (1956) Electrophysiological research in the dominant area in the higher parts of the central nervous system. Proc Int Congr Physiol Sci, 20th, pp 785-786

853. Rusinov VS (1958) Electrophysiological investigation of foci of stationary excitation in the central nervous system. Zh Vyssh Nerv Deiat 8:473-481

854. Rusinov VS (1959) Long lasting excitation, dominant and temporary connection. Proc Int Congr Physiol Sci, 21st, p 238

855. Russell DF, Hartline DK (1978) Bursting neural networks: A re-examination. Science 200:453-456

856. Russell B (1964) A history of western philosophy. Simon & Schuster, New York

857. Russell WR (1948) Studies in amnesia. Edinburgh Med J 50:92-99

858. Russell WR (1959) Brain, memory, learning. Oxford University Press, London and New York

859. Russell WR, Esbir MLE (1961) Traumatic aphasia: A study of aphasia in war wounds of the brain. Oxford University Press, London and New York

860. Ryugo DK, Weinberger NM (1978) Differential plasticity of morphologically distinct neuron populations in the medial geniculate body of the cat during classical conditioning. Behav Biol 22:275-301

861. Sakai M, Sakai H, Woody CD (1978) Intracellular staining of cortical neurons by pressure microinjection of horseradish peroxidase and recovery by core biopsy. Exp Neurol 58:138-144

862. Sakai M, Sakai H, Woody CD (1978) Sampling distribution of morphologically identified neurons of the coronal-pericruciate cortex of awake cats following intracellular injection of HRP. Brain Res 152:329-333

863. Sakhiulina GT, Mukhamedora YeA (1958) Changes in the electroencephalogram of man in the process of motor habit formation. Zh Vyssh Nerv Deiat 8:459-465

864. Sauer FC (1935) The cellular structure of the neural tube. J Comp Neurol 63:13-23

865. Scarpa A, Malmstrom K, Chiesi M, Carafoli E (1976) Letter to the editor on the problem of the release of mitochondrial calcium by cyclic AMP. J Membr Biol 29:205-208

866. Scavio MJ, Jr, Gormezano I (1974) CS intensity effects on rabbit nictitating membrane conditioning, extinction and generalization. Pavlovian J Biol Sci 9:1:25-34

867. Scheibel ME, Scheibel AG (1965) The response of reticular units to repetitive stimuli. Arch Ital Biol 103:279-299

868. Schlaer R, Myers ML (1972) Operant conditioning of the pretrigeminal cat. Brain Res 38:222-225

869. Schlag J, Lehtinen I, Schlag-Rey M (1974) Neuronal activity before and during eye movements in thalamic internal medullary lamina of the cat. J Neurophysiol 37:982-995

870. Schlapfer WT, Woodson PBJ, Smith GA, Tremblay JP, Barondes SH (1975) Marked prolongation of post-tetanic potentiation at a transition temperature and its adaptation. Nature 258:623-625

871. Schmitt FO (1962) Macromolecular specificity of biological memory. MIT Press, Cambridge, Massachusetts

872. Schrier AM (1971) Extradimensional transfer of learning set formation in stump-tailed monkeys. Learn Motiv 2:173-181

873. Schubert P, Kreutzberg GW (1975) [^{3}H]-Adenosine, a tracer for neuronal connectivity. Brain Res 85:317-319

874. Schubert P, Kreutzberg GW (1975) Dendritic and axonal transport of nucleoside derivatives in single motoneurons and release from dendrites. Brain Res 90:319-323

875. Schulman JA, Weight FF (1976) Synaptic transmission: Long-lasting potentiation by a postsynaptic mechanism. Science 194:1437-1439

876. Schwartz A, Entman ML, Ezrailson EG, Lehotay DC, Levely G (1977) Possible cyclic nucleotide regulation of calcium mediating myocardial contraction. Science 195:982-990

877. Schwartz JH, Castellucci V, Kandel ER (1971) The functioning of identified neurons and synapses in abdominal ganglion of Aplysia in absence of protein synthesis. J Neurophysiol 34:939-953

878. Scoville WB, Milner B (1957) Loss of recent memory after bilateral hippocampal lesions. J Neurol Neurosurg Psychiatry 20:11-21

879. Sechenov IM (1863) Refleksy golovnogo mozga (in Russian) St. Petersburg

880. Segal M, Olds J (1972) The behavior of units in the hippocampal circuit of the rat during learning. J Neurophysiol 35:680-690

881. Segundo JP, Roig JA, Sommer-Smith JA (1959) Conditioning of reticular formation stimulation effects. Electroencephalogr Clin Neurophysiol 11:471-484

882. Seidel RJ (1958) An investigation of the mediation process in preconditioning. J Exp Psychol 56:220-225

883. Selfridge OG (1959) Pandemonium: A paradigm for learning. Proc Symp Mech Thought Processes, HM Stationery Office, London pp 511-529; also see Armed Forces Technical Information Agency (ASTIA) AD 236251, 1960, also JA-1140, Sept. 8, 1958

884. Shannon CE, Weaver W (1962) The mathematical theory of communication. University of Illinois Press, Urbana
885. Sharpless S, Jasper H (1956) Habituation of the arousal reaction. Brain 79:655-682
886. Sherrington CS (1898) Decerebrate rigidity and reflex coordination of movements. J Physiol (Lond) 22:319-332
887. Sherrington CS (1906) The integrative action of the nervous system. Yale University Press, New Haven, Connecticut (Reprinted 1947)
888. Sherrington CS (1910) Flexion—reflex of the limb, crossed extension-reflex, and reflex stepping and standing. J Physiol (Lond) 40:28-121
889. Sherrington CS (1941) Man on his nature. Macmillan, New York
890. Shigeki Maeno (1958) Electroencephalographic study of salivary conditioned reflex. Adv Neurol Sci (Jpn) 3:203-217
891. Shik ML, Orlovsky GN (1976) Neurophysiology of locomotor automatism. Physiol Rev 56:465-501
892. Shilyagina NN (1958) Changes in bioelectrical activity of the cerebral cortex during orienting and conditioned reflexes in animals in ontogenesis. Zh Vyssh Nerv Deiat 8:582-592
893. Shimomura O, Johnson FH (1972) Structure of the light-emitting moiety of aequorin. Biochemistry 11:1602-1608
894. Shinkman PG, Bruce CJ, Pfingst BE (1974) Operant conditioning of single unit response patterns in visual cortex. Science 184:1994-1996
895. Shulgina GI (1967) Investigation of the neuronal activity of the cerebral cortex at early stages of elaboration of a conditioned reflex (in Russian). Sovrem Probl Deiat Stroen Tsentr Nerv Syst pp 296-308
896. Shulman RG, Brown TR, Ugerbil K, Ogawa S, Cohen SM, den Hollander JA (1979) Cellular applications of ^{31}P and ^{13}C nuclear magnetic resonance. Science 205:160-166
897. Shumilina AI (1959) Comparative features of the electrical activities in the reticular formation and the cerebral cortex during the elaboration of a conditioned defensive reflex. Sechenov Physiol J USSR (Engl Transl) 45:5-18
898. Shurrager PS, Culler EA (1938) Phenomena allied to conditioning in the spinal dog. Am J Physiol 123:186-187
899. Shvyrkov VB (1968) Form of participation of cortical somatosensory projection neurons in the development of the conditioned defense reflex. Vestn USSR Acad Med Sci (Engl Transl) 23:125-139
900. Siebert WM and Communications Biophysics Group (1959) Processing neuroelectric data. Tech Rep 351 MIT, Cambridge, Massachusetts
901. Siegfried B, Bureš J (1978) Asymmetry of EEG arousal in rats with unilateral 6-hydroxydopamine lesions of substantia nigra: Quantification of neglect. Exp Neurol 62:173-190
902. Siegfried B, Bureš J (1979) Conditioning compensates the neglect due to unilateral 6-OHDA lesions of substantia nigra in rats. Brain Res 167:139-155
903. Siggins GR, Oliver AP, Hoffer BJ, Bloom FE (1971) Cyclic adenosine monophosphate and norepinephrine: Effects on transmembrane properties of cerebellar Purkinje cells. Science 171:92-194
904. Silver CA, Meyer DR (1964) Temporal factors in sensory preconditioning. J Comp Physiol Psychol 47:57-59

905. Simpson I, Rose B, Loewenstein WR (1977) Size limit of molecules permeating the junctional membrane channels. Science 195:294-296

906. Singh J (1966) Great ideas in information theory, language and cybernetics. Dover, New York

907. Sitaram N, Weingartner H, Gillin JC (1978) Human serial learning: Enhancement with arecholine and choline and impairment with scopolamine. Science 201:274-276

908. Skinner BF (1938) The behavior of organisms: An experimental analysis. Appleton-Century-Crofts, New York

909. Skinner BF (1956) What is psychotic behavior? In: Gildea F (ed) Theory and treatment of the psychoses: Some newer aspects. Washington University Press, St. Louis, pp 77-99

910. Skinner BF (1971) Beyond freedom and dignity. Knopf, New York

911. Skrebitsky VG (1974) Plastic changes in activity of cortical neurons. Proc Int Union Physiol Sci 11:463

912. Smith MC (1968) CS-US interval and US intensity in classical conditioning of the rabbit's nictitating membrane response. J Comp Physiol Psychol 66:679-687

913. Smith MC, Coleman SR, Gormezano I (1969) Classical conditioning of the rabbit's nictitating membrane response at backward, simultaneous, and forward CS-US intervals. J Comp Physiol Psychol 69:226-231

914. Smith MC, Gormezano I (1965) Effects of alternating classical conditioning and extinction sessions on the conditioned nictitating membrane response of the rabbit. Psychon Sci 3:91-92

915. Smith S, Holmes G (1916) A case of bilateral motor apraxia with disturbance of visual orientation. Br Med J 1:437-441

916. Snow PJ, Rose PK, Brown AG (1976) Tracing axons and axon collaterals of spinal neurons using intracellular injection of horseradish peroxidase. Science 191:312-313

917. Snyder SH, Bennett JP (1976) Neurotransmitter receptors in the brain: Biochemical identification. Annu Rev Physiol 38:153-175

918. Snyder SH, Childers SR (1979) Opiate receptors and opioid peptides. Annu Rev Neurosci 2:35-64

919. Snyder SH, Matthysse S (1975) Opiate receptor mechanisms. Neurosci Res Program Bull 13:1-166

920. Snyder SH, Young AB, Bennett JP, Mulder AH (1973) Synaptic biochemistry of amino acids. Fed Proc 32:2039-2047

921. Sokoloff L (1977) Relation between physiological function and energy metabolism in the central nervous system. J Neurochem 29:13-26

922. Sokoloff L (1981) The relationship between function and energy metabolism: its use in the localization of functional activity in the nervous system. Neurosci Res Program Bull 19:159-210

923. Somjen GG, Lothman EW (1974) Potassium, sustained focal potential shifts, and dorsal root potentials of the mammalian spinal cord. Brain Res 69:153-157

924. Spear NE, Campbell BA (eds) (1979) The ontogeny of learning and memory. Erlbaum Associates, Hillsdale, New Jersey

925. Spehlmann R, Smathers CC, Jr (1974) The effects of acetylcholine and of synaptic stimulation on the sensorimotor cortex of cats. II. Comparison of the neuronal responses to reticular and other stimuli. Brain Res 74:243-253

926. Spence KW, Norris EB (1950) Eyelid conditioning as a function of the inter-trial interval. J Exp Psychol 40:716-720
927. Spencer RF, Coleman PD (1974) Influence of selective visual experience upon the morphological maturation of the visual cortex. Anat Rec 178:469
928. Spencer WA (1966) Potentiation of recurrent inhibitory action on cat spinal motoneurons. Physiologist 9:292
929. Spencer WA, Kandel ER (1961) Electrophysiology of hippocampal neurons. IV. Fast prepotentials. J Neurophysiol 24:272-285
930. Spencer WA, Kandel ER (1961) Hippocampal neuron responses to selective activation of recurrent collaterals of hippocampofugal axons. Exp Neurol 4:149-161
931. Spencer WA, Thompson RF, Neilson DR, Jr (1966) Response decrement of the flexion reflex in the acute spinal cat and transient restoration by strong stimuli. J Neurophysiol 29:221-239
932. Spencer WA, Thompson RF, Neilson DR, Jr (1966) Alterations in responsiveness of ascending and reflex pathways activated by iterated cutaneous afferent volleys. J Neurophysiol 29:240-252
933. Spencer WA, Thompson RF, Neilson DR, Jr (1966) Decrement of ventral root electrotonus and intracellularly recorded PSPs produced by iterated cutaneous afferent volleys. J Neurophysiol 29:253-274
934. Spencer WJ, Wigdor R (1965) Ultra-late PTP of monosynaptic reflex responses in cat. Physiologist 8:278
935. Sperry RW (1944) Optic nerve regeneration with return of vision in Anurans. J Neurophysiol 7:57-69
936. Sperry RW (1945) Restoration of vision after crossing of optic nerves and after contralateral transplantation of eye. J Neurophysiol 8:15-28
937. Sperry RW (1959) Preservation of high-order function in isolated somatic cortex in callosum-sectioned cat. J Neurophysiol 22:78-87
938. Sperry RW (1964) The great cerebral commissure. Sci Am 210:42-52
939. Sperry RW (1966) Brain bisection and mechanisms of consciousness. In: Eccles JC (ed) Brain and conscious experience. Springer-Verlag, New York, pp 298-313
940. Sperry RW (1970) Perception in the absence of the neocortical commissures. In: Hamburg DA et al (eds) Perception and its disorders. Williams & Wilkins, Baltimore, Maryland, pp 123-138
941. Sperry RW (1974) Lateral specialization in the surgically separated hemispheres. In: Schmitt FO, Worden FG (eds) The neurosciences: Third study program. MIT Press, Cambridge, Massachusetts, pp 5-19
942. Sperry RW, Gazzaniga MS, Bogen JE (1969) Interhemispheric relationships: The neocortical commissures: Syndromes of hemisphere deconnection. Hand Clin Neurol 4:273-290
943. Spira ME, Spray DC, Bennett MVL (1976) Electrotonic coupling: Effective sign reversal by inhibitory neurons. Science 194:1065-1067
944. Spira ME, Yarom T, Parnas I (1976) Modulation of spike frequency by regions of special axonal geometry and by synaptic inputs. J Neurophysiol 39:882-899
945. Spitzer NC (1979) Ion channels in development. Annu Rev Neurosci 2:363-397
946. Spooner A, Kellogg WH (1947) The backward conditioning curve. Am J Psychol 60:321-334

947. Squire LR (1980) Specifying the defect in human amnesia: Storage, retrieval, and semantics. Neuropsychologia 18:369-372

948. Squire LR, Moore RY (1979) Dorsal thalamic lesion in a noted case of human memory dysfunction. Ann Neurol 6:503-506

949. Squire LR, Schlapfer WT (1981) Memory and memory disorders: A biological and neurologic perspective. In: van Pragg HM, Lader MH, Rafaelson OJ, Sachar EJ (eds) Handbook of biological psychiatry Part IV. Dekker, New York, pp 309-341

950. Squire LR, Slater PC (1977) Remote memory in chronic anterograde amnesia. Behav Biol 20:398-403

951. Squire LR, Slater PC (1978) Anterograde and retrograde memory impairment in chronic amnesia. Neuropsychologia 16:313-323

952. Stanbury JB, Wyngaarden JB, Fredrickson DS (eds) (1978) The metabolic basis of inherited disease, 4th edn. McGraw-Hill, New York

953. Standaert FG (ed) (1979) Cyclic nucleotides and synaptic function. Fed Proc 38:2182-2217

954. Standaert FG, Dretchen KL (1979) Cyclic nucleotides and neuromuscular transmission. Fed Proc 38:2183-2192

955. Stanes MD, Brown CP, Singer G (1976) Effect of physostigmine on y-maze discrimination retention in the rat. Psychopharmacologia 46:269-276

956. Starr A (1964) Influence of motor activity on click-evoked responses in the auditory pathway of waking cats. Exp Neurol 10:191-204

957. Stent GS (1973) A physiological mechanism for Hebb's postulate of learning. Proc Natl Acad Sci (USA) 70:997-1001

958. Stern JA, Ulett GA, Sines JO (1960) Electrocortical changes during conditioning. In:Wortis J (ed) Recent advances in biological psychiatry. Grune & Stratton, New York, pp 106-122

959. Sternberger LA (1974) Immunocytochemistry. Prentice-Hall, Englewood Cliffs, New Jersey, pp 18-55

960. Stevens CF (1972) Inferences about membrane properties from electrical noise measurements. Biophys J 12:1028-1047

961. Stevens CF (1974) Kinetics of postsynaptic membrane response at the neuromuscular junction. In: Bennett MVL (ed) Synaptic transmission and neuronal interaction, Raven Press, New York, pp 45-58

962. Steward O, Cotman CW, Lynch G (1973) Re-establishment of electrophysiologically functional entorhinal cortical input to the dentate gyrus de-afferented by ipsilateral entorhinal lesions: Innervation by the contralateral entorhinal cortex. Exp Brain Res 18:396-414

963. Steward O, Cotman CW, Lynch GS (1974) Growth of a new fiber projection in the brain of adult rats: Re-innervation of the dentate gyrus by the contralateral entorhinal cortex following ipsilateral entorhinal lesions. Exp Brain Res 20:45-66

964. Stjärne L, Bartfai T, Alberts P (1979) The influence of 8-Br 3', 5'-cyclic nucleotide analogs and of inhibitors of 3', 5'-cyclic nucleotide phosphodiesterase, on nonadrenaline secretion and neuromuscular transmission in guinea-pig vas deferens. Naunyn-Schmiedebergs Arch Pharmacol 308:99-105

965. Stone LS, Zaur IS (1940) Reimplantation and transplantation of adult eyes in the salamander (Triturus viridescens) with return of vision. J Exp Zool 85:243-269

966. Stone TW, Taylor DA, Bloom FE (1975) Cyclic AMP and cyclic GMP may mediate opposite neuronal responses in the rat cerebral cortex. Science 185:845-847

967. Stoney SD, Jr, Thompson WD, Asanuma H (1968) Excitation of pyramidal tract cells by intracortical microstimulation: Effective extent of stimulating current. J Neurophysiol 31:659-669

968. Stratton GM (1896) Some preliminary experiments in vision withoout inversion of the retinal image. Psychol Rev 3:611-617

969. Streit P, Akert K, Sandri C, Livingston RB, Moor H (1972) Dynamic ultrastructure of presynaptic membranes at nerve terminals in the spinal cord of rats. Anesthetized and unanesthetized preparations compared. Brain Res 48:11-26

970. Struchkov MI (1964) Forward and backward conditioning. Zh Vyssh Nerv Deiat 14:635-643

971. Strumwasser F, Truman JW (1979) Modulation and release of behavioral programs by hormones. Neurosci Res Program Bull 17:623-710

972. Suboski MD, Di Lollo V, Gormezano I (1964) Effects of unpaired exposure of CS and UCS on classical conditioning of the nictating membrane response of the albino rabbit. Psychol Repts 15:571-576

973. Sutherland EW (1972) Studies on the mechanisms of hormone action. Science 177:401-408

974. Swadlow HA, Kocsis JD, Waxman SG (1980) Modulation of impulse conduction along the axonal tree. Annu Rev Biophys Bioeng 9:143-179

975. Swartz BE (1979) The role of cyclic 3', 5'-guanosine monophosphate at muscarinic synapses of the cat sensorimotor cortex. PhD thesis, University of California, Los Angeles

976. Swartz BE, Woody CD (1979) Correlated effects of acetylcholine (ACh) and cyclic GMP (cGMP) on membrane properties of mammalian neocortical neurons. J Neurobiol 10:465-488

977. Swartz BE, Woody CD, Jenden DJ (1978) The effects of aceclidine, a muscarinic agonist on neurons in the sensorimotor cortex of awake cats. Proc West Pharmacol Soc 21:11-17

978. Swett JE, Bourassa CM (1967) Comparison of sensory discrimination thresholds with muscle and cutaneous nerve volleys in the cat. J Neurophysiol 30:530-545

979. Switzer CA (1930) Backward conditioning of the lid reflex. J Exp Psychol 13:76-97

980. Szilard L (1929) Uber die Entropieverminderung in einem Thermodynamischen System bei Eingriffen Intelligenter Wesen. Z Physik 53:840

981. Szlep R (1952) On the plasticity of instinct of a garden spider (Aranea diadenal) construction of a cobweb. Acta Biol Exp (Warsaw) 16:5-22

982. Takeuchi A, Takeuchi N (1960) On the permeability of the end-plate membrane during the action of the transmitter. J Physiol (Lond) 154:52-67

983. Takeuchi A, Takeuchi N (1965) Localized action of gamma-aminobutyric acid on the crayfish muscle. J Physiol (Lond) 177:225-238

984. Takeuchi T, Saito S (1960) The effect of electric shock an an analysis of the variously increased intensity of shock for correct responses in a black-white discrimination in the white rat. Ann Anim Psychol (Tokyo) 10:11-21

985. Talland GA (1961) The amnesic syndrome: A psychological study (AAAS Monograph Prize)

986. Talland GA (1958) Psychological studies of Korsakoff's psychosis. II. Perceptual functions. J Nerv Ment Dis 127:197-219

987. Talland GA (1959) The interference theory of forgetting and the amnestic syndrome. J Abnorm Soc Psychol 59:10-16

988. Talland GA (1960) Psychological studies of Korsakoff's Psychosis. VI. Memory and learning. J Nerv Ment Dis 130:366-385

989. Talland GA (1964) The psychopathology of the amnesic syndrome. Mod Probl Psychiatr Neurol 1:443-469

990. Talland GA (1965) Deranged memory. Academic Press, New York

991. Tarnecki R, Konorski J (1963) Instrumental conditioned reflexes elaborated by means of direct stimulation of the motor cortex. In: Gutmann E, Hnik P (eds) Central and peripheral mechanisms of motor functions. Publ House Czech Acad Sci, Prague, pp 177-182

992. Tasaki I (1956) Initiation and abolition of the action potential of a single node of Ranvier. J Gen Physiol 39:377-395

993. Tasaki I (1968) Nerve excitation: A macromolecular approach. Thomas, Springfield, Illinois

994. Tasaki I (1974) Nerve excitation. New experimental evidence for the macromolecular hypothesis. Actualités Neurophysiol 10:79-90

995. Tasaki I (1975) Evolution of theories of nerve excitation. In: Tower DB (ed) The nervous system, Vol 1: The basic neurosciences. Raven Press, New York, pp 177-195
and energy transfer produced by electric simulation of nerves labeled with fluorescent probes. Proc Jpn Acad 51:7:604-609

997. Taub E, Berman AJ (1960) Movement and learning in the absence of sensory feedback. In Freedman SJ (ed) The neuropsychology of spatially oriented behavior. Dorsey Press, Homewood, Illinois, pp 173-192

998. Tauc L (1965) Presynaptic inhibition in the abdominal ganglion of Aplysia. J Physiol (Lond) 181:282-307

999. Tauc L (1967) Transmission in invertebrate and vertebrate ganglia. Physiol Rev 47:521-593

1000. Tauc L, Hoffman A, Tsuji S, Hinzen D, Faille L (1974) Effect of intracellularly injected acetylcholinesterase on a cholinergic synapse. Proc Int Union Physiol Sci 11:152

1001. Taylor J (ed) (1931) Selected writings of John Hughlings Jackson, Vol 2. Hadden & Stoughton, London, p 60

1002. Taylor JA (1956) Level of conditioning and intensity of the adapting stimulus. J Exp Psychol 51:127-130

1003. Tchilingaryan LI (1963) Changes in excitability of the motor area of the cerebral cortex during extinction of a conditioned reflex elaborated to direct electrical stimulation of that area. In: Gutman E, Hnik P (eds) Central and peripheral mechanisms of motor functions. Publ House Czech Acad Sci, Prague, pp 167-175

1004. Teas DC, Kiang NY (1964) Evoked responses from the auditory cortex. Exp Neurol 10:91-119

1005. Terrace HS, Petitto LA, Sanders RJ, Bever TG (1979) Can an ape create a sentence? Science 206:891-902

1006. Teuber HL (1966) Alterations of perception after brain injury. In: Eccles JC (ed) Brain and conscious experience. Springer-Verlag, New York, pp 182-216

1007. Thach WT (1970) Discharge of cerebellar neurons related to two maintained postures and two prompt movements. II. Purkinje cell output and input. J Neurophysiol 33:537-547

1008. Thach WT (1978) Correlation of neural discharge with pattern and force of muscular activity, joint position, and direction of intended next movement in motor cortex and cerebellum. J Neurophysiol 41: 654-676

1009. Thesleff S (1959) Motor end-plate "desensitization" by repetitive nerve stimuli. J Physiol (Lond) 148:659-664

1010. Thomas DR, King RA (1959) Stimulus generalization as a function of level of motivation. J Exp Psychol 57:323-328

1011. Thomas DR, Miller JT, Svinicki JC (1971) Non-specific transfer effects of discrimination training in the rat. J Comp Physiol Psychol 74: 96-101

1012. Thomas MV and Gorman ALF (1977) Internal calcium changes in a bursting pacemaker neuron measured with arsenazo III. Science 196: 531-533

1013. Thomas RC (1974) Intracellular pH of snail neurones measured with a new pH-sensitive glass microelectrode. J Physiol (Lond) 238:159-180

1014. Thomas RC (1979) Ionic mechanisms of intracellular pH regulation in excitable cells. Delivered at Annual Meeting, Society for Neuroscience, November

1015. Thompson R (1969) Localization of the "visual memory system" in the white rat. J Comp Physiol Psychol Monogr 69:4(2):1-29

1016. Thompson RF (1967) Foundations of physiological psychology. Harper, New York

1017. Thompson RF, Sindberg RM (1960) Auditory response fields in association and motor cortex of cat. J Neurophysiol 23:87-105

1018. Thompson RF, Spencer WA (1966) Habituation: A model phenomenon for the study of neuronal substrates of behavior. Psychol Rev 173:16-43

1019. Thompson SH (1977) Three pharmacologically distinct potassium channels in molluscan neurones. J Physiol (Lond) 265:465-488

1020. Thorndike EL (1913) Educational psychology: The psychology of learning, Vol 2, Teachers' College, New York

1021. Tinbergen N (1951) The study of instinct. Oxford University Press (Clarendon), London and New York

1022. Tosaka T, Kobayashi H (1977) The SIF cell as a functional modulator of ganglionic transmission through the release of dopamine. Arch Histol Jpn 40:187-196

1023. Towe AL (1966) On the nature of the primary evoked response. Exp Neurol 15:113-139

1024. Tower DB (1977) Neurochemistry—one hundred years (1875-1975) (collective review). Ann Neurol 1:2-36

1025. Tremblay JP, Woodson PBJ, Schlapfer WT, Barondes SH (1976) Dopamine, serotonin and related compounds; Presynaptic effects on synaptic depression, frequency facilitation and post-tetanic potentiation at a synapse in Aplysia Californica. Brain Res 109:61-81

1026. Truex RC, Carpenter MB (1969) Human neuroanatomy, 6th edn. Williams & Wilkins, Baltimore, Maryland

1027. Truman JW, Reiss SE (1976) Dendritic reorganization of an identified motoneuron during metamorphosis of the tobacco hornworm moth. Science 192:477-479

1028. Tzebelikos E, Woody CD (1979) Intracellularly studied excitability changes in coronal-pericruciate neurons following low frequency stimulation of the corticobulbar tract. Brain Res Bull 4:635-641

1029. Ueda T, Maeno H, Greengard P (1973) Regulation of endogeneous phosphorylation of specific proteins in synaptic membrane fractions from rat brain by adenosine 3':5'-monophosphate. J Biol Chem 248: 8295-8305

1030. Ukhtomsky AA (1926) Concerning the condition of excitation in dominance. Nov Refl Fiziol Nerv Sist 2:3-15; also see Psychol Abstr 1:581 (1927)

1031. Ukhtomsky AA (1938) On conditioned reflex action. Fiziol Zh SSSR 24:379-385; also see Psychol Abstr 12:516 (1938)

1032. Ukhtomsky AA (1950) Parabiosis and the dominant. Collected works, Vol. I (in Russian). Lzd LGU, Leningrad; also see Ukhtomsky AA (1911) On the dependence of cortical motor reactions upon central associated influences (in Russian). Moscow.

1033. Uttley AM (1966) The transmission of information and the effect of local feedback in theoretical and neural networks. Brain Res 2:31-50

1034. Uttley AM (1970) The informon: A network for adaptive pattern recognition. J Theor Biol 27:31-67

1035. Uttley AM (1975) The informon in classical conditioning. J Theor Biol 49:355-376

1036. Uttley AM (1976) A two-pathway informon theory of conditioning and adaptive pattern recognition. Brain Res 102:23-35

1037. Uttley AM (1976) Simulation studies of learning in an informon network. Brain Res 102:37-53

1038. Uttley AM (1976) Neurophysiological predictions of a two-pathway informon theory of neural conditioning. Brain Res 102:55-70

1039. Valverde F (1968) Structural changes in the area striata of the mouse after enucleation. Exp Brain Res 5:274-292

1040. Van Harreveld A (1978) Two mechanisms for spreading depression in the chicken retina. J Neurobiol 9:419-431

1041. Varon S (1975) Nerve growth factor and its mode of action. Exp Neurol 48:75-92

1042. Vasington FD, Gazzotti P, Tiozzo R, Carafoli E (1972) The effect of Ruthenium red on Ca^{2+} transport and respiration in rat liver mitochondria. Biochim Biophys Acta 256:43-54

1043. Vassilevsky NN (1963) Neuronal mechanisms of the cerebral cortex (in Russian). Meditsina, Leningrad

1044. Verzilova OV (1958) Changes in the cortical electrical activity of the dog in the region of the auditory and motor analysers during the formation and reversal of motor-defensive reflexes. Zh Vyssh Nerv Deiat 8:410-419

1045. Victor M, Adams RD, Collins GH (1971) Wernicke-Korsakoff syndrome. Davis, Philadelphia

1046. von Baumgarten R (1970) Plasticity in the nervous system at the unitary level. In: Schmitt FO (ed) The neurosciences: Second study program, Rockefeller University Press, New York, pp 260-271

1047. von der Malsburg C (1973) Self-organization of orientation sensitive cells in the striate cortex. Kybernetik 14:85-100

1048. von Neumann J (1956) Probabilistic logics and the synthesis of reliable organisms from unreliable components. In: Shannon CE, McCarthy J (eds) Automata studies. Princeton University Press, Princeton, New Jersey, pp 43-48

1049. von Neumann J (1961-1963) Collected works, 6 vols (ed. by AH Taub). Pergamon Press, New York

1050. von Neumann J (1958) The computer and the brain. Yale University, New Haven, Connecticut

1051. Voronin LL (1971) Microelectrode investigation of cellular analogs of learning. Sov Neurol Psychiatr 4:99-125

1052. Voronin LL (1976) Cellular mechanisms of conditioned activity. Zh Vyssh Nerv Deiat 26:705-719

1053. Voronin LL (1976) Microelectrode study of neurophysiological mechanisms of conditioning. In: Woody CD (ed) Soviet research reports, Vol 2. Brain Information Service, University of California, Los Angeles, pp 1-59

1054. Voronin LL (1978) Involvement of cortical neurones in conditioned and unconditioned startle reflex. Neuroscience 3:133-137

1055. Voronin LL, Gerstein GY, Ioffe SV, Kudrioshov IE (1973) A rapidly elaborated conditioned reflex with simultaneous recording of neuronal activity. Zh Vyssh Nerv Deiat 23:636-639

1056. Voronin LL, Ioffe SV (1974) Changes in unit postsynaptic responses at sensorimotor cortex with conditioning in rabbits. Acta Neurobiol Exp 34:505-513

1057. Voronin LL, Kudryashov IE (1977) Long-lasting hippocampal post-tetanic potentiation (PTP) with particular reference to mechanisms of conditioned reflex (CR). Proc Int Union Physiol Sci 13:798

1058. Voronin LL, Skrebitskii VG (1965) An intracellular investigation of the neurons of the cerebral cortex of the unanesthetized rabbit. Bull Exp Biol Med 59:473-477

1059. Voronin LL, Solntseva EI (1970) After-effects of intracellular polarization of single cortical neurons. Neurosci Trans 13:65-74

1060. Vyklicky L (1978) Transient changes of extracellular potassium and presynaptic inhibition. In: Ryall RW, Kelly JS (eds) Iontophoresis and transmitter mechanisms in the mammalian central nervous system. Elsevier/North Holland Publ, Amsterdam, pp 284-286

1061. Vyklicky L, Sykova E, Kriz N, Ujec E (1972) Post-stimulation changes of extracellular potassium concentration in the spinal cord of the rat. Brain Res 45:608-611

1062. Vyskocil F, Kriz N (1972) Modifications of single and double-barrel potassium specific micro-electrodes for physiological experiments. Pfluegers Arch 377:265-276

1063. Waggoner AS (1979) Dye indicators of membrane potential. Annu Rev Biophys Bioeng 8:47-68

1064. Wagner AR, Thomas E, Norton T (1967) Conditioning with electrical stimulation of motor cortex: Evidence of a possible source of motivation. J Comp Physiol Psychol 64:191-199

1065. Walker JL, Brown HM (1977) Intracellular ionic activity measurements in nerve and muscle. Physiol Rev 57:729-778

1066. Warashina A, Tasaki I (1975) Evidence for rotation of dye molecules in membrane macromolecules associated with nerve excitation. Proc Jpn Acad 51:7:610-615

1067. Watanabe A (1972) Macromolecules and excitation. In: Bourne GH (ed) The structure and function of nervous tissue, Vol 6. Academic Press, New York, pp 335-366

1068. Watson J (1968) The double helix, a personal account of the discovery of the structure of DNA. Atheneum, New York

1069. Waziri R (1977) Presynaptic electrical coupling in Aplysia: Effects on postsynaptic chemical transmission. Science 195:790-792

1070. Wedner HJ, Hoffer BJ, Battenberg E, Steiner AL, Parker CW, Bloom FE (1972) A method for detecting intracellular cyclic adenosine monophosphate by immunofluorescence. J Histochem Cytochem 20: 293-295

1071. Weight FF (1979) Modulation of synaptic excitability. Fed Proc 38: 2078-2079

1072. Weight FF, Erulkar SD (1976) Modulation of synaptic transmitter release by repetitive postsynaptic action potentials. Science 193:1023-1025

1073. Weight FF, Padjen A (1973) Slow synaptic inhibition: Evidence for synaptic inactivation of sodium conductance in sympathetic ganglion cells. Brain Res 55:219-224

1074. Weight FF, Petzgold G, Greengard P (1974) Guanosine 3', 5'-monophosphate in sympathetic ganglia: Increase associated with synaptic transmission. Science 186:942-944

1075. Weight FF, Schulman JA, Smith PA, Busis NA (1979) Long-lasting synaptic potentials and the modulation of synaptic transmission. Fed Proc 38:2084-2094

1076. Weight FF, Smith PA, Schulman JA (1978) Post-synaptic potential generation appears independent of synaptic elevation of cyclic nucleotides in sympathetic neurons. Brain Res 158:197-202

1077. Weight FF, Votava J (1970) Slow synaptic excitation in sympathetic ganglion cells: Evidence for synaptic inactivation of potassium conductance. Science 170:755-758

1078. Weinreich D (1971) Ionic mechanism of post-tetanic potentiation at the neuromuscular junction of the frog. J Physiol (Lond) 212:431-446

1079. Weinstein JN, Yoshikami S, Henkart P, Blumenthal R, Hagins WA (1977) Liposome-cell interaction: Transfer and intracellular release of a trapped fluorescent marker. Science 195:489-491

1080. Weisberg TH, McBride KE (1935) Aphasia, a clinical and psychological study. Oxford University Press, London and New York

1081. Whitehouse GE (1973) Systems analysis and design using network techniques, Int Ser Ind Syst Eng. Prentice-Hall, Englewood Cliffs, New Jersey

1082. Wickens DD (1938) The transference of conditioned excitation and conditioned inhibition from one muscle group to the antagonistic muscle group. J Exp Psychol 22:101-123

1083. Wickens DD, Wickens CD (1942) Some factors related to pseudo-conditioning. J Exp Psychol 31:518-526

1084. Wiener N (1933) The fourier integral and certain of its applications. Cambridge University Press, London and New York

1085. Wiener N (1948) Cybernetics. Wiley, New York

1086. Wiener N (1958) Nonlinear problems in random theory. Technology Press of MIT, Cambridge, Mass.

1087. Wiener N (1966) Generalized harmonic analyses and Taubarian theories. MIT Press, Cambridge, Massachusetts

1088. Wiersma CAG (1947) Giant nerve fibre system of the crayfish. A contribution to comparative physiology of synapse. J Neurophysiol 10:23-38

1089. Wiesel TN, Hubel DH (1974) Reorganization of ocular dominance columns in monkey striate cortex. Program Abstr Soc Neurosci, 4th Annu Meet p 478

1090. Wiesel TN, Hubel DH, Lam DMK (1974) Autoradiographic demonstration of ocular dominance columns in the monkey striate cortex by means of transneuronal transport. Brain Res 79:273-279

1091. Wilson VJ (1958) Early post-tetanic potentiation and low frequency depression of some group I reflex actions. J Gen Physiol 41:1005-1018

1092. Wilson WA, Wachtel H (1978) Prolonged inhibition in burst firing neurons: Synaptic inactivation of the slow regenerative inward current. Science 202:772-775

1093. Wine J, Hagiwara G (1978) Durations of unitary synaptic potentials help time a behavioral sequence. Science 199:557-559

1094. Wolbarsht ML, MacNichol EF, Jr, Wagner HG (1960) Glass insulated platinum microelectrode. Science 132:1309-1310

1095. Wolfle HM (1930) Time factors in conditioning finger-withdrawal. J Gen Psychol 4:372-378

1096. Wolfle HM (1932) Conditioning as a function of the interval between the conditioned and the original stimulus. J Gen Psychol 7:80-103

1097. Wong B, Woody CD (1978) Recording intracellularly with potassium ion-sensitive electrodes from single cortical neurons in awake cats. Exp Neurol 61:219

1098. Wood JD, Mayer CJ (1978) Slow synaptic excitation serotonin in Auerbach's plexus. Nature 276:836-837

1099. Woodbury JW (1968) Potentials in a volume conductor. In: Ruch TC et al (eds) Neurophysiology, 2nd ed. WB Saunders, Philadelphia, pp 85-91

1100. Woodson PBJ, Tremblay JP, Schlapfer WT, Barondes SH (1976) Increased membrane fluidity implicated in acceleration of decay of post-tetanic potentiation by alcohols. Nature 260:797-799

1101. Woodward DJ, Moises HC, Waterhouse BD, Hoffer BJ, Freedman R (1979) Modulatory actions of norepinephrine in the central nervous system. Fed Proc 38:2109-2116

1102. Woody CD (1962) Some aspects of information processing in the CNS. Honor's thesis, Harvard Medical School

1103. Woody CD (1967) Characterization of an adaptive filter for the analysis of variable latency neuroelectric signals. Med Biol Eng 5:539-553

1104. Woody CD (1970) Conditioned eyeblink: Gross potential activity at coronal-precruciate cortex of the cat. J Neurophysiol 33:838-850

1105. Woody CD (1974) Aspects of the electrophysiology of cortical processes related to the development and performance of learned motor responses. The Physiologist 17:49-69

1106. Woody CD (1977) Alterations in neuronal excitability supporting sensorimotor integration. Proc Int Union Physiol Sci 12:604

1107. Woody CD (1977) Changes in activity and excitability of cortical auditory receptive units of the cat as a function of different behavioral states. Ann NY Acad Sci 290:180-199

1108. Woody CD (1982) Acquisition of conditioned facial reflexes in the cat: Cortical control of different facial movements. Fed Proc (in press)

1109. Woody CD (ed) (1982) Conditioning: Representation of involved neural functions. Plenum, New York (in press)

1110. Woody CD, Black-Cleworth P (1973) Differences in excitability of cortical neurons as a function of motor projection in conditioned cats. J Neurophysiol 36:1104-1116

1111. Woody CD, Brown KA, Crow TJ, Jr, Knispel JD (eds) (1974) Cellular mechanisms subserving changes in neuronal activity. Brain Information Service, University of California, Los Angeles

1112. Woody CD, Brožek G (1969) Gross potential from facial nucleus of cat as an index of neural activity in response to glabella tap. J Neurophysiol 32:704-716

1113. Woody CD, Brožek G (1969) Changes in evoked responses from facial nucleus of cat with conditioning and extinction of an eye blink. J Neurophysiol 32:717-726

1114. Woody CD, Brožek G (1969) Conditioned eyeblink in the cat: Evoked responses of short latency. Brain Res 12:257-260

1115. Woody CD, Buerger AA, Ungar RA, Levine DS (1976) Modeling aspects of learning by altering biophysical properties of a simulated neuron. Biol Cybern 23:73-82

1116. Woody CD, Carpenter DO, Gruen E, Knispel JD, Crow TW, Black-Cleworth P (1976) Persistent increases in membrane resistance of neurons in cat motor cortex. Armed Forces Radiobiology Res. Inst Sci Rep [February], pp 1-31

1117. Woody CD, Carpenter D, Knispel JD, Crow TJ, Jr, Black-Cleworth P (1974) Prolonged increases in resistance of neurons in cat motor cortex following extracellular iontophoretic application of acetylcholine (ACh) and intracellular current injection Fed Proc 33:399

1118. Woody CD, Engel J, Jr (1972) Changes in unit activity and thresholds to electrical microstimulation at coronal-pericruciate cortex of cat with classical conditioning of different facial movements. J Neurophysiol 35:230-241

1119. Woody CD, Gruen E (1977) Comparison of excitation of single cortical neurons in awake cats by extracellularly and intracellularly delivered current (abstr). Soc Neurosci Symp 3:166

1120. Woody CD, Gruen E (1978) Characterization of electrophysiological properties of intracellularly recorded neurons in the neocortex of awake cats: A comparison of the response to injected current in spike overshoot and undershoot neurons. Brain Res 158:343-357

1121. Woody CD, Gruen E (1980) Effects of cyclic nucleotides on morphologically identified cortical neurons of cats. Proc Int Union Physiol Sci 14:789

1122. Woody CD, Knispel JD, Crow TJ, Black-Cleworth PA (1976) Activity and excitability to electrical current of cortical auditory receptive neurons of awake cats as affected by stimulus association. J Neurophysiol 39:1045-1061

1123. Woody CD, Nahvi MJ (1973) Application of optimum linear filter theory to the detection of cortical signals preceding facial movement in cat. Exp Brain Res 16:455-465

1124. Woody CD, Swartz BE, Gruen E (1978) Effects of acetylcholine and cyclic GMP on input resistance of cortical neurons in awake cats. Brain Res 158:373-395

1125. Woody CD, Vassilevsky NN, Engel J, Jr (1970) Conditioned eye blink: Unit activity at coronal-precruciate cortex of the cat. J Neurophysiol 33:851-864

1126. Woody CD, Wong B (1981) Intracellular recording of potassium in neurons of the motor cortex of awake cats following extracellular applications of acetylcholine. In: Sykova E, Vyklicky L (eds) Ion-selective microelectrodes and their use in excitable tissues. Plenum, New York, pp 125-132

1127. Woody CD, Yarowsky PJ (1972) Conditioned eye blink using electrical stimulation of coronal-precruciate cortex as conditional stimulus. J Neurophysiol 35:242-252

1128. Woody CD, Yarowsky P, Owens J, Black-Cleworth P, Crow T (1974) Effect of lesions of cortical motor areas on acquisition of eyeblink in the cat. J Neurophysiol 37:385-394

1129. Woolacott MH, Hoyle G (1976) Membrane resistance changes associated with single, identified neuron learning. Soc Neurosci Abstr 2:339

1130. Worden F (1959) Comments in the article: EEG studies and conditional reflexes in man by VS Rusinov. In: Brazier MAB (ed) Central nervous system and behavior, 2nd edn. Josiah Macy Jr, Found, New York, pp 270-312

1131. Yarowsky PJ, Carpenter DO (1978) A comparison of similar ionic responses to γ-aminobutyric acid and acetylcholine. J Neurophysiol 41:531-541

1132. Yoshii N (1957) Principes méthodologiques de l'investigation électroencéphalographique du comportement conditionne. Electroencephalogr Clin Neurophysiol [Suppl] 6:75-88

1133. Yoshii N, Hockaday WJ (1958) Conditioning of frequency - characteristic repetitive electroencephalographic response with intermittent photic stimulation. Electroencephalogr Clin Neurophysiol 10:487-502

1134. Yoshii N, Matsumoto J, Hori Y (1957) Electroencephalographic study on conditioned reflex in animals. Int Congr Neurol Sci [Reun Plen] 1:313-334

1135. Yoshii N, Matsumoto J, Maeno S, Hasegawa Y, Yamaguchi Y, Shimo-kochi M, Hori Y, Yamazaki H (1958) Conditioned reflex and electro-encephalography. Med J Osaka Univ 9:353-375

1136. Yoshii N, Ogura H (1960) Studies on the unit discharge of brainstem reticular formation in the cat. I. Changes of reticular unit discharge following conditioned procedure. Med J Osaka Univ 11:1-17

1137. Yoshii N, Yamasaki H (1959) Electroencephalographic studies on de-layed and trace conditioned reflexes of defensive movements. Med J Osaka Univ 10:185-201

1138. Yoshioka T, Pant HC, Tasaki I, Gainer H (1978) Phosphorylation of proteins in the squid giant axon. IBRO News 6:7

1139. Young JZ (1964) A model of the brain. Oxford University Press, London and New York

1140. Young RA, Cegavske CF, Thompson RF (1976) Tone-induced changes in excitability of abducens motoneurons in the reflex path of the rab-bit nictitating membranes response. J Comp Physiol Psychol 90:424-434

1141. Younkin SG (1974) An analysis of the role of calcium in facilitation at the frog neuromuscular junction. J Physiol (Lond) 237:1-14

1142. Yuyama T (1959) Electroencephalograms in formation and abolition of the conditioned avoidance reflex in dogs. Tohoku J Exp Med 70:27-38

1143. Zachar J (1971) Electrogenesis and contractility in skeletal muscle cells. University Park Press, Baltimore, Maryland

1144. Zak R, Martin AF, Blough R (1979) Assessment of protein turnover by use of radioisotopic tracers. Physiol Rev 59:407-447

1145. Zener K (1937) The significance of behavior accompanying con-ditioned salivary secretion for theories of the conditioned response. Am J Psychol 50:384-403

1146. Zernicki B (1968) Pretrigeminal cat. Brain Res 9:1-14

1147. Zeuthen T (1978) Intracellular gradients of ion activities in the epi-thelial cells of the Necturus gallbladder recorded with ion-selective microelectrodes. J Membr Biol 39:185-218

1148. Zieglgansberger W, Reiter CH (1974) A cholinergic mechanism in the spinal cord of cats: Neuropharmacologia 13:519-527

1149. Zucker RS, Kennedy D, Selverston AI (1971) Neuronal circuit medi-ating escape responses in crayfish. Science 173:645-650

1150. Zuckermann E (1959) Effect of cortical and reticular stimulation on conditioned reflex activity. J Neurophysiol 22:633-643

GLOSSARY

(Some of the terms within the Glossary are better defined by the extended definition within the text than by an abbreviated definition herein. The page numbers on which those definitions may be found are given.)

ACh (acetylcholine), CH_3-CO-O-CH_2-CH_2-N-$(CH_3)_3$ A neurotransmitter thought to influence the postsynaptic membrane at nicotinic synapses by directly increasing gNa and at muscarinic synapses by indirectly decreasing gK.

Action potential Fast (e.g., 0.1 to 2.0 msec), spikelike depolarization supported by increased gNa or increased gCa. In mammals the increased gNa is self-perpetuating from point to point in the axonal membrane, thus causing a propagating spike potential.

Adaptation See pages 3, 4, 8-10, 43, 221, 383.

Afferents Nerve pathways leading to or further into the central nervous system; also, nerve pathways carrying sensory labeled messages.

Afterdischarges Spike discharges continuing beyond those elicited directly by a momentary stimulus input.

Agnosia Loss of the ability to recognize the significance of sensory stimuli.

Alexia Loss of the ability to understand written words.

Alpha conditioning See EEG conditioning (of alpha wave activity), page 126.

Amusia Defect or loss of the power of musical expression, especially by song.

Anosognosia An agnosia for (or loss of the ability to recognize that one has) a disease or bodily defect.

Aphasia Defect or loss of the power of expression by speech, writing, etc.; inability to understand the meaning of speech; loss of the ability to use words; see page 298.

Appetitive behavior Behavior directed towards satiety of hunger or thirst.

Apraxia Loss or impairment of the ability to perform a motor act intentionally; see page 297.

Area 17, 18, 19 Each area is a part of the visual cortex (see Brodmann map, page 303).

Association See page 61.

Associative See page 59.

Autotopagnosia Body image agnosia.

Axon hillock The part of the cell body from which the axon originates.

Backward conditioning See pages 35, 79.

Bandwidth The frequency range of a signal or transmission channel.

Brainstem The region at the base of the brain connecting the brain and the spinal cord.

Brun's frontal ataxia A broad-based, staggering gait seen after frontal lesions.

Capacitance See Membrane capacitance.

Cholinergic Releasing acetycholine as a transmitter.

Cholinesterase An enzyme that hydrolyzes acetylcholine.

Classical conditioning Conditioning performed after the manner of Pavlov in which two stimuli are presented in fixed temporal relationship.

Code The *form* of transmission of the information content of a signal—usually systematically applicable to different signals.

Coded message A systematically transformed message.

Conditional probability The probability of occurrence of one event, given that some other event has (or has not) occurred.

Conditioned inhibition See pages 22, 27.

Conditioned response See page 9 (Figure 2.2).

Conditional stimulus See page 14.

Conductance (g) The reciprocal of electrical resistance, related in neurons and other cells to the transport of current across the cell membrane by ions such as sodium and potassium.

Contingency The condition(s) on which a dependent variable depends.

Continuous event An event taking place continuously in time, e.g., a sinusoidal wave.

Contralateral Pertaining to the opposite side of the body.

Convergence The confluence of inputs to a single element such as a neuron.

Delayed conditioning See inhibition-produced delay, page 28.

Dependency Wherein the state of one variable is conditional on the state of another variable (or the same variable at an earlier point in time); see Conditional probability.

Depolarization Any reduction of the transmembrane potential from the resting value toward zero.

Differential inhibition See differentiated inhibition, page 26.

Discrete event An event taking place at a moment in time rather than steadily, e.g., a step function.

Discriminability A measure of the sensitivity of the organism to stimulus differences [473] (see page 95 ff.).

Discrimination Preferential reception of one stimulus (S^+) with respect to another (S^-).

Disinhibition The removal of inhibition, sometimes facilitating the production of a motor response.

Dominance See Reflex dominance.

Dominant hemisphere 1. The hemisphere in which the circuitry critical for performance of a particular function is mainly located (thus, the dominant hemisphere may vary from function to function, the left hemisphere usually being dominant for speech in both right- and left-handed persons, the right hemisphere being dominant for spatial construction and music). 2. The hemisphere serving speech (*and* handedness in right-handed people) is often called *the* dominant hemisphere, since it *appears* to control much of what is going on.

Efferents Nerve pathways leading outward from the central nervous system; also, nerve pathways carrying motor labeled messages.

Electrical synapse See page 197 and Figure 5.25.

Electroencephalogram (EEG) See page 116.

End plate The region of a skeletal muscle fiber that receives synaptic terminals.

Engram A unit of memory; further distinction may be made between units of memory that are (i) transient, (ii) persistent, or (iii) permanent.

Ensemble A set of related elements.

EPSP Excitatory (usually depolarizing) postsynaptic potential.

Equilibrium potential The potential resulting from differences in concentration of an ion (at equilibrium) across a semipermeable membrane.

Escape conditioning The equivalent of instrumental conditioning; see pages 46-48.

Excitation See page 12 (footnote) and page 13.

External inhibition See pages 19-20.

Exteroceptive Concerning the reception of stimuli arising outside the organism.

Extinction See page 24.

Facilitation See page 12.

False peak An other-than-desired "signal" found by hill climbing.

Faraday (F) 96,500 coulombs: the amount of electricity needed to deposit 1 gm equivalent of an element during electrolysis.

Frequency dependency The dependence of a process on the rate of some variable (such as a stimulus or input signal).

Gap junction See page 197 and Figure 5.25.

Generalization gradient The slope of the line linking different (graphed) levels of response performance to different stimuli (also see Response generalization).

Glabella tap A tap delivered at or just above the bridge of the nose (the region of the skull called the glabella); such a stimulus commonly produces an eyeblink.

Habituatory adaptation See page 30.

Higher function See pages 262, 265, 312.

Hill climbing A technique for signal detection employing the maximization of input gradients.

Hyperpolarization An increase of transmembrane potential in the negative direction with respect to the intracellularly measured component.

Ideational agnosia Loss of the special associations which make up the idea of an object from its component ideas.

Imprinting The acquisition of stereotyped behavior following early postnatal exposure to specific stimuli, usually by an entire genus or species.

Inactivation Used herein as a decrease in ionic conductance, usually at or near the limiting of conductance change.

Information   *Generic*: Knowledge of something.

Analytic: The number of possible outcomes of the inverse of the probability of occurrence of a number of possible outcomes.

Inhibition See pages 15, 19.

Inhibition of delay See inhibition-produced delay, page 28.

Instrumental conditioning See page 21.

Internal inhibition The effect of stimulus repetition observed by Pavlov. See page 21.

Iontophoresis Application of a charged ion by passing current through a solution containing the (dissolved) ion.

IPSP Inhibitory (usually hyperpolarizing) postsynaptic potential.

ISI Interstimulus interval (the interval between stimulus presentations).

Isomorphism Similarity of form, content, or meaning.

Language The code of speech (of which words are, generally, the smallest coded messages).

Latent facilitation A facilitation of motor performance arising from repetitive stimulus presentation (see pages 33, 153, 157).

Latent inhibition See pages 24, 157.

Learning See Introduction.

Length constant Another term for the space constant.

Liebnitz monads Elementary, substance-like souls (c.f. [856]).

Linear threshold function ψ is a linear threshold function with respect to Φ, if there exists a number θ and a set of numbers α_φ, one for each φ in Φ, such that

$$\psi(X) = [\sum_{\psi \in \Phi} \alpha_\varphi \varphi(X) > \theta].$$

Line labeling See page 110.

Linguistics The study of speech.

Majority logic Decisions based on agreement among a majority of available inputs or transmission channels.

Membrane capacitance (Cm) Property of the cell membrane enabling electrical charge to be stored and separated (and introducing distortion in the time course of passively conducted signals); measured in Farads (F) [571].

Membrane conductance The inverse of membrane resistance; more specifically, the current carried by ions across the cell membrane with respect to the transmembrane potential.

Membrane resistance (Rm) Property of the cell membrane limiting the passage of electrical current (measured in ohms).

Memory See page 2 and Introduction.

Message Transmitted information; popularly, the specific information content of a signal (though sometimes plus noise).

Metabolic pump See page 206; a process that uses metabolic energy to transport ions across a semipermeable membrane (usually against their natural diffusion gradient).

Minepp Miniature end plate potential.

Monad See Liebnitz monads.

Monogenic CR A single Cr elicited by one CS or a simple stimulus and generated from simple association or reinforcement.

Motoneuron A neuron whose axon terminates on a muscle.

Motor neuron Any neuron that serves a conspicuous efferent function.

Motor unit The motoneuron and the muscle fibers to which it projects.

Multiplexing See page 327.

Network state (See System state) The state of adaptation or the actual transfer functions within a network at a particular moment.

Neuromuscular junction The synapse between axon and muscle.

Nociceptive stimulus A noxious stimulus such as one that produces a sensation of pain.

Noise The content of a transmission that is not the signal.

Normalization Reducing to a specified base or range of operation.

Operant conditioning The equivalent of instrumental conditioning.

Orienting response See page 40.

PAD Primary afferent depolarization (the depolarization of the synaptic terminals of first-order sensory neurons).

Parallel processing Data processing, message handling, etc. that is carried out using two (or more) parallel channels to accomplish the actual transfer or processing operation.

Parametric Pertaining to the parameters employed (e.g., to produce adaptation).

Paraphasia Partial aphasia in which the wrong words are employed.

Pheromone A chemical compound exuded by one animal and capable of eliciting stereotyped behavior in another.

Posttetanic potentiation Facilitation of neural transmission after rapid (often maximally rapid) neural activation.

Predicate A function that has two possible values; i.e., a binary function. (See page 389.)

Preparatory reflex A reflex defined in terms of the behavioral operation for which it is used; some would define it as a reflex that prepares for some other reflex operation.

Preprogrammed response A response that arises from "built-in" features of the transmission network.

Presynaptic inhibition A form of inhibition of transmission at certain synaptic terminals (thought to relate to change in membrane potential, calcium, and local potassium) brought about, classically, by the action of another synapse on the synaptic terminal itself.

Primary afferent depolarization See PAD.

Proprioceptive feedback Transmission to the central nervous system of information concerning movement detected by specialized receptors in muscles and tendons.

Pseudoconditioning See page 35.

Pump, metabolic See page 206.

Reciprocal innervation Neural circuits causing activation of synergistic and simultaneous relaxation of opposing or antagonistic muscles.

Reflex See page 6ff.

Reflex dominance See page 33.

Refractory period That period after initiation of an action potential during which another action potential cannot be produced (absolute refractory period) or can only be produced incompletely or with difficulty (relative refractory period).

Reinforcement See pages 9, 46.

Repetitive adaptation See page 21.

Resistance See Membrane resistance.

Response generalization The ease with which different responses may be acquired or performed in response to the same stimulus.

Reticular formation A group of 98 interconnected brainstem nuclei forming a conspicuous network of nerve fibers.

Second-order conditioning See pages 52, 89.

Sensitization See page 40.

Sensory preconditioning See pages 51, 72, 89.

Serial processing Data processing, message handling, etc. that is carried out by means of a single channel along which various transfer or processing operations may occur.

Signal That part of a message or input that is not noise; see page 255.

Space constant (λ) See page 195.

Specificity *Neuronal*—The sensory and motor line labeling of nerve circuitry responsible for selectivity of reception and effectuation; also, the specificity of neurotransmitter, neuromodulator, conductance change, etc. in neurons which contributes to the selectivity of reception, effectuation, and adaptation.

Of motor response—The selectivity of motor performance resulting from motor line labeling.

Of stimulus reception—The selectivity by which different stimuli will be discriminated (and by which different motor responses may or may not be elicited) resulting from sensory line labeling.

Speech The expression of systematically meaningful vocal discourse or communication.

Stacking Queuing up in time or space.

Stimulus A signal of biological significance, usually defined as capable of eliciting some response.

Stimulus generalization See Generalization gradient.

Stretch receptor A specialized nerve terminal located in tendons or muscles and sensitive to stretch, e.g., a Golgi tendon organ (see page 14 and references 693, 849).

Subliminal fringe Neural elements that can be liminally activated by multiple inputs but not by the same inputs individually.

System state The state of adaptation or the actual transfer functions within a system at a particular moment (see pages 230, 347, and 383).

Tachistoscope An instrument used to deliver a very brief light image.

Tetany Abnormally sustained (maximal) discharge or muscle contraction.

Time constant (τ) The rate of change in transmembrane potential to an applied step voltage, determined by the product of the resistance and capacitance of the nerve membrane.

Trace conditioning See pages 63-69.

Tropism Movement characterized by tight feedback between stimulus and response, often resembling tracking.

Tropismic Motor performance dependent on tight feedback loops resulting in conspicuous tracking or following behavior.

Transmittance The conductance between modes of a circuit or the relationship between mode variables (see page 369).

Unconditional stimulus See pages 14-15.

Venn Diagram A form of notation employing logical diagrams similar or analogous to those used to describe the algebra of events shown on page 396 (see Figure 7.31).

Voltage dependent Influenced by a level of potential (difference) or by a shift in potential.

Word The smallest unit of speech that has meaning.

Index